INTRODUCTION TO THE GIFTED

Psychology and Human Development in Education

NICHOLAS HOBBS, *Consulting Editor*

FRANDSEN   *Educational Psychology*

GINOTT   *Group Psychotherapy with Children*

HARING AND PHILLIPS   *Educating Emotionally Disturbed Children*

HILDRETH   *Introduction to the Gifted*

VAN DALEN   *Understanding Educational Research*

INTRODUCTION TO THE GIFTED

Gertrude H. Hildreth

Professor Emeritus, Brooklyn College
The City University of New York

McGRAW-HILL BOOK COMPANY

New York   St. Louis   San Francisco   Toronto   London   Sydney

INTRODUCTION TO THE GIFTED

28762

234567890 MP 7210698

To the wonderful children
who appear in these pages

We must dream of an aristocracy of achievement arising out of a democracy of opportunity.

THOMAS JEFFERSON

PREFACE

During the past fifty years, particularly in the last decade or so, an unusual amount of attention has been centered on a segment of the child population formerly neglected and little understood—the gifted, talented, and creative individuals whose promise when fulfilled enlightens the world. Close psychological scrutiny and educational experimentation have led to new understanding of these individuals as human beings with the right to self-fulfillment and to the kind of education that makes the realization of their full potential possible. Concern has been shown not only for gifted children from good homes and in excellent schools who immediately stand out from the crowd, but for hidden talent among youths of limited background and opportunity in depressed areas, whether in crowded cities or remote places. Today, in view of the world's needs for expertness in every phase of public life and private enterprise, the need to discover and conserve superior abilities and creative talent has a new urgency.

This book originated in my own personal experience with gifted children in public and private schools, dating back over forty years, in fact, to the time when I first encountered six-year-old Sara in grade 1 assisting the harried teacher with the tots who "couldn't read yet" and a bright Negro boy of eleven with a phenomenal memory who was accelerating rapidly through senior high school. The book is the outgrowth of lectures and discussions in a course on the gifted at Brooklyn College, the City University of New York, of seminars at Hunter College some years ago, and of extramural courses and summer workshops both in the United States and abroad.

All young persons preparing to teach should become familiar with modern concepts of the gifted and their special needs as school learners, even though the prospective teachers scarcely expect to specialize in this work; a teacher may be called upon at any time to pass judgment on a gifted or talented child or give advice about him. *Introduction to the Gifted* has been organized as a general text for use in education and child psychology courses, for courses on the exceptional child, and for training courses preparing specialists in this field.

The book presents a comprehensive survey of developments through the years—the identification and appraisal of the bright and talented and various alternatives in educational adjustments for them. Consideration is given to the personal guidance of bright children with special problems, particularly the so-called under-achiever; to the special measures that must be taken to motivate and challenge the gifted in modern schools; to the nurturing of high creativity in promising young people.

The first few chapters provide an introduction to the topic, a discussion of definitions of the gifted and talented, methods of assessing traits of the gifted as disclosed by scientific studies of these children and their development. From Chapter 7 onward the book deals primarily with educational theory and practice with respect to the gifted and talented in the elementary grades, the secondary school, and college.

Today, educational planning for the gifted is recognized as but one phase of instituting overall programs for individualizing instruction so that every child, whatever his talents, can realize his full potential. There is full discussion of controversial issues, such as ability grouping and acceleration for rapid learners. An attempt has been made to anticipate and to answer typical questions teachers ask about these unusual children and their instruction. Research findings relating to the chief issues and problems that arise when the subject of the gifted and talented is under discussion are fully reported.

Although the book has been designed primarily for those who work with the gifted, the teacher who prefers to think that "every pupil is gifted" will find here an outline of the principles that underlie all good education. In fact, the keynote throughout the book is the need to upgrade the entire level of education so that every child receives the best education the community can provide.

The tremendous upsurge of interest in the gifted starting about fifteen years ago is now leveling off as other pressing problems in education arise. This is to be expected, since many of the recommendations of this book have now become accepted educational practice, but so long as the special needs of the gifted and talented are recognized, interest in their welfare will continue.

One of the basic criteria for judging the effectiveness of college teaching is whether the instructor has brought about new and fuller understanding in the minds of his students. It is my hope that *Introduction to the Gifted* will meet this essential criterion.

In preparing these chapters, I have drawn freely upon the great mass of previously published material on the subject—research monographs, bulletins, and periodical references here and abroad. I owe a special debt of gratitude to my students who, through the years, have supplied anecdotes, descriptions, and references concerning the gifted, and have raised innumerable queries about these super-children, sometimes, hopefully, as parents whose child may be in this category.

Colleagues at Brooklyn College and elsewhere frequently enlarged my vision through deliberations on the issues and problems discussed here.

Acknowledgment has been made throughout the book to authors and publishers for permission to use published material.

My special thanks are due to Dean Walter H. Mais of Brooklyn College who granted me some hours of released time from classroom teaching to prepare these chapters for publication.

Gertrude H. Hildreth

The sketches on the cover, title page, and chapter-opening pages were drawn by students at the High School of Music and Art, New York City.

CONTENTS

Chapter Five

Chapter Six

Chapter Seven

Chapter Eight

Chapter Nine

Chapter Ten

Chapter Eleven

Chapter Twelve

Chapter Thirteen

Chapter Fourteen

Chapter Fifteen

Chapter Sixteen

Chapter Seventeen

Chapter Eighteen

Appendix

Chapter One

A WORLD
OF
TALENT

The development and utilization of a nation's human resources prove to be the best indicators of economic prosperity and social advancement. This principle was recognized by Plato, who observed over 2,000 years ago that the state's gifted leaders are its most valuable asset. They are the ones who make economic and social progress possible. Without them—without the contributions of great minds, the ideas of original thinkers who stand out from the crowd, whose innovations and creative ideas advance the frontiers of knowledge—the world would, indeed, be a barren place. No less important than the conservation of human resources for national and world welfare is the development of every young person's potential for his own self-fulfillment as an individual.

Leaders throughout the Ages

Throughout all the epochs of history there have been people with natural ability and superior training who were as remarkable in their time as our leaders are today. Gifted people at some unknown place in an early civilization invented the alphabet for recording language symbolically. Inspired people wrote the Bible and passed the great work down to us. The Roman emperor Justinian gave us the pattern for legal codes in use today. The great writers of the past five hundred years have expressed man's enduring truths with beauty and sensitivity. Since the beginning of the industrial era, the inventors of the telephone, the radio and television, mechanized transportation, household appliances, and the discoverers of new principles in chemistry and physics have eased the lot of the common people while creating a new era of health and wealth. Some of these leaders have been many-sided, versatile people of enormous gifts who devoted their talents to productive work throughout a long lifetime.

Today there are gifted leaders in all areas of achievement and human relationships—in business, government, industry, education, social and community welfare, family life. Who can estimate the contribution of a modern scientific and social leader of the stature of Albert Schweitzer, who has dedicated his talents to human welfare and world service? Dr. George Washington Carver, an American Negro of lowly birth, became an eminent chemurgist and agricultural experimentalist, one of the great benefactors of humanity. The material progress of the present century is due largely to the growing number of highly trained intellectual workers and technological specialists for every sort of enterprise.

LEADERS FROM THE COMMON PEOPLE IN A DEMOCRACY

Thomas Jefferson asserted that a free world could not survive without trained leadership of the best minds. Life in a free democracy thrives on leadership that derives from the common people; under freedom the full resources of human talent and creativity can be recognized and developed. In the ideal society everyone of ability has the opportunity to rise to the top unhampered by social stigmas. The elite in this society are people of superior aptitudes who lead the way. Talent and intellectual power stamp the aristocrat, and intelligence becomes the badge of the nobility—not dress, manner of speech, wealth, or social position.

America has become a great nation, as Arnold Toynbee pointed out, through the achievements of creative leaders from the founding fathers of the Republic onward. These leaders have pressed for social justice and worked for the uplift of the common people. The emergence of new nations in our century reflects the growing enlightenment of a new generation, forever experimenting to discover new processes and open up new frontiers.

Stepped-up Need for "Idea People"

Today as we enter the thermonuclear age, inventive minds, with an array of scientific tools not dreamed of fifty years ago, can accomplish almost anything within the scope of man's imagination. New problems, too, confront the world on every hand. At the judging and decision-making level in government and industry, and in all phases of our social life, a vast new pool of resource people is demanded with the skills, trained intellect, personality, and integrity to exert national and international leadership.

The older conception of the intellectual man as an impractical visionary who tends to upset the *status quo* with his radical views has given place to fuller appreciation of the accomplishments of the "egg-head," the expert, the specialist. Around the world there is new respect for intellect and the people who possess it, including professionals with specialized aptitudes and training. The affairs of the United Nations and the economic and political problems of the Common Market of Europe are regarded as among the most complex of all times and require the best-trained statesmen.

The individual nations can no longer selfishly hoard their talents, but must participate in a global effort to upgrade human welfare, to lift backward people from poverty, ill health, and ignorance. Experts in international affairs agree that national security depends more largely on education and social progress linked to industrial development than on armaments or military expenditures.

Modern nations have new and enlarging international contacts in business and statesmanship. The foreign service is an expanding field that requires career people of intelligence, sound judgment, and high purpose—people of all races and social classes, women as well as men. The underdeveloped and backward countries need an army of highly trained professional people. For example, the African nation of Nigeria on achieving independence had about 3,000 such persons, but the immediate need was for at least 7,500.

Every community requires the services of citizen leaders, those highly competent persons who, though they may not be in the Hall of Fame category, can direct and manage affairs—the type of person who is voted "Citizen of the Year." Mr. G is this sort of person. He graduated from a small Midwestern college with honors, then went on for graduate study in law and political science. In his profession, he works for an international organization, but he reserves considerable time for outside affairs. Mr. G was recently elected president of the local school board on which he had already served for some years; he is a trustee of his church and is on the board of the town park commission, the college scholarship committee, and the regional orchestra society. He and his wife enjoy social gatherings; they especially like to entertain foreign students in their home. Such people strengthen the life of their communities.

Investment in Talent

The most valuable investment any society can make is the development of the full potential of its human resources. The extent and quality of education a promising youth receives play a major role in shaping his future career as a specialized, productive worker, a high-level professional, a director and decision maker, a social leader. Only through the most thorough intellectual training will capable young people be able to develop their unique abilities. Education, especially the influence of great teachers, opens up wider vistas of opportunity for them.

In modern times most eminent persons have come from a cultural background that provided superior training, either formal or informal, as a foundation for their life work. Thomas Jefferson gave credit to his college professors at William and Mary for fixing the destinies of his life. Dr. John Dewey was a Vermont village boy of ordinary background, but he happened to grow up in a town that contained the state university, and his love of philosophical reflection dated from his teen-age contacts with university professors.

Educational opportunities may compensate for limited background. The story is told of a humble Scotsman who, when strolling near his home one day, rescued a boy mired in a bog. The boy proved to be a nobleman's son. The Scotsman refused the nobleman's offer of a gratuity, but requested instead that his own son be given a good education. This boy eventually graduated from medical school and followed a career of scientific research. He was Alexander Fleming, the discoverer of penicillin.

The American musician, Marian Anderson, had a fine voice but little encouragement until the principal of the high school she attended discovered her gifts and provided for her musical education. Women who have attained eminence or leadership in their professions are as much the product of superior educational opportunities as men, perhaps even more so, because the home and the typical out-of-school environment of women provide almost no stimulus to notable productivity.

The great shortage of trained manpower in the less-developed countries can be attributed, in part, to the shortage of professional leadership, which in turn is due to lack of widespread educational opportunities for talented youth. Early leaders in many under-developed countries, however, began their careers with little formal education.

The many success stories of self-made people who have risen to eminence without benefit of a lengthy formal education suggest that there is more than one route to distinctive achievement. Count Leo Tolstoi observed a hundred years ago that many of Russia's leaders lacked formal education. An outstanding agriculturist in his community had never been to school. A general commanding a cavalry brigade was unable to read or write.

Benjamin Franklin, a universal genius, had only a year at the Boston Latin Grammar School before he started out to seek his fortune. Abraham Lincoln had very little formal education, a few months of school in the winter, frequently interrupted. Michael Faraday, the distinguished British scientist, was largely self-taught up to the time that he became a laboratory assistant to Sir Humphry Davy at the Royal Institution of Great Britain. Thomas A. Edison, though an inveterate reader, had relatively little formal schooling.

Thus it is possible both to underestimate and to overestimate the values of lengthy and formal education for certain individuals. Throughout history, however, rulers and leaders have sought to provide an extended and enriched education for promising youths, and their efforts have brought about periods of remarkable advancement.

Differentiated Education for Gifted Youth

Within the past few years national leaders in education and public affairs have urged that a systematic search be made in every community to locate all young people of exceptional promise and then to provide differentiated educational programs to develop their full potential.

The noted French psychologist, Dr. Alfred Binet, promulgated the idea that the varied capacities and talents of individual children should be the starting point of all educational endeavor, the determiner of educational goals and programs. This viewpoint was also expressed by Dr. Ernst Meumann, an early German psychologist, by Dr. John Dewey, Dr. Edward L. Thorndike, and more recent American educators.

Too often children and youths have been herded together and taught en masse as though all could benefit equally from the same books and lessons. The mentally retarded have fared better than others—their defects so obviously unfit them for mass instruction—but the gifted and talented have received little special attention.

A persistent question is whether we are producing enough specialists with capacities for intellectual leadership. The experts say No; the resources of trained talent today are not great enough to meet the demand in many areas vital to our society.

Where are the young people with leadership potential and creative talents? How early can the unusual abilities of these young people be identified? What sorts of training are best calculated to develop latent gifts and talents? These are questions that urgently require answers.

There are in the United States today at least 2 million children with unusual minds and potential for social leadership, for creativity in the arts, and for scientific productivity. Many times this number growing up in all parts of the world constitute an enormous resource of future talent. When highly talented young people remain undiscovered and untrained, their potential is wasted, and society suffers an irreparable loss.

Educational Opportunity and the Emergence of Talent

Can the number of productive and creative people be increased through the extension of superior facilities to all youths who are able to profit from advanced intellectual training? Will universal popular systems of education tend to increase the number of highly talented young people? The answer to these questions is unquestionably in the affirmative, even though formal education is not the sole determiner of unusual achievement.

Around the world the advantage is clearly with the nations that provide a broad basis of state-supported education. The most progressive nations are those with a tradition of common schooling for all, undifferentiated according to class, and with advanced schooling provided free of expense according to students' individual aptitudes. Dr. John Dewey expressed the view that in a democracy a social return must be demanded from all and opportunities for the development of distinctive capacities must be accorded to all.

Providing the best possible education for everyone guarantees that diverse aptitudes and individual competencies will be fostered. In a democratic society that ensures wide social benefits, more capable young people are apt to come to the fore and receive the education their talents merit. Invention and ingenuity have freer outlet in countries that provide education for all, free of artificial class distinctions.

UNEVENNESS IN EDUCATIONAL OPPORTUNITY

Fortunately for children of unusual promise in the United States, education statutes require that all continue in school until at least age sixteen. By that time capable students are well along in secondary school and their exceptional abilities have probably been discovered. Beyond the secondary school there are unrivaled opportunities for higher education throughout the country.

In backward countries there is little guarantee that a bright child of exceptional ability will receive any formal education; at most, he may be required to attend school for a few years in the lower grades. The result is that many promising children, especially the girls, are never able to develop their gifts and talents. Where state-supported systems of education have not yet been established, parents are often too poor to pay even the small fees demanded for instruction. In the less-developed countries the most acute problem begins at the secondary school level. In the most backward countries it begins as early as the primary grades.

The plight of bright boys of poor parents living in semibackward countries who are denied the advantages of continued education is illustrated in the following case. The personnel of the international headquarters of a large company in a metropolis of the Near East agreed that the little bus boy of the local coffee shop was decidedly above average. There was nothing unusual in his appearance except the expression in his dark-brown eyes. After carrying hundreds of tea glasses and coffee cups to the offices for long hours, he would come in at five o'clock and, closing his eyes tightly, figure out, without ever faltering or making a mistake, how many teas or coffees every individual had ordered. A person would protest in order to mislead him, but then the boy would proceed to give the details, "You had two cups of coffee in the morning, then a glass of tea in the other office in the afternoon, and you ordered a cup of coffee for a visitor," without having made any written record whatsoever. Within fourteen months after he started to work at the shop this boy could speak some Italian, French, Greek, and English in addition to his native tongue. The signal division of the organization with its teletype machines particularly fascinated the boy, and he had soon learned to manipulate these complicated machines.

At the time of these observations, the boy, who was then twelve years old, had received only four years of primary instruction in the public schools. The people who observed his interest in electronics tried to encourage him to undertake some study in this field, if not as a professional at least as a skilled worker. When they got in touch with his father, who was a bus conductor and the head of a large family, they were told apologetically but firmly that the boy was a great help to the family with the generous tips he was getting. If he started to learn a new trade, he would not only fail to earn any money for several years but be a burden to his family. This ended all chances for the unusually promising boy to receive further education and to rise above a lifetime of menial work.

While we in the United States of America lament the loss of talent when capable youths fail to attend college, in the less-developed countries scarcely half of the children attend school long enough to become literate and not more than 4 or 5 per cent complete secondary school. There may be no school, or a capable student may be barred from attending for arbitrary reasons. It seems ironical that in many parts of the world today a bright boy from a family in humble circumstances is denied education, while a mediocre student from a wealthy home is forced to struggle with advanced academic studies.

BROADENING THE BASE OF COMMON SCHOOLING

One way to ensure an increasing number of science specialists and other professional experts is to broaden the base of popular,

tuition-free education. More expert mathematicians might be produced through well-designed courses for all children beginning with
the first grade, with full provisions at the higher levels for specialized and advanced technical training.

Only when the maximum number of young people attend
school continuously can the full range of their gifts and specialized
talents be discovered and developed. The spread of universal common school education has brought a larger proportion of young
people to the gates of the university, fully qualified to pursue
advanced studies. The most insistent problem in higher education
today is to extend facilities to a larger proportion of the most-
capable youth.

The less-developed countries look to the educated nations for
trained personnel and scholarly leadership in all areas of endeavor.
The next decade will see a larger number of our gifted, well-
educated young people going abroad to work on projects of international significance.

ADVANTAGES OF HIGHER EDUCATION FOR CAPABLE YOUTHS

In college young people come into contact with trained minds
in every area of specialization. Here their sights are raised, their
intellectual horizons are broadened, they discover abilities within
themselves they had not recognized previously, their ambitions are
challenged, and new career opportunities are discovered. Ordinarily, the college graduate is of far more value to society than
the young person of equal promise who lacks the intellectual
training that college years provide.

Today, college-educated people head three-fourths of all the
biggest industrial enterprises in the United States. They dominate
the learned professions, increasingly fill the top government posts,
and control the political life of the country. During the present
century they have furnished three-fourths of our national leaders.

The new generation of college-trained people sets the pace
for a higher standard of living, better housing, more and larger
recreation areas, more hospitals and social service agencies, better
schools and child-care services in their communities. If what they
need and want does not exist, they proceed to invent or produce
it.

Dr. James McKeen Cattell, in a study of the backgrounds
of great men of science, found that the opportunity to study with
a great university professor was a prominent common factor in
the early careers of these men. The more mentally stimulating

the educational environment, the more likely the person is to experience enlargement of thought and enrichment of ideas.

Over thirty years ago Dr. William S. Learned, after a thorough study of American higher education, recommended the establishment of programs for gifted youths in public-supported institutions of higher learning. He had in mind a more advanced and thorough type of intellectual training for the top fifth or top fourth of the student body.

Is Differential Provision for the Gifted Compatible with Democratic Principles?

A perplexing question that is raised in conjunction with that of educating the gifted is concern for the principle of equality in education. At the suggestion of searching out talented young people and providing selective educational opportunities, many people bristle up for fear that democratic ideals will be compromised. They argue that the aim of education in a democracy is to raise the whole mass of the people, not to give special assistance to a favored few. All young people have gifts and talents of a sort. Why single out certain ones for special attention? A privileged class might arise, an elite of the intellectually gifted and talented. Do we want to encourage the emergence of an aristocracy of brains, arrogant individuals who would remain aloof from the common people and tend to subordinate them?

The answer to these questions and objections has been given by thoughtful people many times over. Focusing attention on the gifted and talented does not deny the basic principle that every individual is valuable on his own account and of equal concern to society. Democratic education requires equality of opportunity, not identity of schooling (or other opportunity) for all. Everyone has the right to the type of educational opportunity that will develop all his potential. Plato affirmed that in a just society each individual is trained to do the things for which his talents particularly fit him.

Gardner (*Excellence*, 1961) agrees that virtually everyone has some characteristics of excellence in a personal sense, but that the types of excellence are not comparable; in fact, they are decidedly uneven. As Wolfle has expressed it, we can justify the identification and differential education of the most competent youth because their gifts have most to contribute (1960). Any youth of ordinary capacities can be expected to make his own contribution as a citizen and as a worker, but the quality of his contribution is different from that of intellectual leaders. There should be no conflict between recognizing a diversity of abilities and talents and recognizing the peculiar value of certain types of excellence.

Even those who subscribe to the idea that everyone has gifts and talents, large or small, must recognize that our society does not appraise all types of human performance equally. Some talents and accomplishments are rated higher than others as shown by financial rewards or other recognition of significant social and cultural contributions.

The facts about variability in human potential, in aptitude for learning, as well as in goals and interests, suggest the futility of demanding that all be forced through the same training program. Uniformity would leave the majority of children and youths improperly and inadequately educated. Since schooling in America is open to all, concern is necessarily shown for individual variability among students and the adjustment of instruction to the entire range of scholastic ability. It is in our best interest to abandon the fiction that recognizing and fostering exceptional gifts and talents is undemocratic or that special school programs for talented youth are unfair to those not included. Inequalities in talents and learning capacities, whatever their cause, pose intricate problems relating to education and career planning.

A question that persistently bothers educational planners as well as others is: Has the science of individual psychology progressed far enough to determine the extent to which individual talents are developed by educational experiences and to predict success in school and life career? The reluctance to make distinctions between children in educational treatment may be due primarily to fear that a mistake might be made in estimating a child's abilities and predicting his success in learning. Experimentation and research continue, of course, but the present state of our understanding of the gifted provides a firm basis for programs now being advanced.

The weight of evidence suggests the wisdom of taking steps to increase the supply of trained manpower. A first step is to search out the bright and talented in every school and community, so that the most capable boys and girls may have full access to suitable educational opportunities. They should be sought out not later than the early teens so that they and their parents can receive appropriate guidance.

Both boys and girls should be encouraged and assisted to continue their studies in college and in professional or advanced training. Their progress through school should be accelerated where this is practical so that they can make an earlier start on their careers. The community should develop plans for compensating the parents for the temporary loss of the student's financial assistance where need exists.

Programs should be planned for various levels of ability and all kinds of talent, not only for students who are gifted in science and mathematics or music and art.

Later chapters will consider at length the nature of exceptional ability and special talent, and describe educational programs for the gifted at all levels of schooling.

Full Utilization of Woman Talent

Although eminent men grow up in gifted families along with their bright sisters, few women, even those who earn advanced degrees, equal men in creative achievement and social leadership. The reason, it is said, is biological. Women can scarcely be expected to produce great ideas in the arts and sciences and at the same time give undiminished attention to their families.

The Victorians believed that women were weaker than men both physically and mentally. A hundred years ago, however, Matthew Vassar declared his belief that woman had received from her Creator the same intellectual constitution as man, and therefore had the same right as man to intellectual culture and development. The medieval view that women are of lower status than men and less worthy of education still prevails in the less-enlightened countries around the world.

Economists recognize that one means of increasing our resources of trained manpower is to make fuller utilization of womanpower. Although modern industrialization has not altered woman's biological role, it has vastly changed our mode of living, giving women more education and more freedom from household cares, elevating them more nearly to the position of men in civic, business, and social life.

The United States, the countries of Northern Europe, the Soviet Union, and some countries of Southeast Asia have led the way in advancing the status of women and in making more effective use of trained womanpower. Today the alert, well-educated young woman stands in direct contrast to her Victorian sisters and women in less-developed countries. She has been emancipated from the tyranny of ignorance and superstition as well as from a life of physical drudgery. Formerly, an educated woman had little professional outlet for her talents save as a teacher, librarian, or nurse. Today, the fields that professionally trained women enter are practically identical with those of men, including engineering, geology, chemistry, and scientific research in all areas.

The growing number of young women in the United States who enter the professions and occupy posts of local and national leadership is due primarily to expansion of opportunities for higher education in the present century. In the Soviet Union promising women scholars are given every incentive to continue their studies and to take up professional careers. In some countries, women scientists actually outnumber the men. Half of the doctors in the Philippines and Thailand are women, compared with 6 per cent in the United States.

Studies have shown that although few college women in the early years of homemaking carry on full-time outside careers, women today tend to work outside the home on an average of twenty-five years, chiefly after their children are grown. Women also play a prominent part in civic affairs and local government. Better-educated women establish cultured homes which make for community stability and a better life for children.

Steps now being taken to ensure fuller utilization of highly talented young women include advising promising high school girls to take courses that prepare for college and professional careers, assisting the best qualified to work toward advanced degrees, overcoming prejudices toward women in business and the professions, calling the attention of qualified women to job opportunities, providing for refresher training of college women who wish to go on with careers after their children are grown. More information concerning current talent search programs is given in Chapter Sixteen.

References

Gardner, John W.: *Excellence: Can We Be Equal and Excellent Too?* Harper & Row, Publishers, Incorporated, New York, 1961.

Henry, David (ed.): *Education and Manpower,* National Manpower Council, Columbia University, New York, 1960.

McClelland, David C., and others: *Talent and Society: New Perspectives in the Identification of Talent,* D. Van Nostrand Company, Inc., Princeton, N.J., 1958.

Wolfle, Dael: *Diversity of Talent,* Walter Van Dyke Bingham Memorial Lecture, Columbia University, New York, May, 1960.

Chapter Two

ON THE
TRAIL
OF THE
GIFTED

When people discuss the "gifted," they may have in mind quite different types: the precocious kindergartner, the boy scientist or inventor, the talented child musician, a straight-A student in high school, the mechanical genius, the popular social leader, and many others. The common denominator in these different connotations of "gifted" is remarkable performance for a person of that age or unusual ability of a high order.

The gifted, then, must be relatively uncommon individuals of unusual attainments. One man in agriculture is a typical farmer, another becomes a leader in his community in agricultural advancement, but the rare gifted person is the Luther Burbank of his day who develops an improved vegetable or strain of wheat. The ordinary person concentrates on immediate sensory impressions and centers his attention on existing facts, but the unusual person makes a leap from present impressions to some new, original interpretation of the situation. The average person is more comfortable going along accepting things as they are; the unusual person pioneers a new social reform, writes a play or biography, or works out a new mathematical theorem. The average person finds it more congenial to sit down and read about a new idea or invention than to work out the original plan and write up a report of it.

Who Is the Gifted Child?

Through the years various terms have been used to describe unusual children: child prodigy, precocious, gifted, highly talented, creative. In educational literature before 1900, the term "bright" applied to school learners, often in contrast to slow, dull, or stupid. "School brightness" was also commonly used; bright children were sometimes referred to as "mentally exceptional," "children of superior intelligence," and "abnormally intelligent children."

Although the term "gifted child" did not come into popular use until 1917 or 1918, it was used in several reports as early as 1912 and 1913. Dr. Guy M. Whipple used "supernormal children" in his early writing, and Dr. Leta S. Hollingworth used "prodigious child." Dr. Lewis M. Terman used "bright" to designate mentally superior children; later on he used "genius" to describe the most highly endowed intellectually. Today the term "genius" is generally reserved for adults who have made original contributions of unusual distinction. Bright children have also been referred to as "mentally advanced" or "mentally accelerated."

The German adjective, *begabten*, referring to intellectually gifted children as well as to the talented, began appearing in foreign literature about 1905. Dr. William Stern spoke of the *Gutbegabten*, the *Mittelbegabten*, and the *Schwachbegabten*, referring to schoolchildren of high, average, and low mentality. The French expression *bien doué* applied to gifted children has come into use within recent years. In the Soviet Union these children are appropriately referred to as "eagles."

Although "talented" has always had a somewhat different meaning from "gifted," the former term is now used in referring to all sorts of gifted individuals, not only those with specialized talents.

A widely accepted view is that giftedness in young people is primarily a matter of special talents; the gifted child is one who is "specially talented" in music or art, in dancing or dramatics, or in a particular school performance, as in the case of a child who can do complex mathematics computations in his head. In other words, the gifted child is a star performer who can put on a good show. The quiet, studious boy or girl who is absorbed in his books or the solitary young student interested in maps or literary composition is less likely to be thought of as "gifted." The idea that the gifted are those with special talents is more acceptable to most people than the concept of giftedness as all-around intellectual superiority because it seems more fair to the youngsters. The "special talent" category would include more of those who are "not so bright."

What is an acceptable definition of giftedness and talent? The chief problem in arriving at a definition is to draw up a set of basic criteria to distinguish the gifted from others. Is the gifted child one who is accelerated in all-around mental development as shown by reasoning ability, rapidity in learning, precocious linguistic development? Or is he the child who stands out from his classmates in school achievement, particularly in academic studies? Does the term refer to those who exhibit special talents that are shown at an early age, for example, art, music, and dancing? Is the gifted child one who shows a creative bent?

Attempts to arrive at a definition of giftedness lead back to the whole question of mental organization: whether intellectual qualities are specific or general and the extent of correlation between mental traits. An understanding of brightness, giftedness, and unusual mental qualities also requires some understanding of the nature of human variability in developmental traits.

The Concept of Trait Variability

Among the great contributions of modern psychology is the establishment of basic principles concerning variations in human capacities, principles which have far-reaching implications for education. Variability characterizes all qualities—biological, physical, mental, and personal. Research data have confirmed the common observation that every human being is a unique individual not only in physical appearance but in all his characteristic behavior traits.

The studies of Sir Francis Galton on human trait variability proved that human capacities could be objectively studied and that abilities were distributed in the population in an orderly, predictable manner. Children of similar age and background develop at different rates both mentally and physically. Nothing is more apparent to teachers than differences in the capacity to learn. "Stringing out" in achievement is evident from the first lessons and continues all the way through school.

In a cross-sectional class in a large city school a wide array of aptitudes will be found. Here is an exceptionally alert boy who is planning to attend a highly selective high school, planning perhaps to become a scientist or a college professor. Alongside him is a boy of the same age who has difficulty with academic subjects and rates low in verbal intelligence. In between there are many children of average ability and modest attainment in schoolwork. Children in an intermediate-grade classroom may vary as much as six to eight years in mental age and almost as widely in educational achievement. Within a typical class of ten- and eleven-year-olds are a few who rate at a mental level of twelve, fourteen, or even fifteen years, along with a scattering of slow and mentally retarded pupils.

Children themselves recognize differences in brightness. In grade 3, Tommy hesitated about marking the item "Brightest one in the class" in a questionnaire, but his neighbor said, "Go ahead and mark it, Tommy. You know you're the smartest."

THE DISTRIBUTION CURVE

The fact that traits in a large unselected population measured with standard devices conform to the familiar bell-shaped frequency curve first described by the mathematician Gauss is well known to college students. The percentage distribution of cases in the normal probability curve will be found in the Anastasi book on psychological testing (1961) and other standard texts. Meumann described the mental capacities of the child population for any given age as a continuous gradation ranging from very low to extremely high, with those of average ability and achievement massed around the middle of the frequency distribution (1907).

Measures of traits and achievements of schoolchildren and data for army recruits and other wide-range populations have conformed to the normal frequency curve of distribution. A survey of the entire eleven-year-old population in Scotland some years ago yielded a normal symmetrical distribution curve for mental ability (*The Intelligence of Scottish Children,* 1933). Mental test data for French school children, discussed below, also conformed to this general principle. Flanagan's recent surveys of high school students in America have revealed the tremendous variation between students of the same age in aptitudes and school achievement (1962).

The French Survey of 1944   In 1944 the Institut National d'Études Démographiques of Paris made a nationwide survey under the direction of Dr. G. Heuyer, Dr. Henri Piéron, and others (1950). This is the most comprehensive survey ever undertaken: it fully reported the intellectual abilities of schoolchildren in the age range six to fourteen. The Gille Mosaic Test of intelligence, devised by René Gille, was used.

The total number of children tested was 95,237, about half of them boys and half girls, representative of the juvenile population of France, enrolled in both public and private schools. Figure 1 shows the typical curves of distribution for nine-year-olds on the Gille Mosaic Test. Similar curves were found for the other age levels. This survey indicated that mental ability as measured by the Gille Mosaic Test was a continuous variable ranging from extremely low to high scores, with the larger portion of the popula-

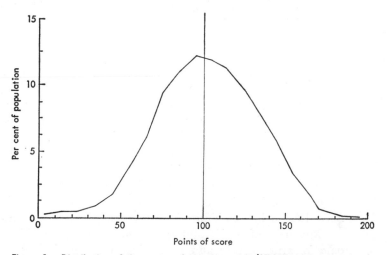

Figure 1. Distribution of the scores of nine-year-olds (17,607 children ranging in age from 103 to 114 months) on the Gille Mosaic Test. (Based on data from G. Heuyer, H. Piéron, and others, *Le niveau intellectuel des enfants d'âge scolaire,* vol. 1, Presses Universitaires de France, Paris, 1950. Used by kind permission of the Presses Universitaires de France.)

tion ranged in the middle. Note that as deviations from the central tendency become wider, the number of individuals rapidly decreases.

What produces the wide variations? The best answer is that a unique combination of fairly constant and interrelated hereditary, constitutional, environmental, and social factors determines where each individual will be on the curve.

A Pyramid of Abilities   Thorndike regarded the altitude of the mental tasks and skills an individual was able to learn or perform—whether high, low, or average—as the most important criterion of intellectual capacity (1927). The structure of the tasks and skills and the ability they require is something like a pyramid. At the base are the simplest tasks demanding the least intelligence, those depending primarily upon physical coordination and mechanical repetition. Everyone who has the opportunity to learn or observe is able to perform them. There are relatively few people who lack sufficient intelligence to "pound sand in a rathole," as the expression goes. Higher up on the pyramid are more complex tasks, still well within the capacities of the average person, but making greater demands on thinking and judgment, such as routine jobs and household activities. Near the apex of the pyramid are the mental tasks and processes demanding the highest level of reasoning, generalization, conceptualization, theoretical problem solving, and original thinking exemplified in the reflections of the mathematician and scientist, the electrical engineer, the composer of music and great literature.

Applying the pyramid principle to the school population would mean that in a cross section of ten-year-olds practically all would be able to perform the basic tasks and acquire the simple learning required at the base of the pyramid, but near the top of the pyramid would be the few ten-year-olds who compose remarkable poetry or can compute algebraic problems in their heads.

Dr. Thorndike's measurement of mental superiority by the altitude of the tasks the child is able to perform is the basic principle on which scaled tests of intelligence are constructed. Although Dr. Thorndike considered altitude of performance the most significant factor in appraising intelligence, he also recognized the significance of breadth or variety in the tasks a person could perform.

For an excellent brief account of the psychology of individual differences, see the article by Symonds (1959). A fuller discussion of individual differences will be found in Anastasi, *Differential Psychology* (1958).

Mental Giftedness as Deviation from the Norm of the Distribution

Mental superiority was defined by Dr. Ernst Meumann and later psychologists as deviation from the midpoint of the distribution in a plus direction, the counterpart of mental retardation. According to this definition, the gifted are those individuals with superior mental aptitudes ranging in the upper reaches of the distribution curve, at the opposite extreme from the backward and mentally retarded. This viewpoint regarded the distribution of intellectual capacity as a continuum and gradually supplanted the older view that a wide gulf separated the mentally deficient from the generality of the population and that child prodigies were freaks rather than the most exceptional deviates.

Various Definitions of Giftedness

The earliest definition of gifted children based on objective criteria was stated in terms of rank or IQ on an intelligence test, most frequently the Binet scale. The gifted child was one whose level of cognitive development was advanced beyond children of comparable age as measured by standard tests.

Virtually all the experimental work on the gifted has been based on this simple formulation. The advantage of the definition is that it is based on clearly defined, measurable criteria; however, its limitations have been pointed out repeatedly and are discussed below in detail.

The IQ obtained from an intelligence test pertains only to mental functioning and conceptual thinking and sets up too narrow a definition of the gifted. Psychologists tell us that only a few of the fifty or more dimensions of the mind are measured by present-day standard intelligence tests. The capacities of remarkable children can scarcely be encompassed by the "high IQ" definition.

The trend today is toward broader definitions of giftedness, based on multidimensional traits and more comprehensive, elastic concepts of unusual ability and superior capacities; not only the "good student" type but also the creative and original are included.

At a conference on the gifted held at Teachers College, Columbia University, in 1940 the following statement was made:

"We may define the intellectually gifted child as one who excels markedly in ability to think, reason, judge, invent or create."

Witty defined the gifted child as "one whose performance is consistently remarkable in any potentially valuable area" (1940). This definition is by implication broader than a definition based on limited test scores, and it includes the talented as well as the intellectually superior. It also points to the social value of superior qualities. The National Council for the Gifted, Inc., includes in its definition of the gifted those young people of high intelligence who, in addition, possess the potential for unusual performance in any creative socially useful area of human concern.

Sumption and Luecking write of giftedness in intellectual terms: "The gifted are defined as those who possess a superior nervous system characterized by the potential to perform tasks requiring a comparatively high degree of intellectual abstraction or creative imagination" (1960).

DeHaan and Havighurst prefer to include all sorts of outstanding talents and aptitudes in their definition: "Gifted children are those individuals from kindergarten through high school age who show unusual promise in some socially useful area and whose talents might be stimulated" (1957). They contend that there are many bright and talented children within the top 20 per cent of the juvenile population—for example, a boy who is clever at working with electricity or a girl who shows talent for interior decorating or dress design. These authorities would distinguish between:

High-level scholastic or academic aptitude, the mentally exceptional
Scientific aptitude
Superior talent in arts and crafts, creative writing
Social leadership
Mechanical ingenuity

In developing criteria for the identification of the gifted, the Portland, Oregon, authorities cooperated with the Quincy, Illinois, Youth Development Commission. In Portland, the definition of the gifted was broadened to include creative talent in art, music, dramatics, the dance, social leadership, and mechanical ability (1959). At the Hunter College Elementary School, Dr. Gerald Lesser and his associates have been exploring early signs of giftedness of various types—linguistic, numerical, scientific, artistic, and social leadership.

Such efforts are in line with Dr. Thurstone's analysis of primary mental abilities. As a basis for educational planning there are several different types of gifted children to be considered:

Those who show all-around mental acceleration for their years, the high-IQ youngsters

Those who excel in some specialized area such as mathematics or studies depending heavily upon verbal fluency

Those with special talents in the arts or with mechanical ingenuity, and so on

Those with exceptional originality and inventiveness, the creative type

The definition would then exclude the young tennis star, the twelve-year-old champion figure skater, as well as the child whose ability is limited to physical prowess and manual dexterity.

Children who rate high on IQ tests have been referred to as the "verbally gifted." There is a question whether thinking and problem solving at a high level are ever possible apart from reasoning in verbal terms, whether the task is inventing a new lawn mower or solving intricate mathematical problems.

Perhaps "gifted" should be used only in conjunction with a modifying or restricting term such as: intellectually gifted, musically gifted, mechanically gifted, and so on. Without such modifiers, the term is too broad and vague to be of much use in educational planning.

"Bright," "superior," "remarkably intelligent," "talented" are all subjective terms which can mean whatever we wish them to mean because they do not refer to any standard or agreed-upon criteria of excellence. "Academically talented" and "rapid learner" may be more useful for educational guidance.

Basic Criteria for Distinguishing the Gifted

In summary, the following criteria serve to distinguish the gifted child or youth:

1. He is superior to his age-mates in traits other than those capacities that are purely physical, physiological, or dependent primarily on muscular development.

2. He possesses the intellectual powers and qualities essential for success with advanced education and training in general or in his specialty.

3. His superior developmental maturation is reasonably consistent from the early years of life to maturity.

4. His unusual abilities may be general or specialized, his superior traits single or multiple.

5. The traits and abilities in which he shows superiority are those that predict unusual achievement or productivity in areas of high social value.

We might generalize by saying that the gifted child or young person is one whose development and behavior—apart from sheer physical superiority—consistently demonstrate unusual traits, capacities, and achievements for his age.

Although some may prefer a different interpretation of giftedness, with more emphasis on specialized talents or nonintellectual tasks, we have, in any event, moved in the direction of a broader definition and at the same time reached agreement on certain criteria.

Different types of giftedness are not mutually exclusive. Some individuals show high correlation in all the traits making up their profiles; others tend to be highly specialized in ability and performance.

Whether there is such a thing as superior "global intellectual ability" comparable to general mental retardation depends upon the correlation of exceptional mental and behavior traits. Evidence on the existence of such ability will be presented in Chapter Four.

Interest in creativity and what is termed "deviant productive behavior" has been growing rapidly, and in time research may prove that creativity is another criterion to be included in a broad definition. For more information on this topic see Chapter Fifteen.

The remainder of the chapter is devoted to three aspects of unusual ability: developmental acceleration, educability for academic work, and nonacademic or special talent.

Developmental Acceleration

According to the criterion of developmental acceleration, a gifted child is one who up to age seven or eight passes more quickly than the average through typical stages in mental development, particularly in such traits as perception, spatial orientation, psychomotor control, language, verbal behavior, and memory, and from then on continues to outdistance others of his age in practical judgment, abstract reasoning, thinking, practical problem solving, memory for facts, creativity, and other mental traits.

The accelerated child's performance on mental tasks resembles that of an older child—for example, a nine-year-old with a mental age of eleven (IQ 122) or twelve years (IQ 133). A high IQ signifies that in the areas sampled by the test, vocabulary, memory, reasoning, presumably adding up to "general intelligence," the child is ahead of his age group.

Acceleration may be shown not only by the individual's response to intelligence test items but also in his school achievement, his demeanor, his conversation, and so on. Popular expressions for this concept are "old for his years" or "old head on young shoulders."

One bothersome question is whether the gifted child's superior mental age indicates that he resembles the maturity level of older children or whether he is merely a plus variant in his own age group. When a ten-year-old earns a mental age of twelve, does he closely resemble a twelve-year-old mentally, or is he just a ten-year-old who is mentally exceptional? The same question is raised regarding the mentally retarded. Another problem is that the final IQ represents the average of several different mental-age levels; the typical bright child, as all the others, tends to "scatter" in his age-level responses rather than to rate uniformly high on all test items.

STATISTICAL DEFINITIONS

Statistical definitions of mental giftedness stated in terms of the percentage of individuals who range above average on standard intelligence and achievement tests derive from the frequency curve of distribution of abilities referred to above. According to this criterion, a mentally gifted child is one who deviates to a substantial degree in a plus direction from the average of his age group.

This definition implies some agreed-upon lower threshold or "cutoff" score. But where should the cutoff point be in terms of IQ or percentile rank? At the top 2 or 3 per cent, the top decile, the upper 15 per cent, the upper quartile (or 25 per cent) of the population? Here there is wide diversity of opinion. The figures stated commonly range from 1 per cent up to 15 or 20 per cent. Dr. Lewis M. Terman, Dr. Leta S. Hollingworth, and other workers in the early period preferred to designate as gifted only those children in the top centile of the distribution curve, those with an IQ of 130 or higher on the 1916 Stanford Revision of the Binet-Simon Scale. The 1940 conference on the gifted held at Teachers College, Columbia University, was in agreement with this statistical criterion.

DeHaan and Havighurst defined the most extremely gifted or the "first order" of giftedness as $\frac{1}{10}$ per cent or 1 in 1,000

of the general population (1961). Conant mentioned 2 or 3 per
cent of high school students as constituting the extremely gifted
or academically talented (1959). Laycock mentioned 5 per cent
of the child and youth population as mentally gifted (1957). Authorities of the Long Beach, California, public schools decided
that 5 per cent of the elementary school children and 3 per cent
of high school students belonged in the gifted category.

If consideration is given to the ultimate value of the social
contributions to be expected of this group, 5 per cent, say the
experts, seems a reasonable figure, because this group has the capacity for the abstract reasoning and mental conceptualization that
is needed in preparing for professional occupations and productive
careers.

Some authorities prefer to think in terms of the "top quarter"
of the school population as gifted. At Public School 208 in Brooklyn
where for a period of years there have been gifted classes for
elementary school children, out of a total enrollment of 1,118
children in 1960–1961, 240 children, or 21 per cent of the population, were considered gifted; but the school as a whole ranks high,
so one would expect to find here a larger percentage of gifted
children than in a typical urban elementary school. At Hunter
College Elementary School where the minimum IQ is 130, the
entire population rates in the top 3 per cent of the general population, the great majority of the pupils in the top 2 per cent.

In a population of 5,000 sixth-grade pupils in Albuquerque,
New Mexico, who were given the California Test of Mental Maturity there were 215, or about 4 per cent, who measured 130
IQ or more, 125 boys and 90 girls. Heuyer, Piéron, and their
associates, who conducted the survey of French schoolchildren,
regarded 10 per cent as the figure marking off the gifted. This
figure strikes a medium between the top 2 or 3 per cent—designated
as the ultrasuperior or supergifted—and the generous estimate of
20 to 25 per cent.

Since about 15 per cent of the population (15.86) is located
at or above one standard deviation (one sigma) of the distribution
curve, corresponding to the 84th percentile, the academically talented have been nicknamed the "super sigma" group. A bulletin
of the New York State Education Department (*Bright Kids—We
Need Them,* 1960) estimates that about 14 per cent of the children
in the state may be considered "bright" by this criterion.

How much difference is there in the functioning of an extremely bright child, a bright child, and a near-bright child? The

differences between the first and third categories are unquestionably very wide, but between the second and third categories there is less distinction. The "near-bright" and the average are even less easily distinguished.

IQ EQUIVALENTS OF STATISTICAL DEVIATIONS

The percentages cited above can be converted into IQ ratings. Terman's 905 standardization cases for the 1916 Stanford-Binet scale were distributed according to IQ levels as shown in Table 1. Those with IQs of 130 and above constitute 2.2 per cent of the total population.

Dr. Frederick B. Davis derived Table 2 from the data for the 1937 revision of the Stanford-Binet scale (1940).

Table 1 Terman's Standardization Cases for 1916 Stanford-Binet Scale

IQ	Percentage of total population
56–65	0.3
66–75	2.3
76–85	8.6
86–95	20.1
96–105	33.9
106–115	23.1
116–125	9.0
126–135	2.3
136–145	0.5

Source: Lewis M. Terman, *The Measurement of Intelligence,* Houghton Mifflin Company, Boston, 1916.

Table 2 Classification of Data from 1937 Revision of Stanford-Binet Scale

Classification	IQ	Per cent
Brilliant	139 and over	0.9
Very superior	128–138	3.7
Superior	117–127	11.0
Bright	106–116	21.3
Average	95–105	26.2

Source: Frederick B. Davis, The Interpretation of I.Q.'s Derived from the 1937 Revision of the Stanford-Binet Scales, *Journal of Applied Psychology,* 24:595–604, 1940.

Dr. Percival M. Symonds prepared a table of frequency equivalents for the distribution of IQs given by Terman and Merrill in their manual for administering the 1937 revision of the Stanford-Binet scale; the data, shown in Table 3, indicate the frequency with which children of a given (or higher) IQ above the mean of 100 will be found in the general child population. According to Table 3, by interpolation, those who test at 125 IQ and over are in the top 5 or 6 per cent of the child population, regardless of age. About 6 children in 1,000 of the general elementary school population rate at 140 IQ and above.

The Psychological Corporation, New York City, has distributed a chart showing the equivalence of standard scores, centiles, and IQs according to the theoretical frequency curve.

VARIATIONS IN IQ STANDARDS FOR SELECTING THE GIFTED

Schools and research workers have adopted varying IQ standards as the lower limit or cutoff point for admission of children to gifted child programs. For example, the standard for admission to the first Opportunity Classes for the gifted in Los Angeles in 1916–1918 was a Stanford-Binet IQ rating of 125. For entrance to the Major Work classes of Cleveland, the minimum IQ requirement standard was

Table 3 IQ Frequencies in General Child Population

IQ at or above	Frequency
160	1 in 10,000
156	2 in 10,000
152	6 in 10,000
148	1 in 1,000
144	3 in 1,000
140	6 in 1,000
136	1 in 100
132	2 in 100
128	4 in 100
124	7 in 100
120	11 in 100
116	16 in 100
112	23 in 100
108	31 in 100
104	40 in 100
100	50 in 100

also set at 125. Dr. Terman's experimental group of 1,000 children was limited to those testing 140 IQ or higher, with a few exceptions. Both Dr. Coy and Dr. Hollingworth restricted their experimental classes for the gifted to children testing 130 IQ and over. This was also the figure adopted in 1941 for admission to the Hunter College Elementary School, as noted above, and the minimum score for subjects in a number of New York City experiments.[1]

The fact that bright children tested a few points higher, as a rule, on the 1937 revision of the Stanford-Binet test than on the 1916 revision must be taken into account in comparing earlier and later designations of "gifted" based on IQ derived from the later revision.

An IQ of not less than 110 is the figure most commonly stated as the minimum for classification of a child as "bright." In Great Britain, according to one authority, an IQ of 110 to 115 distinguishes the mentally gifted child from the average, whereas at the university level, an IQ of 120 to 125 marks the dividing line (Wall, 1960).

A school servicing a small community may set up programs for the gifted beginning at 110 IQ, but, in general, in large cities in the United States and Canada, an IQ of 125 to 130 is most commonly required.

LIMITATIONS OF A STATISTICAL DEFINITION

A number of objections can be offered to the interpretation of juvenile giftedness in statistical terms. The fact that there is no agreement on the cutoff point in test scores and other ratings suggests that the definitions are wholly arbitrary. The number to be included in special programs will always depend upon how many can be recruited or accommodated.

The validity of the statistical definition rests entirely upon the validity and reliability of the measuring devices used and the adequacy of their standardization. The finality of selection on a rigid statistical basis has proved to be questionable in many cases. Although most gifted children are included, others are missed for whom the school should be making special provision. It happens, too, that a child of ordinary talents may be included because of "an error of measurement."

---

[1] In the instances noted above, IQ on a standard test was not the *only* criterion for admission to special classes. Other factors that are considered in selective admissions to programs for gifted children will be discussed in Chapter Eight.

SUPERIORITY IN AN ABSOLUTE AND IN A RELATIVE SENSE

Superior learning ability may be judged in either an absolute or a relative sense. A child with an IQ of 108 might be a failure in a highly selective school with an average IQ of 122 but a success, even a leader, in a school or class that averages 95 IQ.

A teacher in a large urban school drawing its enrollment largely from a low-income population identified a number of children as "well above average" in one of the better sections of the fourth grade. The following year, the teacher transferred to a school in a superior community, and found that the average children in a typical class were fully up to the bright class in her former school, and those in a bright class far outstripped the children she had formerly considered "most gifted." Another kind of relative "superiority" may be seen in the child who is gifted or exceptional in some single trait or talent with reference to his own profile but who in this same trait, ability, or skill rates below the average for his age group.

Educability for Academic Schoolwork

Educators are concerned about formulating a definition of the gifted that furnishes a guide for educational purposes, a definition that serves to distinguish the children who have potential for intellectual problem solving, those who can profit most from advanced academic schooling.

Educability refers to capacity for learning as the result of school experience. Some young people obviously have more "academic talent" than others. Educability in terms of school learning can be predicted from the study of a student's abilities and his past school accomplishments. According to this criterion, the gifted person is one who is more capable of profiting from advanced levels of education and difficult studies than others of similar age.

A definition of giftedness in terms of educability could be stated as follows: The gifted person is one with demonstrated potential for high-level educational attainments in the arts and sciences. At the secondary school level this definition would include those boys and girls who have the ability to study effectively and rewardingly advanced mathematics, foreign languages, and "tough" courses in chemistry and physics (Conant, 1959).

Though scholastic aptitude may be considered but one special type of ability, it is the essential ingredient for academic schoolwork. Some young people obviously have more "academic talent" than others. A distinguishing mark of this type of gifted person is receptivity to instruction and devotion to serious scholarship.

Schooling itself becomes a sorting-out process. Every child in the public school system in this country is exposed to a standard series of educational experiences in the school curriculum as he advances from grade to grade from the first year until well into high school. From one grade level to the next, school tasks become intellectually more demanding, abstract elements become more predominant, a higher level or altitude of reasoning and thinking is required. The ability to use intelligence in problem solving, to generalize, to make inferences and deductions from rules and principles becomes more essential than before. Children of average ability encounter more and more difficulty in meeting these new hurdles.

The ability to solve problems with fractions in arithmetic is a good illustration of a dividing line or discriminative indicator of those pupils who have more abstract reasoning ability and those who have less. In fact, tests in fractions have been used for selecting nursing school candidates, not only because nurses need to work with fractions but because this test has proved to be discriminative of higher-level learning abilities.

Only a small proportion of entering high school students easily complete advanced academic courses as they move on through school. A teacher of a freshman class in algebra discovers at once the intellectual differences that separate the students in both academic aptitude and mathematical talent. In Proctor's early study of high school achievement and scholastic aptitude (1923), algebra was responsible for more academic failure than any other subject. The grade of A in algebra can be considered a sign of exceptional academic aptitude. In a recent British study general intelligence was the best single predictive factor in success in mathematics. Difficulty in learning a foreign language (as an academic study) or mathematics appears to increase as allover scholastic aptitude diminishes.

How far up the ladder a student can move in academic achievement without experiencing difficulty or outright failure and dropout depends increasingly upon intellectual aptitudes, though aptitude alone will not guarantee success. The minimum IQ for continued success in academic high school programs is somewhere around 110 IQ, the top 30 per cent of the school population. To achieve on a higher level requires an IQ of not less than 115, the cutoff point for the top 15 per cent of the population.

The secondary school population in a typical institution rates above the typical lower school in the proportion of high-IQ children because of the dropout of slower learners. That a diligent youth with a modest IQ can by close application and additional tutoring go through high school and be accepted for college only proves that there are other factors than mental ability that contribute to academic success.

A teacher-training instructor was asked to demonstrate a lesson in social studies to a class of slow learners. He found this an interesting experience but difficult, because the children could not think so clearly as brighter children nor see so quickly the points the instructor made. The students lacked the necessary store of basic facts though they had come through the same standard elementary school training as brighter children. An experienced French teacher contends that there is no comparison between a class of selected bright students and ordinary children in foreign language classes.

The principle applies at the college and university level as well as in high school. To earn a degree in arts or science requires several years of stiff academic courses. Few students below the top 5 per cent in educability can hope to succeed in the academic work of the typical college, even though the institution is not highly selective with respect to entering classes. Those in the lower range of educability more frequently tend to drop out earlier. Even a university program in hotel management or forestry, primarily technical subjects, requires basic training in academic studies: the sciences, economics, sociology, psychology, not to mention foreign languages and English.

STUDIES OF EDUCABILITY

IQ levels on reliable tests show substantial correlation with levels of educability throughout the child and youth population.

In an early study of California high school students by Proctor, 87 per cent of those who did not complete their high school course were in the lower half of the ability distribution: median IQ 94 (1923). The school achievement of these students was also below average: median school mark C—. The median IQ of those who graduated from high school but did not go on to college was 107 (group test); their median school mark was B—. The median IQ of the high school graduates who continued their studies was 121 for boys and 119 for girls. The average school mark for these boys was B, for the girls B+. There was also a direct relationship between social status, as measured by parents' occupation, and tendency to continue schooling.

Wolfle derived the following table of educational expectancies for fourteen-year-olds in the United States at mid-century (1954); the scores were made on the Army General Classification Test, 100 representing the average:

SCORE 80
60 chances in 100 of entering high school

23 chances of graduating

SCORE 100
85 chances in 100 of entering high school

60 chances of graduating

18 chances of entering college

8 chances of graduating

SCORE 120
98 chances in 100 of entering high school

90 chances of graduating

37 chances of entering college

25 chances of graduating[2]

IMPLICATIONS OF THE EDUCABILITY CRITERION

According to the educability criterion, a student who shows talent in arts and crafts, in using tools, even in learning to speak foreign languages would not qualify as gifted unless he also showed high potential for mastering the theoretical aspects of these studies. A youth with aptitude in manual construction and keen interest in mechanics says he wants to become a bridge builder. How far will he go with this ambition? Assuming that he continues to be strongly motivated, the answer depends largely upon his educability for an engineer's career. Although one youth has the capacities and aptitudes that will carry him far in scientific studies of an academic and abstract character, another impresses everyone as being more practical minded; that is, he learns better through direct experience and responds to the type of training needed for practical and manipulative skills.

A highly educable person does not always become highly educated; a person lacking high academic potential cannot profit from advanced high school and college studies. Our future scientists

[2] Dael Wolfle, *America's Resources of Specialized Talent*, Harper & Row, Publishers, Incorporated, New York, 1954. Used by permission of the author and publisher.

and other professionals will continue to come only from those identified as highly educable, because the required background studies are primarily academic and abstract.

Research is needed on problems of educability. Questions are: Who is educable for what? What proportion of students at any school level are educable for the next level? What are the intellectual demands of the different subject areas? What sort of diversification in curriculum offerings is needed to accommodate students of high academic attitude?

Teachers inquire whether a child may properly be considered gifted if he stands out in one area of school achievement, for example, in mathematics or creative writing, but is not a high-ranking student in general. The answer can only be given in terms of other information about the individual. Is he a highly intelligent individual in his general approach to problems quite apart from school studies? What are the reasons for discrepancies between the area of special excellence and other school studies? Is the child capable of better work in other studies but neglectful of them because of lack of interest or motivation? Is too much attention centered on school marks as evidence of superiority and not enough on other evidences of interest and achievement, especially in the case of adolescent boys? The problem of underachievement is considered at length in Chapter Fourteen.

Special Talent

The term "talent" is most commonly applied to exceptional performance in such nonacademic areas as sports, dramatics, dancing, music, arts and crafts, mechanical skills, and social leadership. By definition, a talented child or youth stands out from his age-mates in some special activity. A youth with a flair for costume design or club leadership may be regarded as talented though he seems quite ordinary otherwise. A nine-year-old girl may show unusual dramatic talent, interest, and enthusiasm in putting on plays, though her schoolwork is nothing out of the ordinary. Such a child is undeniably talented. A twenty-year-old Dutch girl won the world's figure-skating championship with a dazzling performance. She must certainly be considered highly talented.

Mechanical trades and vocations offer other illustrations of talented performance: skill in machine-shop design, draftsmanship, automobile repair work, welding, plumbing, and the whole array of crafts.

Talent for social leadership means that the individual has outstanding social qualities and that his qualities are admired and accepted by the group.

As someone has said, "Talent is an intelligence of its own"; this suggests that special talents do not depend upon the same kind of intelligence as academic achievement and intellectual accomplishments. The juvenile jazz orchestra member is considered talented though he may be a mediocre student and intellectually undistinguished. High motivation, capacity for self-discipline, and drive to succeed may in themselves be considered forms of talent.

Dr. William Stern distinguished between talent as a special gift on the one hand and general high intelligence on the other in contrast to "untalented" and "unintelligent" (1928). Dr. Samuel Laycock, a Canadian psychologist, also draws a distinction between the terms "gifted" and "talented." He applies the first of these terms to persons with a high degree of general intellectual capacity, the latter to specific achievements that are largely the result of special training (1957).

The dictionary makes no clear distinction between the two. *Webster's Collegiate Dictionary* says: Gift—"special talent or aptitude"; Talent—"the abilities, powers, and gifts bestowed upon a man; natural endowments; . . . Pre-eminent aptitude, superior intelligence and ability, as for business, or artistic pursuits; . . . a natural capacity or gift; as, musical *talent*."

The term "talent," strictly speaking, refers to specific performance rather than to potential. The level of talent even within the same field varies from the individual who has some show of talent to the one who consistently wins prizes and finally to the virtuoso of highest distinction.

ARTISTIC TALENT IN CHILDHOOD

Since most children find satisfaction in art instruction and since art materials are everywhere to be had at little expense, it is difficult to detect consistently high talent in art before the junior high school years. The exception is the child who shows high creativity. Although most young children are interested in color and design, the child who is talented in art shows more maturity for his years, longer sustained interest, and more persistence in experimenting with art forms on his own initiative.

A five-year-old has recently come into possession of plasticine in different colors. He reproduces any object he sees, using originality in choice of colors and background settings for the objects he molds. He has set up on a piece of cardboard a miniature garden with a scene of flowers, benches, fountain, domestic animals, birds, and ornaments. He is certainly talented for his age in this medium. Another child, a five-year-old ornithologist, has painted her own original bird book. She must be considered both talented and precocious.

F is an eight-year-old boy who already shows special artistic talent. He has not been given an intelligence test, but his teachers consider him a remarkable boy. His special talent is paper tearing. At the age of two when he manifested unusual interest in animals, his aunt showed him how to make the different animals by tearing figures from sheets of paper. His outstanding traits in following this hobby are his close observation of animals and other figures before he makes them and the great care he exercises during the work. Even when he was very small his mother noted that when he saw a horse, he might stand looking at it for two hours at a stretch. One summer at the farm he spent so much time watching the chickens and going about the hen house that the rooster pecked him. When he tears paper he does not go by trial and error, but works cautiously, thinking all the while. He has identified the "hard part" of each animal—for example, the bony protecting eyebrows of the crocodile—and prefers to do this part first. Then he finds that the rest follows easily. Horses are his specialty and he has studied them thoroughly. He also seems to understand the anatomy of the pig (a heavy creature on four short legs), the alligator, sheep, and others. In doing a cutout of a sheep jumping over a hedge, his comment was, "He left his back legs." The notable quality of this boy's work is that he has not fallen into the stereotypes children of his age usually show in representing figures. Instead, he has continued to make steady progress in cutting out figures which show movement and vitality, as well as in composition and color when he mounts the figures to make a picture. Will this boy become a true artist, perhaps a remarkable one? All we can say at this stage is that he is exceptionally talented.

Both William Blake and the artist Whistler showed early talent in drawing and received early instruction so that they continued to develop their art talents as they matured. At the age of five, Edwin Landseer, the celebrated English animal painter, made drawings of dogs and other animals that were recognized as exceptional. At the age of eight he made a remarkable sketch of a ferocious wolf which he said was "from his own ideas." In later years he became a virtuoso in animal drawings noted for their wonder-producing vitality.

TALENTS AND GENERAL INTELLIGENCE

Specialized talents vary in their intellectual demands. One type of talent may require more abstract verbal intelligence than another. The ping-pong expert, the skilled teletype operator, the tightrope walker, even an unusually skilled taxi driver may be considered talented, though their jobs may not require a college education or an IQ of 115 and over. Thus, an individual of modest intellectual equipment may have a highly developed special talent.

An eleven-year-old boy in the fifth grade in a public school, a year older than his classmates, is a slow learner who is not interested in academic studies, but his teacher has discovered that this boy shows exceptional ability in metalwork. He made a copper tray with an original design for his mother's birthday, and says he plans to go into metalwork as a vocation. There is no doubt that work in crafts may be a promising field for this boy, but he may not have the capacity to go beyond a level of technical competence in this field. Some children are both specially talented and gifted academically.

The fullest development of talent in some areas unquestionably requires intelligence of a high order: reasoning, thinking and inventing, planning, ability to learn from reading, and social sensitivity. Children who develop consistently in special talents leading to promising careers tend to be the brighter learners, the more intelligent children on the whole.

At the 1940 conference on the intellectually gifted held at Teachers College, the following statement was made concerning the nature of special talents and high intellectual capacity:

> Technical or executive skill in music and graphic art seems to be relatively separate from general intelligence. The one may appear with or without the other. As in the average group, a certain proportion of the intellectually gifted are found to possess in addition specialized talents. However, it does appear that a high degree of intellect is necessary for great creative work in these fields. Specialized musical (and perhaps artistic) talent is likely to make itself manifest at an early age.

Dr. Terman's gifted subjects were more talented in art than children with average IQs. In the survey of French schoolchildren conducted by Heuyer, Piéron and others, the authors stated: "The artistic disposition shows most frequently in the brightest subjects, those students in the first and second percentiles, and decreases regularly by centiles" (1954).

Dr. Joseph E. Maddy, President of the Interloehen Arts Academy in Michigan, discovered that talented youths were also bright students as demonstrated by their ability to learn at a rapid pace. These students, he found, have both the energy and interest span essential to the concentration required for the development of high talent.

A high school art teacher commented that his most talented students had the highest IQ of all those enrolled. An elementary school teacher who has had wide experience with talented children observed that the bright children did the best art work. The relationship between exceptional talent and superior intelligence shows up more clearly in older students than in the younger ones.

Sometimes early talent in art or music or mechanical ingenuity is the first sign that a child is highly gifted all-around. The special talent may ultimately disappear as other interests come to the fore or as intellectual training opens new vistas for professional work. The boy musician may decide to become a doctor and have no trouble realizing his goal. Music then becomes his recreation.

Talent in a child who is also intellectually gifted seems to turn out differently from talent in children with ordinary mentality. At an early age M showed exceptional talent at the piano and interest in studying the instrument. The school she attended in New York City gave her released time in the afternoon to study at the Juilliard School of Music. This child's IQ on the Binet rated in the high 160s. She has since become a concert star and an expert piano teacher. A boy of seven attending the same school was considered exceptionally talented in violin playing. He had an excellent teacher who gave him every encouragement to develop his talent. Although the child practiced faithfully, the teacher began to express disappointment in the results and finally when the child was ten refused to have him as a pupil. His IQ on the Binet test was slightly over 100, and his schoolwork was never above average. Unfortunately, the boy was blamed for failure to profit from the instruction given him.

Exceptional literary work in student years is largely done by bright and intellectual young people. Mr. A, a New York City junior high school teacher, says that he obtains the best work and the most creative ideas from the higher-IQ students. He finds that wealth of creative talent and intellectual ability go together.

Children with special talent are chosen to participate in the All-City Orchestra of Evanston, Illinois, each year. Of the small number chosen for this honor from the sixth grade, 19 per cent, a substantial proportion, are intellectually gifted judging from results of standard tests.

In the representative and performing arts—music, the graphic arts, dramatics—one should distinguish between those young people whose potential does not extend beyond high executive skill and those with higher-level creative talent, those who are far advanced in an understanding of art principles and the academic phases of art study. For children of mediocre general aptitude but specialized talents, continued expert training may lead to a trade or vocational skill.

Superior intellectual qualities combined with excellent instruction enable the talented person to develop his gift to a remarkable degree. A distinguished musician who has had extensive training in the best schools or with leading masters of musical art is certain to be a highly educated person, well-informed, alert, and interested in various aspects of life that affect him as a person and as a professional musician. He could scarcely have reached the heights without developing social sensitivity and acquiring cultural breadth.

The High School of Performing Arts in New York City enrolls an array of "fabulous kids," in the words of a former principal. Every one of the students is highly talented or he would not be there. The IQ of the student body averages around 121. Teachers report a high correlation between special talent in dramatic art and music and general intellectual ability. Many applicants are not accepted because of low scholarship or limited intelligence ratings. Officials say the school can scarcely afford to invest in children who cannot benefit from the academic program provided for them along with specialized training in the arts.

In dancing, too high an IQ is something of a disadvantage, because intellectual geniuses generally refuse to be regimented. Here the problem is one of physical endurance. The talented dancer who carries both the specialty and a program of academic work tends to become overloaded.

ORIGINS OF TALENT

Formerly, talent was thought to be God-given, a divine trust, unquestionably inherited; but this viewpoint has been modified because of the frequent disappearance of early talent and the facility with which talent can be developed in almost any area when the learner receives intensive training and works consistently to improve his performance.

A newspaper headline stating that it takes ten years and $40,000 to make a good figure skater suggests that special talent in sports depends primarily on specialized training and practice from an early age. Talent declines rapidly when direct training slackens. This may explain why an infant prodigy may turn out to be an ordinary performer.

One should distinguish genuine talent, which is the result of native ability, early spontaneous interest, and good training, from pseudotalent, which is a mere projection of parents' wishful thinking.

Some effort has been made through the "backward look" technique to study the careers of successful artists to try to determine the origin of their talent. One such study was made of actors (Lane, 1960). What kind of children were they, and what experiences shaped their careers? Through such studies we may eventually obtain more insight into the origin and training of special talent.

References

Anastasi, Anne: *Differential Psychology: Individual and Group Differences in Behavior*, 3d ed., The Macmillan Company, New York, 1958.

Anastasi, Anne: *Psychological Testing*, 2d ed., The Macmillan Company, New York, 1961.

Bright Kids—We Need Them, Bulletin of the New York State Education Department, Board of Regents, Albany, N.Y., 1960.

Conant, James B.: *The American High School Today*, McGraw-Hill Book Company, New York, 1959.

Davis, Frederick B.: The Interpretation of I.Q.'s Derived from the 1937 Revision of the Stanford-Binet Scales, *Journal of Applied Psychology*, 24:595–604, 1940.

DeHaan, Robert F., and Robert J. Havighurst: *Educating Gifted Children*, rev. ed., The University of Chicago Press, Chicago, 1961.

Flanagan, John C., and staff: *Characteristics of High School Youth*, vol. 2 in a 3-vol. series, Houghton Mifflin Company, Boston, 1962.

The Gifted in Portland: A Report of Five Years of Experience in Developing a Program for Children of Exceptional Endowment, Portland, Ore., Public Schools, 1959.

Heuyer, G., H. Piéron, and others: *Le niveau intellectuel des enfants d'âge scolaire*, vol. 1, 1950; vol. 2, 1954, Presses Universitaires de France, Paris.

The Intelligence of Scottish Children: A National Survey of an Age Group, Scottish Council for Research in Education, publication no. 35, University of London Press, Ltd., London, 1933.

Lane, Yoti: *The Psychology of the Actor,* The John Day Company, Inc., New York, 1960.

Laycock, Samuel R.: *Gifted Children: A Handbook for the Classroom Teacher,* The Copp-Clark Publishing Company, Toronto, Canada, 1957.

Meumann, Ernst: *Vorlesungen zur Einfuhrüng in die Experimentelle Pädagogik,* vol. 2, W. Engelmann, Leipzig, 1907.

The Nature of Giftedness: Some Issues and Problems Raised by the Conference on Education for the Gifted, *Teachers College Record,* 42:8–12, 1941.

Norman, Ralph D., Betty P. Clark, and David W. Bessemer: Age, Sex, I.Q. and Achievement Patterns in Achieving and Nonachieving Gifted Children, *Exceptional Children,* 29:116–123, 1962.

Proctor, William M.: *Psychological Tests and Guidance of High School Pupils,* Public School Publishing Company, Bloomington, Ill., 1923.

Seashore, Carl E.: Musical Inheritance, *Scientific Monthly,* 50:351–356, 1940.

Social Implications of the Scottish Mental Survey, Scottish Council for Research in Education, publication no. 35, University of London Press, Ltd., London, 1953.

Stern, William: *Die Intelligenz der Kindern und Jugendlichen und die Methoden Ihrer Untersuchung,* Johann Ambrosius Borth, Leipzig, 1928.

Sumption, Merle R., and Evelyn M. Luecking: *Education of the Gifted,* The Ronald Press Company, New York, 1960.

Symonds, Percival M.: What Education Has to Learn from Psychology, VIII: Individual Differences, *Teachers College Record,* 61:86–98, 1959. Reprinted in *What Education Has to Learn from Psychology,* chap. 8: Individual Differences, Bureau of Publications, Teachers College, Columbia University, New York, 1963.

Terman, Lewis M.: *The Measurement of Intelligence,* Houghton Mifflin Company, Boston, 1916.

Terman, Lewis M., and Maud Merrill: *Measuring Intelligence,* Houghton Mifflin Company, Boston, 1937.

Thorndike, Edward L.: *The Measurement of Intelligence,* Bureau of Publications, Teachers College, Columbia University, New York, 1927, pp. 33–36.

Thorndike, Robert L.: Problems in Identification, Description, and Development, of the Gifted, *Teachers College Record,* 42:402–406, 1941.

Wall, W. D.: Highly Intelligent Children: The Psychology of the Gifted, *Educational Research,* 2:101–110, 1960.

Witty, Paul A.: Some Considerations in the Education of Gifted Children, *Educational Administration and Supervision,* 26:512–521, 1940.

Wolfle, Dael: *America's Resources of Specialized Talent,* Harper & Row, Publishers, Incorporated, New York, 1954.

Chapter Three

THE STORY
OF THE
GIFTED

Interest in gifted children and their education goes back to ancient times. Plato made proposals for selecting potentially gifted children in early childhood, testing them, and training them for leadership. In the *Republic* he proposed that the children of laborers or artisans be elevated to the rank of magistrates or warriors if they came into the world with a "vein of gold or silver." This view was in direct contrast to the concept that leadership was the prerogative of hereditary social classes. In the ideal state the most competent intellectually would become the aristocracy. To detect future leaders, Plato suggested that promising juveniles be watched from their youth upward and made to perform actions in which they are most likely to forget or to be deceived, "and he who remembers and is not deceived is to be selected, and he who fails in the trial is to be rejected."

Attention to the Gifted throughout History

Among the earliest records of talented children is the story of Daniel and three other remarkable boys recounted in the Bible. These boys were among the most promising children taken captive in Jerusalem and sent to Babylon at the command of King Nebuchadnezzar to be educated at the palace. The idea was said to stem from Plato. The story of the Child Jesus in the temple at Jerusalem as recounted by the physician Luke portrays a twelve-year-old boy of exceptional maturity. He tarried behind, and when his parents returned, they found him in the temple "sitting in the midst of the doctors both hearing them and asking them questions. And all that heard him were astonished at his understanding and answers" (King James Bible).

The Emperor Charlemagne is said to have urged the education at state expense of promising children among the common people.

In the fifteenth century a great Turkish sultan, Mehmet the Conqueror, founded a palace school in Constantinople for the tribute children of the conquered Christian nations. Emissaries were sent throughout the empire to select the fairest, strongest, and most intelligent boys without regard to social class. The palace school of the tribute children became one of the most notable educational experiments of history. The objective of the training was to create "fine minds in hardened bodies." The school featured intensive education and a doctrine of service to the government. A robe of honor was bestowed on a boy for exceptional work. The employment of the most able graduates of this school in high government posts was said to explain the amazing rise to power of the Turkish Empire during the fifteenth and sixteenth centuries.

Comenius, writing in the seventeenth century, made frequent reference to students of unusual aptitude for learning and advocated financial aid for bright students from poor homes.

Early in the eighteenth century Thomas Jefferson proposed a bill for the "Diffusion of Education" providing for the education of promising youths at public expense at a university where they would receive the training in the arts and sciences that leadership in the New World required.

In his "Notes on the State of Virginia" Jefferson proposed the strengthening of our natural aristocracy of virtues and talents by the establishment of rigorously selective tests in the grammar schools through which "the best geniuses will be raked from the rubbish annually" and sent to William and Mary College at public expense. By this means, said Jefferson, "We hope to avail the State of those talents which nature has sown as liberally among the poor as the rich, but which perish without use, if not sought for and cultivated." In these proposals Jefferson, too, was influenced by the ideas of Plato.

Interest in gifted and talented youth was for some time concentrated on the child prodigy, but the rise of scientific interest in the latter part of the nineteenth century shifted attention in new directions. The testing movement focused attention on mental variability, provided objective means for the appraisal of giftedness and superior achievements, and stimulated interest in special education. The movement has concentrated on the discovery and conservation of talent, reappraisal of the meaning of giftedness and talent, recognition of creativity, the development of new techniques for the appraisal of talent, and various curriculum adjustments for gifted students.

Although the United States has taken the lead in conducting research and exploring possibilities in educating the gifted, other nations have not been far behind. The identification and training of talented youth have worldwide significance in view of the rapid emergence of new nations and the sudden need for a larger supply of trained leadership.

THE ERA OF THE CHILD PRODIGY

The child prodigy, the *Wunderkind*, the child with exceptional talents, prodigious powers, and remarkable achievements, has always attracted public attention. Around 1550, in the later years of the reign of the sultan Suleiman the Magnificent, there was a remarkably gifted boy poet, Baki, the son of a muezzin, who, it was said, could write words that pulsed with life. Many people could not believe that a child wrote the poems because they expressed things a boy would hardly know. The same surprise was expressed at the precocious work of Edgar Allan Poe.

Parents' reports of child prodigies appeared in the literature from 1800 onward. The number of these reports increased as interest in the new field of child psychology grew. In American psychological literature, the term "genius" was applied to children as early as 1897, and an American "arithmetical prodigy" was reported in 1900. Dr. Leta S. Hollingworth wrote a comprehensive account of early child prodigies, both American and others, in 1926.

Karl Witte, the German child prodigy who was ready for college when most children are in the primary grades, received the degree of doctor of philosophy from the University of Leipzig at the age of fourteen. Christian Heinrich Heiniken, the "miracle baby" from Lübeck, was tutored by his parents from the age of ten months. At age four, shortly before he died, he read German, knew French, and had memorized fifteen hundred sayings in Latin. Lord Kelvin, who was tutored by his father, entered college at the age of ten and won distinction at the University of Glasgow before he was twelve.

These children usually cropped up in the families of educator parents who were competent drill masters and most apt to write up accounts of their precocious children.

Dr. Alfred Binet, the French psychologist, took great interest in child prodigies and people of remarkable talent: phenomenal mathematicians, lightning calculators, chess players, juvenile writers, and others. He devoted considerable time to the exploration of their capacities, and his early writings reflected the prevailing notion that the highly talented were freaks of nature, abnormal individuals in a class by themselves.

The talents of the child wonders were no less remarkable than the unchildlike way in which they were treated. At the age of five John Howard Payne was taken to Boston by his father to work on a juvenile magazine. Such children were kept long hours at difficult abstract tasks, trundled about in all seasons for display at public exhibitions and late evening parties, fondled by members of the aristocracy, who had the privilege of commanding performances. One reads of the child Mozart, the pet of Austrian royalty, enjoying the rhythmic sounds of long, rough stagecoach rides and attending banquets where he "sang for his supper." Such children were required to perform feats far beyond their strength, and of course only the strongest among them could survive.

A change in the popular conceptions of gifted children has come about in large part as a result of general enlightenment and improvement in child-rearing practices in the present century. Precocious children are less often treated like miniature adults today, but can live and play and grow up as normal human beings.

THE SCIENTIFIC ERA IN THE STUDY OF THE GIFTED

The scientific era in the study of giftedness and talent begins with the work of the English scientist, Sir Francis Galton, who was himself a child prodigy. Galton's contribution in the latter years of the nineteenth century was the objective observation and measurement of human traits and the invention of statistical methods for summarizing data. He devised the use of percentiles for indicating an individual's rank in the population and demonstrated that trait variability conformed to the normal distribution curve. Galton appears to have been the first scientific writer to furnish a comprehensive description of the traits of gifted children and to furnish information about the origins and development of genius.

The scientific study of the gifted in America began in the early years of the present century with the publication of Terman's *Genius and Stupidity* (1906). In France, at the turn of the century, Dr. Alfred Binet introduced to pyschology several important new concepts: first, evidence for the existence of general aptitude for learning; second, the educational significance of differences in mental functioning in children; and third, the possibility of measuring general learning ability with a series of developmental tests built on the principle of sampling an array of intellectual performance.

In Germany, from 1910 onward, psychologists and educators showed increasing interest in intellectually gifted children and their school careers. An article by Stern published in the *Journal of Educational Psychology* in 1911 aroused much interest in the subject.

The movement was carried forward in succeeding years in England by Dr. Cyril Burt, psychologist of the Education Officer's Department of the London County Council, with improved techniques for measuring the abilities and achievements of schoolchildren. Some remarkable children attracted Dr. Burt's attention, along with the dull and backward.

The new era was characterized by psychological studies of the nature of giftedness and talent, the use of standardized mental tests for the identification of the gifted, and experimentation with special educational programs and curricular adjustments for gifted children.

Early Studies of the Gifted

Before the advent of mental testing, bright children were identified primarily on the basis of their performance in and out of school.

With the publication in 1916 of Dr. Terman's Stanford Revision of the Binet-Simon Scale, a tool was available for the more accurate identification of children designated as gifted in terms of mental acceleration. This scale could be used for comparative ratings and was relatively free of the subjective biases of an observer. The subsequent wide use of the Binet scale in America demonstrated the variability of learning aptitudes among schoolchildren in the general population and paved the way for research studies of high aptitude and talent.

In working with the Binet scales, Dr. William Stern took the next logical step beyond Binet when he computed the ratio of mental age to actual age and obtained a quotient of intellectual status, the IQ. Binet had not taken this step, possibly because he concentrated on testing mentally retarded children, many of whom were nearing their teens and hence reaching their limit in mental development. A statement of mental age was sufficient for general classification purposes.

In his early studies Dr. Terman was impressed with the significance of word definitions on vocabulary tests as measures of intelligence and mental maturity. By 1915, Dr. Guy M. Whipple had become interested in the use of mental tests in identifying and assessing bright children in contrast to slow learners. Through these efforts the notion that bright children were queer little freaks gave way to the fuller understanding that they were part of the general child population, but unusually mature for their age.

More attention was paid at first to children who rated extremely high; then studies were broadened to include the bright, the near-bright, and all types of talented children.

In 1921, Dr. Terman, with financial assistance from the Commonwealth Fund, inaugurated a long series of investigations concerning gifted children (1926). His plan was to locate 1,000 mentally superior boys and girls in California, and to follow up their school and life careers. This first follow-up report was published in 1927–1928, a second in 1945, and a third in 1955. Dr. Terman's study was a fact-finding enterprise, with no intention of devising improved methods of educational treatment for gifted children.

Considerable attention was also given to the study of individual children through the clinical approach. Dr. Harvey Zorbaugh established a clinic for the study of the gifted at New York University in 1926. He said that he first became interested in gifted children in 1924 when he encountered a juvenile safecracker in a Chicago gang. This boy with an IQ of 168 spent his spare time reading up on explosives in the public library.

Beginning in 1924–1925, Dr. Paul Witty collaborated with Dr. Harvey C. Lehman in a study of the play behavior of gifted children. In the following years Dr. Witty conducted extensive research relating to the traits, interests, and achievements of the gifted as compared with average children (1930). He called attention to cases of gifted Negro children and others of limited background.

The scientific study of the gifted continued intermittently through the 1930s with little change in approach.

Educational Experiments with the Gifted

With the advent of graded elementary schools a century ago, many plans were proposed for grouping children according to ability. William T. Harris, Superintendent of the St. Louis Public Schools, recognizing the problem of differences in aptitude for school progress, introduced a plan of flexible promotions in 1867 to permit bright children to advance through the graded system at a stepped-up pace. The plan provided for promotion every five weeks throughout the school year when such promotion was justified in terms of achievement.

The Cambridge plan some years later provided two parallel sections in each class. Rapid learners covered six years' work, grades 4 to 9, in four years. Other successful multiple-track plans were operated in Elizabeth, New Jersey, Santa Barbara, California, Batavia, New York, and Detroit, Michigan. A comprehensive summary of experiments in ability grouping in the United States is given by Sumption and Luecking (1960).

Plans for individualized instruction were also proposed to offset the limitations of uniform curricula and standard texts for each grade. Superintendent Frederic Burk's self-instruction plan for individualized teaching, which originated in San Francisco in 1912, became the forerunner of other plans of individualized instruction, particularly Dr. Carleton Washburne's program in the Winnetka, Illinois, schools a few years later.

SPECIAL CLASSES FOR BRIGHT LEARNERS

Although rapid-advancement classes for bright pupils were started in New York City and Worcester, Massachusetts, as early as 1900, by 1911 only five cities in the country were known to operate such classes. Between 1916 and 1925 however, special classes for the gifted were organized all over the country in cities both large and small. The *Twenty-third Yearbook of the National Society for the Study of Education* (Whipple, 1924) gave a full account of these developments. Special classes for gifted children were somewhat analogous to systems of classes for the mentally retarded, which had rapidly multiplied with the introduction of Binet testing in the schools.

At first, the grouping of children for these classes was done entirely on the basis of school accomplishment and teacher judgment. Later on, with the development of testing programs, scores on intelligence and achievement tests were combined with other ratings in sectioning pupils for ability groups. Dr. Henrietta Race reported favorably on a class for superior children established in Cincinnati, Ohio, in 1916 (1918).

DR. WHIPPLE'S EXPERIMENTS WITH SPECIAL CLASSES

Dr. Guy M. Whipple urged that instead of parading the prodigious child, one should work out for him a systematic, comprehensive school and home program. In the summer of 1917 Dr. Whipple received from the General Education Board through its representative, Dr. Abraham Flexner, an appropriation to be expended for experiments with gifted children during the ensuing academic year. His effort and that of his associates were originally directed toward answering the question: What mental tests are most valuable in selecting bright pupils from ordinary public school classes for training in special classes for the gifted?

The first class was conducted in the Leal Elementary School in Urbana, Illinois. This appears to have been the first experiment in which matchees for the selected class of gifted children were used as controls. Later on, Dr. Whipple published a report on classes for gifted children established under his direction in collaboration with Dr. T. S. Henry, Dr. H. T. Manuel, and Dr. Genevieve Coy (1919). Dr. Manuel made a special study of children and youth who were talented in drawing. At about this same time Dr. C. E. Seashore of the University of Iowa was at work on his studies of musical aptitudes and the construction of tests for measuring musical talent. Meanwhile, Dr. Henry made an analysis of classroom problems in working with gifted children and published his doctoral thesis on this subject (1920).

The second experiment under Dr. Whipple's supervision was a special class conducted by Dr. Coy in Columbus, Ohio, in 1918. All the pupils in three schools from which the gifted were to be drawn were screened by means of a group intelligence test arranged by Dr. E. L. Thorndike of Teachers College, Columbia University. Teachers were also asked to name the five or six brightest children in each room from which the gifted were to be selected. Thirty-five names were proposed and twenty-six of these children were given the Binet test because of high group test scores. The report pointed out that the selection of bright children on the basis of their teacher's recommendation alone would have resulted in ignoring half of the bright-testing children but that the accuracy of selection was increased slightly by the addition of teacher judgments. When the class selected by Dr. Coy opened in the fall of 1918 it consisted of eighteen children, seventeen of whom had IQs of 117 or higher. These children averaged six months younger than typical children in grades 4 and 5, and their average mental age was on a par with children in the middle of grade 6.

As a result of his experiments and observations, Dr. Whipple recommended that classes for the gifted should be restricted to the top 5 per cent of the child population, those with IQs of 120 and above, with not more than twenty such children in a special class. The next best plan was to include the upper 10 per cent in IQ, those with IQs of 115 and over. As an alternative to a single class for a given grade level, if there was an insufficient number of children, Dr. Whipple recommended making up the class from 15 fifth graders and 15 sixth graders in a school having about 150 children to select from.

OTHER EXPERIMENTS WITH SPECIAL CLASSES

Classes for the gifted in the Los Angeles elementary schools organized early in 1918 were originally called "Opportunity Classes" for bright children. They were referred to as "workshops in which children experience purposefully." The Stanford-Binet test was used along with other criteria for selecting the children for these classes, according to the report of Stedman, who supervised the work (1924). Similar classes were established for bright children in various cities throughout the country. In Rochester, New York, a plan of special classes was adopted, and two classes were set up in 1920. Pupils with IQs of 120 and above were eligible.

One of the most ambitious programs of special classes for gifted children was set up in Cleveland, Ohio, in 1921. The objective of the program, according to its originators, was to find the children of highest intelligence in the elementary schools, separate them so that they would not be impeded by slower learners, and then educate them for leadership by the best methods that could be devised. By 1940 more than 1,200 bright children were enrolled in seventeen Major Work centers (the name given these classes) in Cleveland. For more information about the Cleveland Major Work classes see Chapter Eleven.

In 1922–1923, Dr. Leta S. Hollingworth of Teachers College, Columbia University, working with Mr. Jacob Theobold, the principal of Public School 165 in New York City, assisted by a committee from the school, initiated a project for the study and instruction of gifted children in the elementary school. This project was supported by a three-year grant from the Carnegie Corporation. At this time Dr. Hollingworth also began to offer a course on the study and education of the gifted at Teachers College.

Before concentrating her attention on gifted children, Dr. Hollingworth collected information about special talents and defects in schoolchildren, which was published in a book containing considerable information about the nature of special talents in music and art, mechanical aptitude, and achievement in the school subjects (1923).

In collaboration with Dr. Benjamin Greenberg of the New York City schools, Dr. Hollingworth began a new project in 1935 with two classes of gifted children at an experimental center known as Public School 500. From that time on, classes for gifted children were established in other New York City public schools, and honors classes were provided for exceptionally capable students in the city's high schools.

Miss Phoebe Ebling, principal of Public School 208 in Brooklyn, New York, exerted leadership on behalf of gifted children from 1926 onward by providing special classes with enrichment in foreign languages and other activities for the intellectually superior pupils in her school. Research studies relating to the gifted were also fostered in this school.

In the larger school systems, such as Rochester, New York, and Detroit, Michigan, classes for the gifted were placed under the supervision of the department of special education along with previously established classes for the mentally retarded.

EXPANDING PROGRAMS FOR THE GIFTED

From a rather narrow pattern of special class organizations and curriculum plans, classes and programs for gifted children, in both elementary and high schools, have been organized in dozens of different ways, worked out to fit the particular school and the community in which it is located.

Separate schools enrolling only gifted children have also been set up, but these are rare because they require a high-level population in a limited school transportation area, a condition found chiefly in certain residential areas of the largest cities. The Hunter Elementary School, which served as a demonstration school for Hunter College, New York, was reestablished in 1940 as a school for gifted boys and girls from nursery school through the sixth grade. The Hunter High School for Girls was designated in 1955 as a school for gifted girls. Philadelphia and other cities have experimented with the idea.

Although the Horace Mann School of Teachers College, Columbia University, and later the Lincoln School under the same auspices were never designated as schools for the gifted, as other campus schools at university centers they enrolled a population of which 75 per cent or more of the children rated bright or gifted according to the Stanford-Binet standards. The Townsend Harris High School, formerly operated in connection with the College of the City of New York, enrolled only boys selected for high promise and achievement.

Other efforts to individualize instruction within regular classrooms should be mentioned. Superintendent Frederic Burk's program of individualized instruction was inaugurated in San Francisco in 1912. Dr. Carleton Washburne, an associate of Burk, began a more extensive program of individualized instruction in the schools of Winnetka, Illinois, in 1920. These programs aided the gifted along with the slow learners since the pupils could work on individual assignments independently and proceed through the elementary school program at an accelerated pace. Miss Parkhurst's Dalton plan, originated at the Dalton School, New York, also featured individualized study programs throughout the grades and high school.

COLUMBIA CONFERENCE ON THE GIFTED

In December, 1940, a conference on the education of the gifted was held at Teachers College, Columbia University, commemorating the work of Dr. Leta S. Hollingworth. In addition to general sessions there was a series of seminars on the following topics:

Who Is the Gifted Child?

What Special Problems Are Encountered by the School Administrator in Providing for the Education of the Gifted and How May These Problems Be Solved?

What Is the Place of the Gifted in Modern Life?

Gifted Children: Their Educational Needs

Education of Gifted Pupils in Secondary Schools

How Can We Better Educate Teachers for Work with Gifted Children?

What Are the Physical and Mental Health Problems of the Gifted and How Can They Best Be Met?

Home Guidance of the Gifted Child

How Can We Release the Creative Energies and Develop the Creative Capacities of the Talented Gifted Child?

Research Problems in the Study of Gifted Children

How Do the Intellectually Gifted Evaluate Their Own Educational Experience?

What Provisions Should Be Made for the Education of Gifted Persons at the College Level?

How Should a School Be Organized to Provide for the Most Effective Education of the Gifted?

The findings of the conference were published in the *Teachers College Record* (1941).

Present-day Developments

A new tide of interest in the gifted and talented followed on the close of World War II. After a term of service abroad, Dr. James B. Conant warned audiences in the United States that we were in danger of losing out as a world power unless more concern was shown for the training of all promising youths for professional careers in science and other areas. This was in 1947.

The spectacular launching of the first artificial earth satellite in the Soviet Union ten years later aroused public interest in education to a greater extent than before. Whether we were doing as effective a job in education as the Russians was a persistent question. As a result, there were new developments in all directions, but particularly in connection with the discovery and training of scientific talent.

The earlier studies by Terman and others had focused on children in the age range nine to twelve or fourteen, possibly because of prevailing interest in the Binet test; more recent experiments have centered primarily on young people of high school and college age. The movement has expanded, so that educators everywhere have become sensitized to the needs of the gifted. The upsurge of interest in this special topic in all its ramifications is unparalleled in the entire field of education.

The movement is not only broader and more extensive than in previous years, but better organized and more widely supported by persons of influence both within and outside the teaching profession.

Study of the gifted now includes many different types of unusual children—those with all sorts of special abilities and talents as well as creative tendencies. Increased attention has been given to background factors as determiners of achievement, interests, and ambition; and there have been new experiments with educational programs conducted on a research basis.

Today there is less confidence in a single test score, such as the Binet, and a trend toward "broad-band" methods of identification, that is, the use of a wide array of tests and evaluation techniques.

Research on creativity and "divergent behavior" has been moving forward at a rapid pace within the past decade. Studies have explored the nature of creative talent, measurement of creativity and invention, as well as educational factors that foster creativity and divergent thinking.

Considerable attention has been given to a problem mentioned in Chapter One, the resources of specialized manpower, and the fuller conservation of potential for creativity and leadership. A committee was appointed by the Associated Research Councils to plan and conduct a series of inquiries into the nation's supply of natural scientists, social scientists, humanists, and members of other professions. Results of this report are given in Chapter Sixteen.

Talent search programs are widely supported. The objective of these programs is to identify promising young people with high academic aptitude and special talents who should be encouraged to continue their education beyond secondary school. Details of talent search programs are also given in Chapter Sixteen.

There has been experimentation with curriculum organization for superior students at all educational levels with emphasis on greater breadth and depth in teaching. In some elementary schools attention has shifted from special classes for the gifted to provision for bright pupils within regular classes. Several experiments have combined regular class instruction and special groupings; there has also been experimentation with individualized instruction and afterschool, weekend, and summer programs. Special class programs in the larger cities have expanded and at the same time have been thoroughly appraised. Adapting the program for gifted children to local needs of the schools and community has been given serious attention.

In the December, 1959, issue of the *Review of Educational Research* on the gifted and talented, Fliegler and Bish traced the following developments in this field during the 1950s: research studies concerning the nature and development of the gifted, new educational experiments, the growth of organizations promoting the study and education of the gifted, increased participation of the separate states and the Federal government in the identification and education of gifted and talented youth, improved communication through organizations and publications.

The high schools have made progress in recognizing and providing for the gifted in many directions:

The organization of honors divisions and classes for abler students in high school

Experiments with sectioning according to ability

The provision of advanced college-level courses for mature, competent students

Special attention to the needs of students with aptitude for science and engineering

Increased acceptance of acceleration as an approved means of adjustment in high school

Increased effort to keep all capable young people in high school and to encourage more of them to continue on to college

Experimentation with the use of teaching machines and audio-visual aids in individualizing instruction

An inordinate amount of research effort has been devoted to the study of the "underachiever," the student who fails to come up to his capacity in schoolwork, particularly in the senior high school.

Counseling and guidance programs now devote more attention to gifted students in high school and college.

More concern is shown today about social factors, obstacles, and influences that divert capable and talented young people from continuing their education and achieving success in their chosen fields. There are projects aimed at unearthing hidden potential among disadvantaged urban children. The Higher Horizons Program in the New York City junior and senior high schools is an example. For details of these projects, see Chapter Seven.

Programs of teacher preparation for work with the gifted have received special attention. Mrs. Romaine P. Mackie undertook a study for the United States Office of Education on the competencies needed by teachers of the gifted. College and university programs

at both undergraduate and graduate levels have been developed
for teachers specializing in work with the gifted; programs for
the retraining of teachers in science and mathematics have been
provided.

At the college level, progress is noticeable in more selective
admission policies, financial grants to able students, and experiments with programs for selected college youths. Provision for gifted
college students have included experimentation with advanced-
placement programs for capable high school graduates and early
admission of bright high school students before graduation, joint
high school–college programs, honors seminars and courses, and
independent study.

A useful summary of advancements in the study and education
of the gifted within recent years will be found in a publication
by Gowan (1961).

SUMMARIES OF RESEARCH ON THE GIFTED AND TALENTED

The number of extensive and well-planned research studies on
the nature of giftedness and talent has steadily increased. Summaries of current research appear triennially in the *Review of
Educational Research*. One summary was prepared by Fliegler and
Bish, as mentioned above, and another by Birch and Reynolds
in February, 1963. Other summaries appear annually in the *Elementary School Journal*. Miles summarized material on this subject
up to the middle 1940s in a comprehensive article in the *Manual
of Child Psychology* (1946).

The spectacular development in this field since the late 1940s
is indicated by the volumes of publications that have appeared
on every aspect of the subject: reports of programs; follow-up
studies; curriculum outlines and materials of all sorts; doctoral
theses; a series of bulletins put out by the National Education
Association; reports of studies resulting from foundation grants;
textbooks for teachers of the gifted; reports of college programs;
bulletins, yearbooks, and other publications of educational organizations; periodical editorials and articles; and newspaper publicity.

Probably twenty times as much material was published on
this subject in the decade 1950–1960 as in any previous ten-year
period. The bibliography compiled by Gowan for this period lists
nearly 800 different references, including books, bulletins,
pamphlets, and articles (1961).

A report of twenty-seven research projects on children with
special abilities supported by the Cooperative Research Program

of the U.S. Office of Education between 1956 and 1960 was prepared by Carriker and Asher (1960).

INCREASED FINANCIAL AID

Increased financial support for work with the gifted has been furnished by the Federal government, state and local organizations, and private foundations. A notable example is the National Scholarship Service and Fund for Negro Students. Grants for graduate study are also on the increase. One illustration is the Woodrow Wilson awards for selected students preparing for college teaching.

The national government as well as a number of states have allocated funds for developing programs for promising youth and for providing scholarship aid. In the summer of 1958, President Eisenhower signed a bill for Federal aid to education, the National Defense Education Act, to support improved programs in mathematics and science teaching in the high school, improved foreign language programs, and the extension of guidance and counseling services in the secondary school.

The U.S. Office of Education organized the Talent Development Project under the direction of Dr. Ned Bryan, with a professional committee that establishes programs of action through state departments of education. Twelve states and Puerto Rico, as of 1962, had full-time directors of programs for the gifted. Money has been allocated for research related to the gifted at all educational levels.

A decade ago the Connecticut State Department of Education appointed a committee on the gifted to draw up a report on present and prospective programs. The New York State Education Department has had a director of work with the gifted for several years. Oregon, Pennsylvania, California, New Jersey, Illinois, and others have also organized on a statewide basis to further the cause of the gifted. A three-year study of gifted children in the elementary grades and high schools of California was begun in 1957.

New York State in 1958 allocated $200,000 to encourage local communities to establish experimental programs for students above average in scholastic ability. In North Carolina a commission to study the public school education of exceptionally talented children has been appointed.

A group of twelve Southern states organized a leadership training project designed to train supervisory personnel for setting up educational programs in the different states. This project was inaugurated in 1960, headed by Dr. Virgil S. Ward of the University of Virginia, and financed by the Carnegie Corporation of New York (Ward, 1961).

PROGRAMS BY UNIVERSITIES AND PRIVATE FOUNDATIONS

Programs of research and experimentation sponsored by public and private universities have expanded in recent years. The universities are now cooperating with schools in the community to provide expert assistance in identifying the gifted and establishing programs for them.

Under the direction of a staff from the University of Chicago, talented child surveys and longitudinal studies were organized in an Illinois city to continue over a ten-year period. The University of Illinois has cooperated in a number of statewide projects relating to the gifted and talented under the direction of Dr. T. Ernest Newland.

In 1953 the Talented Youth Project was organized by Horace Mann–Lincoln Institute of School Experimentation at Teachers College, Columbia University, under the direction of Dr. A. Harry Passow. The project had three principal objectives: (1) to assemble existing research results in this field, (2) to assist school systems in conducting their own research for finding and developing talented children, and (3) to study the nature of talent itself.

A program of studies for gifted children in regular elementary school classes of Austin, Texas, is carried on under the supervision of the University of Texas. The University of Rochester is cooperating with the high schools of Monroe County, New York, in what is known as the Wide Horizons Program.

Private foundations as well have generously supported experimental work with the gifted and talented. For a period of ten years or more The Fund for the Advancement of Education of the Ford Foundation has sponsored a number of studies:

Support of Ford scholars and a study of their progress. These are high school students admitted to college before graduation.

Studies of the admission of students to college with advanced standing.

The development and evaluation of seminar-type teaching and programs of enrichment in high school.

The fund has also financed a summer program of study in high school subjects in private boarding schools in New England. The various programs for the superior student supported by The

Fund for the Advancement of Education are described in a report by Paschal (1960) and will be discussed in later chapters.

THE WORK OF ORGANIZATIONS

Another trend at mid-century has been the founding of organizations devoted to the study of the gifted and talented. The first of these was the American Association for the Study of the Gifted, founded in 1946, with membership confined to a number of leaders in the field and those who favor promoting the cause of the gifted. This organization, with headquarters in New York City, answers questions relating to gifted children, distributes published materials, sponsors programs, and has furnished some scholarship aid. It also sponsored a book on the gifted under the editorship of Witty (1951).

The Metropolitan New York Association for the Study of the Gifted, organized in 1950, has a growing membership of professional people within the metropolitan area. This organization sponsors annual programs of interest to teachers, parents, and others.

The National Association for Gifted Children, founded in Cincinnati in 1954, publishes *The Gifted Child Quarterly*, which is distributed to members of the organization.

In 1958 a clearinghouse on the education of the academically talented was set up by the National Education Association in Washington, D.C., under the direction of Dr. Charles Bish and financed by the Carnegie Corporation. This center provides consultation services for state and local school systems, colleges, and universities as well as local, state and national education groups. It maintains up-to-date records of experimental and research projects, has developed a comprehensive collection of materials on all aspects of the subject, makes plans for needed research in the field, and organizes study conferences on related topics. A newsletter is issued periodically by the program director.

The Association for the Gifted established by the International Council for Exceptional Children, a division of the National Education Association, publishes a newsletter and provides other services on behalf of the gifted.

The National Council for the Gifted was organized privately by a group of prominent educators and industrialists to undertake programs of research and advisory work in the education of the gifted at all school levels, including college. The council hopes to encourage leaders in business, industry, and the professions to cooperate with schools in developing educational activities for gifted and talented young people. The headquarters of the organization are in West Orange, New Jersey.

The Inter-University Committee on the Superior Student, in Boulder, Colorado, has been financed by the Carnegie Corporation. This organization publishes a bimonthly newsletter that devotes much of its space to college honors programs.

There are also a number of organizations operating on a state-wide basis; among them are the Pennsylvania Association for the Study and Education of the Mentally Gifted and the Ohio Association for the Gifted.

The work of the Philadelphia Suburban School Study Council illustrates the activities of a group locally organized to promote the study and education of gifted children. The New York Board of Regents Council on the Readjustment of High School Education now gives more attention to the bright and talented student.

A complete list of organizations in the United States working in behalf of the gifted up to 1960 was included in the publication by Gowan (1961).

Progress has been made in recognizing the gifted in programs of professional organizations, particularly meetings and conferences of the National Education Association, the American Educational Research Association, the American Psychological Association, and Division Q of the American Association for the Advancement of Science.

A lectureship in honor of Dr. Walter S. Bingham was established in 1954 for the purpose of advancing the cause of the gifted through an invited annual address by an expert. The first lecture was given by Dr. Lewis M. Terman; another was given by the British psychologist, Dr. Cyril Burt.

Developments in Other Countries

While experiments were going forward in America, psychologists and educators abroad were also conducting school surveys for the identification of gifted children and experimenting with schools and classes for the gifted. Mention was made above of the early interest shown by English and German scientists in the nature of individual differences in learning capacity.

Beginning in 1917, Dr. William Stern, in collaboration with Dr. Otto Weigmann of Hamburg, Germany, undertook the selection of gifted youths by means of intelligence tests developed in the Hamburg Psychological Laboratory. A report of similar work in

Berlin was made by Professors Moede, Piorkowski, and Wolffe in 1918. This trend increased during the 1920s and 1930s, reaching its height in the Third Reich. A report on Berlin schools for gifted children appeared in 1923 (Meyer).

The survey of French schoolchildren by Heuyer, Piéron, and others was described in Chapter Two; this research had significant implications for the evaluation and education of gifted children.

Abroad, as in the United States, educators have become concerned about the gifted as a precious resource of leadership and unusual productivity.

The most comprehensive report of programs for the gifted throughout the world will be found in the 1961 and 1962 editions of the *Yearbook of Education,* edited by George Z. F. Bereday and Joseph A. Lauwerys. These volumes contain descriptions of the work in Britain, Australia, New Zealand, Belgium, Bulgaria, Canada, France, Italy, Japan, Poland, Pakistan, Switzerland, the U.S.S.R., the United States, and the emerging new nations.

IN ENGLAND

Special classes for bright elementary (primary) school pupils were established in England as early as 1912, but after that little more was heard of them. Through the years, however, the larger tax-supported schools have provided for grouping or "streaming" of elementary school pupils according to ability.

For children from age eleven onward, public education in England is selective. At the age of eleven students enter one of three types of secondary schools; the grammar school, which prepares for the university, the technical schools, which emphasize mathematics and science, and the secondary modern school. Selection for each type of school is made on the basis of scholarship ratings in the lower school. Admission was formerly on the basis of the "eleven-plus" standard, objective-type school-leaving examinations, but these tests have gradually been abandoned in favor of other means of evaluating pupil aptitudes and achievement.

About 25 per cent of all pupils enter the grammar schools, about 65 per cent the secondary modern school, and some 10 per cent the technical schools. The grammar schools, which cater primarily to boys and girls of high intellectual ability regardless of social class, conduct a rigorous academic program. Only the brightest 10 per cent complete the sixth form, the last year of the grammar school. Normally, the secondary modern school does not give access to the university. There is, however, a trend in the direction of establishing the comprehensive type of secondary school catering to all types of students as in the United States.

Students of unusual qualities may also be admitted to the great "public" secondary schools; these schools offer scholarships to some students who are unable to pay their tuition fees. As the grammar schools, they prepare students for admission to the university. The new head of Eton College, which has been patronized largely by the upper classes, plans to enroll more working-class boys.

There are exacting entrance requirements for admission to the British universities, which enroll about 4.7 of the age group. Each student accepted is entitled to a government grant according to need for the whole of his university career. Obviously, too few of Great Britain's bright youths have access to education beyond the secondary school. Dr. Cyril Burt estimated that 40 per cent of the non–fee-paying secondary school students who did not go on to the university had ability equal to that of the average university student. Long-range plans are now being made to ensure that all capable youths have access to advanced studies regardless of social-class distinctions. There is a prospect of raising the total university enrollment from less than 5 per cent of the age group to nearer 12 per cent.

IN FRANCE

Before the French child enters grade 6, around age twelve, decisions are made regarding his educational and vocational future in the light of his interest and educational potential. Grants-in-aid made by the departments since the war have enabled gifted youths, regardless of social class, to enter the academic secondary schools, the only route to the university and preparation for the learned professions.

IN THE SOVIET UNION

Although scholars in the Soviet Union apparently have rejected the concept of individual differences in intellectual capacity and they disclaim making any special provisions for the gifted throughout the educational system, the entire educative process is sharply selective. Only those with high marks are permitted to continue schooling full time beyond the eighth grade, and only the most promising can hope to take studies that prepare for the university. Selection for the university and other advanced institutions is even more rigid. These facts are reflected in comparative data for secondary and higher education in the United States and in the Soviet Union. In 1959, 26.4 per cent of the population in the United States over fifteen years of age had completed secondary education; in the Soviet Union, 12 per cent. In the United States 6.8 per cent had completed college; in the Soviet Union, 2.5 per cent.

Looking toward the Future

At the present, support of programs for the gifted is still rather sketchy in most parts of the United States. In some communities there is apathy or even opposition to such programs. And in others, different kinds of educational problems divert the attention of school and civic authorities. Appropriations for the mentally retarded and the rehabilitation of delinquents, for example, far surpass the funds allocated for the gifted. Although there has been growing attention to the needs of the gifted in recent years, friends of the gifted and talented hope to see more generous support for their advancement in the future.

BASIC QUESTIONS

Both within and outside the teaching profession, people who are interested in knowing more about gifted and talented young people and in furthering their careers have asked the following questions:

What can science tell us about the traits of the gifted?

What are the distinguishing characteristics of these chldren?

What are the best means of identifying them and how early can they be identified?

Are intelligence tests fair to bright children of low-income groups?

How do gifted children turn out in adult life?

Are special programs for the gifted compatible with life in a democracy?

What sort of schooling is best for children of exceptional ability and special talents within the framework of our public school system?

What are the best means of individualizing instruction so that exceptionally promising children can receive better-adapted education?

What measures should schools take to develop creative talent?

What happens when gifted children are placed in separate classes and given special attention? What are the attitudes of the gifted children themselves? Of the nonselected children?

What sorts of research projects should be undertaken to advance knowledge of the gifted and their education?

Through a period of forty years or more, considerable evidence has been accumulating from child study, psychology, sociology, and education that relates to these questions. Results of the chief studies will be found in subsequent chapters.

References

Bereday, George Z. F., and Joseph A. Lauwerys (eds.): *Concepts of Excellence in Education: The 1961 Yearbook of Education,* Harcourt, Brace & World, Inc., New York, 1961.

Bereday, George Z. F., and Joseph A. Lauwerys (eds.): *The Gifted Child: The 1962 Yearbook of Education,* Harcourt, Brace & World, Inc., New York, 1962.

Bertrand, François Louis: *Alfred Binet et son oeuvre,* Librairie Félix Alcan, Paris, 1930.

Birch, Jack W., and Maynard C. Reynolds: Education of Exceptional Children, *Review of Educational Research,* 33:83–98, 1963, chap. 6.

Burk, Frederic: *Remedy for Lock-step Teaching,* Department of Education, San Francisco Normal School, no date.

Burwell, Elizabeth P.: Instruction in Mathematics for Gifted Pupils, *Pedagogical Seminary,* 24:569–583, 1917.

Carriker, W. R., and William Asher: Research Related to Pupils with Special Abilities, *School Life,* 42:19–23, 1960.

Coy, Genevieve L.: The Daily Programs of Thirty Gifted Children, *Journal of Genetic Psychology,* 37:123–138, 1930.

Coy, Genevieve L.: *The Interests, Abilities and Achievements of a Special Class for Gifted Children,* Teachers College Contributions to Education, no. 131, Bureau of Publications, Teachers College, Columbia University, New York, 1923.

Coy, Genevieve L.: The Mentality of a Gifted Child, *Journal of Applied Psychology,* 2:299–307, 1918.

Downes, F. E.: Seven Years with Unusually Gifted Pupils, *Psychological Clinic,* 6:13–17, 1912.

Educational Policies Commission: *Education of the Gifted,* National Education Association, Washington, D.C., 1960.

Everett, Samuel (ed.): *Programs for the Gifted: A Case Book in Secondary Education,* John Dewey Society Yearbook, Harper & Row, Publishers, Incorporated, New York, 1961.

Fliegler, Louis A., and Charles E. Bish: The Gifted and Talented: The Education of Exceptional Children, *Review of Educational Research,* 29:408–450, 1959, chap. 2.

Freehill, Maurice F.: *Gifted Children: Their Psychology and Education,* The Macmillan Company, New York, 1961.

French, Joseph L. (ed.): *Educating the Gifted: A Book of Readings,* Holt, Rinehart and Winston, Inc., New York, 1959.

Gallagher, James J.: *Analysis of Research on the Education of Gifted Children,* State Department of Education, Office of Public Instruction, Springfield, Ill., 1960.

Goddard, H. H.: *School Training of Gifted Children,* World Book Company, Tarrytown-on-Hudson, N.Y., 1928.

Goldberg, Miriam: Recent Research on the Talented, *Teachers College Record,* 60:150–163, 1958.

Gowan, John C.: *An Annotated Bibliography on the Academically Talented Student,* NEA Project on the Academically Talented Student, Washington, D.C., 1961.

Henry, T. S.: *Classroom Problems in the Education of Gifted Children: Nineteenth Yearbook of the National Society for the Study of Education,* part 2, Public School Publishing Company, Bloomington, Ill., 1920.

Heuyer, G., H. Piéron, and others: *Le niveau intellectuel des enfants d'âge scolaire,* vol. 1, Presses Universitaires de France, Paris, 1950.

Hollingworth, Leta S.: *Gifted Children: Their Nature and Nurture,* The Macmillan Company, New York, 1926.

Hollingworth, Leta S.: *Special Talents and Defects,* The Macmillan Company, New York, 1923.

Meyer, A. E.: Berlin Schools for Gifted Children, *Pedagogical Seminary,* 30:205–210, 1923.

Miles, Catherine C.: Gifted Children, chap. 16 in Leonard Carmichael (ed.), *Manual of Child Psychology,* John Wiley & Sons, Inc., New York, 1946.

Miller, Barnette: *The Palace School of Muhammad the Conqueror,* Harvard University Press, Cambridge, Mass., 1941.

Moede, W., C. Piorkowski, and A. Wolffe: *Die Berliner Begabtens Schulen: Ihre Organisation und die Methoden Schülerauswahl,* Beyer und Söhne, Langensale, 1918.

Paschal, Elizabeth: *Encouraging the Excellent: Special Programs for Gifted and Talented Students,* The Fund for the Advancement of Education, New York, 1960.

Passow, A. Harry: *Secondary Education for All: The English Approach,* International Education Monographs, no. 3, Ohio State University Press, Columbus, Ohio, 1961.

Passow, A. Harry, and Miriam L. Goldberg: The Talented Youth Project: A Progress Report, 1962, *Exceptional Children,* 28:223–231, 1962.

Passow, A. Harry, Miriam L. Goldberg, A. J. Tannenbaum, and W. French: *Planning for Talented Youth*, Bureau of Publications, Teachers College, Columbia University, New York, 1955.

Pidgeon, D. A.: Selection for Grammar Schools in England and Wales, *California Journal of Educational Research*, 9:204–207, 214, 1958.

Race, Henrietta V.: A Study of a Class of Children of Superior Intelligence, *Journal of Educational Psychology*, 9:91–98, 1918.

Rickover, H. G.: *Education for All Children: What We Can Learn from England, Hearings before the House Committee on Appropriations*, 87th Cong., 1962.

Shaer, I.: Special Classes for Bright Children in an English Elementary School, *Journal of Educational Psychology*, 4:209–222, 1913.

Some Issues and Problems Raised by the Conference on Education for the Gifted, *Teachers College Record*, 42(5), 1941.

Stedman, Lulu: *Education of Gifted Children*, World Book Company, Tarrytown-on-Hudson, N.Y., 1924.

Sumption, Merle R., and Evelyn M. Luecking: *Education of the Gifted*, The Ronald Press Company, New York, 1960.

Terman, Lewis M.: Genius and Stupidity, *Pedagogical Seminary*, 13:307–373, 1906.

Terman, Lewis M., and others: *Genetic Studies of Genius*, vol. 1, *Mental and Physical Traits of a Thousand Gifted Children*, Stanford University Press, Stanford, Calif., 1925.

Ward, Virgil S.: *Educating the Gifted: An Axiomatic Approach*, Charles E. Merrill Books, Inc., Columbus, Ohio, 1961.

Ward, Virgil S., and others: *The Gifted Student: A Manual for Program Improvement*, Charlottesville, Va., 1962.

Whipple, Guy Montrose: *Classes for Gifted Children: An Experimental Study of Methods of Selection and Instruction*, School and Home Educational Monographs, no. 1, Public School Publishing Company, Bloomington, Ill., 1919.

Whipple, Guy Montrose (ed.): Report of the Society's Committee on the Education of Gifted Children, *Twenty-third Yearbook of the National Society for the Study of Education*, part 1, section 2: Special Studies, Public School Publishing Company, Bloomington, Ill., 1924.

Witty, Paul A.: *A Study of One Hundred Gifted Children*, State Teachers College Studies in Education, vol. 1, no. 13, Emporia, Kans., 1930.

Witty, Paul A. (ed.): *The Gifted Child*, D. C. Heath and Company, Boston, 1951.

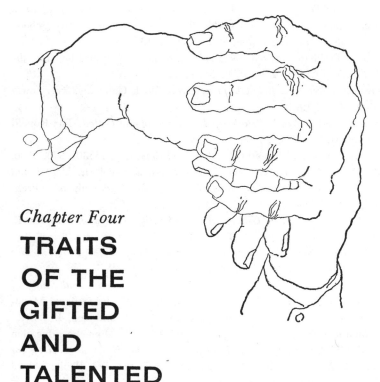

Chapter Four
TRAITS OF THE GIFTED AND TALENTED

The traits of precocious children were first described by Sir Francis Galton in the late nineteenth century. Since that time, there have been investigations covering all aspects of the behavior of bright children. The results of the major studies will be summarized in this chapter.

What traits or combinations of traits distinguish the most promising children? We are interested in knowing not only in what traits the gifted excel, but also in discovering common patterns of behavior shown by individual children. Another question concerns the consistency of development in individual children. Is the promise of early superiority fulfilled in youth and in adult life? Data relating to the first question are reported in this chapter; those relating to developmental tendencies in the next.

Most studies of gifted children pertain to those who have been identified through mental tests, more particularly, the Stanford-Binet test; hence, the largest store of information about the gifted relates to those who were initially selected on the basis of intellectual superiority. The traits of children identified as gifted on the basis of high test ratings and other criteria have been described by Terman (1925), Hollingworth (1926, 1942), Witty (1930), Carroll (1940), Strang (1960), Barbe (1955), Hildreth (1938, 1954), and other authorities cited in the preceding chapter.

The largest source of objective information about traits of the mentally gifted is Terman's study of 1,110 California children who were in the middle childhood years when first identified. The first volume by Terman and associates in the five-volume series, *Genetic Studies of Genius,* was devoted mainly to a description of the mental and physical traits of 1,000 children who rated at or above 140 on the Stanford-Binet test (1925).

In our discussion, the traits of the gifted will be described in several categories, even though there is considerable overlap among them: physical traits and health; mental qualities; command of language; reading; writing; special interests, talents, and aptitudes; academic skills and attainments; and personal, social, and character traits. Finally, we shall consider sexual, racial, and socioeconomic influences.

WIDE–RANGING ABILITIES

In considering the nature and traits of the gifted, several general points, discussed here and in the following sections, should be kept in mind. The first is that these children differ as much among themselves as children of ordinary abilities. There is no such thing as a typical gifted child. No one child would be a composite of all the traits and characteristics to be described. A gifted child usually shows a range of ability within his own profile; he may be outstanding in one trait and less distinguished in others, or his abilities may be quite uniformly superior.

Gifted children tend to show wider variation in characteristic traits than others because of the multiplicity of their talents. One child may be most successful in the traditional type of lesson learning, another may be inventive and original, show more independence in thinking, more originality in problem solving. At the same time the gifted child, sharing the traits, immaturities, and tendencies typical of his age group, has much in common with all other children.

Social traits tend to follow the usual developmental age patterns in such characteristics as interest in playing with other children, in organized group games, team organization, association with the opposite sex, and so on.

Traits of the gifted vary with the age of the child. Obviously, children of equal superiority will show different traits at age five, ten, and sixteen. A younger child who shows special mathematical aptitude cannot be described in the same terms as an older child who is mathematically inclined. Differences will be found in the behavior and interests of gifted children in different environments— large urban centers, suburban communities, or small villages and rural areas.

A POPULAR MYTH EXPLODED

The myth of the gifted child as a queer, physically weak little prodigy who became neurotic and was apt to burn out quickly persisted for many years. This stereotype can no longer be accepted. Instead of being puny, nearsighted little misfits, these children are sturdy, vivacious, fun-loving, well-adjusted youngsters.

In delineating the traits of remarkable children, early writers tended to highlight the intellectual traits and academic achievement, even the adultlike behavior of the child prodigy, to the neglect of personal qualities. The fact that the child was a delightful person with attractive human qualities attracted less attention than his reputation as a "brain" or intellectual robot.

There is a close connection between unusual mental qualities and energy and vitality, according to Havelock Ellis who made an analysis of British genius. "Lively" and "energetic" are two words that well describe the behavior of the gifted. These children seem to have surplus energy which they are able to direct toward self-determined goals. They show enthusiasm for new experiences and are self-motivated in pursuing their interests. A teacher of gifted children commented, "Their self-starters are in good working order." Characteristically, they have drive and perseverance.

Louisa May Alcott's father discovered when his daughter was very small that she had exceptional energy and understanding, was creative and inventive and more precocious than her older sister had been at the same age. Her father noted in his journal that the child "realizes all she conceives. She manifests uncommon activity and force of mind, and has both creative imagination and practical talent."

The childhood of Nikola Tesla, the electrical inventor, and that of Lawrence of Arabia, military genius, suggest anything but reclusive, owlishly bookish, socially inept individuals. Their seriousness of purpose and mature demeanor gave these people as children an impression of maturity beyond their years. They showed independence and liked to take the initiative.

CORRELATION AMONG SUPERIOR TRAITS

The question is often asked, "Isn't the bright child one of the poorest, if not a failure, when away from his books and memory work?" This attitude reflects the notion of inconsistency rather than correlation of traits in the gifted individual. The popular notion that the typical gifted child usually excels in some one trait or talent and is inferior in others is not borne out by the facts. The individual who rates high in one area tends to rank above average in others as well.

Data from Liddle's study of the characteristics of sixth graders (1958) indicate that the top 10 per cent in intelligence test scores were within the top 45 per cent in leadership ratings, and they were also within the top 33 per cent in art expression and drawing. The coefficients of correlation obtained ranged between .50 and .70.

The child who scores high in mathematics is more likely than an average achiever to be a good reader and to score high in other studies such as French. General high intellectual ability is found to be related to social leadership and artistic talent. A positive correlation among traits in the individual's profile is also the general rule for average children, as well as for the mentally retarded.

On the whole, the abilities of younger children tend to be more highly correlated then those of older boys and girls. As children mature, they tend more and more to direct their attention toward specialized interests that absorb their time and attention.

An English schoolboy who later graduated from Cambridge University described himself as "lamentably intelligent, and good at games." He won a scholarship at Trinity College, Cambridge, and there he enjoyed tremendously the companionship of his fellow students. He said that he had intellectual curiosity and enjoyed intensely a large number of very different things: the smooth working of his brain on difficult material, playing cricket or any game, omnivorous reading, particularly the works of great writers, bicycling and walking, working, and attempting to write. This must be accepted as the usual picture of a bright young man—a completely human, acceptable person.

Terman's studies indicated that correlation rather than compensation characterized trait relationships in the gifted individual. The typical gifted young person has multidimensional abilities of high order. Terman's gifted subjects were superior in physical characteristics, school achievement, maturity of interests, and social and personal traits. The only exception was average ratings in mechanical aptitude (1926).

Hollingworth considered the question of the relationship between capacities in the individual, the extent to which a high or low rating in one trait or capacity is related to high or low ratings in others (1923). On marshaling the available data, she concluded that measures of different mental function yield positive correlations, but in varying degree. Some individuals are high all around, others have pronounced special aptitudes and defects.

An early inquiry into the intellectual traits of children conducted by the English scientist, Karl Pearson, revealed that highly intelligent children were more conscientious than others, possessed of greater athletic ability, and characterized by more robustness.

Japanese children who rated above 130 IQ on the Wechsler Intelligence Scale were superior to average-rating children in both physical and mental traits (Mori, 1959). The gifted were heavier in birth weight, superior in motor capacities, earlier in starting to read and write, and more active in extracurricular life.

Reports of Individual Children   Consistency in superior traits was obvious in three gifted boys studied by the author (1954). Gifted child A was outstanding in a wide array of talents: mathematics, science, reading, poetry, story and play writing, even arts and crafts. This boy, who was the most superior mentally of the three, was also top scorer in a test of manual dexterity, a finding that runs contrary to the view of the mentally gifted as inept in motor control.

Typical of the intellectually gifted is Paul, who was nine years old at the time the following report was made. This boy has shown precocity in all aspects of development from his earliest years. The results of several intelligence tests have yielded IQs between 140 and 150. On the New York City Reading Test at the end of grade 2 his grade score was 6.5; on the Stanford Achievement Reading Test, 5.7. At the end of the second grade he was skipped to fourth grade because of his accelerated accomplishments. This placed him with children a year older than himself. Science is his chief interest, then mathematics and social studies; but he excels in all. In reporting his science fair project, an explanation of "heavy water," he spoke more like a high school student than a boy of nine. His teacher says, "You feel you could sit down with him and talk man-to-man." In expressive writing this boy is also well ahead of his years.

Ronald, a sixth grader, with a Binet IQ of 136, is the largest boy in his class and outstanding in accomplishment. His manner is easy and engaging, and he moves about with poise and confidence. This boy is looked upon as a leader because of his ability to direct other children in group work on projects. His special interest is science, to which he devotes much of his reading and study time. His classmates respect him for his vast fund of knowledge and are generally willing to follow his suggestions. In conversation he reveals a fine mind; his arguments are logical, his manner persuasive. He has been skipped twice in the elementary school, at the end of the second grade and again at the end of the fourth.

Bright teen-agers, too, tend to be well-rounded individuals. They are not necessarily book worms or social isolates whose top-heavy intellect prevents them from mingling socially, but wide-awake young people, often with poise and charm. A junior high school teacher noted that his mentally gifted students were not only high achievers in schoolwork, but also had a broad range of interests, including art, music, and sports.

Edward, thirteen, whose father described him as a "regular" boy who enjoys fishing and likes to play handball, prefers the study of pure mathematics to all other pursuits. He has already finished junior high school and has been accepted for a selective academic high school next fall. Sara, a precocious high school student, not only earns honors rating in all her studies, but shows versatility in out-of-school interests as well. She enjoys piano and ballet lessons and finds foreign language study interesting. Socially, she is among the most popular in her class.

George is another bright teen-ager, whose specialty is mathematics. As the result of travels abroad he is adept in two languages in addition to his mother tongue. As a young child his paintings seemed remarkable to his teachers as well as to his parents. Recently he has gone back to art, and his paintings are soon to be exhibited in a public gallery, although he maintains that his artwork is only recreational. Now he is studying chemistry at the university to prepare for a teaching career. In the meantime he enjoys the theater, concerts, art, and social life.

A high school senior known to the author, a mature youth of eighteen, excelled in areas as widely varied as chemistry, public speaking, French, social studies, English composition, and baseball throughout his school career and succeeded in capturing top awards in them all.

A Study of Young Bright Children   The author made a comparative study of intellectually gifted children and those of average ability in a private school in Brooklyn with a predominantly Jewish population (1938). Included in the superior group were those testing 130 or above in IQ; in the average group, those rating between 90 and 110. Fifty children in each group were matched for age and sex. Analysis of the results revealed nearly five times as many favorable notations of intellectual, personality, and character traits for the gifted group as for the controls. The gifted group were superior to the control group in energy, physique, language, information, judgment and reasoning, sense of humor, willingness to face difficulties. They fatigued less quickly than the average group, had more experiences to relate, showed more skill and originality in the arts, were more active and vivacious, more independent and self-assured. More of the gifted knew and used a foreign language in addition to English. All these distinguishing traits were obvious at the five-year level in chronological age.

For comprehensive reports of children testing very high on the Stanford-Binet test, see Hollingworth's book *Children Who Test above 180 I.Q.* (1942).

Physical Traits, Dynamic Energy, and Health

Mentally gifted children tend to be mature for their years in size, physiological development, and motor control. In thirty-seven different anthropometric tests Terman's gifted subjects proved to be superior to the norms for children of comparable age in height, weight, lung capacity, and muscular strength (1925). Fewer were feeble and defective than in the general population, and they tended to be more precocious in physical maturation at adolescence.

Hollingworth and Taylor reported that high-IQ children were larger and stronger than their age-mates (1924). There was a consistent relationship between physical characteristics of height and weight and intelligence. It has also been shown that male science talent search candidates are taller and heavier than Army inductees of the same age.

The physical superiority of the bright and gifted may be due to favorable environmental conditions. Indeed, when the socioeconomic factor is held constant, the differences tend to disappear. In a longitudinal study of three mentally accelerated children and a matchee average child, the writer found no difference in physical status between the high-rating boys and the boy of average ability who came from an equally superior home (1954).

Although the health of mentally superior children tends to be above average, mentally superior children in the lower-age groups observed at the Lincoln School of Teachers College of Columbia University, New York, suffered from asthma, allergies, and respiratory and feeding problems associated with the conditions and strains of urban living.

Intellectual Traits

By definition, children with precocious intellectual development are certain to show unusual mental traits. Questions are: How do they think and conceptualize? How well do they reason in planning and in problem solving? What are their powers of perception and memory? How original and ingenious are these children? In problem solving, how well do they succeed in transferring knowledge from the original situation to a new one? Do they learn only at a faster rate than other children, or do they also learn in different ways?

Highly gifted children show mental precocity from an early age. A four-year-old announced that he intended to become a scientist. He proceeded to explain the physical properties of water, telling about things that float and why water freezes, all the while using a vocabulary well in advance of his age. A six-year-old who developed a keen interest in astronomy during the sputnik launchings drew pictures of a sputnik, adding all the nine planets in the solar system, naming each one, and volunteering information such as the distance from the earth to the sun. Another boy of four has been asking his neighbor, a science teacher, about dinosaurs and early man. He remembers all the scientific terms easily and uses them: brontosaurus, antediluvian, Neanderthal. One day he led a troop of his friends along the street shouting these terms at the passing sanitation truck, which had, in his fantasy, turned into a dinosaur.

The gifted child tends to become immersed in a given topic and to study it in complete detail, showing maturity in making and carrying out plans. He may become obsessed with the idea of learning about the world's great rivers or about the planets, how an adding machine works, how ancient people told time. One child wanted to learn Egyptian hieroglyphics; another insisted on being taught the French language.

Henry at the age of six was so well posted on the subject of gravity that he knew why some children fell on the playground slide. Although he was afraid to go down the slide himself, he would stand alongside and explain, "Don't lean over so far; your center of gravity is wrong."

Mentally gifted children have a strong disposition toward intellectual activity, a liking for reflective and abstract thought and ideas, and interest in scholarly pursuits. According to Dr. Terman, signs of youthful intelligence are intellectual curiosity and imagination, extensive knowledge, superior verbal comprehension, rich vocabulary, ability to assimilate and generalize, and interest in number relations, the atlas, and the encyclopedia.

A gifted child may show scholarly tendencies very early. One precocious six-year-old had his own little worktable in a corner of his grandfather's study where he kept his book collection, his stones, and other treasures. There he was often observed studiously bent over his paper drawing railroad maps or recording data in bold lettering.

These children master scholarly skills early: the use of a slide-rule and compass set, a high-powered microscope, a dissecting set, mathematical tables, maps, and reference resources of a library.

INTELLECTUAL CURIOSITY

In speaking of gifted children in the Cleveland Major Work classes, Theodore Hall remarked that the gifted displayed two main qualities: first, a sense of wonder and curiosity, and second, creativeness, the desire and power to invent something new (1956). These were also characteristic of young children at the Hunter Elementary School. Although the gifted child shows his superiority to others in a number of different traits, the degree of superiority is greatest in intellectual interests, in originality, and in school achievement, according to the findings of Wall (1960). The typical bright child shows an eagerness to learn, though this interest is not necessarily directed toward school tasks.

Although all normal young children show a sense of wonder and curiosity about their surroundings, and even display some creative ability and invention, the gifted child shows these qualities to a more pronounced degree and in advance of his age. The gifted children studied by Dr. Terman proved to be more intellectually curious and imaginative than other children. These children excelled in the ability to structure their own thinking in problem solving, whether of a verbal nature or in a practical situation.

INDEPENDENT LEARNING

Incidental learning or spontaneous learning from clues in the environment without direct instruction appears to be a characteristic of young gifted children. A comment frequently made of a gifted child is, "He learned by himself," or "I don't see how he learned to count (or draw, or recite rhymes from memory); we certainly didn't teach him." These children learn a great deal spontaneously and independently because of their general alertness and their questioning attitude. They seek and demand facts—for example, the use of gauges for measuring.

The eight-year-old child artist referred to in Chapter Two, whose special talent is tearing paper in the shape of animals, has instructed himself by closely observing the animals he represents in this original way.

PHILOSOPHICAL LEANINGS

The gifted child shows an interest in moral issues and social problems that ordinarily do not appeal to others of the same age. He is fascinated by questions of time and space, origins, destiny, life and death. A remarkable boy of six years old told his teacher he was terribly confused because the Bible and his book on astronomy differed about the beginning of the world. "What am I to believe?" he solemnly asked. Dr. Terman reported that his subjects were often concerned with philosophical problems. This was also true of the young Goethe and many other eminent persons in childhood.

As all others, the gifted ask incessant questions, but their questions reveal more advanced thinking for their age; they tend to wait for answers and pursue the point until they are satisfied. A representative of UNICEF visited a third-grade class one day to tell about the work of that organization abroad. A bright youngster persisted in wanting to know all about his work, how the organization got its name, where the countries mentioned were located, and so on.

THINKING, LEARNING, AND CONCEPTUALIZING

The outstanding trait of children who rate high in intelligence is their ability to think, reason, and generalize beyond their years. The ability to reason logically is the distinguishing characteristic of young people who have unusual scientific aptitude.

The mentally bright are characterized by superior generalizing power, the ability to apply an operation to a variety of relevant tasks, for example, computing fractions with problems having different denominators, or computing areas of different shapes and sizes because the principles of computation are known and understood. These children show precocity in thinking abstractly and forming generalizations apart from perception of concrete situations or representations. An intelligent boy or girl generalizes fluently and spontaneously, seeing the relationship between old and new experiences, generalizing and making effective transfer from the learned to the unlearned. This means that he can solve problems through thoughtful reasoning on the basis of past experience. He can grasp and apply principles in problem solving on an advanced level.

In the author's study of three gifted boys and a control case of average ability, the responses of A, the most gifted boy, to a series of science information questions and demonstrations were invariably mature for his age and far superior to the reasoning of an average child. In one of the problems two coins were displayed with the comment that one of them was a lucky coin. The child is told: "A sports manager said his team won because he carried this lucky coin." A's response to this comment was, "Certainly not because of the lucky coin! I don't believe in those superstitions. Bad luck once came to me when I had a 'lucky' coin." B, the next brightest boy, said, "He had the best men. The men that won the game." C, the third boy in rank, was slow in answering. Then he pointed to a feature of the coin and said, "Does it have something to do with this?" D, the boy of average ability, responsed by saying, "Because this one is round, and he had the best one [coin]."

When the boys were about nine years of age they were asked without any preliminary instruction to draw a bicycle, then a steam locomotive (at that time diesels had not yet supplanted steam). Each boy was tested separately. The results clearly indicate the difference in level of conceptual thinking and understanding of the highly gifted boy A and the normative control case D (see Figures 2 and 3).

The trait of the gifted child that seems most uncanny is the speed with which he makes inferences and arrives at solutions to problems. This trait is most obvious in work with mathematics. From preliminary findings Flanagan estimated that the top 5 per cent in ability among high school youths learn twice as fast as others in preferred subjects (1962).

The gifted child organizes his thinking more effectively than typical like-age children. He catches on to "the system," the rules and principles which help him organize ideas. The case of Karl Friedrich Gauss is illustrative of this trait. When Gauss was a ten-year-old schoolboy the teacher required the class to add all numbers from 1 to 100. The first one to finish the assignment was to place his slate on the teacher's desk. Karl obtained the answer almost at once using the formula he had figured out for the sum of a series of numbers. The bright child's trial-and-error efforts in problem solving do not involve physical manipulation of materials so much as visual and intellectual manipulation. He economizes overt trials through reflection (mental tricks).

INTUITIVE REASONING

Equally interesting is the intuitive way in which bright children go about getting answers to questions. The first-grade class was figuring out attendance for the day. The first child said, "Six are out with chicken pox." The second child said, "No, Sally and Billy are back." A bright child spoke up quickly, "Then there are twelve here today, because there are sixteen altogether in our class."

In another class the problem was to find 58×16. "Well," said a thoughtful youngster, "it can be $50 \times 16 = 800$ plus $8 \times 16 = 128$. That makes 928."

Another problem was to find 36 per cent of 122.40. One pupil took 30 per cent of the number, then twice that amount, pointed off each term properly, then added the two numbers for the answer, 44.064.

Paul, who had mastered division with a one-place divisor, solved $3\sqrt{96}$ and $3\sqrt{369}$ immediately without error. Could he, without further instruction, apply the principle of division in a problem

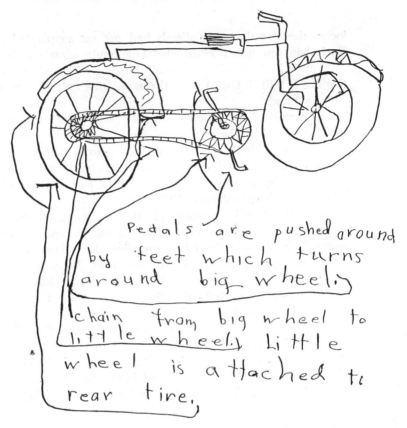

Pedals are pushed around by feet which turns around big wheel. chain from big wheel to little wheel. little wheel is attached to rear tire.

Bicycle drawing, boy A.

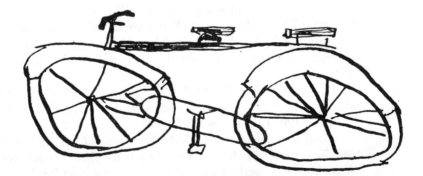

Bicycle drawing, boy D.

Figure 2. Bicycle drawings by a gifted boy A and an average boy D. (Gertrude Hildreth, Three Gifted Children: A Developmental Study, *Journal of Genetic Psychology,* 85:239–264, 1954. Used by permission of the publisher.)

with a two-place divisor? His teacher, who tried the experiment, reports that he succeeded in working through 18 $\sqrt{13,113}$ without error, even though there was an unanticipated remainder.

A nine-year-old girl reasoned out the mid-score in an assorted list of grades ranging from 78 to 100 when her father asked her if she could find the middle score of a set of marks. First she arranged the papers in order, then she counted to the middle

Locomotive drawing, boy A.

Locomotive drawing, boy D.

Figure 3. Steam locomotive drawings by a gifted boy A and an average boy D. (Gertrude Hildreth, Three Gifted Children: A Developmental Study, *Journal of Genetic Psychology,* 85:239–264, 1954. Used by permission of the publisher.)

score, all without any instruction or previous demonstration. Instead of thinking this problem was hard, she asked for more arithmetic problems.

A bright boy of five ceased to believe in Santa Claus, but he did not tell anyone for fear of upsetting his younger brother. Later he reported that his loss of faith occurred when he began making computations of the time required for travel distances on his globe. He concluded that even at the highest rate of speed Santa could not fly down from the North Pole and encircle the globe leaving presents for everyone all in one night.

PRODIGIOUS MEMORY

The prodigious memory of exceptional children in the early years—memory for unusual words, poems, scientific nomenclature, musical scores, arithmetic facts, and all kinds of unassorted information—may be the most obvious sign of precocity. A kindergartner could say the entire " 'Twas the night before Christmas" after hearing his older sister read it several times. A twelve-year-old with a surprisingly good memory knows his lesson by heart after reading it through twice. A French teacher at the Hunter College Elementary School observed how easily the children remembered new vocabulary the first time they heard the words. A ten-year-old who showed unusual knowledge of railroading could give the track mileage of all the main railroads in the country, and showed remarkable talent for map making and drawing engineering plans.

These children learn easily without prolonged drill and remember what they learn not only because they are attentive and comprehend instructions easily, but also because they understand what they are learning.

Control of Language and Verbal Behavior

Mentally gifted children tend to range above average and ahead of their years in linguistic development and control of verbal behavior. They are accelerated in use and understanding of vocabulary, in maturity of sentence structure, and in originality of expression.

ACCELERATED DEVELOPMENT IN ORAL LANGUAGE

Two recent studies have confirmed the fact that bright children tend to be ahead of others in the use of oral language. In the analysis made by Loban of all forms of language used by a wide cross section of elementary school children in California, the highest correlation was between results of the Kuhlmann-Anderson test administered in the second grade and an oral vocabulary test, .844 by the product-moments method (1963). Bright children use longer, more complex sentences and more mature expression than other children of their age (Strickland, 1960).

Gifted children of nine or ten may seem quite grown-up in conversation. Their preference for older companions may be due to their mature use of language.

Accelerated children are often leaders in class discussion; they express ideas effectively, enjoy using big words, study dictionaries for word meanings, and participate vigorously in debate. Although verbal fluency is a characteristic of the intellectually gifted, an occasional shy child may hesitate to speak before a group. The three gifted boys described by the author provided many illustrations of linguistic precocity. All three maintained their relative superiority in language usage throughout the seven-year observation period. Terman's gifted subjects were rated by teachers as superior in debating and public speaking.

To what extent is verbal facility a reflection of home background? Some research effort has been directed to this question. Davidson and Balducci studied social-class and sex differences in the verbal facility of very bright children, but results were inconclusive (1956). Loban's study disclosed a consistent relationship between the children's maturity in language usage and their socioeconomic level.

Relatively little is known about the gifted child's talent for learning foreign languages. Is this a special talent? High intelligence is unquestionably a factor, but what are the other components? A good ear for language? Interest in speaking as a foreigner? Studiousness in general? These questions require investigation.

Although all normal young children catch on to a new language without formal instruction when they are suddenly plunged into a new language world, the bright child catches on faster than usual. Helena, a bright five-year-old visitor to the United States, knew only her mother tongue. Within seven months after entering kindergarten, she could use fluent, idiomatic English. "You have a new rug upstairs. It's nice and thick," she commented. Helena solved the irregular-verb problem by generalizing; at first she used the "-ed" form for the past tense of all English verbs, "runned," "bringed," "catched," etc.

Reading Habits of the Gifted

On the whole, the gifted outdistance their age-mates in learning to read. Often they cannot recall how they learned to read or remember a time when they were unable to read. One day when Marie Curie's older sister was faltering over her reading lesson, the four-year old Marie grew impatient, seized the book, and read aloud the opening sentence. Then panic overcame her and she apologized, saying that she had done it only because reading was so easy.

Not all intellectually gifted children are addicted to books, however. Some of them prefer to concentrate on inventive projects and experiments in which, for the time being, books play little part. One bright boy who specialized in mechanics and science experiments never did care much for reading and was slow in developing skill in written expression, to the despair of his parents and teachers.

Bright children sometimes do not learn to read easily, and even require remedial help. Such children may be overlooked by teachers who are unaware of constitutional, linguistic, or emotional problems that may prevent the child from advancing rapidly.

EARLY BEGINNINGS IN READING

Nearly half of Terman's gifted subjects had learned to read before entering school; 20 per cent, before they were five years old. They were great readers; nearly 90 per cent of them read more, and none of them less, than average children of the same age (1925).

Durkin identified in a population of over 5,000 school beginners 49 children with some reading ability at the time of school entrance. In IQ they ranged from 91 to 161, with a median of 121 (1959). In a second investigation conducted in New York City, Dr. Durkin found that 157 children, about 3½ per cent of 4,000 tested, had learned to read before going to school. Although there was a wide range of intelligence in this group, the mean IQ was 133.

Bright girls are somewhat ahead of boys in reading according to the results of Barbe's study of 103 high school students with a mean IQ of 135: 47 per cent of the girls and 33 per cent of the boys had learned to read before entering school.

EARLY READING BY EMINENT PERSONS

An early start in reading and writing characterized many notable people in their childhood. Once they learned the trick and grasped the significance of reading, they fairly devoured books, discovering in reading unlimited resources for study and for creative imagination. This was true of Milton, Benjamin Franklin, Marie Curie, Albert Schweitzer, and other great figures.

Benjamin Franklin described his early interest in books in his autobiography: "From a child I was fond of reading and all the little money that came into my hands was ever laid out in books. Pleas'd with *Pilgrim's Progress,* my first collection was of John Bunyan's works, in separate little volumes. I afterwards sold them to enable me to buy R. Burton's Historical Collections. My Father's little library consisted chiefly of books in Polemic Divinity, most of which I read. Plutarch's Lives there was in which I read abundantly, and I still think that the time spent to great advantage." Franklin goes on to say that his early reading gave him a "turn of thinking" that perhaps had an influence on some of the future events of his life.

The young Milton poured over his books until midnight, even before he was in his teens. Balzac's biographer described him as an exceptionally rapid reader in his youth. The boy's extensive reading of a heterogeneous mass of material excited his imagination so much that he suffered physically from "congestion of ideas." According to Balzac's own testimony, the images he gained from books at the age of twelve were as clear and real as if he had actually had the experiences he was reading about.

Many a gifted youth with access to a good library has found in reading the means to his own private education. Walt Whitman began reading early and never stopped, because he said that he met superior minds in the books he read.

READING, A FAVORITE RECREATION

A characteristic picture of the gifted child shows him with a book in his hands, whether he is up in a tree munching an apple, reading in the garret on a rainy afternoon, or flat on his stomach in the grassy park. Stephen Vincent Benét as a teen-ager was often seen bicycling home from the library with a load of books, and William Faulkner said that he got his early education from reading in his grandfather's library.

Gifted children read with depth of understanding and keen appreciation. Their preference is often for books that satisfy intellectual interests beyond their years.

A bright child, once started on reading, may become a "chain" reader, devouring one book after another in quick succession or reading several books at a time, and reading continuously once he picks up a book. Bright children are more apt to have library cards and to use the local public library more consistently than others.

Reading is a popular pastime because it feeds the child's intellectual needs without requiring too much physical exertion. Bright children find in books an outlet for their imaginative language and the satisfaction of their interests: tracing the itinerary of Marco Polo, exploring the preglacial period in North America, investigating the physiology of the heart, learning about insects or fossils.

The bright child is usually a faster reader, and he is aware of the use of books for obtaining information. Any child's knowledge and use of books, however, depend upon the kind of instruction he has received. Acceleration in reading is associated with superior home background and a literary environment. Gifted children from intellectual homes do a great deal of reading at home and often have built up their own libraries from an early age.

Nine-year-old children in Dr. Terman's study read three times as much as ordinary children of the same age. They read fewer books of adventure and mystery or emotionalized fiction than their age-mates, perhaps because they had access to plenty of mentally challenging books on science and history as well as biography, poetry, and other types of literature. Boy A studied by the author usually preferred science, history, and other informational material, but from time to time he read the fairy tales and nonsense stories that other children of his age enjoyed.

ILLUSTRATIONS OF ACCELERATION IN READING

Acceleration in the gifted child's reading habits is shown in his demand for reading material ahead of his years. This was characteristic of boy A studied by the author; he showed a preference for adult books well before reaching the teens.

A precocious second grader in an elementary school where the central library is reserved for pupils in third grade and above decided one day to stop by the library just to make an inquiry. The place proved to be so fascinating that he stayed on for a visit with the librarian. She decided, as a special privilege, to give the boy a book to take out; but the first one she selected for him proved to be the wrong choice. He had already read the book. "Reading biography," he said, was his chief hobby. This was the type of book he always chose for reports in class. He read these books not only rapidly, usually returning a book selection within two days, but with excellent comprehension and good retention of details. When a copy of the junior edition of *Profiles in Courage* was added to the school library collection, the book was saved for him. "I enjoyed that book very much," he said. "My daddy took it out of the public library for me." Then he went on at length commenting about prominent people in public life. He found unusual words for himself by consulting the large *Webster's* in the school library.

One day a visitor strolled over to the shelf of new books in a school library, picked out a book, and leafed it through. An alert ten-year-old stepped right up. "Here's a better book on horses than that one," he commented. "It has beautiful pictures." He exclaimed over details in the book, then picked out several others rapidly. "My favorite picture—lions in the jungle," and he sketched the story rapidly. The visitor turned the page, commenting on the next picture, "Leopards, no, wildcats." "Oh, no," said the boy, "those are cheetahs." "Have you read all these books?" inquired the visitor, indicating a row of 200 or 300 volumes. "Well, not quite all of them [modestly], but I know what most of them are about." This boy's reading achievement on standard tests measured at the college level.

During his first year in junior high school a precocious twelve-year-old was reading simultaneously *The Odyssey, The World of Susie Wong, Mathematics for the Millions, Catcher in the Rye,* and *Paradise Lost.*

Written Expression

Literary juvenilia is a fascinating study and has received considerable attention. Wonderful illustrations of the writing of gifted juveniles will be found in Walter De la Mare's *Early One Morning in the Spring* (1935). Illustrations of the dictated stories and writings of young gifted children at several different age levels are contained in the book by Herbert Carroll (1940). Creative writings of adolescents will be found in *Creative Youth,* by Hughes Mearns.

Here is a journal jotting by precocious Marjorie Fleming, age eight, in the summer of 1810: "I am now going to tell you about the horrible and wretched plaege that my multiplication gives me you can't conceive it—the most Devilish thing is 8 times 8 & 7 times 7 it is what nature itselfe can't endure."

A teacher met one of her pupils, a child of nine, musing along the hall. "I'm writing a book review right now," she told the teacher. "It's in my head." This child says she plans to become a writer. A book of poems by a French child, Minou Drouet, eight, received favorable publicity several years ago.

Girls enjoy writing notes to their friends, and both boys and girls write stories of imaginary worlds and fantastic creatures. Older boys and girls, particularly, keep voluminous diaries of the minute daily happenings that seem so important to the adolescent.

ILLUSTRATIONS OF LITERARY PRODUCTIVITY

A record of the literary productivity of the three gifted boys, A, B, and C, compared with child D of average ability, showed that the most gifted far outdistanced the others in the writing of stories, poems, science and mathematics notebooks, and other material (Hildreth, 1954). A's early scribblings filled one notebook after another. A record of this boy's writings done at school between the ages of five and ten are included in the report of the study. At age eight A's school file contained a story, "Chris Columbus," a poem that appeared in the school paper, limericks and other poems, four book reviews, original stories, a quiz, a report of summer experiences, science notes, the report of a trip to the New York World's Fair (1939), and a scrapbook of collected writings. By contrast, the boy of average ability had a notebook containing only four entries and a story relating to summer experiences that appeared in the school paper.

Boy A made extensive science jottings in his notebooks. Here are two illustrations:

BULLHEAD SNAKES

In the American Museum of Natural History we saw a bullhead snake. She was five feet long, seven years old, and came from Arizona. She was white with black spots and a little black forked tongue with which she feels.

[Drawing of a wriggly snake with plenty of spots]

First they called her Oscar, but one day when she laid eggs they had to change her name to Esmeralda. Miss Friend opened the cage and took her out. I stroked her and she felt dry and cool.

LODESTONE

Lodestone was found to be magnetic 600 years ago. When electricity was discovered it was found that in motion it produced a magnetic field. If a piece of hard steel is stroked by a piece of lodestone it becomes magnetized, or when it is placed in a powerful magnetic field. The magnet pulls little iron bits to itself mainly in two points.

[Drawing of a magnet with lines radiating from it labeled "Lines of Force"]

K is another wide-awake boy, in the third grade. Although he is equally successful in all phases of schoolwork, including arts and crafts, he is exceptionally talented in expressive writing. This boy has vivid recollections of his life out West, and he takes keen delight in regaling his classmates with tales of his exploits—riding over the plains on his pony, finding caves for games of Indians, cowboys, and "bad men." Then he proceeds to write the stories in his notebook, using diction and sentence structure far beyond his years, inventing a style of literary expression all his own. His teachers predict that if his interest and skill in written expression continue to mature, this boy might become one of the country's leading literary lights; but it is too early to know whether his talent will become a permanent professional interest or whether it is merely an expression of the boy's alert imagination and superior intelligence.

Interests and Activities of Mentally Advanced Children

Children who are mentally advanced tend to reveal interests that are in accord with their precocious development. Their hobbies often have an intellectual flavor—stamp collecting and arranging, studying flight schedules or railroad timetables, looking up facts in the encyclopedia, making up games, inventing puzzles, and so on. One energetic eleven-year-old started a hectographed medical and science journal for himself and his friends. Such activities reach the virtuoso level in the adolescent years.

The bright and gifted may be more inclined to spend their spare time in pursuit of individual interests than in typical after-school club activities. Gifted children often prefer sedentary games of some complexity because these appeal to their intelligence and provide association with older companions.

REPORTS OF SURVEYS AND CASES

Terman's gifted children proved to be more interested than others in abstract subjects, literature, discussion, dramatics, and ancient history (1925). They enjoyed activities typically followed by older children, and preferred tranquil games rather than amateur sports. A large proportion of the children showed specific aptitudes in music, mathematics, science, mechanics, experimentation, art, and dramatics.

In a study of fifty gifted children begun in 1924–1925, Witty and Lehman reported that these children engaged in the same number of play activities as the control group, but avoided the more competitive and more social activities (1927).

A special interest often becomes the center of the universe for gifted children. They become singularly absorbed and pour all their concentrated energy into it, whether it be writing stories, creating unusual costumes, working with chemistry, or editing the school paper. The gifted child has a strong urge to seek out experience and knowledge that feed his craze for information about subjects that interest him.

Seven-year-old Allen became deeply interested in prehistoric monsters, but instead of being satisfied with typical children's books on the subject, he made numerous trips to the Museum of Natural History in New York City to study dinosaurs. There he made a series of twenty watercolors illustrating these fascinating creatures. Then, after delving into the school library to obtain material for his report, he proceeded to give his class a lecture on the subject that would have done credit to an advanced student.

A gifted child may explore many fields before settling down to more permanent interests and hobbies. One week he will concentrate on repairing clocks, the next he will read about the history of clockmaking; another time he writes stories about how the ancients told time. Eventually, he will specialize in a particular subject, possibly mathematical games and puzzles or science writing.

Claude, a highly verbal child of twelve now in the top section of his class in junior high, is addicted to "monsters," an interest that developed from his studies of early man in the primary grades. He is an avid collector and maker of both "monster" pictures and literature. Currently he subscribes to a junior magazine called *Cyclops* edited by a Midwestern teen-ager who has chosen Claude to be vice-president of his organization. Claude predicts that eventually this interest will wane as he gets into senior high school and begins to specialize more definitely in anthropology as a science, a field in which even now he reads widely.

In Dr. Whipple's early studies, bright children were asked what they wanted to be when they were grown. Practically everything was listed that children in grades 5 and 6 would normally mention: farmer, soldier, mechanic, dressmaker, carpenter. Similarly, the vocational aspirations of the mentally exceptional children studied by Hollingworth revealed nothing unusual (1926). Whether differences would be found in gifted children of contrasting socio-economic backgrounds remains to be determined.

Academic Achievement and School Accomplishment

As a general rule, there is substantial positive correlation between children's intelligence as measured by reliable tests and school achievement. On the whole, rapid progress at school characterizes the mentally accelerated pupil, the rate of progress corresponding somewhat to the degree of acceleration indicated by the IQ. In the major studies of Terman, Hollingworth, and others, high-IQ children were accelerated in basic skills—reading, arithmetic, and language—and in the content studies. Terman's subjects were 44 per cent in advance of the norms in grade scores for academic achievement in basic areas, though they were no more than 14 per cent accelerated in actual grade placement (1925). At the time of Terman's initial inquiry, 85 per cent of the children were advanced in school studies for their chronological age; none of the children were retarded. By the end of the primary period they were a year ahead of their age-mates, on the average. Results of the Stanford Achievement tests proved that over half of the children had achieved a level two years higher than their grade placement at the time of the tests. Some were three or even four years advanced. These results are not surprising since intelligence tests contain items closely related to school learning.

A CASE OF UNUSUAL ACADEMIC TALENT

Laura was just eleven when she entered a seventh-grade junior high school class composed of children with IQs of 120 and above and reading scores of ninth-grade level or higher. On a group intelligence test Laura's IQ touched 168, and her reading grade score was 12.5. She impressed her teachers as being a well-poised, well-liked girl. She earned marks in the upper nineties during her high school years; owing to an exceptional memory for facts and figures and a keen interest in original research, her marks in science were as high as in other academic subjects. Laura represented her school year after year in mathematics contests and spelling bees. In addition she was an accomplished musician. Teachers found that their chief problem with this student was to provide her a sufficiently challenging program of studies.

Table 4 Stanford Achievement Test Results for Three Groups

	Lowest group							Middle group							Brightest group						
Grade	2	3	4	5	6	7	8	2	3	4	5	6	7	8	2	3	4	5	6	7	8
READING																					
Median score	2.6	3.9	5.4	6.6	8.3	9.4	10+	3.8	5.0	7.4	9.1	10+	10+	10+	4.5	5.4	8.8	10+	10+	10+	10+
Number	38	47	48	45	32	28	22	37	50	50	41	36	31	23	22	34	34	33	30	19	8
ARITHMETIC																					
Median score	2.5	3.2	4.4	5.4	6.9	7.1	8.7	3.0	4.4	5.4	7.4	8.8	10.	10+	3.0	4.4	5.7	7.9	10+	9.6	10+
Number	38	47	48	44	332	8	22	39	50	50	41	36	29	20	22	34	34	33	29	20	8
SPELLING																					
Median score	2.6	3.1	4.6	5.3	6.4	7.9	8.5	3.1	4.6	5.5	6.8	7.8	9.7	10+	3.8	4.8	6.3	7.4	8.5	9.7	10+
Number	38	47	47	45	32	28	21	39	50	50	40	38	28	17	22	34	34	32	29	19	8

Source: Gertrude Hildreth, Educational Achievement of Gifted Children, *Child Development*, 9(4):365–371, 1938. Used by kind permission of the publisher.

A CUMULATIVE STUDY OF ACHIEVEMENT

A study of the cumulative achievement records for children of different ability levels at the Lincoln School of Teachers College, Columbia University, revealed characteristic differences in achievement from grades 2 through 8 (Hildreth, 1938). One group consisted of children with IQs on the Stanford-Binet test averaging 126, another group had IQs between 118 and 122; while a third scored 110 and below, with an average of 106. How did the three groups compare? The median grade scores in achievement measured by the Stanford Achievement tests in reading, arithmetic, and spelling will be found in Table 4.

These results are shown graphically in Figure 4, where the curve labeled A represents the lowest group, G1 the middle group, and G2 the highest group. Individual achievement progress curves for five pupils in each group based on the total score of all three tests combined are shown in Figure 5.

The bright group (average IQ 126, 17 cases) achieved fourth-grade standards at the end of second grade and eighth grade or higher at the end of the sixth grade; the average pupils (average 1Q 106, 19 cases) rated at second-grade and sixth- to eighth-grade

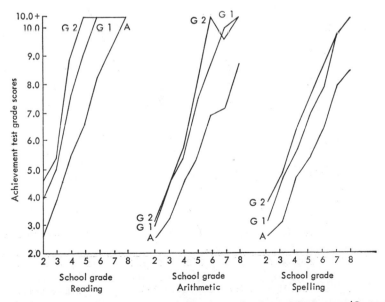

Figure 4. Stanford Achievement test median curves for three ability groups. (Gertrude Hildreth, Educational Achievement of Gifted Children, *Child Development*, 9(4):365–371, 1938. Used by permission of the publisher.)

standards, respectively, at these two periods. All the pupils had
had similar instruction and reading opportunities at school. They
had been taught together in regular classes, not in segregated
groups.

The consistent superiority of the brightest group was greatest
in reading, with these children reaching the ceiling of the test
as early as fourth grade. Differences were least marked in spelling,
although consistently in favor of the brightest group. In all tests
at all levels the groups maintained their respective ranks except
for arithmetic achievement at grade 7, where the middle group
exceeded the brightest group.

A COMPARISON STUDY OF INDIVIDUALS

Achievement test results for the three gifted boys in the author's
study, A, B, and C, and the control boy D are shown in Table
5. The brightest boy of the three showed remarkable acceleration
in reading ability from the beginning.

The results of the French survey mentioned earlier revealed
a substantial relationship between scholastic aptitude as measured
by the Gille Mosaic Test and success in school achievement.

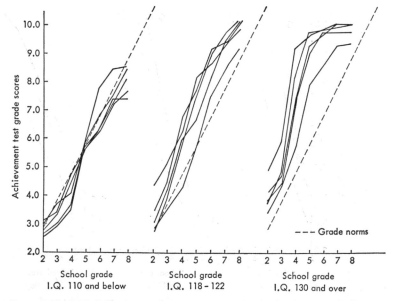

Figure 5. Individual Stanford Achievement growth curves at three IQ levels. (Gertrude
Hildreth, Educational Achievement of Gifted Children, *Child Development*, 9(4):365–371,
1938. Used by permission of the publisher.)

In New York City the children chosen as most talented for the special high schools prove to be academically talented as well. In a two-year study of gifted pupils in the New York City elementary schools, Dr. Joseph Justman found a high correlation between IQ levels and subject achievement in all groups (1953).

From two-thirds to four-fifths of students in independent private schools whose IQs average 115 to 125 surpass in scholastic achievement the norms for public school children. A recent British survey indicated that general intelligence was the single most important factor in success in mathematics (Wrigley, 1958). A study of young college students proved that educational acceleration appears to be closely associated with superior intelligence, natural science interests, and achievement motivation.

Louisa May Alcott said that she learned to think, but never to spell very well, and she was vague on figures. The fact that the mentally accelerated are not necessarily ahead of their agemates in spelling, handwriting, and manual skills has been verified by a number of studies, including those of Terman.

THE UNDERACHIEVER

In general, mental acceleration as measured by intelligence tests is prognostic of high scholastic achievement. Accomplishment is not necessarily uniform, however, and in some cases there is a wide gap between ability and achievement.

Many intellectually gifted children are studious and work with a high degree of concentration on projects related to their special

Table 5 Achievement of Three Gifted Boys and a Control

Pupil	Detroit Word Recognition (beginning of grade 1)	Metropolitan Reading (end of grade 1)	Haggerty Reading (beginning of grade 2)
A	38	4.2	44
B	0	2.8	41
C	1	3.1	26
D	0	1.7	4
	Expected score, 0; perfect score, 40	Expected score, 1.9; no perfect score	Expected score, 6; perfect score, 45

Source: Gertrude Hildreth, Three Gifted Children: A Developmental Study, *Journal of Genetic Psychology,* 85:239–262, 1954. Used by permission of the publisher.

interests, but they may not be particularly studious at school. They may be impatient of detail and dislike routine, traits that are inimical to high scholarship. The prediction of rapid educational progress is not always borne out, because school success depends so largely on a student's motivation, his study habits, his reponse to the teacher, the extent of his outside interests, and other factors.

Considerable attention has been paid to gifted children referred to as underachievers—those students, particularly in high school, who fail in their studies or achieve results below standard for ability. The causes for the discrepancy between high potential and actual achievement and the steps to be taken to bring the two more nearly into line are considered more fully in Chapter Fourteen.

Some of the world's eminent people heartily disliked school and failed to learn their lessons except under compulsion. These people may have been too much preoccupied with their own thoughts to concentrate on anything so remote as Latin grammar or even the grammar of their mother tongue. Creative-minded children prefer to work at the inventions of their own imagination and according to their own time schedules.

Oliver Goldsmith's teacher said, "Never was so dull a boy," although this "dullard" was writing verses at seven and reading Latin poetry at eight. Henri Fabre, the famous naturalist, skipped out of school at every opportunity to follow his own pursuits and to carry out experiments. Charles Darwin's teachers were down on him because he carried insects and small animals in his pockets. W. B. Yeats said, "Because I had found it difficult to attend to anything less interesting than my thoughts, I was difficult to teach." It is not surprising to learn that Mark Twain disliked school. Edvard Grieg hated school so much that he tried to get thoroughly wet in the rain one day so that his teacher would send him home. Picasso had difficulty learning his letters because he was interested only in their shapes, not in their sounds. Winston Churchill is the case most frequently cited of a school-dull, life-bright individual, practically a failure at Harrow at age thirteen. Stephen Vincent Benét took little interest in school, preferring the out-of-doors, reading, and writing.

In a survey of 400 prominent modern world figures, Dr. and Mrs. Goertzel discovered that although these remarkable people loved learning, three out of five were poor performers or maladjusted at school (1962).

Personal and Social Traits of
the Intellectually Gifted

Dr. Terman ascertained the personal traits and qualities of gifted children in California through a series of questionnaires and check-lists. He found the gifted children as a whole to be above their age level in all the traits studied. The gifted nine-year-olds were rated as equivalent to children of fourteen in character development; they showed a better spirit of cooperation than other children, were neither domineering nor egotistical, showed respect for authority and intellectual discipline, were less easily influenced by suggestion than their age-mates, and proved to have a sense of humor. They rated high in earnestness, trustworthiness, honesty, and emotional stability, as well as in capacity for objective self-appraisal. Although most of Terman's subjects were superior in personal adjustment, there were some cases of serious maladjustment (1925).

The question has been raised whether Terman's subjects were better adjusted, on the whole, than average children because the IQ criterion tended to select children from socially advantaged classes with more favorable influences for good adjustment than a cross-sectional sampling of all the children in the community.

Some interesting conclusions about the contrast in personality between bright and dull children were reached by Lightfoot, who compared children selected on the basis of the Stanford-Binet test in a variety of traits (1951). The superior traits of the gifted were comparable to Terman's earlier findings. The hundred gifted children tested by Witty turned out to be equal to the general population in emotional maturity, in the ability to adapt to conditions they could not change, and in the number of behavior problems they exhibited (1930).

The personal and social traits of elementary school children in grades four and six were extensively explored by Liddle, who surveyed all the children in these grades in an entire community from 1951 to 1952 (1958). The traits investigated were aggressive maladjustment, withdrawn maladjustment, social leadership ability, artistic talent, and intellectual ability. Intellectual talent was found to be significantly related to other talents and negatively related to maladjustment. The trait of leadership, judged from the measurement devices used, proved to be more constant from one year to the next than did indications of maladjustment.

Boehm investigated the development of moral judgment in children through the use of little stories in which children were tested for their judgment of right and wrong behavior (1963). In comparisons between academically gifted children and those of average ability and achievement, the gifted were more mature in their moral judgments concerning distinctions between the intentions and outcomes of an action. Dr. Boehm also found that upper-middle-class children developed earlier in this respect than working-class children.

The gifted French writer, Ernest Renan, tells in his autobiography that he would ask ten times a day, "Mama, are you satisfied with me?" an indication of unusual sensitivity at an early age.

POPULARITY OF THE GIFTED

How popular are gifted children in a typical school class? Gallagher summarized eight studies having a bearing on the attitudes of other children toward those recognized as gifted (1958). These studies were based chiefly on sociometric techniques. On the whole, the gifted are well-liked by their classmates and are often among the most popular because they are attractive individuals who are helpful, outgoing, and demonstrate leadership qualities. Barbe reported that bright children were better liked and were more frequently chosen by average children as friends than slow learners (1955).

In Liddle's study mentioned above, the children in grades four and six were given a who-are-they test requesting them to nominate children in two categories: the leaders in the class and those with good ideas of interesting things to do. According to the results, the children in the top 7 to 10 per cent in ability received half of the nominations.

Another study designed to answer the question, "Is the gifted child a social isolate?" was conducted by Grace and Booth (1958). Of 294 children, grades 1 through 6 in urban schools, 8 of the most popular were among the most gifted; none of the most popular were among the least gifted. On the other hand, twice as many unpopular children were among the least gifted as among the most gifted. The gifted child did not prove to be a social isolate in the elementary school.

In a study of social acceptance of gifted children, Williams found a positive correlation between group acceptance and academic performance (1958). Those achieving up to ability or beyond were more popular in the group. There was also a marked relationship between social performance and acceptance. The most pronounced relationship was between total acceptance and total performance.

At Public School 115 in Brooklyn, New York, bright children are grouped in special classes part of the day, but share assembly periods with all others in the school and have some studies on a departmentalized basis. A fifth-grade teacher of a bright class sought to determine personal preferences of the children for others in the school by asking all pupils in the five fifth-grade classes to write on a slip of paper the names of the three children they would like to be with in a school play. They were asked to list first, second, and third choices in order of preference, giving the child's name and his class. The children were mainly from good middle-class families living in private homes, chiefly of Jewish or Italian background.

The results showed that children in the IGC class (brightest group) and those in the G class (bright children, but not rating quite so high as the IGC) were among the most popular. The gifted were chosen overwhelmingly as preferred associates by children in other classes. Slower learners and the socially deprived were less popular.

THE SOCIAL ADJUSTMENT OF SUPERIOR HIGH SCHOOL STUDENTS

Are intellectually superior high school students social misfits? Miss Gloria Hoberman, a New York City social studies teacher, decided to explore this question in two classes in a New York City high school. In classs A there were 34 students, 19 girls and 15 boys; in class B, 34 students, 17 boys and 17 girls of typical high school caliber. On a secret ballot the students were asked to name the member of the class of their own sex with whom they would most like to be friendly. In class A, the girls chose sixteen-year-old Bonnie, IQ 146, a pretty, chic-looking girl, with a vibrant personality, who studies music and is a cheerleader. A close runner-up was Leslie, fifteen, a pretty girl, who shows art ability and has an IQ of 144. The boys in this particular class chose Joe, sixteen, IQ 131, a tall, good-looking, well-built boy. In class B, the girl chosen by her classmates was fifteen and a half with an IQ of 151. She is a member of the debating team, a cheerleader, and a member of Arista, the honor society. The most popular boy was Richard, IQ 121, a good-looking, athletic youth, a member of Arista and of the football team.

According to the results of a sociometric–personal preference test, Paul, a well-rounded gifted boy, was the most popular in his class, in spite of the fact that he was the youngest; he was also most often chosen for leadership posts. Boy A, studied by the author, was not so popular as another bright boy in his class who was kind and calm, but both boys were chosen for class positions that best fitted their particular talents.

Usually the gifted prefer older associates. In one study, whereas 25 per cent of gifted children expressed preference for older comrades, only 9 per cent of average children did so (Williams, 1958).

THE QUESTION OF SOCIAL ADJUSTMENT

Whether the gifted young person is socially well-adjusted or, on the contrary, lonely and isolated depends upon how well the social side of his life has been developed, and how he responds to pressures in the family environment. A pair of highly gifted sisters showed intense sibling rivalry. The younger sister was fully as capable as the older, but she was reserved and had feelings of inferiority. The social difficulties of exceptional children appear to be most marked in the middle years of childhood and to lessen as the range of their social contacts increases.

The musically gifted youngster can hardly expect to lead a normal social life because he must spend so much time practicing. An only child who is closely attached to his parents may have few friends and scarcely sense the lack of them. This was true of one fifteen-year-old girl who was ill at ease with her contemporaries and preferred the company of adults. Another case is that of an only son who had associated mostly with his parents and their sophisticated friends here and abroad. In school he found himself a social misfit with other fourth graders because his interests and even his conversation seemed odd to them.

Dr. Hollingworth pointed out that extremely gifted children who are young for the grade may have problems in social acceptance and group identification because a child who is obviously younger than the others, physically smaller, inclined to be bookish, not interested in sports, and tending to be hypercritical is apt to be rejected by his classmates. His status may improve as he goes on through high school and into college where he finds more congenial associates who can appreciate his unusual abilities.

Is isolation necessarily a characteristic trait of extremely bright children? Isolation in twenty-eight children testing 170 IQ and above who were under twelve years of age was investigated by Dr. Paul M. Sheldon at the Consulting Center for the Gifted, New York University (1959). Rorschach tests, psychiatric examinations, and observations of play behavior were employed. The popularity of these children with their classmates was observed by teachers, and the attitudes of other children toward them was assessed. Feelings of inferiority and some tension were reported in the majority of cases, but most of the children were well-liked by or even popular with their age-mates in general.

Bright children, just as all others, have individual temperaments. Some are bold and domineering, given to ordering people about; others are reclusive and retiring. Shy children, in spite of their talents, may suffer from feelings of inadequacy and be rejected by children of their own age.

ATTITUDE OF THE GIFTED TOWARD OTHER CHILDREN

The popular notion is that gifted children are conceited, arrogant little show-offs who are snobbish toward persons less talented than themselves. The results of attitude tests as well as informal observations indicate that the gifted are not necessarily conceited or inclined to think of themselves as superior to others. In fact, they more often display modesty and generous feelings. According to Dr. Florence Brumbaugh, children in the Hunter College Elementary School disclaimed having any exceptional ability. Instead of feeling snobbish, these children were more apt to feel modest about their accomplishments, and might name another child who could "do it better."

In Williams's study, none of the children showed concern about himself as a "big brain." None sought special attention on the grounds of unusual intellectual capacity (1958). The situation may, of course, be quite the opposite. A college student said that when he was in junior high school all the children knew their IQs. The bright ones scorned a boy with a low IQ and would scarcely speak to him, but they all looked up to a girl known to have a very high IQ.

Cliquishness among gifted children was investigated by Silverstein, who tested the hypothesis: Of the cliques involving intellectually superior children in regular classes, as many cliques will include less gifted children as will not include them (1962). The subjects were 169 boys and 181 girls in thirteen fifth-grade classes in eleven schools in middle-income areas in New York City. A modified form of the Ohio Social Acceptance Scale was used in the study. The results confirmed the hypothesis. The intellectually superior pupils were not more cliquish than their classmates.

Notwithstanding all this evidence, teachers report that children do frequently exhibit cockiness when placed in special classes for bright students. There is plenty of conversation about who is in the smart class and which ones have been placed in the dumb section. The bright pupils would not think of associating with the others, or even speak to them. Obviously, these attitudes are picked up from adults, even from teachers whom the children over-hear lauding the bright class and disparaging the slow-learner group.

For more information on the traits of gifted adolescent youths see Chapter Twelve. For a fuller discussion of the adjustment problems of gifted children see Chapter Fourteen.

Comparison of Boys and Girls in Mental Superiority

Are there essential differences or only incidental distinctions between the sexes in mental capacities and talents? Plato raised this question in proposing plans for the education of all citizens in the ideal state. The fact that eminent men far outnumber eminent women suggests that men are smarter than women.

Test data for the childhood years prove that bright boys and girls are found in nearly the same proportions. No difference in the incidence of IQs above 140 was found for boys and girls grades 9 to 12 in the population reported by Witty (1930). The ratio was the same as the proportions of the sexes in the general population, 104 boys to 100 girls.

Hollingworth reported the ratio of boys to girls in those testing above 140 IQ to be 111 to 110 when allowance was made for the slightly greater proportion of boys in the general population. In Terman's studies the ratio of boys to girls in the initial identification was 121 to 100. In the school population from which these children were drawn the ratio of boys to girls was 104.5 to 100. In the nominations of gifted children made by teachers the ratio was 109.7 boys to 100 girls. Terman concluded that in the general population high intelligence as measured by the Stanford-Binet test was somewhat more frequent among boys than among girls.

In the French survey of 1944, no differences were found in the percentages of boys and girls scoring at the same levels on the Gille Mosaic Test. In the age range six to fourteen in the total population tested, 95,273 pupils, about half were boys and half girls.

In the Albuquerque, New Mexico, survey mentioned in Chapter Two, boys testing 130 IQ and above were more numerous than girls in this category, 125 boys as compared with 90 girls.

The traits of 4,529 children in grades 4 to 8, all of whom scored in the upper 10 per cent on the Kuhlmann-Anderson Intelligence Test, were analyzed by Lewis (1940). These children were enrolled in schools from 310 different communities in 36 states. Descriptions of personality traits, emotional stability, extracurricular activities, hobbies, educational achievement, and family background were obtained from questionnaire data supplied by teachers. Comparisons were made between the gifted group and comparable data for a normative population. Many of the findings were similar to those of Terman, Witty, and others; but they differed somewhat from these earlier studies because more of the children were living in small communities. The larger proportion of girls to boys in this study, about 10 to 7, may reflect some bias in the test favoring the girls, possibly the reading factor.

By late adolescence boys outdistance girls in tests of mathematics and science. Boys far outnumber girls in the science talent search contests, but this is partly because boys more frequently enroll in advanced high school science courses.

Although test differences favor the boys, girls earn higher grades on the whole both in high school and college; they are also more frequently listed as honor students. Gifted boys, however, display their originality and inventiveness more clearly and forcefully than girls. Among children appearing on the quiz kid programs the boys are younger than the girls and far more numerous.

The Question of Racial Differences in Mental Ability and Special Talents

Are there racial differences in giftedness, originality, genius, and talent, as Dr. Ernest Kretschmer and other social scientists contended a half century ago? This question is continually kept alive with new findings. One set of figures contradicts another. With upward mobility of a racial group, the children in one generation rate higher than those in the preceding one. Northern Negroes score consistently higher than Southern Negroes, probably because of a differential in educational opportunities.

The children in the Terman studies were Scottish and Jewish in larger proportions than the general population of the California city areas from which the children were drawn. When public facilities such as libraries are set up in urban communities, the proportion of Jewish youths using the facilities outnumbers those of other races who have equal access to them. Is this because Jewish children are smarter than others, or because these children and their parents are more apt to take advantage of educational and cultural opportunities?

How can one account for the growing ascendancy of the non-white races in the present century? With educational and cultural opportunities equalized, the myth of racial superiority in intelligence may vanish.

De Craecker, a Belgian psychologist, observed that families of immigrants in a new country produce more than the expected proportion of notables and distinguished persons compared with the natives of comparable background and educational opportunity (1951). This proved to be true of the high school students in the French survey referred to above, and the same thing is true of political leaders in South American countries. Is this due to the migration of the stronger, more independent members of a community; or does migrating, which forces the immigrant to make adjustments in a new community, draw out talent to the fullest degree?

The Socioeconomic Background of Gifted Youth

Bright and talented children come from every type of home and background. The socially superior classes, however, furnish more gifted children as well as more potential leaders and professional workers than others. Sir Francis Galton found chances of eminence much higher among children of upper-class and professional families. With quality of education held constant, bright children tend generally to come from better-class homes and neighborhoods. They more often grow up in communities that offer superior schooling and other cultural advantages, and the parents of these children are better educated than average.

A universal finding is that IQ is directly proportional to socioeconomic status. Children who rate high on intelligence tests are relatively more numerous in middle- and high-income families. In Terman's studies the professional classes furnished far more gifted children than their proportion in the general population; the families of unskilled and semiskilled workers furnished far fewer than their respective proportions. Ten times as many (31.4 per cent) of Terman's original group of gifted children came from professional families as would be expected from the number of professionals found in the general population. These parents had had a better education than the generality of the population, their annual income was far above average, and, in spite of their relative youth, they occupied responsible occupational posts.

High-occupation fathers tend to have high-IQ children, and the reverse is true of fathers of low occupational status. Gifted children are often members of gifted families where both parents are highly educated, the father and perhaps the mother, too, being professional people. The other children in the family are also bright. These "massed talent" families are frequently found in university communities. In the families of children testing over 180 IQ reported by Hollingworth, twelve cases in all, ten of the fathers were professional men, and five of the mothers were college graduates, figures that are exceptional compared with parents in the general population.

It is estimated that only 6 per cent of slum children have IQs of 125 or higher, whereas 25 per cent of suburban schoolchildren rate at or above this level.

REPORTS OF SURVEYS

Heuyer, Piéron, and their associates found a close association between socioeconomic factors, the father's occupation, the economic level of the home and community, the number of children in the family, and the age-level scores of children who rated in the top decile on the Gille Mosaic Test (1953). There was an inverse ratio between a child's test level and the number of children in the family.

In a survey of sixth-grade pupils in public schools of a medium-sized Midwestern town, the upper and upper-middle social classes produced 1.8 times as many children in the upper quarter of the IQ distribution as they would if all social classes had been equally represented; the lower-lower social class, only 0.4 times as many. In a study of high school seniors in a city of 500,000 population, the number of superior graduates was roughly proportional to the socioeconomic level of the parents (Havighurst, 1961). British children who come out on top in the "eleven-plus" examinations at the end of elementary school tend to come from a superior environment.

In a statewide survey of gifted children in California in 1957, data for 929 children were collected. About half were in the elementary school grades and half in junior and senior high school. Of these children, 478 were boys and 451 were girls. The mean Stanford-Binet IQ was 140.1. Of these children 40 per cent came from the upper (professional-managerial) class, 48 per cent from the middle economic group, and 2 per cent from the lower socio-economic group (Martinson, 1960).

An analysis of the records of students selected for the Early Admissions to College Program of The Fund for the Advancement of Education showed that 76 per cent of the students came from families of professional, government, and business occupations, and the remainder from homes of laborers and farmers (1957).

The question arises whether superior socioeconomic factors, cultural and educational advantages, are the result or the cause of children's high-level aptitudes and ultimate achievements. Is a child brighter for having attended a better-than-average school, one with a reputation for high standards?

Some people hold the view that the terms "gifted" and "socially favored" are interchangeable, on the assumption that superior cultural advantages account for the difference between bright children and others. Others insist that those who live in high-standard homes and communities are people of high intelligence to begin with who demand and obtain for themselves the better things of life. There is no conclusive evidence that moving from slums to high-class suburbs improves children's intellectual capacities to an appreciable degree.

Those who believe that talent is primarily the product of a good environment have launched programs to uncover hidden talent in children living in poor neighborhoods; they feel that if living conditions could be improved and these children could have the advantages upper-class children enjoy, they would display a surprising amount of intelligence and creative talent.

The Higher Horizons Program organized in New York City represents such an effort. It will be some years before the full effects of the program have been demonstrated. For more information on this subject, see Chapter Seven.

References

Barbe, Walter B.: Characteristics of Gifted Children, *Educational Administration and Supervision,* 41:207–217, 1955.

Barbe, Walter B.: A Study of the Reading of Gifted High School Students, *Educational Administration and Supervision,* 38:148–152, 1952.

Boehm, Lenore: The Development of Conscience: A Comparison of Upper Middle Class Academically Gifted Children Attending Catholic and Jewish Parochial Schools, *Journal of Social Psychology,* 59:101–110, 1963.

Carroll, Herbert A.: Generalization of Bright and Dull Children: A Comparative Study with Special Reference to Spelling, *Journal of Educational Psychology*, 21:489–499, 1930.

Carroll, Herbert A.: *Genius in the Making*, McGraw-Hill Book Company, New York, 1940.

Davidson, Helen, and Dom Balducci: Class and Sex Differences in Verbal Facility of Very Bright Children, *Journal of Educational Psychology*, 47:476–480, 1956.

De Cracker, R.: *Les enfants intellectuellement doués*, Presses Universitaires de France, Paris, 1951.

De la Mare, Walter: *Early One Morning in the Spring*, The Macmillan Company, New York, 1935.

Durkin, Dolores: A Study of Children Who Learned to Read Prior to Grade One, *California Journal of Educational Research*, 10:109–113, 1959.

Durr, William K.: Characteristics of Gifted Children: Ten Years of Research, *Gifted Child Quarterly*, 4:75–80, 1960.

Flanagan, John C., and staff: *Characteristics of High School Youth*, vol. 2 in a 3-vol. series, Houghton Mifflin Company, Boston, 1962.

Gallagher, James J.: Peer Acceptance of Highly Gifted Children, *Elementary School Journal*, 58:465–470, 1958.

Goertzel, Victor H., and Mildred G. Goertzel: *Cradles of Eminence*, Little, Brown and Company, Boston, 1962.

Grace, Harry A., and Nancy Lou Booth: Is the Gifted Child a Social Isolate? *Peabody Journal of Education*, 35:195–196, 1958.

Hall, Theodore: *Gifted Children: The Cleveland Story*, The World Publishing Company, Cleveland, 1956.

Havighurst, Robert J.: Conditions Productive of Superior Children, *Teachers College Record*, 62:524–531, 1961.

Heuyer, G., H. Piéron, and others: *Le niveau intellectuel des enfants d'âge scolaire*, vol. 2, Presses Universitaires de France, Paris, 1954.

Hildreth, Gertrude: Characteristics of Young Gifted Children, *Journal of Genetic Psychology*, 53:287–311, 1938.

Hildreth, Gertrude: Educational Achievement of Gifted Children, *Child Development*, 9(4):365–371, 1938.

Hildreth, Gertrude: Three Gifted Children: A Developmental Study, *Journal of Genetic Psychology*, 85:239–264, 1954.

Hollingworth, Leta S.: *Children Who Test above 180 I.Q. Stanford Binet: Origin and Development*, World Book Company, Tarrytown-on-Hudson, N.Y., 1942.

Hollingworth, Leta S.: *Gifted Children: Their Nature and Nurture*, The Macmillan Company, New York, 1926.

Hollingworth, Leta S.: *Special Talents and Defects*, The Macmillan Company, New York, 1923.

Hollingworth, Leta S., and Grace A. Taylor: Size and Strength of Children Who Test above 135 I.Q., in Guy Montrose Whipple (ed.), *Twenty-third Yearbook of the National Society for the Study of Education,* Public School Publishing Company, Bloomington, Ill., 1924.

Justman, Joseph: *A Comparison of the Functioning of Intellectually Gifted Children Enrolled in Special Progress Classes in Junior High School,* unpublished doctoral dissertation, Teachers College, Columbia University, New York, 1953.

Lewis, William Drayton: *A Study of Superior Children in the Elementary School,* George Peabody College for Teachers, Nashville, Tenn., 1940.

Liddle, Gordon: Overlap among Desirable and Undesirable Characteristics in Gifted Children, *Journal of Educational Psychology,* 49:219–223, 1958.

Lightfoot, Georgia P.: *Personality Characteristics of Bright and Dull Children,* Contributions to Education no. 969, Bureau of Publications, Teachers College, Columbia University, New York, 1951.

Loban, Walter D.: *The Language of Elementary School Children,* Research Report no. 1, National Council of Teachers of English, Champaign, Ill., 1963.

Martinson, Ruth A.: *Educational Programs for Gifted Pupils,* State Department of Education, Sacramento, Calif., 1960.

Mearns, Hughes: *Creative Youth: How a School Environment Set Free the Creative Spirit,* Doubleday & Company, Inc., Garden City, N.Y., 1925.

Miles, Catherine C.: Gifted Children, chap. 16 in Leonard Carmichael (ed.), *Manual of Child Psychology,* John Wiley & Sons, Inc., New York, 1946, pp. 886–953.

Mori, Shirgetoshi: Basic Study of the Characteristics of Intellectually Gifted Children: I. General Developmental Characteristics, *Japanese Journal of Educational Psychology,* 7:131–141, 1959.

Parkyn, G. W.: *Children of High Intelligence: A New Zealand Study,* Council for Educational Research, Wellington, New Zealand, 1948.

Sheldon, Paul M.: Isolation as a Characteristic of Highly Gifted Children, *Journal of Educational Sociology,* 32:215–221, 1959.

Silverstein, Samuel: How Cliquish Are Intellectually Superior Children in Regular Classes? *Elementary School Journal,* 62:387–390, 1962.

Strang, Ruth: *Helping Your Gifted Child,* E. P. Dutton & Co., Inc., New York, 1960.

Strickland, Ruth G.: *The Language of Elementary School Children,* Bulletin of the School of Education, Indiana University, 34, no. 4, Bloomington, Ind., 1960

Terman, Lewis M.: An Experiment in Infant Education, *Journal of Applied Psychology,* 2:219–228, 1918.

Terman, Lewis M., and others: *Genetic Studies of Genius,* vol. 1, *Mental and Physical Traits of a Thousand Gifted Children,* Stanford University Press, Stanford, Calif., 1925.

They Went to College Early, Evaluation Report no. 2, The Fund for the Advancement of Education, New York, 1957.

Wall, W. D.: Highly Intelligent Children: The Psychology of the Gifted, *Educational Research,* 2:101–110, 1960.

Whipple, Guy Montrose: *Classes for Gifted Children: An Experimental Study of Methods of Selection and Instruction,* School and Home Educational Monographs, no. 1, Public School Publishing Company, Bloomington, Ill., 1919.

Williams, Meta F.: Acceptance and Performance among Gifted Elementary School Children, *Ohio State University Educational Research Bulletin,* 37:216–220, 224, 1958.

Witty, Paul A.: *A Study of One Hundred Gifted Children,* State Teachers College Studies in Education, vol. 1, no. 13, Emporia, Kans., 1930.

Witty, Paul A., and Harvey C. Lehman: The Play Behavior of Fifty Gifted Children, *Journal of Educational Psychology,* 18:259–265, 1927.

Wrigley, Jack: The Factorial Nature of Ability in Elementary Mathematics, *British Journal of Educational Psychology,* 28:61–78, 1958.

Chapter Five

DEVELOPMENTAL STUDIES OF THE GIFTED

What kind of people have yesterday's gifted children become? Does a gifted youth usually realize in adult life the promise of his early abilities? How consistent is the development of the exceptional individual? Were eminent persons mediocre or undistinguished as children? Answers to these questions will be found in long-range follow-up studies of gifted children and in investigations of the early lives of eminent persons.

Follow-up studies are of two kinds: reports of data in terms of group averages and intensive studies of individual children over a period of years. Longitudinal follow-up studies have some analogy to birdbanding studies, in which birds are caught and banded when young, and are then reported on at intervals as they are captured and released. Similarly, the children are "caught" early and studied at intervals.

Follow-up studies of human subjects are expensive and time-consuming, because the children are on the move with their parents from year to year, in and out of school, and finally off to a job. These studies require an inordinate amount of painstaking effort on the part of research workers and a willing cooperation from the subjects.

Terman's Follow-up Studies

Up to the time of Dr. Lewis M. Terman's follow-up studies no one knew with any certainty what became of children who had been identified as gifted by scientific procedures. The only developmental material was that found in biographical sketches of a few precocious children and several accounts of the origins of great men.

In undertaking his extensive investigations, Dr. Terman observed that cross-sectional studies must be supplemented by full-length longitudinal studies of the gifted from earliest childhood to late maturity. There was need, too, he pointed out, for "backward-looking studies," the systematic collection of early biographical data for the great figures of history and persons of distinction.

Dr. Terman and his associates conducted three follow-up studies of nearly 1,500 gifted children identified in California in 1921–1922. The studies covered more than thirty years. Only the chief findings will be reported here. Growth was described in terms of group changes, but some developmental studies of individuals were included in the published reports.

TERMAN'S FIRST STUDY, 1930

Between 1923 and 1926, Terman received a good response from parents and schools on periodic follow-up report blanks, and in 1927 field workers began testing the children and interviewing the parents. In 1927–1928, data were systematically collected for the first extensive follow-up report (Terman and others, 1930). The authors hoped to check on the original findings and obtain a picture of gifted youth. The chief question was: Is the nature of the mental and behavioral deviation observed in the follow-up the same as that observed in the initial study? This first follow-up gave conclusive evidence that generalizations made about the exceptional qualities of these children in 1921–1922 were also true in 1927–1928.

At the time of the initial tests the children tended to be two years accelerated in age-grade school placement according to the Ayres-Strayer standards. Seven years later, according to the same standard, 74 per cent of the boys and 84 per cent of the girls continued to be accelerated in age-grade placement: the children were about two years younger, on the average, than the mean age of those in high school with whom they were compared.

Intelligence Test Results   The group retested in 1928 with the Terman group test averaged lower scores on the whole (IQ 130 to 135) than when they were initially tested with the Stanford-Binet. For the entire group there was an average drop of 9 points. The distribution of changes in individual IQs was of greater significance than changes in means. On the Terman test the group exceeded the 99th percentile for the general high school population.

On retests of intelligence, the boys tended to maintain their relative superiority. The girls more often showed a drop in IQ.

In processing his follow-up data, Dr. Terman experienced difficulty in making valid comparisons; he found the general population in high school much more selective than in the elementary grades because school dropout and failure had automatically screened out many of the less competent students.

In the follow-up study, students in the fourteen- to seventeen-year age group were given Thorndike college entrance tests, and their scores exceeded the means of students entering Stanford University in previous years.

School Achievement and Other Ratings   School achievement tended to remain high, in line with the original findings, but there was some tendency to regress to the mean of the general population. In the senior high school year the gifted tested above the 90th percentile on the Iowa High School Content Examinations or from 1.5 to 2 standard deviations above the mean of high school seniors in general.

As to the interests of these youths in 1928, both boys and girls preferred reading to all other occupations. They took part in a wide range of extracurricular school activities, however, and gained recognition in several.

The children tended to remain above the average of the general population in health and physique. The death rate was lower than the expected actuarial figure.

Teachers' ratings of personal traits placed these young people a little lower than on the earlier ratings, but they were still above the average of normative controls in nearly all cases. The social and personality traits of the youths in 1928 were similar to those reported in 1922. Responses on checklists and other devices were similar to those of other well-educated groups, well above the norms for the general population. By 1928 more girls than boys had developed interest in the opposite sex. The highest-ranking individuals had more difficulty in social adjustment than more typical members of the gifted group. Serious behavior or personality problems proved to be about half as great as among unselected youths of corresponding age.

The specialized abilities and interests of the boys included mathematics, science, debating, public speaking, and mechanical arts; the girls showed greater interest or ability in art, writing, dramatics, dancing, household arts, and music.

Brief portraits of a number of gifted individuals revealed the ways in which the vicissitudes of fortune arising from home conditions, personality difficulties, school problems, and other factors affected their progress. An exceptionally promising individual might not have been able to maintain his high status because of unfavorable circumstances.

Terman and his associates stated that the most important conclusion of the first follow-up study was that the composite portrait of the group had changed only in minor respects over a period of six or seven years.

TERMAN'S SECOND STUDY, 1947

By the end of 1946 Terman and his associates were prepared to answer the question: How well do mentally gifted children turn out? (Terman and Oden, 1947).

The results of the second follow-up study proved that after twenty-five years the people originally selected as gifted continued to be superior in physical development, educational achievement, intelligence, and personal traits. However, the degree of superiority was less marked for traits indicative of emotional stability and social adjustment than for intellectual traits.

One hundred ninety-four of the subjects graduated from high school before age sixteen, and 554 before seventeen. More than

90 per cent of the gifted boys and 86 per cent of the gifted girls went on to college, although some lost interest, and 30 per cent of those who entered failed to graduate. Of those who by 1928 had graduated from college, three times as many had been elected to Phi Beta Kappa honorary scholastic society as in the general college population, and twice as many had graduated with distinction or with great distinction. The typical gifted student who graduated from college did so a year earlier than is typical, and a substantial number went on for advanced degrees.

Although average college grades for these highly selected students were, on the whole, superior, the findings indicated that intellect and achievement were far from perfectly correlated. An analysis of eighty students who had failed in college disclosed a number of causes to account for their difficulties.

A quarter of a century after their selection, 86 per cent of the group placed among the upper occupational levels. They were, in fact, following professional occupations nine times as frequently as the generality of the population, owing no doubt to the preponderance of college people. There were 71 per cent of the gifted in professional, semiprofessional, or managerial occupations compared with 13.8 per cent of the California employed population in general, and 55 per cent for all college graduates. Their average income was also higher than that of the typical college graduate.

In the group were scientists of recognized status or of great promise, outstanding physicians, lawyers, successful writers, and a number of leading business executives, as well as an impressive number of university teachers. The higher the individual's mental level, the more likely he was to follow the career plans he had announced in childhood, e.g., chemist, artist, etc.

In this second follow-up study Dr. Terman compared a productive group with a less productive group from his original gifted population. The former showed superiority in persistence in accomplishment of ends, integration toward goals in contrast to drifting, self-confidence, and freedom from inferiority feelings; they undertook more extracurricular and leadership activities in high school and did superior schoolwork. Factors in the family background more clearly differentiated the successful and unsuccessful gifted.

On the whole, these people did not prove to be one-sided in their development. They had broad interests and they become superior citizens with better-adjusted home life than people of comparable education in the general population. Marital adjustment was above average.

TERMAN AND ODEN'S THIRD STUDY, 1959

The results of a third follow-up study in 1955 represented responses to questionnaires received from 93 per cent of the original group (Terman and Oden, 1959). Their intellectual, scholastic, and vocational achievements were especially noteworthy. Of the scientists, forty-seven were listed in the 1949 edition of *American Men of Science.*

By age forty the men had published 67 books and more than 1,400 scientific, technical, and professional articles. They also had more than 150 patents to their credit. This is many times the frequency of occurrence for adults in the general population. However, as many as 20 per cent had not accomplished anything out of the ordinary. Less than half the gifted women were reported to be working outside their homes.

The great majority of the original subjects continued to be well adjusted socially; the rate of antisocial behavior was far below that of the general population.

CRITICAL EVALUATION OF THE STUDIES

Everyone is indebted to Dr. Terman for his tremendous contribution to our knowledge of gifted youngsters and how they grow. Nevertheless, a number of questions arise concerning the validity of the findings. These center about the criteria used for the original selection of the cases, the nature of the controls, and the analysis of the causes of deviation from initial status.

Selection Criteria   The validity of the Terman studies hinges upon the validity of the initial selection of subjects. The method, in brief, was as follows: In the initial sifting, teachers were asked to list the three most intelligent pupils in their classes, grades 3 to 8, and to indicate the reasons for making nominations. They were also asked to list the youngest child in each grade or half-grade in the room. These children constituted about 6 to 8 per cent of the population in their schools, grades 3 to 8. The second step was the administration of the National Intelligence Test. The third was the administration of an abbreviated Stanford-Binet test to those ranking high on the group test and nominated by teachers as most intelligent or youngest in the class. Those who earned an IQ of 130 or higher on the abbreviated test were then given the full Stanford-Binet test. The lower limit for inclusion in the experimental group was 140, with a few exceptions made for children rating below this figure. The Terman group test was given to the few children in grade 8 who were fourteen years of age or older.

Dr. Terman attached most significance to the intelligence test ratings as the final criterion for selection but he realized that a few highly intelligent children might have been missed by this screening process or that a few of lesser intelligence might have been included through errors of measurement. What are the chances that a child was overrated or underrated? Taking into account the probable error of the 1916 revision of the Stanford-Binet test, statistically there was 1 chance in 16 that a measured IQ of 130 was actually 140, and 1 chance in 7 that a measured IQ of 135 was actually 140, and vice versa. "Broad-band" selection through a combination of tests and ratings, including several successive ratings, might have yielded different results in the follow-up appraisals of these subjects.

Matched Controls   The "controls" used in the Terman studies were primarily normative group scores and ratings of population averages rather than matched cases of average ability given the same tests and rated with the same devices. The tendencies in two different populations were compared in the follow-up series—the population of highly intelligent individuals and the general population. The higher selectivity in older age groups created difficulties in follow-up comparisons, which Dr. Terman recognized. Longitudinal studies with matched controls from the beginning obviate some of the hazards of mass comparisons.

A Socially Favored Group   Dr. Terman did not attempt to take into account the effects of different types of environment affecting the gifted. This requires initial and follow-up studies of children with a wide variety of abilities and talents growing up under diverse environmental conditions. The fact that so many of Terman's group went on to college and remained to graduate at a time when liberal college scholarship grants for high-ranking students were less common than today reflects the high socioeconomic status of his subjects. A group such as this had advantages that favored good health, wholesome adjustments, emotional security, and life success. A bright group, less favored socially, might not have shown such consistent superiority.

Regression to the Mean   Groups chosen on the basis of extreme test scores tend to regress toward the mean of the population on retests, which accounts for part of the drop in IQs on retests in the Terman study. At several points in the early reports Dr. Terman indicated his awareness of this problem. For further information on this topic see Thorndike (1948); also Clarke, Clarke, and Brown (1960).

Other Follow-up Studies

Hollingworth   Hollingworth and Kaunitz reported on the intellectual status of 116 gifted children ten years after their initial selection (1934). These young people, who had an average age of eighteen years, six months, were given the Army Alpha examination. Ninety-five of the gifted subjects reached the top percentile on this test; 82 per cent of the group were at the same percentile on the Army test that they had reached when initially tested with the Stanford-Binet. The remaining 18 per cent approached this status. None regressed to average status. However, the girls showed greater tendency to regress than the boys.

A later report on these subjects was made by Lorge and Hollingworth (1936). Eighteen of the original group were given Thorndike's CAVD college-level tests. On these tests the gifted group with IQs above 140 fell within the upper quartile of the college population.

Another report was made by Hollingworth of twelve very exceptional children testing over 180 IQ, who were observed over a period of time, some for as long as twenty-three years (1942). These individuals maintained their high intellectual status as they matured.

Lamson conducted a follow-up of 56 children of Hollingworth's early study who had been given Stanford-Binet tests at the age of nine (1930). These children were chosen at random from a larger group of 148 children testing over 133 IQ. Teachers gave their judgments of the children in self-control, intelligence, personal appearance, conceit, sustained effort, general deportment, general quality of schoolwork, and popularity with schoolmates. By the time the children were in senior high school, they were significantly superior to a control group of average-rating children with respect to intelligence, general quality of schoolwork, and sustained effort. The mean IQ of the gifted group on the first test was 153, on the second test, a year later, 157. On a third test, again a year later, the average was still 157. These results showed that the intellectual development of this group as measured by tests was remarkably consistent. When chronological age was held constant, the children were in the top decile of the high school population as judged by the Army Alpha examination. This is equivalent to being in the top percentile for an unselected group of like-age youths. These children graduated from high school at an average chronological age of sixteen.

Although the children originally studied by Dr. Hollingworth went on to high school and college with good records, now, after a period of from thirty to forty years, few of them have been heard from as notable leaders or creative thinkers. One amazing boy who set records in accelerating through school, college, and graduate studies is a college professor, but not otherwise distinguished. Some who came from low-income families were unable to move ahead in their school careers, possibly for economic reasons.

Witty   Witty made a follow-up study of fifty gifted children, beginning in 1924–1925 and continuing to 1939–1940. These children, who were attending public schools in the Middle West, grades 3 to 7, when first identified, all rated above the 99th percentile on the National Intelligence Test and all had Stanford-Binet IQs of 140 or over, with a mean IQ of 153. The average age of the children, 26 boys and 24 girls, at the time of the first test was ten years, five months. Control cases ranging in IQ from 90 to 110 were paired with each gifted child in sex, age, and race (Witty, 1940).

The traits of the gifted children and their family background proved to be similar to those reported by Terman. In physical status the children were above average as a group and in vigorous health; they proved to be well adjusted in school life. There was more English, Scottish, and Jewish stock in their ancestry than in that of the control group. Most of the gifted children had had the advantages of stimulating cultural influences at home. Their parents averaged thirteen years of formal education, and the fathers rated above average in occupational status.

Although the mean IQ of the children was 153, the mean educational quotient (EQ) was 136—an accomplishment quotient of 88 indicating a substantial degree of "educational retardation." The interests of the children reflected their general superiority, versatility, and vitality. They were more solitary and sedentary in their play than their matchees of average ability. In ratings and tests of character the gifted were above the average of the controls.

A follow-up study five years after the initial testing showed that these children had maintained their superior mental ability.

The mean on the Terman Group Test of Mental Ability was 136, with the entire group falling within the upper 5 per cent of college students. The rank on both early and later tests was similar, as shown by a positive correlation of .66. The lack of ceiling for the most gifted children of high school age on the Terman group test, however, tends to reduce the correlation.

These students maintained a high level of school achievement in spite of the school's neglect of them. Aside from one boy who rated average, all others were above average in school marks. The boys rated slightly below the girls in the follow-up evaluation. At the time of a second follow-up study, most of the students were in college. Half of the boys and 70 per cent of the girls earned marks of A in their school studies. On the whole, they maintained their high level in general information and all-around academic attainment. They participated fully in school life and received more honors than average students.

Failure to respond well to discipline increased during the interval between the two follow-up studies. Boys were more often offenders than girls. Maladjustment also tended to increase.

Lincoln   In a study of bright children reported by Lincoln, 109 children, 45 boys and 64 girls, with initial IQs ranging from 119 to 145 were reexamined after intervals of five to eight years (1935). Nearly half the boys and about one-third of the girls gained in points of IQ.

Hildreth   The Lincoln School of Teachers College, Columbia University, New York, enrolled some remarkable boys and girls during the years of its existence, 1918 to 1948. Although there was no minimum IQ for admission to the school, through the years the average Stanford-Binet test IQ in the elementary school years was around 120, with the middle range between 115 and 130. Gifted Lincoln School students grew up in gifted families; their parents were, on the whole, well-educated, cultured people with wide social and professional interests. At one PTA meeting the families of thirty lawyers were represented.

In 1942 the author made a follow-up study of Lincoln School graduates by means of a questionnaire requesting information about further education and present employment. A comparison was made of the reports for a mentally superior group, 52 graduates with IQs of 130 or higher on all mental tests given before the age of thirteen, and a group of 52 students of relatively less ability, with IQs below 120. The median for the high-IQ group was 140, for the low group 111. Parental occupations were similar for the two groups. The college-going record showed that of the gifted group 30 graduated from Ivy League colleges and 5 attended without graduating, whereas of the low group, 11 graduated from Ivy-type colleges and 2 attended without graduating. Of the high group 21 went on for graduate work, compared with 4 of the low group. There were 10 master's degree graduates and 7 Ph.D.s among the gifted, compared with 4 master's degree graduates and no Ph.D.s from the low group. There were 4 M.D.s in the high group, none in the lower group. In the gifted group 17 had average college marks of A or A—, but none of the lower group had earned such high average marks. Among the gifted, 16 had entered professional careers, in contrast to 6 of the lower group.

Teachers who were well acquainted with the Lincoln School graduates went over the lists of those who had graduated by 1942, indicating students they considered outstanding because of scholarship or distinguished contributions to school life. They also checked students who for any reason had been considered problem cases. Sixty graduates were listed as outstanding; twenty-two were listed as problems. The median IQ for the outstanding group was 136, with a range from 105 to 159; the median for the problem group was 114, with a range from 88 to 149.

Since then, judging from informal reports, the graduates now in their forties and fifties have given a good account of themselves. Among Lincoln School graduates are leading writers, musicians, college and university professors, college deans and department chairmen, business executives, statesmen, linguists, and professionals of every description. The number of notables among them far exceeds the incidence of distinguished people in the general population. A particularly precocious youth, a science major, finished high school at sixteen. After graduating from a leading medical school, he was appointed to teach there; he died heroically in World War II during the Battle of the Bulge. The women as well as the men have earned distinction beyond the average in teaching, library work, science, and other fields—in some cases, along with their careers as homemakers.

Some of the most promising, like those in Terman's group, are solid citizens but in no way remarkable; a few have been thwarted by ill health, emotional problems, and disaster of one kind or another. On the whole, however, gifted Lincoln School graduates have fulfilled their early promise as capable, productive adults.

Wilson   Dr. Frank T. Wilson, in reporting on retests of Hunter College Elementary School children, found that when these boys and girls reached adolescence they generally maintained their place at the top centile for their age groups and continued to be versatile, healthy, well-adjusted individuals.

D'Heurle   A seven-year study of seventy-six gifted elementary school children yielded substantial intercorrelations in trait superiority over the growth span (d'Heurle, Mellinger, and Hapgood, 1959).

Havighurst   Children growing up in a Midwestern city of 45,000 population were studied continuously from sixth grade to early adult years (Havighurst and others, 1962). Factors found to be related to high rating on initial adjustment were high intelligence, acceptance by others, and high family social status.

UNIVERSITY HIGH SCHOOL, COLUMBUS, OHIO

In 1938, the University High School of Ohio State University graduated its first class to complete the full six years of junior-senior high school at University High. In their senior year the students, working under the direction of faculty members, wrote and published a book entitled *Were We Guinea Pigs?* (1938), in which they recounted their experiences in the school. Instead of following the traditional high school curriculum and instructional procedures, the program was experimental. This school was one of thirty high schools participating in an eight-year study to determine the relative value of traditional and newer types of programs, particularly with reference to college preparation. The book title arose from the fact that the children were often referred to as Guinea Pigs in an educational experiment.

Most of the students came from established families of good social status, all white, living in a university community. There were no illiterate, backward, or financially poor families represented in the group. The school itself was located in a corner of the Ohio State University campus. There was considerable range in intellectual aptitude in the student body, but the intelligence level was well above that of the typical public high school. Relatively few of the students fell in the low-normal category. There is some resemblance between this population and that of the Lincoln School of Teachers College, New York (also a campus school), in the same era, a school which was also a member of the eight-year study.

A follow-up study of the 1938 class of the University High School was begun in the mid-fifties. This study eventuated in a publication, *The Guinea Pigs after Twenty Years* by Margaret Willis, a faculty member of the school (1961).

There were 54 students in the 1938 graduating class. The mean IQ from scores on the Otis Self-administering Test of Mental Ability available for 50 of the students was 115. This is well above the typical public school average, but slightly below the Lincoln School average of 117 to 118 for the same test. Scores on the Ohio State University Psychological Examination required for admission to the university were available for 43 of the 54 students. The median score was equivalent to the 63d percentile, a rating well above average for high school graduates.

Ratings and Comparisons for a Highly Gifted Group   A special study was made of the most highly gifted students in the class, selected on the basis of combined ratings. First, the entire class was divided into quintiles. The top quintile, the "highly gifted" group, was subjected to intensive study, and the results were compared with Dr. Terman's findings from the California studies.

Twenty-four (44 per cent) of the fifty-four graduates were identified as highly gifted. Some of these young people were on a par with Terman's subjects. This top quintile ranked at the 76th percentile on the Ohio State University Psychological Examination.

College-going Trend. Rates for college going and graduation from four-year institutions were exceptionally high. The data for the Guinea Pigs and comparison with Terman's subjects are given in Table 6. Terman's data were taken from *The Gifted Child Grows Up* (Terman and Oden, 1947). Some of the differences between the Guinea Pigs and the Terman cases are probably due to the difference in size of the two groups—nearly 1,500 cases in Terman's study in contrast to only 24 Guinea Pigs. The higher college-going rate of the Guinea Pigs in comparison with Terman's subjects is due to several factors: the location of the University High School on a college campus, the advice given the students by faculty members, and increased college-going rates in general during the late 1930s and 1940s.

Ratings for the Class as a Whole   Other analyses were made to compare the entire graduating class with Terman's cases and with other appropriate data. A remarkable fact is that every member of the 1938 graduating class was living at the time of the survey twenty years later. Self-ratings on health and physical condition in categories from "very good" to "very poor" indicate that the graduates tended to be in good physical condition (see Table 7). There is remarkable similarity here between percentages for the Guinea Pigs and the Terman cases.

Mental Health. In self-ratings of mental health, 35 of the Guinea Pigs indicated that they had encountered no special adjustment problems. Of 16 who mentioned emotional disturbances some had sought therapy, but in the main, the problems had disappeared or had been overcome. The evidence suggests that the Guinea Pigs grew up to become normal, well-adjusted people.

The adult Guinea Pigs rated high on appraisals of self-direction, self-realization, and creativity; those rating in the highest quintile in intelligence rated highest in creativity. The group as a whole rated very high in social sensitivity in face-to-face relationships and fairly high in the scope of their social world. Creative thinking

Table 6 Higher-education Percentages for the Guinea Pigs and Terman's Group

		Percentages	
		Men	Women
Graduates from four-year colleges			
	Guinea Pigs	80	100
	Terman's group	69.5	66.8
Graduate degrees beyond the A.B.			
	Guinea Pigs	62.5	14
	Terman's group	51.2	29.3
Bachelor's degree with distinction of membership in college honorary society			
	Guinea Pigs	87.5	37.5
	Terman's group	39.8	32.5
Phi Beta Kappa members			
	Guinea Pigs	87.5	7.0
	Terman's group	39.8	19.4

Source: Reprinted from *The Guinea Pigs after Twenty Years: A Follow-up Study of the Class of 1938 of the University School at Ohio State,* by Margaret Willis. Copyright 1961 by the Ohio State University Press. Used by permission of the author and the publisher.

defined as the method of intelligence used in problem solving was more characteristic of the academically gifted students than of others.

The Guinea Pigs, twenty years out of school, had healthy interests and enthusiasms; they knew how to use their leisure time to good advantage. In self-ratings they indicated interests similar to those of Terman's cases, but the small size of the Guinea Pig group makes comparisons here unreliable. The Guinea Pigs appeared to be more interested in literature, music, and politics and less interested in religion than Terman's subjects.

On the whole the Guinea Pigs rate as good citizens, taking an active part in community activities and voluntary organizations. They find their family relationships satisfying and are excellent parents, judging by their reports of child-rearing practices.

The great majority of the Guinea Pigs are in white-collar occupations. Here is the new "diploma set," with the men and women tending to marry within their own college-going group. Three-fourths of the women married college men and nearly four out of the five men who graduated from college have wives with college degrees.

THE CLEVELAND MAJOR WORK CLASSES

The follow-up study of the Cleveland Major Work class graduates made by Sumption (1941) and a later study by Barbe (1953, 1956) furnish clear evidence of the successful accomplishments of these young people. Barbe obtained completed questionnaires from

Table 7 Health Status

| Self-rating | Per cent of men | | Per cent of women | |
	Terman's group $N = 700$	Guinea Pigs $N = 27$	Terman's group $N = 563$	Guinea Pigs $N = 25$
Very good	52.3	52.0	44.7	64
Good	38.6	40.6	39.0	32
Fair	7.3	—	12.8	—
Poor	1.0	3.7	3.2	4
Very poor	0.9	3.7	0.5	4

N = Number.
Source: The Guinea Pigs after Twenty Years: A Follow-up Study of the Class of 1938 of the University School at Ohio State, by Margaret Willis. Copyright 1961 by the Ohio State University Press. Used by permission of the author and the publisher.

456 graduates (65 per cent) with a mean age of twenty-five years and found that the accomplishments of the group in college and afterward were impressive. In Cleveland a large percentage of all highly intelligent high school graduates go on to college, but college going was more common among the Major Work class students than among others.

THE FRENCH STUDY

A follow-up study was made by Heuyer, Piéron, and their associates at the University of Paris of French children in the age range six to eleven who had been identified as gifted on the Gille Mosaic Test in 1944 (1954). At the time of the follow-up study some of the subjects were still in the primary school (elementary school), some were in technical or secondary school, early or advanced grades, and some were at work. In 1951, when the children were in the age range thirteen to eighteen, they were checked for progress in school studies and the types of jobs they had undertaken.

Children were selected who had rated in the first decile on the original tests; a comparison group consisted of children who had rated at the 46th to 55th percentile level on the original tests, that is, the top 10 per cent and the middle 10 per cent of all children tested seven years before. A sampling of half these cases was used for the follow-up study. (Actually, 45.5 per cent of the students were in the top decile and 54.5 per cent in the middle 10 per cent on the original tests.) In the follow-up study, information concerning scholastic ratings, diplomas obtained, and factors that might have interfered with school studies was sought. Usable returns were received for over 5,000 of the children or 58 per cent.

Of the children rated as bright on the Gille Mosaic Test, 73 per cent pursued school studies beyond the age of fourteen, in contrast to 47 per cent of those rated as average. Of those who went on beyond age fourteen, 78 per cent rated at centiles 1 and 2 on the test; 65 per cent at centiles 9 and 10, still in the upper tenth of the entire group.

Ratings of Scholastic Achievement Teachers were asked to rate the students in scholastic achievement according to a fivefold scale: excellent, good, average, poor, very poor. Ratings were obtained at the end of the primary (elementary school) period, and also at the end of the secondary period for those who continued their education. The teachers who made the ratings did not know the purpose of the study and had no knowledge of the students' earlier test.

Over 2,000 replies relating to school achievement were received for secondary and technical school students, of which 1,383 were usable. Half of these students were boys and half girls. Results in terms of percentages of the two groups were as follows:

	Excellent	Good	Average	Poor	Very poor
Gifted children	10	32	41	15	2
Average children	3	24	42	26	5

Source: Le niveau intellectuel des enfants d'age scolaire, vol. 2, Presses Universitaires de France, Paris, 1954. Used by kind permission of the Presses Universitaires de France.

After age fourteen, those students who rated in the top decile on the original intelligence test most often obtained ratings of "excellent" or "good" in schoolwork. They less often experienced hindrances in their work such as medical problems. However, these high-rating students had as much difficulty with mathematics as others. Ratings of scholarship in 1951, at the end of the eighth grade, showed no appreciable difference between boys and girls.

The results prove that the gifted (those in the top decile on the original intelligence test) succeeded better in school than the average student, but the correlation was lower in secondary school than at the end of the primary school period. With the passage of time there was a steadily decreasing correlation between the success in school and the student's ability as measured by the early intelligence test. The scholastic results were uniformly better for those in the top centile than for those in the lower centiles of the highest decile.

Some students rated high on the original intelligence test but did not rate high in achievement in the follow-up study seven years later. The reasons for poor achievement given by teachers were illness, family breakup, lack of interest in intellectual work, social problems, and other conditions, such as distance from school. Another reason was the higher selectivity of students in the upper grades. Competition for high ratings was thus more severe. A child rated superior in the lower grades might rate no higher than average in his secondary school studies. The bright students rated higher in technical school than in the academic secondary school studies. These results are shown in Figure 6.

Among those over eighteen years of age, over half in the high group (51 per cent) continued their schooling in contrast to 32 per cent in the average group. Of those continuing their schooling after fourteen years of age, two-thirds went on to *lycées,* colleges, and normal schools, one-third to technical schools and the like. Of those in the professional and intellectual classes, nearly all pursued academic studies. Fewer gifted children whose parents were listed as "cultivators" went on to secondary school after age fourteen than average-rating children of professional people. Among the bright children of professional and intellectual families, there were no cases of scholastic failure.

Long-range Studies Under Way

In a long-range study organized by Dr. John C. Flanagan, which includes 440,000 boys and girls, a cross-sectional sampling of the entire youth population in the United States will be followed up for a period of twenty-five years (1962). Ninety thousand of the

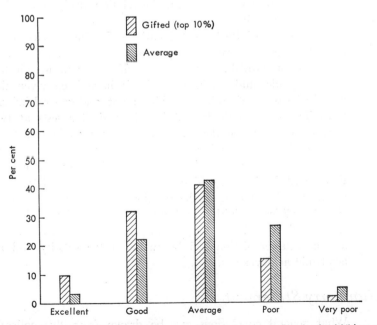

Figure 6. School achievement ratings of gifted and average French schoolchildren who continued their education after age fourteen. (From *Le niveau intellectuel des enfants d'age scolaire,* vol. 2, Presses Universitaires de France, Paris, 1954. Used by permission of the publisher.)

original population tested were given a follow-up questionnaire subsequent to their graduation from high school for the purpose of ascertaining later schooling and occupational success. Reports from this questionnaire should reveal some significant information about members of the group who rated in the highly intelligent, gifted, and talented categories. Additional follow-up studies are planned for five-, ten-, and twenty-year intervals.

A study of all the high school graduates in the province of Ontario, Canada, was begun in 1955–1956. This is known as the Atkinson Study of the Utilization of Student Resources and is supported by funds from the Atkinson Foundation (Brehaut, 1962). The purpose of the study is to determine the talents and aptitudes of high school graduates and then to follow them up for a decade to see how they use their talents and what becomes of them. An especially intensive study is being made of the top 10 per cent of the group. An unusually large number of responses has been received from the graduates, and institutions of higher learning that the students entered have been exceptionally cooperative in supplying follow-up information. It is too early, however, to determine what this study will show about the relationship between high-level capacities and ultimate career success.

In the fall of 1961 the Educational Testing Service of Princeton, New Jersey, began an eight-year study of academic prediction and student growth. Over 40,000 fifth-, seventh-, ninth-, and eleventh-grade students in 170 schools have been given the first round of a series of aptitude, achievement, and general information tests. The same students will be given similar tests at two-year intervals through the eleventh grade. All the students will also fill out periodic questionnaires on their activities in and out of school. In grade twelve they will be given the College Entrance Examination Board Achievement Tests. Outcomes of the study will provide a better understanding of the relation of academic growth to individual abilities, activities, and different types of school programs. Results will also indicate how early in the student's school career an accurate prediction can be made of the quality and rate of academic achievement.

A Summary Statement

What general conclusions can be drawn from this collection of information? Just as there is always some resemblance between a person's appearance in advancing years and his early photographs, so is there considerable consistency between his early and late profiles of performance.

Children who are accelerated learners to begin with tend to continue in this pattern, but any prediction on an individual basis is likely to be far from perfect. Early intelligence tests predict school performance more successfully than development in personal traits and other growth characteristics.

Success in school and in life as a whole is dependent not merely on good intellect but on certain personal qualities as well—ambition to do well, drive to achieve, determination to succeed in chosen enterprises. A high IQ alone does not guarantee success.

Family background appears to be a determining factor in how well a bright child realizes his early promise.

Gifted children of equal ability as measured by tests show wide divergence in personality, interests, and achievement as they mature.

Regression to the mean is to be expected in data from repeated intelligence tests of gifted exceptional individuals.

Follow-up studies indicate that children who showed early precocious mental ability are less likely to develop neurotic or psychotic symptoms than other people.

Although there are essentially no sex differences in general intelligence in the early years, test results show that in the teens and beyond gifted girls regress more than gifted boys. That girls are less frequently identified in the gifted youth population during high school and college suggests the influence of social factors in the emergence of high ability and talent.

Developmental Studies of Individual Children

There are relatively few reports of continuous longitudinal studies of individual children identified early as mentally gifted or talented. Hollingworth included the developmental history of E, an exceptionally gifted boy, in her book *Gifted Children: Their Nature and Nurture* (1926), and in subsequent reports. Considerable continuous case history material is also found in her report on children who tested above 180 IQ (1942).

The author made a seven-year longitudinal study of three gifted boys and a like-age matchee of average ability, all enrolled at the Lincoln School of Teachers College, Columbia University, New York (1954). This study confirmed the general principle of positive correlation of traits during the growth period. Retests indicated perfect consistency in relative rank on the Stanford-Binet test over a seven-year period (see Table 8). Figure 7 shows the mental ages for the four boys throughout the test series. The brightest boy invariably rated highest on successive tests, and the average boy was always fourth, with his IQs varying closely around 100 for the seven-year period. Up to the end of the sixth grade the four boys maintained their respective rank order in scholastic standing, literary productivity, the use of library books, and other characteristics. These results indicated that superior intelligence and other outstanding traits observed as early as four or five years of age persisted throughout the childhood growth period.

The following conclusions were drawn from this study: The Stanford-Binet test IQs remained relatively constant. In physical

Table 8 **Stanford-Binet IQs**

Age	A	B	C	D
3-0				
				100
4-0				
	170			
		137		
5-0				
			125	
	171			
6-0				
	200			
				101
7-0				
		153		
			145	
				100
8-0				
		151		
9-0				115
	183		144	107
10-0				
		158		
11-0				

Source: Gertrude Hildreth, Three Gifted Children: A Developmental Study, *The Journal of Genetic Psychology,* 85:239–262, 1954. Used by permission of the publisher.

development and health, the average control case was equal to the gifted boys. This may be due to the fact that all four were from families of superior socioeconomic status. All three gifted children showed unusual linguistic skills, and they rated above the normal in manual dexterity and motor skills. All showed wide variation in personal characteristics.

Intensive studies of two gifted children reported by Ketcham indicated earlier and more rapid mental development and achievement than their age-mates (1957). Acceleration was shown in objective measures as well as in qualitative ratings. These results are summarized in a number of charts in Ketcham's publication.

A CHILD PRODIGY WHO IS STILL PRODIGIOUS

In the summer of 1939 nine-year-old Lorin Maazel conducted a youth orchestra in a public performance at the New York World's Fair. The music was Mendelssohn's "Italian Symphony." Shortly before, the young conductor had made his debut with the student orchestra at the Interloehen Music Camp in northern

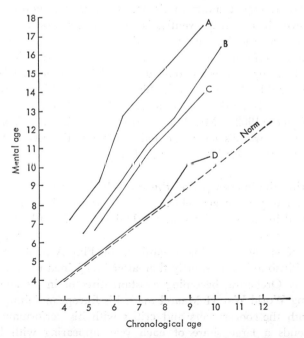

Figure 7. Mental ages derived from repeated Stanford-Binet tests (Gertrude Hildreth, Stanford-Binet Retests of Gifted Children, *Journal of Educational Research,* 37:297–320, 1943. Used by permission of the publisher.)

Michigan where he had been studying, conducting from memory a repertoire that included symphonies by Haydn, Schubert, Mozart, and other great composers. The following year he was invited to conduct the leading orchestras of the country, including the New York Philharmonic at Lewisohn Stadium and the Los Angeles Philharmonic in the Hollywood Bowl. The following year Arturo Toscanini approved his conducting the NBC Symphony Orchestra, considered the greatest of them all. These performances were continued at Lewisohn Stadium in 1942 and 1943 when the boy was twelve and thirteen years of age. At these concerts he directed the works of Mozart, Beethoven, and Tchaikovsky, all without a score before him.

At first the music critics were skeptical. A good, well-trained orchestra could do tolerably well even without a conductor. The critics soon became convinced that the boy knew what he was about, however, and agreed that he was directing with exceptional skill. Leading musicians, on hearing the boy conduct, declared that he was a genius. The musical instrument on which this boy not yet in his teens performed was an organization of eighty to one hundred expert adult musicians. Skill in conducting an orchestra even in the early twenties is considered precocious.

Reporters eagerly sought out the boy conductor, and after each major performance there were extensive write-ups in the city papers. The boy's successes continued until he reached adolescence when the public lost interest in him. As Maazel himself realized, he had lost his market value as a child prodigy. At thirty-two years of age (1962), Mr. Maazel reappeared in New York City as one of the world's most talented musicians, the second-highest-paid orchestra leader in the world. The public was interested once more.

During the interim period the youth had continued his musical studies, making a concert debut at sixteen as a violinist. He showed intellectual interests, studying at the University of Pittsburgh, in his home city, taking courses in philosophy and foreign languages. At the age of seventeen he had organized the Fine Arts String Quartette of Pittsburgh, and shortly thereafter had joined the Pittsburgh Symphony Orchestra, becoming assistant director in his late teens. Following World War II Maazel made his European debut, electrifying both the concertgoers and critics with his performances. He now spends a large share of each year appearing with leading symphonies in the world's major cities and at musical festivals here and abroad. In May, 1963, Maazel was accorded a tremendous ovation when he conducted the Moscow State Symphony Orchestra. The players and critics alike were struck by his skill in conducting the music without scores.

What influences produced one of the foremost musical prodigies of our time? What features of Lorin Maazel's early career fore-shadowed the great professional musician? Most seemingly pre-cocious performers fail to fulfill their early promise. Why did this boy's talent continue to ripen? What were his characteristic mental and personal traits during childhood and youth?

Mr. Maazel's grandfather was a violinist and concertmaster in Moscow at the age of fourteen. Later he became first violinist with the Metropolitan Opera Orchestra in New York. Lorin was the second son of musically talented parents. His father was a professional singer, his mother a pianist. They discovered when the boy was four that he had a sense of absolute pitch, one of the rarest gifts. From his earliest years he showed intense interest in everything musical. At the age of five, he showed great interest in the violin and began taking violin lessons. He wanted to play the piano, and was taught by an aunt who was a concert pianist. The parents decided to limit his practice, allowing him extra time at the piano as a reward for his best behavior.

The child got his start at conducting through play-conducting simplified orchestral scores and then by reading full scores along with recordings by great conductors. His mother, realizing that the boy might have special talent for conducting, took him to a leading musician for instruction. When the boy was seven, a musical director in Los Angeles accepted him as a student in conducting and continued to guide his studies for a period of years.

In addition to having a remarkable ear for music, the boy had an exceptional memory for complicated scores. He gained extensive musical knowledge early. His memory was phenomenal for other material as well. He showed keen intelligence both in learning and in musical performance. Outstanding traits were an eagerness to learn, a powerful energy drive, a capacity for serious study, a sense of responsibility for accomplishment, and skill in tactful leadership.

At the age of nine he enjoyed baseball, football, and tennis; he also liked to swim, but his real hobby was astronomy. The boy was accelerated a full year for his age in elementary school even though he attended school only 1½ hours daily in order to have plenty of time for music. Later on in private schools in

Pittsburgh he continued to advance rapidly. Reading was one of his favorite occupations. Throughout his youth, the boy's tastes ran to books, the arts, and sciences in the broad sense of these terms. He learned foreign languages easily and can now use six major languages fluently.

Young Lorin's talents unfolded naturally in the musical environment of his home. It would seem that he pushed his parents more than they pushed him toward a musical career. As a child conductor, he was poised and affable; he had a warm smile and seemed sure of himself. He was able to command the respect of a body of trained, sophisticated musicians, exhibiting poise both at rehearsals and in public performances. As an adult he has the reputation for being socially distant from his colleagues, owing no doubt to his early training and experiences, which tended to separate him from others of his age.

When Mr. Maazel was queried recently about his attitude toward the early exhibition of precocious talent, he said that he considered it an unhealthy experience to have performed before gushing adults at a tender age. He is definitely against public appearances for child prodigies, and wonders why a young musical prodigy should be required to perform before audiences any more than a youthful mathematician or a precocious juvenile writer. (*New York Times Magazine*, 1939, 1941, 1962.)

IQ Constancy on Repeated Tests

A number of studies have been made of changes in intelligence test scores when the same children are tested at intervals. One of these studies made by the author some years ago involved children at the Lincoln School of Teachers College, Columbia University, who rated 130 IQ or above on their first Stanford-Binet test (1943). The interval between the first and later tests ranged from one to ten years. Results were grouped in three categories: children who had the 1916 revision of the Stanford-Binet on both initial and retest; those who had the 1916 revision on the first test and the 1937 revision on the second; and those who had the 1937 revision test only. For the first two categories the interval between tests averaged a little over three years; for the third group the median interval between tests was four years. Results are shown in Table 9.

The median changes for children in the three categories were found to be, respectively, 6.5 points gain (219 cases), 19.75 points gain (29 cases), and 15.4 points gain (39 cases), omitting comparisons for children who were over ten years of age at the time of both tests. Possible explanations of differences between these median changes are given in the original report of the study (Hildreth, 1943).

Table 9 IQ Changes of Gifted Children

Points of IQ change	Group I 1916–1916 Tests			Group II 1916–1937 Tests			Group III 1937–1937 Tests		
	1 Both tests under 10 yrs.	2 One test over, one under 10	3 Both tests over 10 years	1 Both tests under 10 yrs.	2 One test over, one under 10	3 Both tests over 10 years	1 Both tests under 10 yrs.	2 One test over, one under 10	3 Both tests over 10 years
Over 50	—	—	—	1	—	—	1	—	—
48	—	—	—	—	—	—	—	—	—
46	—	—	—	—	—	—	—	—	—
44	—	—	—	—	—	—	—	—	—
42	—	—	—	1	1	—	—	—	—
40	—	—	—	—	—	—	—	—	—
38	1	1	—	—	—	—	—	—	—
36	1	1	—	1	—	—	1	1	—
34	—	—	—	—	1	—	—	1	—
32	1	—	—	1	—	—	—	—	—
30	1	1	—	1	—	—	1	—	—
28	3	—	—	2	—	—	—	2	—
26	—	1	—	—	—	—	—	1	—
24	—	4	2	2	—	—	—	1	—
22	4	—	—	—	—	—	1	2	—
20	6	2	—	3	—	—	2	4	—
18	5	3	2	1	—	—	1	1	—
16	3	7	1	2	—	—	—	—	—
14	6	4	1	—	1	—	1	3	—
12	5	7	1	1	—	—	1	1	—
10	10	6	1	2	—	—	—	3	—
8	9	9	—	1	—	—	—	—	—
6	9	4	2	1	—	—	1	—	—
4	5	4	3	—	—	—	—	—	—
2	7	7	1	—	—	—	1	—	—
0	6	8	8	1	—	—	1	1	—
-2	6	7	9	—	—	1	—	1	—
-4	4	2	8	—	—	—	—	—	—
-6	5	3	9	1	—	—	1	—	—
-8	4	7	3	—	—	—	—	1	—
-10	3	—	7	—	—	1	—	—	—
-12	3	6	7	1	—	—	—	—	—
-14	4	1	6	—	—	—	2	—	—
-16	1	2	1	—	—	—	—	—	—
-18	—	3	5	1	—	—	—	1	—
-20	—	1	4	—	—	—	—	—	—
-22	—	—	2	—	—	—	—	—	—
-24	—	1	—	—	—	—	—	—	—
Over -24	2	3	1	—	—	—	1	—	—
Total	114	105	84	24	3	2	16	23	—
Medians	6.8	4.75	-5.0						

	Columns 1 and 2	Columns 1 and 2	Columns 1 and 2
Highest positive difference	39	54	56
Q_3	13.6	29.75	22.6
Median	6.5	19.75	15.4
Q_1	-2.6	10.25	2.25
Highest negative difference	-55	-17	-37
Q or semi-interquartile range	8.1	9.75	10.18
Total number	219	27	39

Source: Gertrude Hildreth, Stanford-Binet Retests of Gifted Children, *Journal of Educational Research,* 37:297–302, 1943. Used with kind permission of the publisher, *Journal of Educational Research.*

Dr. E. A. Lincoln made a study of the Stanford-Binet test IQ changes of superior children on retests after periods of two years and five years, respectively (1935). The subjects were 21 boys and 21 girls. For the total group of 42, the median gain was 6.79 points; the median loss, 10.16 points; the median change, disregarding the direction, 8.06 points.

There is some evidence that retest data become more stable and consistent in the upper ranges. Perfect IQ constancy is not to be anticipated because of factors of unreliability in the tests and changes that take place in the subjects. As would be expected, results obtained by two different examiners varied more than the results of two tests given by the same examiner.

BRIGHT CHILDREN WHO "FADE OUT"

The studies reported above do not lend support to the notion that bright children identified by mental tests generally "fade out." On the contrary, the evidence supports the conclusion that early giftedness is a continuing trait. On the whole, highly intelligent children, as they mature, retain their rank among the most capable intellectually in the general population of their age groups.

What is the basis for the myth that the infant prodigy shines brightly and then burns out around the onset of adolescence? The truth is that genuine precocity does not burn out, but public interest dies down. As soon as the precocious musician or child poet reaches adolescence, he ceases to be a *Wunderkind* in the eyes of the public and is no longer worth making a fuss over.

Child prodigies whose performance consists in imitating the actions of older people soon fade out because there is no intellectual involvement in the activity from which permanent talent can be built. This seems to be true particularly of children who are the product of hot-house forcing by parents—the infant mathematical wizard, the baby elocutionist, the kindergartner reciting the Greek alphabet.

Ambitious parents often mistake the natural mimicry and tenacious memory of the young child for precocity; for example, the two-year-old who can identify his favorite phonograph record in a large pile or the child who can repeat a rhyme verbatim after hearing it once or who can sing in perfect tune and rhythm is often mistakenly called a "little genius." Parents can easily make a pseudo prodigy of a young child through special drill that builds on his natural tendencies. As Dr. Norbert Wiener commented, the quiz kid is trying to perform as an adult without an adult's seasoned experience; hence, he is nothing more than an intellectual robot.

One explanation for the fading out of pseudo prodigies is that the forcing of their talent tends to fix performance at an immature level of mechanical behavior, preventing the talent from developing step by step in a normal way. This premature pressure and exploitation prevent the child's creative imagination from ripening, and interfere with his learning independently through self-initiated experimentation. The bright child can scarcely skip normal developmental steps in growing up and become a competent, outstanding performer or productive worker. Every child needs to live the full life of a child as preparation for adulthood.

If the child is mentally accelerated because of pressure to learn beyond his natural tendencies, he is doomed to revert sooner or later; but if acceleration is due to his own spontaneous urge to learn, to invent, to describe, and to perform, early promise is more apt to be fulfilled. In some cases, the truly gifted musical prodigies fare better than others because they attract the attention of good teachers who discourage premature forcing of talent.

Precocious boys such as Goethe or Lord Kelvin did not burn out in early youth. Why? Probably because their early environment had a stimulating allover effect on development of imagination and intellectual achievements.

THE "LATE BLOOMER"

The idea that gifted children are often "late bloomers" has a popular appeal. This is what we should like to believe—that children who show no special promise in their early years tend to blossom out with maturity. This concept satisfies the notion that success in life is due largely to chance factors and that unpredictable events shape an individual's destiny. "He may surprise you later" is the common remark when a child appears to have no special or unusual qualities.

How many ordinary children blossom out later and supply the ranks of the great or near great? How many ordinary children remain ordinary in adult life? How many people in college or later life achieve distinction quite out of proportion to early predictions? These are questions that need to be answered.

No doubt there are individuals who fit the "late-blooming" category, even dull children or school laggards. Intelligence is so largely judged by what children learn and their interest in learning that any factors conditioning learning, motivating them to learn or causing failure to learn, enter into judgments of ability.

These "late-blooming" cases must be the exception rather than the rule, judging from the efforts made by parents and teachers to stimulate and improve children's learning abilities and performance. In unselected school groups, there are still only one or two who emerge as truly gifted although the slower children receive the same or even more attention from the teacher.

Unquestionably, there are children whose intelligence and achievement spurt after a period of early latency, but the chances are largely against this probability. The results of the French survey cited above tend to refute the contention that average children in the lower grades became exceptional scholars later on. Efforts to make children brighter through intensive drills and special coaching are generally disappointing.

One explanation for a "late bloomer" may be that no attention was paid to a child who was diligent but shy and withdrawing in the early years; his true abilities may not have been fully recognized or appreciated. In other cases an actual change may take place in the mental functioning of the child as the result of his abilities' being drawn out and stimulated.

In order to substantiate or refute the contention that the gifted are simply ordinary children who blossom out, cumulative biographical studies are needed for an unselected sampling of the population extending from early childhood to late maturity.

DEVELOPMENTAL IRREGULARITY

There is little evidence concerning irregularity and unevenness in the developmental histories of gifted children. To what extent do certain individuals gravitate back and forth between superiority and mediocrity during the course of development? Are there periods of virtual cessation in mental growth—plateaus in development? We know that physical growth is not entirely consistent. By analogy, there is no reason to assume that mental development is. The problem here is to disentangle aspects of mental growth from superficial evidences of achievement in or out of school; this is an insuperable problem. A gifted child's development might be one-sided, due to gaps in his training and background or to the dominance of special interests—for example, an obsession with mapmaking or collecting.

A Look Backwards: Eminent Persons as Children

Exploring the early lives of distinguished persons is another means of tracing the development of exceptional individuals. Do the childhood activities and achievements of famous people foreshadow their later careers or give any prediction of remarkable accomplishment? Can we find the roots of genius in the childhood of eminent people? What were the goals of these persons as youths? By what methods did they learn? What type of education did they receive? What sorts of teachers did they have? What were their early interests? What were the effects of being reared in a particular cultural climate? Do the records tend to support the idea that most eminent persons were mediocre as children, even slow and backward at school? Answers to these questions would serve to establish the facts concerning the roots of eminence and creativity.

We are all familiar with the accomplishments of Thomas A. Edison, Henry Thoreau, and Edward MacDowell, who were admitted to the New York Hall of Fame in 1960. Were these just any boys who by luck and chance earned lasting fame because of their remarkable contributions? Were there any evidences in childhood of the remarkable men to come? Can we assume that a certain life-style and distinctive behavior patterns must have been evident in early childhood? These questions can be answered in part by the records distinguished people have made of their early years: early diaries or autobiographies and records of observations in youth.

The chief limitations of biographical studies are that the early records may be sparse, inaccurate, or biased. Furthermore, since biographical records of children are not usually kept in permanent form, there is no way of knowing who, among all the average people, may have been exceptionally gifted or talented as children.

EARLY YEARS

Several comprehensive studies have been made of the lives of eminent persons in childhood. Yoder's investigation of the boyhood of great men was among the first (1894). The most comprehensive research investigation and the most widely quoted is that of Dr. Catherine Cox Miles, who reported the early traits of 301 eminent people of history (Cox, 1926). Dr. James McKeen Cattell made a statistical study of eminent men, and Hollingworth summarized reports of eminent adults (1926).

This evidence indicates that eminent people were somewhat unusual as children. Yoder found that the keen play interests of children who became eminent adults were often of a solitary or unusual kind—reading, calculating, designing, compiling statistics, making maps, constructing things. Many of them enjoyed physical activities, and a number were unusually tall. Yoder found no cases of weak or sickly childhood in the eminent. The age range of the parents of the eminent was from twenty-one to forty-five years. The families were of superior socioeconomic status, and they averaged five siblings each, which is in marked contrast to Hollingworth's data reported a hundred years later. Yoder found in families of more than one child a strong tendency for the great man to be in the elder half of the siblings.

The 301 eminent persons whose biographical material was explored by Cox lived between 1450 and 1850 (1926). The individuals were selected on the basis of the attention accorded to them in biographical dictionaries. Cox concluded from her study that people who achieved eminence had superior advantages in their early environment; their behavior in childhood indicated an unusually high degree of intelligence; they were characterized by persistence of motive and effort, confidence in their abilities, and great strength of character. Cox reports a wealth of fascinating information about the childhood and youth of great figures of history.

Dr. Victor H. Goertzel and his wife undertook an extensive study of 400 world figures of the twentieth century (1962). Most of these persons obtained considerable informal education; they were avid readers and enjoyed in youth close association with intelligent and stimulating adults. Strong and persistent drives were common to both the children and their parents. As children they had more freedom to travel, to read, and to engage in self-initiated projects than did more conventionally reared children of their day.

Wagenknecht compiled an anthology of childhood biographies of famous people that adds to our knowledge of gifted children, particularly those who became literary figures (1946).

All these reports support the theory of developmental consistency rather than haphazard origins of giftedness. On the whole, biographical records suggest that remarkable adults were remarkable as children even though their parents and teachers may not have been aware of their budding genius. In childhood, almost without exception, they showed unusual vitality, originality, and intellectual maturity. Exceptional ingenuity was evident in their games, in their choice of activities and companions, and in other behavior. On the whole, these eminent people as children showed more tendency to initiate their own projects and to carry them through to completion.

Gifted men became interested in their life occupations at an early age. By the age of ten the playwright had composed and staged his first amateur production. The notable physicist or chemist had begun conducting experiments by the fifth grade. The successful journalist was most likely a young newspaper editor, and perhaps an energetic newsboy as well. A leading expert and writer on the subject of ships first became interested in boats and shipping in early boyhood. Although not all promising music students become great musicians, no case is known of a renowned musician who was not a child prodigy in music. The records of leaders prove that they had the basic knowledge of their "trades" well in hand by age eighteen, whether they became celebrated writers, artists, scientists, or professional people such as doctors.

There is a close correspondence between early expression of scientific interests and subsequent success in a science career (Roe, 1953).

Might the early development of people who were undistinguished in adult life show some of the same traits exhibited by notable persons? Such questions as this can only be answered with detailed longitudinal studies of an unselected population.

A study of 600 national science talent winners over a two-year period indicated that these talented young people made their decisions to become scientists when they were in elementary school (MacCurdy, 1956). A cumulative science service study of 1,306 finalists at the national science fairs reveals these facts: About half the group had developed their initial interest in science as early as the fifth grade; almost 90 per cent of them were oriented toward science well before they had been introduced to senior high school courses in physics, chemistry, biology, and mathematics. Almost 10 per cent of them had become novice scientists by the time they were fourteen years old.

A seventeen-year-old New York City boy who was the only student among 150,000 contestants to attain a perfect score on a difficult mathematics competition test given in 1958 began his serious study of mathematics at the age of eight. He attributed his success on the test primarily to his speed in handling the large number of problems within the time limit.

Origins of Giftedness and Talent

"Some are born great, some achieve greatness, and some have greatness thrust upon them," said the Bard of Avon. What accounts for differences in mental ability among individuals of the same age? Why has one person special talents that others do not possess? Why is one student gifted in mathematics or languages while another who has been exposed to the same instruction remains ordinary?

Galton, Terman, and other early observers of the gifted had a firm belief in the genetic origin of superior mental capacities. They assumed that a gifted child is one who is born with a superior nervous system. Just as it is possible for a child to be born with a nervous system so defective or inadequate as to leave him incapable of performing typical physical responses or learning basic skills, so is it possible for a child to be superior biologically, with unusual powers of memory and perception, of thinking and judgment.

William James expressed a fundamental truth when he said, in discussing the forces of heredity and environment in human development, "Minds inhabit environments which act on them and on which they react." People are not and cannot be equal in development, because they are biologically unequal to begin with, and the resulting interplay with environmental forces makes for still greater differentiation. Capacity for learning is dependent upon the maturation of the nervous system in response to the outer environment. Each person is affected differently.

Dr. Cyril Burt, the British psychologist, after a lifetime of study, concluded that general intelligence is largely innate, genetically determined (1959). Biological inheritance is a weighty factor in causing individual differences, but mental differences are the product of many interrelated, interdependent factors. Burt believes that there are differences in mental potential that cultural advantages do not erase. He has summarized evidence that refutes the belief that environmental opportunities alone or to a major degree account for individuals of superior ability (1961).

Others contend that superior talents and remarkable gifts are largely, if not wholly, the result of social conditioning and cultural influences. Placed in a superior environment, any ordinary child could become a gifted, talented, or creative individual. In contrast to Burt's view is the contention of the Soviet psychologist, Prof. Alex Luria, that innate intelligence and inherited abilities simply do not exist. IQ tests, the search for the gifted child are therefore futile and meaningless objectives. In Luria's view, mental backwardness is a physical disorder, a medical problem rather than a deviation in a continuum of ability. Giftedness and talent owe all to superior environment.

THE CURRENT VIEW

The currently accepted view is that variability in intellectual potential is subject to the genes controlling inheritance, as height or weight, but that intelligence reaches its ultimate development only through environmental stimulation. Intelligence, then, is developed ability, but limits to mental development are set by heredity.

Favorable environmental circumstances are so influential that it would be misleading to ascribe unusual capacities solely to heredity; on the other hand, without good mental endowment, a superior environment may give the individual no special advantage. As an old Turkish savant expressed it, "Great qualities are partly the gift of God, partly the result of good training and effort." Given good innate qualities of mind and body, the shaping and strengthening of potentials are due primarily to experiences in family life, at school, and elsewhere. Certainly the combination of inborn and environmental factors that operate to produce people of unusual abilities and accomplishments is unique in every case.

Pressey believes that too much emphasis has been put on giftedness as constitutional endowment and that too little attention has been paid to the concomitance of favorable factors operating throughout the growth years (1955). People of genius level or marked superiority almost invariably had unusual environmental opportunities to develop their abilities and special talents, whether at home or in school. Pressey believes that a practicing genius is produced by starting a precocious and capable youngster on the right track by giving him encouragement, intensive instruction, continuing opportunity as he advances, a congruent stimulating social life, and a cumulative success experience. He points out that in musical training as in physical education, the advantages of special early intensive and continuous training of talented young people produce the master or champion. Lorin Maazel, discussed above, is a case in point.

Pressey thinks that it is entirely possible to step up the number of highly productive and creative people through giving more attention to training and the cultivation of high abilities. When the learner is bright and interested and the instruction is superior, results are apt to be exceptional.

GIFTEDNESS AS A DEVELOPMENTAL TRAIT

Giftedness, talent, and high achievement in adult years are the result of continuous development throughout all the years of growth. From birth to maturity, the child is undergoing continual transformation as he reacts to his environment. The uniqueness of his behavior and character arises from the complex interaction of all the maturational forces and educative influences that have affected him. The research cited in the foregoing sections, as well as records of child growth in general, confirms this hypothesis. Information from follow-up studies and other sources suggests that (1) superior abilities emerge by successive growth stages; (2) the force of chance combinations of circumstances influences the direction the course of growth may take, just as chance circumstances affect the course of a meandering stream; (3) giftedness and talent can be fostered by direct control of the individual's home and life experiences, by educational and cultural influences from infancy onward. With increasing maturity, the individual takes a larger hand in controlling the circumstances of his own growth.

In her studies, of the growth of children from infancy, Bayley observed that some children got off to an early start, then dropped back; others moved ahead slowly or picked up speed later (1955). She proposed the theory that intelligence consists of a series of separate but related abilities which mature in sequence. Each ability can begin to develop only when the preceding ones have prepared the way. If one ability is inhibited for any reason, the succeeding development will be delayed.

The initial momentum started by a train of favorable circumstances tends to "snowball" with favorable effects that are not only cumulative but reinforcing. For example, a bright child who catches on to reading and writing early not only gains in vocabulary and powers of self-expression, but rapidly amasses a store of information lying beyond immediate experience.

All things considered, a child tends to keep on growing in the direction taken early in life; slow, fast, or highly individualistic. In childhood, the different aspects of intelligence do not emerge at the same time or grow at the same rate; one kind of ability moves foward while others are apparently dormant for a while. There may be no compelling motive to keep on growing at the same speed or in the same direction as before. Training and education assist by triggering the next stage of development through providing appropriate motivation.

Enthusiasm, zeal, ambition characterize all high-talent people who succeed. Incentives as well as a powerful drive to achieve motivate the gifted young person to seek out the training opportunities that he requires for the realization of his plans. Any circumstances that increase the drive, vitality, and interest of the individual tend to increase his potential abilities. The cultural values of society are so influential that they may result in a clustering of genius at a certain epoch, as in the Italian Renaissance artists.

These newer concepts imply that giftedness in childhood and youth is not a trait or combination of traits that can be identified once and for all at any stage. Rather, we speak of the individual's developed abilities at successive stages of growth, and trace through the picture for significant trends.

References

Barbe, Walter B.: Career Achievement of Gifted Students, *Personnel and Guidance Journal,* 34:356–369, 1956.

Barbe, Walter B.: *A Follow-up Study of the Graduates of Special Classes for Gifted Children,* unpublished doctoral dissertation, Northwestern University, Evanston, Ill., 1953.

Bayley, Nancy: On the Growth of Intelligence, *American Psychologist,* 10:805–818, 1955.

Brehaut, Willard: *The Atkinson and Carnegie Studies of Student Talent in Ontario,* Department of Educational Research, The University of Toronto, address at the American Educational Research Association, Atlantic City, N.J., February, 1962.

Burt, Cyril: General Ability and Special Aptitudes, *Educational Research,* 1:3–16, 1959.

Burt, Cyril: The Gifted Child, *British Journal of Statistical Psychology,* 14:123–139, 1961.

Clarke, A. D. B., Ann M. Clarke, and R. I. Brown: Regression to the Mean: A Confused Concept, *British Journal of Psychology,* 51:105–117, 1960.

Cox, Catherine M.: *Genetic Studies of Genius,* vol. 2, *The Early Mental Traits of Three Hundred Geniuses,* Stanford University Press, Stanford, Calif., 1926.

d'Heurle, Adma, Jeanne C. Mellinger, and Ernest A. Hapgood: Personality, Intellectual and Achievement Patterns in Gifted Children, *Psychological Monographs,* 73(483), 1959.

Flanagan, John C., and staff: *Characteristics of High School Youth,* vol. 2 in a 3-vol. series, Houghton Mifflin Company, Boston, 1962.

Girard, Alain, and Henri Bastide, La détermination et l'avenir des bien doués, chap. 10 of *Le niveau intellectuel des enfants d'âge scolaire,* vol. 2, Presses Universitaires de France, Paris, 1954, pp. 251–269.

Goertzel, Victor H., and Mildred G. Goertzel: *Cradles of Eminence,* Little, Brown and Company, Boston, 1962.

Havighurst, Robert J., and others: *Growing Up in River City,* John Wiley & Sons, Inc., New York, 1962.

Hildreth, Gertrude: Results of Repeated Measurement of Pupil Achievement, *Journal of Educational Psychology*, 21:286–296, 1930.

Hildreth, Gertrude: Stanford-Binet Retests of Gifted Children, *Journal of Educational Research*, 37:297–302, 1943.

Hildreth, Gertrude: Three Gifted Children: A Developmental Study, *Journal of Genetic Psychology*, 85:239–262, 1954.

Hollingworth, Leta S.: *Children Who Tested above 180 I.Q. Stanford Binet: Origin and Development*, World Book Company, Tarrytown-on-Hudson, N.Y., 1942.

Hollingworth, Leta S.: *Gifted Children: Their Nature and Nurture*, The Macmillan Company, New York, 1926.

Hollingworth, Leta S., and R. M. Kaunitz: The Centile Status of Gifted Children at Maturity, *Journal of Genetic Psychology*, 45:106–120, 1934.

Ketcham, Warren A.: Growth Patterns of Gifted Children, *Merrill-Palmer Quarterly*, 3, Spring, 1957.

Lamson, Edna E.: *A Study of Young Gifted Children in Senior High School*, Contributions to Education, no. 424, Bureau of Publications, Teachers College, Columbia University, New York, 1930.

Lincoln, E. A.: A Study of the Changes in the Intelligence Quotients of Superior Children, *Journal of Educational Research*, 29:272–275, 1935.

Lorge, Irving, and Leta S. Hollingworth: Adult Status of Highly Intelligent Children, *Journal of Genetic Psychology*, 49:215–226, 1936.

MacCurdy, Robert D.: Young Scientists Studied, *Science Newsletter*, 69:38, 1956.

McClelland, David C., and others: *Talent and Society: New Perspectives in the Identification of Talent*, D. Van Nostrand Company, Inc., Princeton, N.J., 1958.

Articles in *The New York Times Magazine*, July 30, 1939, Aug. 17, 1941, Sept. 30, 1962.

Pressey, Sidney L.: Concerning the Nature and Nurture of Genius, *Scientific Monthly*, 81:123–129, 1955.

Ratchford, T. E.: *The Brontës Web of Childhood*, Columbia University Press, New York, 1941.

Roe, Anne: *The Making of a Scientist*, Dodd, Mead & Company, Inc., New York, 1953.

Sumption, Merle R.: *Three Hundred Gifted Children: A Follow-up Study of the Results of Special Education of Superior Children*, World Book Company, Tarrytown-on-Hudson, N.Y., 1941.

Terman, Lewis M., and Melita H. Oden: *Genetic Studies of Genius*, vol. 4, *The Gifted Child Grows Up*, Stanford University Press, Stanford, Calif., 1947.

Terman, Lewis M., and Melita H. Oden: *Genetic Studies of Genius*, vol. 5, *The Gifted Group at Mid-life*, Stanford University Press, Stanford, Calif., 1959.

Terman, Lewis M., and others: *Genetic Studies of Genius*, vol. 3, *The Promise of Youth*, Stanford University Press, Stanford, Calif., 1930.

Thorndike, Robert L.: An Evaluation of the Adult Intellectual Status of Terman's Gifted Children, *Journal of Genetic Psychology*, 72:17–27, 1948.

University High School, Ohio State University, Class of 1938: *Were We Guinea Pigs?* Holt, Rinehart and Winston, Inc., New York, 1938.

Wagenknecht, Edward C.: *When I Was a Child*, E. P. Dutton & Co., Inc., New York, 1946.

Willis, Margaret: *The Guinea Pigs after Twenty Years: A Follow-up Study of the Class of 1938 of the University School at Ohio State*, Ohio State University Press, Columbus, Ohio, 1961.

Witty, Paul A.: A Genetic Study of Fifty Gifted Children, in *Intelligence: Its Nature and Nurture: Thirty-ninth Yearbook of the National Society for the Study of Education*, part 2, pp. 401–409, Public School Publishing Company, Bloomington, Ill., 1940.

Yoder, A. H.: The Study of the Boyhood of Great Men, *Pedagogical Seminary*, 3:34–56, 1894.

Chapter Six

THE ASSESSMENT OF UNUSUAL ABILITIES

Talent searchers are on the lookout for children who show intellectual and academic aptitudes of a high order, originality and creativity, special interests and talents, and leadership potential. The planning of educational opportunities and specialized services for these children depends upon reliable methods of identification and continuous appraisal of each individual.

The decision that a child is gifted or talented is the outcome of many observations and the use of a variety of testing and screening techniques by more than one person through a continuous time span. An attempt should be made to bring together all pertinent data—a developmental record—for the child who has been so identified. Definitions given in Chapter Two and descriptions of traits of the gifted in Chapter Four provide guidelines for recognizing the unusual child.

Appraisal is essentially a diagnostic process involving a variety of fact-finding techniques that provide the evidence for sound judgments. The problem is to find the best combination of measures that will most fairly and reliably distinguish the gifted from others in the same age range.

An actuarial appraisal can be made on the basis of mental test data—the child scores at a superior level reached by only a small percentage in the population (see Chapter Two). Or a clinical type of assessment and diagnosis can be made for more intensive study of the individual's skills and aptitudes. Best of all is the comprehensive developmental study that reaches back into earliest childhood and spans the school life of the individual.

Broad-band Studies

Formerly, superior children were assumed to be reliably identified by means of an hour-long standardized intelligence test; but today the simple formula of "giving a Binet" and deciding where to "draw the line" no longer suffices. If giftedness is viewed as developed capacities and unusual performance in a wide range of skills and achievements, the identification of the gifted and talented requires a many-sided study of the individual's intellectual abilities. Typical of broad-band identification is Flanagan's study of high school students (1962). The purpose of this study is to discover how well some 120 to 130 variables predict success in learning throughout the high school years. The study will indicate what sorts of abilities the superior individuals show and which elements in the testing program are predictive of unusual development. McGuire and others collected information about 1,242 junior high school students in Texas in a broad-band study that included 40 variables (1961).

How Early Should the Talent Search Begin?

How early can gifted and talented children be identified? School people recommend starting the talent search early in order to have the maximum span of time for continuous observations, for special educational planning, and for effective guidance of children and their parents. Otherwise, bright youngsters may be held down to a level of mediocrity or they may get "lost in the shuffle." If identification is delayed beyond age twelve or fourteen, less time remains for educational planning on an individual basis.

Even in kindergarten the child's spontaneous response to the learning opportunities of his environment becomes evident. He may be observed doing unusual problem solving with blockbuilding; he may show originality in storytelling, dramatization, or musical invention. The craze for books can be seen even in the nursery school.

A mother described her kindergartner as follows: "She can count to one hundred and beyond with no difficulty, and write the numbers to 25. She recognizes every letter of the alphabet, can print each letter in large and small letters, and also prints about three dozen words. She has taught herself to pick out tunes on the piano after hearing them once or twice. Her memory is remarkably keen, too." Here, at least, are some indications of mental acceleration and early academic talent.

In the La Mesa, Spring Valley, California, program conducted in cooperation with the State of California Gifted Child Program, the children were tentatively identified in kindergarten for study and further observation in kindergarten and grade 1 (Martinson, 1960).

The study of three gifted boys made by the author reported in Chapters Four and Five proved that unusual abilities were recognizable by the time the children were four years of age, even as early as three. The Hunter College Elementary School has been successful in identifying gifted children as early as four and five years. The more unusual the child, the more likely are his abilities to be evidenced early.

OBSERVATIONS DURING THE EARLY ELEMENTARY YEARS

The period from five to ten years of age during which rapid growth takes place under the stimulus of school experience is an excellent time to watch for unusual ability and all sorts of talent. The school environment affords an opportunity for comparative ratings of individual abilities. Here is a girl nearing ten who seems unusually bright to her teachers and parents. She rates far above fifth-grade average in all her schoolwork, checks her work carefully, begs the teacher for harder problems in mathematics, and is recognized as a class leader. She must be highly gifted, her teacher and parents believe. This will do for a tentative guess, but it should be verified through checks and evaluation from now on. By the time she is twelve or thirteen the evidence will be more clear-cut. Just as the gifted ballplayer is more positively identified at age seventeen than at age seven, so are judgments about children more accurate after continued observation over a period of time.

APPRAISAL IN THE UPPER–ELEMENTARY AND JUNIOR HIGH SCHOOL PERIOD

The period from ten to fifteen years of age furnishes numerous clues to the direction the child's development is taking. By this time the child has his basic skills of learning well in hand, his special talents and interests are taking more definite shape, he has been able to demonstrate such originality as he possesses. His predominant character and personal traits are now at a more mature stage of development than in the earlier years, and he has been continuously subjected to the tests of school and life.

By age twelve to fourteen, growth is fairly well stabilized, so that observations in these years have considerable reliability for predicting academic achievement and special aptitudes.

Screening and Selection of the Gifted and Talented

In this day of objective-type electronically scored tests schoolchildren and adults alike are continually subjected to "screening" for one purpose or another—for special groupings, scholastic honors, scholarships, job applications, the Army, Civil Service, and so on.

The identification of the gifted and talented moves in two directions: (1) Screening or sifting the entire school population, or at least the most promising segments of it, through making a systematic, inclusive survey, and (2) selection of the most promising or the brightest by nominations and recommendations of teachers for subsequent testing and more intensive study. The common practice is to use group intelligence tests for preliminary sifting, and then to recheck selected cases with an individual intelligence test and supplementary ratings. A cutoff score in terms of IQ or percentile rank is set up in advance or determined by the proportion of the school population to be selected. Achievement tests may be used as part of the original screening battery or for a later check-up.

Another common procedure for selecting exceptional children of any type—bright, dull, speech defective, the physically handicapped, and others—is to request teachers to list pupils in these categories and to refer the cases for further diagnostic study. Teachers include with their nominations supporting data such as information about school performance, past records, significant incidents in the child's behavior, and home information.

PLANS FOR THE SELECTION OF GIFTED SCHOOLCHILDREN

The selection procedures adopted by Terman were outlined briefly in Chapter Five. The full account is given in *Genetic Studies of Genius* (vol. 1, pp. 19–38, 1925).

Laycock recommended the following plan for the diagnosis of giftedness in a general or special sense (1957):

1. Observations by the teacher, who is guided by a twenty-item checklist

2. Results of standard achievement tests

3. School records

4. Results of standard tests of mental ability

5. Individual intelligence tests

6. Tests of special abilities

7. Informal tests and procedures, results of memory games and contests

8. Information gained from conferences with parents and other informants[1]

In Portland, Oregon, children are screened for high scholastic ability as well as talent in art, music, creative writing, dramatics, and social leadership through the use of standard intelligence and achievement tests, combined with teachers' observations and ratings.

In the Quincy, Illinois, project for the early discovery of talent, teachers are guided in systematic observations by means of a handbook developed by the Science Research Associates of Chicago (Kough and DeHaan, 1956). Teachers are directed to watch for children who show special intellectual talent, social leadership, and ability in fine arts, graphic arts, mechanics, dramatics, and rhythms. Other techniques for identification include contests, game-tests, and observations of children in the wider community.

The National Merit Scholarship Program has been able to identify intellectually and academically promising high school youths with considerable success. For more details on high school talent search programs and procedures see Chapter Sixteen.

Although class marks furnish the most obvious indication of superior academic talent, they should be supplemented with objective information provided by standard achievement tests in basic skills and subject areas. For the purpose of identifying all high-

[1] Samuel Laycock, *Gifted Children*, The Copp-Clark Publishing Company, Toronto, Canada, 1957. Reprinted with the kind permission of Dr. S. R. Laycock and The Copp-Clark Publishing Company, Toronto, Canada.

potential students, comprehensive scholastic aptitude and achievement tests should be administered on a uniform basis to everyone.
The latter include measures of reading comprehension, written
expression, mathematics, science, and social studies. Most school
authorities give considerable weight to reading achievement in
evaluating students of high promise because advanced studies depend so largely on the capacity to absorb knowledge from books.
Few schools adhere strictly to any elaborate set of criteria for
screening the gifted and talented. The judgment of teachers and
principals carries much weight along with other criteria.

Teachers who have daily contact with children are in a good
position to make judgments of their abilities, to observe signs of
giftedness and talent, to study their records, and to collect new
information about them. An elementary school teacher described
two children, a boy of 11 and a girl of 6½, who were considered
celebrities in the school because of their remarkable accomplishments.

People outside the school may also assist in identification: club
leaders, librarians, social workers, church-school teachers, music
teachers, pediatricians, and other specialists. Child guidance clinics
can assist the school in identifying the gifted and talented by reporting on children whose diagnostic records and tests give indications
of exceptional ability.

THE RELIABILITY OF TEACHERS' JUDGMENTS

How well can teachers spot the gifted child? The answer depends
somewhat upon what is meant by "gifted." The task is similar
to that of identifying the problem child. Certain talents and special
aptitudes are more obvious than others. The "exhibitionist" talents
and talent for social leadership make more of an impression on
teachers than talents that flourish in solitude and isolation. In
the early years the distinction between pseudo precocity due to
coaching and pushing and true talent is not so clear-cut as it
becomes later.

Unless teachers are given criteria for judging, their nominations
may not agree with those of the mental-hygiene experts. If the
term "gifted" means only "high IQ," teachers may fail to identify
those the tests select because teachers are better judges of present
achievement than of academic potential. Dr. Guy M. Whipple
was among the first to call attention to this fact when in 1919 he
and Dr. Genevieve Coy administered mental tests to gifted children nominated by teachers and the school principal. In Dr.
Whipple's control group of twenty "average children," six were
found to have IQs higher than the median IQ of the special-class

group, but were definitely characterized as "average in schoolwork." Dr. Whipple discovered that teachers were more accurate in spotting the dull than the bright, because the dull were so obviously unable to learn as fast as the others. Whipple concluded that the selection of the gifted for special classes must be made on the basis of performance on mental tests because the selection by teachers on the basis of classroom impressions and school marks results in the inclusion of some who are unsuited for a special speeded-up program. Dr. Coy reported that half of the brightest boys and girls selected for special classes set up in Columbus, Ohio, would have been missed if she had depended only upon teachers' judgments in selecting the children.

Only 15.7 per cent of the children nominated for Dr. Terman's study as "most intelligent in the class" by 6,000 elementary teachers were qualified in terms of the required Stanford-Binet IQ. However, 19.7 per cent who were listed as "youngest in the class" were qualified in terms of the test IQ. In an investigation conducted by Varner, from 20 to 40 per cent of the bright-test children were identified by teachers without prior knowledge of test results, and 50 to 60 per cent of the dull (1922). Teachers had less difficulty selecting the bright in older age groups.

In tests of 1,400 junior high school students in Pittsburgh, investigators found that teacher nominations missed more than half of the gifted, and about one-third of those nominated proved not to be gifted according to the standards set up. The honor roll listed 73.6 per cent of the academically gifted, but it also included large numbers of less gifted children. Group intelligence tests failed to distinguish between those who were somewhat above average and those who were highly gifted. Seven screening devices or selection criteria were used in this investigation (Pegnato and Birch, 1959).

Children tend to be overrated in intelligence by teachers who are impressed by conspicuous talents. Dr. Genevieve Coy mentioned one child whom the teacher sent to a special class for the gifted because he could draw cartoons, play the ukulele, and sing. His test IQ proved to be 114, whereas the gifted class rated above 130 IQ.

Explanation of the Discrepancies   Teachers' judgments rest largely on impressions—on feelings or ratings that may be biased or even prejudiced. Furthermore, teachers' ratings of aptitude and achievement are contaminated by nonintellectual traits and behavior symptoms. A teacher who is asked to select the most promising or superior student is inclined to choose the attractive, agreeable, lively, or glib student and to pass over the nonverbal child or the young rascal who gets into difficulties over his cleverness. On the whole, bright girls are marked higher than bright boys because good conduct and social conformity, which are more characteristic of girls, influence the teachers' marks.

Terman noted the tendency of teachers to neglect the age of the child in making estimates of ability. Ratings of a child's behavior and achievement as superior or average in comparison with others in his class will be inaccurate if the child's age is neglected in the evaluation. A younger child in the class tends to be underrated, but the younger pupils tend, on the whole, to be brighter than others. Similarly, intellectual parents may misjudge a child because they lack a basis for comparison with others of his age.

Another source of discrepancy in teachers' ratings is failure to consider the relative ability of the group with whom the child is being compared. The teacher who neglects "age-norms" of behavior and accomplishment rates a child with reference to the class rather than with reference to universal standards for children of comparable age. A mark of A or "excellent" does not mean the same in a class where achievement is low as it does in a class where achievement is above average. In the selection of bright children for a junior high school class, school marks may prove to be a misleading criterion for admission when the children come from low-rating sixth-grade classes. This problem was discussed more fully in Chapter Two.

Improvement of Teacher Ratings   Teachers can become more expert in identifying the gifted by studying child behavior in terms of growth norms and by learning how to appraise developmental records and recognize symptoms of giftedness in the child's everyday behavior. Most teachers can improve their professional knowledge by learning what research has to say about gifted and talented children, their traits and tendencies. Seminars led by psychologists and guidance workers can give teachers deeper insight into the use of trait ratings, measures of ability, and other indications of talent.

CLASS MARKS

Class marks are invariably included in any present-day list of criteria for identifying and assessing the gifted. These marks have most value in predicting the student's educability. They will not necessarily pick out the children with the most creative minds, avid curiosity, and eagerness to explore or those with special talents that do not depend on school achievement. Schools marks will predict future school marks better than anything else. The combination of high marks and superior ratings on standard intelligence tests will separate the bright high achievers from hard workers of ordinary aptitude.

School marks are not entirely satisfactory as indicators of academic achievement, because, as noted above, they are "contaminated" with nonintellectual factors. Furthermore, marks vary with the teachers' grading standards.. One teacher might give great weight to accuracy in spelling when grading school compositions, whereas another might attach more importance to freshness and originality of expression.

Highly significant in the study of the gifted is the record of the courses and subjects the student enjoyed and the success he had with them.

Just as in the case of the slow learner, the test of daily schooling through the elementary years and high school serves to establish the gifted child's relative mental status in the general population of children his age. Success in school from one grade to the next is the best test of academic aptitude, provided the student has had normal opportunity to learn. Schooling tests the child's ability to profit from instruction and to make use of what he has learned, i.e., to transfer his new skills and knowledge. In the early school years, distinctions in ability are not so clear-cut as they will be by grade 7 or 8. Tentative judgments may change with continued study of the child. By grade 8 the record of the child's past school performance is clear enough to afford a sound prediction of his future academic success. The longer the period of observation the better, but the record of one year's experience in an academic high school is valuable in picking out the academically talented. This point was discussed in Chapter Two under the topic of educability as a criterion of academic talent.

The Use of Standardized Tests

Selection of the gifted, as selection of the tallest or the strongest, is impossible without some objective basis for comparing one child with another. Standardized tests have the merit of being uninfluenced by the teacher's judgment in evaluating aspects of ability and achievement. They provide a means of ranking a child above or below the established norms for the general child population, and they furnish a comparable set of observations independent of the type of school the child attended or the marking system used. Conduct ratings which affect school marks cannot influence the standardized test scores. Valid tests will discriminate effectively between those who have varying amounts of the capacities tested. Finally, standardized tests are practical and economical to use. The problem is to find the best combination of measures to reduce testing time to the minimum for initial screening.

The chief types of standardized tests are group and individual intelligence and scholastic aptitude tests, achievement tests in a wide range of subjects, and tests of aptitudes such as music, manual dexterity, mechanical ingenuity, and other specialties.

INTELLIGENCE TESTS

As the discussion in Chapter Three indicated, standardized intelligence tests provided the first objective evidence of individual differences in learning capacity. They have been used for nearly fifty years as a tool for the identification and analysis of mental aptitudes.

Formerly, intelligence tests were assumed to measure a student's inborn potential, but today they are commonly believed to measure the individual's developmental maturation in intellectual qualities and his achievement at the time of the test. They usually include subtests of verbal ability and language comprehension, abstract reasoning, and numerical skills, all of which are capacities developed through schooling and therefore good predictors of further academic achievement. The sampling of these abilities sums up the individual's general mental level.

New data on the value of mental and educational measurement in the identification of bright and dull children have been provided in a study by Klausmeier (1959). Among a wide array of measures of physical, mental, and personality traits, those which ranked highest in predicting the school achievement of boys and girls who averaged 113 months of age (about 9.3 years) in the fourth grade were:

Intelligence test results
Achievement test results
Strength of grip (a measure of vitality)

Intelligence Tests as Predictors of Academic Promise   A substantial, though not perfect, correlation is found between the results of intelligence tests and school marks or other evidences of school success. The predictive value of a test is higher for some subject-matter areas than others. It varies with the nature of the test and is higher for short-range than for long-range prediction. Furthermore, the prediction of achievement is imperfect to the extent that the child has special abilities or special disabilities not fully measured by a general test of intelligence.

Follow-up studies prove that measures of school performance and mental aptitude test scores together predict future achievement more accurately than either does alone. College aptitude tests administered to high school students yield results that correlate higher with subsequent college grades than do school marks or any pattern of preparation for college.

The Degree of Mental Acceleration Indicated by the IQ   According to one of the definitions given in Chapter Two, the gifted child is one who is mentally accelerated according to the results of standard intelligence tests. The amount of mental acceleration is relative to the child's chronological age, as the figures of Table 10 indicate. This table shows the degree of mental acceleration for a given IQ in 10-point intervals, starting at 100, for chronological ages from five to fifteen years. The table is read as follows: A child who is ten years old chronologically (10-0) and has an IQ of 130 determined by an intelligence test would have at that age a mental age of 13-0 years, or mental acceleration of three years. A child who is 10-0 and has an IQ of 150 has a mental age of 15-0 years, mental acceleration of five years. A child of 9-0 with an IQ of 170 would have a mental age of 15-4 (fifteen years and four months). A child of 10-0 with an IQ of 115 would have a mental age of 11-6 years, by interpolation of the table.

Table 10   Determination of Mental Age

IQ	Chronological Age										
	5-0	6-0	7-0	8-0	9-0	10-0	11-0	12-0	13-0	14-0	15-0
100	5-0	6-0	7-0	8-0	9-0	10-0	11-0	12-0	13-0	14-0	15-0
110	5-6	6-7	7-8	8-10	9-11	11-0	12-1	13-2	14-4	15-5	16-6
120	6-0	7-3	8-5	9-7	10-10	12-0	13-3	14-5	15-7	16-9	18-0
130	6-6	7-10	9-1	10-5	11-8	13-0	14-4	15-7	16-11	18-2	19-6
140	7-0	8-5	9-10	11-2	12-7	14-0	15-5	16-9	18-3	19-7	
150	7-6	9-0	10-6	12-0	13-6	15-0	16-6	18-0	19-6		
160	8-0	9-7	11-2	12-10	14-5	16-0	17-7	19-2			
170	8-6	10-3	11-11	13-7	15-4	17-0	18-8				

Some Limitations of Intelligence Tests   Although intelligence testing has been widely accepted in school practice and educational research, the limitations of the tests must be recognized. Too much finality has been attached to a single test score; some bright children would be missed if mental tests alone were used for appraisal. The score on a brief group intelligence test is not sufficiently reliable for placement of pupils in special classes at the time of the test; it is even less reliable after the lapse of several years.

In the interpretation of intelligence test results, the reliability of the particular test needs to be taken into account, that is, the accuracy of the measuring device. The reliability of an intelligence test score is expressed in terms of the number of points a duplicate second test score differs from the first. An IQ of 115 should actually be stated as 115 plus or minus the number of points of probable error. If the probable error is 7 points, the truer statement is: The child's true IQ ranges between 108 and 122.

Since the spread of IQs or converted scores varies for different tests, comparisons of results for two or more tests may be misleading. Scores on four different tests given to nineteen elementary school children are shown in Table 11. The average of all four measures probably gives a more reliable measure than the score on any one test.

A brief test, even though it taps a variety of mental traits is inadequate for complete analysis of a gifted child's potential. Even a comprehensive intelligence test can yield no more than a limited sampling of information about an individual's capacities.

The validity of paper-and-pencil intelligence tests for identifying the mentally gifted is suspect because these tests depend so largely upon reading ability. The bright child with a language handicap or mediocre reading achievement would be disadvantaged if his intelligence were judged on a verbal test.

The question is asked whether IQ tests identify only the intellectually superior and fail to identify the child of high creativity. This question is considered in Chapter Fifteen.

The Influence of Socioeconomic Factors on Test Scores   On a group intelligence test question which asked children to choose two words that belonged together, the son of a migrant worker chose "cup" and "table" rather than the correct answer "cup" and "saucer." This illustrates what many critics of mental aptitude tests say—that the tests reflect nothing more than the socioeconomic background of the child. Improve the background, and the IQ will rise, runs the argument. In selecting candidates for classes for the gifted in a large city school with a low-income clientele, teachers were told to overlook the recorded IQs and to use the child's performance level as the guide in making nominations. The reason was that children from culturally deprived homes were lacking in basic experiences common to typical children. Many had language barriers to overcome; hence, it seemed unfair to consider the test IQ a valid indicator of ability.

To circumvent the problem of cultural bias in the tests, some authorities recommend depending entirely on teachers' recommendations of the most promising children in different categories: the children from superior homes, the Negroes, the foreign-born, those from low-income families. Eventually, however, all must be rated

Table 11   IQ Data for an Elementary School Class

Child	Pintner Cunningham (beginning grade 1)	Otis Alpha (beginning grade 3)	Thorndike Lorge Verbal	Nonverbal (grade 4)	Otis Beta (beginning grade 6)
A	134	117	140	125	110
B	118	122	136	123	132
C	104	100	127	123	115
D	114	113	125	121	124
E	111	95	121	111	111
F	126	117	112	107	117
G	128	103	112	91	113
H	139	117	111	—	111
I	99	116	111	109	105
J	100	94	106	93	97
K	102	96	106	79	96
L	87	85	106	99	101
M	109	86	105	107	103
N	98	99	103	86	110
O	107	91	87	96	95
P	106	92	103	94	—
Q	109	93	97	104	—
R	110	99	114	108	—
S	80	95	105	105	—

on an objective comparative basis because academic programs in high school and college will severely screen out those youths who lack systematic knowledge of our common heritage. By this time the academically talented must have demonstrated their capacity to deal with abstract ideas and to handle problems of increasing complexity.

As children grow older, regular schooling, various media of communication in and out of school, and free access to cultural resources, such as libraries, tend to even up their backgrounds. Then poor results on standard tests cannot necessarily be ascribed to limited background.

Is it possible to devise some sort of universal culture-free test? This has been tried, but the attempts proved disappointing because the authors of the tests soon ran out of difficult discriminative items. More recently, there has been considerable experimentation with "culture-fair" tests, notably by Allison Davis and others at the University of Chicago. The results have also been disappointing in view of their original purpose because children from better homes and communities still do better on the tests—in about the same proportion as on traditional types of intelligence tests.

Identifying the Gifted Child from a Foreign Language Background   Children are handicapped in taking any sort of verbal test that is not in their own language. In the French survey, foreign children rated consistently lower than native French children on the Gille Mosaic Test, because all items were given orally in the French language.

The question was raised about the precocity of a clever little Persian girl, now five and a half years old, who lives in Istanbul, Turkey, and is rapidly learning the Turkish language. How bright is she? If she rates average on the Turkish version of the Binet test, she may nevertheless be an exceptionally bright little girl.

It is unfair to attempt to rate non-English-speaking children with English language tests. A teacher reported that José, a Puerto Rican boy in her class, got a low score on an intelligence test. This is too bad, she said, because the boy appears to be quite bright. The mistake was in subjecting the child to an inappropriate test in the first place. A continuous record of his behavior should be kept until his reading ability and comprehension of English enable him to respond freely to English language tests.

Nonlanguage tests and performance tests that require a minimum use of language are more discriminative in younger age levels than later on. By the time a child reaches age ten or so, nonlanguage tests are not difficult enough to discriminate between bright and average children. An exception is the Raven Progressive Matrices Test, which is nonlanguage but requires a high level of insight and reasoning ability. At the Lincoln School of Teachers College, New York, the progressive matrices furnished corroborative evidence of high intelligence, as did the Alexander Passalong Test, though the IQs did not run so high as those on pencil-and-paper tests. Children with more aptitude in spatial relations and a high interest in geometry did relatively better on the Raven Progressive Matrices Test. The use of abstract problems presented in symbolic terms seems essential for distinguishing older students of superior aptitudes.

The Present View of IQ Tests   Today we seem to have reached an intermediate position between the two extremes of unquestioned acceptance and complete rejection of intelligence test results. The modern viewpoint is that intelligence tests and measures of differential aptitudes arc indispensable in the study and analysis of individual potential and achievement. Now with machine scoring, the convenience of wide-range objective-type tests is appreciated more than ever. Two or three hours spent in administering group tests to a school will yield valuable information about individual capacities that cannot be obtained so accurately and conveniently in any other way. There is no point in discrediting the tests because of a small percentage of inconsistent results due to errors of measurement. This is to be expected in the use of any measurement device.

Psychologists may argue that a single test score is better than no score at all, but this can be true only if teachers and school officials recognize the tentative nature of test scores. It is shortsighted to depend on test information alone in screening the gifted for special educational programs. In the last analysis the only safeguard is to regard the test score or IQ as but one item of information along with various indications of a child's developmental status.

Dr. Roger J. Lennon, Director of Test Research and Service of Harcourt, Brace & World, Inc., recommends that all standardized testing should be part of a carefully planned and well-integrated guidance program—not a haphazard affair left to the individual teachers or a special program isolated from other school services in child study and record keeping.

Identifying the Gifted through Individual Tests Psychologists place more confidence in individual intelligence scales than in pencil-and-paper tests because of their diagnostic value. In an individual examination, the tester can observe the individual's performance in a face-to-face situation, elicit verbal response, and time the responses—diagnostic features that are lacking in group tests. The mentally advanced child can be recognized through an individual intelligence test as early as the kindergarten years.

It is doubtful whether the Stanford-Binet test, in spite of the extended range of abilities it covers in the upper levels, or any other individual intelligence test can possibly probe the mind of the budding genius. Dr. Henry Garret of Columbia University expressed this view some years ago, and it seems to be borne out in observations of the gifted. Brief intelligence tests cannot measure a sufficient number of the dimensions of intellect to be adequate measures of the gifted child's general intelligence, the richness of his imagination, his originality, the speed and quality of his thinking processes, and other unusual traits. Better than a single brief test is a thorough study of many aspects of the child's mental life.

Repeated Binet test IQs of dull or backward individuals have always shown more consistency than results for the bright, because the dull less often get into the upper levels of the test. Furthermore, they do not branch out into so wide an array of different interests and hobbies, and schooling does not have so much effect on the test results in these cases.

The extent of IQ fluctuations on repeated tests over an interval of time was reported in Chapter Five. Gifted children above elementary school age who are given both individual and group tests tend to lose as much as 20 or 30 points on the latter because of greater restriction in the distribution of IQ scores. In the California State Department of Education study conducted by Ruth A. Martinson, group IQs ranged downward as low as 100 for individuals whose Stanford-Binet IQs were 130 or higher (1960).

Coaching for IQ Tests During the early years of the testing movement, parents and others outside the teaching profession were scarcely aware of the existence of standard tests, their nature and use. Now almost everyone is familiar with them. Coaching manuals and courses exist for the purpose of cramming students for these examinations. A drill book has been published consisting of sample test exercises for pupils who want to "improve their IQs." When anything seems so desirable to parents as having a child accepted for a special class for the gifted or so unfortunate as having the child rejected, they will go to any lengths to help the child pass the required tests.

The results of standardized tests may be invalidated when children are given preliminary practice at home or at school because tests are standardized on results for children who have not had recent direct drill on the test items. Special coaching may result in a spuriously high IQ, with the result that the coached child placed in a gifted class or group may later prove to be a disappointment.

Coaching on group intelligence tests is not too serious unless the child is coached on precisely the same test he will be given for screening purposes, because these tests have several different forms, with a large number of items in each. Coaching on individual tests is more serious, because they are less likely to have alternate forms, there are fewer items, and the items are easy to recall.

ACHIEVEMENT TESTS

From the time of Dr. Terman's first studies, results of standardized achievement tests have been used to check on the school progress of the gifted child. Today there is scarcely an area of school study for which an appropriate achievement test cannot be found, whether for first graders or high school and college students.

The great advantage of standardized achievement tests used for studying the gifted, apart from their convenience and objectivity, lies in their wide range. If the appropriate form of the test is given, the child can go as high in responding to questions and problems as he is able, whether or not he has covered the material in school.

The New York City schools regularly require that children entering the seventh grade of special progress junior high schools meet certain school achievement standards as determined by standardized tests: a reading test grade score of 8.5 (equivalent to the middle of grade 8) and an arithmetic score of 8.0. In schools where the authorities prefer to select students for bright classes primarily on the basis of achievement test results rather than on IQ scores, the children may be disappointing academically because the age factor is not taken into account in achievement test results as it is in intelligence testing.

Special aptitude tests and achievement tests are similar in form and overlap in content. For example, a science aptitude test would be little different from a science achievement test.

IDENTIFYING SPECIAL TALENTS AND CREATIVITY

Bright and talented youngsters are forever winning prizes that are awarded on the basis of the judgment of experts, e.g., for the best essay on "Liberty" or "Democracy" or "Why I Want to Go to College," for the best painting or piece of modeling in an exhibit, and for the best performance at the local music festival. Are there any aptitude tests that disclose budding talent in these areas?

Predictive tests of special talent in the arts, social leadership, creative writing, and even science are not highly reliable because the traits, talents, or achievements displayed in these activities are not static, fixed, or set once and for all; they are, on the contrary, developed through experience and training. Identifying special talents is also difficult because there are no agreed-upon standards of judging excellent performance, and popular opinion is not of much aid.

Are there any measures that predict which young people now in school are most apt to become highly creative workers in the future? Although extensive research is now going on, both in devising new testing instruments for measuring specific qualities and in planning long-range studies, results so far are tentative.

Dr. Paul Witty made use of a symbolic and imaginative film entitled *The Hunter and the Forest* to stimulate creative expression in elementary school children and to identify those who were most talented in creative writing (1956). After viewing the eight-minute film, the children wrote their own original stories and poems based on the film theme.

In evaluating writing talent, teachers should guard against overrating superficial aspects, e.g., correct spelling, grammar, and punctuation, and overlooking the more essential qualities in a composition such as diction, style, creative imagination, excellent reporting, and the like.

How can genuine talent in the arts be recognized? Before they attain fluency in written expression, all children use drawing more or less as a form of expression. Consequently, the artwork of children up to the age of eight years is more likely to reveal mental qualities and developmental acceleration than special talent. Until the child has had an opportunity to respond to art instruction by a competent teacher, it is difficult to distinguish the genuinely talented from those who will soon turn from this form of expression to other interests. Toward the beginning of adolescence, however, special talent is more definitely revealed; children are more outgoing, and their genuine interests and capacities are more fully expressed. The extent to which the student will be able to profit from advanced training is now more clearly demonstrated.

Whether or not a student has special talent in music, art, science, mathematics, creative writing, crafts, or technical skills can be determined in part by the way he tackles lessons and other learning opportunities in the respective areas. Note should be taken of the child's interests, as shown on field trips, in the school laboratory, and in extracurricular activities and the use he makes of spare time for these interests at home. Ask the child what he likes to do most, also what he seems to do most easily and well. In the case of one young girl the answer was, "Make costumes." A boy may show special ingenuity with tools and machinery or a craze for studying insects. A girl may devote all her spare time to story writing or musical composition. One child showed special interest in studying tropical fish. For more information on the subject of creativity and the identification of creative talent see Chapter Fifteen.

Science Talent   Considerable attention has been given within recent years to the identification of science talent. In one study a list of forty-nine characteristics of children gifted in science was drawn up (Hone, 1959). Lesser and Davis conducted a research investigation on the identification of gifted elementary school children with exceptional science talent. They devised special tests for space conceptualization, vocabulary, number ability, reasoning, and scientific knowledge (1960). Marshall has drawn up a twenty-one-point science-talent checklist (1961).

Other Devices for Identifying the Gifted

Devices that have been used experimentally for identifying the gifted include trait checklists, self-rating scales, observation guides, sociometric devices, situations tests, anecdotal records, and the "critical-incidents" technique in which the teacher records a student's behavior in specific situations. Use is also made of reading records, interest inventories, and autobiographies, as well as evaluations of the children's productions in art, writing, mechanical invention, and other areas.

Some use has been made of projective devices, such as the Rorschach, sentence completions, TAT, draw-a-person, and so on, but there is little evidence concerning the special value these tests may have in studying the intellectual capacities and emotional stability of the gifted. Dr. Harvey Zorbaugh who used the Rorschach with children referred to the New York University Clinic some years ago did not find that the results added much to information gained through interviews.

OBSERVATION OF BEHAVIOR

Observations of children's everyday behavior provide a wealth of information about their past experience, current interests, and unusual traits. What guidelines serve as aids to teachers in identifying the bright and talented in their classes through informal observation?

The teacher should note the child's ability to learn from his environment, his capacity to remember new things, the way he handles problems, how well he uses language, his progress in learning to read and in making use of reading, indications of any special hobbies of an intellectual sort, the ease and rapidity with which he completes assignments, his degree of attention and concentration when social responsibility and other matters are discussed, his interest in a challenging study task. The teacher should always be on the lookout for the child who has more ability than he uses in school studies. This pupil may be the most promising of all.

In some schools extensive use is made of anecdotal records as a means of building a comprehensive record of the child's performance and abilities. As time permits, the teacher jots down notations on slips of paper, with the child's name and the date. Later these slips are filed in the child's individual folder. Here are several illustrations:

Billy, a boy of nine in fifth grade, told the class one day that they should have a class newspaper, and he outlined his plans for the paper.

Barbara, at the beginning of the term, showed the class the watercolors she had made on a summer trip and the illustrated notebook she had kept of travel with her family.

This is the sort of information that begins to build the picture of children of unusual promise. The cumulative record of such incidents is more significant than isolated items. Did Billy go on with his plans for the paper? Did he get the cooperation of the other children? In the child's file would go copies of the newssheet that originated from Billy's suggestion. Did Barbara persist with her artwork and writing? Did she display unusual talent continuously from year to year?

Talent for social leadership is evaluated best through observation of the individual's everyday behavior. Sociometric tests are used to supplement clues to unusual traits obtained from other sources. In responding to the guess-who test, the pupil indicates social preference. He would be asked:

Which classmate he would prefer to work with

Which one he likes best

Which one he would choose as a leader

Judgments about bright and talented children can also be made from their self-ratings and the statements they write about themselves, their interests, and their occupations. The high school student's self-ratings might contain questions such as:

Do I like school study? Which studies do I like best?

Do I seem to have more ability than others?

Do I work up to my potential?

What are my strong points? What appear to be my limitations?

Checklists and Observation Guides   In stock judging, the experts who rate the animals are guided by a checklist of traits and features that distinguish superior specimens. The experienced judge, with this list in hand, appraises each animal, grading on a point scale adding up to 100. Is it possible for an expert judge of child behavior, having in hand a list of traits that characterize mentally superior and talented children, to check a given child, even to assign ratings with the purpose of identifying the mentally superior? Such checklists have been prepared by a number of authorities.

Laycock drew up a twenty-item list (1957). He suggests that the teacher be on the lookout for the pupils who:

1. Possess superior powers of reasoning, of dealing with abstractions, of generalizing from specific facts, of understanding meanings, and of seeing into relationships

2. Have great intellectual curiosity

3. Learn easily and readily

4. Have a wide range of interests

5. Have a broad attention-span that enables them to concentrate on, and persevere in solving problems and pursuing interests

6. Are superior in the quantity and quality of vocabulary as compared with other children of their own age

7. Have ability to do effective work independently

8. Have learned to read early (often well before school age)

9. Exhibit keen powers of observation

10. Show initiative and originality in intellectual work

11. Show alertness and quick response to new ideas

12. Are able to memorize quickly

13. Have great interest in the nature of man and the universe (problems of origin and destiny, etc.)

14. Possess unusual imagination

15. Follow complex directions easily

16. Are rapid readers

17. Have several hobbies

18. Have reading interests which cover a wide range of subjects

19. Make frequent and effective use of the library

20. Are superior in arithmetic, particularly in problem solving[2]

Jack Kough of the Science Research Associates, Inc., Chicago, has drawn up a list of twelve items recommended for the use of teachers in discovering the most promising students in their classes in upper elementary grades and high school (Kough and DeHaan, 1956). The teacher is asked to consider:

Which of your students stands out from the rest of the class in these characteristics?

1. Learns rapidly and easily

2. Uses a great deal of common sense and practical knowledge

3. Reasons things out, thinks clearly, recognizes relationships, comprehends meanings

4. Retains what he has heard or read without much rote drill

5. Knows about many things of which most students are unaware

6. Has a large vocabulary which he uses easily and accurately

7. Can read books that are one or two years in advance of the rest of the class

8. Performs difficult mental tasks

9. Asks many questions, has a wide range of interests

[2] Samuel Laycock, *Gifted Children*, The Copp-Clark Publishing Company, Toronto, Canada, 1957. Reprinted with the kind permission of Dr. S. R. Laycock and The Copp-Clark Publishing Company, Toronto, Canada.

10. Does some academic work one or two years in advance of his class

11. Is original in his thinking, uses good but unusual methods

12. Is observant and responds quickly[3]

A fifteen-item list was prepared for the use of teachers and guidance workers as an aid in the study and identification of gifted children in the public schools of Portland, Oregon. Teachers were requested to rate the children for each trait in one of four categories: (1) outstanding, (2) very good, (3) average, or (4) below average (Freehill, 1961).

Science Research Associates, Inc., Chicago, has published a checklist of ability and talent, with from seven to twelve items under each of these nine categories:

Scientific ability	Dramatic talent
Leadership ability	Musical talent
Creative ability	Mechanical skills
Artistic talent	Physical skills
Writing talent	

This checklist was used in the study of gifted and talented students in Quincy, Illinois (Kough and DeHaan, 1956).

The author prepared a checklist consisting of sixty-five items based on research reports of the traits of the gifted. Fifteen of the points relate to the child's background and early experiences. The items are grouped in five categories:

Mental traits, intellectual qualities

Command of language

Academic skills and attainments

Special interests, aptitudes, talents

Personal and social traits, character qualities

This form is found in the Appendix. An abbreviated version of this checklist has been prepared for younger children in the five- to ten-year age range.

No child is expected to show all the traits in any list, but the more checks he earns and the higher his ratings in these traits, the more exceptional he proves to be. Teachers can be requested to rate all pupils whom they consider to be in the upper 5 per cent in aptitude, and then to collect test information and other data as a check on their ratings. This procedure gives the

[3] Jack Kough and Robert F. DeHaan, *The Teacher's Guidance Handbook,* vol. 1, Science Research Associates, Inc., Chicago, Ill., 1956. Used by permission of the authors and publisher.

teachers a part in identification procedures and at the same time focuses their attention on points to be used in school and home guidance of these pupils.

Effective use cannot be made of a checklist unless the rater has a reasonably good idea of the normal behavior traits and performance of like-age children in general. The use of these lists requires considerable skill on the rater's part in observing the child, knowing how to judge him, and knowing how to obtain the information needed on which to base judgments. No one need be discouraged in these attempts, however, because expert judging requires training and long experience.

For other checklists see the publications of Abraham (1958), and Brumbaugh and Roshco (1959).

Psychologists have devised "readiness" questionnaires for rating the developmental status of kindergartners and school beginners. These questionnaires and checklists serve much the same function as checklists for identifying the gifted. See, for example, the readiness questionnaire prepared by Banham (1950).

Other suggestions for the more comprehensive study of children's aptitudes and performance will be found in the book by Prescott (1957).

SITUATION TESTS

Young people demonstrate their strengths and weaknesses in problematic or critical situations that call for prompt decisions, good planning, originality, and independence of thought and action. Dr. John C. Flanagan has described what he terms the critical-incidents technique for studying and recording pupil behavior. How does the individual handle himself in critical situations? For example, discipline in the class has broken down. "We need to do something about this matter," the teacher may say. "What do you suggest?"

In one case a child was seriously injured on the playground when no teacher was present. A student demonstrated immediate grasp of the situation, and his prompt action probably saved the child's life. In another case, the children in one of the lower grades were planning a spring picnic, but their funds and resources were limited. Several children in the group showed initiative and good judgment in suggesting ways to have a good picnic without going over their budget.

When the senior class in one school visited the state capitol and were invited by their legislator to attend a legislative session, an outstanding student rose and with poise and well-chosen words responded to the legislator's invitation, all without any affectation and as though he were doing nothing more than was normally expected of him.

Continuous Appraisal: The Developmental Record

The chronology of development revealed through observations and multiple evaluations made continuously over an extended period serves better than any single device or "once-for-all" rating to assess the abilities of the exceptional individual. Comprehensive biographical records also provide the types of information needed for individual guidance through the school years.

The use of life-history records becomes increasingly significant as the gifted students plan their future education and look forward to their life careers.

Observation of children over a period of years is the only means of distinguishing between those who are *consistently remarkable* and the ones who show superficial, sporadic flashes of talent as a result of pushing and coaching. Such records also aid in distinguishing young people of general all-around ability from those with highly specialized interests and talents that have persisted over a period of time.

A continuous record should be kept of the gifted child's special interests and hobbies, his purposes and goals, and his educational and career plans. What do the records reveal about tendencies that have been showing up with each new step in growth? Has mental acceleration been noted as a continuing trait? What special interests are becoming more apparent? In what direction is the child's purposing leading him?

Keeping track of the most promising students all the way through school requires some special attention to record keeping. Dr. Carleton Washburne's teachers in the Winnetka, Illinois, schools placed a "blue flag sheet" in the child's folder to signal an individual of unusual abilities. Whenever a teacher discovered a pupil with the qualities and traits that satisfied the definition of "gifted" or "exceptionally promising," information validating the observations was placed on a blue sheet which was sent to the principal's office, where it was placed in the child's permanent dossier. Teachers in subsequent years added their observations in turn. Through these records consistency or inconsistency in cases of unusual development could be discovered.

The suggestion to look beyond the child himself, to give some thought to the child's home and his parents as a means of confirming impressions of the gifted child, is not farfetched, since the emergence of remarkable achievement can often be attributed to favorable circumstances in the child's home environment.

References

Abraham, Willard: *Commonsense about Gifted Children*, Harper & Row, Publishers, Incorporated, New York, 1958.

Anastasi, Anne, M. J. Meade, and A. A. Schneiders: *The Validation of a Biographical Inventory as a Predictor of College Success*, Educational Testing Service, Princeton, N. J., 1960.

Banham, Katharine: *Readiness Questionnaire*, Educational Test Bureau, Minneapolis, 1950.

Brumbaugh, Florence N., and Bernard Roshco: *Your Gifted Child: A Guide for Parents*, Holt, Rinehart and Winston, Inc., New York, 1959.

Burt, Cyril: The Examination of Eleven Plus, *British Journal of Educational Research*, 7:99–117, 1959.

Chauncey, Henry: Measurement and Prediction Tests of Academic Ability, in James B. Conant (ed.), *The Identification and Education of the Academically Talented Student in the American Secondary School*, conference report, National Education Association, Washington, D.C., 1958.

DeHaan, Robert F., and Robert J. Havighurst: *Educating Gifted Children*, 2d ed., The University of Chicago Press, Chicago, 1961.

Flanagan, John C., and others: *The Talents of American Youth: I. Design for a Study of American Youth*, Houghton Mifflin Company, Boston, 1962.

Freehill, Maurice F.: *Gifted Children: Their Psychology and Education*, The Macmillan Company, New York, 1961.

Hone, Elizabeth: Identification of Children Gifted in Science, *California Journal of Educational Research*, 10:64–67, 1959.

Klausmeier, Herbert J.: Identifying Children through Measurement, *Education*, 80:167–171, 1959.

Kough, Jack, and Robert F. DeHaan: *The Teacher's Guidance Handbook*, vol. 1, Science Research Associates, Inc., Chicago, 1956.

Krugman, Morris: Identification and Preservation of Talent, *Teachers College Record*, 61:459–463, 1960.

Laycock, Samuel R.: *Gifted Children: A Handbook for the Classroom Teacher*, The Copp-Clark Publishing Company, Toronto, Canada, 1957.

Lesser, Gerald S., and Frederick B. Davis: *The Identification of Gifted Elementary School Children with Exceptional Scientific Talent*, Hunter College Educational Clinic, New York, 1960.

McGuire, Carson, Edwin Hindsman, F. J. King, and Earl Jennings: Dimensions of Talented Behavior, *Educational and Psychological Measurement*, 21:3–38, 1961.

Marshall, J. Stanley: Science in the Elementary School, chap. 5 in Louis A. Fliegler (ed.), *Curriculum Planning for the Gifted*, Prentice-Hall, Inc., Englewood Cliffs, N. J., 1961.

Martinson, Ruth A.: *Educational Programs for Gifted Pupils*, State Department of Education, Sacramento, Calif., 1960.

Martinson, Ruth A., and Leon M. Lessinger: Problems in the Identification of Intellectually Gifted Pupils, *Exceptional Children*, 26:3–38, 1961.

Orr, David B.: Opportunities for Research on the Education of Gifted Students, in *The Gifted Students: Cooperative Research*, U.S. Department of Health, Education and Welfare, Office of Education, Washington, D.C., 1960.

Pegnato, Carl W., and Jack W. Birch: Locating Gifted Children in Junior High School: A Comparison of Methods, *Exceptional Children*, 25:300–304, 1959.

Prescott, Daniel A.: *The Child in the Educative Process*, McGraw-Hill Book Company, New York, 1957.

Sumption, Merle R., and Evelyn M. Luecking: *Education of the Gifted*, The Ronald Press Company, New York, 1960.

Terman, Lewis M., and others: *Genetic Studies of Genius*, vol. 1, *Mental and Physical Traits of a Thousand Gifted Children*, Stanford University Press, Stanford, Calif., 1925.

Varner, G. F.: Can Teachers Select Bright and Dull Pupils? *Journal of Educational Research*, 6:126–132, 1922.

Whipple, Guy Montrose: *Classes for Gifted Children: An Experimental Study of Methods of Selection and Instruction*, School and Home Educational Monographs, no. 1, Public School Publishing Company, Bloomington, Ill., 1924.

Witty, Paul A.: The Use of Films in Stimulating Creative Expression and in Identifying Talented Pupils, *Elementary English*, 33:340–344, 1956.

Chapter Seven

EDUCATIONAL PROVISIONS FOR THE GIFTED AND TALENTED

The childhood years are remarkable for rapid growth in all aspects of development. During these years the individual's mental powers mature, he is transformed into a rational social being, and he acquires his own distinctive personality. The questions to be considered in this chapter are: How can the growth process of the gifted and talented child be facilitated through school instruction? What sort of mental training is best for students who will in the future be grappling with problems of great complexity? Obviously the world of tomorrow will present challenges that are unknown today. What kinds of educational programs produce the original thinker, the talented artist, the intellectual leader, the highly trained professional person? A chief concern of school people is to discover the conditions that foster the development of exceptional abilities and to use this information in educating young people of unusual promise.

Distinctive Needs and Special Requirements of the Gifted

The teacher of a fifth-grade class containing a number of bright children asked a typical question: "How can a better program of lessons and activities be worked out for these children? They complete an assignment I had planned for a forty-minute period within a few minutes, and then they lose interest. They do not like to review an arithmetic lesson after they have once completed all the problems. What can be done to challenge them more fully?"

Intellectually superior children think, generalize, and solve problems on a more mature level than other children and they require different emphases in their schooling. The bright can learn at a faster pace than their age-mates and are ready to explore wider areas of knowledge and to go farther afield with their inquiring minds. First-grade pupils in a typical school vary in mental and developmental age all the way from three years of age to ten, with the most capable of them able to learn twice as fast as the slower children.

Teachers tend to direct instruction toward the middle-ability group in the class, with the result that rapid learners may be held down to the pace of this group. A bright first grader dutifully followed his teacher's instructions to draw the number of flags necessary to correspond with the number 9, but after making the flags he insisted on coloring them so that they represented nine different countries. He consulted the encyclopedia for the information he needed and on his own initiative went far beyond the regular class assignment.

BETTER TIMING OF EDUCATIONAL EXPERIENCES

In the initial stages of instruction, whether the learning task is reading or writing or studying algebra or economics, academically talented students are at a higher level of readiness than others. Therefore, to economize learning time the mentally gifted should be exposed to basic concepts and introduced to fundamental skills earlier than others. Difficult concepts can be introduced earlier, depending upon the maturity of the student. A gifted pupil may be ready for dictionary work or map study well ahead of others his age. An unusual fifth- or sixth-grade student may need certain equipment—for example, a slide rule or a drafting set—long before his classmates have any interest in using it; he may need certain books of information and other resources that most children would not care to use until high school, if at all.

Undifferentiated programs of schooling are wasteful of time and talent. Each student needs an optimal program for learning in which he begins at the point he has actually attained and then proceeds at his own pace.

Our standard graded curriculum with uniform texts and assignments is too rigid for the bright, rapid learner. A boy of eleven who finishes his work quickly and has nothing to do while the others are still studying may seem to be content to sit and wait, but actually he revolts by withdrawing into his own world where his fertile imagination can be exercised. One boy deliberately gives wrong answers to attract attention. In sheer desperation, teachers give active bright youngsters any occupation to keep them busy— running errands, coaching slow learners, straightening out the book shelves, and doing other routine jobs.

Providing for the gifted means setting up programs that deviate widely from standard practices, grade for grade. For these children the standard grade-level concept should be separated from chronological age or class grade placement. A bright child of ten may be capable of a standard of work ordinarily set for the typical twelve-year-old. Bright children should be able to move rapidly through basic schooling with adjusted programs and special adaptations of the curriculum.

LEARNING THROUGH SELF–DIRECTION

Another consideration is that gifted students are often more capable of self-directed learning than others. These children easily acquire factual information on their own. They may be given the responsibility of setting up an exhibit or looking up facts in reference sources while others are still working on basic skills. They are capable of greater independence in problem solving. They come up with original ideas which lead to research projects requiring time and space, books, and equipment for further exploration. They seek answers to complex problems not even recognized by their age-mates. Bright pupils engage in long-range assignments, they show more independence in choosing and planning their studies, and they are often more capable of self-evaluation than others.

Incidence of Gifted Pupils
in the School Population

How many gifted children are there in the general juvenile population, say from age six to eighteen years? The answer to this question has practical bearing on planning educational programs and community facilities; quite specific information is needed for grouping and sectioning students, planning for enrichment activities both in school and out, providing for advanced courses in high school, supplying guidance facilities, and other purposes.

The incidence of gifted children in the general population must be stated in terms of the definition adopted and the criteria used, as suggested in Chapters Two and Six. Test score criteria have been most frequently used—the upper 2 per cent, the upper 15 per cent, or whatever cutoff point is used. When some standard in terms of mental test scores has been adopted, the actual number of bright and talented children varies with the size of the total school age population and the type of community. A city of 350,000 population with 50,000 children of school age would have about 1,000 children in the top 2 per cent, whereas a community with 5,000 school-age children would normally have no more than 100 in the top 2 per cent, and a community with 500 pupils would theoretically yield only 10 children of this level. The corresponding figures for the top 15 per cent of the school population would be 7,500, 750, and 75, respectively.

In a typical elementary school enrolling about 500, there will be about 50 unusually capable children (10 per cent), but many more who are bright and specially talented. These children will be found scattered throughout all the grades, perhaps 2 or 3 in a class of 30 or 35.

These computations assume comparability among different-sized communities, but actually, the proportion of gifted children in a community varies with the socioeconomic and cultural level of the particular community and the type of clientele represented in the school population.

VARIATIONS IN DIFFERENT TYPES OF COMMUNITIES

The tremendous variation in level of academic aptitude in different types of communities—industrialized urban centers, high-class suburbs, rural areas, and cities of varying size and economic status—has been confirmed by the results of Flanagan's survey of high school youth and their schools (1962). There may be several times as many children rating over 125 IQ in a suburban community as in a typical urban school enrolling a more heterogeneous population. A backward community may have few children who rate in the top 2 per cent on the theoretical curve, whereas a superior suburban center may have five or even ten times the national average in this category. High-class communities that send 80 to 90 per cent of their high school graduates to college have a selected school population to begin with and a smaller proportion of slow learners who require individual attention.

Schools in the slums are found to rank below the standard of those in better-class communities. Bright children from poor homes may be shunted into narrow vocational studies in high school instead of being advised to prepare for a college and professional career. High class suburban schools are often better because the residents pay higher local taxes and there is a higher per capita expenditure for school support. These schools attract better teachers; they have smaller classes, better facilities, a cooperative parent group, more intelligent educational leadership, better libraries, and community supplementation. New Trier Township High School, in Winnetka, Illinois, is rated among the country's leading high schools. With exceptional students from cultured homes, this school is able to achieve superior results.

College and university-related schools for elementary and high school students, the so-called "campus" schools, invariably attract many families with exceptional children, sometimes with faculty families predominating unless a broader selection policy is adopted. The Ohio State University School referred to in Chapter Five is an illustration of the superior campus school.

The independent private schools also reflect a high correlation between social selectivity and intellectual ratings of the students. As a general rule, the more prominent the school and the higher the tuition rates, the higher the intellectual level of the student body. The reputation for being a "good school" is due as much to the high caliber of the students as to the teaching methods and superior facilities. Children in these schools rank far above average on mental test scores, particularly when minimum standards in scholastic ability are set for admission. Tuition schools usually offer scholarship aid to families who cannot pay all or part of the tuition, but such assistance is usually extended only to the most capable applicants whose achievements will reflect credit on the school. Although the less prominent independent schools do not possess the financial resources of the larger prep schools, they attract a selected clientele, have small classes, and permit freedom and elasticity in instruction. The programs in these schools are primarily college preparatory.

Efforts to improve schooling for promising children from impoverished homes and to enrich their cultural background have resulted in what is known as the Higher Horizons Program in the New York City schools and similar programs elsewhere. Details of these developments are given later on in this chapter.

The Identification Phase

Experts agree that every school should conduct a planned, continuous search for gifted and talented children. One of the first steps is to set up an identification system and to prepare a roster of the children tentatively identified. In Cleveland, Ohio, Quincy, Illinois, Portland, Oregon, and other places, teachers take an active part in this phase of the program, at least by nominating the most promising children in their classes for further study.

Identification of children to be included in the program should extend through all levels of the school no matter what particular ages or grade levels are to be involved in the initial program. School authorities, teachers, and parents, working together, may decide on the criteria to be adopted in selecting children for special programs. This avoids the charge that only limited criteria were used and that the opinions of people in the best position to make judgments were disregarded. Procedures most commonly used to identify the gifted and talented were described in Chapter Six. In an all-out effort to locate the gifted and talented, teachers and school officials should be assisted by leaders of children's work in the community, social agencies, librarians, and others. The school should set up a permanent register of the children who are identified as gifted in order to keep track of the children year by year through school and beyond. The file of information for each student distinguishes between bright and promising children, the specially talented, and the truly remarkable ones. This record is used as the basis for conferences and discussions with the school staff and parents. In high school the record provides a guide to college and career planning.

State Support for Gifted Child Programs

The growing trend to establish programs for the gifted on a statewide basis was mentioned in Chapter Three. In a number of instances, the state department of education has taken an active part in developing programs for the gifted in conjunction with school people in local communities. Teacher-training opportunities have been supported, and published information on the subject has been made available. California established a statewide program in 1957 under the direction of a coordinator who has developed the instructional program and directed the evaluation (Martinson, 1960).

In the planning stage, meetings are held in local communities. Plans for a program of several years' duration are drawn up; local people are appointed to undertake the direction in cooperation with the state director through occasional conferences and other means of communication. Records of local projects are kept which become part of the periodical reporting that must be done. Local school people are assured of the services and support of an educational expert as the plans emerge and the program gets under way.

A survey was undertaken in 1955 in the state of Connecticut to determine what was being done for children of exceptional intellectual capacity. As an outcome of the survey, recommendations were made to improve educational services for gifted children everywhere in the state.

In Racine, Wisconsin, experts from the state university joined the school staff in developing arrangements for pupils of superior learning ability (Klausmeier and others, 1961). A study was made of 120 fourth graders, some of whom were placed in segregated classes, others in special classes one day a week, and the rest in regular classrooms. Special classes and other instructional arrangements were tried out in the fifth grade; instructional teams and other special provisions were explored in the seventh grade.

School and Community Planning for the Gifted

When the question of "doing something for the gifted" first arises in a community, the commonest gesture of parents and school authorities is to set up afterschool and Saturday club groups for the "exhibitionist" type of talents, particularly art, music, and dancing. This is good as far as it goes, but it reveals failure to recognize the more comprehensive meaning of the terms "gifted" and "talented." Catering chiefly to artistic talent may even divert attention from a wide array of aptitudes that should be provided for in science workshops, literary and library hobby groups, nature study programs, and so on.

The urgency of long-range educational planning for the gifted comparable to what has been accomplished through the years with the retarded and handicapped is generally recognized. Total school planning tends to offset any tendency of administrators and teachers to deal with these children as isolated cases.

Educational programs for the gifted should be in harmony with the character of the community and the facilities of the local school system, and they should be planned as a part of the ongoing school program.

Formerly, providing for the gifted meant nothing more than skipping them ahead in school or putting them on a fast-moving track or in a special class. Today, provisions for the gifted have become endlessly diversified; a wide variety of programs, administrative devices, and instructional techniques and devices has been tried out. These range all the way from giving special assignments to one or two exceptional children, working with a small cluster of bright youngsters or part-time groups, up to organizing an entire school for exceptional children.

School planning for the gifted and talented is part of the larger problem of adjusting instruction to individual differences. In individualizing instruction for the benefit of the gifted, the first requirement is to think in terms of a differentiated program of educational services throughout the school system for all the children, in all areas of instruction, all the subjects in the curriculum, and in the life of the school beyond classroom studies.

FIRST STEPS IN PLANNING

An initial step is to evaluate present educational offerings and facilities to determine how far the school is already prepared for some special effort on behalf of bright children. The authorities should consider what features of the total educational program need strengthening. The first step in developing the Portland, Oregon, program was an examination of existing procedures and facilities with a view to improving them. Are all the children receiving the best instruction the schools can provide? If so, the program for the gifted is already under way, and the problems of making special provisions for the gifted are already partly solved.

Planning for the gifted should include the entire range of schooling from the elementary grades through high school; it may originate, however, either on a community-wide basis or in a particular school.

Passow and Brooks have made the following recommendations for improving provisions for the gifted (1960) :

Set up a workshop for studying various aspects of educating the gifted.

Design a research experiment relating to any aspect of work with the gifted.

Organize in-service courses dealing with instructional programs for the gifted.

Modify school policies affecting the gifted.

Assign a committee to work on the problem of instructional materials.

Establish committees to revise curriculum provisions for the gifted.

In setting up school and community services for the gifted, the first year is largely exploratory. Working committees are formed of administrators, parents, community leaders. Professional help is solicited. Valuable consultant and cooperative services can often be obtained from a neighboring college, the state university, or the state department of education. Even before a full year has elapsed, the community and the school system may be ready to move ahead. In that case, plans can be speeded up.

The second year a coordinator should be employed to set up workshops for in-service teacher training and inaugurate a pilot program. Summer school teacher-training opportunities may be organized. This work should be planned in terms of total educational improvement as suggested above. Curriculum enrichment materials and equipment are obtained and classified or prepared for teachers' use. Plans are made for continuous record keeping and long-range evaluation of the program. The next step is to put the experimental program into action in pilot schools or demonstration classes, while maintaining the activities of workshops and committees.

One or more schools should be set up as demonstration centers for experimental classes and programs, in both elementary grades and high school. The pilot program might involve, first of all, those teachers who have shown most enthusiasm for the idea.

The principal may appoint a steering committee from the faculty or a single faculty member to coordinate the work with the gifted. Participating teachers serve on a part-time basis to organize the program.

One effort to reach the gifted in small elementary schools has been described by Dr. Walter B. Barbe, who served as coordinator of work with the gifted during a two-year experiment in Portage County, Ohio (1963). Special plans for gifted children were developed in every elementary school in each of the ten local districts. Special-class programs were developed in five districts with the combination of two grades where there were too few children to form a class in each of the respective grades. In the other five districts some type of organized program was set in operation in every elementary school. Supervision of these programs was devoted largely to conferences, visits, and demonstrations.

Larger city school systems, attempting to include all schools in the program, may employ a full-time specialist or coordinator and a permanent staff to carry on the work, supported and supplemented in some cases by local agencies such as the PTA, community clubs, museums, libraries, church groups, and resource persons in the community.

A series of excellent articles on school planning for the gifted was prepared by Pritchard (1951).

Further Recommendations   Other suggestions for organizing programs for the gifted are:

Set up committees to work on different phases of the program: curriculum planning, pupil selection, grouping problems and organization of special classes, teaching methods and materials, the training of teachers for the program.

Hold a seminar or institute to acquaint teachers with the nature of the program, to explore possibilities, and to provide a "workshop" training program, with reading, observation, demonstrations, and other features.

From the outset, a program of training for teachers and specialists working with the gifted should be in operation, consisting of institute and university courses, summer workshops and institutes, afterschool local conferences, and training groups.

Teachers in the California program felt that the in-service activities had made them better teachers, and they appreciated the extra materials provided for their use. In workshop groups there is discussion of principles of curriculum development, methods of instruction, selection and use of materials, program planning, record keeping, and other pertinent topics.

To initiate a program of courses and activities for the gifted in high school, pilot projects should be set up in one or more high schools and within several curriculum areas so that studies of the merits of alternative plans can be made.

Another recommendation is to establish a guidance program for student counseling or to strengthen the existing program. A well-qualified person should be made responsible for seeing to the direction and counseling of gifted children all the way through school. Guidance personnel in larger schools are prepared to perform this function and to furnish information from the school's records for individual students.

Additional materials and equipment are needed to enrich instruction throughout the school: more library books, reference works, advanced textbooks, audio-visual aids, such as slides and projector, filmstrips, video tapes, phonograph and records, duplicating equipment, and supplies for arts and crafts.

A college scholarship fund administered by a committee of responsible citizens is another means of providing for the academically talented.

Work of the Coordinator   The responsibilities of the coordinator include working closely with teachers who need help with individual children, filling teachers' requests for speakers, arranging field trips, and supplying illustrative materials and other information. The coordinator's office locates and catalogs available resources, organizes their use, and advises teachers about them. In the coordinator's office the teachers will find curriculum materials, resource units, and reports of experimental programs, which they are free to study.

In a small community, a teacher placed in charge of work with the gifted spends time in each school conferring with teachers and working with gifted groups.

Programs for the Gifted

There are several criteria to guide the establishment of programs for the gifted and talented: Provisions are made for a wide variety of superior traits, capacities, and talents; the selection of students for special programs is based on reliable developmental criteria such as those outlined in Chapter Six; there is planned continuity in whatever program is undertaken. The best thinking should guide curriculum development so that bright and talented students will be sufficiently challenged.

The kinds of provisions for teaching the gifted have usually been summarized under the three terms: ability grouping, acceleration, and enrichment. Such a classification is misleading because it suggests that the three are mutually exclusive. Instead, they are more often interrelated and interwoven. There is usually some type of ability grouping within the regular class, and partial grouping is practiced more often than complete segregation. There is plenty of enrichment in special classes as well as in regular classes.

Ability grouping is more widely practiced today than before, following a period of neglect when administrators succumbed to the argument that tracking (or "streaming," as it is termed abroad) was unfair to slow children and produced unfavorable side effects. Some schools prefer part-time or partial grouping.

Early entrance to first grade and skipping one or more grades are possible adjustments in the primary grades.

Another device is compression of studies into a shorter than average period—for example, covering the work in the upgraded primary school in two years instead of three, or a sequential program in junior high school condensed to two years from the usual three-year span. A New York City school principal has termed this "accelerichment."

Special classes for the gifted continue to be popular in the elementary schools of larger cities where a class for the gifted may be the top section in a track plan of grouping. Special schools for the gifted and talented, however, are scarcely feasible outside the largest cities.

PROGRAMS IN CALIFORNIA

Seventeen somewhat different administrative and instructional approaches were tried out in the California experimental programs for the gifted from 1957 to 1960 (Martinson, 1960). The following types of adjustments were made:

Elementary School

First grade:

Enrichment in regular classes

Putting bright children ahead

Ungraded primary classes

Cluster groups in the school or classroom

Higher grades:

Enrichment in regular groups

Special-interest groups

Cluster groups

Special classes

Saturday classes

Eighth grade:

Rapid progress

Special classes

Community-sponsored activities

Senior High School

Special classes

Independent study

Honors classes

Articulation with junior college and the university

Acceleration to the university and junior college[1]

An attempt was made to set up suitable programs for the different grade levels in a variety of schools.

In the final appraisal after three years, a higher level of achievement was obtained by the gifted children than by matched controls for whom no special provisions were made (Simpson and Martinson, 1961).

Other Provisions   The ungraded school, which eliminates standard grade designations and moves children ahead at varying rates, has been widely adopted in the primary grades, 1 through 3. More recently the idea has been extended to the upper grades and junior high school. One suburban school system near New York City has set up a "middle school" for all pupils in grades 6 through 8 in which the children progress according to their own rate and readiness. The pupils are "on their own" for at least 25 per cent of the time, receiving individual help from the teacher and working at study tasks independently.

Afterschool club groups are often used to provide for the hobby interests of bright and talented children. Similar programs have been set up in summer camps. Some elementary schools have organized seminars or study clubs which meet during afterschool hours.

Departmentalization, with the use of various subject-matter specialists rather than a single person who teaches all the basic subjects, has been the prevailing plan in large urban elementary schools, particularly in the upper grades, for many years. Nearly 40 per cent of all elementary schools are now departmentalized. In spite of certain limitations, this administrative device offers one means of individualizing instruction in the skill subjects.

The discovery and encouragement of children's driving interests are imperative because early enthusiasm might be stifled in a standard program of formal school studies. In providing for spe-

[1] Ruth A. Martinson, The California Study of Programs for Gifted Pupils, *Exceptional Children*, 26:339–343, 1960. Used by the kind permission of the author and publisher.

cialized talent, the school has a distinctive role to play, particularly for children interested in art, music, creative writing, science, mathematics, and other intellectual pursuits. At the same time the gifted nonspecialized child whose life will be enriched by having some background in these subjects must be cared for.

SOME WAYS OF INDIVIDUALIZING INSTRUCTION

Since gifted children are scattered all through the school with no great concentration of numbers in any given age level, individualized adjustments are usually made within the regular classroom through independent work and special-interest groups.

A list of possibilities for individualizing instruction includes:

Small-group work within the regular class

Independent study of problems related to pupil interests

Unit teaching and the core curriculum

Schoolwide activities such as school publications, assembly programs, exhibits, etc.

Interest groups meeting during the school day

Pupil teams working on various projects

Out-of-school projects and activities

Afterschool club groups

The use of school libraries

The use of self-instructional materials: workbooks, teaching machines, audio-visual equipment

Some years ago, Dr. Elise Martens, of the U.S. Office of Education in Washington, compiled a description of curriculum adjustments for the gifted which is pertinent to curriculum planning today (1946). A bulletin by DeHaan and Kough gives an account of programs provided for the gifted in many parts of the country at all educational levels, elementary through high school (1956). Paschal has prepared a comprehensive report of the various types of programs for the gifted and talented supported by The Fund for the Advancement of Education (1960).

The Gifted: Educational Resources, published by Porter Sargent, Boston, contains a list of existing programs for the exceptionally intelligent in some 800 private and public schools, with a description of the methods and procedures used. The New York State Education Department has published a useful bulletin entitled *Curriculum Adaptations for the Gifted* (1958). Other bulletins are listed in the references at the close of this chapter.

PLANNED CONTINUITY IN SCHOOLING FOR THE GIFTED

A comparatively recent development in programs for superior students is planned continuity throughout the different levels of schooling. Such planning ensures better integration of studies from year to year and smoother acceleration for rapid learners.

The transition points at the end of the elementary school period, age eleven or twelve, at the end of junior high school, age thirteen or fourteen, and at the close of the secondary school period, age seventeen or eighteen, pose special problems not only of educational and vocational guidance, but also of articulation in studies from one school unit or level to the next.

More attention is now given to sequence and long-range continuity in the various subjects—for example, in geography, mathematics, or literature. The lessons are not planned for a short time span and then broken off for new undertakings, but the early learning prepares for more advanced study in spiral sequence. Elementary arithmetic prepares the pupil for an understanding of algebra. Elementary geography is the prelude to more intensive scientific studies of the world and its inhabitants.

The schools of Hicksville, New York, have been experimenting with continuous foreign language studies in grades 1 through 12. Hicksville has also developed a science program based on the assumption that children are ready for instruction in science earlier than has been supposed. A three-year chemistry sequence has been developed for grades 4 through 6, and a two-year sequence in junior high school, grades 7 and 8.

Results of the Hicksville junior high school program indicate that 97 per cent of the students were able to pass the regents examinations in senior high school chemistry. A similar program is now being developed in physics. Administrators of the program think that the most capable students should be able to complete the usual twelve-year elementary and high school sequence plus two years of college within twelve years.

In Fort Lauderdale, Florida, an ungraded school has been set up for ages from kindergarten through college. The children will progress through school at individual rates.

In the Pittsburgh area, a coordinating education center was set up in 1960–1961 as a joint enterprise of the University of Pittsburgh, the Pittsburgh Board of Public Education, Schenley High School, a junior high school, and two elementary schools to ensure better continuity in the education of promising students from kindergarten through graduate school. This enterprise has been financed by a grant from The Fund for the Advancement of Education. The curriculum puts greater responsibility on the student and allows for different rates of progress according to ability. At each level some students are to be admitted to advanced experimental classes in Schenley High School taught by members of the University of Pittsburgh faculty. This is the continuation of an earlier cooperative experiment carried on by Schenley High School and the University of Pittsburgh.

The advantage of joint programs covering the entire span of formal schooling is that waste due to duplication at consecutive school levels is eliminated. The students advance from elementary school to college more rapidly, without breaks or gaps in their progress.

PROBLEMS ENCOUNTERED IN PLANNING

Excellent ideas about educating the bright and talented are plentiful, but many of the programs that have been set up have been poorly planned and the outcomes never thoroughly evaluated. Some of the experiments have been disappointing. Part of the difficulty has arisen from failure to define specifically the type of child to be included in a program for the "gifted." Teachers have not always understood how a given child of high promise or marked talent differs from typical children in the classroom. Children have been put together into a so-called special class or group indiscriminately, without planned selection on the basis of recognized criteria.

The notion that a "new deal" in program and methods is required for teaching the gifted is short-sighted, because practices that are already an established part of good teaching are too often minimized, such as making full use of library resources and encouraging recreational reading.

Some efforts at enriching the gifted child's studies have dwindled into trivial additions to the children's everyday assignments, without offering any real or new challenge. Too often the gifted have been turned loose on their own without sufficient guidance or direct instruction. The squabble over special classes versus enrichment in regular classes has not advanced the cause.

Unless programs for the gifted become an integral part of public education, their continuance is uncertain. In the capital city of a foreign country, a program for gifted children was begun with Wednesday and Saturday afterschool classes in art and music.

Teachers and parents were enthusiastic and worked zealously to support the program, which flourished for several years, but was then abandoned.

In spite of all the enthusiasm and interest that have been generated on behalf of the gifted during the past two decades, relatively few schools today make any special provision for brighter-than-average children in the elementary school, and not much of significance is done in high school beyond classifying students as college preparatory material or noncollege.

The problem that has complicated curriculum planning and school adjustments for the gifted is the relatively small number of children to be considered in typical communities, even though liberal standards are set up for screening. Larger schools and school systems are more apt to have planned programs for the gifted than small schools, according to a report by Durr (1962). Some schools in large systems, however, say they scarcely need planned programs because they have too few exceptional pupils to warrant attention. The larger schools make more use of group intelligence tests as a means of identifying the gifted. Smaller school systems may lack the financial resources to establish these programs.

There is also the problem of providing for a group of children who are highly individual in character and range widely in ability and achievement even though they are all considered gifted.

The chief problems that teachers of the gifted encounter, as reported in the 1957–1960 California study, are pressure of time in certain programs and problems created by the wide range of ability in a class. Class size presents obstacles as does the need for complete and continuous communication between members of the school staff regarding program development. The problem most frequently mentioned by the California teachers was the need for reduction in class size. Individualized instruction and small-group work are not feasible in very large classes.

One report on the adaptability of school systems showed that the most adaptable systems tend to have smaller classes; they employ on the average 18 nonclasssroom professionals for every 100 pupils, assigned either to the elementary or to the high school, not to both; and they have more clinical and guidance personnel for every 1,000 children (Lambert, 1960).

Regimentation increases in direct proportion to class size. Classes for slow learners and for the socially handicapped are invariably reduced in size, but in most places, school administrators say that they cannot justify classes for the bright unless class size is kept up to the standard of regular classes—30 to 40 pupils.

A GUIDE FOR RATING PROVISIONS FOR THE GIFTED

Passow and Brooks have prepared a guide for rating provisions for the gifted in secondary schools that is equally applicable to other levels of schooling (1960). This is a device for self-examination by the school personnel in preparation for improving the school's provisions for the gifted. The device was tried out in 266 schools in New York State and in 20 selected urban schools throughout the country.

The guide consists of ten major sections with subpoints under each heading. The main points are presented in the form of the following questions:

1. How clearly have the areas of talent to which attention is given for program planning been defined and the purposes of the program clarified?
2. How adequately are standardized tests and inventories used specifically for the identification of talented students?
3. How adequately are nonstandardized tests and procedures specifically used for the identification of talented students?
4. How adequate are provisions for continuous assessment, specifically for identifying, teaching, and counseling talented students?
5. How adequate is articulation with other schools from which students come or to which they go for purposes of identifying and planning for the talented?
6. How adequate are administrative grouping modifications for the talented?
7. How adequate are the provisions for administratively accelerating talented students?
8. How adequate are the instructional adaptations made for talented students?
9. How adequate is the overall balance in the instructional program for the talented?
10. How adequate are the provisions for special equipment and facilities needed for the talented?[2]

When teachers who were attending a graduate course on the gifted were asked to rate their own schools (mostly in metropolitan New York or on Long Island) according to this schedule, a number remarked that the best things more often went to the retarded and disturbed children than to the gifted.

[2] A. Harry Passow and Deton J. Brooks, Jr., *A Guide for Rating Provisions for the Gifted,* Bureau of Publications, Teachers College, Columbia University, New York, 1960. Used by permission of the authors and publisher.

EVALUATION OF OUTCOMES

Passow and Brooks also listed several criteria for evaluating educational programs and outcomes for the gifted (1960). These are:

1. Increased achievement
2. Increased interest in and improved attitudes toward school activities
3. Improved social status of the gifted
4. Improved personal adjustment
5. Improved teaching
6. Improved community attitudes
7. Follow-up studies of students[3]

In spite of all the discussion on the subject, there has been little objective study of outcomes under the different educational plans and schemes such as those outlined in this chapter. The next decade should see the general spread of education for the gifted throughout the entire range of schooling and more extensive research efforts to evaluate results.

The Contribution of an Excellent School to the Development of the Gifted

The continual upgrading of every feature of common schooling is the basis of sound education for gifted and unusual children. The school that aspires to do "something for the gifted" could well begin by checking its assets as an educational institution equipped to provide the best possible education for all the children on a differential basis. School patrons and the general public are more ready to give support to total educational improvement plans than to a program designated specially for the gifted. Programs for the gifted come and go, whereas the upgrading of educational facilities is a continuing process in all progressive communities.

A well-equipped school with a competent staff, flexibility in grouping and programming, classes of reasonable size, full guidance services, and good community support is already well prepared to work with all sorts of unusual children including the gifted and talented.

---

[3] A. Harry Passow and Deton J. Brooks, Jr., *A Guide for Rating Provisions for the Gifted,* Bureau of Publications, Teachers College, Columbia University, New York, 1960. Used by permission of the authors and publisher.

Today in the better schools the teacher in charge of a self-contained classroom spends more time giving the children individual help and less time giving whole-group lessons with a uniform textbook or blackboard demonstration. The accent is on teacher-pupil planning, individual action, small-group discussion, individual and group study projects, self-responsibility.

A good school seeks out competent, well-trained teachers who are able to establish a warm, friendly relationship with each student and to understand his problems as an individual.

Specialist teachers and resource consultants, those, for example, who supervise the work in music or science, work with other teachers in enriching curriculum offerings; their function is also to advise students about study projects, for example, the construction of puppets or the study of glaciers. A science expert may be appointed to help with the children's science interests that range far beyond the standard curriculum and the usual textbook coverage. Similarly supplementary instruction may be offered in foreign languages, arts, crafts, music, shopwork, dramatics, creative writing, and other areas.

In all well-run schools today there is expert guidance work by trained specialists at all levels of schooling, but particularly in the high school. For more information on this topic see Chapter Fourteen.

SPECIAL PERIODS FOR INTEREST CLUBS AND HOBBY GROUPS

In a good school program, time and space are allotted for the boys and girls to work at their special interests and hobbies. The club groups cut across age and grade lines to some extent. The groups may meet in double periods once or twice a week under the leadership of a teacher, a special consultant, or a parent leader. Even though the groups are unrestricted in their membership, bright and ambitious boys and girls find opportunities in club work for original contributions and group leadership.

The value of a science center or corner for free-time experiment and study, with the children taking responsibility for setting up the center and maintaining it, has been demonstrated time and again.

In some cases the school day has been extended to provide more time for club groups and other activities, but this arrangement is less satisfactory than scheduling all school-supervised programs during the regular school day.

Community-wide Programs for the Gifted and Talented

There is tremendous educational value for the gifted and talented in well-planned out-of-school experiences. Programs held after school hours, on Saturday, and during the summer extend opportunities for these children to work on advanced studies and hobby interests. Talent groups may be sponsored by adult civic groups; they may be extensions of well-established community services—for example, the children's own library or museum—or they may be cooperative school-community enterprises.

Membership in youth organizations appeals to some gifted youth; boy scouts, sea scouts, and the corresponding groups for girls, 4-H clubs, and others provide valuable practical experience as well as personal enrichment. Since membership is voluntary, boys and girls are free to choose the groups that fit in best with their special hobby interests.

In Brooklyn, New York, children throng the Brooklyn Children's Museum after school and on Saturdays. In New York City, the Natural History Museum and the Metropolitan Museum of Art also offer comprehensive programs for children. Although admission is not restricted to youngsters of proven mental superiority, these programs cater to the wide-awake, intellectually curious type of child. Often promising children have gained new incentives through the stimulus of a class at the museum. Talented students may be excused from regular afternoon classes to take private lessons in music or language at the parent's request.

The Dallas, Texas, public library conducts an afterschool program for talented children who are interested in literature and creative writing. Two classes are held for elementary pupils and one for high school students. Here the children are encouraged in their writing efforts and directed to good reading.

When schools must operate on a half-day session because of overcrowding, the best arrangement is to set up a program of community-supervised activity and recreation clubs so that the children can spend their free time in worthwhile activities under competent supervision.

In the Soviet Union nearly all children between ten and fourteen years of age belong to the Young Pioneers organization. Each child chooses a "circle" in line with his special interests. He may spend as much as four to six hours two or three days a week after school in these club activities. Aside from the political objectives of the groups, they are a source of enrichment in many phases of youth activity. Gifted adolescents serve as leaders of Young Pioneer platoons.

A number of cities in the United States have been moving in the direction of eleven-month schools and Saturday classes in order to maintain fuller supervision of children through the year and to allow more time for school studies. This trend obviously offers advantages in planning enrichment of studies for the gifted.

SUMMER PROGRAMS FOR THE GIFTED

A recent development is the creation of summer school and camp programs for children who have been selected on the basis of intellectual advancement and special talents. Summer camps for gifted music students have long been in operation; now there are both summer day schools and camps catering to high school students as well as younger children who want to advance more rapidly with schoolwork or develop their special talents. Today it is not unusual during the summer months to see a bright boy or girl headed down the street or getting into the bus with a load of books in hand ready to take off for the local summer school accelerated program.

An organization known as Science and Art Camps, Inc., was established in 1960 by Dr. Hertzel Fishman of Darien, Connecticut, with support from the Carnegie Corporation. In the summer of 1960, over 200 fifth-, sixth-, and seventh-grade children from seven communities attended a six-week summer session conducted at the Darien High School. The children were chosen on the basis of school records indicating promise in intellect and creativity or leadership. This program of both day and residence camps has been extended to other Connecticut centers and to Long Island, New York. The purpose of the program, as explained by one of its supporters, is to broaden the horizons of bright youngsters, strengthen intellectual fiber, and raise the leadership caliber of a democratic society.

The program emphasizes the individual child and his talents rather than group work. The children have work in science, communications (language), Russian, mathematics, philosophy, political science, art, and music, balanced with recreational activities. Duplication of regular schoolwork is avoided. Classes are taught by local teachers and adult specialists. Many of the youngsters in the summer program have continued their studies in Saturday groups conducted under the same auspices during the following year. Although tuition fees are charged, there is liberal provision for scholarships.

Reports of summer programs for the gifted have also come from North Carolina and other parts of the country. The use of some of the New England boys' preparatory schools during the summer for selected boys and girls is another phase of this development. Here is a movement that will probably expand rapidly during the coming years.

Meeting Objections to Special Programs for the Gifted

Public sentiment may be definitely against making special provisions for gifted children in a community where differentiation of any kind is interpreted as discrimination. This problem was mentioned in Chapter One. When a special class for the bright was first proposed in Los Angeles, in 1918, objection was voiced against the proposal on the ground that such a class would be undemocratic; and this argument has been regularly voiced ever since.

Sorting out children according to all-around intellectual capacity or academic promise is definitely unpopular, chiefly with the families of those not selected. Since these school patrons will always be far more numerous than those whose children are selected for special programs, through sheer force of numbers they are often able to defeat any special measures on behalf of the gifted.

When the question of separating out the gifted children arose in one city, the school superintendent stated that he did not want to divide children into classes, a practice reminiscent of Nazi Germany. Dr. George Z. F. Bereday of Teachers College, Columbia University, has asked whether we can reconcile selective education with our policy of improving the general quality of education for all.

Another argument is that giving special attention to a small favored group may be detrimental to other children. The brighter-than-average student will become that much brighter, and run away with the golden opportunities open only to a selected few. In the meanwhile, nothing has been done to help the average individual become any brighter. This does not seem like a fair deal.

Many people regard the school as an agency for evening up abilities, for equalizing the level of achievement among all the pupils, not for separating out groups already favored. They contend that any special educational provisions should be aimed at evening up abilities and helping children overcome their handicaps. The idea of a summer camp for the gifted seems unfair when there are so many backward and underprivileged children who would benefit from educational summer programs.

It is difficult to controvert the argument that a child or youth who shows no special promise may surprise us by blossoming out later. Many parents who easily accept variability in physical development have difficulty accepting evidence of differences in intellectual capacities. These same people voice no objection to special instruction or awards for the child who is talented in art, music, crafts, dramatics, dancing, chess, or athletics, because no stigma is attached to a child's lack of such talent.

What of the argument that the gifted require no special consideration at school because they can "take care of themselves"? The fact is that the unusual child who is capable of taking care of himself probably has an exceptional home background that has fostered independence.

School people are aware that parental attitudes toward special sectioning and grouping of the bright tend to change as children advance through school. In the elementary school years when mothers have close contact with the school, parents are likely to demand the same treatment for all. By the time their children reach grade 6 or 7, parents adopt a more realistic attitude as the result of the testing out of the children's aptitudes during the preceding years. A number of teachers who were asked whether this was a correct observation, however, admitted that even in high school rivalry among parents persists.

Some parents feel that special programs for the gifted provide the best of everything for a selected few and neglect everyone else. Parents of the nonselected children would have just cause for complaint if their children were denied library privileges and access to other resources that should be available to all. What the experts are saying, however, is that every student should have the educative experiences, courses, and programs best suited to his abilities. The test of any school in a democratic social order is how well it provides for the individual talents and capacities of every student. There need be no conflict between providing the best education for every child and making special provisions for the most promising, for example, the child who races ahead of the sixth grade class in arithmetic or the language-gifted adolescent in high school,

Opposition to programs for the gifted can be met by avoiding invidious distinctions such as playing up "special provisions for our intellectually superior children" or calling attention to elite groups in the school. Instead, we should stress the excellent features of the school that are shared by all—the massive efforts to help the disadvantaged and to search out and accommodate every type of student, bright or slow, talented or undistinguished. Opposition is less apt to arise in communities where flexibility in school programming and differentiated instruction have long been accepted as normal. Installing and publicizing a program for promising children from lower-income groups, such as the Higher Horizons Program, can go far in allaying the fear that most of the children are being neglected at the expense of a few.

The size and resources of the community largely determine what sorts of programs are provided. All special programs cost more than average ones because teachers trained for special work cost more, as do improved equipment and small-group instruction. Even so, programs for the gifted cost a fraction of the outlay for individualized remedial work for slow learners and all the "hidden costs" of teaching and counseling problem children. The extra expense of educating the gifted is fully justified, because these young people will repay society in the largest measure.

Fortunately, programs for the gifted tend to raise the entire level of schooling in the community, because improvements instituted for the gifted will be demanded for the children in general—better library services, more time for free reading, more trips and excursions, provisions for work in laboratories and art studios, and so on.

More details concerning programs for the gifted in the elementary years will be found in Chapter Nine, and for those in junior and senior high school, in Chapters Twelve and Thirteen. The topics of acceleration, ability grouping, and special classes are considered in Chapters Ten and Eleven.

Finding and Conserving Talent in Depressed Urban Areas

Concern has been expressed over the failure to identify and to utilize in science, industry, and the professions the full human resource potential among people of lower socioeconomic strata, the talents of children from poor homes and neighborhoods, children of uneducated parents, Negroes and other minority groups, often foreign-speaking, living in depressed areas, particularly in crowded urban centers.

Among children of exceptional promise from impoverished homes may be a future college scholarship winner, a potential careerist of eminence. If children from culturally limited groups fail to develop their full potential because of accidental impoverishment, our resources of trained expert manpower are thereby reduced. There is no question that some remarkable people have risen from homes of poverty and ignorance; young people, surmounting severe social handicaps, have fought their way to the top.

The personal-social environment of lower-class families often fails to give children the supportive encouragement and training that those in better-class homes enjoy. High school dropouts are most likely to come from poor homes. Children from better homes ordinarily finish high school; they are more likely to go on to college than those from lower-class homes, unless the latter receive special recognition and counseling. Through the years the social settlements organized in the great cities have brought out and developed the talents of children of immigrants and others in limited circumstances, enabling many a poor youth to go on to higher educational levels, perhaps to become a distinguished leader.

In most parts of the country, children from poor homes and middle- or upper-class homes attend the same schools and receive the same quality of education. But in urban communities with vast slum areas where people take little interest in education, schools in neighboring districts or even in the same district may vary considerably. Today most of the country's large urban centers have undergone a striking population change as the better-class families have migrated to the suburbs and left lower socioeconomic groups to occupy the dilapidated housing. Even when bright young people of limited background are discovered through a talent search, their future is uncertain because of adverse influences in home and community life. Persuading these boys and girls to remain in school is often the first hurdle. For the bright boy or girl from a limited background and ignorant home, education affords practically the only means to better his condition and to develop his potential.

THE HIGHER HORIZONS MOVEMENT IN NEW YORK CITY

The Higher Horizons movement represents a new departure in the search for talent and its cultivation. The movement seeks to aid the underprivileged child of exceptional promise through special

programs designed to broaden his cultural background. The idea
was originated by a far-sighted school principal, Dr. Daniel
Schreiber, of Junior High School 43 on the border of Harlem
in New York City (1958). The demonstration guidance project,
as it was called, the pilot program of the Higher Horizons movement, was established in 1956. The special program that was set
up in junior and senior high school sought to cultivate whatever
special abilities the children might have, to encourage them to
complete high school and, if possible, to go on to college.

Dr. Schreiber was struck by the contrast between the cultural
advantages his own children enjoyed and those of the children
in his school. Junior High School 43 had a student body that
was 48 per cent Negro and 40 per cent Puerto Rican at the
time the program was launched. Some of these children were from
families who had recently come from the South or from Puerto
Rico. Many of them had had no regular schooling before coming
to New York, and a substantial number spoke limited or substandard English. The result was that even the brighter children
were behind in skill subjects, particularly in reading.

Before Dr. Schreiber's program was inaugurated, only half the
school's graduates had been able to finish senior high school; 10
per cent of the children were chronically in trouble. Few were
considered capable of learning a skilled trade or of going on to
college. The question the principal and other leaders were asking
was whether these youngsters must forever remain victims of the
slums into which they were born. Was it possible for the school
to counteract the negative influences of socioeconomic limitations?
Could it become a more potent factor in helping talented students
overcome the limitations of their environment?

In 1956, over 600 boys and girls, selected as the school's most
promising material, became subjects of a six-year experiment in
educational motivation. Two of the special features of the Higher
Horizons Program were extracurricular enrichment and extensive
individual guidance. In afterschool hours and on weekends the
children were taken to concerts, art galleries, museums, football
games, swimming meets, and other youth activities they might
not ordinarily attend if left on their own initiative. The leaders
of these excursions were university students and other volunteers.
There were educative trips for small, selected club groups of those
who could appreciate and enjoy the experience together.

Teachers attempted to raise the cultural sights of the children
with a program which included stimulation through wide reading,

good films and music, inspirational assembly programs, learning about the city and its resources for study and culture, understanding themselves, their abilities, and the prospects ahead for capable learners. The Higher Horizons Program brought additional personnel into the school for instruction in mathematics, science, art, remedial English, and other areas.

The Demonstration Project Students in Senior High School   After finishing junior high school, the students went on to George Washington High School, New York, where arrangements were made for a planned sequence of studies to carry the children through the high school years, and guidance services were provided to stem the dropout trend. A total of 356 pupils entered the special program for graduates of Junior High School 43; 54 per cent were Negro, 26 per cent Puerto Rican, 18 per cent white, and 2 per cent Oriental. The outcomes of this project have been summarized in a report by Henry T. Hillson, principal of George Washington High School (1963).

In the beginning, all the students were placed in the academic course in high school with the aim of preparing for college. To ensure the most favorable learning conditions, the students were grouped homogeneously in all major subject areas on the basis of test data and school records, classes were kept small, and special guidance services were provided. New motivation was needed for the students to overcome background influences that were largely lacking in educational values. Arrangements were made for individual tutoring, small classes in English and other subjects were organized, a program of intensive psychological counseling and college advisement was set up.

What were the accomplishments of these youths from depressed areas in New York City? Two and a half times as many earned academic diplomas as in the past; more than three and a half times as many went on to higher education.

Of 108 pupils who graduated from George Washington High School with academic diplomas, 89 per cent went on to higher education; also, 43 per cent of those graduating with general course diplomas were admitted to some institution of higher learning.

The annual cost for additional services in high school for each pupil was $250 beyond the usual allocation.

Extensions of the Higher Horizons Movement   In New York City the Higher Horizons Program now involves over sixty elementary and junior high schools, involving some 33,000 students. Some authorities rate the movement as the single greatest development in American education today.

Queens College of the City University of New York has inaugurated a program called "Bridge" to set up and supervise this type of program in junior high school. The National Scholarship Service and Fund for Negro Students has sponsored and supported a demonstration project in a New York City junior high school to identify children of good scholastic promise and encourage them to aim for college.

More recently the Higher Horizons Program in New York City has been diverted from its original purpose of spotting and encouraging the most capable students among disadvantaged children in slum areas to improvement of schooling and remediation for disadvantaged children in general, including slow learners and the retarded.

THE HIGHER HORIZONS MOVEMENT IN OTHER CITIES

Other cities have taken up the challenge to improve educational opportunities and cultural advantages for children living in depressed urban areas. Washington, D.C., has a program in which selected Negro pupils are given enriched courses of study, necessary remedial instruction, extensive guidance and counseling, and cultural enrichment of out-of-school life.

In the suburban community of White Plains, New York, the schools have given the most promising children from poor homes educational guidance as well as supplementation in schooling, such as the background of a good home would normally provide. In spite of extra counseling and special help directed toward raising the children's school marks, after an initial spurt of interest, the students tended to fall back to their original status. This situation suggests that there is no simple solution to the problem of cultural uplift.

Pittsburgh inaugurated what is known as the Hill Project inspired by the New York City Higher Horizons Program. This project, supported by a half million dollar grant from the Fund for the Advancement of Education, searches out talent among students in a region largely inhabited by Negroes and culturally disadvantaged families, in order to give promising children incentives to stay in school and to seek college opportuntities.

The film *A Desk for Billie* portrays a child of migrant workers in the Southwest who succeeds in going through school and getting into college with the constant encouragement of teachers and community leaders.

In Israel, two experiments are under way with gifted children from economically undeveloped strata (Smilansky, 1962). In one study 80 boys and girls have been selected from various parts of the country and placed in a boarding home maintained by the government. The children are enrolled in a regular four-year secondary school where they attend academic classes in the morning. In the afternoon the boarding home conducts a program of practical activities suited to the interests and needs of teen-agers. In a second project, to continue for three years, an attempt is being made to identify gifted children from undeveloped strata at an earlier age in their school career and to give them special preparation for secondary school studies. In this project there are about forty grade-6 classes in three urban areas. Ordinarily, few of the children from these areas obtain school marks qualifying them to enter the country's secondary schools.

EVALUATION OF HIGHER HORIZONS PROGRAMS

Although the final appraisal of these programs must come from analysis of continuous follow-up studies of the youths enrolled in them, it is obvious that the programs have raised the entire level of schooling where they have been introduced. They have brought into the schools many excellent facilities they should have had right along, features that schools in good neighborhoods accept as a matter of course. One teacher commented of the Higher Horizons Program in her school, "This is what we've always needed, more personnel, enrichment materials, smaller classes, tutorial instruction for remedial cases, afterschool activities, parent education."

The question that remains to be answered is whether such programs can make up for the lack of a supportive home and community life in the early years—whether the extra cost and effort expended can offset the deleterious influences of slum life on the child before he reaches the junior high school and throughout the adolescent years.

References

Administration: Procedures and School Practices for the Academically Talented Student, National Education Association, Washington, D.C., 1960.

Baker, H. J.: An Experiment in the Education of Gifted Children, *Exceptional Children*, 9:112–114, 120, 1943.

Barbe, Walter B.: *As If the Chart Were Given: Report of a Demonstration Project for Gifted County Elementary School Children*, Division of Special Education, Columbus, Ohio, 1963.

Curriculum Adaptations for the Gifted, Bureau of Elementary Curriculum Development, New York State Education Department, Albany, N.Y., 1958.

DeHaan, Robert F., and Jack Kough: *Helping Children with Special Needs*, Secondary School Edition, vol. 1, 1955; Elementary School Edition, vol. 2, Science Research Associates, Inc., Chicago, 1956.

Durr, William K.: Provisions for the Gifted in Relation to School Size and System Size at the Elementary Level, *Journal of Educational Research*, 55:149–158, 1962.

Education for Gifted Children and Youth: A Guide for Planning Programs, Bulletin no. 77, Connecticut State Department of Education, Hartford, Conn., 1956.

Education of the Gifted: A Manual for Program Improvement, A Report of the Southern Regional Project for Education of the Gifted, Southern Regional Education Board, Atlanta, Ga., 1962.

Educational Policies Commission: Education for All American Youth: A Further Look, National Education Association, Washington, D.C., 1952.

Flanagan, John C., and others: *The Talents of American Youth: I. Design for a Study of American Youth*, Houghton Mifflin Company, Boston, 1962.

Gallagher, James J.: *Teaching the Gifted Child*, Allyn and Bacon, Inc., Boston, 1963.

The Gifted: Educational Resources, Porter Sargent, Boston, 1961.

The Gifted in Portland: A Report of Five Years of Experience in Developing a Program for Children of Exceptional Endowment, Portland, Ore., Public Schools, 1959.

Glyn, Morris: Helping the Mentally Superior Child in Rural Areas, *Exceptional Children*, 22:161–162, 174, 1956.

Hamilton, Norman K.: Attitudes toward Special Educational Programs for Gifted Children, *Exceptional Children*, 27:147–150, 163, 1960.

Havighurst, Robert J.: Community Factors in the Education of the Gifted, chap. 17 in *Education for the Gifted: Fifty-seventh Yearbook of the National Society for the Study of Education*, part 2, The University of Chicago Press, Chicago, 1958.

Havighurst, Robert J., E. Stivers, and Robert F. DeHaan: *A Study of the Education of Gifted Children*, The University of Chicago Press, Chicago, 1955.

Hildreth, Gertrude: School-wide Planning for the Gifted, *Educational Administration and Supervision*, 41:1–10, 1955.

Hillson, Henry T.: *The Demonstration Guidance Project, 1957–62,* Board of Education, City of New York, 1963.

Johnson, W. H.: Programs for Conserving Our Superior Elementary School Students, *Educational Administration and Supervision,* 29:77–86, 1943.

Klausmeier, Herbert J., and others: *Results of Experimentation with Acceleration in the Third and Fourth Grade, Special Classes and Other Instructional Arrangements in the Fifth Grade, Instructional Teams and Other Instructional Arrangements in the Seventh Grade,* Wisconsin Improvement Program, Madison, Wis., 1961.

Lambert, Sam. M.: Educational Growth and Change, *Journal of the National Educational Association,* 49:45–47, 1960.

Laycock, Samuel R.: *Gifted Children: A Handbook for the Classroom Teacher,* The Copp-Clark Publishing Company, Toronto, Canada, 1957.

Martens, Elise: *Curriculum Adjustments for Gifted Children,* U.S. Office of Education, Bulletin no. 1, 1946, Washington, D. C.

Martinson, Ruth A.: The California Study of Programs for Gifted Pupils, *Exceptional Children,* 26:339–343, 1960.

Martinson, Ruth A.: *Educational Programs for Gifted Pupils,* California State Department of Education, Sacramento, Calif., 1960.

Paschal, Elizabeth: *Encouraging the Excellent: Special Programs for Gifted and Talented Students,* The Fund for the Advancement of Education, New York, 1960.

Passow, A. Harry, and Deton J. Brooks, Jr.: *A Guide for Rating Provisions for the Gifted,* Bureau of Publications, Teachers College, Columbia University, New York, 1960.

Practical Programs for the Gifted, Science Research Associates, Inc., Chicago, 1960.

Pritchard, Miriam: Total School Planning for the Gifted Child, *Exceptional Children,* 18:107–110, 128; 143–147, 174–180, 1951.

Schreiber, Daniel: Identifying and Developing Able Students from Less Privileged Groups, *High Points,* 40:5–23, 1958.

Simpson, Ray E., and Ruth A. Martinson: *Educational Programs for Gifted Pupils: A Report to the California Legislature,* State Department of Education, Sacramento, Calif., 1961.

Smilansky, Moshe: Israel, chap. 5 in Educational Research in Countries Other than the United States, *Review of Educational Research,* 37:280–293, 1962.

Special Programs for Gifted Pupils, Bulletin of the California State Department of Education, 31(1), January, 1962.

Ward, Virgil S.: *Educating the Gifted: A Manual for Program Improvement,* Charlottesville, Va., 1962.

Williams, Clifford W.: Organizing a School Program for the Gifted, chap. 18 in *Education for the Gifted: Fifty-seventh Yearbook of the National Society for the Study of Education,* part 2, The University of Chicago Press, Chicago, 1958.

Wilson, Frank T.: A Survey of Educational Provisions for Young Gifted Children in the United States and of Studies and Problems Related Thereto, *Journal of Genetic Psychology,* 75:3–19, 1949.

Wrightstone, J. W.: Discovering and Stimulating Culturally Deprived Talented Youth, *Teachers College Record,* 60:23–27, 1958.

A number of cities have prepared bulletins for use of local teachers in working with the gifted. Typical of these bulletins are *Challenging the Able Learner,* Cincinnati, Ohio, 1957, and *Guiding Your Gifted: A Handbook for Teachers, Administrators and Parents,* published by the Philadelphia Suburban Schools Study Council, and the School of Education, University of Pennsylvania, Philadelphia, 1954.

Chapter Eight

TEACHING
THE GIFTED
AND
TALENTED

In this chapter, the basic aims of education for the gifted and principles of curriculum making as they apply to programs for gifted and talented students will be outlined. Areas of subject matter will be described briefly, together with suggestions of ways creative teachers can meet the challenge of gifted minds.

Goals for the Education of the Gifted

The basic goals of education are identical for all children, but the interpretation of the goals is somewhat different in the case of the gifted because of the unique potentialities these children possess. Faculty members of the Ohio State University High School analyzed five major objectives which can serve as guides for the education of gifted and talented children in any school (Willis, 1961). These are self-direction, social sensitivity, democratic living, "use of the method of intelligence" in problem solving, and creativity.

In educational planning, consideration should be given to the foundation needed for the careers exceptional students are likely to follow. What sort of early preparation best serves a professional career? Can we anticipate the careers students are likely to be following twenty-five years from now?

CREATING THINKING ATTITUDES

Ralph Waldo Emerson observed that the chief aim of education is to create thinking attitudes. This means, in the education of the gifted, devising a program of studies and learning experiences that will maximize the students' abilities to think critically and work creatively. The school must foster an interest in learning and whet the child's curiosity to find out, to explore, to seek answers.

One of the major objectives of the Ohio State University High School was to develop in students the ability to use intelligent thinking to the fullest in dealing with all problems of human concern. By the phrase "use of the method of intelligence," teachers in the school had reference to the use of critical thinking and reflective thought in problem solving to reach valid conclusions, the method of scientific inquiry.

The "method of intelligence" in problem solving includes the following aspects:

1. Recognizing problems
2. Formulating hypotheses
3. Discovering and organizing data; getting the facts
4. Arriving at tentative conclusions and acting on them

DEVELOPING INDEPENDENCE OF THOUGHT AND ACTION

As gifted children mature, they must depend more and more upon themselves for their own education in areas of special interest. This means that they will need to learn habits of independence and resourcefulness in seeking answers to problems. Equally important, they must develop faith in their capacity to achieve results.

The gifted and talented should have freedom to work on self-selected projects reflecting their special interests, for example, the writing of a play, construction of scenery and sets, designing costumes for the actors, making puppets, and operating a puppet theater. The gifted student may take the lead in planning and directing an assembly program, preparing an exhibit for a science fair, writing a report on new discoveries in astrophysics, atomic energy, electronics, prehistoric animals. A student with a flair for writing and group management may become editor of the school paper.

The gifted student needs time for independent study during the school day, time to muse and reflect in order to gain new insights. His studies in some respects may be more self-directed than teacher-directed.

A leading educator has said that it does not matter so much what children learn at school, if only they learn how to find out whatever they need to know. By learning early how to learn for themselves they are better able to work independently. Children can be taught how to teach themselves through reading, observing, experimenting, obtaining and recording information. Gifted children have the ability to gain information by drawing people out in conversation; they will sense the importance of using the library or of turning to resource people in the community for assistance.

ACQUIRING SCHOLARLY HABITS

The school can enhance a child's scholarly tendencies by encouraging him to think and work as a scholar—that is, a person who has his materials at hand, who keeps them in good order for quick reference, who concentrates his energy and attention on the job he is doing until he is satisfied with his results. The scholarly person marshals his data in an orderly way and produces something in the way of a report, whether in writing or otherwise. Gifted children can begin learning in their early school years the skills of observation, investigation, and experimentation.

Although the gifted may appear to learn easily, they, as all others, need to develop serious attitudes toward work tasks, toward their mental chores at school and after school. Some of these tasks are boring and not much fun, for example, practice in order to improve spelling, punctuation, or piano technique; but they must be accepted by anyone who expects to develop expertness. When this responsibility was pointed out to one bright youngster, he observed cheerfully, "Certainly, the dessert is your reward after eating vegetables."

SETTING HIGH ACHIEVEMENT STANDARDS

If much is expected of bright children, much can be achieved. Related to the development of scholarly habits is the matter of setting high goals and standards of achievement for the gifted, challenging them to work up to their capacity, to put forth full effort.

Dr. Louis T. Camp, principal of the Hunter College Elementary School, asserted that we do not demand enough of capable children. They are eager to learn, the potential is there, but it is not realized because of the laissez-faire attitude we take toward them. The bright child needs intellectual work that is a stimulus to his inquiring mind, that enables him to work up to his level of mental acceleration. This may require a speeded-up program of some kind, individually or in groups, as well as more effective incentives to achieve.

The gifted child may need to be shown what it means "to learn" something. Otherwise, he may have the notion that success will always come easily, and he will be disappointed when first challenged by an intricate skill or difficult problem. The older student may be given some insight into the nature of the learning process so that he will better understand what genuine learning involves: concentration of attention, systematic practice to improve skills, extra effort to surmount unusual difficulties.

EDUCATING THE WHOLE CHILD

John Dewey's doctrine that the whole child must be educated has particular bearing on teaching the gifted, whose special talents and competencies tend to be exploited at the expense of all-around development. Those responsible for training the gifted must be concerned not only with high standards of scholarship, but also with the child's growth as a stable personality, as a person who is acquiring the inner controls essential for self-discipline.

The gifted student who is wrapped up in his own interests may encounter difficulties in handling social relationships. He may need advice about cultivating the social side of his personality, getting along with others, learning to participate as a member of a group. For his own good he needs to avoid drawing into his shell; instead, he should learn to use his intelligence in dealing tactfully with his associates.

Since many promising children are destined to become leaders in their professions and in their work with other people, they can be given training that will equip them more fully for leadership roles—learning what true leadership requires and what the desired qualities in leaders are. They can be given opportunities to exert leadership at school and elsewhere.

Gifted children will not become bookworms if they live a balanced life, alternating book study with recreation, home tasks, group activities, and hobby interests, learning practical things, and becoming acquainted with a world of experience outside their special interests. Even an unusually brilliant individual can attain well-balanced development without sacrificing his achievement goals.

BUILDING GOOD CHARACTER

No matter how bright a person may be, if he grows up lacking honesty, sympathy, and integrity, his life may come to naught. To develop the character of a good and worthy person with the highest ethical standards is a basic objective of education for all children; it is especially significant for the gifted.

Children need to be directed toward values outside their own self-centered goals; they need to develop traits of courtesy, concern for others, tolerance toward those who are not so fortunate as themselves. The vision of true greatness as service to humanity is particularly appropriate for the gifted, who have capacity for leadership.

The school must seek to inculcate in the minds of the gifted strong adherence to democratic principles; it must provide experience in democratic living so that unusually bright young people will think of themselves as members of the entire human family, not as a privileged group.

LEARNING ABOUT PHYSICAL FITNESS

Physical fitness is a goal for the gifted just as it is for everyone else. Often a bright young person, intent upon his enthralling studies, fails to keep in good physical condition. Here the advice of the school health people will be invaluable. A precocious boy, the young Theodore Roosevelt was a sickly child, but he built up his health by determining in his youth to improve his physical condition through exercise and outdoor life.

Curriculum Making for the Gifted

Realizing these goals in educating the gifted and talented is primarily a matter of wise curriculum planning. Administrative devices, groupings, and special programs serve merely as the framework for curriculum design. The curriculum is viewed as a continuum from first grade through high school and even into college, a sequential series of studies and learning experiences spanning the years of formal schooling. Educating the whole child as well as training his special competencies requires more breadth than is possible with a limited array of offerings in formal subjects.

School studies should be organized in terms of the types and levels of problems, exercises, and experiences that will enrich the students' minds and serve to develop their special aptitudes. The children should share in the planning of their studies; in this way, they can make independent discoveries, exercise initiative, solve problems in the choice and use of materials, participate in evaluating outcomes, and relate school studies to their out-of-school interests.

Curriculum planning for the gifted should include the entire program of school studies. Even though the student is a gifted writer or musician, his school experience must embrace work in all the major subject-matter areas. The curriculum design should focus on the basic concepts and major problems in each area.

The well-designed curriculum includes experiences for learning about human adjustments and social living. The student gains insight concerning civic life and community responsibilities. His concepts of the nature of common things, of the world, of the past, of natural phenomena, of people, their life and customs, and of human relations are enlarged and deepened through his program of studies.

The school should impart to all students the world view, that is, the ability to see ourselves as but part of many great interrelated nations and societies, reaching out to Pakistan and Japan, Indonesia, Kenya, and South Africa, and gaining an understanding of the United Nations in world affairs.

In recent years science studies have held a prominent place in the curriculum for the gifted, but equal attention should be given to the cultural content of other subjects, particularly language and literature.

Even though most academically talented students are headed for college, their course of study should not be limited to academic subjects. Students need the enriching experience of music and art as well as mechanical skills. Children can do expressive writing with good quality in any study area—science, social studies, the arts.

The current trend in schooling is to introduce the basic concepts early, and then to reintroduce them at each successive grade level. For example, body chemistry and the science of nutrition follow the earlier experiences related to foods and health; decimal fractions follow ordinary fractions; working with algebraic equations is an outgrowth of earlier problem solving in arithmetic.

THE MEANING OF ENRICHMENT

"Enrichment" means any modification of class instruction that provides more challenge for the gifted mind than regular classwork affords. Enrichment chiefly involves teaching the pupils how to learn and study independently with books and other materials that are made available to them. Capable students who are freed from class routines can go beyond the usual assignments and explore topics outside the standard curriculum. Enrichment is most commonly thought of as parallel study for bright children on a more advanced level than that being done by the rest of the class; while the class is studying a piece of great literature, the gifted child may make an intensive study of significant themes in world literature, or he may read a biography of the author whose work is being studied and report on it.

"Enrichment" for the gifted refers both to the special provisions made for those who remain in the regular classroom and to the study in greater depth for those in special classes. Enrichment is considered an alternative to assigning children advanced work. For example, instead of assigning an algebra text to a ten-year-old with the mental age of fourteen, the teacher enriches the mathematics concepts being studied in the child's fifth- or sixth-grade class.

Although enrichment is usually considered an alternative to acceleration, putting children ahead is actually a form of enrichment; also, putting children into special classes is a way of enriching the regular school experience. In fact, one of the purposes of special-class instruction is to provide more breadth and depth in studies for the exceptionally competent.

Too often enrichment has been nothing more than trivial or repetitive work: an extra set of the same arithmetic problems, a longer list of spelling words, an extra review lesson, another composition, or an assignment to do the next lesson.

True enrichment occurs when pupils are challenged to undertake problem solving and original work beyond the interests and abilities of the rest of the class. In arithmetic this might mean having the pupil compose some original problems, working out the mathematics of construction in kite making, combining a science project with mathematics, investigating the science of missile projection, working with a computing machine, solving mathematical puzzles, checking answers by different methods. Enrichment may be provided by introducing more extensive materials for study or by assigning more advanced reading. A university scientist, a museum director or staff member, a local musician or artist may be invited to talk to the class; afterward, he may hold interviews with talented students. A good illustration of genuine enrichment will be found in the regular elementary classes of the Portland, Oregon, public schools.

Ideas for enrichment may be found not only in the regular classroom but in the larger life of the school. Talented students may take the lead in planning an assembly program or a program for parents.

Full use should be made of audio-visual aids, filmstrips, slides, moving pictures, phonograph records, and radio and television programs. A talented child may learn to operate the equipment; he may plan and conduct a program for the class.

In a subject-centered curriculum, in contrast to a unified approach to teaching content and basic skills, enrichment is provided within each subject, whether it is geography, literature, or spelling. Teachers may ask their supervisors for assistance in putting "more depth" into the lessons for bright pupils.

The difficulty in providing enrichment in the regular class is that the teacher can scarcely spare the time to prepare genuine enrichment exercises for a few bright students and do justice to the others as well. True enrichment requires released time for the teacher, curriculum consultants, and semitutorial approaches. The services of specialist teachers in certain areas is indispensable.

UNIT TEACHING AND THE CORE PROGRAM

The core program provides for the study of basic problems of human experience without confinement to one particular subject-matter area. In the core program a problem may cut across several subject fields as widely divergent as social studies, science, and music. A project on the modern uses of rubber or plastics, for example, moves students away from textbook study in a single subject area. A study of modern industry or modern agricultural methods could well include material usually allocated to social studies, science, mathematics, statistics, geography. The core or block-time program allows for a longer period of work on significant problems in related areas.

Core teaching was illustrated in the elementary and junior high school classes of the Lincoln School some years ago in study units on Latin America and China. These units were described in two publications, *South of the Rio Grande* (grade 6) and *Western Youth Meets Eastern Culture* (junior high school), both published by the Bureau of Publications, Teachers College, Columbia University, New York.

In the lower grades, work on a project with marionettes could include material from history, literature, music, arts and crafts, and even the scientific aspects of illumination. A broad study theme in the primary grades might be "How animals prepare for winter"; in the upper grades, "Good nutrition." A core theme such as modern inventions and the industrial era would be appropriate for the junior high school, or the role and work of the United Nations organization for mature students.

Studies organized on the basis of broad themes or problems that cut across several subject areas usually provide for greater student initiative and individual experimentation than separate-subject teaching. Research work on a problem in the unit may carry one student far beyond the others. For example, in a food unit, a bright child may go farther than his classmates in making experiments in nutrition, in exploring the relation of food to health, in reporting on the science of agriculture. Several students may take the lead in writing a play for the class to perform at the end of the unit. They may make illustrations for posters and prepare charts summarizing information.

CONCRETE EXPERIENCE FOR THE GIFTED

One issue in educating the gifted concerns whether they, as other students, should have firsthand learning experiences in such studies as fractions, natural science, or social studies. The answer is definitely "yes," judging from the ways the gifted themselves tackle their own learning problems. Firsthand experience—for example, learning fractions with cubes or "pies"—is one of the best ways of coming to grips with a new problem, regardless of the student's age or level of mental maturity. This experience is the prelude to working with abstract symbols.

INDIVIDUAL PROJECTS AND INDEPENDENT STUDY

The laboratory plan of study, with work on an individual or small-team basis, has many advantages for gifted children who need incentive to put their talents to full use. Independent work requires initiative on the part of the student rather than the teacher.

Bright children can often manage their own studies quite well under the guidance of a good teacher. They need assistance in planning from week to week in terms of long-range projects, but they can be counted on to suggest original ideas both for their own projects and for the class. A fifth grader may explore clocks and their history; a seventh grader, "Styles and Costumes through the Ages." The students may conduct original experiments in science and work on special projects in creative arts and writing; they may do independent reading and report on their topics or problems. At times they may hold conferences with adult specialists and other resource people in addition to the teacher.

STUDENT PARTICIPATION IN PLANNING AND PROGRAM MAKING

Instead of having official curriculum makers or the teacher make all study plans in advance, students themselves may share in the planning of programs, study projects, and activities. This approach may necessitate continual planning and revision of plans from week to week, even from day to day. With flexibility the keynote, topics of current interest can be woven into the schedule; there is more leeway for adjusting the program of studies to emerging pupil interest and individual talent. An opportunity may arise to hear a noted explorer recently returned from distant lands; perhaps a downtown bank has put on a coin exhibit to celebrate a centennial; or a moving picture that relates to class studies in science, history, or literature is to be shown at a local theater. These opportunities can be accommodated in a flexible program. The teacher who favors flexibility does not worry about "covering the ground" in the syllabus, since his objective is to aid the students in problem solving and to bring about clear understanding of facts and principles.

What of the Outcomes?   A parent observed, "School life is so much more interesting for children today, and they gain competence so early. Why, even my nine-year-old boy gets right up in class and talks about his topic. It's remarkable how this new type of school draws out the individual child. We were tongue-tied when I was in school, always *afraid of doing something wrong*." A young musical prodigy was asked to express his opinion of modern education. He replied, "The schools have very good methods these days. They will give you, for instance, a project on farming. You learn botany, arithmetic, a little geology, and many other things all at once. It goes quickly that way."

Education through School-life Activities

The entire life of the school enriches learning: the assembly programs, student government activities, musical events, school publications, science fairs and exhibits, contests of various kinds, programs for national holidays, films, book fairs, social service and welfare projects, club activities, plays, managerial work, library duties, and so on. These activities serve to develop traits and insights that will prove invaluable later on in school or life careers. The school world may be considered a youth society in which young people develop their skills as leaders through shared experiences in such groups as the student government and organized clubs.

Some schools set aside double periods once a week for children to work on their hobby interests, individually or in small groups. Clubs and recreational activities are an integral part of school life, instead of extracurricular activity.

In San Diego, California, school clubs for talented elementary students are well attended. There are clubs for science, mathematics, slide rule, chess, creative writing, and creative dramatics. A professional mathematician from an aircraft concern, a parent of one of the children, provides guidance for the mathematics club which meets twice a week. The science club enjoys working on physics problems using a high school textbook.

Basic Skills in the Curriculum for the Gifted

ORAL LANGUAGE AND LITERACY

All children require training throughout their school years in the use of their mother tongue. Expert command of one's native language is the basis of creative expression and practical writing for every purpose. Language skills are developed functionally in the regular curriculum and in special projects, such as class or school newspapers, reports of experiments and research studies, and book reports. In every subject, there are ideas that deserve a write-up, that would be interesting or fascinating to attempt to express on paper.

READING AS AN INTELLECTUAL RESOURCE

The precocious interest of gifted children in reading was referred to in Chapter Four. This skill is the gifted person's time-tested resource for intellectual stimulation and independent study. Books stand second only to teachers in stimulating learning and the desire to learn; books may even surpass the teacher when the child's mind is running ahead into fields with which his teacher is unacquainted. Through the use of books, bright young people can study at a level more in line with their mental maturity than would otherwise be possible. Boys and girls also experience personal development through reading as they gain an understanding of themselves and others. Biographies may inspire gifted young people to emulate famous and distinguished persons. Books provide information about career opportunities and about personal and emotional problems. Reading is one of the best means of broadening the backgrounds of children from poor homes and limited circumstances.

Reading instruction for the gifted has several objectives:

Gaining proficiency in the techniques of reading and refining these skills in each successive year

Learning how to use books for study projects: outlining, summarizing, and reporting on information gained from reading

Exploring the wide world of reading, discovering the best books for every possible purpose and the books of special interest to the individual reader

Learning how to use the facilities of the school library

Becoming acquainted with the best literature and learning to appreciate the value of reading great books

Unless the child actually dislikes reading and rates low in basic skills, the teacher need not be concerned about how much time he spends in reading or what he reads. The bright and mentally advanced should not be required to read only those books adults think are good for them, but they should be encouraged to read widely. A mature child may prefer reading materials intended for an adult audience. The child's special interests lead him to read books on the topics he most enjoys—space exploration, early man, wild animals, mathematical puzzles, the history of ancient times.

Children should have the opportunity to read newspapers, periodicals, biography. They should be taught at an early stage how to use reference sources: the encyclopedia, an atlas, yearbooks, biographical references, and other materials in this category.

Bright children need to be taught only those reading skills in which they show an inadequacy. They should not be required to participate in classwide drills in exercise books or to use standard readers of limited educational value for them.

Plenty of time should be allowed for children to share what they have learned from books and what they have enjoyed reading. Sharing can be done through individual reports, panel discussions, dioramas, tape recordings, displaying and making book jackets, dramatizing reading selections, and in other original ways the children will think of themselves.

Subject-matter Areas in the Curriculum

Each of the major subject-matter areas is discussed at length in later chapters—Chapter Nine for the elementary division, Chapter Thirteen for junior and senior high school. A brief discussion is in order here, however.

THE STUDY OF LITERATURE

The extension of literary experience is a goal of English instruction for the gifted all the way through school. What can the study of great literature do for the gifted? As J. B. Priestley pointed out, Western man has in the past 500 years achieved in literature the clearest and most complete expression of his nature, his needs, his ideas, his ideals, his fears, and his love. Great literature is a means of understanding human life in all epochs; consequently, the study of literature leads to understanding one's self. For this reason, the study of the classics should be part of the experience of every intelligent person.

All children are not equally fond of juvenile classics. In fact, modern boys and girls, with a tremendous array of good reading to select from, are inclined to leave the classics on the shelves, while they wear out modern adventure stories and informational books. Their appreciation of great books can be developed, but not forced, by a teacher who knows and loves the best in literature. One reason that the habit of using the library is so important is that the library shelves contain a minimum of trash.

SOCIAL STUDIES

The social studies permeate every aspect of life and relate to every study in the curriculum. The objective of social studies for children is to present facts and concepts about the past and the present, about people of other times and of today, in a way that they can understand. These studies—history, geography, civics, political science, and economics—offer tremendous possibilities for enrichment of learning for the gifted, with plenty of intellectual challenge and rich problem-solving opportunities.

Experience in social studies is extended through participation in school and class government, school-life activities, and school-related community projects; in the exploration of social phenomena in the community; and in the study of local government, sanitation, industry, welfare, and housing, to name a few topics.

Gifted students enjoy preparing dramatic productions of scenes in history. They can construct dioramas of historical events and prepare materials for exhibits. Groups or individuals can take trips to places of historical interest and to museums housing significant materials that enrich the study of history. Biographies of famous men and women offer an interesting way to learn about different epochs in history.

Throughout the school and even in college, geography is receiving much attention today because of the expansion in international communication, the increased mobility of people throughout the world, and the study of our own earth in relation to outer space. There are unlimited explorations in this field for the gifted of all ages who enjoy scholarly research.

Map study has tended to be a neglected area in the social studies. Bright pupils may be ready ahead of others to learn how to interpret maps; they can be taught how maps are made, and then they can make their own maps for many purposes, using original ideas in the process. The study of maps may well include map-making projects—city, county, and state, as well as the United States, foreign countries, and the world. The study of history is enriched through maps that depict the life and times of other periods.

Economics is another social studies subject that offers a challenge to the bright mind. This study can start with the child's immediate experiences—earning money, buying and selling things, care of equipment, conservation—and then move into such topics as wages, credit buying, insurance, investments.

SCIENCE

The modern child has an affinity for scientific studies, which is encouraged by advertising, news items, museum exhibits, and fascinating science books of every description. Even though a student does not plan to become a scientist, science studies encourage scholarly thinking that is valuable in other areas.

The modern curriculum wisely requires some work in science in both the elementary grades and high school; thus the students not only grasp the great principles of the physical world, but become acquainted with scientific methods of thinking and problem solving.

Science relates to and permeates virtually all other areas of the curriculum. In any number of topics, such as modern transportation or life in outer space, for example, it is difficult to say where social studies leave off and science begins.

Plenty of time should be devoted to science so that the students can keep abreast of the swiftly changing scene and new developments in the scientific field.

MATHEMATICS

Mathematics offers a supreme challenge to the student's mental processes, engaging all his powers of reasoning in abstract problem solving. In mathematics the gifted should not be taught processes and operations mechanically, but should be required to discover the reasons for the computations they make. This holds true for problem solving in algebra, for constructing lines and angles in geometry, for working with measurement and proportion, for studying perspective.

The bright student discovers the application of mathematics to many fields of study and life experience—in science, music, art, and architecture, in domestic science, in sports and games.

The child with a flair for numbers can be introduced earlier than other children to the mysteries of geometry and work with algebraic concepts. Exploring number games and learning shortcuts in computation make mathematics more interesting for him than following routine textbook lessons.

FOREIGN LANGUAGES

Modern foreign language study is a source of enrichment for the gifted because it furnishes not only intellectual enrichment, but an understanding of foreign cultures. Knowledge of a foreign language is also invaluable for bright young people who are likely to need languages for college and in their future careers.

The alert student may find in foreign language study the incentive to explore linguistic science. He will enjoy discovering the interrelationships of various languages and exploring the origin and derivation of words in his own and other languages.

THE ARTS

Children benefit from developing any abilities they may have in artistic expression. The gifted careerist, whether a doctor, a writer, a teacher, a chemist, or an engineer, will find art training of value in his professional life; and the study of art appreciation brings out new meanings in life as represented in form and color through the eyes of a great artist.

Music is a form of language, which, though wordless, conveys emotions, feelings, ideas, and pictures that add a rich dimension to daily life. Leaders in music education find that nearly everyone has some musical talent, which needs only to be discovered and developed.

Music study can be of interest to the gifted child who may not be especially talented in music, even for one who has never studied an instrument. With good instruction he can enjoy singing and learn to play a simple instrument such as the recorder; musical rhythms can be related to dancing and dramatization. If none of these activities seem to appeal to the student, perhaps his interest can be aroused in music appreciation, the study of the classics and the lives of great musicians. The study of theory and harmony and acoustics may appeal to the mathematically gifted student.

Classes in art, music, dramatics, and foreign languages should be part of the student's regular daily program, instead of an extracurricular activity for a few exceptionally talented children. Today individual instruction in music and art is sometimes included in the school's program.

Drill for Skill

Too often the assumption is made that the gifted student learns by intuition, that creative work and drill are antithetical, whereas the opposite is true. Great achievements are the end product of long, sustained study involving practice to perfect the necessary skills.

The gifted child may be impatient with drills for skill in reading, writing, arithmetic, and art, but he will not be able to advance in intellectual work without them. Spelling may seem stupidly erratic, but there is no escape from practice for mastery of conventional forms.

The gifted student should realize the importance of drill for perfecting performance and achieving permanent learning. Often enough, the bright learner will discover his need for drill as he gets farther into his experimental problem solving. Usually, he will need certain skills ahead of others of his age; for example, he will need to learn how to mount his specimens or work with algebraic formulas.

A common error in teaching skills is wrong placement or timing. A gifted child may know the skills before they are taught, e.g., multiplication or spelling or punctuation rules. Bright children seldom need the same drills, usually not as much drill, as others. Drill can be meaningful or meaningless, interesting or dull, depending on its purpose for the student and his readiness for learning.

The modern curriculum provides for efficient learning of basic skills through the use of many devices—programmed drill books, games, contests, mechanical aids, teaching machines—all of which are as valuable for a rapid learner as for any other child.

With individualized instruction, a rapid learner can undertake skill-related studies when he is ready for them instead of waiting for others to catch up. The more mature student assumes the responsibility for knowing what level and amount of practice he needs. He gives himself an assignment, takes a practice test, checks and notes the results, then makes a graph of his improvement day by day. He learns to diagnose his own difficulties and then takes measures to correct them.

The Role of the Teacher

Although the typical gifted student is animated with a zest for learning, he is often given ready-made answers, ideas, and opinions to be memorized and recited rather than real mental stimulation. The student's mind is cluttered with random, unrelated facts, and criticism is given and marks meted out strictly according to the teacher's standards of correctness.

Lessons in a standard uniform text, with assignments that require answering a few questions, filling in some blanks, and then reading a selection or answers aloud to the class, do not provide sufficient intellectual stimulation for the gifted. Catching and repeating a slick jargon has little to do with genuine understanding. Having to memorize and give back obscure textbook paradigms can be a stultifying experience for the intellectually gifted child. Quick memorizing and quicker forgetting are wasteful under any circumstances. No child retains much by sheer memorizing without meaningful associations. The teacher's primary goal is not to impart information, but to show the student how to learn as he responds to thought-provoking problems.

Instruction should result in comprehension of broad principles rather than the accumulation of detached facts. Factual information is meaningful only in relation to problem solving. The facts are most easily learned and retained when they are meaningfully organized in terms of basic concepts and generalizations. The teacher is advised to reduce the amount of explanation, to make more use of the principles of application, to experiment with freer and more individualized types of assignments. Then the students should be able to learn with greater interest and understanding.

GUIDED LEARNING

Teaching the gifted requires rethinking the concepts "to teach" and "to learn." The art of teaching the gifted resides in releasing and challenging their energies, arousing enthusiasm for learning, with the children taking a large share of responsibility for their own learning.

In the opinion of teachers at the Hunter College Elementary School, gifted children need guidance rather than dictation. A teacher in another school said that his role was to set the stage so that students would become alert and interested in pursuing ideas; then he would step aside and let them move "full steam" ahead. When interest is aroused, students become inquisitive and seek answers to questions. Teachers are advised to let the gifted take the initiative in deciding what they will learn, so far as practical.

Primarily, the teacher's work is to open up new vistas, encourage frank questions, setting the stage for explorations of a high order. Raising issues, demonstrating, evaluating—all bring about greater understanding of relevant problems. Student-teacher planning of study projects is a feature in all good schools.

Instead of requiring group conformity, teachers should reward bright students for originality in thinking. A permissive atmosphere encourages further exploration of problems through the use of many resources. The development of special talent requires a finely balanced program of direct instruction, opportunity for self-expression, exploration, and experimentation.

The gifted need time to discuss their ideas with the teacher and others who can follow their thinking; they should be trained to discuss, to inquire, to state their views, and to support them in debate. Bright children do not require as much step-by-step instruction as others, but they do need advice about finding and using materials, locating information, summarizing and reporting their findings.

LEARNING THROUGH DISCOVERY

According to an old Chinese proverb, "Those who can think learn for themselves and not from the sages." Teachers no longer assume that all a student needs to know can be learned by word of mouth or even from the study of a basic textbook. Instead, the student is required to seek out information for himself, and then to use the facts in problem solving.

As Dr. Jerome Bruner has pointed out, helping the student discover facts for himself is more time-consuming than presenting selected facts and requiring students to learn them, for example, in mathematics, fractions, ratio, proportion. The economy lies in the development of the student's capacity for thinking (1960).

Experimental "tries" are the basis of all effective learning. Through repeated trials the student becomes aware of his successes and failures, overcomes his difficulties, and improves his performance.

Methods of instruction should lead the pupil to discover for himself important relationships and processes, whether he is working in a particular school subject or on experiments of his own. This means that experimental work and firsthand investigation have priority in the student's modes of learning. Instead of handing the student everything ready-made for his science experiments, the teacher advises him to bring in his own equipment or to construct it. In carrying on experimental projects, the student may work individually or in a small group with a student leader. Reporting the results of his study projects is the culminating phase of the work.

A good rule is never to put a ceiling on the achievements of the gifted by suggesting that some problem or material is too advanced for them. There is no telling what bright children can do until they try.

Educative experiences other than those gained through direct teacher contacts include discussion, informal instruction from adults and associates, observation and looking up facts, self-initiated experiments, independent reading, participation in cultural events such as lectures and concerts, visiting the museum, going to the theater, visiting a fair or science exhibit, and so on.

Is the idea of student self-exploration opposed to the idea of discipline? On the contrary, thinking flourishes best in the atmosphere of intellectual discipline that good teaching provides.

PROBLEM SOLVING

Teaching children to solve problems by the use of the method of intelligence was mentioned above as a major aim in educating the gifted. In pursuing this aim, teachers attempt to develop understanding of the problem-solving process—thinking critically, reflectively, and objectively. As a result the student understands relationships and acquires new concepts. He learns to arrive at sound decisions through his own reasoning powers and to solve problems with imagination and originality.

In problem solving, the student learns the bases of evidence, the nature of objectivity in thought, the sources of fallacies met in reading. He learns the scientific method of thinking: statements must be substantiated with evidence. He develops the habit of asking: How do you know that? What are the facts? Where did you get your evidence?

Locating the problem, setting up a hypothesis, marshaling the supporting data, drawing conclusions, and reporting objective results—all are within the abilities of bright students in the upper elementary grades and high school. They will need guidance in finding materials for problem solving however.

The subject of teaching for creativity is considered in Chapter Fifteen.

Instructional Facilities for Work with the Gifted

Frequent mention has been made of the expanded facilities and equipment that enriched teaching requires. Superior equipment will not make children brighter or increase the number of competent students, but it will encourage those who show unusual aptitudes. Whatever is required in the way of special equipment for the gifted and talented will enrich the school experience of all children.

Individualized instruction is more feasible in a school with multipurpose architectural features and flexible classroom furnishings that permit small-group seating and adequate work space.

A well-equipped elementary school classroom has a science table, a reading and library corner, a writing center, and areas for art projects. In the newer schools there is often a small room adjoining the classroom where groups of children can work separately. The children should have access to shops, studios, the science laboratory, the home economics room, and other facilities their studies require.

Some provision must be made at school, at least at the secondary level, for semisecluded study and work; a quiet library with cubicles, alcoves, or "islands" for individual and small-group work is particularly important for students who have little privacy or work space at home.

Some communities have experimented with the "school in the round": a large circular area in the center is used for assemblies, and opening off from this are classrooms, workshops, study rooms, and laboratories, shared by different grades and classes. There is also an instruction materials center, actually an enlargement of the school library, not to mention outside space for play, sports, and recreation.

LIBRARY FACILITIES

The school library and materials center, staffed by trained librarians, serves as a research center for the entire school. Every child, beginning in the first grade, should learn how to use the library and have some time during the school week to enjoy the good books to be found there. For more detail on this topic, see *Teaching Reading* (Hildreth, chap. 22, 1958).

Public community libraries add to the school's resources. The City-County Library of Yuma, Arizona, has excellent library facilities, including a bookmobile that serves children in the city. A substantial amount of money available to the library each year goes into children's books.

STUDY RESOURCES

Gifted and talented students, as all others, need tools and construction materials for arts and crafts, maps and a globe, charts and graphs, pictures, slides, films and filmstrips, tape recorders, record players, headphones, books of classified information, and self-help instruction manuals. They need materials for making their own maps and charts, pictures, murals, dioramas, and exhibits. They should be informed of local materials and resources that will enrich their studies, such as collections of specimens and pictures.

To add interest to regular classroom work, the pupils can use a computing machine to check arithmetic, card games for geography facts and historical events, records and tape recordings for foreign language study. The children themselves can prepare their own drill materials—lotto or bingo cards for reading drill, crossword puzzles for spelling, multiplication tables, a simple slide rule for arithmetic, conversion charts for centigrade and Fahrenheit thermometers, vocabulary-picture drill cards, and short-answer or multiple-choice tests.

The modern self-instruction exercise books are recommended for independent work on an individual basis. Through self-administering check tests, the student can determine whether or not he has mastered a given unit and is ready to proceed to the next. Special problems requiring systematic drill can be cleared up with such self-teaching devices.

Portable science laboratories for children offer a new resource for imaginative play and serious study as well. Microlaboratories now available include equipment for constructing engines and materials for studying mathematics, earth sciences, fossils, atomic principles, light and energy, etc. There are a beginner's microscope set, an electronics workshop, a pre-electricity physics laboratory, a computer laboratory. A child's interests and intellectual advancement alone will determine when he is ready for a miniature laboratory and what use he will make of it.

Lessons recorded on tapes with the teacher's instructions provide another means of enriching instruction on an individual basis. The use of recordings and tapes has virtually revolutionized the teaching of foreign languages because the initial stress is on oral experience rather than written work. These devices individualize instruction and reduce the need for teacher contacts because they are used by the students independently and provide self-corrective exercises.

Some gifted children enjoy preparing tapes for reporting class performances and for sharing musical programs, reports, plays, poetry readings, games, and current events with other classes.

Educational television programs enrich learning in all areas, but especially in foreign languages, science, and mathematics. A French language program is now broadcast twice a day during the school year in the United States on Wednesdays and Fridays. A new trend is to link educational television with reading by having librarians and school consultants prepare reading lists related to selected programs. Airborne television is the latest development in televised programs. The Midwest program which is based at Purdue University has a potential audience of 7 million students in 13,000 schools within a 200-mile radius.

TEXTBOOKS

What place do standard graded textbooks have in the gifted child's studies? How should they be used? Textbooks are next to useless if the bright child is limited to those designed for his grade. The best practice is to upgrade the texts in all subjects of study, both skill and content subjects; to have on the classroom bookshelves many different texts from different publishers; and then to teach children to use the books much as they do library reference materials, by looking up specific topics.

Too often textbook study has been a cut-and-dried perfunctory performance leading to verbalism—the mouthing of meaningless generalities. The correction lies, in part, in combining other methods of study, such as direct experiencing and the use of audio-visual materials, models, and experiments, with textbook work.

The New York City schools have recently abandoned the use of uniform basal textbooks in classes for the intellectually gifted. Although not all teachers are resourceful enough to find substitutes for textbooks, the best plan is to require children to look up their own materials in a wide array of books the school supplies for them. The pupils need intensive instruction in the use of library resources from the primary grades onward so that they can find information for themselves in reference sources as well as in other sorts of printed matter—books, magazines, pamphlets, newspapers, bulletins, and mimeographed materials.

TEACHING MACHINES

Teaching machines for programmed learning have proved their value in instructing the gifted because these devices individualize the drill phases of instruction. The student selects the problems, practices or drills himself, and self-checks his answers, all without teacher aid. There are now programs in virtually every skill subject and content area—mathematics, science, history, foreign language, English, spelling.

Whether or not teaching machines are bane or blessing remains to be seen. At this stage it seems clear that they have a number of advantages in work with the gifted. Programmed teaching speeds up learning for a bright child, motivation is usually high, and the student's attention is well sustained. With drill for skill out of the way, the student has more time for genuine problem solving. Since gifted children learn to handle gadgets easily and can work independently with the machines, the teacher's time is spared for other duties and for more time with individual students.

TEACHING TEAMS

Team teaching now being tried out in various centers has much to contribute to programs for the gifted. Under this arrangement, two or more teachers have joint responsibility for a class. The head teacher or chairman is assisted by two or three associates, among whom may be beginning teachers, student teachers, and nonprofessionals who serve as aids. The group as a whole plans the program, but individual teachers may be responsible for carrying out various aspects of it.

Another interpretation of "team teaching" is instruction given by a group, with the classroom teacher and teacher specialists working cooperatively with the children on their projects. In this way the strengths of different teachers are fully utilized.

In Hicksville, New York, teachers who are specialists travel from school to school giving children individual help with their special projects. Itinerant teachers give individual music instruction in San Diego, California. The chief advantage of these arrangements lies in better provision for individual instruction.

Evaluation of Progress and Achievement

What happens when studies for the gifted and talented are conducted in line with the principles outlined in this chapter? What do these capable students accomplish? Answers to these questions can be given only through wide-range, scientifically designed research studies. In the meanwhile, continuous evaluation by teachers and the students themselves will serve as a guide to curriculum modification and provide information for individual student counseling. Full use is made periodically of standard tests and ratings, teachers' observations, and records as outlined in Chapter Six.

The gifted student can turn his superior abilities to good account in evaluating himself because he is able to reflect on his goals and accomplishments and to verbalize the outcomes of his reflections.

References

Bruner, Jerome: *The Process of Education,* Harvard University Press, Cambridge, Mass., 1960.

Cutts, Norma E., and Nicholas Moseley: *Bright Children: A Guide for Parents,* G. P. Putnam's Sons, New York, 1953.

Fliegler, Louis A. (ed.): *Curriculum Planning for the Gifted,* Prentice-Hall, Inc., Englewood Cliffs, N.J., 1961.

French, Joseph L., (ed.): *Educating the Gifted: A Book of Readings,* Holt, Rinehart and Winston, Inc., New York, 1959.

Gallagher, James J.: *Teaching the Gifted Child,* Allyn and Bacon, Inc., Boston, 1963.

Hildreth, Gertrude: *Child Growth through Education,* The Ronald Press Company, New York, 1948.

Hildreth, Gertrude: *Teaching Reading,* Holt, Rinehart and Winston, Inc., New York, 1958.

Hildreth, Gertrude, Florence N. Brumbaugh, and Frank T. Wilson: *Educating Gifted Children at the Hunter College Elementary School,* Harper & Row, Publishers, Incorporated, New York, 1952.

Osburn, W. J., and Ben J. Rohan: *Enriching the Curriculum for Gifted Children,* The Macmillan Company, New York, 1931.

Strang, Ruth (ed.): A Symposium on the Gifted Child, *Journal of Teacher Education,* September, 1954.

Ward, Virgil S.: *Educating the Gifted: An Axiomatic Approach,* Charles E. Merrill Books, Inc., Columbus, Ohio, 1961.

Willis, Margaret: *The Guinea Pigs after Twenty Years: A Follow-up Study of the Class of 1938 of the University School at Ohio State,* Ohio State University Press, Columbus, Ohio, 1961.

Chapter Nine

TEACHING THE GIFTED IN THE ELEMENTARY SCHOOL

From age five or six up to adolescence is a golden period for learning. At no other time will a child learn skills so easily and enjoy learning them so much; at no other time will he pick up assorted information so quickly or grow so rapidly in social outlook and understanding. During these years the gifted child's interests are reaching out in all directions; intellectual curiosity is insatiable. Now is the time for acquiring the skills and scholarly habits to prepare for a life of high achievement.

The developmental tasks of gifted children are quite similar to those of all others. They include:

Gaining mastery of the skills of oral language, literacy, and number usage

Learning essential facts about common things

Gaining a wide range of new concepts

Learning how to think scientifically

Learning how to work and study as a true scholar

Learning to become a socialized person

Learning how to plan and carry out a program of activities and learning to cooperate with others in planning

Teachers can begin at once, as alert teachers have always done, to spot incipient talent in the children they work with and to think through the special, individual requirements of these children as rapid learners. All the general suggestions given in Chapters Six to Eight have a bearing on elementary school instruction at one point or another.

TEACHING GIFTED CHILDREN IN THE SELF–CONTAINED CLASSROOM[1]

Although ability grouping, special-class programs, and departmentalized instruction have been widely adopted, the self-contained classroom continues to be the commonest administrative unit in the elementary school. When the school enrollment is small, with comparatively few gifted children in any one grade, or when public sentiment is opposed to special-class programs, gifted children must be provided for in regular classes.

In the self-contained classroom all the major curriculum areas are in the charge of one teacher, while instruction in such areas as music and art, crafts, science, and foreign languages is usually handled by teacher specialists.

Providing for gifted children in the regular elementary school classroom is entirely feasible. Competent teachers of typical grade groups have always managed to make some provision for unusual children through special assignments and individual guidance.

The planning committee in Long Beach, California, concluded that neither special groupings nor acceleration best answered the question of what to do with unusually bright and talented children in the elementary school (Freese, 1953). Enrichment for these children in regular classrooms seemed the best arrangement. Ad-

[1] On the subject of special-class instruction for the gifted, see Chapter Eleven. Questions concerning acceleration of the gifted child are considered in Chapter Ten.

Although the modern public elementary school ordinarily terminates at grade 6, the statements in this chapter apply equally well to teaching the gifted in the regular classroom through grade 8.

vantages are that a minimum of extra administrative effort is required, charges of unfair discrimination are avoided, a bright child in a regular class can have experience in leadership, and the gifted child does not feel himself isolated from other children his age.

CONDITIONS FOR SUCCESSFUL WORK IN REGULAR CLASSES

Teaching the gifted in the regular classroom can be successful if the teacher is highly competent to begin with; if the class is not too large, preferably not above thirty children; if the teacher is allowed plenty of leeway in organizing class work, apart from the daily schedule of the entire school; and if there is a good supply of instructional materials that can be adapted to individualized teaching.

Providing for gifted children in their own grade classrooms is generally most successful when other members of the class are capable learners or when there are enough bright children to form a group for special work. Under these conditions, the teacher can give considerable attention to the gifted and talented.

Sometimes teachers give the two or three gifted pupils in the class the books and assignments of the grade ahead, but this is not usually the best arrangement. Teachers of higher classes have a right to object, because certain features of the books and lessons may be patently unsuited for younger children in spite of their high IQs.

Challenging the gifted while not undermining the confidence of the less-able pupils is possible only when every child in the class is made to feel that he is an integral part of the whole, that his achievements, no matter what their quality, count for something in the ongoing projects of the class.

Teachers find that their chief difficulty in attempting to enrich studies for gifted children in a regular elementary class is lack of time to prepare materials and to outline special study projects. Often there is a shortage of necessary equipment, even when children are prepared to learn on their own responsibility. Teachers also confess that they do not have the technical "know-how" needed to guide the gifted child in the study of his special interests, for example, atomic energy or missile weapons. Teaching the child who has exceptional talent in music, science, or languages or unusual interest in advanced reading on any topic calls for specialized teaching talent together with a trained librarian in the central school library.

One teacher who finds time for the gifted along with all her regular class duties says that she first becomes thoroughly acquainted with every child; she learns about his abilities, skills, hobbies, and special interests. She visits the child's home and consults the school records to obtain as much information as possible. Then she keeps her attention centered at all times on the child, not on the textbook or the conventional standards of the course of study, except as a minimum requirement.

What stage has this child now reached in his mental growth? What is his state of readiness for new concept development in history and social studies, in science and mathematics? How well can he handle an assignment independently? This information furnishes the basis for enrichment of the child's studies.

FLEXIBLE GROUPINGS AND INDIVIDUAL WORK

Individualization of assignments, materials, and activities is the basis of enrichment in the self-contained classroom. Gifted children benefit from flexibility in groupings within the class as well as opportunities for individual work. Recommendations are:

Provide whole-class experiences in which the gifted pupils participate.

Organize the class into subgroups, teams, or committees to work on special projects or experiments. Plan library work for small groups or for individual students.

Set up individual activities and projects for gifted children in terms of their special interests. Provide for individual use of textbooks and other resource materials.

When the teacher feels that she knows the child thoroughly, she is ready to plan in terms of his particular requirements, assigning him to a special group, encouraging him to contribute to the sharing periods by giving reports on books, TV programs, trips, hobbies, and other interests. The pupil may be a leader in organizing a hobby show or book fair for the school.

The gifted child in the elementary school is challenged by having to lead and participate in class discussion, by working on study projects with a small group having a common interest, by carrying on independent "research studies," by participating in club activities—music, art, mathematics, reading, science, or foreign languages—during the school day or in afterschool groups under school auspices or privately arranged.

Primarily, the teacher's task is to open up new frontiers for the gifted child so that he can make full use of his unusual abilities.

For example, in studying a topic such as soil erosion, the superior student goes farther than others into the social implications and the scientific principles involved. He may be able to report results in statistical form, using charts and graphs he has constructed himself.

Talented children can set up and take care of the science table. Children with literary inclinations will enjoy working on the class or school paper. Mathematicians can prepare charts and graphs to accompany class studies. One exceptionally talented child wrote and staged an original puppet show for the class. Bright third graders compiled a dictionary of common words and greetings in several foreign languages.

The children work on individual or small-group projects growing out of class activities but related to their own specialties. Bright children with a flair for investigating facts serve as resource persons for the class. A fifth-grade teacher appointed a boy who was considered a history expert the class historian, referring to him any difficult points that needed to be looked up.

A gifted child may be carrying on a weather or nature study or calendar project independently because it outdistances what the rest of the class can do with the same themes or may not be relevant to their classroom work at the time. He may be exploring current events with a thoughtful, analytical approach. The mentally mature child will be using books for his special studies that the rest of the class could not read easily or enjoy reading. A gifted child with a highly developed interest in invention or some phase of biology may read extensively on this subject and then report to the class the results of his study.

A resourceful teacher can enrich the learning of the bright child by having the right materials on hand when the child is ready to use them, for example, butterfly specimens from the museum, along with readable books.

The pupil who has learned to do research through library resources and reference materials—dictionary, encyclopedias, gazateer, thesaurus, style books, almanac, and various yearbooks—can help himself to facts. He is prepared to explore all sorts of topics and go as far as he likes.

WORKING INDEPENDENTLY

Even though bright children are encouraged to work independently, this does not mean that they have no supervision or that they work alone. On the contrary, there are frequent pupil-teacher contacts during which the teacher coaches the children in the best use of their time, the proper use of materials, and the importance of maintaining high standards of work.

Children who work on individual projects should be taught the specific techniques they will need in carrying on an independent piece of work, whether making a mural, using the typewriter, looking up information in a reference book, or working with electric batteries.

Skills and habits of independent work can be learned even as early as the first grade. In fact the earlier they are learned, the more competent the child will become in managing his study tasks. These skills include learning to use time wisely, to seek out the information required for a project, to read critically, to take notes, to remember facts. Another essential skill is learning to work congenially with others in group projects. The teacher should take pains to check completed assignments as well as projects under way.

A fourth-grade teacher with a good background in science described how she worked with a bright nine-year-old boy who was already far ahead of the others in her typical classroom. As soon as she discovered his special interests, she proceeded to give him as much help with them as possible. She brought in books and equipment he needed, gave him a special assignment in connection with the science fair, demonstrated procedures, leading him on step by step, for example, in advanced lessons in arithmetic.

Contrary to what one might expect, working independently did not make this boy an isolate. Instead, he was helpful and considerate, even popular with his classmates, because the teacher worked with the class in establishing good relationships among all the pupils.

At the same time that the gifted child is working on his individual projects he needs recognition and support from the class; in turn, he must be ready to recognize the worth of what the rest of the class is doing. The work of a cluster group can be related to the ongoing activities of the whole class.

THE LABORATORY PLAN OF STUDY

Experiments with elementary school children have proved that they can learn the skills and attitudes needed in research, usually with good results. The laboratory plan of instruction in which small cluster groups or individuals work on simple experiments has advantages over the usual textbook assignments. Or there may be independent problem solving, with the pupils using the textbook as a guide. These groupings are more tentative and informal than the special-class and part-time grouping plans described in Chapter Eleven.

The distribution of the gifted pupil's time, as he explores his special topics, will vary from the regular time allotted for the rest of the class. He may need less time or want twice as much for arithmetic as the others.

The teacher of an average fourth-grade class in a large city school said that it took the first six weeks of school for small-group teams with pupil leaders to establish routines for getting out materials, taking instructions from the leader, checking one another's work, and collecting and replacing materials. By the end of this time the children were prepared to handle their assignments or independent projects with little teacher supervision.

Plans for flexible grouping and individual study require classroom furniture that permits a variety of seating arrangements—a group around the teacher, a group around the library table, partners working together, the teacher with one pupil alone. The best arrangements for seating and work space can be worked out by the teacher and pupils together.

The chief problems are the number of groups (how many such groups can a teacher manage at one time?), the training of children for group work, and the kinds of activities a small group can carry on with a minimum of teacher supervision. Teachers report that trying to enrich the studies of a gifted cluster in the general classroom is a difficult task because of the need to supervise each child more or less individually. It is not sufficient simply to tell the children to go ahead on their own responsibility.

A beginning can be made by forming a small cluster group of several children who are bright learners, well ahead of the rest of the class. The group is formed either by the teacher on the basis of her knowledge of the achievement of individual pupils or through pupil choices. Regroupings take place very frequently, but without using labels. Groups change according to the schedule of activities. One hour it is arithmetic; next, the class moves on to committee work for the social studies theme. The children are regrouped for drill on specific skills; they work on various study projects, on service and housekeeping jobs, or follow special interests, such as science or puppetry. They do advanced work in arithmetic, carry on special projects in art or music, do science experiments, have recreational reading or a library period.

At other times the bright children work with buddies or part-ners, for example, in checking spelling. There may be a period in the day when the teacher works with a small group while the others work individually or with buddies. Or the teacher may work with a large group while individual children or a small group works on special projects or goes to the library.

OTHER SUGGESTIONS

Marion Schiefele has made a number of valuable suggestions for working with gifted children in classrooms enrolling a typical cross section of school children (1953). She recommends that the gifted child have four types of experience:

He should enter fully into the life of the classroom, sharing in group projects.

He should do advanced work on an individual basis in skill subjects according to his level of advancement.

He should have the opportunity to work on his own hobbies and interests on an individual basis or in a club group.

He should participate fully in the life of the school—in dramatics, student gov-ernment, charity drives, school publications, club groups.

These are all practical suggestions that fit into the work of the typical modern elementary school.

For the child who quickly finishes an assignment and wonders what to do next, the teacher keeps a list of all the special projects on which an individual pupil might work when he has time to spare: He might work on the next edition of the school paper, index the classroom library and make index-card notations about particular books, use reference books for looking up certain topics, work on a scrapbook of pictures and clippings, complete written work, prepare posters, mount pictures and reports, make illustra-tions and maps, prepare an almanac or weather reports. Other suggestions for individual activities are:

Plan and conduct a panel discussion

Write scripts for radio programs or a play

Practice to improve in letter writing

Study word derivations

Undertake story writing

Act as class parliamentarian

Prepare reports of individual projects

Work on an assembly program

Teachers in the Portland, Oregon, schools compiled a book of ideas for classroom teachers to use with gifted children in seven curriculum areas: arithmetic, arts and crafts, language arts, health, music, science, and social studies. The suggestions for each area describe the enriching activity or project, list the materials to be used, and give know-how notes, references, comments, and suggestions (Norris, 1958).

FEATURES OF PUBLIC SCHOOL PROGRAMS

In the Portland, Oregon, elementary schools especially talented pupils participate fully in schoolwide projects in terms of their individual talents, exploring topics of special interest through the use of the encyclopedia and other sources of classified information (Norris, 1958). The pupils learn library skills and how to locate information in reference books; they assume leadership roles in school and class activities and develop skills in the workshop and art laboratory.

A pupil with a flair for music, mathematics, and invention constructed a model of a music staff with removable notes, and demonstrated for the class the values of notes and their relation to fractions.

A bright girl in the sixth grade, in charge of the classroom library, instructed the class in replacing their books properly on the shelves according to the classification numbers. She became an expert in the Dewey decimal classification and in the use of classified guides to information. She was able to direct her classmates in the use of an index to periodical literature.

Sometimes arrangements are made for the gifted child to visit an advanced class when topics allied with his special interest are under discussion, or he may give reports to other classes on subjects on which he is well informed.

In Plainfield, New Jersey, gifted pupils in grades 4, 5, and 6 are given a program which stresses study skills and the desire to learn. The children are trained to use reference sources in the library; they are encouraged to read as much as possible and to select individual projects which they would like to explore. In Erie, Pennsylvania, children of exceptional ability and talent are released from regular classrooms for an hour each day to pursue special interests requiring intensive study.

Enrichment for elementary school pupils can also be achieved through expansion within conventional subject areas. In the Indianapolis elementary schools, bright children are given additional work in literature, science, history, and social studies. The regular subject matter of the grades is expanded through special research projects, individualized instruction, teacher-pupil conferences, educational excursions. The children prepare, with the teacher's aid, some of their own reading material, study guides and workbooks, which are kept on file for reference use.

In the regular classes of an Austin, Texas, elementary school connected with the University of Texas, bright children use media of learning and communication that range far beyond basic textbooks in the areas of science and social studies, arithmetic, art, and music (Otto, 1955).

Some elementary schools teach subjects not ordinarily offered for all pupils—foreign language, algebra, creative writing, etc. Many other valuable suggestions for enriching studies for individual children and small groups in the regular classroom will be found in the publications listed at the end of this chapter.

Special Interests and Hobbies As Sources of Enrichment

The bright child's special interests can be used to enrich his studies and save his time, according to a report made some years ago by Osburn and Rohan (1931). The authors advocated hobby groups and club programs for child-initiated activities growing out of special interests.

In any ordinary classroom will be found the budding playwright, the young artist or mathematician. Others may be specialists on birds, rocks, or insects. An older child may be interested in word origins and find the study of words deeply satisfying as well as a bridge to foreign language study. The teacher is alert to draw out talented children, the one who can play the guitar, give science demonstrations, give a report on his travels, or tell the class about his interest in pets, and so on.

One young scholar composed a play for the class, but older children wrote it down for him because he was not yet a fluent penman. A nine-year-old was deeply involved in the study of taxidermy. An eight-year-old spent every Saturday morning at the museum studying dinosaurs. One upper grader was fascinated by "codes"; after reading a book on the subject, he invented a code and taught it to his friends. Later on he gave a class report on this topic. An eleven-year-old playwright spent an hour each day in a secluded room adjoining the school library where she worked on her plays. A seventh-grade girl worked up an extensive report on her hobby—styles through the ages.

Using children's special interests in their school life was the subject of a study undertaken by Durrell and his associates in the schools of Dedham, Massachusetts (1956). The program involved individual projects carried on by high achievers as an integral part of their class study. No less than 1200 specialties came to light. In grade 6, children were interested in weather forecasting, strange fish, levers and wedges, fabrics, birds of prey, the dry cell, and many other subjects. Some of the interests pertained to history, others to science and geography. A number involved artwork and related to other areas in the curriculum.

As part of the program, children gave ten-minute reports, using graphic materials to improve reporting and to save time. In such a program the children exercised initiative and self-discipline; they read widely and developed new skill in organizing material for oral and written reports.

Unit Teaching in the Elementary School

Unified studies and the core or block-time program were mentioned in Chapter Seven as a means of individualizing instruction. To enrich studies for the gifted in typical elementary classrooms, teachers are advised to organize the curriculum in terms of broad, unified study themes or projects.

Through unit studies, the work of the gifted child, as well as the depth and breadth of his contribution to the central theme, can be differentiated from that of the other pupils. Children can contribute in terms of their own interests and capacities, working with a small group or individually, conducting experiments, doing independent reading, and then reporting to the group. The talented can make fuller use of their special abilities, for example, in doing historical research, in producing maps, charts, or other illustrations, or in discussion groups.

The unit theme might be "Pioneers on the Westward March," a social studies project enriched through work in literature, written expression, science, arts and crafts, and music. The possibilities of enrichment for the gifted pupil in such themes seem limitless.

A fourth grade launched into the project of making weather vanes. Instead of telling the pupils exactly what to do, the teacher helped them search out the information they needed, allowing plenty of time for this stage of their planning and study. Another fourth grade studied the beginnings of the earth and recent advances in sending a rocket to the moon.

A favorite unit for children in New York State is "The Erie Canal." One sixth-grade class traced the roots of American freedom. Another spent the entire year studying "Our Latin American Neighbors."

Elementary school children in New York City who studied the early Indian settlements on Manhattan Island visited Inwood Park, the site of an early settlement, for some of their information. A class of junior high school children interviewed members of the city department of sanitation to learn about this branch of civic operations. A seventh-grade class studying the making of a modern newspaper took a trip to the newspaper branch of the public library and went on a guided tour of a newspaper publishing establishment.

The Hunter Elementary School program is organized around themes or study topics, disregarding formal sequence of subject matter in the curriculum, but requiring that each child demonstrate competence up to minimum grade standards in academic skills.

The curriculum of the Portland, Oregon, public schools centers about unified themes, with the pupils contributing to the central theme in terms of their individual talents and abilities. The plan is similar in most respects to other programs of unified teaching. In an upper-grade unit on "The Middle Ages," pupil teams and others working alone or in small groups developed special topics growing out of the larger theme. In a unit on South America several creative children made a map of the world, showing the South American continent in its global setting. Another group worked on astronomy, making a colorful map of the solar system based on information gained from a shelf of books on the subject.

Unit studies extend beyond school walls into the community as the children go on trips, participate in civic projects, visit rural areas, exchange visits with students from other places, all under school auspices. The teacher posts on the bulletin board notices of museum programs, concerts, and other opportunities for enrichment, some of which are free of charge.

In unit teaching, the teacher does not pretend to be an expert in every subject that contributes to the unit, but skillfully guides the pupils in seeking out the information they need to bring the unit to a successful conclusion.

THE SERVICES OF SPECIAL TEACHERS

The regular class teacher welcomes the services of specialist teachers and expert consultants to assist the highly gifted children with their projects. Special teachers are particularly valuable in extending the children's learning experiences in science, music, arts and crafts, or other areas related to comprehensive curriculum studies. In one class, a science specialist aided the children in constructing a miniature glacier model; in another, she supervised the construction of a balanced aquarium. Specially trained teachers also handle the work in foreign languages.

One school reports that when a play is to be put on, all the special teachers cooperate. The sixth graders who were studying "The West" decided to dramatize what they had learned. They planned and made their own costumes and scenery. At one point they introduced a scene from a gypsy camp and sang gypsy songs. One can easily visualize the part of the special teachers in all this activity.

Gifted Children in the Lower Grades

Unusually mature children in kindergarten and first grade—the quick, alert ones who are already well along in basic skills or have displayed special talents—may be too young to be put ahead a year, but they are ready for learning experiences beyond the standard curriculum.

Some people are opposed to doing anything about the gifted below the intermediate grades on the ground that it is still too early to tell for sure whether they are gifted; furthermore, singling them out so early may cause them anxiety or prevent good social adjustment. Then, too, there is a temptation for parents and teachers to stress acceleration in reading at the expense of other skills and activities. The child's parents may get an inflated notion of his abilities; they may be disappointed later if the diagnosis of giftedness was incorrect, or they may intensify the child's home training with unfortunate results. If these problems can be avoided, the school can enrich the curriculum and foster the strengths of the young scholar to his benefit.

Recommendations concerning young gifted children are:

Watch for these children even as early as kindergarten, and begin recording reports on their development.

Study the children from day to day to observe what their special capacities appear to be. Since versatility of interests and curiosity in many directions are characteristic of young children generally, pay more attention to the traits in which development seems unusual.

Provide broad experiences for gifted children in the primary grades so that they do not become specialists too soon. Keep open the whole world of knowledge and experience to provide a broad base from which they may take off in whatever direction their talents carry them.

Train the children early in self-responsibility and independence. Give them the opportunity to make choices. This can be done in a "choosing time" when they select from a list of activities suggested by the teacher what they will do during a particular period. If interest centers are set up in the classroom, with an artwork area, a library corner, an area for building, another for dramatic play, the children soon learn to use the materials independently. Train the children to work in little groups of two or three. Also, let them select their own books and read to themselves.

Do not emphasize acceleration in academic skills at the expense of other learnings, such as using a hammer, working with paper, clay, paint, wood, setting up a display, sewing, playing indoor and outdoor games, and singing.

SHOULD BRIGHT CHILDREN LEARN TO READ EARLY?

Bright children can learn to read before they enter school, but is it a good thing? There has been considerable debate over this issue. Evidence indicates that between one-third and one-half of all highly gifted children have already learned to read by school age. Usually they learned informally with parents or older children, saying over the simple text in picture books and remembering the words until they were able to read easy books independently. Often children who learn to read without formal lessons are the most fluent and natural readers in the class.

These children are not harmed in any way by precocious reading; however, reading can become such an absorbing occupation that normal play life is neglected. Even though the child is liked by others, he may fail to develop his social personality. Then, too, he may find school activities not involving reading uninteresting. If a child gets far ahead in reading before much attention is paid to spelling or writing, he may consider these skills irksome and unimportant, and may have a struggle catching up in them later on. Another problem is that the school beginner who is a precocious reader is assumed to be equally mature in other traits and skills, whereas he usually is not.

If a young child can read well for his age, there is no point in pushing him to read better or to read more. This will come naturally. Instead of trying to improve his reading, the teacher should turn some of his attention to oral and written expression. The ability to write legibly and correctly is not only as important as the ability to read, and even more interesting to the bright school beginner, but it also facilitates the interpretation of language in print.

Here are other suggestions for guiding the younger bright child.

In these early stages let special talents develop normally without forcing or intensive drill. If the child is younger than the rest of the group, do not force him to try to compete with the best skaters, folk dancers, or softball players, but compliment him on his effort to perform well.

Help the child learn the value and importance of sharing and teamwork to offset tendencies toward solitariness. Even from the first grade children can become accustomed to working in small activity groups.

Additional suggestions will be found in the books by Cutts and Moseley (1960) and Darrow and Van Allen (1961).

Individualized Teaching of Skills

All instruction in skills for the bright learner should be put on an individual basis as the result of a diagnostic inventory indicating the pupil's status in achievement. The preliminary survey may indicate that the pupil can dispense with daily drill in spelling, that he no longer needs practice for speed in reading, that he is ready for computation with fractions, and so on.

The bright child who is weak in some skill area may become impatient if he is advised that he must drill to improve. Other learning has come so easily that the idea of working intensively to improve his performance is discouraging. He may scarcely have been aware of the drudgery of practice in music or swimming or ice-skating, because of his driving interest in these pursuits, but now in school he must face the requirement of coming up to the standards of an educated, literate person. In reading, in spelling, arithmetic, punctuation, correctness in written expression, handwriting, there are conventional forms that must be mastered.

In the early 1920s an individualized plan of learning and instruction in the basic subjects was developed in the Winnetka, Illinois, public schools by the superintendent, Dr. Carleton Washburne, and his associates, which enabled the pupils to progress at their own rate (1932). The Winnetka individualized teaching program required extensive use of specially constructed self-administering materials in order to ungrade the teaching of the skill subjects.

Today, there are many self-help devices for mastery of basic study tools individually. The Hunter College Elementary School children drill themselves on arithmetic with workbooks and computers, learn to type, check their own spelling words, and use workbooks for word study.

The teacher should have on hand individual sets of drill materials with self-checking answer keys which are virtually self-teaching. Then the pupil can select the level of material he needs and go to work.

Team Learning As an Aid to the Bright Student

Team learning in which two or three children of similar ability work together can be used to individualize instruction in the skill subjects. Durrell found that with team learning it was possible to differentiate instruction in skills for the brighter, more advanced students in the class (1959). They completed assignments in arithmetic computation and spelling rapidly when they worked in small teams, saving time for other work. First, all the necessary levels of instruction were identified; then the children were formed into small teams and given assignments suited to their level. The children worked together, teaching and checking up on one another.

Although team learning can be carried on in departmentalized classes or in special classes, it is especially helpful with the typical cross section of pupil abilities found in the self-contained classroom.

In Dr. Durrell's experiment, teams of two or three pupils who were high or average achievers were organized for spelling, arithmetic, and reading, freeing the teacher for more attention to slow learners. There were also five-member teams heterogeneously grouped following whole-class presentation of a topic.

The teachers constructed job sheets for language skills, self-directing and self-correcting, for children working in teams of two or three members. Each child kept a record of his own progress. When it was time to introduce a new topic, the teacher would work with one group at a time.

The program in arithmetic included adjustments in regular textbook assignments by the use of job sheets, with self-direction

and self-correction of problems. Each pupil first worked the example alone, then checked with his partner. In the study of
written problems, one pupil read the problem, and his partner
worked it.

In spelling, personal spelling lists became the key to individualized learning. The children centered their attention on collecting twenty words each week or every other week that they needed
in writing but did not know how to spell. Working with a classmate
of fairly equal ability, high achievers tested each other on these
word lists. There were sequential lessons for words of special difficulty and systematic reviews about every two weeks. Each pupil
kept a personal list of words misspelled in language activities and
in spelling lessons. His attainment was recorded on a progress
chart. All the spelling test sheets were kept in the pupil's individual
folder.

Team learning worked particularly well in spelling because
of the ease of checking on spelling needs and determining the
results of study. Dr. Durrell found that high achievers completed
the required spelling for a thirty-six–week lesson series in four
to seven weeks.

Although team learning required considerable planning and
careful training of the pupils, once established, the plan operated
smoothly. Regrouping was found to be necessary throughout the
year. The children preferred to work in pairs or small groups,
rather than with the whole class or alone. Results proved that
there was more active participation in small teams and the teams
functioned best when the members were of nearly equal ability.

The study activities of pupil teams may or may not be integrated with ongoing curriculum projects, depending on what they
undertake and how the projects are organized. In a comprehensive
study project, one member of the team may act as a recorder, with
the group summary presented orally to the entire class. Ordinary
subject texts can be used by pupil teams without the necessity
of processing special-unit materials.

Group work not only guards against the isolation of a gifted
student, but also utilizes children's capacity to learn from each
other and provides some competition. There are many opportunities
in science, in foreign language study, and in other areas when
two students of comparable ability can profitably work together.

Is it "enriching" for a bright or talented student to assist
a slower learner? Since the student cannot explain things to others
unless he himself understands the intricate points, assisting others

enlarges his own understanding. Also, the practice tends to be socially valuable. Teachers should, however, guard against having a gifted student tutor others merely to fill up his time.

Programs of instruction for elementary school pupils in special classes and part-time groups are described in Chapter Eleven.

Enrichment through Reading and Literature

Typically, the elementary school child reads for recreation, to find out things he wants to know, and to study problems growing out of the curriculum. The particular values that reading has for the gifted were discussed in Chapter Seven.

Once the mentally advanced child catches on to the trick of moving his eyes across the lines of print to get the meaning, catching clues to words from the context and from familiar word roots, he moves ahead independently without special drills. As soon as he has reached this stage, he can proceed at his own rate, so long as plenty of good reading material is available and books continue to hold his interest.

Bright boys and girls in the upper elementary grades will demand teen-age books and adult reading. They may be able to read as well as adolescents, and their reading interests may be exceptionally mature. A bright child who asks for *Treasure Island, Two Years before the Mast, Green Pastures, Red Badge of Courage, Moby Dick, Dr. Jekyl and Mr. Hyde, Lorna Doone* in the elementary grades should not have to wait until high school to enjoy them.

READING EXPERIENCES FOR THE GIFTED

Both academic and recreational reading experience should be provided on an individual basis. With ungraded reading material, the brighter pupils are not held back by standard grade reading requirements.

There may be as many as seven reading levels in an ordinary cross section of the class group. The children in the upper levels can spend their reading time in the library; others can read their assignments independently; while others can work with partners for the improvement of reading skills.

Every child should have access to a wide range of materials on a variety of subjects—good story books, the best in children's literature, informational books, biographies, how-to books, poetry, humor, juvenile periodicals. School shelves seldom hold enough to meet the needs of every child.

Gifted children in the elementary school should choose freely according to their own interests and preferences—the tales of Cooper, the works of the great English novelists, or selections from the less distinguished, mass teen-age literature of today. The elementary school boy who expects to become a scientist, the girl who is headed for a career in costume design or historical research, should be free to follow these interests independently in the school library. These children will know how to use their time when turned loose in the library for browsing, or "grazing," as one youngster termed it. The younger children should have books that discuss advanced concepts in which they are interested in simple terminology. If the books these children want are found only outside of school, why not bring them to school and use them there?

Through simple techniques, books in the classroom library can be identified and grouped according to subject matter and reading level.

Since bright boys and girls of elementary school age are still children, they gravitate back and forth between advanced books and those more typical of their actual age. If the children make their own choices from among good books, they can scarcely go wrong.

In an older day bright children were devoted to the *St. Nicholas Magazine* and *The Youth's Companion.* Today child and youth periodicals touch all interests: *Story Parade,* the *Horn Book Magazine, Junior Red Cross, American Boy* and *American Girl, The Young Elizabethan* (British), among others. The livelier adult magazines also have a strong appeal to bright youngsters with good reading ability: *The National Geographic Magazine, Life* and *Time, Nature Magazine, Popular Science, The Reader's Digest,* and the specialized periodicals devoted to stamp collecting, numismatics, and other youth interests.

The most difficult problem is to provide enough good reading to satisfy the eager minds of the bright and gifted. Teachers are advised to draw upon the whole world of children's literature to be found in every good school library, every children's reading room in a public library, in the children's homes, in the bookstores. Children's book clubs are another source of the best juvenile literature. Parents should be advised to give children books as gifts, selected with the advice of a teacher, a librarian, or a store clerk who knows the children's book field.

Since few schools, even those with a good central library, can supply every class with sufficient reading material, every child should have a library card so that he can make full use of the community library resources. A book club that meets after school once a week or at the library on Saturday will bring great books to the attention of gifted children when they are ready to appreciate them.

A gifted reader may become addicted to certain types of books, those in his area of interest, or a book series. Although any good reading is beneficial, the teacher and librarian should encourage a balanced reading diet by suggesting alternatives in the book collection, baiting the children in reading-aloud sessions.

The gifted child's reading skills improve coincidentally with daily reading that is tied in with school studies and outside interests. Although fluent silent reading is the chief objective, the bright also need to practice fluent oral reading so as to be prepared to read orally with self-assurance.

Learning to use the dictionary for word meanings is one route to independence in using more difficult books. If children are introduced to the dictionary early, they can learn to help themselves to the new vocabulary they meet in their reading and to other items of information as well. The teacher should demonstrate the use of the dictionary and other reference resources commonly found in libraries, giving children practice in their use.

BIOGRAPHY FOR THE GIFTED CHILD

The reading of biography as a source of enrichment for the gifted was mentioned in the preceding chapter. Biography gives children insights into the lives of people whom they identify with through their own interests. Studies have shown that biography is a favorite form of reading for children who have access to the best books of this type. Dr. Hollingworth made extensive use of biography in study units developed for gifted classes at Public School 500 in New York (Hollingworth, 1924, and Greenberg, Bruner, 1941). The study of biography ramified into every branch of knowledge and coordinated with ongoing projects in science, music, art, commerce, history, and others. The children in these experimental classes were given the opportunity to study "the lives of interesting people who really lived." Each child selected his "real person," and then collected from various sources whatever information he considered significant about the person and wrote an account to read to the class. Following the reading, he conducted a discussion on the person he had studied. Teachers avoided dwelling at length on the inspirational features of these lives or pointing out the moral lessons they taught. One criterion guided the development of these units: the fact that people are the most important environmental factor in experience. The books gave the pupils new consciousness of the role people have played in the evolution of common things of life.

In another school a bright boy chose as his social studies project the comparison of an eminent person of an earlier period with a present-day celebrity, using biographical material for this enterprise. For a more extensive discussion of biography as a valuable source of reading material for the gifted see Chapter Thirteen.

BOOK REVIEWS

It would be a fatal mistake to require the precocious reader to write reviews of all the good books he reads. Fewer books could be enjoyed if he had to make out formal reports on every one. Book reports should be optional, but the child should be invited to express his opinion about any books he reads. If the question is how well he is reading, this is checked by his success in reporting on reading done in conjunction with study projects.

One suggestion is to allow more time in class for informal discussion of books. Bright children clustered in a special literature group in the upper grades made oral reports each week on the reading they had done, with the aid of their notebooks. Other possibilities are dramatizations of book characters and incidents in assemblies for the entire school and tape recordings for reports of good reading to be broadcast. One school librarian had gifted readers review new books as they came in. The students prepared a book review index containing their comments on each book for the benefit of future readers.

READING PROBLEMS

Gifted children are not always ahead in reading or invariably fond of reading as a pastime. Occasionally a gifted child prefers other activities and does little reading apart from school assignments. One bright boy who said that he had lost interest in reading in the third or fourth grade had fallen considerably behind by grade 5. However, with persistent help from the teacher, he came out well ahead on the final tests.

Bert was a primary grade pupil who had a high IQ but preferred mechanics to all else, following in the footsteps of his engineer father. By the time he was ready for high school, the boy had done all the required work in reading and literature, but he read practically nothing on his own initiative except certain sections of the newspaper. His mother wondered when he would ever read the classics she had enjoyed in school. Now, long out of college, he never has.

Special attention may need to be given to reading as a study skill. Perhaps in time a smoothly operating teaching machine will take care of all the drill that any child needs. In the meanwhile, a checkup will show where there is need for improvement in basic skills such as word recognition, reading for precise meanings, fluency and rapidity, and familiarity with reference sources.

Drill time can be economized through the use of self-administering, self-correcting test exercises consisting of sets of graded pamphlets used on an individual basis. The pupil works at his own level, proceeds at his own speed, and uses answer keys to check his responses. He keeps his own record, making a graph of daily improvement.

THE BOOKWORM

Both parents and teachers become concerned about the child who at one period or another cares for nothing but reading. Sometimes books serve as a means of escape from real life. This becomes morbid, however, only when the child is unable to make social contacts or withdraws completely into a world of fantasy. Wise handling at home and in school will help children develop other interests which may offset the bookworm neurosis.

Isn't excessive reading hard on the child's eyes? Not usually, because a good reader grasps meaning by inference from partial clues to the print without painstaking inspection of every word.

More complete information on the subject of reading will be found in a wide assortment of professional books and articles such as those in the following list.

Barbe, Walter B.: Guiding the Reading of the Gifted, *The Reading Teacher,* 7:144–150, 1954.

Commission on the English Curriculum: *Language Arts for Today's Children,* vol. 2, National Council of Teachers of English, Appleton-Century-Crofts, Inc., New York, 1954.

Hildreth, Gertrude: *Teaching Reading,* Holt, Rinehart and Winston, Inc., New York, 1958, chap. 24. Contains many practical suggestions for reading instruction of the gifted.

Hollingworth, Leta S.: Introduction to Biography for Young Children Who Test above 150 I.Q., *Teachers College Record,* 26:277–287, 1924.

Larrick, Nancy: *Parents' Guide to Children's Reading,* Doubleday & Company, Inc., Garden City, N.Y., 1958. An excellent source of information about children's literature.

Laycock, Samuel R.: *Gifted Children: A Handbook for the Classroom Teacher,* The Copp-Clark Publishing Company, Toronto, Canada, 1957, chap. 8.

Munson, Grace: Adjusting the Reading Program to the Gifted Child, *Exceptional Children,* 11:45–48, 1944.

Reading and the Gifted Child, *The Reading Teacher,* 9, 1956. Contains many practical suggestions for instruction.

Robinson, Helen M. (ed.): *Promoting Maximal Reading Growth among Able Learners,* Supplementary Educational Monographs, no. 81, The University of Chicago Press, Chicago, 1954.

The School Library and the Gifted Child, *American Library Association Bulletin,* 52:73–152, 1958.

Strang, Ruth: *Helping Your Gifted Child,* E. P. Dutton & Co., Inc., New York, 1960. Contains a list of children's book clubs.

Other excellent professional texts are listed throughout this chapter, following discussion of the particular subject-matter area to which they have especial relevancy. They contain many suggestions for teaching bright and talented pupils.

Written Expression

Written expression should be related to ongoing curriculum units in all subject areas instead of being limited to formal theme writing in language or English classes. The gifted child will also be doing extensive writing as an expression of his special interests. Creative writing offers an outlet for the child who enjoys putting his original ideas on paper in the form of stories, poems, plays, magazine articles, and reports. Writing not only is satisfying to the young student, but also serves to enliven and enrich class projects. It is, as well, valuable preparation for adult years, whether or not the student becomes a writer by profession. From the gifted who make an early start in expressive writing come the story writers, the producers of literature, along with the specialists in reportorial and scientific writing.

Written expression is related to reading because the ability to write grows with extensive reading. In fact, a child's interest in expressive writing may grow out of his pleasure in reading good literature.

A first-grade teacher in suburban New York was convinced that her pupils could enjoy expressive writing as soon as they gained a little skill in writing and spelling. By taking advantage of every opportunity that would evoke original oral expression, the teacher prepared the children to express their ideas in writing, first as a group and then individually. Initially, the teacher wrote the children's exclamations, sentences, and rhymes on the blackboard, often using colored crayons to express the mood of the moment. Soon the children were able to do a little writing for themselves with help on spelling from the teacher or a classmate. The story or poem was rexographed, and copies were given to each child to illustrate and then to bind in a little book. The finished booklets were placed on display in the classroom, and finally taken home to share with parents.

Here are some of the situations the teacher used to draw out the children's ideas in preparation for expressive writing:

What we did last summer, and what we liked about the summer months

The changing season, the falling leaves, getting ready for winter

Halloween, pumpkins, ghosts and witches, and other scary things

Why we celebrate Thanksgiving, and what we did during this holiday

The first snow

Getting reading for the Christmas party

Some experiments with air

Through these lively, meaningful activities every phase of language experience was developed simultaneously—reading, writing, and oral expression.

CORRECT FORM IN WRITING

Should the budding author be permitted to go ahead even though his spelling, grammar, and punctuation are scarcely equal to his verbal fluency? The child whose alert mind overflows with original ideas may find drills in spelling, punctuation, capitalization, and sentence structure annoyingly tedious. Practicing spelling seems remote from his objectives in writing.

The habits of writing freely and expressively cannot wait for perfection in the conventions of written form. Young children become discouraged if mechanics are overstressed. The mechanics are bound to improve if the child persists in writing freely, recognizes the need of improvement, and responds to the teacher's constructive criticism.

The question is how to help the child improve in the mechanics (including handwriting) without killing his interest in expressing his thoughts freely on paper. Meaningless drill for which a bright child sees no purpose becomes a bugbear.

Drill for improvement in written expression should be planned on an individual or small-group basis. The children make something of a game of it to see who can win the contest. All drill for skill should be related to the actual job of writing. There should be frequent opportunity for written expression in connection with school studies. The teacher should give the child constructive criticism, pointing out how he is improving and noting the items that need correction. The child does not need to recopy every paper; instead, he should tackle another writing task, attempting to use what he has learned in a new situation.

Spelling improves when the child feels a real need to write something correctly. Teachers should avoid the practice of assigning a bright achiever the spelling lists for the next grade. It is better to have him keep his own individual list of words he needs to write but cannot spell.

The gifted, along with the others, need to work on vocabulary enrichment. The use of the dictionary for finding the right word, for looking up the correct spelling, and for syllabification, is all a part of language study.

The children themselves will have good ideas to offer about games and drills to make practice more interesting. They can invent their own vocabulary and spelling games. Crossword puzzles help with spelling and word meanings. The bright child can use his ingenuity in making up word puzzles for his classmates to work out.

For more detail on the subject of written expression, the reader is referred to the excellent professional books and articles listed below.

Applegate, Mauree: *Easy in English,* Harper & Row, Publishers, Incorporated, New York, 1960.

Baldwin, Michael: *Poetry without Tears,* Routledge & Kegan Paul, Ltd., London, 1959.

Burrows, Alvina T.: *Teaching Composition: What Research Says to the Teacher,* Bulletin no. 18, Department of Classroom Teachers, American Educational Research Association of the National Education Association, Washington, D.C., 1959.

Burrows, Alvina T., Doris C. Jackson, and Dorothy O. Saunders: *They All Want to Write: Written English in the Elementary School,* 3d ed., Holt, Rinehart and Winston, Inc., New York, 1964.

Cole, Natalie R.: *The Arts in the Classroom,* The John Day Company, Inc., New York, 1940.

Jackson, Doris: Poetry-making with Children, *Elementary English,* 20:129–134, 1943.

Marksberry, Mary Lee: *Foundation of Creativity,* Harper & Row, Publishers, Incorporated, New York, 1963.

Strickland, Ruth G.: *The Language Arts in the Elementary School,* D. C. Heath and Company, Boston, 1957.

Weil, Truda T., and Margaret B. Parke: *Developing Children's Power of Self-expression through Writing,* Curriculum Bulletin 1952–1953 Series, no. 2, Board of Education of the City of New York, 1953.

Wilt, Miriam E.: *Creativity in the Elementary School,* Appleton-Century-Crofts, Inc., New York, 1959.

The Social Studies

The social studies—history, geography, and civics—occupy a large block of school time in the elementary grades because of the range of problems these studies introduce that have a bearing on present-day life. The social studies begin in the primary grades with the study of common things and their use, of family relationships, of life in the community and the larger world. In schools that follow a unit plan of curriculum organization, the social studies unit furnishes more good themes than any other. Science is a close second, although it is often difficult to determine where social studies leave off and science projects begin. The subjects of housing and climate, for example, can scarcely be confined to social studies or science, but must be related to both.

A UNIT ON "THE FAR EAST"

In a summer demonstration class for gifted children, grades 4 to 6, conducted by Dr. Hilary Gold at Brooklyn College, New York, the unit theme chosen for study was "The Far East" (1962).[2] This theme covered many aspects of life in the Far East and encompassed a number of subject-matter areas in addition to the social studies. The focus of instruction was on enrichment of meanings and understanding, with freedom for creative expression.

[2] Hilary Gold, Report on the Practicum: The Psychology and Education of the Gifted, unpublished staff report, Brooklyn College, New York, 1962.

The keynote of the program was flexibility. Instead of everything being rigidly planned in advance, plans for activities evolved during the term. The children had freedom of choice in selecting individual topics for study and in working out their own ideas for research projects. When the teacher asked the class for ideas on the study theme, the children's interests covered art, music, religion, symbolism, geography, food, clothing, shelter, and other topics.

Highlights of the children's study of the Far East included a visit by two members of the Indonesian consulate, an exploration of Chinatown, and a trip to the Chinese museum. A presentation was given by a member of the consulate of India, followed by a demonstration and interpretation of Indian dances. There was a trip to the Japanese garden in the Brooklyn Botanical Gardens and a visit to exhibits at the Brooklyn Museum of Art. A number of films, filmstrips, and recordings were used to enrich the program. The showing of *Child across the Sea,* a film about Hong Kong, was accompanied by discussion led by a junior high school student who had recently come to the United States from the Far East. Japanese visitors gave a demonstration of traditional Japanese music. Before the end of the month, the children were writing haiku, the seventeen-syllable Japanese poems.

Individual and group reports were given of the research studies. One report was accompanied by a demonstration of oriental music, a Kabuki dance. A report on the evolution of rocketry required the use of the college athletic field for a demonstration. Other activities were not necessarily related to the study of Asia. One day the author of a popular book for children addressed the class.

At the end of the term the pupils were asked, "How is summer school [the demonstration class] different from regular school?" Responses were: more interesting, 11; more fun, 7; liked working with individual teachers (the graduate students associated with the demonstration class), 6; more freedom, 5; open discussions, 4; don't have to wait for other children, 4; a more creative program, 1.

ECONOMICS

One aspect of social studies that can be developed with bright children in the elementary school and related to work in mathematics is economics—the study of our resources and their efficient use. This can begin with the study of the care of our possessions, the sources of the things we own and buy, the question of good purchasing, and move on to more advanced problems. A bright child who chooses such a topic for an independent project will educate himself, the class, even the teacher, perhaps, with the results of his research on consumer buying or his studies of world trade.

In one social studies class, the textbook selection for the lesson related the story of a man who went West in pioneering days and took up a farm of 240 acres for which he paid $25 an acre. The questions that arose were: How much money did the farmer have to pay for his land? Was this a good deal of money or very little? What would you have to pay for the same farm land today? What does farm land cost in our part of the country?

For further teaching suggestions, see the references below.

Gavian, Ruth (ed.): *The Social Education of the Academically Talented,* National Council for the Social Studies, Curriculum Bulletin 10, Washington, D.C., 1958.

Goldberg, Janice B.: Enrichment in Social Studies in an Enriched School, *Elementary School Journal,* 61:418–423, 1961. Describes ways of enriching the social studies for the gifted student in the elementary school.

Kenworthy, Leonard S.: *Guide to Teaching the Social Studies,* Wadsworth Press, San Francisco, Calif., 1962.

Michaelis, John U.: *Social Studies for Children in a Democracy,* 3d ed., Prentice-Hall, Inc., Englewood Cliffs, N.J., 1963.

Seegers, J. Conrad: Teaching Bright Children, *Elementary School Journal,* 49:511–515, 1949.

Arithmetic and Mathematics

Arithmetic reasoning problems offer a good test of a child's general reasoning ability. For bright children in the elementary school, mathematics is more of a specialty than a skill such as reading or written expression. Some highly intelligent children develop no interest in mathematics and never do well in it; more often these nonmathematical children are girls, largely because of differences in the social conditioning of boys and girls.

Arithmetic is a basic skill that all must acquire for dealing with numerical computation in daily life; but mathematics for the gifted child is far more than a drill subject. It is a mode of thought, a tool for scientific thinking. Therefore, in teaching mathematics to bright elementary school pupils, teachers stress the discovery aspect, the meaning and understanding of principles.

The gifted child uses his intelligence when he searches out facts for himself in arithmetic and solves problems in various ways, getting answers through shortcuts, without having to put everything down on paper. He invents his own problems and number games, thinks up new ways to check answers, works out applications of arithmetic processes. He uses intelligence in estimating and approximating answers; for example, in decimals, he estimates the approximate answer and uses the approximation as a guide in pointing off. He is ready to think about the meaning of proportion before the rest of the class has come to the topic. In working on this topic, he is guided in understanding the meaning of proportion and its practical applications, instead of spending all his practice time on computation problems.

Mathematics begins even in the kindergarten. When a child told the teacher he was out of long blocks, another tot directed, "Take two short blocks. They make one long one." Bright children in the elementary grades accomplish remarkable feats in arithmetic. A nine-year-old was confronted with a special mathematics problem around Christmas time. He helped his mother cut out a gingerbread house but wanted one for himself one-fourth the size of the large one. This kept his active mind busy with mathematics for the entire morning. Next he wanted to know how many *hours* old he was. More lengthy computation.

Ten-year-old Mary, who was asked to add $29 + 28 + 27$, said after a moment without benefit of paper and pencil, $90 - 6 = 84$. Another child showed quick understanding of fractions and decimals: $3.5 \times .4$ will be less than 2 because .4 is less than $\frac{1}{2}$, he observed.

SUGGESTIONS FOR TEACHING THE BRIGHT MATHEMATICS STUDENT

What should be done about the pupil who quickly moves ahead of his age or grade group in arithmetic? How can the study of mathematics be enriched in the elementary school? The abler pupils should proceed to more advanced levels of mathematical operations and make use of mathematics wherever possible in ongoing class projects. Assigning more long-division problems is not enrichment, but trying out a new method of getting the answer or finding shortcuts to checking answers and applying the long-division process to new problems are challenging tasks for the bright student.

Dr. Charlotte Junge has made the following recommendations for teachers who want to further the abilities and interests of the gifted mathematics student in the elementary school:

1. Have the pupil diagram problems and show proof of solutions. This requires that the child have a clear mental picture of textbook problems.

2. Provide opportunities for the child to investigate topics in the encyclopedia and other reference books:

The weather	Wages, credit, insurance
The globe	Aviation flights
Fractions in industry	Measuring instruments in cars
Scores in sports	Money and foreign exchange

3. Provide problems requiring the gathering, summarizing, and analyzing of data.

4. Prepare statements of actual problems arising in school, at home, in shops, and indicate how to solve them.

5. Do mental problem solving; that is, work problems without pencil and paper. Estimate answers instead of working the problems out.

6. Make use of maps, charts, graphs, tables, diagrams, and solve problems using these devices.

7. Give exercises to develop the mathematics vocabulary and to fix it in mind.

8. Relate the work in arithmetic to science problems in the social studies, art, and music. The gifted student can help others with these problems.

9. Use number tricks and puzzles.

10. Help the student learn to attack all sorts of problems such as those which arise in constructing a raft that will float, a kite that will sail, a bird feeding station, or learning how to predict the weather.[3]

Arithmetic can be enriched through experimentation with numbers, measurement, geometry. The pupils may enjoy constructing number tables, a slide rule, number blocks for the demonstration of fractions and other arithmetic concepts.

The pupils bring in mathematics items and problems found in newspapers or magazine articles. A gifted child may devise his own experiments for determining the ratio of the diameter to the circumference of a circle; he may make use of mathematics, geometry, and science through constructing a hexagonal kite. A gifted "cluster" in the class may study banking, use computing machines, do mathematics games and puzzles, or make graphs while the rest of the class is doing the regular assignment. Sixth graders who are accelerated in mathematics may form a small group for studying algebra.

The abacus, the Cuisenaire blocks, and other devices for learning about the number system through objects aid the younger

---

[3] Charlotte Junge, The Gifted Ones: How Shall We Know Them? *The Arithmetic Teacher,* vol. 4, pp. 41–46, 1957. Used by the permission of the author and publisher.

bright child in discovering arithmetic facts through his own experiments instead of merely memorizing the number facts. (See references to the Cuisenaire method and the Catherine Stern's methods on page 264.)

Bright children can use a simple slide rule for addition and subtraction as early as grade 1. At the Hunter Elementary School, the children check their answers with commercial computers after first computing answers with pencil and paper.

A special mathematics program for pupils who complete the regular course of study before the end of the sixth grade has been worked out in Norwalk, Connecticut. The program avoids repetition of drills in fundamentals the children have already mastered, and at the same time avoids overlap with the program of the high school. Under the direction of their regular teachers, the students spend three periods each week studying a different approach to many of the processes of arithmetic. Another period, taught by a special mathematics teacher, carries the students into new areas of mathematical thinking. They are encouraged to make discoveries about topics that are new to them and to look for the mathematics implication of problems that come up in other studies and in daily life. Students are admitted to the group on the basis of tests indicating their arithmetic proficiency. One period a week is spent working on skills that tests have indicated need review. In Santa Barbara, California, the gifted pupils benefited from individualized arithmetic drill followed by a small-team work session.

The "scavenger hunts" described by Parsons appeal to the children's love of games and the chance to team up with a partner and add zest to problem solving and fact finding in arithmetic and other school studies (1961). The children look up the information they are seeking in the *Information Please Almanac* or a standard encyclopedia.

For more information on enrichment of mathematics teaching for the gifted, see the excellent modern professional books and articles for teachers on this subject among the references on page 264).

Science

Elementary school children usually show marked enthusiasm for science studies. Frequently, interest in science coincides with interest in mathematics. Formerly, elementary school children had to satisfy their scientific curiosity largely through their own home laboratory experiments, but today science has become a regular part of the curriculum. Investigations have proved that science concepts presented in simple terms and derived from everyday experience can be comprehended by all children of elementary school age. Those with special ability move rapidly into the vast world of scientific phenomena.

It is possible to spot the child who has special talent in science and mathematics as early as age ten or eleven. This child is identified by his high IQ, his skill and interest in reading, his general and technical vocabulary. He shows intellectual curiosity and has considerable scientific knowledge. His interest in science topics is quite obvious. Lesser and Davis have devised a series of tests for the identification of science talent as early as the third grade (see the references at the end of this section).

Science studies for the talented begin when very young children observe the changing seasons, ice and snow, growing plants, animals, the moon and stars, the operation of machinery. Exceptional interest is manifested in the child's avid questioning.

In the elementary school, a child begins forming the attitudes of a scientist by developing an inquiring mind, being open-minded, learning to use the scientist's method in experimental problem solving, making careful plans before beginning to work, learning the difference between facts, opinions, and unfounded beliefs, and recognizing the value of expert opinion. The emphasis is not so much on storing up factual information as on science as a way of thinking, starting with exploration and study of scientific phenomena. Teachers are advised that important things for a young scientist to learn are the ability to read scientific material, to apply mathematical processes in problem solving, and to make effective reports.

Such topics as the weather, the earth in space, living things, electricity, transportation—all offer limitless experimentation for the science-talented youngster. Nature-study trips taken any time of year, beginning in the lowest grades, introduce children to the world of nature; even the child who makes his own explorations gains added incentive and understanding from going on teacher-guided trips.

Children with a special interest in science should have simple laboratory work with apparatus they can obtain or make for themselves. School projects in science may carry over to the home laboratory; in turn, home projects may be brought to school. A school science fair gives the pupils an outlet for their special interests.

The best results are obtained in schools that employ a science teacher or a consultant trained for elementary school work. Science experts in the community, e.g., an astronomer, a chemist, or a biologist, may be willing to advise the children on their projects.

The more capable students are ready for serious work in science much earlier than we used to think. In the Hicksville, New York, elementary schools a three-year sequence in chemistry has been developed for grades 4 through 6, which includes preliminary experiments and study of principles, and is followed by a two-year sequence in the junior high school. In this program, test results at the end of the sixth grade showed that 54 of the 93 sixth-grade pupils who had completed the three-year sequence did as well as or better than the median grade for high school seniors on a national basis. About 9 per cent of the sixth graders were at the 90th to 94th percentile on the test.

In the Dual Progress plan originated by Stoddard, selected elementary school children meet with the science coordinator in afternoon groups (1961, in references at end of chapter).

In New York City, museums have lecture programs, movie showings, and Saturday morning classes for elementary school children interested in science. One program offered at the Hayden Planetarium was entitled "Astronomy in the News."

The child who enjoys reading has a wide array of science books to choose from. The biographies of scientists, explorers, discoverers, and inventors furnish enrichment as well as inspiration to young scientists. The newer textbooks also contain material that is suitable for enriching science studies. For example, in the series by Schneider and Schneider for kindergarten through the eighth grade, published by D. C. Heath and Company, every unit contains stimulating problems for the more-able pupil.

Under the auspices of the American Association for the Advancement of Science, a traveling elementary school library science service was set up in 1957 comparable to similar provisions made earlier for the high school. Participation is limited to those schools with central library collections in the school building.

Nature and Science is a periodical for children in the middle elementary grades, published by the American Museum of Natural History, New York.

In the Soviet Union children become interested in science early through reading popular books for juveniles on science. Sci-

ence films are shown everywhere. Young naturalists, future
mechanics, chemists, and mathematicians join afterschool science
centers and clubs.

The reader is referred to the following list of excellent books
and articles on enrichment of science and mathematics in the
elementary school:

Arey, Charles K.: *Science Experiments for Elementary Schools,* rev. ed., Bureau
of Publications, Teachers College, New York, 1960.

Cuisenaire, G., and G. Gattegno: *Numbers in Color: A New Method of Teaching
Arithmetic in Primary Schools,* William Heinemann, Ltd., London, 1954.
(The Cuisenaire materials are obtainable from the Cuisenaire Company
of America, located in New York City.)

Junge, Charlotte, The Gifted Ones: How Shall We Know Them? *The Arithmetic
Teacher,* 4:41–46, 1957.

Lesser, Gerald S., Frederick B. Davis, and Lucille Nahemow: The Identification
of Gifted Elementary School School Children with Exceptional Scientific
Talent, *Educational and Psychological Measurement,* 22:349–364, 1962. Also
in *The Gifted Student,* U.S. Office of Education, Cooperative Research
Monograph no. 2, Washington, D.C., 1960, pp. 19–32.

Marshall, J. Stanley: Science in the Elementary School, chap. 5 in Louis A.
Fliegler (ed.), *Curriculum Planning for the Gifted,* Prentice-Hall, Inc.,
Englewood Cliffs, N. J., 1961.

Parsons, Cynthia: Unusual Arithmetic, *The Arithmetic Teacher,* 8:69–74, February,
1961.

Schneider, Herman, and Nina Schneider: *Elementary Science Series,* Grades
Kindergarten through Eight, D. C. Heath and Company. Boston.

Spitzer, Herbert: *Practical Classroom Problems in Enriching Arithmetic,* Houghton
Mifflin Company, Boston, 1956.

Stern, Catherine: *Children Discover Arithmetic,* Harper & Row, Publishers, Incorporated, New York, 1949.

UNESCO (comp.): *700 Science Experiments for Everyone,* Doubleday & Company, Inc., Garden City, N.Y., 1958.

Visner, Harold, and Adelaide Hechtlinger: *Simple Science Experiments for the
Elementary Grades,* Franklin Publishing Company, Palisade, N.J.

Foreign Languages

Sixty years ago, German, French, and Spanish were taught in
the elementary schools largely for their practical value in communities with a large foreign-speaking element. As this need de-
clined, foreign language instruction all but disappeared from the
elementary school curriculum. In the late 1940s a strong revival

of interest in teaching modern foreign languages developed and has gathered momentum each year; interest is especially high now, with the world situation calling for more people who are competent in at least one language besides their mother tongue.

The study of foreign languages in the elementary school has made marked gains since 1953, when it became a popular movement known as FLES (Foreign Language in the Elementary School) sponsored by the Modern Foreign Language Association. From a total of only 145 communities and fewer than 150,000 pupils in 1953, elementary school foreign language instruction now reaches over 8,000 communities and 1,250,000 pupils.

There are many issues involved in foreign language teaching in the elementary school. Pertinent questions are:

Is linguistic ability a special talent or an indication of high mental ability in general?

Does talent for language study require a high IQ?

Are there some children, not necessarily the most gifted intellectually, who have more language learning talent than others?

Should all the children study foreign languages or only the most talented?

How early should foreign language study begin?

What languages should be taught?

What methods of teaching should be followed?

Where shall we obtain teachers with the training for this work?

How should the children be selected for foreign language study?

How can instruction in a foreign language contribute most to the pupils' cultural appreciation?

There are problems involved in the continuity of foreign language study once it is begun as well as articulation between elementary and secondary school.

Usually the time available for foreign language study in the elementary school is not more than a brief period several times a week. Not much can be accomplished in periods lasting only fifteen to thirty minutes. Usually, too, there is a problem of correlating foreign language study with other topics and areas of the curriculum, for example, history and geography, art and music.

From their inception, the Major Work classes for gifted children in Cleveland, Ohio, have offered French as a second language. French was taught in the experimental elementary school classes for the gifted at Public School 165, New York City, in the 1920s and at Public School 208, Brooklyn, New York. In the Hunter

Elementary School, instruction is given in French, Italian, and German. At the Colfax School, Pittsburgh, there are classes in German.

The Desauze method of oral-auditory instruction developed for the Cleveland Major Work classes has been adopted in many elementary schools. When methods are highly informal, the children scarcely realize that they are learning a foreign language. At the Hunter School one day during recess, a child proposed to the group, "Let's play Italian."

Dunkel and Pillet have prepared a progress report on a five-year experiment in teaching French at the University of Chicago Elementary School (1962). The report contains information about language aptitude in relation to general brightness, and the teaching methods that were tried out.

PUBLIC SCHOOL PROGRAMS

In the larger cities where there are special classes for the gifted, foreign language study is usually begun by the fourth grade. New York City has approximately 6,000 intellectually gifted children in grades 4 through 6 who are enrolled in foreign language classes. Instruction is given in French, Spanish, and Italian by audio-lingual methods exclusively. In classes meeting three times a week, approximately 90 minutes a week is given to language lessons in grades 4 and 5, 100 minutes in grade 6. Public School 208 in Brooklyn has a well-equipped language laboratory for this work.

In some schools, children with special interest in foreign language study are formed into cluster groups or language study clubs meeting at convenient times of the day or on Saturday with trained language teachers. In the Stoddard Dual Progress plan, one of the afternoon classes that pupils may elect is foreign language study.

The public schools of Hicksville, New York, have an extensive program of foreign language instruction in the elementary schools for pupils in the highest level of a three-track system. Capable children begin the study of a foreign language in the first grade, either French, Spanish, Italian, or German. The same language is to be continued for twelve years, through high school. The expectation is that with early exposure to the language by the audio-oral method, followed by instruction in reading and writing beginning in the fourth grade, the student will be able to study foreign literature by the time he enters high school, reading foreign books in the original language.

These selected elementary school pupils spend twenty to thirty minutes a day, five days a week, in foreign language study. In 1962 there were 1,200 pupils, grades 1 to 6, in the program. Criteria set up for admission to the program are: an IQ of 120 or higher, ability to read at or above grade level, a favorable showing on the local foreign language aptitude test, and the classroom teacher's recommendation. The pupils must maintain language grades of 85 or higher to remain in the program.

A comparison study is now under way to determine the effectiveness of the Hicksville program, to discover whether there is an optimum grade level for beginning the program, and to ascertain the most suitable class size (Campbell, 1962). So far, boys have not done so well as girls in the program. Of the 46 per cent who drop out during the first three years, approximately two-thirds are boys. In a follow-up study of the Cleveland Major Work classes, some of the students, particularly boys, thought that the study of French in the elementary school was of doubtful value.

Schools are warned against introducing foreign language study without provision for a planned sequence of lessons over several years. Experts agree that a smattering of the language in the intermediate years when children have no out-of-school opportunity to use it may be a waste of time. If language study is begun one year and dropped the next or if after two years another language is introduced, the early learning may not be lasting. Results are unsatisfactory unless the teacher uses oral imitation methods, acting out and dramatizing the language study.

It seems rather absurd to push a child into foreign language study if he is a low achiever in his own language. Foreign language should be postponed until native language skills are well advanced; otherwise, the child may not become efficient in using any language.

One suggestion is that, instead of spending half an hour or more a day learning a foreign vocabulary, elementary school children should study *about* foreign languages as they work on themes in geography and history relating to people in foreign countries, their life and customs, music, arts, and crafts. Foreign language study can be introduced in word study and word building in connection with reading and oral and written expression. Where does a word such as "photograph" or "culinary" come from? Here is a tie-in with dictionary study.

While studying "Our Neighbors in Latin America," a sixth-grade social studies class at the Lincoln School of Teachers College,

New York, picked up many Spanish words and phrases. The children learned Spanish songs, gave a program requiring some use of Spanish, read articles and stories about Latin Americans, and had personal contacts with Spanish-speaking people. This might be termed "language readiness" rather than language study proper.

For futher information about FLES programs, see the excellent book by Andersson and the other publications listed below.

Andersson, Theodore: *The Teaching of Foreign Languages in the Elementary School*, D. C. Heath and Company, Boston, 1953.

Campbell, William J.: Foreign Languages in the Elementary School: *Report of the Metropolitan Association for the Study of the Gifted*, New York, 1962.

Dunkel, Harold B., and Roger A. Pillet: *French in the Elementary School*, The University of Chicago Press, Chicago, 1962.

Hildreth, Gertrude: Learning a Second Language in the Elementary Grades and High School, *Modern Language Journal*, 43:136–142, 1959.

Thompson, Elizabeth, and Arthur Hamalainen: *Foreign Language Teaching in the Elementary Schools*, Association for Supervision and Curriculum Development, Washington, D.C., 1958.

Art

Although artistic ability, as musical talent, depends upon certain capacities that appear to be inborn, there is overwhelming evidence that early experience under expert training is requisite for the emergence of high artistic talent. The clever eight-year-old paper tearer described in Chapter Three was the nephew of an art teacher, who, without giving the boy formal lessons, encouraged him to observe animals and to see things in proper proportions.

Art instruction in the elementary school is not intended to produce geniuses, but to give children an understanding of the meaning of art in life and the satisfaction that can come from artistic expression.

Through the centuries crafts work has been the folk art of the common people: rug weaving, wood carving, house decorations, embroidery, quilt making, and other practical art forms. Work in crafts should be a normal part of every child's education. For the gifted, crafts work is extremely valuable as a form of self-expression and as a physical outlet to offset bookishness. Art experience is a source of invention, as the children work with various media in painting, drawing, modeling, etc. The children's creative ideas are expressed in experimenting with cloth, printing, designing, weaving, lettering, and other art forms.

School instruction in the graphic arts can enhance the talents of the artistically gifted child only if it frees him for creative work instead of confining him to the teacher's models or textbook illustrations. Art experts urge safeguarding the budding artist from premature adult instruction. Artistic talent needs to ripen unhurriedly; otherwise, the results are superficial and false. The child's own ideas should take the lead in every form of art expression. A truly original child needs opportunity to experiment rather than formal instruction. A teacher who is willing to let the children experiment with art media fosters budding talent without jeopardizing their creative sensitivity. The main thing is to supply the needed materials and make the children feel comfortable about experimenting with their own ideas whether with ceramics or Japanese water color.

The children should practice art skills not only in art periods, but whenever they have occasion to use art media. Art study ties in with all phases of school study; for example, perspective and proportion make use of mathematical principles; color mixing ties in with science. In the larger schools, music and art teachers and the classroom teacher work together to make the children's art experiences and projects an integral part of regular school studies.

Art instruction may be provided outside of school for talented children. Classes are held at the Metropolitan Museum of Art in New York City, at the Corcoran Gallery in Washington, D.C., in Cleveland, and in other large cities. Services include instruction, art lectures, and museum visits.

Teachers will find a number of helpful books on teaching art in the elementary school, some which are listed at the end of the section on play making. Two of the newer books are those by Barkan and Jefferson.

Music

Parents and most teachers still cling to the notion that a child cannot be expected to go far in learning to sing or play an instrument unless he shows early talent. Actually, thousands of bright children have proved that this notion is false. A bright fourth-grade child who began to study the song flute quickly caught on to this simple instrument and went on to other instruments. The child's parents commented, "We didn't know he had any musical talent. He certainly didn't show it at home."

For the young, a sense of rhythm is perhaps the most important component in musical language, rhythm of sound and tone, the backbone of every musical composition. To convey this sense of rhythm, of variations in time patterns, is a basic requirement in musical education. Gifted young musicians, in contrast to average learners, either have an innate sense of rhythm or they have been precocious in developing it—hearing the rhythm of a train, a mother crooning, the workmen singing, the sledgehammer falling, etc. Expert musicians put the development of a keen sense of rhythm ahead of instruction in harmony and theory for children.

Composition can begin in the lowest grades, as the school beginners dance and tap out rhythms or try out simple melodies. These can be jotted down in a simple 1-2-3 notation by the teacher; before long, the children will be able to write them down themselves.

Music study for the gifted need not begin and end with dreary exercises. Here, as in every other phase of learning, children gain mastery over technical difficulties by learning to perform interesting little pieces or to sing happily or by listening to records that show how the music goes when good musicians perform.

Musical creativity takes the form of telling a story in music, creating original songs and dances, composing the themes and motifs for characters and scenes in a fairy tale or a space rocket story. Music, crafts, and science studies can be linked in projects in which children make simple musical instruments.

A notable example of creative music teaching in the elementary grades was the work done by Mrs. Satis N. Coleman, who introduced creative music at the Lincoln School, New York, many years ago. Even the younger children appreciated rhythms, bells, and all manner of instruments for making musical sounds. The talented youngsters wrote their own melodies, jotting down musical ideas in a simple musical notation demonstrated by the teacher. Upper-grade children made their own marimbas in the school workshop and then played them in groups or individually. For class projects, particularly for programs, children composed sound effects and song melodies.

At the Iowa State Teachers College Demonstration School, Cedar Falls, even kindergarten tots and primary school pupils learn to play real musical instruments, not toys, working in small groups.

Again, the reader is referred to the references at the end of the following section.

Play Making

Like all other forms of aesthetic expression, dramatization is a natural part of the child's play life, an outlet for phantasy, a source of invention and creative expression, an emotional experience, and a mode of learning. Informal creative dramatization is also a wonderful activity for enriching the meanings gained from books.

Relatively few of the children who show "dramatic talent" in the primary grades are going to become professional actors, movie stars, radio or TV personalities; but all can gain valuable lessons from impromptu performances that illustrate stories they have been reading or express their original ideas.

Dramatic expression in kindergarten and primary grades leads in the upper grades to play production. In creative dramatics, meaningful experiences are acted out by the younger children as they improvise their own dialogue and action. There is no plot and no audience except the rest of the class. The play may be entirely in pantomine.

The meaning of holidays is brought to life in the children's experiments with creative dramatics. Dramatizing the lives of famous people grows out of the study of biography. Through dramatization of foreign scenes, children gain a deeper understanding of people of other lands.

Bright children have more than enough ideas if only the teacher will encourage self-expression, and then make suggestions when help is requested. Instead of putting on stereotyped productions of commercial plays, children should exercise their ingenuity in thinking up plots, in writing their own scripts, in designing the costumes, scenery, and staging.

Teachers have discovered many values of puppetry and marionette plays as an outlet for creative thinking and linguistic expression. No one expects the puppets to be professional or the puppet play to be a finished production. Instead, puppetry is a simple device through which children of all ages can express their original ideas in language and dramatic play.

For more information on art, music, and dramatics for children, see the following publications:

Barkan, Manuel: *Through Art to Creativity: Art in the Elementary School Program,* Allyn and Bacon, Inc., Boston, 1960.

Cole, Natalie R.: *The Arts in the Classroom,* The John Day Company, Inc., New York, 1940.

Coleman, Satis N.: *Creative Music for Children,* Lewis E. Myers. Valparaiso, Ind., 1927.

Fox, Lillian M., and L. Thomas Hopkins: *Creative School Music,* Silver Burdett Company, Morristown, N.J., 1936.

Jefferson, Blanche: *Teaching Art to Children,* Allyn and Bacon, Inc., Boston, 1959.

Lewis, Hilda P.: *Art Education in the Elementary School: What Research Says to the Teacher.* Department of Classroom Teachers, American Educational Research Association of the National Education Association, Washington, D.C.

Löwenfeld, Viktor: *Creative and Mental Growth,* 3d ed., The Macmillan Company, New York, 1957.

Maazel, M.: What to Do about the Child Prodigy? *Étude,* 68:12–13, 60–61, 1950.

Mendelowitz, Daniel M.: *Children Are Artists,* 2d ed., Stanford University Press, Stanford, Calif., 1963.

Sheehy, Emma Dickson: *Children Discover Music and Dance,* Holt, Rinehart and Winston, Inc., New York, 1959.

Slade, Peter: *Child Drama,* University of London Press, Ltd., London, 1954.

Ward, Winifred: *Play Making with Children,* Appleton-Century-Crofts, Inc., New York, 1957.

References

Barbe, Walter B.: *As If the Chart Were Given,* Report of a Demonstration Project for Gifted County Elementary School Children, Division of Special Education, Columbus, Ohio, 1963.

Challenging the Able Learner, Curriculum Bulletins nos. 301 and 401, Cincinnati. Ohio, Public Schools.

Cutts, Norma E., and Nicholas Moseley: *Bright Children: A Guide for Parents,* G. P. Putnam's Sons, New York, 1953.

Cutts, Norma E., and Nicholas Moseley: *Providing for Individual Differences in the Elementary School,* Prentice-Hall, Inc., Englewood Cliffs, N.J., 1960.

Darrow, Helen Fisher, and R. Van Allen: *Independent Activities for Creative Learning: Practical Suggestions for Teaching,* no. 21, Bureau of Publications, Teachers College, Columbia University, New York, 1961.

Dunlap, James M.: Gifted Children in an Enriched Program, *Exceptional Children,* 21:136–137, 1955.

Durrell, Donald D. (ed.): Adapting Instruction to the Learning Needs of Children in the Intermediate Grades, *Journal of Education,* 142:2–78, 1959.

Durrell, Donald D., and Leonard Savignano, Jr.: Classroom Enrichment through Pupil Specialties, *Journal of Education,* 138:1–31, 1956.

Education for the Gifted: Fifty-seventh Yearbook of the National Society for the Study of Education, The University of Chicago Press, Chicago, 1958, p. 246.

Freese, Theron: The Challenge of the Gifted Child, *Educational Leadership,* 11:156–159, 1953.

Gallagher, James J., and Thora Crowder: The Adjustment of Gifted Children in the Regular Classroom, *Exceptional Children,* 23:306–312, 317–319, 1957.

Gray, W. S.: Education of the Gifted Child with Special Reference to Reading, *Elementary School Journal,* 42:736–744, 1942.

Greeman, Gladys: *Independent Work Periods,* Bulletin of the Association for Childhood Education, Washington, D.C., 1941.

Greenberg, Benjamin B., and Herbert B. Bruner: *Final Report of Public School 500 (Speyer School),* Board of Education of the City of New York, Division of Elementary Schools, 1941.

Hildreth, Gertrude: *Child Growth through Education,* The Ronald Press Company, New York, 1948.

Hildreth, Gertrude, Florence Brumbaugh, and Frank T. Wilson: *Educating Gifted Children in the Hunter College Elementary School,* Harper & Row, Publishers, Incorporated, New York, 1952.

Hollingworth, Leta S.: *Gifted Children: Their Nature and Nurture,* The Macmillan Company, New York, 1926.

Hughson, Arthur (ed.): *Providing for Our Gifted,* Bulletin 1961, Board of Education, New York City, 1961.

Huston, Isabelle C., and Isabel C. McClelland: Classroom Enrichment, *Education,* 80:161–163, 1959.

Laycock, Samuel R.: *Gifted Children: A Handbook for the Classroom Teacher,* The Copp-Clark Publishing Company, Toronto, Canada, 1957.

Lewis, Gertrude M.: *Educating the More Able Children in Grades Four, Five and Six,* U.S. Office of Education, Bulletin 1961, no. 1, U.S. Department of Health, Education and Welfare, Washington, D.C., 1961.

Maybury, Margaret W., and Gerald S. Lesser: Program for Gifted Children, *Elementary School Journal,* 64:94–101, 1963.

Mearns, Hughes: *Creative Power,* Doubleday & Company, Inc., New York, 1929.

Norris, Dorothy: Programs in Elementary Schools, chap. 11 in *Education for the Gifted: Fifty-seventh Yearbook of the National Society for the Study of Education,* part 2, The University of Chicago Press, Chicago, 1958.

Osburn, W. J., and B. J. Rohan: *Enriching the Curriculum for Gifted Children,* The Macmillan Company, New York, 1931.

Otto, Henry J. (ed.): *Curriculum Enrichment for Gifted Elementary School Children in Regular Classes,* University of Texas, Austin, Tex., 1955.

Rex, Buck R., Jr.: The Gifted Child in the Heterogeneous Class, *Exceptional Children,* 19:117–120, 1952.

Roberts, Helen E.: *Current Trends in the Education of the Gifted,* California State Department of Education, Sacramento, Calif., 1954.

Saunders, David C.: *Elementary Education and the Academically Talented Student,* National Education Association, Washington, D.C., 1961.

Schiefele, Marion: *The Gifted Child in the Regular Classroom,* Bureau of Publications, Teachers College, Columbia University, New York, 1953.

Stoddard, George D.: *The Dual Progress Plan: A New Philosophy and Program in Elementary Education,* Harper & Row, Publishers, Incorporated, New York, 1961.

Strang, Ruth: *Helping Your Gifted Child,* E. P. Dutton & Co., Inc., New York, 1960.

Sumption, Merle R., and Evelyn M. Luecking: *Education of the Gifted,* The Ronald Press Company, New York, 1960.

Washburne, Carleton: *Adjusting the School to the Child,* World Book Company, Tarrytown-on-Hudson, N.Y., 1932.

Wilson, Frank T.: Salvaging Gifted Students in Regular Classrooms, *Educational Administration and Supervision,* 41:462–466, 1955.

Chapter Ten

SCHOLASTIC ACCELERATION FOR BRIGHT STUDENTS: SOME ISSUES AND PROBLEMS

Gifted learners are by definition mentally advanced for their years, ready for more advanced studies than their more typical age-mates. They sometimes pose a problem for teachers, as was pointed out in Chapter Seven.

In the graded public school system children normally advance by annual promotion one grade a year. According to standard age-grade placement, children enter school at age six, finish the first six grades by age twelve, and graduate from senior high school by age eighteen. A few children have to repeat a grade, and fewer still skip one grade or more.

Gifted Children as School Laggards

Fifty years ago a noted educator, Dr. Leonard S. Ayres, observed that the true "laggards" in our schools were not the overage slow learners who had repeated a year or more, but the gifted children who were not being promoted rapidly enough. He found that mentally accelerated pupils were seldom advanced as far as their rapid development would warrant; grade placement was closer to their chronological ages than to their mental ages. Ayres contended that bright children were held back by the standard graded curriculum, uniform textbooks, and rigid promotion practices, and that age-grade stratification prevented the gifted from advancing according to their true mental potential.

Through the years, schools have followed conservative policies about promotion and grade advancement. A slow learner is more apt to be left back than a bright child to be put ahead. Dr. Terman's gifted children were accelerated in their studies by 40 per cent as measured by standard achievement tests, but in age-grade placement they were accelerated by not more than 25 per cent (1925). This finding was confirmed by both Hollingworth and Witty. Recent studies of age-grade status prove that the gifted tend to be "at grade" corresponding to life age but that their accomplishment is generally above the level of their grade placement.

The failure of bright children to advance in proportion to their mental acceleration was a matter of concern to Dr. Terman. He believed that the exceptionally bright student who is kept with his age group finds little to challenge his intelligence and may develop habits of laziness that later wreck his college career. He recommended that students with IQs of 135 or above should be advanced more rapidly through school so as to enter college by the age of seventeen or even sixteen.

Rapid Advancement

The term "acceleration" has commonly been applied to any means of advancing students through school faster than the standard pace of a year for each year of age. For a number of years Dr. Sidney L. Pressey has been urging educators to relate school advancement more closely to the intellectual level of the student (1949). He has led the movement urging more study of the problem of getting the bright through school at an accelerated rate.

Dr. Pressey's interest in this subject was aroused through studies of eminent persons who completed basic education early and produced their masterpieces in their thirties. The success of young people who finished school early has convinced him of the value of acceleration. He believes that superior students are capable of far more advancement in their studies than has been assumed, and he has characterized our fixed grade system as ridiculous. Some school people urge that the conventional plan of annual promotions be abandoned and each student be permitted to advance at his own pace from first grade through the university.

Authorities point out that we are needlessly wasting some of the best years of the bright student's life by prolonging his preparatory education unduly. Superior students in the top 10 to 15 per cent of the population should be able to complete the usual twelve years of schooling in ten years and be ready for college by the age of sixteen. The high school and college sequence could be cut down from eight to six years for a substantial proportion of high-ranking students without any serious loss to their education. About 20 per cent of all high school students should be able to complete the six years of junior and senior high school within five regular school years.

If even 5 per cent of school entrants completed grade school and high school in ten years, the estimated financial saving would be 163.5 million dollars, figuring from the basis of a school-entering population of 3.7 million children. The money saved would pay the salaries of superior teachers and counselors to advise gifted students and to individualize instruction.

RAPID SCHOOL PROGRESS OF NOTABLE PERSONS

Advocates of acceleration point out that few of the notables of history spent twelve years in elementary and secondary education. Jonathan Swift, who could read any chapter of the Bible at the age of three, matriculated at Trinity College, The University of Dublin, at the age of fifteen. Martin Luther, John Milton, Thomas Mann, Alexander Hamilton, Immanuel Kant, Sigmund Freud, and many other great men all finished school early.

Benjamin Rush, eminent physician and signer of the Declaration of Independence, graduated from Princeton at eighteen and became a professor at twenty-four. Scholastic records of many eminent Britishers show that they finished Oxford or Cambridge in their teens; they entered school early, had individual tutoring or made rapid progress through preparatory schools. The older private school tradition permitted students to go through school according to their ability to learn.

The distinguished writer Mark Van Doren is a good illustration of a gifted youth who went through school at an accelerated pace without experiencing any handicap. The story is told in his autobiography. As the result of entering grade school early and skipping fourth grade, the boy entered a four-year Illinois high school at the age of twelve, wearing short pants in an era when such gear was a differential age symbol. In high school he devoured academic courses, made many friends, all older than himself, and led an active social life. Although he spent most of his free time with older boys, he was a leader of the group, and his initiative sparked most of their fun and plans. In his senior year he was elected to the senior honor society, edited the school magazine, and became president of the senior class.

Dr. Harold Brown, high-ranking science authority at the Pentagon, graduated from the Bronx High School of Science at the age of fifteen, then graduated from college at seventeen, winning half the awards for scholarship at the same time.

CASES OF YOUNG ACCELERATES

High school seniors who win Westinghouse science contest awards and National Merit Scholarship competition awards tend to be "underage" for grade. A recent award winner in the American National Merit Scholarship competition is a high school senior of fifteen with special aptitude in mathematics. During his last year in high school, he was placed in charge of tutoring students in his school. Michael E. Lesk, a fifteen-year-old high school senior, made the top score among all competitors in the New York State Regents Examinations in 1961.

Brooklyn College has accepted a number of students from a neighboring high school before graduation. One of these students, a boy who entered college at the end of his junior year in high school, made a straight-A record in his freshman year.

Greta, who is completing the sixth grade at the age of 10 years, 8 months, is one of the recognized leaders in her class. This girl, who earned an IQ of 148 on the Stanford-Binet test, is reported to be ambitious and full of original ideas. She goes at a tremendous pace all the time, but sets high standards for herself and is eager to do a good job. She is far ahead of her class in arithmetic. One of her interests is writing original stories and illustrating them. Greta becomes impatient with the commonplace ideas of her classmates; for this reason she works best alone.

A bright, attractive girl known to the writer entered the ninth grade at the age of twelve. At this time she was physically mature, as tall as her mother, in excellent health, energetic, an accomplished musician, and interested in older boys. Although she disliked study, she proceeded through high school with no difficulty. She was socially popular and became accompanist for all major musical events of the school. On entering college at sixteen, she majored in Latin and French, maintaining a good scholastic record. Through four years in college she became accompanist for leading college musical events, organist in a local church, and a member of the girls' glee club and the debating society. Because of her good looks and social popularity, she carried off the May Queen honor in her junior year.

As early as 1919, able students at the University of Chicago junior-senior high school were able to take precollege training in five years instead of six; the more able were further advanced by taking special courses in their senior year in what was known as the junior college. Many of these students covered the senior high school year and the freshman college year in one, graduating two years ahead of schedule.

Students at the Lincoln School of Teachers College, Columbia University, averaged a median IQ of 121–122 and were about three-fourths of a year accelerated in school for chronological age. The brightest showed even more acceleration in age-grade placement. Many bright youths graduated from the Harris Townsend High School for gifted boys in New York City at the age of fifteen or sixteen and finished the City College of New York three years later.

Various Provisions for Acceleration

Some people have asked: Why not put bright students ahead instead of planning special programs for them? This solution is a simple and obvious one, but there are a number of additional ways in which the educational level of these children can be brought more nearly into line with their mental advancement. They can enter first grade early or be placed in a rapid-advancement class or section; they can take extra courses, even college courses, in high school. They can be allowed to move ahead on an individual basis in ungraded classes; and there can be short-term promotions in the lower grades and a lengthened school year. These are all means of acceleration.

Is enrichment of studies superior to acceleration? This is not a fair question because acceleration results in enrichment unless it is patently nothing more than skipping a grade. Enrichment and acceleration are not necessarily mutually exclusive educational practices. Acceleration of isolated bright students is chiefly by grade skipping or doubling up in schoolwork. Acceleration of groups is usually accomplished through rapid-advancement classes. In one school in New York City an entire fourth-grade class has been formed of "skipped" children.

Instead of accelerating the pupils, schools sometimes accelerate the children's studies by providing special classes, setting up activities in interest groups, devising programs of individual study, and other measures. One of the main objectives of early multiple-track plans was to move students through school at different rates.

Some special classes and rapid-advancement classes provide a program which ensures continuous acceleration through the grades. A child may save a year in the first three grades, a year in the upper elementary grades, or a year in junior high school, covering the usual grades in less time and even going beyond the regular work of these grades. Both in New York City and in Baltimore, Maryland, children in special progress classes in junior high school can cover three years' work in two.

THE DEBATE OVER ACCELERATION

Through the years the pros and cons of acceleration for rapid learners have been vigorously debated. School administrators have often been opposed to rapid advancement of brighter students. When Dr. Terman explored the attitudes of school people, he found that about half of all school administrators were in favor, but the other half were definitely opposed. In a survey made in 1940 by the National Education Association research division, only 12 to 15 per cent of the junior and senior high school principals responding believed that students of superior ability should complete the division in less time than average. The National Association of Secondary School Principals at first vigorously opposed the Ford Foundation plan of early admission to college on the ground that gifted students, as the others, needed a full four years in high school; but results have proved that when these students are carefully selected and fully prepared, they can take college in stride and even achieve outstanding success in their studies (Paschal, 1960).

The debate over acceleration for the gifted centers around two issues: the desirability of grade skipping and the social problems created when a gifted teen-ager is considerably younger than his classmates. There is widespread belief that a gifted child in a group or class of older students will become a social misfit, that getting out of high school and into college ahead of schedule will cause social and emotional imbalance. People become exercised over the occasional child prodigy who "blows up."

WHAT DOES RESEARCH SAY ABOUT RAPID ADVANCEMENT?

Administrative decisions about acceleration based on general opinion are less valuable than judgments based on factual evidence and the apprasial of individual cases. What are the facts? Terman reported that 84.9 per cent of his elementary school group had skipped at least one grade. Of the high school group, 43 per cent of the boys and 55 per cent of the girls had been accelerated, graduating from high school over a year ahead of average for California students (1947).

The following table shows the mean age at graduation for boys and girls as reported by Terman.

| | Mean Age | |
Graduated from	Boys	Girls
Eighth grade	13.10	12.10
High school	16.10	16.8
College	20.9	20.5

Studies reviewed by Dr. Terman convinced him that the dangers of maladjustment from rapid progress through school were less than had commonly been believed.

Follow-up studies prove that acceleration has little if any adverse effects on the children. Keys confirmed the fact that accelerated students did as good academic work and were as well adjusted socially as others going through school at the normal or standard rate (1938). Keys found that the young gifted students tended to surpass those of average age in school marks and in scholastic honors. The underage group equaled or surpassed the equally gifted control cases in participation in student activities. Keys concluded: Acceleration is favorable to social as well as to educational adjustment.

Morgan has collected considerable evidence on acceleration in the elementary school (1957). She reported that many gifted children could stand from one to two years' acceleration in age-grade status provided they were socially mature and could hold their own with older children. Morgan made an assessment of twenty-five bright children five years after twelve of them had been accelerated by one year. Comparisons between the accelerated and nonaccelerated children indicated that accelerates equaled non-accelerates in school achievement and surpassed them in academic distinction and social leadership. The accelerated also tended to have better emotional adjustment. The findings confirmed the adequacy of certain criteria previously determined by the author as predictors of subsequent achievement and adjustment. Morgan found that maladjustment of a gifted child was less often the result of grade acceleration than of personal traits. The child who lacked purpose and self-assurance would be a misfit under any circumstances.

As the result of studies of acceleration in New York City schools, Justman concluded that there were many advantages in acceleration for selected children and that difficulties were at a minimum (1954).

In Racine, Wisconsin, superior second-grade pupils were placed in the fourth grade following attendance at a special summer school. Outcomes at the end of the year showed that these children fared well compared with regular nonaccelerated pupils (Ripple, 1961). Elwood reported an experiment in accelerating gifted children in grades 4 to 7 in an eight-year elementary school. Those who were accelerated in groups had little difficulty in making normal social adjustments (1958). In another study, Moore found that students who graduated from high school at the age of fifteen maintained their academic supremacy throughout the college years, according to results of comprehensive examinations taken in the sophomore and senior years (1933).

Pressey was inclined to scoff at the "maladjustment bugaboo." His investigation at Ohio State University, 1939–1940, showed that 50 per cent of those entering at sixteen graduated, in contrast to 38 per cent of the eighteen-year-olds of equal ability who followed similar programs. The accelerates also seemed more successful in their subsequent careers (1949).

A study of the youngest Harvard College graduates in the years 1952 to 1957 proved that acceleration was most strongly associated with superior intelligence, natural science interests, and achievement motivation. The younger students had better academic records and received more honors. These findings have been confirmed by studies in other colleges and universities (Kogan, 1955).

Reports on experiments sponsored by the Fund for the Advancement of Education have proved that the performance of students entering college early is superior to that of regular-entrant matchees (1957). An additional year or two of growth and high school preparation did not put the regular college entrants ahead of the younger scholars. Through the years the fund's scholars have outranked the comparison students in the top tenth, fifth, and third of their classes. Some of the boys attending accelerated programs in the men's college mentioned that their chief trouble was "getting dates." Through the four years of college, however, they gradually gained in social acceptance. Bright girls sometimes admitted regret at having gotten into college early because they felt the need of more social maturity to participate fully in college life along with girls from one to three years older than themselves. On the whole, the students did not feel that they had begun college too early.

Research has shown a lack of correlation between achievement in a school subject and the amount of time a student devotes to it; that is, a student who studies little may actually make a better showing than one who studies a lot. The general belief is that speed and quality of learning are incompatible. The contrary is true. There is a substantial positive correlation between rate of learning and excellence. This was put to a test by Dr. Harry Passow and his associates of the Horace Mann–Lincoln Institute of Teachers College, Columbia University. In a study of mathematics teaching in the junior high schools of Cheltenham, Pennsylvania, rapid-progress pupils achieved high-quality work. Passow concluded that acceleration is actually one form of enrichment.

SOME QUESTIONS TO CONSIDER

What criteria serve to determine how much acceleration a particular child can sustain?

If there is evidence that two years can be saved in the bright student's educational program, where in his schooling should the time be saved?

What is the best age for entering high school if a student is obviously in advance of other children his age?

Every decision about rapid advancement must be an individual one, because every child is different. How much and when to accelerate will also depend on the provisions made for rapid learners in the school, whether there are special consultants to guide them and teachers who are experienced in working with them. A bright student would not ordinarily be placed at the level of his mental age, but somewhere in between his actual age and his mental age. For example, a ten-year-old who measures up to a fifteen-year mental level would not usually be placed with the fifteen-year-olds. A child with mental grasp ahead of his years is not identical with an older child of average aptitudes. An eight-year-old with a ten-year-old's mentality is still immature physically; his motor-muscular coordination is below that of the typical ten-year-old, and his firsthand life experience more limited.

There is wide diversity of practice from one community to another. In St. Louis, Missouri, there is no acceleration for rapid learners, but students enter high school and college with advanced standing in French, mathematics, and English.

RAW GRADE SKIPPING

Skipping refers to moving a pupil ahead one or more grades or part of a grade without his having done the work of the grade, thus giving him an extra promotion. Skipping a grade is the simplest way of bringing a mentally advanced child into closer alignment with his achievement and potential.

Abrupt grade skipping has always been open to question. In general, the practice is frowned upon; in some places it is prohibited by law. Skipping was fairly frequent some years ago, but it went out of style because it created problems for the school administration and because new ways were devised for rapid advancement of bright children. Generally, a fast-track plan or rapid-advancement class is considered superior to giving a double promotion. Skipping is more common in the elementary school than in high school where the students accelerate in terms of separate academic subjects.

Most authorities agree that skipping a pupil to a higher grade and then giving him the regular work of this grade is not the best arrangement even if he can handle the work. In mathematics, for example, the pupil might be better off doing original problem solving at his own level of experience in terms of his interests and insights.

Skipping may cause serious disjunction in the child's school studies and social contacts. Unless a child is well developed and mature, he may find himself out of place with children a year older. The most serious objection to grade skipping is that gaps in learning may result. The pupil may miss important concepts. Skipping is especially hazardous in this respect in the intermediate and upper elementary grades.

Another difficulty is that the work of an advanced grade may be too heavy. The pupil may find that he is actually behind the others in some subjects. A bright eight-year-old who was skipped from second to fourth grade because he was a good reader was pushed too fast. As a result, he became anxious and fearful, unable to do good work because he had trouble with advanced textbooks.

A Moderate Amount of Skipping   Witty and Wilkins summarized the literature on the subject and concluded that a moderate amount of grade skipping seemed justifiable (1933). Later on Trusler recommended more frequent grade skipping for children with IQ's of 125 and over (1949).

Klausmeier and Ripple sought to determine the effects of accelerating bright elementary school children who skipped from grade 2 to grade 4 at the end of the summer vacation (1962). No unfavorable academic, social, emotional, or physical correlates with the year's acceleration were observed. These findings were confirmed by Klausmeier, who made a follow-up study of the children when they were nearing the end of the fifth grade (1963).

Today, schools are reconsidering their conservative policies and prohibitions concerning grade skipping. Now with the use of comprehensive standard test data, school authorities can back up their recommendation either that a child is eligible for a double promotion or that he should not be skipped.

If a pupil in the elementary school has been skipped a grade or has entered a first-grade class ahead of the usual age, this acceleration may be all the adjustment that is needed to bring school tasks into line with the child's mental development.

Questions commonly asked regarding grade skipping are:

Under what circumstances should a child skip a grade?

At what point in his school career can he safely skip?

How much skipping can a child tolerate in the elementary school?

What type of child can successfully bridge over the skipped year or term?

Should a child ever skip more than one grade?

Under what circumstances is grade skipping not advisable even if the pupil is exceptionally bright?

Here again, the answers depend upon the age and traits of the child, his present accomplishments, the type of school he is attending, and the quality of the teaching. Skipping in the earlier grades is preferable if the child is ahead in reading. Usually he should not skip more than one year in the elementary school.

Children who have been skipped a term or a year may need some individual tutoring for certain subjects, especially basic skills they may have missed, for example, in arithmetic or English fundamentals.

EARLY ENTRANCE TO GRADE ONE

Should bright children be permitted to enter first grade ahead of the age schedule? In view of new light on the subject of readiness for school and increased interest in speeding up the progress of bright children, this question requires thoughtful consideration.

Occasionally five-year-old kindergartners are advanced immediately to the first grade. On entering kindergarten, Carl impressed the teacher as being exceptionally mature for a five-year-old. He was the largest of all the children and had already learned to read. After consultation with the parents, the teacher recommended that he be allowed to enter first grade immediately. The boy did well in school and is now a distinguished surgeon.

Most schools have rigid policies concerning the minimum chronological age at school entrance. Unless a child reaches six by a specified date shortly after the fall term begins, he is ineligible for grade 1 until the next term or school year begins. These school statutes serve to bar the entrance of children who are too immature and to restrict the age range of the school entrants.

Elementary school people have been experimenting with early admission to first grade for children who are substantially ahead of their years in all-around mental, social, and physical development. A child whose sixth birthday comes a little too late for the minimum statutory first-grade admission age can save a year if he is sufficiently mature for classification with the six-year-olds. In the first grade he will be placed more nearly with his mental equals. One advantage of getting bright children into school early is that this may take care of the need for grade skipping later on. Studies have shown that bright children do well both academically and socially when they are admitted to school early.

Worcester has been a strong advocate of advanced placement in first grade (1956). He recommends this practice in individual cases of children who show all-around maturity comparable to that of typical school beginners.

On September 1 of a given year the median age of first-grade entrants will normally be around six years and three months, with the youngest about five years and nine months, and the oldest about six years and nine months. Since in these early years every month marks a substantial increment in the child's mental and psycho-motor development, the question of early admission for a child less than five years and nine months old must be decided on an individual basis. The recommendation is that admission standards for grade 1 include special provisions for bright children who are younger than average.

For early admission to the first grade a child should be mentally mature for his age, as shown by readiness for learning to read and write; he should be above average in muscular coordination and show the linguistic capabilities of a typical six-year-old.

In the Nebraska studies, children were admitted to first grade as early as age five years, three months, when the results of an individual intelligence test indicated that the mental age was fully a year ahead of chronological age. Children who entered first grade early on this basis made good progress on the whole (Miller, 1957).

A Mature Kindergartner   A child below the minimum entrance age for grade 1 but with more maturity than the typical kindergartner is illustrated in the case of Julie, whose birthday falls on March 1. Since she was only five-and-a-half at the beginning of school in September and the school statutes required at least five years, eight months, for first-grade entrance, the child was placed in kindergarten. There the teacher found her to be a thoroughly delightful child with the maturity of a second grader in many respects. Even as a baby, Julie wanted to do everything without assistance, such as feeding and dressing herself. The teacher observed that the child accomplished easily any task she set out to perform. She was mature socially as well as mentally and in excellent health.

Even prior to entering kindergarten, Julie had voluntarily practiced writing words, and shortly before her fifth birthday, she wrote a little letter to her parents away on vacation, with assistance in spelling the words she wanted to use. Recently (age five years, ten months) she wrote down all the words she could think of, then asked for others to round out the list to twenty words. Each word was spelled correctly, but the letters were a mixture of capitals and small print. During the summer a teacher helped with reading at the child's insistence. In learning to read, she showed quick grasp of the principles of sounding and other clues to words, and was able to use this knowledge in story reading. Now she is in the fourth book of a primary reader series, but is ambitious to finish the series so that she can read something more interesting, such as *The Wizard of Oz*. Julie enjoys recognizing the neighborhood signs containing familiar words.

This child has also made progress in arithmetic largely on her own initiative. She solves easily the simple problems in addition, subtraction, and multiplication that people write down for her. Not only is the work done correctly and neatly, but the child applies her arithmetic knowledge in real-life situations. Julie paints freely and likes to explain the ideas in her paintings. She has also picked up some knowledge of piano from her older sister.

This agreeable youngster is well liked by everyone because of her natural charm and tact. Rather than offend an opponent who is apt to lose a game, she will make intentional errors during the play. "So that the other person won't feel so bad" is her explanation. She compliments other children on their paintings to make them feel good, regardless of the quality of the production. Children enjoy her company and flock to her; visiting with her friends is, in fact, a favorite pastime. Away from home, Julie is happy and gets along with everyone. At summer day camp last year she was voted "best all-around camper," and received a handsome trophy. Should this child be put ahead into first grade? Her parents say they are reluctant to push her because she is happy and fully occupied with her own self-initiated studies. Perhaps they will approve of a skip next term when Julie is scheduled to enter the first grade.

Objective Standards   In schools where early entrance is permitted, objective standards have usually been set in order to avoid the charge of favoritism. The requirement may be an IQ of 120, a mental age of six and a half or seven, and a certain minimum chronological age, perhaps five and a half, in order to exclude "mere babies." The use of individual intelligence tests such as the Stanford-Binet supplements the teacher's judgment in screening underage children for early admission.

The New York City public schools permit early admission of children who prove to be mentally accelerated according to tests (IQ at least 120), who are in excellent physical condition and able to make satisfactory social adjustments in a class of six-year-old beginners.

Table 10 (page 156) shows the mental age corresponding to a given chronological age for children of various IQ levels. For a five-year-old with an IQ of 120, the corresponding mental age is six years; for a child who is five and a half with an IQ of 120, the mental age is over six and a half.

A review of studies on early school admissions of exceptional children is presented in the report by Reynolds (1962).

EARLY ENTRANCE TO KINDERGARTEN

Related to the question of early entrance to grade 1 is the proposal to admit to kindergarten bright children who are below the regulation age of five years. Birch's study in Pittsburgh (1954) gave strong evidence of good progress and adjustment when younger than average bright children were admitted to kindergarten. Birch listed five advantages of accelerating at the beginning of kindergarten and first grade.

Hobson's study of 550 children in Brookline, Massachusetts, admitted to kindergarten early proved that they retained their superiority through high school (1948). Children who entered kindergarten and first grade early showed favorable adjustment according to a study of Hamalainen (1952). Bright children have also entered kindergarten early in Nebraska with good results (Worcester, 1956).

ADVANCED PLACEMENT OF SCHOOL BEGINNERS

Advanced placement, or skipping part of the first year fairly near the beginning of the term, is another means of bringing school experience more nearly into line with the mature development of a bright beginner, provided the child has already made a beginning in reading, writing, and numbers. Children who have been to kindergarten, who are fully six, and show all-around maturity can safely be accelerated at this point. With short-period promotion a child stays only a month or two or a few weeks in first grade and then is skipped ahead to second grade without losing an entire year in either grade.

Lynn is a mature six-year-old who is not only mentally accelerated but as large and mature physically as a child a year older. She learned to read in kindergarten. On entering first grade, she was promptly put into the second grade because the school had no other means of accommodating a child who was so far advanced on school entrance.

UNGRADED PRIMARY CLASSES

The ungraded primary class or "primary pool" makes it possible for rapid learners to save a year's time in the primary grades.

With this plan, grade distinctions are abolished in the first three grades, and pupils are grouped according to ability within the class; or separate classes are formed for brighter and slower learners. The bright complete the regular schedule in two years; the slow require four years. Mature children enrolled in the ungraded school have the advantage of joining a group with others of similar maturity during a continuous span of two or three years. Milwaukee has ungraded primary schools in which bright children can complete the primary school in four or five semesters, and then enter grade 4.

ABILITY GROUPING AND SPECIAL CLASSES

Acceleration through placement in a rapid-advancement section or special progress class is a means of challenging the rapid learner, while avoiding the disadvantages of grade skipping. Acceleration in rapid-learner classes, unlike grade skipping, does not leave gaps because the work is planned for continuous progress at a rapid pace. In some separate classes and "special-track" plans the children complete the work of one or more grades ahead of the regular schedule. In rapid-progress classes, time is saved by means of unit teaching, with integration of skills and subject matter.

Rapid-progress classes for the gifted in the elementary schools in New York and other cities telescope the work of grades 4 through 6 into a two-year sequence. In some communities the standard junior high school program of three years can now be completed in two, three, or four years, depending on the student's capacities and progress. In San Diego, California, there is carefully planned group acceleration of gifted junior high school children in grades 7 and 8.

Once children start on an accelerated program, they must continue with it; otherwise, new difficulties arise in readjusting to a regular program. If there are no rapid-progress classes in junior high school, and no special provisions for a gifted student beyond that point, pupils who have been in rapid-advance classes may be misfits in regular classes because they will be younger than the average student and well ahead in school achievement.

In the Mineola, New York, public schools, gifted pupils have been grouped together and accelerated by means of an eleven-month school year. From fifth grade onward, by attending three full school years and four weeks each summer for four summers, a group completed grades 5 through 8 in three years. A comparison study showed that the achievement of this group equaled that of a control group a year older. Parents expressed satisfaction with the program, but one difficulty was that teachers were inclined to treat these children exactly like those a year older.

The organization and work of special classes is described in Chapter Eleven.

RAPID PROGRESS IN HIGH SCHOOL

High school authorities are concerned about getting the ablest students through school at an optimum pace to prevent wasting their time and to give them an earlier start in college. Speeding up can be accomplished through permitting the student to carry an extra course, or permitting him to skip elementary work and go directly to more advanced studies in special subject fields. He can be placed in rapid-progress advanced-learning sections in academic studies such as mathematics, biology, or foreign languages. A two-, three-, or four-year sequence may be set up in mathematics or foreign language which the ablest students complete in less time than standard courses require.

In some cases, admission to honors courses results in speeding up the program in mathematics, science, foreign languages, and other subjects. In seminar courses, superior students progress at their own pace through independent study. A mature student may enroll in advanced courses for which colleges give exemption credit, take Saturday or summer courses for high school or college credit, or be tutored in special subjects such as Latin outside of school.

In the advanced-placement plan students take college subjects while still in high school, and on admission to college are given advanced standing. By taking analytic geometry and calculus in high school, students can enroll in second-year mathematics on entering college.

Rapid advancement is also possible through entering college after two years of senior high school instead of three without waiting for graduation.

A student may be exempted from certain required courses if he shows sufficient maturity. One bright boy in a Chicago high school carried two high school courses simultaneously at his own suggestion, attending the courses on alternate days.

Students who attend a college preparatory school where there are small groups and tutorial instruction, as well as individual guidance, move through school more rapidly than usual without any awkward breaks or gaps. Surveys prove that children in private schools tend to be accelerated almost a year compared with standard age-grade public school children, either because they enter school early or move along faster on an individual basis.

Programs of early admission to college and advanced placement are described more fully in Chapter Seventeen.

Advantages and Disadvantages of Acceleration

The advantages of acceleration may be summarized as follows:

Accelerating a child will bring the demands of his schoolwork more nearly into line with his capacities, and at the same time move him through school faster. Acceleration takes up some of the slack that occurs when the bright are given busywork to fill up their time. It holds students to a higher level of accomplishment and gives them more mental stimulation. With an accelerated study program there is more challenge for bright students at every step and less emotional frustration.

With accelerated progress a student can enter high school earlier where he has more challenging studies. There he has access to the books and equipment he needs for scholarly work and independent studies.

Advanced work provides more intellectual stimulation, a richer fare, and permits earlier specialization.

If an unusually gifted child is kept with his age-mates, he may find the work too easy and develop poor study habits. Although there has never been any conclusive proof that putting the bright ahead improves their marks or motivates superior achievement, there is no question that in a regular class with like-age children of ordinary ability they become bored and waste their time.

There is a financial saving both for the school and for parents when a rapid learner is able to finish school early.

More of the highly gifted accelerates remain in college and go on to graduate school.

One of the main arguments in favor of acceleration is that the student enters on graduate studies and his life career at an earlier age, and has a longer span of years for public service and creative work. Extra professional man-hours are thus released for the sciences, engineering, medicine, and other fields.

Acceleration of gifted children up to a maximum of two years when they are physically normal and well adjusted is not harmful; on the contrary, it may be beneficial. The opportunity of working with older students may improve their sense of purpose and responsibility.

The success of accelerates, according to Dr. Morgan and others, largely hinges on careful selection of those to be accelerated. If care is exercised in the selection of students, the danger of maladjustment is minimized. A sixteen-year-old girl who is now a senior in a New York academic high school reported that although she had been skipped a year in the elementary grades, she has never felt any ill effects from having been accelerated in this way. In her opinion, "It all depends on the individual student."

A considerable number of bright children can tolerate a year's rapid advancement by the time they are ready to enter high school, two years by the time they are ready for college, but only when other conditions are favorable to good adjustments at early graduation. For the child with an IQ of 130, one or two years of acceleration appear to be optimum.

The disadvantages of acceleration include the following:

In general, children are better off with their own age group. If a child goes ahead in a rapid-advancement class, he may first sense age differences on entering high school or college. When bright children are accelerated more than two years, problems tend to increase and eccentricities may become more marked. So here is the dilemma: If the student remains with his age-mates, he is misplaced mentally; if he goes ahead with older students who are more nearly his mental equals, he may become a misfit socially.

The chief danger in grade skipping is that gaps may be left in the pupil's skills and information. A young teacher reported that because she was bright in school, she skipped the second grade; this skip hampered her mastery of important processes in arithmetic; today she is still shaky in simple computation. Another bright student who was rapidly advanced through junior high school found that her knowledge of literature was inadequate as a foundation for advanced work.

One problem concerns the attitude of older children toward younger bright children in their classes, "the sharp little kids." In making a study of the social acceptance of accelerated and nonaccelerated boys, Ripple asked each student to name his five best friends in the class (1961). Nonaccelerated boys had higher social acceptance than accelerated boys. Other evidence on this point was given in Chapter Four.

Dr. Leta S. Hollingworth believed that the dangers of acceleration may have been exaggerated, but that the effect on the personality of the child could not be ignored. Certainly it is inadvisable to skip a child who would be disadvantaged because of his size or appearance, social immaturity, shyness or aloofness, no matter how high his IQ. The risk of becoming a social misfit may be too great a price to pay for a year or two saved in high school or college. In such cases, some sort of broadened program, with enrichment or extra studies, would be better than acceleration.

There is some evidence that the social and emotional problems created by rapid advancement in school are likely to be more serious around the onset of adolescence. The junior high school student who has been advanced in school may—in dress, manners, voice, and deportment—resemble his age-mates more than his present classmates, thus reducing his chance of social success. An underage high school student is in mortal fear of being dubbed a "baby" or a "little kid." He may be overlooked in the selection of leaders and feel frustrated in social situations; in the upper grades and high school, school leaders are more often chosen on the basis of physical size and social popularity than brains.

The tendency of some parents to push a child ahead to satisfy their own pride may do real harm, as case studies have proved. A student who skipped several terms in elementary school and another half year in high school graduated from high school at fifteen. This skipping was approved by his parents largely for prestige. After high school the youth floundered about in college and left at the end of a year and a half seriously confused. The boy had become overconfident and had not acquired the study habits and the ability to concentrate that college work requires.

Acceleration is considered more disadvantageous for girls in the adolescent years than for boys. Dr. Hedwig Pregler, principal of the Colfax School, Pittsburgh, believes that finishing high school at fifteen or sixteen is unfortunate for the bright girl who goes right on to college. Graduation at too early an age may leave youngsters confused and undecided as to what to do. Maturity brings confidence and better understanding of one's capacities.

Students themselves say they feel the adverse effects of acceleration most keenly in athletics and in the social life of high school and college. If the gifted youngster can "tolerate fools bravely" and not be disconcerted by the track stars and social queens, if he can find some compensation in high marks, he will have a reasonably satisfying school life.

Pupils in the Hunter College Elementary School have been advanced as much as a year or two years ahead of their normal age-grade status, but difficulty occurs when the children leave the school at the end of the sixth grade. They may find themselves much younger than the typical student in junior high school and, in spite of some remarkable qualities, have a tough time making all-around adjustment. Because of this problem, higher minimum age standards were set for each grade in the fall of 1961, six to nine months higher than the previous standards at the Hunter School.

A gifted child in a class of older students will have more difficulty learning anything that depends largely on motor skill—handwriting, sports, some of the work in arts and crafts—simply because he is younger.

College authorities do not consider advanced placement an unmixed blessing because students who have been given credit under this plan may have missed important areas of knowledge and show signs of immaturity.

Compressing the bright child's schoolwork may cause overstimulation and anxiety. Teachers and parents would prefer to give the children more time for growing instead of requiring them to spend so much time on textbook study. The total experience of living is important in the child's development, a process that cannot be hurried.

Another problem is that a high mental age as revealed by intelligence tests does not necessarily indicate that the student will learn, work, or achieve at school on that level. He may lack motivation for schoolwork because of outside interests or for other reasons. Furthermore, a bright student is not necessarily equally talented in all study areas.

Since acceleration through school signifies "brightness" and lends prestige, parents of nonaccelerated children object to this special distinction shown to a few.

The opponents of acceleration point out that there are other ways of bringing a child's schoolwork into line with his mental maturity without putting him ahead of his age group or moving him rapidly through school.

In conclusion, whether a child who is advanced for his years in school is advantaged or disadvantaged depends primarily on the traits and characteristics of the individual. The implication is that all decisions about accelerating students should be made on an individual basis in the light of reliable information about the particular student. Establishing wholesale policies for or against acceleration would seem to be unwise.

References

Birch, Jack W.: Early School Admission for Mentally Advanced Children, *Exceptional Children*, 21:84–87, 1954.

Bridging the Gap between School and College, Evaluation Report no. 1, The Fund for the Advancement of Education, New York, 1953.

Conant, James B.: *1958 Conference on the Academically Talented Student,* National Education Association, Washington, D.C., 1958.

Cutts, Norma E., and Nicholas Moseley: *Teaching the Bright and Gifted,* Prentice-Hall, Inc., Engelwood Cliffs, N. J., 1957.

Elwood, Clarence: Acceleration of the Gifted, *Gifted Child Quarterly,* 2:21–23, 1958.

Hamalainen, A. E.: Kindergarten-Primary Entrance Age in Relation to Later School Adjustment, *Elementary School Journal,* 52:406–411, 1952.

Hobson, J. R.: Mental Age As a Workable Criterion for School Admission, *Elementary School Journal,* 48:312–321, 1948.

Hollingworth, Leta S.: *Gifted Children: Their Nature and Nurture,* The Macmillan Company, New York, 1926.

Individualizing Instruction: Sixty-first Yearbook of the National Society for the Study of Education, part 1, The University of Chicago Press, Chicago, 1962.

Justman, Joseph: Academic Achievement of Intellectually Gifted Accelerants and Nonaccelerants in Junior High School, *School Review,* 62:142–150, 1954.

Justman, Joseph: Personal and Social Adjustment of Intellectually Gifted Accelerants and Nonaccelerants in Junior High School, *School Review,* 61:468–478, 1953.

Keys, Noel: Should We Accelerate the Bright? *Exceptional Children,* 8:248–254, 1942.

Keys, Noel: *The Underage Student in High School and College: Emotional and Social Adjustments,* University of California Press, Berkeley, Calif., 1938.

Klausmeier, Herbert J.: Effects of Accelerating Bright Older Elementary Pupils: A Follow-up, *Journal of Educational Psychology,* 54:165–171, 1963.

Klausmeier, Herbert J., and Richard Ripple: Effects of Accelerating Bright Older Pupils from Second to Fourth Grade, *Journal of Educational Psychology,* 53:93–100, 1962.

Kogan, Nathan: Studies of College Students, *Journal of Consulting Psychology,* 2:129–136, 1955.

Laycock, Samuel R.: *Gifted Children: A Handbook for the Classroom Teacher,* The Copp-Clark Publishing Company, Toronto, Canada, 1957.

Miller, V. V.: Academic Achievement and Social Adjustment of Children Young for Their Grade Placement, *Elementary School Journal,* 57:257–263, 1957.

Moore, Margaret Whiteside: *A Study of Young High School Graduates,* Contributions to Education, no. 583, Bureau of Publications, Teachers College, Columbia University, New York, 1933.

Morgan, Antonia Bell: Critical Factors in the Academic Acceleration of Gifted Children: A Follow-up Study, *Psychological Reports,* 5:649–654, 1959.

Morgan, Antonia Bell: Critical Problems in the Academic Acceleration of Gifted Children: Hypotheses Based on Clinical Data, *Psychological Reports,* 3:71–77, 1957.

Paschal, Elizabeth: *Encouraging the Excellent: Special Programs for Gifted and Talented Students,* The Fund for the Advancement of Education, New York, 1960.

Passow, A. Harry: Enrichment of Education for the Gifted, chap. 10 in *Education for the Gifted: Fifty-seventh Yearbook of the National Society for the Study of Education,* part 2, The University of Chicago Press, Chicago, 1958.

Pressey, Sidney L.: *Educational Acceleration, Appraisals and Basic Problems,* Bureau of Educational Research, Ohio State University, Columbus, Ohio, 1949.

Reynolds, Maynard C. (ed.): *Early School Admission for Mentally Advanced Children,* Council for Exceptional Children, National Education Association, Washington, D.C., 1962.

Ripple, Richard E.: A Controlled Experiment in Acceleration from the Second to the Fourth Grade, *Gifted Child Quarterly,* 5:119–120, 1961.

Shannon, Dan C.: What Research Says about Acceleration, *Phi Delta Kappan,* 39:70–72, 1957.

Terman, Lewis M.: *Genetic Studies of Genius,* vol. 1, *Mental and Physical Traits of a Thousand Gifted Children,* Stanford University Press, Stanford, Calif., 1925.

Terman, Lewis M., and Melita H. Oden: *Genetic Studies of Genius,* vol. 4, *The Gifted Child Grows Up,* Stanford University Press, Stanford, Calif., 1947.

They Went to College Early, Evaluation Report no. 2, The Fund for the Advancement of Education, New York, 1957.

Thompson, J., and L. H. Meyer: What Research Says about Acceleration, *Journal of Secondary Education,* 36:301–305, 1961.

Trusler, J. W.: Pupil Acceleration in the Elementary Schools, *Grade Teacher,* 67:16–17, 1949.

Twelve Years of Early Admissions to Schools in Nebraska, University of Nebraska Bulletin, Lincoln, Nebr., 1962.

Tyler, Leona: Studies on Motivation and Identification of Gifted Pupils, *Review of Educational Research,* 27:291–399, 1957.

Weiss, Rosalie G.: The Validity of Early Entrance into Kindergarten, *Journal of Educational Research,* 56:53–54, 1962.

Wilkins, W. L.: High School Achievement of Accelerated Pupils, *School Review,* 44:268–274, 1936.

Wilkins, W. L.: The Social Adjustment of Accelerated Pupils, *School Review,* 44:445–455, 1936.

Witty, Paul A., and W. L. Wilkins: The Status of Acceleration or Grade Skipping as an Administrative Practice, *Educational Administration and Supervision,* 19:321–346, 1933.

Worcester, Dean A.: *The Education of Children of Above Average Mentality,* University of Nebraska Press, Lincoln, Nebr., 1956.

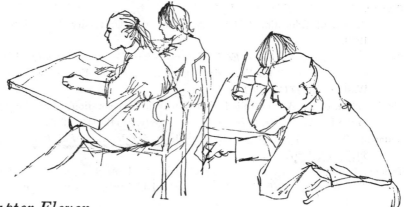

Chapter Eleven

GROUPING STUDENTS ACCORDING TO ABILITY AND INTERESTS

In a graded school system, where children tend to be grouped by age level, problems of instruction and adjustment arise because of wide differences among the children in maturity, achievement, interests, and background. Although the diversity of the middle 50 per cent in the grade may not be very wide, the typical class contains deviates who range far above or below the class average in many traits and capacities. The variability found in the primary grades becomes even more striking in intermediate and upper classes; in high school, wide diversity in talents persists in spite of the adolescents' urge toward group conformity.

Through the years, various experiments have been tried to break up the rigidity of the graded school system and to individualize instruction. Some form of ability grouping is usually adopted in large urban schools. Special classes in the elementary school and honors classes in high school represent the commonest practice in providing for the academically talented.

Schoolwide Ability Grouping and Multiple-track Plans

"Ability grouping" or "homogeneous grouping" means the classification of children for instructional purposes in terms of capacity for learning and demonstrated achievement. The purposes of grouping—and the advantages—are that it narrows the range of ability in the classes and permits the differentiation of curriculum offerings for bright and slow learners. In England the equivalent terms are "streaming" and "tracking."

Experimentation with multiple-track plans has had a long history in American education. Some indication of this experience with respect to the gifted was given in Chapter Three. A comprehensive report of the movement is presented by Sumption and Luecking (1960).

In 1929, 23 per cent of the elementary schools had some form of ability grouping; in 1958, 49 per cent; and today even more. In 1929, 56 per cent of all secondary schools had some form of ability grouping; in 1958, 86 per cent.

There are various interpretations of "ability grouping"; they range all the way from a small group within a class to special schools for exceptional children. There are multiple-track grouping plans, full-time special or separate classes with children largely segregated from their more typical classmates, separate courses or sections as in high school, partial grouping of the gifted and talented for part of the program or certain hours in the day. Usually there are three sections in a grade—bright, average, and slow; but in the larger multiple-track schools there may be six or more sections. A large junior high school in New York City has thirteen sections in the seventh grade, grouped according to ability. The top group is known as the SP or special progress class.

Numbers are assigned to sections for administrative purposes (but without revealing the relative ability of the separate sections) in an attempt to avoid the stigma of "special classes" for the slow and objections to segregation of the bright. Total grade sectioning takes care of the entire range of learning variability in a comprehensive school, both the rapid and slow learners.

Grouping is done according to various criteria. The pupils may be sectioned according to subject areas or according to allover ability combined with ratings of allover achievement. Sectioning may be confined to the respective grade levels, e.g., three separate sections for rapid, average, and slow learners in the fourth grade; or it may cut across grade boundaries, e.g., all the pupils of a given level of reading ability in grades 3 and 4.

In the elementary school, some grouping may be confined to separate subjects such as music, science, or foreign language with a teacher specialist in charge. In the high school, separate subject sectioning is far more common than overall ability grouping, though in the junior high school, gradewide ability grouping is often found.

The three-track grouping plan now in effect in New York City enables rapid learners to complete the six years of elementary school in five years; children of average ability require the full six years, and slow learners take seven years to finish six grades of work. Teachers begin in the kindergarten watching for bright children to place in a mature grade 1. In the first grade, shifts are frequently made to form a group of the most rapid learners. In grade 2 this group completes the second-grade work in January and begins third-grade work in the spring term. Then the children are ready to begin the regular fourth-grade work the following fall. They are given the achievement tests for the third grade while they are still second graders.

A three-track plan of grouping in basic subjects in a large high school is considered the only way to care for rapid learners and not discourage the slow. The eager mind of a bright mathematics student can scarcely be challenged in a heterogeneous class. Sectioning students in mathematics according to ability enables the talented to go through the basic courses and undertake advanced studies ahead of the regular schedule. In special sections students can have advanced work in physics and chemistry that other students may never take. In high school, the stiff demands of advanced courses make for high selectivity among the students enrolled.

A multiple-track plan presents certain difficulties for both the school and the parents. The administration must justify to the school patrons any separation of children according to ability. Parents of students and the students themselves are concerned about any stigma attached to being in the lowest group; and the bright are concerned about the grades they will receive in a top section where there is more competition with superior students. In any tracking plan, grouping must be flexible and tentative; otherwise, mistakes in placement will be made and parents will condemn the scheme.

What are the bases of grouping or sectioning? The most common practice is to group all the pupils in a given grade according to group intelligence test scores, school marks, achievement test results in academic subjects, particularly in reading, and the teacher's final judgment. The school principal exercises the privilege of making final decisions in consultation with parents. Although these combined ratings materially narrow the range in ability and achievement in the class, a wide range in aptitudes and achievement will still exist.

Special Classes

Special classes for the gifted represent an effort to group together children of high potential and to adjust instruction to their particular requirements. Special classes make provision for independent study and enable pupils to move ahead at an accelerated pace, with enrichment of studies in line with special interests and talents. In Dr. Leta S. Hollingworth's program at Public School 165 in New York City, set up in 1922, students were able to enter senior high school around the age of thirteen.

Special classes for bright and academically talented students have been in operation in American schools since 1914. Although interest in special classes developed slowly, by 1920 the movement was well under way, and since the early 1050s the number and variety of special-class programs for the gifted have rapidly multiplied. Special full-time classes for bright children in the elementary school are quite common in the larger American cities today.

Classes for intellectually gifted children (IGC classes) have been in operation in the elementary schools of New York City for many years, and there is a steadily increasing number of such classes in the junior high schools there. In Cleveland, the Major Work classes, first established in the elementary schools, have been extended into the junior and senior high schools.

Through the years, special classes for the gifted, unlike those for the mentally retarded, have led an uncertain existence, depending upon community sentiment or the initiative of school administrators and the school board. Too often classes for the bright have been set up without adequate overall planning. In some cases the character of the school population has changed, bringing in a larger group of slow learners.

For more information about the special-class movement relating to the gifted see the publications of Laycock (1957), Sumption and Luecking (1960), and *Education for the Gifted: Fifty-seventh Yearbook of the National Society for the Study of Education,* part 2 (1958).

QUESTIONS ABOUT SPECIAL CLASSES

Many questions arise concerning the nature, organization, programs, and outcomes of classes for the gifted.

What are the purposes of grouping? For what ages and grades are special classes practical? What criteria should be used in selecting the pupils? How many children should be enrolled in a class?

What is the nature of special-class instruction for the gifted? What sorts of programs are carried on? How are classes organized and conducted? How do teaching and learning in these classes differ from regular classes? What special resources are needed? Do the teachers need to be specially trained?

What happens if a child who has been attending a special class in the elementary school transfers to a high school where there are no special classes or fast-moving sections?

Is there any research evidence to justify separate classes or sections for the bright? What are the objections to special classes? How can they be answered? Does attendance in special classes make snobs of gifted children? How should school marks be assigned in special classes?

An attempt will be made to answer these and other questions in the following pages.

SECTIONING AND SCHOOL SIZE

Special classes for the gifted are feasible only in cities with a sizable population and convenient transportation to a school center. When the elementary school enrollment is below 500, special classes are scarcely practical. In a large elementary school there will be enough bright children in the fourth and fifth grades, for example, to recruit a combined fourth- and fifth-grade class of thirty or more gifted children. If there are not enough children for a class in one school, children from several schools may be brought together in a central location.

Sectioning high school students in basic subject-matter courses according to ability is only feasible in large city high schools or in consolidated high schools where the student body reaches at least 500. In smaller schools there would be an insufficient number of students for any type of sectioning for those subjects with small enrollments, such as foreign languages or second-year mathematics.

In a high-level community with superior schools and the best of facilities there is less need for special classes for bright students, because classes tend to be smaller than in crowded urban areas and instructional facilities are better.

Placement in a special class for the gifted or talented may or may not imply rapid advancement. In some cases, children in special classes may gain a year in school; more typically, the curriculum of these classes is enriched in many ways, and the children progress through school at the standard age-grade pace.

Grouping children in special classes does not take care of individualization automatically because fast learners differ as much among themselves as they do from the typical child in regular classes. Here the work must be even more largely on an individual basis.

STANDARDS FOR ADMISSION

Membership in special classes or sections for the gifted is restricted to those children who have demonstrated unusual learning capacities on intelligence tests and in school achievement. Grouping is done first of all on the basis of evidence of developmental advancement and superior intellectual capacities. The criteria most commonly adopted are superior rating on a standard intelligence test, superior ratings on achievement tests, good marks, the teacher's recommendation, acceptable health status, and the parents' approval.

Although there may be a minimum IQ standard for admission, as indicated in Chapter Two, IQ is seldom made the sole criterion for admission, and even the IQ minimum may be waived in individual cases if other ratings are uniformly high.

Unless the basic qualifications are expressed in standardized terms such as certain minimum test scores and grade average, the selective process will seem unfair and it actually may be. To limit selection to test-high children will also be unfair, however, because of fallacies in ratings based on test scores.

Too often the selection of students for special classes has been haphazard, or the criteria have been uncertain. One school admits the children chiefly on the basis of their reading scores; in another, the decision rests largely on the teacher's judgment. Teachers report that when tests and ratings of mental acceleration are disregarded in selecting children for "talent" classes, and the chief reliance is placed on achievement ratings, particularly high reading scores, the range of ability of those selected is too wide for effective enrichment work.

Whether the minimum IQ level for special classes is set at 110, 120, or 140 is determined on a practical basis, according to the general level of the school's enrollment or in terms of the number of children to be accommodated. The scheme adopted in some districts in New York City is as follows:

IQ 130 or above
IQ 120 to 130, plus high reading scores
IQ 110 to 120, plus high reading scores and superior class marks

For admission to special progress classes in the New York City junior high schools (grade 7), students are required to have an IQ of at least 120 on standard tests, a reading grade on standard achievement tests of at least 8.5, a mathematics grade score of 8.0, and the recommendation of the sixth grade teacher. The student must also be at least eleven years of age and in good health.

Universal standards cannot be adopted for admission to special classes because of variation in the proportion of bright learners from one community to another. In a university town a group of extremely bright children can be recruited for a special class in the upper elementary grades; in a small town without an unusual concentration of rapid learners, the children in the special class will be composed of the bright and near bright. The New York City school system has set up what are known as "G classes," a level just below the IGC classes, with more flexibility in selection of the pupils who are above average.

In the high school as well as in the elementary grades, care must be taken to see that only the highly qualified are included in an advanced or rapid-progress class. If selection is made on partial information or superficial judgment, errors will be made, the misfits will fail, the bright be held back.

There are various degrees of flexibility in sectioning and grouping the gifted. In some schools, the grouping is more or less permanent, with little changeover to regular classes. In other schools, grouping is considered highly tentative; the pupils are transferred in and out of classes as need requires. In some schools, the gifted are held together in the same class throughout the school day; in others, the special class or group meets for only half a day or for only certain periods during the week.

THE CLEVELAND MAJOR WORK CLASSES

The Major Work classes of the Cleveland public schools provide an outstanding example of a special-class system for the gifted that has been in continuous operation since 1921, chiefly because of good planning from the beginning and expert supervision since 1940 under the leadership of Dr. Dorothy Norris. In the early 1920s Cleveland already had a system of special classes for various types of deviant children; consequently, setting up separate classes for the gifted caused little comment (Hall, 1956).

The Major Work program has been extended and expanded through the years. The name "Major Work" was a fortunate choice, implying that far more was to be expected of children in this program than of those in regular classes. Any school that had a nucleus of gifted children and was accessible to public transportation could become a Major Work class center. If there were too few bright children in one school to form an entire class with an age range no wider than two or three years, the class was set up in a centrally located school. Responsibility for a child's transportation was assumed by parents when the child was enrolled.

At present there are approximately 600 elementary school children and 300 junior and senior high school students in Major Work classes. There are three junior high schools and three senior high schools in the city to which graduates of the Major Work elementary school classes are directed. Practically all of the elementary school graduates of Major Work classes go on to these selected high schools, though some prefer to attend high schools nearer home.

Selection of Students In the selection of candidates for the Major Work classes, the results of annual standardized intelligence and achievement tests are scanned to discover those pupils not overage for the grade who have made high scores. These children are later checked with individual Binet intelligence tests. Those with IQs over 125 are considered for placement in special classes. In evaluating the children, other factors are considered, such as emotional maturity, social adaptability, and health. The teacher's judgment is exercised in nominating children for individual check testing.

Enrollment is not restricted to children with superior academic records. There are usually some who definitely need to be challenged, whose school marks in regular classes may have been below average. Others may have been misfits in their former classes for various reasons. Children from several grades are grouped in one classroom, usually grades 1 to 3 in one class, grades 4 to 6 in another, but any workable grouping is acceptable. More than three grades in a room has proved to be impractical. The largest number of these classes in any one school at present is four. Enrollment may take place at any time in the child's school career, but experience shows that the earlier the placement, the better for the child.

Children in the Major Work classes have daily contacts with others in the school, since they participate in the regular gymnasium classes, club periods, orchestra, crafts work, and student government councils.

One of the basic aims is training for responsibility, preparing the children for independence and leadership. Some of the responsibilities the children learn to accept early are budgeting their time, being ready for a class discussion or for a morning talk, and evaluating their own presentations and those of their classmates.

Guiding Principles of the Program   A number of guiding principles have been followed in curriculum organization and instruction. The program is intent on:

Increasing the range of knowledge and skills of the students

Developing alertness

Developing initiative and creative power

Developing critical thinking

Developing power to work independently, to plan, to execute, and to judge

Developing increased ability to share in an undertaking

Developing leadership

In these classes there is less teacher direction of each student, more opportunity for self-discipline and responsibility for control of behavior, more opportunity for pupil participation in planning, sharing, discussing, and evaluating. Emphasis is on social development and adjustment as well as other developmental needs of the children.

The program adheres to the principle of enrichment rather than rapid advancement; however, no two teachers or two classes enrich the program in exactly the same way. Enrichment results from broadening the regular courses of the elementary school curriculum and deeper study of topics than is common in regular classes.

Work is planned in large units and is often related to group projects. The students themselves formulate the outline for a broad topic, for example, "The Mound Builders," which is used as the basis for a series of discussions.

Classroom activities include discussion, elementary research, short-term research activity, long-term research study, and research projects carried on by a group of students. Short-term research projects terminate in "morning talks," given by individual students, limited to five or ten minutes. To show when they expect to be ready to report on their topics, the children sign a large "morning talk calendar," posted in a prominent place in the room. They are then responsible for having their reports ready on time. The children select their topics in line with school studies and their own interests, both for these reports and for long-range research projects, which employ similar study techniques.

Wide-range reading experience and improvement of reading skills are taken care of largely through a "Reading Club" in which children share with others ideas gained from their reading. Importance is attached to critical reading, what the children think and how they feel about what they read. The pupils prepare reviews of books and write stories, articles, and editorials for the school newspapers. They are taught to type to facilitate written expression.

Arithmetic is done largely on an individual basis. The classes provide special instruction in art, intensive work in language and literature, and opportunity for writing and producing plays. French is taught daily by special teachers trained in the Desauze conversational method in which games, songs, and dramatization are used.

Each child in these classes keeps his own folder containing all records of progress from the time of his entrance into the class, and he carries this folder along with him until he graduates from high school. These records are helpful to the guidance counselors in the secondary school in planning programs for advanced work in the child's strongest subject areas.

In high school, the enriched program is continued. Pupils are grouped according to major subjects as far as is possible; but in senior high school, as interests become more definite and diversified, ability grouping is impractical. In some cases, honors courses have been provided in English, mathematics, and science.

Teachers of Major Work classes are aided through monthly meetings at which they present reports on successful activities, unit studies, and procedures. A file of teaching units that have worked well is kept in the curriculum library of the central office.

A more comprehensive report of the Major Work classes will be found in the book by Hall (1956) and in *Education for the Gifted* (1958).

PROGRAMS IN OTHER CITIES

At Public School 208 in Brooklyn, New York, where classes for the gifted have been in operation for thirty years or more, the program now consists of two classes each in grades 4, 5, and 6, for 240 children. The children who are specially selected come from the neighborhood and other sections of Brooklyn. The regular course of study is followed, but the program is amended and expanded to adjust to the children's mental maturity.

A program of special classes was inaugurated in the St. Louis, Missouri, elementary schools in the fall of 1955. To enter these classes, fourth graders must score 130 IQ or above on an individual test, and show performance at least equal to the grade in reading, language, and arithmetic. The school principal recommends a pupil for the class on the prospect of good adjustment, and with the parents' consent. There is no grade acceleration in these classes, but pupils enter high school with advanced standing in French, algebra, and English.

Special classes for the gifted in Indianapolis supplement the regular curriculum in literature, science, history, and social studies. The regular subject matter is expanded through teacher-pupil conferences, educational excursions, research projects, and individualized instruction, much as in the Cleveland Major Work program. The study of French begins in the fifth grade, typing in the seventh and eighth grades.

A pilot program for children and youths of superior ability was launched in Milwaukee in the fall of 1958 in cooperation with the University of Wisconsin research services (Raasch, 1959). Admission to the program is on the basis of intelligence test data, school achievement, the teacher's nomination, and parents' consent. Provisions for grade 5 and above include special classes in three centers, part-time classes for children in their own schools, and enrichment in regular classes. The public is kept informed about these special provisions through radio and TV programs, meetings, published reports, and in-service courses.

THE PROBLEM OF ARTICULATION BETWEEN ELEMENTARY CLASSES AND HIGH SCHOOL

Children who have attended special classes in the elementary division may have "nowhere to go" when they reach the junior or senior high school. They find themselves thrown back into regular classes with students considerably older than themselves, where much of what they have gained may be lost and where no one is specially interested in their welfare. The lack of transition classes proves to be an impediment to the continued rapid progress and enrichment of studies for these children through high school.

For more information on the subject of grouping the gifted and the organization of special classes, consult the list of references at the close of this chapter.

Ungraded Groups and Classes

Another means of adapting instruction for bright pupils is to set up intergrade groupings in a two- to three-year age range, bringing a few young bright children into contact with older pupils for types of activities a bright child can manage, for example, a fourth grader working with sixth graders in science or foreign language. The ungraded school in which there is intergrade classification ensuring continuous progress for every child, but at different rates, has grown in favor as a means of differentiating progress and instruction for like-age groups.

The ungraded school divides the six grades of the elementary school into three-year blocks, permitting pupils to advance without the artificial barrier of grade placement or yearly promotions. In some places the idea has been extended to the junior high school, where pupils go through the three-year sequence in two, three, or four years, at their own pace.

In the ungraded plan, the pupil is assigned to a particular teacher rather than to a grade, and he may remain with the same teacher for two years. A pupil remains in each division, primary or upper grades, for two, three, or four years according to his rate of progress, and then he goes on to junior high school.

In one of the elementary schools of San Angelo, Texas, the top pupils in grades 1 and 2 are grouped together, with good results. The children move ahead at the end of the year without formal promotion. In ungraded classes, the requirements of the regular graded courses of study for a given grade are disregarded, and study projects are organized for pupils in terms of intellectual maturity and academic progress. Such a program requires flexible use of all instructional materials for every group or class.

Part-time Groupings

Through the years the concept of "grouping" gifted children as an administrative policy has broadened from total segregation in special classes or fast-moving sections to various types of groupings for many purposes, on a part-time or temporary basis. There are part-time groups that meet for a period of a day, for half a day, or perhaps twice a week for work on skill subjects, academic studies, or special-talent areas such as art, crafts, music, and writing. Special groups made up of children from several grades may work on the school paper, a musical program, a school play, or other activities or projects.

The elementary schools of Wantagh, Long Island, have an Enrichment Center program for gifted children who come together in groups of ten for an hour each day. During the week there are two group activities, two independent study periods, and one period for individual interests. Ideas for projects come both from the curriculum and from the children. This program has meant much to the children, judging from their informal comments. The first group to enter the program is planning for a reunion on Mars in 1982, which will include all the children who have been in the program since it was established.

In the Bay Shore, Long Island, schools three special teachers are provided in the areas of language arts, social studies, and mathematics. These teachers work with groups of gifted children twice a week on special projects. In Erie, Pennsylvania, children are released from regular classes an hour each day to pursue their special interests and to work intensively on their studies.

In a junior high school where there are three sections in the eighth grade, each containing thirty-two students, the following flexible grouping plan is followed: On Tuesday and Thursday the classes are broken up into six sections meeting for one hour and fifteen minutes each. On Tuesday there is a choice of shop, homemaking, an accelerated course, or remedial work in mathematics and English. On Thursday three accelerated groups meet as well as a class in remedial language, one in special library work, and one in crafts. Parents and students alike are enthusiastic about the plan.

THE DUAL PROGRESS PLAN

A plan of semigrouping has been developed experimentally by Dr. George Stoddard of New York University in collaboration with school officials in Long Beach, Long Island, and Ossining, New York (1961). The "Dual Progress plan," as it is called, represents another effort to break the "lockstep" for children of different abilities and to provide interest groups, particularly in mathematics and science, foreign language, and art and music for mentally advanced and talented children. In the morning session social studies, reading, and language arts are carried on with the whole class in the homeroom. Work in reading and spelling skills is individualized so far as possible. In the afternoon, ungraded club groups are formed for work in all other studies and activities, the sciences, mathematics, and art talent groups. Slow learners are put in separate sections, and the others are grouped in terms of interest and aptitude. The Dual Progress plan provides the services of five specialist teachers in art, music, science, mathematics, and physical education, in addition to the homeroom teacher of social studies and language communication.

Parents approve these special-interest groups because they can easily recognize and accept differences in the special talents of individual children. Furthermore, they are accustomed to the idea of special releases from school for religious instruction, for music or reading lessons, for speech therapy, and other purposes.

Evaluating the benefits of the plan is difficult because of the problem of controlling variables in a matched group experiment. A three-year study of this program reported no distinctive advantages over other arrangements, but the plan is successful in preventing the more-able students from remaining at a standstill.

Other schools that make no pretense of providing for gifted children actually do so through club groups that meet once a week for a double period or through afterschool club groups and recreation activities.

Afterschool club groups may also be considered a form of grouping on a part-time basis. These groupings have the advantage of adjusting learning opportunities for the bright and talented, while preserving nonsegregated group experiences for the children in the school day.

Today in towns and cities where special classes have never been established, the trend is toward part-time grouping for gifted and talented children according to activity interests. Special classes for dull and retarded children, however, still operate on an all-day basis because these children require a closely supervised school program.

THE COLFAX PLAN

A highly successful partial-grouping plan to care for gifted children has been developed and supervised by Dr. Hedwig Pregler, principal of the Colfax School in Pittsburgh, Pennsylvania. The Colfax School enrolls about 1,200 children in the kindergarten and first six grades. The school is located in a good community with a school population varying from 109 to 115 IQ on the average. Children selected for special "workshop" classes have IQs of 130 and over on individual intelligence tests and advanced-achievement ratings. Children who are identified as having high mental ability are brought together in workshops for their academic work, but remain with other children in regular classes for the rest of the school day. There is a workshop class in the school for grades 1 and 2 combined and one such class for each other grade. The purpose of the workshops is to develop mentally gifted children in all aspects of their giftedness—individually, and as members of the special group. In the Colfax plan there are group activities, individual projects, and drill for skills largely on an individual or small-group basis.

In the primary grades all children spend the first half of the morning with their regular classes, at which time social activities, sharing of experiences, music, games, and safety instruction are provided for the entire group. Midway through the morning, when the children move into their skill subjects, the mentally superior children leave for their workshop classes. In the upper grades the school is run on the platoon plan. The gifted children leave their class when the group goes to the academic teacher and rejoin it for special subjects such as art, music, and physical education.

In workshop groups, material that is beyond the grasp of average learners is studied avidly. There is extensive cooperative planning by the children and their teachers. The gifted children acquire the fundamental skills early and go ahead with advanced work. They do critical, analytical thinking within the range of their interests and abilities. In these classes the children learn to do an elementary type of research work similar to research studies in the Cleveland Major Work classes. By the sixth grade the pupils produce written reports summarizing the term's work. They receive training in the critical evaluation of the material they gather and are taught how to make effective reports. Even in the primary grades the children learn to use resource materials for their studies and projects. At first they observe and take note of things as a group; later they concentrate more and more on their individual projects.

UNIVERSITY CITY, MISSOURI

Dunlap has described the plan of special groups he devised for elementary school children in the public schools of University City, Missouri (1955); see also Norris (1958). In University City, cur-

riculum enrichment and individualization have always been provided in the schools. Therefore, this extension of service for certain
children on a part-time basis aroused no more concern than provision for remedial reading for those in need of special help. No
publicity was needed or given for the acceptance and development
of this program.

Ten per cent of the children in grades 3 through 6 are enrolled
in a program of part-time enrichment groups. There are 250
children in thirty of these groups conducted by three special
teachers. All the children rate at 140 IQ and above; 85 per cent
of them have IQs of 150 or over. The program is quite different
from the Colfax partial-segregation plan described above because
the part-time enrichment groups are more numerous and no strict
line is drawn between grouping for academic studies and all other
types of activities in the elementary schools.

The plan is as follows: Groups of eight to ten children meet
twice a week for periods of 40 to 50 minutes with a special teacher.
Usually the groups include only children of similar age level, though
sometimes younger children are included. The work of the groups
may be an extension of a class project, or it may be unrelated
to a class, but of particular interest to the children themselves.
Many activities are group undertakings; some, however, are individual projects. The children are most apt to choose topics not
included in their regular classwork, such as astronomy, mythology,
prehistoric times, science, children in other cultures, and so on.
The sixth-grade children in these groups carry out certain projects
connected with the spring camp week conducted for all the children.
Their activities take the form of research reading, discussion,
written and oral reports, lectures by outside authorities, trips for
firsthand observations, experiments, the construction of models and
equipment, the preparation of maps, charts, illustrations, graphs,
art work, etc.

Because of the breadth and depth of the program, teachers
of unusual versatility and competency are required and are chosen
from among the most able in the school system. Although the
teachers recognize the abilities of the children, at the same time
they understand the limitations and special requirements of elementary school pupils.

The director of the project and the teachers believe that the
particular projects the children work on are less significant than
the attitudes and habits being established: the interests that are
aroused and broadened, experimental methods of learning, work

and study habits befitting the budding scholar, the use of books for many purposes, the development of library skills, and the ability to use special equipment properly.

THE PORTLAND, OREGON, PROGRAM

The schools of Portland, Oregon, have had unusual success in recognizing talented children and developing their abilities largely within the setting of the regular classroom. The program for gifted children in Portland extends through the twelve grades (*Education for the Gifted*, 1958).

The children in the special program of the Portland project are selected in the fifth grade through a combination of teacher ratings, results of the California Test of Mental Maturity, and scores on comprehensive standardized achievement tests. Following this screening, the selected children are given the Thurstone Primary Test of Mental Abilities.

Today in the Portland, Oregon, program, the typical elementary school experience of an exceptionally capable youngster would be as follows: normal self-contained homeroom four-fifths of the time, special classes one-fifth of the time. The typical high school program of such a student would be: normal heterogeneous classes three-fifths of the time, advanced section or seminars two-fifths of the time.

Although, as a matter of policy, capable children are not grouped separately, special-talent groups are formed in such areas as mathematics, science, mechanical comprehension, foreign languages, creative writing, art, music, rhythms, creative dance and drama, and social leadership. These groups meet for short periods two or three times a week.

According to Mr. Clifford Williams, director of the Portland project, the program and procedures in classes for students participating in the program vary, depending on the community, the school, the faculty, and the children. Emphasis is placed on a variety of materials and techniques, especially independent exploration, critical thinking, and training in leadership.

An appraisal of the Portland, Oregon, programs for the gifted compared groups of children enrolled in these programs and those not enrolled. Overwhelming approval of the programs was expressed by parents, teachers, and the children themselves (Hamilton, 1960).

In a number of cities where libraries have been installed in the schools or where a branch of the public library adjoins the school, all the pupils spend at least one period a week in the library.

This plan results in more voluntary reading and wiser selection of books, a provision from which all the children derive benefit and an arrangement that is invaluable for the gifted.

COMMUNITY—SPONSORED GROUPS AND CLASSES

Agencies other than the school have supplied supplementary enrichment for the gifted in some communities. In a large city in Texas, the public library conducts two classes for gifted children during afterschool hours, one for elementary school pupils, the other for high school students. The activities of these groups relate to enjoyment of literature and creative writing. The plan of releasing certain children from their regular classes for two hours a week to work in small groups with master teachers in literature, art, music, mathematics, foreign languages, and other interests of the more intellectual sort has met with success in other communities.

San Diego, California, has set up special Saturday art classes for talented children in the upper elementary grades and high school. Classes are conducted in several parts of the city and are free of charge. There are workshops in painting, mosaics, and ceramics, each conducted by a specialist in the field. For students in grades 7 through 12 interested in creative writing there are also workshop groups on Saturday mornings.

CLUSTER GROUPINGS

In communities where there is objection to segregated classes for the gifted, or where there are not enough children to form a special class, several bright children within a regular class are instructed as a "cluster," a term adopted by the California Gifted Child Program. A cluster may consist of three or four children or as many as ten or twelve.

School administrators have found that teachers can manage cluster groupings of the gifted and supervise individual projects more successfully when the slowest learners are removed from the regular class beginning with the first grade. In some cases, a few transfers of pupils within the school will create clusters without any wholesale regrouping. This arrangement also benefits the slow learners who can be placed in smaller classes and receive more individual attention.

In the La Mesa—Spring Valley school district in California several mentally advanced children were grouped together in one class from which an equal number of slow and backward children had been removed. The bright children had IQs of 140 and over.

The services of specialist teachers or teaching aides working along with the regular class teacher will greatly facilitate instruction of cluster groups.

Special Schools

Separate schools for the gifted and talented represent a further step beyond special-class programs. The great "public" schools of England, the Gymnasiums of Germany, the *lycées* of continental Europe, by the very nature of their classical curriculum, were essentially schools in which only the academically talented could survive. Campus schools conducted by university teacher-training centers have tended to enroll a student population far above average—the University of Chicago elementary and high schools; the former Horace Mann and Lincoln School of Teachers College, Columbia University; the demonstration high schools at the Universities of Ohio, Illinois, Texas, and others. The Hunter College Elementary School and Hunter High School operating within the New York City university system enroll only intellectually gifted children selected according to certain objective criteria. New York City also has several academic high schools with population restricted to the academically talented. Some years ago the city of Baltimore established the Homewood demonstration school for children of superior ability. In Philadelphia, the Masterman School accepts bright and gifted children of elementary school age from all over the city. Abroad, the Maadi Secondary School in Iraq accepts only outstanding pupils.

Rickover has advocated the establishment of special schools to provide a more challenging and intellectually demanding program of studies for the ablest students (1962). He recommends searching for the most talented children, not later than age ten or eleven, and educating them through specially planned programs. Whether special schools rather than comprehensive institutions better serve the purposes of the gifted remains to be determined.

The Pros and Cons of Ability Grouping

There are wide differences of opinion concerning the wisdom of separate-class groupings for gifted children. Is it better for a bright but mentally lazy boy to be put in a special class where he will receive more stimulation from the teacher and more competition from high-powered classmates than to remain in unselected class groups? The possible advantages or disadvantages for slower learners of having the bright withdrawn from regular classes must also be considered. Do the advantages of special-class placement outweigh the disadvantages?

Arguments for and against ability grouping have been summarized by many authorities. Laycock listed ten points in favor and five against (1957). Sumption and Luecking also discussed the advantages and disadvantages of special-class grouping (1960).

Some teachers voice strong objection to the removal of gifted children from regular classes and even to the sectioning of pupils according to ability, because they consider the bright a stimulus to the dull and morale builders for the whole class. Others contend that both the bright and dull pupils are benefited by sectioning, that the gifted need the challenge of other gifted children to "keep on their toes." Both groups admit, however, that grouping may result in the development of unfavorable social attitudes on the part of the children.

Authorities point out that some aspects of instruction, though not all, can be better adapted to the gifted when they are grouped. Skills and subject matter, apparently, can best be taught in separate groups. Activities such as singing, folk dancing, trips, radio programs, enjoyment of literature, art appreciation, gymnasium, and recreation are best suited to like-age groups.

POINTS IN FAVOR

Special groupings make differentiation of instruction for the gifted more efficient and practical. The gifted child tends to be neglected in overcrowded classes in large schools. In regular classes teachers must concentrate on the more numerous children of average ability; the bright must largely shift for themselves. In special classes, it is possible to adjust the level of work to the abilities of the children. The teacher can help a student with his individual problems while the others work independently on their own activities. The entire program can be more completely individualized, with emphasis on independent study. Consequently, special talents and creative aptitudes are more likely to emerge.

Special classes afford a means of steadily accelerating the child's studies without the disadvantages of grade skipping.

Enrichment through problem solving on the child's intellectual level is more possible in special classes.

Special classes provide opportunity for the exercise of student initiative under the guidance of skillful teachers.

In classes formed on the basis of ability there is more conversation on a give-and-take basis between the members of the group.

An integrated program can be organized that is planned in terms of the special abilities and interests of the children. The fundamental skills can be mastered in much less time with individualized study.

The bright child has to exert more effort when he is grouped with others of exceptional ability. He sizes up his abilities more realistically in a special-class group, and he is more fully appreciated by his classmates, who also have high goals and intellectual interests.

A bright child benefits from close contact with children who have minds as alert as his own. In a class composed of mentally advanced students the bright child is challenged to work up to his ability. Gifted children working together stimulate one another in creative thinking. Competition is more wholesome than in a regular class where the bright child stands far ahead of the others.

In special classes, young bright children are not competing in motor skills and arts and crafts with older children who have more physical strength and dexterity.

The specialist teachers of classes or sections for the bright and talented are expertly trained for this work, and are able to show respect for the unusual child's original questions and statements, instead of censoring him for nonconforming behavior. The special class for the bright affords exceptional opportunities for teachers of unusual ability.

OBJECTIONS

There are both theoretical and practical objections to special classes and ability grouping for the bright and talented. These may be summarized as follows.

The charge of favoritism toward children already favored is sure to be made. Separate classes for the intellectually gifted tend to become a status symbol in the eyes of parents, as owning a high-powered car or wearing custom-made clothes. Since special classes spell social prestige, ambitious parents will demand that their children be enrolled in these classes.

Separation of the bright from regular classes means that the selected children are likely to have fewer contacts with other, less gifted children at school. Also, grouping by ability brings together children predominately of a superior social class, thus widening the gap between these children and those of minority groups in the community—those speaking foreign languages, Negroes, and others.

Special-class separation is hard on those left out. Every child likes to be thought bright whether he is or not. Children have difficulty accepting the idea of differences in school ability. Serious emotional harm may be done to a child who is nearly accepted, but not quite.

A practical objection is that the bases for selection may be unreliable. Some children will be included who should not be, and others who should have been included will be missed. To fill up the classes, children may be enrolled who are not strictly up to the accepted standards.

Parents are inclined to push their children into special classes with accelerated programs that are beyond the children's capabilities. Parents have been known to have their children tutored so that they will show up well on the entrance tests. The test-coaching problem has become a real threat to the reliability of test results as a criterion for admission.

If children are selected for homogeneity in one trait, such as verbal thinking, they will not necessarily be homogeneous in others, such as mathematics; this objection can be answered if selection for special classes is based on all-around ability, determined by tests that average out the differences.

In special-class programs there is danger of overemphasis on subject matter at the cost of well rounded development.

Competition in a class of gifted children may be too severe; even the rapid learners may be academically overloaded.

The students become unduly concerned about marks. They expect to earn the A's they would have received in a regular class, yet here they are competing with an entire class of A-grade students.

A problem is sometimes created for siblings in the family when one of them is selected for a special class. A teacher learned that the mother of a bright girl who was accepted for a special progress class in junior high school gave an elaborate dinner party for all the relatives to celebrate the event. In the meanwhile, a younger child in the family was threatened with dire consequences unless he "ponied up" in his studies to keep up with his big sister. Brothers or sisters not accepted may show resentment.

There is some evidence that children placed in gifted classes may become arrogant, snobbish, boastful. They are inclined to make invidious distinctions and to ridicule the less gifted who are not included.

There is also the problem of staffing the classes with competent teachers. All the teachers in the school feel that there should be rotation so that everyone can have a turn with the bright pupils. This means lack of continuity in the instructional staff.

What Does Research Indicate Concerning Ability Grouping?

Opinion is freely expressed on the question of special classes for the gifted. What does research actually show? Special classes for the gifted were just getting under way when studies were begun to test their effectiveness. Early reports were made by Hollingworth (1926), McCall and Jones (1926), Worlton (1928), and others. Goldberg has summarized more recent research findings (1958). A review of experimental studies has also been reported by Ekstrom (1959). Ekstrom was unable to discover any consistent pattern of effectiveness for homogeneous grouping related to age of the pupils, ability level, course content, or methods of instruction (1959) So far, there are no experimental results that furnish a basis for sound generalizations concerning ability grouping, pro or con. The alleged desirable or undesirable results have so far eluded scientific verification.

In spite of the general assumption held by educational leaders for sixty years or more that concentrating pupils of superior ability within a classroom is beneficial for the students, there is no clear-cut evidence that this is necessarily true. Much depends upon the nature of the program and the quality of teaching.

There is some evidence that ability grouping produces slightly greater academic achievement in comparison with instruction of the bright in regular classes, but this is not invariably the case. Aside from superior marks, the achievements of the special-class children are undistinguishable from those of the regular classes.

The chief value of special-class groupings in the elementary and junior high school may reside more in instructional convenience than in any remarkably significant outcomes from separate instruction.

There is no evidence, however, that, on the whole, grouping of bright children for educational programs has produced any lasting harmful effects.

FOLLOW-UP STUDIES OF THE CLEVELAND MAJOR WORK CLASSES

An early report of the Cleveland Major Work classes and the progress made by pupils in these classes was published by Goddard in 1928. These children in comparison with those in regular classes working with similar subject matter accomplished more because they branched out farther in a program suited to their age and interests.

In 1941 Sumption published the report of a follow-up study of graduates of the Cleveland Major Work classes, the most comprehensive investigation undertaken of the results of special classes for the gifted with regular-class graduates as controls. A later study of Major Work class students was reported by Barbe (1953).

The respondents of Sumption's investigation were 328 former students of the Cleveland public schools, all of whom were in their early twenties at the time of the study. The special-class students were matched with regular school graduates on the basis of age, IQ, place of birth, sex, nationality, and racial background. At the time the respondents attended the Major Work classes, the classes did not extend beyond the junior high school.

Sumption inquired of the graduates of the special classes, first, what parts of their education had been most helpful and satisfying; second, what parts had been of little or no value; and third, what subject materials had proved to be most useful. A group of 65 individuals, 34 women and 31 men, who had IQs over 120 in the elementary school but had not had Major Work class experience were matched with the special-class graduates.

Sumption concluded that a student was definitely not disadvantaged in any way by attending these classes. Results proved that the Major Work class experience did not cause any neglect of the fundamental knowledges and skills in order to provide time for other activities, nor did it impair the health of the students in any way. The longer the period in Major Work classes, the more effective the results. Advantages of attendance in these classes were found in the development of leadership ability, in reading interests and activities, in the sense of social responsibility the students acquired, and in the discovery and development of individual aptitudes. Major Work graduates proved to be superior in the area of self-expression, in developing qualities of leadership, in critical thinking. Compared with regular-class graduates, they were more ambitious with regard to professional careers. These are significant findings although the numbers of individuals questioned was small and the differences were not very great.

Students in the Major Work classes liked the socialized procedures, the guidance they received in good reading, opportunities for creative work, field trips, their excellent teachers who had been specially trained for this work. According to the graduates, the program tended to limit the social contacts of the students, because the special classes were largely isolated from other classes in the school.

A charge had been made that the Major Work program placed undue emphasis on going to college. The data proved that more of the graduates of these classes entered college and earned degrees than was true of the control cases.

Over 84 per cent of the respondents reported that they approved of special classes for the gifted; 8 per cent disapproved; in some cases the disapproval was qualified. The preponderance of approval expressed by the graduates and gratitude for the privilege of having attended these classes attests to the success of the program.

Barbe's follow-up study of the 456 adults who had attended the Cleveland Major Work classes was made by means of a questionnaire sent to the graduates from both elementary and high school classes (1953). Over 90 per cent of the men and 63 per cent of the women entered colleges or universities. Normally, even in socially favored communities, the proportion is scarcely over 50 per cent. Over 70 per cent of the male graduates are now in professional and managerial occupations, whereas only 40 per cent of their fathers were in similar occupations. The educational program of these classes was presumably a factor in stimulating the boys to prepare for high-level occupations. Most of these men have had regular employment records and have received satisfactory promotions. Over 60 per cent of the graduates, both men and women, reported social adjustment as better than average. Marital adjustment was good, 80 per cent rating it above average, and the divorce rate was low. Over half are members of some community organization. About one-third of the men and two-fifths of the women said that some person had been a strongly determining influence in their lives.

OTHER REPORTS OF ABILITY GROUPING

In an elaborate study of ability grouping in the New York City elementary schools conducted in 1956–1958, Goldberg and Passow, in cooperation with Dr. Joseph Justman of the Board of Education, sought to determine the effects of ability grouping on school achievement (1962). Forty-five elementary schools cooperated in organizing some 3,000 pupils into eighty-six fifth-grade classes beginning in September, 1956. The pupils were divided into five ability levels with IQs from 76 to 181.

The purpose of the study was to learn the effects of grouping on achievement in all the elementary school subjects, as well as on social and personal behavior, without any systematic variation in content or teaching methods.

An analysis of the results showed that average achievement across all subjects was greatest in classes with pupils of four or five ability levels, but no one grouping pattern proved to be best for all ability levels in all subjects. The effect of the teacher on the achievement gains of the class proved to be more potent than the effects of pupil intelligence, ability range, or relative position. In the gifted group, particularly, most teachers achieved far better results in one or two subjects than in others.

In this experiment, ability grouping by itself did not have any positive effect on the academic attainment of the pupils. Gains in achievement were influenced more strongly by teacher and group differences in individual classrooms than by the presence or absence of gifted pupils, the range of ability in the class, or even by the intellectual ability of the pupils.

The conclusion is that narrowing the ability range without specifically designing varied academic programs for the various ability levels does not result in consistently greater academic achievement. There is no telling what might have happened had the teachers in the experiment adjusted the program to the gifted students instead of teaching the same curriculum in the usual way without planned differentiation in terms of pupil abilities.

In another study by Lorge, gifted children in special progress classes in New York City junior high schools made significantly superior gains in achievement in comparison with their peers in regular classes, and the superiority was not at the expense of their personal adjustment (1954).

A check-up of children who have completed work in the special progress classes of New York City junior high schools proved that though these students accomplished three years' work in two, they were scarcely distinguishable from other students in senior high school classes.

A follow-up study of the Los Angeles Opportunity Classes for the gifted showed that in comparing 284 gifted students from these classes with 381 gifted pupils from regular classes, the opportunity group had earned more A and B marks in high school, a higher average on grade points for all marks, and fewer failing marks than the control group (Savard, 1961).

Results have been reported of a controlled study in which children in programs for the gifted in California extending from

1957 to 1960 were compared with matchees not in any program (Martinson, 1961). The areas of evaluation were achievement growth; effects on personality; social relations; attitudes of parents, pupils, and teachers. The pupils were matched for initial achievement. Ten out of twelve experimental groups in grade 1 and in grades 5 and 6 made significant gains in mean score achievement compared with control groups. The conclusion is that the pupils benefited academically from the experimental year. The children in the experimental classes showed significant gains in friendship choices and social status in the group. Fears that special programs for the gifted, either in special classes or in regular-class groups, would penalize the gifted child socially proved to be unfounded.

Two research studies of outcomes in special centrally located classes for the gifted in Canadian schools were made by Howsam and Rennie in theses done under the direction of Dr. Samuel Laycock. Howsam asked the following questions:

1. Are choices of friends and work made by students in special classes different from choices made by those in regular classes?

2. Are special-class children accepted by the rest of the school population as well as they are by their classmates?

3. Are special-class children as well accepted in neighborhood play groups?

Answers to these questions were as follows: (1) no, (2) yes, and (3) yes. Attendance in special classes was not socially detrimental to these children.

In Rennie's check of graduates of these classes, the majority said they were in favor of them. They cited the many advantages of attending the classes but noted the following limitations: removal from their own neighborhood school; lack of special-classes continuation into high school; feelings of superiority engendered in the children; insufficient mastery of arithmetic, English, and other fundamentals; entrance into high school at too early an age; unwise utilization of spare time; need of more mental discipline; feeling of being different from other children; loss of desire to participate in sports; jealousy on the part of mothers of children not enrolled in the special classes.

In a summer program recently conducted at the State College of Iowa at Cedar Falls, children who had completed the fifth grade and earned an IQ of 120 or higher on the Henmon-Nelson intelligence test were divided into three groups of sixty pupils each for a comparison study of special-class grouping. One set of sixty children constituted the experimental population for a special summer program; the other children served as controls. At the end of the six-week program, in spite of the short time, results in achievement and adjustment were in favor of the experimental groups (Hampton, 1962).

In a comparative study by Drews of bright junior high school students, the teacher's participation was found to be different in homogeneous and heterogeneous classes (1959). In classes for the brighter students, the teacher did less reporting than in other classes. The pitch of the lessons, even the teacher's vocabulary, was higher in classes for bright students. For the greatest student interaction, homogeneous grouping was better. When left in heterogeneous classes the bright received higher ratings for less work than in separate classes. Being in a class with a substantial number of bright children was disadvantageous for the slower ones because the gifted communicated more often, did more reciting, and were more frequently chosen as leaders. This study disclosed the strong preference of bright junior high school students for homogeneous class placement. The results of the study indicate that whether or not the bright are grouped separately, the slow learners should be removed from the regular class to improve their opportunities for participating and sharing. The bright students with their quickness and originality instead of stimulating the slow, as one might suppose, actually limit their responsiveness.

In England, school authorities regard "streaming" of elementary school pupils as of more benefit to slow learners; gains for the bright are less evident (Daniels, 1961). Ability grouping proved to be more advantageous for average and below-average learners than for above average groups, according to a two year study made by Savard (1961).

Children's Attitudes   A question that keeps cropping up is whether gifted children in special classes become conceited. In a large junior high school, children in the special progress classes tended to keep entirely apart from other children in the school. A visitor noted that there were emotional outbursts from children who received less than 100 on daily tests. Children in the special classes did their best to prove that they knew more than other children and looked down on those who were less bright than themselves. Children not in these classes commented, "They think they're superior."

Coy reported that there was little evidence of conceit among the seventeen children in the class she organized, except in the case of one child who had acquired the attitude before he entered the class (1923). The question whether gifted children tended to become snobbish when they were placed in special classes was examined in Portland, Oregon. Results of a questionnaire study showed that 80 per cent of the gifted students said they saw nothing different in the relations of students in special classes to others. Although 15 to 20 per cent felt that special classes gave added prestige, less than 2 per cent reported that their special-class status made them unpopular.

A study by Luchins and Luchins revealed some interesting facts about children's attitudes toward homogeneous classes for children of different mental ability (1948). Their information was gained by asking each child a number of questions that indicated his feelings. Most children would prefer the bright class, even those in the average and dull groups. Most of them stated that their parents would prefer to have them in the bright class. Among the gifted children, 94 per cent stated that they would prefer to remain in the gifted class even though they could transfer to another class with a "better and kinder teacher." Some 91 per cent of the bright said that they would not play frequently with those in the average class. Most of the children in the bright class insisted that their best friends were in the same class.

References

Adams, Mary A.: Homewood Demonstration School for Superior Children, *Baltimore Bulletin of Education,* 18:10–13, 1940.

Barbe, Walter B.: Evaluation of Special Classes for Gifted Children, *Exceptional Children,* 22:60–62, 1955.

Barbe, Walter B.: *A Follow-up Study of the Graduates of Special Classes for Gifted Children,* unpublished doctoral dissertation, Northwestern University, Evanston, Ill., 1953.

Brumbaugh, Florence: A School for Gifted Children, *Childhood Education,* 20:325–327, 1944.

Carlson, E. A.: Project for Gifted Children: A Psychological Evaluation, *American Journal of Psychiatry,* 15:648–661, 1945.

Coy, Genevieve L.: *The Interests, Abilities and Achievements of a Special Class for Gifted Children,* Teachers College Contributions to Education, no. 131, Bureau of Publications, Teachers College, Columbia University, New York, 1923.

Daniels, J. C.: The Effects of Streaming in the Primary School, *British Journal of Educational Psychology,* 31:69–78, 1961.

DeHaan, Robert F., and Robert J. Havighurst: *Educating Gifted Children,* 2d ed., The University of Chicago Press, Chicago, 1961.

Drews, Elizabeth M.: *The Effectiveness of Homogeneous and Heterogeneous Ability Grouping in Ninth Grade English Classes with Slow, Average and Superior Students,* Office of Education, U.S. Department of Health, Education and Welfare, Cooperative Research Program, Project no. 608, Washington, D.C., 1959.

Dunlap, James M.: Gifted Children in an Enriched Program, *Exceptional Children,* 21:135–137, 1955.

Education for the Gifted: Fifty-seventh Yearbook of the National Society for the Study of Education, The University of Chicago Press, Chicago, 1958, part 2, chaps. 11 and 12.

Ekstrom, Ruth B.: *Experimental Studies of Homogeneous Grouping,* Educational Testing Service, Princeton, N.J., April, 1959.

Goddard, H. H.: *School Training of Gifted Children,* World Book Company, Tarrytown-on-Hudson, N.Y., 1928.

Goldberg, Miriam L.: Recent Research on the Talented, *Teachers College Record,* 60:153–154, 1958.

Goldberg, Miriam L., and A. Harry Passow: The Effects of Ability Grouping, *Education,* 82:482–487, 1962.

Goodlad, J. I., and R. H. Anderson: *The Nongraded Elementary School,* Harcourt, Brace & World, Inc., New York, 1960.

Greenberg, Benjamin B., and Herbert B. Bruner: *Final Report of Public School 500 (Speyer School),* Board of Education of the City of New York, Division of Elementary Schools, 1941.

Hall, Theodore: *Gifted Children: The Cleveland Story,* The World Publishing Company, Cleveland, 1956.

Hamilton, Norman K.: Attitudes toward Special Educational Programs for Gifted Children, *Exceptional Children,* 27:147–150, 163, 1960.

Hampton, Nellie D.: *Effects of Special Training on the Achievement and Adjustment of Gifted Children,* State College of Iowa, Cedar Falls, Iowa, 1962.

Hildreth, Gertrude, Florence N. Brumbaugh, and Frank T. Wilson: *Educating Gifted Children at the Hunter College Elementary School,* Harper & Row, Publishers, Incorporated, New York, 1952.

Hollingworth, Leta S.: *Gifted Children: Their Nature and Nurture,* The Macmillan Company, New York, 1926.

Howsam, R. B.: *A Comparative Study of Children Attending Special Classes for the Mentally Gifted and Those Attending Ordinary Classes in the Public Schools of Saskatoon,* unpublished master's thesis, University of Saskatchewan, Saskatoon, Canada, no date.

Justman, Joseph: *A Comparison of the Functioning of Intellectually Gifted Pupils Enrolled in Special Progress and Normal Progress Classes in Junior High*

Schools, unpublished doctoral dissertation, Columbia University, New York, 1953.

Kelly, Florence C.: The Ungraded Primary School, *Educational Leadership,* 18:79–81, 1960.

Laycock, Samuel R.: *Gifted Children: A Handbook for the Classroom Teacher,* The Copp-Clark Publishing Company, Toronto, Canada, 1957.

Lorge, Irving: Social Gains in the Special Education of the Gifted, *School and Society,* 79:4–7, 1954.

Luchins, Abraham S., and Edith H. Luchins: Children's Attitudes toward Homogeneous Groupings, *Journal of Genetic Psychology,* 72:3–9, 1948.

McCall, William A., and V. A. Jones: A Comparison of the Educational Progress of Bright Pupils in Accelerated and in Regular Classes, *Teachers College Record,* 27:825–832, 1926.

Martinson, Ruth A.: *Educational Programs for Gifted Pupils,* California State Department of Education, Sacramento, Calif., 1961.

Nelson, Edwin A., and Edith E. Carlson: Special Education for Gifted Children: III. Evaluation at the End of Three Years, *Exceptional Children,* 12:6–13, 24, 1945.

Norris, Dorothy: Programs in the Elementary School, chap. 11 in *Education for the Gifted: Fifty-seventh Yearbook of the National Society for the Study of Education,* part 2, The University of Chicago Press, Chicago, 1958.

Passow, A. Harry: The Maze of Research on Ability Grouping, *The Educational Forum,* March, 281–288, 1962.

Pregler, Hedwig O.: Adjustment through Partial Segregation, *Journal of the National Elementary Principals' Association,* 32:241–246, 1952.

Pregler, Hedwig O.: The Colfax Plan, *Exceptional Children,* 20:98, 201–222, 1954.

Pregler, Hedwig O.: The Colfax Plan, chap. 11 in *Education for the Gifted: Fifty-seventh Yearbook of the National Society for the Study of Education,* part 2, The University of Chicago Press, Chicago, 1958.

Raasch, Mildred: Milwaukee's Pilot Program, *Education,* 80:143–146, 1959.

Rennie, R. A.: *A Study of Children Who Were Enrolled from 1932 to 1943 in Classes for Mentally Gifted Children in the Saskatoon Public Schools,* study at the University of Saskatchewan, Saskatoon, Canada, no date.

Rickover, H. G.: *Education for All Children: What We Can Learn from England,* Hearings before the House Committee on Appropriations, 87th Cong., 1962.

Savard, William G.: An Evaluation of the Second Year of an Ability Grouping Program, *California Journal of Educational Research,* 12:62–66, 1961.

Stoddard, George D.: *The Dual Progress Plan: A New Philosophy and Program in Elementary Education,* Harper & Row, Publishers, Incorporated, New York, 1961.

Sumption, Merle R.: *Three Hundred Gifted Children: A Follow-up Study of the Results of Special Education of Superior Children,* World Book Company, Tarrytown-on-Hudson, N.Y., 1941.

Sumption, Merle R., and Evelyn M. Luecking: *Education of the Gifted,* The Ronald Press Company, New York, 1960.

Sumption, Merle R., Dorothy Norris, and Lewis M. Terman: Special Education for the Gifted, in *The Education of Exceptional Children: Forty-ninth Yearbook of the National Society for the Study of Education,* part 2, The University of Chicago Press, Chicago, 1950.

Woolcock, Cyril W.: *New Approaches to the Study of the Gifted,* Silver Burdett Company, Morristown, N. J., 1961.

Worlton, J. T.: The Effect of Homogeneous Classification on the Scholastic Achievement of Bright Pupils, *Elementary School Journal,* 28:336–340, 1928.

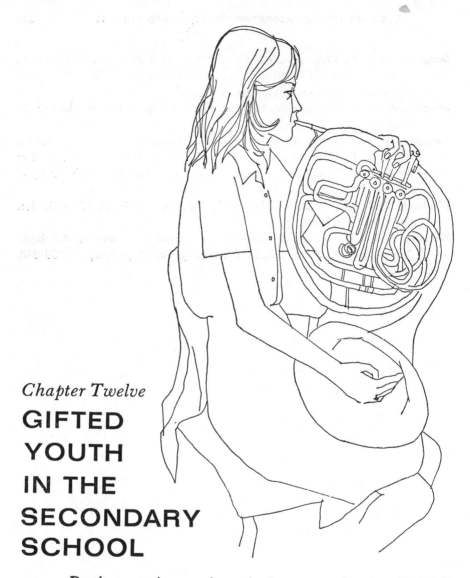

Chapter Twelve

GIFTED YOUTH IN THE SECONDARY SCHOOL

Developments in secondary school programs for the gifted will be considered in this chapter and the next. Leaders in education view this period as the most crucial for the conservation of a nation's resources of intellectual talent. The senior high school years provide a kind of proving ground for the discovery of students with the aptitudes needed for success in college and professional careers. This is the last opportunity for the public schools to identify the gifted and to develop their special competencies.

By the ninth grade, the distinction between a genuinely talented child who has shown a consistent pattern of superior development and one whose early displays of talent have subsided is clearer than ever before. During high school, the adolescent's interests and study preferences are taking a more definite shape, his habits are becoming fixed, and his aptitudes and talents are emerging more clearly. The high school youth is reaching more mature stages in thought and action. More accurate predictions can now be made of success in future schooling than was possible during the elementary school years.

The gifted youth, particularly the student from a home that offers little intellectual stimulus, must depend increasingly on the school as the main source of intellectual training. Gifted students are now in need of educational and career guidance on an individual basis. Personal counseling is as important for them as classroom instruction (see Chapter Fourteen).

SELECTIVE POPULATION

The typical American high school has always had a more selective population, in intellectual talent, than the elementary school. Although this is less true today with the junior high school bridging over from elementary school to senior high, it is still a correct generalization, especially in communities where the high school program is largely academic and dropouts in senior high school are frequent.

What proportion of secondary school youth belong in the category of bright and gifted? As explained in Chapter Two, the upper 15 or 16 per cent of high school youth are recognized as academically talented in terms of aptitude and achievement test scores (the top sigma of the total distribution of high school youth), and the top 2 or 3 per cent are regarded as exceptionally gifted or remarkable.

Who Is the Gifted Adolescent?

Gifted adolescents show the physical and behavioral characteristics typical of all young people in this developmental period as well as certain distinguishing traits. Through the use of the California Psychological Inventory, Lessinger and Martinson found gifted eighth graders to be nontypical of a random selection of like-grade students in personal traits (1961). Gifted students in secondary school reached psychological maturity earlier than their norm population age-mates and tended to resemble each other in basic traits. Gifted students in both junior and senior high school displayed exceptional personal and social maturity.

High school students tend to show initiative in self-selected tasks that are in line with their chief interests. The youth's ambitions, yearnings, and strivings determine his actions. Adolescents drive themselves at a furious pace when the objective satisfies these ambitions. They are keen about new impressions, able to reason in quite mature fashion, to remember, and to reflect on what they have learned. It is only natural to show greater independence in actions and choices at adolescence than before. Although young people now have more self-assurance, they reveal uncertainties about plans for life following high school.

Smith compared superior and average adolescent groups (forty-two students each) matched for social class, chronological age, sex, religion, and nationality (1962). The two groups were selected on the basis of percentile scores on a group intelligence test. The only clear difference between the two groups was in independence and dominance shown by the gifted group.

The scholarly type of gifted student in high school enjoys academic studies that force him to think: mathematics, science, social studies, foreign languages; and he manages to get marks well above average if not the highest in the class. Mathematics was voted the favorite subject in a survey of 1,500 class presidents in New York State high schools. This subject was slightly more popular among boys than girls. The next most popular subject was science for boys and English for girls. Foreign language ranked at the bottom, preferred by only 5 per cent of the boys and 13 per cent of the girls (Bulletin of the Bank of Savings, New York, 1960).

A substantial relationship has been found between mental and social maturity during the adolescent years except in cases of individuals who have been overaccelerated. A seventeen-year-old high school senior was sometimes taken for a teacher because of his poise and businesslike manner. A girl of seventeen, also a high school senior, who enrolled in the Columbia University Science Honors classes meeting on Saturday, associated easily with nineteen- and twenty-year-old students, was accepted by them, and found herself talking easily with others in the group about their mutual interests.

The adolescent development of gifted girls follows somewhat different trends from that of boys. Boys of high ability in high school stand out more than girls in the student population. In the opinion of teachers, girls tend to be more conforming, less original and imaginative, less inclined to experiment in new directions. Girls are inclined to ask, "What shall I do next?" "What do you want me to do?" while the boys are going ahead trying out their own ideas. Goals for schooling and careers beyond high school are also less clear-cut in the case of girls. More often, too, a girl dislikes being thought bright or intelligent by her classmates.

The adolescent with high aptitude and well-rounded interests is illustrated by A, an attractive, socially mature Turkish girl. Although not yet sixteen. she has been chosen from a large number of other candidates for a scholarship to study in America. This girl is equally fluent in English and Turkish and shows all-around superiority in science, mathematics, writing, drama, sports, and other interests. She showed modesty in appraising her attainments, disclaiming abilities superior to others in her class. She plans to finish college before deciding on her life career. A comes from a better than average home. The father is a high-level professional worker; the mother is known for her good sense in training children. The parents have always encouraged the girl to make her own decisions and to assume responsibility for her behavior.

One remarkable boy who attended a special progress class in a New York City junior high school won top honors in all five majors at the end of the ninth grade. Then the family moved to the suburbs, and the boy again won highest honors on graduating from a community high school. He also won more than 80 per cent of all the prize money offered for various awards, a sum amounting to about $300. Friedenberg's book, *The Vanishing Adolescent* (1959), gives sketches of several remarkable adolescents, among them Stanley, the high school student "too good to be true."

Drews made a trait analysis of 500 gifted adolescent boys and girls and observed several different personality types (1963):

1. The studious type, who work for approval or marks. These graduates make excellent employees.
2. The school- and social-leader type, who make good corporation executives and clubwomen.
3. The true intellectuals, the book buyers who like academic studies, constituting about 20 per cent of the gifted. They attend plays and concerts and will give the teacher an argument. These youths belong to the "long-haired" set.
4. The rebels or nonconformists, a small group. These are the "how to do it" fans, who may rate high on tests, but rate average in studies. They become expert mechanics and are good in electronics, technical, or radio work.

In childhood the gifted individual has potential to excel in a variety of school studies as well as interests outside of school. As these young people move on toward adulthood, they normally tend to concentrate more and more on special interests leading to a vocation and to neglect other interests that formerly engrossed them. A bright high school student was torn between piano virtuosity and a medical career. He excelled in science studies, and following college was accepted by a leading medical school. In the meanwhile, he gave up the idea of becoming a concert pianist although he had great difficulty making his decision.

Bright young people in their early teens may become obsessed with an interest that leads to a distinguished career. This was true of a boy who became enamored of the French language because his mother's ancestry was French. In the upper elementary grades he made his first acquaintance with the language; then in his early teens he decided on a career in foreign language teaching, especially the Romance languages. In spite of family poverty, he persisted in this aspiration; on completing college, he traveled in France to perfect his accent. He did a distinguished Ph.D. thesis in his chosen field and went on to become a college department head. All the while his tremendous drive to achieve these goals overshadowed all other desires and immediate concerns.

The peer group dominates the adolescent's ideas and his behavior. What others think of him, his looks, his actions, his ideas, is of utmost importance to normal development. The adolescent would not be true to his nature if he did not seek protection in his crowd, gang, or like-age associates. In growing toward adulthood, the gifted adolescent goes through much the same crises as others in his age group, even though he is able to think and act more independently.

The typical adolescent is striving for social recognition, emancipation, and influence. Anything that enhances these ambitions is certain to be popular with a teen-ager. Although a youth may not wish to be thought bright or intellectual, winning top honors scholastically or being awarded a college scholarship carries almost as much prestige today as getting an athletic award, winning a popularity contest, or starring in a school entertainment.

Goals for the Gifted

Goals for the gifted listed in Chapter Seven apply in general to all levels of schooling, to young children and high school seniors alike. The more specialized aims for the gifted in high school will be described in the following sections.

The purpose of high school education is to enhance the all-around maturity of the individual student by providing a broad background as a basis for later professional work or specialization. High school life serves to develop the unique strengths and traits of each individual.

There is need, on the one hand, for thorough intellectual training of the gifted to ensure disciplined minds capable of coping with the complex problems of our time. On the other hand, there is the necessity of training gifted youths to become adaptable, well-rounded, wholesome human beings. Neither of these tasks is the sole province of the school. Community living and family life have a large share in the youth's all-around education.

LEARNING SCHOLARLY HABITS AND ATTITUDES

The abler students in high school should be cultivating a taste for learning and acquiring the characteristics of a scholarly mind: objectivity in searching out facts and in reaching valid conclusions, a scientific attitude of mind, a sense of detachment in explorations, a love of truth.

To become a scholar, the youth needs to learn to use the scholar's tools; he must develop skill in tackling a difficult problem or a broad project, in using books and library facilities for study, in being able to plan ahead and to organize work. The high school youth should have extensive practice in using classified sources of information: encyclopedia, dictionary, atlas, bibliographical sources, biographical indexes, yearbooks, and other reference works. Technical competence in mathematics will be required of those who are headed for scientific careers. The fundamental skills in arts and crafts are essential for those with special aptitude in art and design. Foreign languages may be needed as tools for specialized study.

For the gifted scholar, competency in oral and written communication—oral reporting, debate, note taking, outlining papers, essay writing, expository writing—is no less important than skill in science and mathematics.

Young people must be taught to make the most of their abilities; guidance can help them to recognize their strengths and weaknesses, to develop a positive attitude toward achievement, and to make full use of their unusual assets as learners and talented individuals.

Teachers should help the student develop a high sense of independence and self-responsibility. They should show respect for the special abilities of the individual pupil so that his unique traits and capacities can be conserved and developed.

THE SOCIALIZATION PROCESS

Since the gifted adult must ordinarily associate with his fellows in various relationships, considerable thought should be given to socialization processes in adolescence. In the case of the Turkish girl mentioned above, socialization was no problem; it may be a serious matter, however, for a talented youth with tendencies toward reclusiveness or extreme aggression.

In the course of a lifetime, a person must have dealings with many, many people and with all sorts of people. A prominent person—a director, a boss, a leader in government, or the head of an industrial enterprise—has more social contacts than the average. These contacts are not solely face to face, but by telephone and correspondence, extending throughout the nation, perhaps around the world. The ability to communicate, to "get along with others," helps one build prestige and gain support for new enterprises.

The gifted youth will be better balanced to the extent that he broadens his social contacts, learns to accept and to be accepted by his fellows—a two-way process. The gifted need to learn to work cooperatively with fellow members of class and club groups or on a team with a common group goal.

DEVELOPING QUALITIES OF LEADERSHIP

True leadership requires, above all, qualities of integrity, honesty, tact, and sympathy. The skills and attitudes for effective leadership are developed through participation in group activities, through sharing and working cooperatively. The youth who learns the skills of leadership in high school is that much better prepared for college life and for his later career. The qualities of leadership develop as students are placed in managerial positions that give them practice in getting along with people and in dealing with problems requiring decision making and resourcefulness.

DEVELOPING A STABLE CHARACTER

The gifted can learn academic work at double-quick time. Why shouldn't the youth with a head start in reasoning and judgment learn to apply his intelligence to the ordinary problems of life with courage and integrity—not merely knowing their meaning as terms or acknowledging their importance, but demonstrating them as traits in everyday behavior? Unless the gifted sense their responsibility to live purposefully and serve others, rather than living lives of selfish exploitation, where is the gain for humanity?

MAINTAINING GOOD HEALTH

Learning to keep physically fit is essential for gifted youth because of the stresses and strains to which modern life subjects its leaders. The health problems of the brain worker are different from those of others. Because the studious youth tends to neglect sports and outdoor exercise, the school should emphasize physical fitness. All students need some time for outdoor activities daily, not only for good health, but to reduce tension and maintain a sense of well-being. Sports and recreation provide a balance wheel for the brain worker.

Curriculum Adjustments

A National Education Research Division survey of school practices in 1958–1959 showed the growing tendency of urban school systems to make some provision for the gifted in high school. Almost eight in ten school systems had special programs for gifted students in both junior and senior high school. The extent of the provision being made was directly proportionate to the size of the school system; 100 per cent of the largest cities had special programs, 66 per cent of towns over 5,000 population, and about 57 per cent of smaller places. The number of high schools offering major programs or special guidance services for the gifted, however, still runs considerably behind the number offering driver education or special courses for slow learners.

Educators agree that a rich and challenging high school program is extremely important for academically talented students. All the conventional subject areas should be included in such a program, but the courses should be given at advanced levels, with more freedom for the student to explore problems on his own initiative.

Questions to be considered are:

What types of secondary programs are best for the well-rounded education of the gifted? What subjects should they pursue? What particular combinations of studies should be planned for students with special interests and talents? What type of subject-matter organization is best in teaching the gifted? How far should the students go in advanced studies before entering college? How can more flexibility be introduced into the high school program to accommodate the unusual student.

Among the different types of programs for the gifted student in high school may be mentioned:

Ability grouping or sectioning in basic courses required of all students

Independent study on an individual basis

Advanced-placement programs

Honors programs

Special seminar courses

Small workshop and laboratory classes

Cluster groups within the regular classroom in different courses

Afterschool club activities and special classes

Televised programs and courses

Cooperation of community resources, libraries and museums in offering programs for the gifted

Variation in academic load is another means of individualizing instruction in the high school. A bright student may be able to carry an extra subject.

In the larger schools advanced electives and honors work are offered in science, mathematics, literature, foreign languages, and other subjects. There are broad, inclusive subjects, such as world literature, international area studies, current issues and problems, and specialities, such as creative writing. Anthropology, world culture, sociology, psychology, specialized history studies, philosophy, and other courses formerly not taught until college are now being introduced as enrichment for advanced students.

Special seminar groups are organized for superior students with like interests, for example, in creative writing or the study of foreign relations.

Gifted students work on projects in the core curriculum, which combines several studies such as history, literature, and art.

There are enrichment opportunities through school programs, attendance at concerts and lectures. The students engage in school-life projects and programs such as science exhibits, assembly programs, school publications, library service.

Loading the more able students with homework assignments is less helpful than permitting them the use of their outside time on special studies and reports related to study projects they have initiated.

Conferences are arranged with professional people in the community who are interested in conferring with a talented youth about his special interests.

The gifted high school student finds an outlet in joining a scholastic team—debating or public speaking, mathematics, and others. His intellectual life is enriched through participation in afterschool club groups, museum courses and lectures, Saturday courses conducted by a neighboring college, summer work in such areas as the humanities, biology, art, music, or mathematics.

High school programs for the gifted were, at first, geared largely toward the production of scientists and mathematicians because it was feared that we were falling behind in meeting the demands of the new technology. Now that this need is being met, school administrators avoid concentrating unduly on science and mathematics at the expense of liberal studies.

The scientists themselves recognize that the training of a chemist or engineer should not be narrowly limited to training in science. A scientist needs to be aware of the social implications of his work. Equally broad intellectual training should be provided in the literary student's program. There is intellectual enrichment for him in studies outside his major interest and beyond the array of academic studies he is required to take.

During the summers of 1958 and 1959, the North Central Association of Colleges and Secondary Schools set up a project on the Guidance and Motivation of Superior and Talented Students, supported by a grant from the Carnegie Corporation of New York. The reports of the ten conferences and of four programs have been published by Shertzer (1960).

The improvement of offerings for talented students has been described by Copley in a report of visits he made to high schools in Michigan and elsewhere (1961). He reported on ability grouping, enrichment, acceleration, advanced placement, and matters relating to grades and credits, as well as the role of teachers and their selection. Special programs for the gifted cost more than regular instruction, but the added cost is small; and people are convinced that the extra expenditure is justified.

Enrichment opportunities for gifted students in high school are suggested in a bulletin of the New York State Education Department (1958).

MORE EMPHASIS ON "SOLID" SUBJECTS FOR THE INTELLECTUALLY GIFTED

Too often the gifted have sailed through high school with little effort, marking time in courses designed for the average student. Instead, in the opinion of Dr. James B. Conant, Dr. Arthur Bestor, Vice-Admiral Rickover, and others, our best students should have the toughest mental training they can take. Even when advanced academic work is offered, many qualified students seem to prefer the easy, more trivial studies.

The U.S. Office of Education reported the results of a survey concerning the kinds of high school programs students of different academic talent were carrying (Greer and Harbeck, 1961). The information was obtained from questionnaires completed by high school principals and from transcripts of credits for a sampling of students in graduating classes of 1958. In schools with large enrollments, approximately 54 per cent of pupils in the upper 15 per cent in ability completed programs with high academic content; in medium-sized schools, 40 per cent completed programs of this type; while in the smallest schools, only 19 per cent completed such programs. The same trend held for the group in the top 25 per cent in ability. In the smaller schools, enrollments in foreign languages were lower, probably because of lack of offerings in this field.

Other findings were as follows: Among the top quarter in academic ability, the median student had less than two years of science and two years of foreign languages. Only 42 per cent of the students had more than two years of mathematics. Only 63 per cent of the upper 5 per cent in ability and only half of the upper 25 per cent were enrolled in the college preparatory curriculum.

Grave concern was expressed about the possible talent loss implied in these figures. There are indications today that an increasing number of the most competent students are enrolling in "solid" academic subjects that prepare for advanced education.

A survey of high school students in Maryland with IQs of 120 and above indicated that two-thirds of the boys in half the schools were taking seven years of mathematics and science, and that virtually all able boys were taking at least six years of these studies (Conant, 1959, appendix E). The story for the girls was quite different. In only 11 per cent of the high schools were virtually all the able girls taking seven years of science and mathematics. In 70 per cent of the high schools, however, at least half the able girls were taking six years of these subjects. Very few of the good students of either sex were taking more than two years of a foreign language. In only half a dozen schools were half of the able boys or two-thirds of the bright girls taking three years of a language.

Competent girls are not so well represented in science and

mathematics courses in typical American high schools as boys. When girls do go in for science, they tend to specialize in biology rather than the physical sciences. We have only to look in the direction of the Soviet Union to realize that when girls are strongly motivated, they try out for science studies in every area in almost the same proportion as boys.

The tendency of girls to avoid the tougher intellectual studies reduces their chances for college entrance and college success. The result is that half the most promising students are scarcely represented in the fields requiring the highest level of expertness.

Ordinarily, students in private preparatory schools complete more units in mathematics, science, and language than students in public high schools.

Dr. Conant recommended that the academically talented student take five "solid" subjects in the senior high school. This might work well in a boarding school, but it is a heavy schedule for students who would like to go out for band, sports, dramatics, or other activities that interfere with the load of homework.

Dr. Conant believes that those who have the ability and energy to handle both mathematics and a foreign language should take these subjects through the four-year high school program. He recommends that schools check annually to make sure that their abler students are not shirking hard subjects. The more able and highly talented students can be expected not only to learn faster but to explore a wider range of problems and to delve into them more deeply.

Ensuring a Balanced School Program for the Gifted

Some people may argue that high school hours are too precious for gifted students to waste on practical skills and nonacademic school-life activities. As a matter of fact, the gifted, as all others, benefit from a well-balanced school program. Participation in recreational and social activities counteracts a tendency toward excessive bookishness or isolation.

A recommendation of the Educational Policies Commission is that secondary schools should allow abler students to carry heavier loads so that they can satisfy their wide intellectual and cultural interests. The bright young person entering the teens needs to try out his powers in many fields. Specializing in mathematics or English literature or any other field too early is a mistake. A broad program of studies opens up new fields of interest and affords better preparation for college. Students attending our large urban high schools seldom have the balanced program of study, sports, and recreation provided by the preparatory boarding schools.

Dr. Clarence Faust, president of The Fund for the Advancement of Education, observed that what the superior high school students needed was not solely stiffer courses that make demands on them intellectually, but more flexibility to permit them to exercise more initiative, imagination, and originality in their work. In our best public high schools, such as the Evanston Township High School in Illinois, students do not concentrate on academic studies alone, but engage in a wide array of school-life and recreational opportunities.

In contrast to earlier years, more attention must be given in the high school to determining the student's special strengths in different subject areas. Relatively few high school youths can carry a program of advanced academic studies in such widely diverse fields as science and mathematics, foreign languages, social studies, and English literature, but they are able to excel in one or two of these areas.

SPEEDING UP

Authorities estimate that from 15 to 20 per cent of all high school students should be able to complete the six-year junior-senior high school span in five years with speeded-up programs, enrichment of courses, independent study, summer programs, and other provisions.

Ninth graders admitted to the special accelerated program in science and mathematics at Cass Technical High School in Detroit do five years' work in four, allowing more time for elective subjects and specialized subjects not ordinarily taught in high school. Students are screened for the program through an intelligence test, superior grades in school subjects, and teachers' recommendations.

The Hicksville, Long Island, pilot program enables the gifted to complete the usual secondary school science program plus two years of college-level science work by the end of the twelfth grade.

REPORTS OF CITY PROGRAMS

The program for the gifted in the schools and colleges of Portland, Oregon, supported by The Fund for the Advancement of Education, grew out of the interest of teachers in developing better methods for extending educational experiences for bright children (*The*

Gifted Child in Portland, 1959). Special programs for the gifted in the secondary schools of Portland include advanced sections of regular classes, seminars in certain academic subjects, comprehensive seminars, and special talent classes. The emphasis is more on broadening and enriching the student's education than on shortening his time in school. Time is saved in the Portland program through school-college cooperation.

The school system of Pittsburgh has instituted new programs to encourage maximum achievement and scholarly development of students ranking in the top 10 to 20 per cent of the student body. Ability grouping is provided during the junior and senior high school years, subject by subject, but with opportunity for students to "cross-track" according to their progress. The Directed Studies Program provides a rigorous academic curriculum for the academically talented, stressing sequential learning rather than samplings here and there in many different areas. Juniors and seniors meet once or twice a week for a unifying course that cuts across departmental lines, with guest lecturers introducing each unit.

SOME PROBLEMS AND ISSUES

Numerous pressures militate against special provision for the abler students in typical high schools. Overcrowding cuts down the amount of time teachers can give to individual students; there is a shortage of competent teachers, particularly in science and mathematics, and to some extent in foreign languages; school guidance personnel are obliged to devote most of their time to slow learners and problem cases.

Small classes for the gifted are criticized as uneconomical. There is the old fear that the gifted will receive benefits that other children, except the slowest learners, are denied. In the rigidly scheduled daily program, more flexible block-time studies or assignments on an individual basis are difficult to schedule.

One of the most serious issues concerns the type of program to be provided for gifted youth headed for college. College entrance requirements tend to constrict the senior high school curriculum; courses are often geared to the content of the comprehensive college entrance examinations. College-bound students are not apt to elect noncredit courses. In one senior high school class observed by the author, cramming for college entrance examinations consumed all the time in the English program. A literature course consisted of memorizing titles, plots, and characters in the classics of English literature.

How a Good High School Ensures Excellent Schooling for the Gifted

The quality of a high school, which is disclosed both by the caliber of its teaching staff and by its physical facilities, will largely determine whether the school can do justice to gifted and talented students. Every countrywide survey of public-supported high schools has shown the great diversity of these institutions, even within the same community. Substandard schools with limited offerings in crowded industrial areas are in marked contrast to schools in the better sections and suburban areas. The latter may have a student population averaging around 115 IQ, with 60 per cent or more of the students planning on college.

The features of a good school and the way in which it works in the best interests of the gifted were outlined in Chapter Seven. It is sufficient to mention here the importance of flexibility and adaptability in scheduling, sectioning, and programming. There should be provision for the abler students to accelerate in their studies, if this seems desirable. The best schools have a relatively small ratio of students to staff.

In his report on the American high school, Conant made a number of recommendations for improving secondary schooling, some of which apply particularly to the gifted (1959). The chief points are:

Set up an adequate counseling and guidance system

Provide individualized programs of study

Require certain basic subjects of study for all students, but provide for the grouping of children in subject areas according to ability

Improve the work in English composition

Set up a special program for the academically superior students

Make special provisions for the most highly gifted through advanced-placement college-level courses

Provide for an academic inventory of every student that will indicate whether the gifted are following courses that challenge their abilities and prepare them for the university

If a student has won academic honors, indicate this fact on his diploma

Provide instruction in developmental reading, including library skills

Offer summer school courses for bright, ambitious students

Extend and improve instruction in modern foreign languages

Strenghten science courses, work in physics and mathematics

Set up a social studies course centering around American problems for senior-year students

THE CORE CURRICULUM—BLOCK—TIME STUDY

Most high schools operate on a departmentalized basis, but there has been a growing trend during the last thirty years to combine two or more academic areas for core teaching or block-time study. The core curriculum cuts across subject-matter boundaries, combining subjects such as social studies, art, and literature, or science and mathematics.

The advantage of core studies and projects is that the student concentrates on problems related to the broad core theme instead of studying textbook lessons in isolated subjects. The students select problems in the core, then through their study and research seek to understand the broad implications of the problems. Cooperative planning is required by the student and his teachers all the way through the study of a core theme.

The core program can be adjusted to the wide range of abilities in a regular class through small-group and individualized studies growing out of the core. Team teaching in which instructors representing several different subject areas work together is the ideal arrangement for core instruction.

Administrators find that scheduling difficulties tend to beset the core curriculum in the high school. Another problem is that teachers need more time than they can usually spare to work with other teachers in the core team for developing the unit resource materials.

The core program at the University School, Columbus, Ohio, was described by Everett (1961). More information on the core program for junior and senior high schools will be found in professional books on the high school curriculum. Some illustrations of topics for core programs are given in later sections of this chapter.

The Comprehensive High School: Its Contribution to the Education of the Gifted

The comprehensive high school is a secondary school attended by all the youths in a typical community regardless of differences in academic or vocational interests and talents, whether college-bound (about 35 to 40 per cent of the enrollment) or not.

The comprehensive American high school stands in contrast to the older preparatory type of school that offers a limited array of academic subjects, and to academic secondary schools abroad that prepare for the university—the Gymnasium of Germany and middle Europe and the *lycée* in Europe and many countries around the world.

In the comprehensive high school all students pass through the same portals, but they move out into a variety of courses and programs according to their interests and abilities.

How does the comprehensive high school serve the gifted? In contrast to schools for separate social classes, it gives youths of exceptional intellectual capacity a chance to rise above an inferior social status. There is more chance that the undiscovered gifted, especially those who might otherwise have been sidetracked into a vocational-training cul-de-sac, will receive the training that leads to distinguished careers. There is also less chance that mediocre students will try academic studies beyond their ability instead of following courses in which they can succeed.

The wide array of course offerings available to all students is more apt to draw out and to display the special talents of gifted students than a school with stratified or limited courses. The comprehensive high school, by not making a hard and fast division between the academic-minded and vocational students in early adolescence, reduces the likelihood of the gifted's concentrating solely on academic courses.

In small communities, much the same courses are followed by all students, but in the larger cities, comprehensive high schools usually have three (or four) separate programs: academic or college preparatory, commercial, and general (sometimes vocational or trades). The choice of a program is usually made at the point of high school entrance on the basis of student interests or parental preferences without much attention to the student's academic aptitudes.

Instead of distinctly separate high school courses or curriculum tracks—the traditional college preparatory, the commercial or business course, a general course, and vocational courses—authorities today recommend opening all subject areas to all students, but with provision for grouping in common required subjects according to the student's past school success and general academic ability. The brighter students are placed in top sections of these basic courses and are steered toward more challenging advanced courses as they progress through school.

During the past few years, the newer type of secondary school with more comprehensive offerings and a flexible program and curriculum has been established in a number of foreign countries in place of the stratified, academic type of school attended by relatively few youths in the high school–age population. Such schools not only provide a better-balanced school experience, but they also serve to break down class distinctions.

A criticism of the comprehensive high school is that it offers a common level of instruction for all that is not sufficiently challenging for the gifted; neither is it suited to those of limited ability who need training in skills to fit them for gainful employment. These criticisms are more likely to be valid in a small school, the only one in the community, than in large urban schools that can offer every type of course a large school population requires.

DISADVANTAGES OF THE "TOO SMALL" HIGH SCHOOL

The "too small" high school that cannot afford to employ the teaching staff for the wide range of studies offered in a large city school has definite limitations for the gifted. Surveys have disclosed that a school with less than one hundred students in the graduating class cannot offer the advanced academic studies needed by the gifted to prepare for college. In a large high school, multiple-track plans are feasible, as well as advanced electives and special seminars, because in these schools there are enough talented students to make up regular-sized class groups.

Consolidation of smaller high schools has the advantage of bringing together a nucleus of gifted students large enough to form groups for advanced studies. A greater variety of courses can be offered and better-trained teachers employed. In his appraisal of the American high school, Dr. Conant recommended that schools with fewer than one hundred students in the high school graduating class should consolidate to form a comprehensive high school for a wider district. The school could then provide ability groups on three levels in each major curriculum field.

Recently, fifty boys and girls, the total enrollment of two small-town high schools in Iowa, found themselves at the opening of school in September in a large, newly organized, consolidated high school. Here they could study modern foreign languages, take a fourth year of English, advanced courses in mathematics and science, shorthand, and driver education. There was also a part-time music teacher in the school.

To suggest that outstanding scholars are graduated only from large high schools would be misleading. Both the valedictorian and salutatorian in the 1963 graduating class of a Midwestern university were graduates of small high schools. However, the mother of one of these young people was a teacher of Latin; the father of the other was a scientist.

Educational television is a great boon to smaller schools where there are too few students to form special-interest groups and where travel to a consolidated school is inconvenient. In Nebraska, lessons in subjects that were previously unavailable to students in smaller schools are now beamed from the University of Nebraska station.

In Hancock High School, 30 miles from Hagerstown, Maryland, students are now enrolled in an advanced college-level TV course in mathematics. The students have TV lessons three times a week plus personal instruction from an instructor who makes the rounds of the seven participating high schools. Foreign language classes, too, are now taught by experts via TV. Classes conducted by airborne television represent a new departure in Midwestern communities. Purdue University in Indiana conducts programs televised by experts.

ENRICHMENT THROUGH SCHOOL–LIFE ACTIVITIES

Participating in school-life affairs and projects is a means of providing the balanced program that is so desirable for every adolescent. A rich program of school and extracurricular activities enables students to develop more self-responsibility and to learn and practice leadership skills. These activities prepare for fuller participation in college life, as well as for a well-rounded life in later years.

The gifted adolescent finds outlets for his talents in art, music, public speaking, newspaper editing, and school government. School-wide projects such as book week, exhibits, school programs, and dramatic performances provide scope for original thinking, planning, and leadership experience.

Grouping and Sectioning Students

In the typical high school where all students are required to take common required courses in English, history and citizenship, mathematics, and science, it has become a common practice to set up different sections for the more able students, for a middle group, and for slower learners, the latter including those requiring special remedial instruction, review work, or terminal courses. Depending on achievement, a student might be in the top group in one or two subjects, but not in others. The work is paced according to the progress and specific interests of the students.

An advantage of sectioning or "tracking" in high school is that it prevents the exclusion of slow learners from academic work in science, mathematics, or foreign languages. Instead, slow learners are given such work at a more elementary level. With slower learners taken care of in their own sections, the highly competent students can move ahead more rapidly; some may be able to do advanced work of college level.

Grouping students in basic courses according to three academic levels is about as far as the typical good-sized high school can go with sectioning. Even a three-track plan for all the basic subjects is practical only in high schools with around 500 or more students. Below this figure there are too few students to compose a normal-sized advanced group.

The high school must be prepared to deal with parents who insist on the placement of a slower learner in college preparatory work or a mediocre student in high sections and advanced courses. Sectioning loses its specific function when the unqualified are included along with the highly talented.

Just as in the elementary school, part-time groupings and small-group work within the class are a means of breaking up uniformity and drawing out the interests and abilities of individual students (see Chapter Eleven).

ILLUSTRATIONS OF GROUPING PLANS

In some schools a compromise with grouping, sectioning, and special courses has been worked out. Cubberly High School, Palo Alto, California, has a scheme that gets around scheduling difficulties yet provides for maximum ability grouping and individualization of instruction. The 400 seniors are placed in the charge of a team of teachers. The students meet in groups of 100 or less. The teaching teams include teaching interns, who are graduate students at Stanford University.

In St. Louis, Missouri, incoming ninth-grade students are screened for programs suited to three ability levels in an effort to avoid repetition for the talented and prevent slow learners from holding back the bright. Students in all three levels work without danger of certain failure, on the one hand, or underachievement, on the other. Bright students in the program take extra units in English, social studies, mathematics, science, foreign languages, and two additional units of electives. They are also encouraged to participate in extracurricular activities.

In Evanston Township High School the students are ability-grouped to provide the maximum amount of intellectual stimulation for bright students without neglecting average and less-capable learners. Groupings are by subjects; a bright student in the top section in mathematics might be in an average or even a remedial section in English. There are as many as eight different levels in senior English. Entering freshmen take any one of five courses in mathematics on the basis of aptitudes shown on initial ratings.

The community of San Angelo, Texas, introduced a three-rail curriculum project supported by The Fund for the Advancement of Education (Paschal, 1960), with three parallel courses in English, science, mathematics, foreign languages, and social studies in grade 12, and two-level courses in grades 7 to 11. Between 10 and 20 per cent of the children are in the top-rail program. A student may be in the fast rail in one or more subjects. From time to time students shift from one rail to another, if a change is warranted. Results indicate that the top-rail students have more challenge, teaching has improved, and the general level of work is higher.

In the Plainfield, New Jersey, High School, students are selected for a special program on the basis of ability and originality. There is a special class in English for gifted students; students remain in the class for two years. In Portland, Oregon, there are special classes for the gifted and part-time special classes in studies such as German or advanced mathematics. A senior high school in Washington, D.C., has inaugurated a four-track plan adjusted to different levels of ability.

San Bernardino, California   A special program was introduced in the San Bernardino, California, public schools, with the purpose of identifying various intellectual abilities and talents and providing educational programs to develop these abilities to the maximum (Paschal, 1960). The program began with grades 7 and 10. A list was compiled of the gifted and talented who would benefit from individual counseling. Each year new groups of about 20 per cent of the incoming seventh and tenth graders are started in special programs. Students with high nonacademic potential are included in the program, but not necessarily in an accelerated program.

Ability grouping on a subject basis has resulted in improved opportunities for the academically talented in high school. In the senior high school, the more capable students are grouped for mathematics, science, English, and foreign languages, and in one of the junior high schools, for music. Students show great interest in these classes, and considerable prestige is connected with them. Students can now qualify for advanced standing in mathematics as the result of courses taken in high school, and these opportunities are to be extended.

In a junior high school drawing students largely from a lower socioeconomic stratum, capable students have resisted placement in gifted classes. Through counseling with parents and through work with students, abler students from this type of background are being more successfully challenged.

Emphasis has been placed on the involvement of faculty and administration in new programs of in-service training of teachers. Teachers believe that in order to do justice to students in the top section, they should be given lighter teaching loads.

College-level Courses

In a growing number of high schools selected students take introductory college courses for which they may earn advanced-placement standing in college. These courses enable the student to avoid needless duplication of college freshman work and provide a more demanding learning experience in the senior year of high school. They have also helped raise the scholastic level and improve the academic atmosphere of the high school. With the increased cost of going to college away from home, there is a real financial gain for a student who can earn part of his college credit in the local high school. Even before this movement became popular, a few selected students in the smaller private schools managed to receive college credit for advanced work in mathematics or language done with an instructor alone or in a small group. Before 1930, gifted students at the Lincoln School of Teachers College, New York, occasionally studied advanced mathematics courses for which they received college credit.

Through the years, capable graduates of the University of Chicago Laboratory School, comparable to the Lincoln School students, have taken examinations for exemption from college courses. In 1932 the University of Buffalo established an examination program for course exemptions in the freshman year as a means of accelerating gifted students through college.

The most rapid development in advanced-placement programs has taken place since 1950. In 1962, college-level courses taken in high school were offered in 46 per cent of large high schools and in 13 per cent of the smaller schools. These courses are chiefly in the larger Eastern independent preparatory schools and in the better suburban high schools. They tend to be offered only in the better-equipped schools enrolling a large proportion of college-bound students.

In the spring of 1950, the Oregon Council on Advanced Placement was formed to assist Oregon high schools in offering college-level courses (*The Gifted Child in Portland,* 1959). The Portland–Reed College program was designed to enrich the educational experiences of gifted high school youth through cooperation with faculty members of Reed College in Portland. Beginning in 1952, faculty members of the college cooperated with Portland high school teachers in offering advanced work for able students. Since 1957 the program has been supported entirely by regular school funds. Now the council is working to increase the number of these courses: it is providing consultants for in-service training of high school teachers and urging school administrators to consider the advantages of this type of program.

NEW YORK CITY SCHOOLS

In New York City during 1961–1962 there were thirty-eight high schools with 135 classes in all subject areas in the Advanced Placement Program. The courses given included English, American history, European history, French, Spanish, German, mathematics, biology, chemistry, and physics.

Admission to the Advanced Placement courses is open only to superior students who are strongly motivated to work at a high achievement level. Priority is given to those who have demonstrated a strong interest in the subjects offered in the program. The students must have high intelligence and reading ability, have regular twelfth-grade standing, have indicated willingness to complete the full year's course, and be able to work well with a small group of superior fellow students.

The curriculum content of the courses credited in the program is described in a book published by the College Entrance Examination Board. The New York State Education Department has also issued Advanced Placement Program booklets in a number of subject areas.

Although the abler students may have college-level minds, the school avoids treating them like mature college students. Instead, they are assigned lessons and explore problems with the superior mentality of bright adolescents. On entering college, these students make excellent academic records and, on the whole, have a satisfying school experience.

In any number of high schools today college-level courses are offered for selected students via TV. In Washington County, Maryland, students who take a special televised mathematics course earn credit for advanced placement in college mathematics. Students also complete beginning work in biology, chemistry, and physics before grade 12, leaving the senior year for advanced courses.

PROS AND CONS OF ADVANCED–PLACEMENT PROGRAMS

Although there is general agreement that these programs offer bright students the challenge of advanced study, that they serve to keep the college goal in focus and save time in college, some possible disadvantages have been pointed out.

In a recent New York City conference, participants discussed the pros and cons of the Advanced Placement Program and drew up a list of proposals for improving it. Conference members observed that the program challenged students by opening up new areas of knowledge and inspiring them with new insights; the curriculum was enriched in several directions; teachers were stimulated to experiment; and the transition from high school to college was improved.

On the other hand, there was evidence that acceleration was sometimes at the expense of needed enrichment; in some cases the program leaned too heavily on standard courses rather than experimenting with curriculum offerings. There tended to be undue preparation for examinations and college work which cannot always be adjusted to the ongoing high school program.

The high school may not be the most favorable setting for college-level courses. Other problems arise from the fact that not all the students who undertake advanced courses complete them or go on to take exemption examinations to receive credit for the work toward a college degree. The college may have nothing special in the way of courses or programs to offer these students once they are in college with advanced standing.

There is a question as to whether the courses offered in advanced-placement programs should be aimed toward preprofessional specializations or should include only general education courses. Some concern about the College Board Advanced Placement Program has been expressed because of the expense of maintaining small classes, scheduling difficulties, and the uncertain policies of some colleges regarding the program.

Joint High School–College Programs

In some schools, as in Portland, Oregon, there has been coordination between a high school and a local college through the cooperation of the college staff and use of college facilities. In 1960, advanced science students were taking college-level courses in 137 college centers across the country. By taking some work at a college center while still in high school, the student has a foretaste of college life and can realize the necessity of good study habits.

Under the University of Connecticut Cooperative Plan for Superior Students, students do college-level work in various subjects in addition to their regular high school work in the same field. The textbooks used are those of introductory courses at the university. The high school teachers are supervised by a member of the university staff. If the student is successful, he is granted credit for the equivalent of the college freshman course. On entering the university, he may accelerate or take other courses for enrichment.

Bright high school girls in the New London, Connecticut, area have been invited by Connecticut College to take freshman college courses tuition-free. The students are accepted for college studies on the basis of their high school records and the school principal's recommendation. They then may choose any regular freshman course meeting three times a week and receive full college credit for satisfactory work.

Superior high school seniors are permitted to take one or two courses in the College of Arts and Sciences at the University of Arkansas concurrently with their studies in high school. The program is similar to that at the University of California at Los Angeles. A bright boy of sixteen who won a four-year scholarship to the university at the end of his junior year in high school proceeded to take both high school and college courses simultaneously the following year.

Miami University in Ohio has made college-level courses available to superior high school students from cooperating schools. These new opportunities are open to students who rank in the top one-fourth of the class, are in the top quartile on standardized college aptitude tests, and are recommended for the program by the school principal. Selected students attend summer school on the college campus in the junior year of high school and one or more classes during their regular senior school year.

There is a somewhat similar plan at the University of Akron, where college-level courses are provided for selected high school students in the community. Satisfactory work in these courses is accepted for college credit. Under this program students from twenty-seven to thirty-one high schools in Akron took advantage of this plan in 1959 and 1960. The results were generally favorable; student achievement corresponded with the maturity level of the students enrolled.

The Carnegie Institute of Technology, Pittsburgh, has cooperated with the local public high schools in setting up advanced-placement courses in English, social studies, and mathematics-science, with Carnegie professors giving instruction in the high schools. The advanced-placement program now in its fifth year has enrolled 1,200 students in thirty-four public and private secondary schools in Pittsburgh and environs. In several schools the scores earned on the Advanced Placement Examinations have been among the best of any public school in the nation.

The objectives of Pittsburgh's "Project English" are to develop composition and reading programs for grades 10 through 12 that will lead to excellent work in college. A long-range goal of the program is to establish sets of standards for high school English for colleges to use in revising freshmen offerings so that learning will be sequential and cumulative. Project social studies involves the preparation and testing of a new sequential and cumulative curriculum in social studies for able students in grades 9 through 12. For the mathematics-science project, new courses have been developed for able students in biology, chemistry, and mathematics, including advanced-placement work in biology in the eleventh grade and in chemistry and calculus in the twelfth grade.

Presently, the University of Pittsburgh, the Pittsburgh public schools, several neighboring colleges, and nearly a hundred school systems in greater Pittsburgh have united in a Learning Research and Development Center to provide continuous learning experiences through which able students can progress on an individual basis without the restraints of the traditional lock-step graded system.

MacMurray College and Jacksonville High School in Illinois cooperate in offering a course in philosophy for superior senior-year high school students. The course is planned by the college and taught by a college faculty member.

The Westminster Schools, a group of independent schools in Atlanta, Georgia, cooperate with three universities in the Atlanta area in offering joint programs during the last two years of high school and the first two years of college in five content areas, affording a continuing experience in high school–college education.

For details of advanced-standing procedures in the colleges see Chapter Seventeen.

EXEMPTION FROM STUDIES IN HIGH SCHOOL

The plan of exemption from studies now commonly practiced in the colleges has been extended to the high school. In the George School, Pennsylvania, and in other secondary schools students may receive credit for a subject on the basis of an examination without attending the class.

Honors Courses and Programs

Honors courses have been referred to as "the school within a school," a program of studies which able students in the senior high school may enter voluntarily. Before honors programs and independent study were introduced in the secondary school, the most capable students had to enrich their education outside of school. Honors work in high school provides the intellectually gifted students with a liberal arts, precollege education. These courses go far beyond typical high school courses in the respective fields.

Plans were made for honors work in Monroe High School, Rochester, New York, as early as 1938. Students selected for honors courses rated in the top 1 per cent in intelligence according to aptitude tests, and they maintained superior scholarship records for each grade level, 9 through 12. Details of the curriculum and instructional policies, reporting, and evaluation are given in a publication by Burnside (1942).

NEW YORK CITY HIGH SCHOOLS

For thirty years the New York City schools have made provisions for the intellectually gifted in high school through organizing honors classes, districtwide, or within one high school; programs of honors classes; and enrichment for gifted students by subjects. Practically all New York City high schools, except the trade schools, have some form of honors program or honors classes.

At Erasmus High School in Brooklyn, honors classes in English provide enriched work in writing for talented boys and girls. These classes include work in poetry, short story, and essay writing, journalism, radio script writing, radio production, dramatics, and discussion techniques. In the Richmond Hill, New York, senior high school, admission to honors courses is on the basis of rating on scholastic aptitude tests, past achievement, academic and college orientation, school citizenship, and favorable personal traits.

A New York City high school honors program has been described and evaluated by the director, Milton M. Klein, who undertook research to refine techniques for identifying able students, to improve the instructional program, and to strengthen counseling services (1958). Mr. Klein cooperated with the teachers in developing special curriculum materials for the classes, conducted in-service training seminars for the teachers, and experimented with instructional techniques better adapted for promising students. He also planned and supervised an experimental program for bright "underachievers." The results of a survey of 150 graduates which was made to obtain student evaluation of honors programs were published in two articles (Klein, 1957, 1958).

In Washington, D.C., students entering the honors program in the tenth grade have been required to take additional work in science and foreign languages. New requirements for honor students in the junior high school also provide for more work in language, mathematics, and social studies.

In the Far Rockaway High School, New York, there are two honors classes: Corps I, consisting of the thirty "top sharks" in the school, among whom a third are girls, and Corps II, the next highest group of thirty students. Selection is rigorously competitive, and students who cannot keep the pace are dropped.

The high school in Summit, New Jersey, conducts honors classes in mathematics, science, English, foreign language, and social studies and a laboratory program on Saturday mornings. In Buffalo, New York, two types of honors courses are offered in certain high schools: regular courses that have been revised to add more breadth and better pacing for rapid learners and new, special advanced courses.

A brief account of programs for superior high school students in various communities in different states will be found in *The Superior Student,* the newsletter of the Inter-university Committee on the Superior Student, November-December, 1963, vol. 6, no. 1.

SOME QUESTIONS AND PROBLEMS RELATING TO HONORS WORK

Who should be selected for honors work? A high school principal recommends that students should not be selected until they have completed one or more terms of a subject within the regular school program; then selection is certain to be more reliable.

One shortcoming in honors courses is that no uniform standard for selection is used among the schools. An honors student in one school might be little better than average in another.

One of the persistent problems is to promote a better student attitude toward honors work. Unless the high school gives sufficient rewards for scholastic excellence, students will scarcely be interested in trying out for honors. A highly eligible student may prefer not to enter honors courses because of the greater amount of work required. Students are concerned about getting lower marks than they would earn in courses outside the honors program, because they are headed for college and must make every mark count.

The traditional system of numerical or letter grades is inapplicable to high school honors students because the lower part of the student distribution has been eliminated. Some schools require that students in honors classes be given marks above average; marks below a B or a grade of 85 are prohibited. In other cases a record is made of the mark with an additional symbol signifying that the grade was earned in an honors class. In addition, a record is kept of the student's status in terms of percentile rank on standard achievement tests.

How do honors course graduates fare compared with other students in college? Dr. David A. Abramson of the Bureau of Educational Research of the New York City Board of Education made a follow-up study of high school graduates through their freshman and sophomore years in college (1960). One group had been in honors classes in high school for one or two major subjects, another group had been in honors classes for most of their work, the third group had been in special schools for gifted high school students in New York City, and the fourth group had had no honors class or special school experience.

The results showed there was no statistically reliable difference in any instance in the college grade-point average of these students. High school students who had not taken enrichment courses held their own with students who had been enrolled in enriched programs. The overall achievement of the students was associated with their level of intelligence rather than with the type of school or classes they had attended. This report criticized the curriculum and teaching methods in special programs for gifted students, pointing out that more research was needed on the most suitable type of high school program for the academically talented.

In response to questions about their satisfaction with school studies, honors students in one high school reported that they had got a great deal out of their experience, but some of their studies were routine, too formal, repetitive, not stimulating.

Seminars and Independent Study

Small-group seminars and independent study furnish other means of enriching and accelerating high school studies. The advanced-standing courses described above may be offered on the seminar plan, with the group meeting twice a week or more often.

As in college seminars, the work involves wider reading and a deeper study of problems. Students learn how to find out things for themselves, they learn to think scientifically, and they develop their talent for reporting and creative writing. In one high school seminar, a teacher's explanation of Archimedes' principle of buoyancy started members of the class off on their own intellectual discoveries in science. In science clubs conducted on the seminar basis, advanced students have worked with various members of the school science department, setting up laboratory equipment, preparing exhibits, working at photography, and so on.

Students are encouraged to seek out information in original source materials and to arrive at their own conclusions regarding issues and problems. The student may be required to make a study of historical research—a project that requires finding relevant materials, taking notes, reaching conclusions in the face of conflicting evidence, and, finally, preparing oral and written reports on the study. Sometimes a promising student is called on for a demonstration lesson, in which he himself teaches the class. A high school in California has set up a daily two-hour work period for gifted students working on extensive study or research projects.

Seminar Study in Portland, Oregon, and Elsewhere   The high schools of Portland, Oregon, have experimented with seminars modeled on the college plan of small groups and tutorial instruction (*The Gifted Child in Portland,* 1959). The students engage in small-group discussion with the instructors or work on individual study projects. Seminar groups, open only to the most capable students, are formed on a voluntary basis. Intellectual curiosity is aroused, there is free discussion, and thinking is richly stimulated. The students report enthusiastically on ideas gleaned from extensive reading in advanced materials. The work is conducted largely through student initiative and responsibility as seminar members bring up for discussion ideas met in their reading and investigating. The students exercise a large measure of independence in selecting problems. They have expressed preference for seminar discussions in the humanities and social sciences, and for individual projects in the natural sciences.

In an English seminar, advanced students may focus on a careful reading and discussion of the *Iliad*, along with the reading of modern narrative. The student may try his own hand at creative writing, working at the same time on a variety of literary enterprises involving extensive reading and reviewing of books, expressive composition, library reference work, and basic research.

A seminar group in the social studies may delve into the work of the United States Supreme Court, the challenge of Soviet Russia, the evolution of modern democratic government, civic government in the local community, urbanization in modern life, and other topics proposed by the students.

The talented science student carries on individually selected projects in the school laboratory, sometimes before or after the day's program if the laboratory is not otherwise available. The science student is encouraged to broaden his interests through participation in other comprehensive seminars, instead of concentrating in one area.

The chief administrative problem in seminar work is scheduling small groups and student-teacher conferences in a crowded daily program. Another difficulty is that with college entrance examinations looming ahead for most of the students, teachers are afraid to depart from the standard syllabus.

INDEPENDENT STUDY

High school administrators and teachers have identified students from time to time who have gone beyond the offerings of the school before graduation and have given these students individual tutoring or assigned them independent work. A teacher in a foreign secondary school who was asked how he managed to assist the most gifted students in his large classes said that he directed them in independent studies which would prepare them for entering the technical university. An English teacher found that putting gifted students to work on independent study projects was the best way to individualize their instruction in a large class. Through independent study the student is freed from uniform, dictated assignments on required course work he has already completed. He is directed to carry out his own exploration of special projects and deal with problems he himself discovers.

Exceptionally capable students are required to attend only such class sessions and small-group meetings as their teachers consider necessary. The rest of their time is devoted to individual projects and study programs. In this way, the unusual student can advance at his own pace in pursuing his special interests. His studies are not only enriched, but at the same time he is preparing for independent study in college or the university.

Outstanding students in Melbourne High School, Florida, pursue advanced independent study in a particular field under a program called "Education by Appointment." Candidates must demonstrate high aptitude, superior achievement, initiative, curiosity, purpose, and creative ability to enter the program. The student submits a one-page description of the study he wishes to carry out and what he expects to gain from it. Then he is assigned to a "directing teacher" who supervises the study and evaluates the results. The student budgets his own time, working out his own schedule. He makes two appointments each week with his consultant and a third with the program coordinator to check on progress.

Erasmus Hall High School in Brooklyn, New York, has been notably successful in turning out Westinghouse science talent winners—five in a single year. At the school is a devoted biology instructor who directs students in working on their own laboratory projects and writing up the reports. In Pittsburgh high schools a tough directed studies program has been devised for the top 10 to 20 per cent of the students in academic aptitude. High school students in Los Angeles are given job sheets as guides to independent study; students proceed to the next job in sequence when the first is satisfactorily completed.

In independent schools, tutorial courses for able seniors may be offered, in which one or two students meet with the teacher once a week for instruction. The student proposes a field of study and research that is approved by the instructor, and then the instructor guides the student's work individually throughout the term. The study topic might be the history of science, Greek drama, short story writing, the study of a classical or modern novelist. The level of work carried on is comparable to work done by college students.

The English department of the Grosse Pointe University School, in Michigan, gives students in the junior and senior years opportunities for independent study. In this program are two-week directed reading sessions that take place about every six weeks throughout the year. During the two-week reading periods the students report to a reading room instead of going to regular English classes. With this plan, more time is allowed for teacher-student conferences, especially for discussion of work in composition.

The Dalton Plan of Individual Instruction   The contract plan of study originated by Miss Helen Parkhurst at the Dalton School, New York, some years ago provides a program of individual study which enables upper-grade and high school students to move ahead on a block of assignments independently (1922). At the beginning of the month, a unit of study is outlined for each student who contracts to complete the unit within a month's time. The nature and level of the individual projects free the student from the traditional lockstep of uniform textbook assignments.

Self-study Aids   Self-study aids used in independent study programs include:

Records and tape recordings for foreign language study and speech improvement
Recordings of music, drama, literature
Machines for improving perception and speed of reading
Educational moving pictures
Museum exhibits and resources
Libraries and book collections
Free pamphlets, maps, materials
Radio and TV programs

Specialized High Schools

Special high schools for the gifted and talented in public school systems are comparatively rare. Although such schools are largely concentrated in New York City, there is a growing interest in them elsewhere, both in this country and abroad.

Stuyvesant High School in New York provides a program of academic studies for intellectually gifted boys. The program of the Hunter High School for Girls has been described by the principal, Dr. Cyril Woolcock (1962). The Brooklyn Technical High School, enrolling boys headed for college and offering a strong program in mathematics and science, has established an enviable record in the achievements of its graduates.

Illustrations of specialized high schools for the talented are the Bronx High School of Science, the High School of Music and Art, and the High School of Performing Arts, all in New York City. The High School of Music and Art enrolls over 2,000 talented youths who are preparing for careers in the music and art fields. The High School of Performing Arts, which specializes in drama and dance, also offers some music courses. Students admitted to these schools have demonstrated high aptitudes not only in specialized areas but in scholastic ability and all-around achievement as well.

The Bronx High School of Science has been keeping track of its graduates who have received National Science Foundation fellowships, established in 1952. Over 17 per cent of all recipients of these fellowships in New York State have been graduates of this one school.

In a book on high school programs for the gifted, edited by Everett, descriptions are given of the programs of the Bronx High School of Science, the Evanston Township High School, the U.S. Grant High School in Portland, Oregon, the Germantown Friends School, Philadelphia, and the Ohio State University High School (1961).

What these special schools actually accomplish is still uncertain. Matchee graduates of other schools where adequate provisions are made for the gifted in groups or on an individual basis appear to fare about as well in their later careers. Consequently, there has been some agitation to do away with these expensive schools with their specialized curricula.

INDEPENDENT SECONDARY SCHOOLS

The independent schools, privately supported and charging substantial tuition fees, tend to enroll a student body of superior caliber. These schools select the students they want on the basis of ability, scholarship, and other traits. Aptitude test findings are commonly used in the selection process. Since scholarships are restricted to the most capable students, a school with a liberal scholarship plan attracts a substantial number of outstanding young scholars with superior records.

Classes in these schools, usually smaller than in large public high schools, provide a setting for tutorial work, with a group of twelve to fourteen students meeting with the teacher around a conference table. Study is more often on an individual basis than in the large public schools. The academic programs of the independent schools, formerly strictly classical, now include many of the subjects offered in any modern high school.

Within these schools some special provision is made for the most gifted. For example, Phillips Exeter Academy offers a special program in mathematics for the gifted. The work of the German-town Friends School, Philadelphia, is outlined in Everett's book (1961).

Afterschool and Saturday Classes

Afterschool and Saturday classes offer further opportunities for the talented. There are programs conducted in out-of-school hours by volunteer teachers who have distinguished themselves in their professions. In Easthampton, Long Island, selected groups work in volunteer programs in creative writing, science, modern dance, and other subjects, with the recommendation of guidance people in the high school.

In Palo Alto, California, local professional scientists meet with selected students in a three-hour session once a week after school or in the evening. These seminar groups consist of four or five students led by an expert on a topic of particular interest to the group. At Niles Township High School, near Chicago, professional men conduct evening seminars in science for promising, interested science students. Seniors in San Diego, California, receive a semester's credit in zoology when they spend two or three afternoons a week working at the zoo.

The Boston Museum of Fine Arts conducts a Saturday afternoon art program for several hundred teen-agers selected as the most talented from high schools throughout New England. This "Senior Prize Program," as it is called, offers these promising youths expert instruction by the museum staff with full use of the museum facilities in various art media.

There is a growing movement to make more use of local colleges and their staffs for after-hours and Saturday instruction for students who are still officially in high school. This is another means of preparing the gifted more fully for college and saving their time in the high school–college sequence.

The University of Washington has been experimenting with special weekend seminars for selected high school students since 1961. Supported by a number of grants, eight honors seminars conducted by university professors in off-campus sites have proved to be highly successful.

Columbia University Science Honors Program   A Science Honors Program has been conducted on the Columbia University campus in a series of Saturday classes for talented high school science students since

1958. The students are selected from a list of nominees sent in by more than 300 high schools within a 100-mile radius of metropolitan New York. Offered by Columbia's School of Engineering and Applied Science, this program supplements regular science courses for the students by offering more-advanced studies than typical school programs provide. The students attend classes and laboratory sessions and devote much of their time to original research projects.

A thirteen-year-old boy from Queens, New York, was one of the winners among more than 1,000 high school students who took the competitive examinations to attend these Saturday science classes. He was in the top 10 per cent of all competitors, ranking well among the 200 young people who were accepted for the program. The youngest of forty winners of the 1964 nationwide Westinghouse science talent search was fourteen-year-old Ralph Linsker, a senior at Forest Hills High School, New York, who enrolled in the Columbia University Science Honors Program.

Officials recognize that this type of program is needed most by gifted students from high schools that are limited in their science offerings. Reaction to the program by students, Columbia faculty members, and other school officials has been extremely favorable. High school teachers from the New York metropolitan area who serve as teaching fellows in the program receive training in teaching the gifted. Students who have completed these courses have earned awards in science talent competitions and New York State regents scholarships.

Catskill Area Project Twenty-two schools in three rural counties in the Catskill, New York, area have combined to enrich the high school curriculum for able students through a program of weekly seminars held on Saturday or in the evening. The project, which began in 1958, is assisted by the College of Education at Oneonta, New York. Courses in science, mathematics, humanities, world affairs, Russian language, and logic have been taught by college faculty members. Students use material programmed in teaching machines. The content of the courses is close to the level of college work. Students are encouraged to study independently and to improve their confidence in group participation.

Colgate University Program In 1959 Colgate University established an after-hours program of study for gifted students in the third school district of Oneida County, New York. The students selected for this program went to the college once every two weeks for lecture-discussion sessions with members of the Colgate faculty. Astronomy, foreign affairs, and psychology were the courses offered.

Neighborhood reading groups were developed as an extension of the summer program. These were conducted in the evening for high school students. Elementary school children met one afternoon a week for discussions and study hours led by librarians and assisted by volunteers. Over forty students worked on science research projects, and some sixty worked in a foreign language laboratory course. These students also took courses in either foreign policy or interpretation of literature, creative writing, speech, and dramatics. Teams composed of a college teacher and a high school teacher conducted the courses.

Other Programs   In Westfield, New Jersey, the senior high school has Saturday classes in advanced science, physics, and mechanics taught by instructors from neighboring New Jersey colleges. Bennett College has established a Saturday school for gifted high school students with a grant from the Carnegie Corporation.

Summer Programs

Today about half of all summer day school students are talented young people taking enrichment courses, often noncredit, to extend their knowledge in certain study areas. The programs are conducted by local school authorities or under the auspices of the state department of education. Some are sponsored by a neighboring college or university. A number of summer programs for the gifted have been supported by grants from The Fund for the Advancement of Education.

During the summer of 1962, twenty-six talented high school biology students were selected from New York and other Eastern cities to undertake biology experiments during a four-week program at Columbia University, a project sponsored by the National Youth Science Foundation. The students worked in close association with outstanding scientists, including Nobel prize winners. The purpose of the summer programs sponsored by the National Youth Science Foundation at Columbia and elsewhere is to provide talented students an incentive to undertake advanced studies.

Since 1956 summer programs in science and mathematics have been offered at colleges in Texas for carefully chosen students from some 200 Texas high schools. Although the work is not taken for credit, students can often qualify for advanced placement on entering college. Many have earned scholarships and other awards. Since 1958 this work has been supported by the National Science Foundation.

During 1962 the foundation sponsored summer programs for about 6,000 high-ranking science and mathematics students in 153 colleges, universities, and research organizations. None of the work duplicated courses the students had taken in high school.

Selected high school students have enrolled in summer courses at Union College, Schenectady, for college credit. Trinity College in Connecticut offers summer programs at the college with opportunities for early admission and advanced placement. These students have found it possible to complete the eight-year high school–college span in seven years.

The University of Pittsburgh has set up a program for high school juniors and seniors that makes it possible for qualified students to earn up to six credits in a six-week summer session.

In the summer of 1961 outstanding high school students were able to spend six weeks, tuition free, at City College, New York, in special science and mathematics classes. This work was supported by a grant from the National Science Foundation. Results proved that the students did as well as or even better than their college-age classmates.

A four-week course, "Astronomy and Space Science," has been offered by the American Museum–Hayden Planetarium, New York, free of charge during the summer for 200 high school students of unusual ability. This program, too, is sponsored by the National Science Foundation.

The Governor's School in Winston-Salem, North Carolina, was founded in 1962 by Governor Sanford with a program for gifted high school students carried on during the summer months. Junior and senior students are selected from all over the state for concentrated work in eight curriculum areas including the performing arts. An integrated program is carried on for eight weeks, Monday through Saturday, in the morning. In the afternoon all follow a course entitled "Essential Ideas."

Another unusual summer program is offered at the Interlaken Arts Academy in Michigan under the auspices of the National Science Foundation and the Committee on Education of the American Society for Microbiology. The program provides a course in modern microbiology for high school students of high ability and strong scientific background. The course is offered at the college level and provides ample opportunity for independent study.

The Telluride Program   The Telluride Association located at Cornell University, Ithaca, New York, is a perpetuating educational trust set up to support programs for superior students. The trust maintains summer programs for a small group of outstanding high school students in the junior and senior years. These programs offer an unusual social and intellectual experience for the six-week summer session. In 1963 there were two programs operating in Ithaca and one at Princeton University. There is keen national competition for these summer program awards; hence, the selected participants are extraordinarily able and highly motivated young people. A college admissions application that bears the notation "Participant in Telluride Association Summer Program" ordinarily receives favorable consideration. Those who participate in the program are regularly invited to accept Telluride college scholarships on completion of their high school studies.

PUBLIC SCHOOLS

In Newton, Massachusetts, high school teen-agers from ten cities around Boston take an intensive six-week summer course in one subject such as biology or history, covering a year's work in this time. A summer program for one hundred bright high school juniors is conducted in St. Paul, Minnesota, for a six-week term.

The Mark Twain Summer Institute, which meets in the Clayton High School, Missouri, enrolls high school juniors and seniors for training not available in their regular high school programs. Each summer, several hundred students take part in lectures and discussion groups on such subjects as Russian, Greek, German, English literature, mathematics, music appreciation, biology, zoology, physics, advanced chemistry, political philosophy, economic theory, and sociology. The students, who come from both public and private schools and from other states as well as Missouri, are screened from a large number of applicants.

At Sewanhaka High School, Floral Park, Long Island, a summer high school is conducted for the gifted, offering units in biology, chemistry, English 2, modern mathematics insights, and others.

Oneida County Summer Program   The Oneida, New York, first school district has experimented for several years with summer school classes on a volunteer basis and without credit for able students who have shown unusual interest in academic studies. The program, supported by The Fund for the Advancement of Education, has been directed by Dr. Madeline Coutant.

Although the students are not selected for this program solely on the basis of mental ability, the opportunity is open only to those rating above average. The classes are organized according to interest groups. By the end of the second year, the program had offered twenty-one units of study varying in length from two to six weeks. The units chosen in the sciences, the humanities, and the arts capitalized on the resources of the locality and centered around skills, concepts, and content not offered in regular school courses. Long trips were scheduled that would not have been possible in the regular school year. Units included citizenship in Oneida County, earth science, electronics, field botany, foreign policy, mathematics, music theory, ornithology, physics, French, German, Russian, Latin, and Greek. A similar program has been conducted in a suburban high school near Utica, New York. Five school systems in suburban Utica were included in the program on a cooperative basis.

The Oneida County program has been evaluated by Colgate University. Questionnaire responses of students revealed that they were highly satisfied with the work. The students were eager, industrious, and gave exceptional performance. Graduates of the program were strongly motivated toward higher education, and they experienced unusual success in college. The New York State Education Department is now supporting this program.

INDEPENDENT SCHOOLS

In 1956, the headmaster of St. Paul's school, Concord, New Hampshire, originated the idea of opening a private preparatory school during the summer for selected students, both boys and girls, from high schools in New Hampshire. Ever since, the school, aided by a grant from The Fund for the Advancement of Education, has offered a summer program in which students concentrate a year's course in a six-week period and earn credits toward college admission. Scholarships are available for those who need them. Similar coeducational programs on a noncredit basis are now offered at Phillips Andover and at Mount Hermon. In the latter school, fourteen major courses are offered, with emphasis on the humanities, science, and mathematics. Lectures are given by college professors.

A cooperative summer program in science and mathematics has also been conducted by St. Mark's School and the Worcester Foundation for Experimental Biology in Massachusetts. This precollege program has served to launch promising young people in science teaching careers and in medicine.

Thayer Academy in Massachusetts conducts a ten-week summer program for talented eleventh-grade students; this cooperative program includes orientation sessions at the academy followed by work in university and industrial laboratories. Here the students obtain a clearer understanding of the difference between science and technology, and they are more apt to seek liberal education in college as preparation for graduate work.

At the Summer Science Institute of the Pingry School, Hillside, New Jersey, forty biology and chemistry students hear distinguished guest lecturers and make a full-day field trip to research laboratories where they engage in rigorous laboratory work.

Out-of-school and summer programs provided by colleges for highly selected students have been described in Appendix B of the bulletin edited by Drews (1961).

References

Abramson, David A.: *The Effect of Special Grouping of High Ability Students in High School upon Their Achievement in College,* Publication no. 144, Bureau of Educational Research, Board of Education, City of New York, 1960.

The Academically Talented Student in the American Secondary School, National Education Association, Washington, D.C., 1958.

Bereday, George Z. F., and Joseph A. Lauwerys (eds.): *The Gifted Child: The 1962 Yearbook of Education,* Harcourt, Brace & World, Inc., New York, 1962.

Burnside, Lenoir H.: An Experimental Program in Education of the Intellectually Gifted Adolescent, *School Review,* 50:274–285, 1942.

Conant, James B.: *The American High School Today,* McGraw-Hill Book Company, New York, 1959.

Conant, James B.: *The Identification and Education of the Academically Talented Student in the American Secondary School,* conference report, National Education Association, Washington, D.C., 1958.

Copley, Frank C.: *The American High School and the Talented Student,* The University of Michigan Press, Ann Arbor, Mich., 1961.

Cornog, William H.: Initiating an Educational Program for Able Students in the Secondary School, *School Review,* 65:49–59, 1957.

Drews, Elizabeth M.: The Four Faces of Able Adolescents, *Saturday Review of Literature,* Jan. 19, 1963.

Drews, Elizabeth M. (ed.): *Guidance for the Academically Talented Student,* NEA Project on the Academically Talented Student, National Education Association, Washington, D.C., 1961.

Education for the Gifted: Fifty-seventh Yearbook of the National Society for the Study of Education, part 2, The University of Chicago Press, Chicago, 1958.

Everett, Samuel (ed.): *Programs for the Gifted: A Case Book in Secondary Education,* John Dewey Society Yearbook, Harper & Row, Publishers, Incorporated, New York, 1961.

Fashew, L. D.: Advanced Study for Exceptionally Able High School Students, *Exceptional Children,* 23:50, 89, 1956.

56 Practices for the Gifted from Secondary Schools of New York State, University of the State of New York, Education Department, Albany, N.Y., 1958.

Flanagan, John C.: *The American High School Student,* American Institute of Research, Pittsburgh, Pa., 1963.

Fliegler, Louis A. (ed.): *Curriculum Planning for the Gifted,* Prentice-Hall, Inc., Englewood Cliffs, N.J., 1961.

Friedenberg, Edgar: *The Vanishing Adolescent,* Beacon Press, Boston, 1959.

The Gifted Child in Portland: A Report of Five Years of Experience in Developing a Program for Children of Exceptional Endowment, Portland, Ore., Public Schools, 1959.

Gilroy, Lewis W.: Educating the Most Able High School Students in Indianapolis, *Education,* 79:25–27, 1958.

Greer, Edith S., and Richard M. Harbeck: *High School Pupil Programs,* Section IV: Program Patterns of the Academically Able Compared with Those of the Less Able, U.S. Department of Health, Education and Welfare, Office of Education, Washington, D.C., 1961.

Hansego, Ian E., and Gordon L. Mowat: Alberta Composite High Schools and Gifted Youth, *Alberta Journal of Educational Research,* 5:23–30, 1959.

Jensen, Barry T.: An Independent Study Laboratory, Using Self-scoring Tests, *Journal of Educational Research,* 43:134–137, 1949.

Klein, Milton M.: Educating Gifted Youth: The Record and the Promise, *High Points,* 39:25–36, November, 1957.

Klein, Milton M.: What Honor Students Think, *High Points,* 40:5–12, March, 1958.

Lessinger, Leon M., and Ruth A. Martinson: The Use of the California Psychological Inventory with Gifted Pupils, *Personality and Guidance Journal,* 39:572–575 1961.

Mosso, Asenath M.: An Experiment with and for Pupils of Superior Ability, *School Review,* 52:26–32, 1944.

Mosso, Asenath M.: A Seminar for Superior High School Seniors, *School Review,* 53:464–470, 1945.

Parkhurst, Helen: *Education on the Dalton Plan,* E. P. Dutton & Co., Inc., New York, 1922.

Paschal, Elizabeth: *Encouraging the Excellent: Special Programs for Gifted and Talented Students,* The Fund for the Advancement of Education, New York, 1960.

Passow, A. Harry: The Comprehensive High School and Gifted Youth, *Teachers College Record,* 58:144–152, 1956.

Passow, A. Harry, and Deton J. Brooks, Jr.: *A Guide for Rating Provisions for the Gifted,* Bureau of Publications, Teachers College, Columbia University, New York, 1960.

Shertzer, Bruce: *Working with Superior Students,* Science Research Associates, Inc., Chicago, 1960.

Smith, Donald C.: *Personal and Social Adjustment of Gifted Adolescents,* NEA Council for Exceptional Children, Research Monograph no. 4, National Education Association, Washington, D.C., 1962.

Thompson, L. C.: Honor Units: My Plan for Superior Students, *Clearing House,* 16:426–428, 1942.

Trimble, Vernon E.: Special Provisions for the Gifted in California Public Secondary Schools, *Dissertation Abstracts,* 16:83–84, 1956.

Willis, Margaret: *The Guinea Pigs after Twenty Years: A Follow-up Study of the Class of 1938 of the University School at Ohio State,* Ohio State University Press, Columbus, Ohio, 1961.

Wilson, J. A. R.: Some Results of an Enrichment Program for Gifted Ninth Graders, *Journal of Educational Research,* 53:157–160, 1959.

Witty, Paul A., and Samuel W. Bloom: The Education of the Superior High School Student, *Bulletin of the National Association of Secondary School Principals,* 39:15–22, 1955.

Woolcock, Cyril: *The Hunter College High School Program for Gifted Students,* Vantage Press, New York, 1962.

Yates, Dorothy H.: A Study of Some High School Seniors of Superior Intelligence, *Journal of Educational Research,* Monograph no. 2, 1922.

Chapter Thirteen

TEACHING THE GIFTED AND TALENTED IN THE SECONDARY SCHOOL

The teacher's task in working with the gifted in high school is to awaken the students to the larger issues of life and to develop their ability to think. Instead of concentrating solely on the accumulation of knowledge, students should learn to use facts in problem solving. This means less dependence on textbooks and lecture notes; it means greater use of a wide range of resources, more questioning, and open discussion of ideas.

Instead of covering routine academic subjects superficially, superior students need to explore selected topics in depth in order to attain real mastery. Learning with understanding is more likely to result when the teacher arouses students to ask questions and raise issues in discussion and then turns these back to the students for exploration. For example, the question is raised: What measures are taken in our community to safeguard public health? Investigation of the subject concentrates the students' attention on problem solving rather than on superficial memorizing of factual material.

The criticism is heard that regular classroom teachers do not sufficiently encourage students to use their creative imagination or to develop initiative in pursuing study projects. For this reason, gifted students of high school age are better off in seminar-type classes where they are freer to carry out their own ideas and do independent reading related to their chosen interests.

For information on conserving and developing creativity see Chapter Fifteen.

Suggestions for enrichment of course offerings for gifted high school students will be found in *Education for the Gifted,* chap. 12 (Michael, 1958), and the books by Everett (1961), Laycock (1957), Fliegler (1961), Woolcock (1962), and others, listed at the end of this chapter.

The Project on the Academically Talented Student of the National Education Association, Washington, D.C., has published a series of pamphlets on instruction in different subject areas. The series includes:

Mathematics for the Academically Talented Student, 1959

Science for the Academically Talented Student, 1959

English for the Academically Talented Student, 1960

Modern Foreign Languages and the Academically Talented Student, 1960

Social Studies for the Academically Talented Student, 1960

Music for the Academically Talented Student, 1960

The following sections outline instruction aids in a number of subject areas.

Communication Skills: Oral and Written English

One of the most important tools of a scholar or educated person is an expert command of his mother tongue: ability to converse intelligently, to speak before a group, to report orally, to read with discrimination and understanding, to record ideas clearly, and to make effective written reports. The talented student who speaks and writes well is more likely to impress others with his scholarly work and to gain acceptance for his original ideas than one who lacks proficiency in the language.

Skill in using one's native language is required in every field of study, and every promising student should master this skill by the close of the secondary school period. The responsibility lies with the teacher for quickening the gifted student's sensitivity to refinements in using language, in choice of words and correct forms of expression to fit the occasion.

The "split-half" plan for teaching large high school English classes is certain to strengthen instruction for the best students along with the others. According to this plan, devised by Dr. Paul Diederich of the Educational Testing Service, the class is divided into two sections. The teacher meets with one section on Monday and Tuesday while the other section goes to the library for independent reading under the supervision of teacher aides. On Wednesday and Thursday the sections switch. On Friday the classes meet with qualified teacher aides while the regular class teacher is free for individual student conferences. This plan has been operating successfully in over 250 school systems.

IMPROVEMENT IN ORAL EXPRESSION

Many careers depend on the individual's ability to project ideas to a group. Instruction in speech and experience in debates and dramatics will give the student the self-assurance he needs for addressing an audience. Skill in public speaking will also advance the student's position as a leader in school affairs. Here, too, are new opportunities for creative talent.

The gifted student who is college-bound, but has limitations or handicaps in speaking, should have speech improvement work on an individual basis. An English language laboratory is as effective for speech improvement as the foreign language laboratory is for learning a new language, and the equipment for individual study is identical. The tapes and records used in such a laboratory are to a large extent self-teaching devices.

PRACTICAL WRITING

Every college student needs to be able to write essays and reports clearly, to use correct grammar and punctuation. In commenting on his high school education, a student at M.I.T. said that more attention should have been given to teaching the students how to write. This would require, according to his judgment, that they be made to work harder at English composition in all subject areas. The star science or mathematics student who contends that expert writing is not his forte might be reminded that the world's great scientists, as well as other remarkable people outside the literary profession, wrote with clarity and conviction, among them Darwin, Freud, and Van Gogh.

Instead of relying on formal drill exercises (e.g., Which is correct, sentence A or sentence B?), basic skills of expression should be developed and improved through oral and written reports relating to the student's special interests; a drama enthusiast might report on stage lighting, costume design, Greek drama, the modern theater, the stage in Shakespeare's day.

At the Ohio State University High School, Columbus, work in English is integrated with unified studies and core courses. Little time is spent on abstract rules of organization, sentence structure, and punctuation. Grammar is learned primarily through experience in writing and rewriting. Research papers are prepared under the supervision of English teachers.

The study of semantics—word meanings and word usage—is an inviting field for adolescents, particularly those who show talent for writing and may go on with linguistic studies. A high school teacher reported that her most gifted students benefited from the study of formal grammar more than others because of their ability to analyze and to systematize their thinking. The gifted were better able to "transfer" what they had learned to new situations; for example, they were able to apply the rules of grammar to their own compositions—in the structure of complex sentences or the use of sentence complements. In studying language, students work on enrichment of vocabulary, word derivations and changes in word meanings, forms of oral and written English used by cultivated people, and modern English grammar.

Since the problems of no two students are the same, improvement in written expression requires a great deal of individual guidance. The student can handle his own vocabulary improvement problems, in part, on a self-study basis.

CREATIVE WRITING

A sure sign of literary giftedness in the adolescent is the urge to express his ideas in writing. Not everyone can aspire to be a poet or literary light; this requires a rare combination of imagination and originality, as well as artistic use of words. Teachers often obtain remarkable results, however, when they arouse the children's interest in creative expression.

Expressive writing derives from freedom in oral expression, from conversation and class discussions, and from reflecting on what to say and how to say it. Beginning with the student's earliest school experience, teachers should encourage imaginative expression without too much concern over matters of technique; otherwise, the free flow of ideas may be impeded.

Michael Baldwin, British poet and schoolmaster, believes that the child who cares to try his hand at poetry writing during school hours should not be considered an idle dreamer, but should be guided in learning the poet's craft. The same thing holds true for other forms of expressive writing.

Hughes Mearns, an English teacher at the Lincoln School of Teachers College, Columbia University, New York, reported the results of a four-year experiment in encouraging high school students in literary productivity (1925). Mr. Mearns went far beyond the traditional courses in high school literature in awakening the students' interest in creative composition.

READING AND THE STUDY OF LITERATURE

For the superior student as for all others, reading is the most convenient means of acquiring recorded knowledge and checking on factual information. Of even greater value, perhaps, is the stimulation an alert young person receives from the recorded thoughts of great minds. A further value of independent reading is that it aids the child in the pursuit of his special interests. Although a child's craze for reading everything may subside with the onset of adolescence, reading remains an absorbing pastime, a favorite recreation, for many youths.

The typical adolescent's independent reading interests are closely tied to his life aspirations as well as to his current emotional involvement, his personal need for escape or fulfillment. For this reason students are likely to gain the greatest satisfaction from books they themselves select.

In the Realm of Great Literature   In great literature the perceptive reader comes face to face with all the basic themes of human living and motivation. He encounters other people like himself and sees that he is not alone in his fantasies and dreams. Literature provides an emotional outlet for pent-up feelings, for doubts, fears, and uncertainties. The reader can evaluate his own experiences in the light of the experience of others who have met and conquered obstacles. In the reading of great literature, the gifted student gains stimulation for his own studies in the humanities and for creative writing.

The student who forms a taste for good reading will find great literature immensely rewarding. Through reading he can enjoy many a luxurious trip abroad, visiting interesting people and localities within the covers of books such as *Buddenbrooks, Anna Karenina, The Cloister and the Hearth, Henry Esmond, Wuthering Heights,* the works of Jane Austen, the world of Honoré de Balzac, the writings of Henry James or James Fenimore Cooper. The study of literature should include foreign literature in translation as well as English and American works.

The Question of Required Reading Lists   Is there a "must read" list of the classics with which every student who goes ahead for advanced studies should be acquainted? Required reading lists, based on college entrance requirements, have been the backbone of high school literature courses since time immemorial. Today, however, it is recognized that students need to have access to a wide range of current material, along with standard works, books that are appealing to all tastes and interests, adult, as well as teen-age literature. One student may thoroughly enjoy reading *Henry Esmond,* whereas another devours everything from Thomas Wolfe.

What if the student shows no predilection for reading the rows of standard literary classics that line the school library shelves: Scott, Dumas, Dickens, Henry James? Even if he never opens one of these books, he can still become an educated person and have a distinguished career, but the literature teacher is duty-bound to expose the academic type of student to the world's great literature, pointing out the riches of Shakespeare, the thoughts of Emerson and Thoreau, the varied characterization in Balzac, Turgenev, or Dickens, the satire of Chekhov, the dramas of Moliére or Eugene O'Neill. Whatever the student's reading preferences may be, he should have some acquaintance with the world's treasure of great literature. Book reviews should not be made perfunctory; otherwise, the student may be inclined to write up the movie version of the book.

Questions have been asked about the suitability of adult literature for adolescent youth. There was never a time when bright boys and girls did not take pleasure in reading their elders' books. This is one aspect of their yearning to become acquainted with the grown-up world. Should a junior high school student be reading *Exodus* or *Gone with the Wind;* a sophomore, *The Sun Also*

Rises? The answer to this question as to so many others is that it depends on the individual, his all-around maturity and emotional stability, his breadth of experience and depth of understanding. The best rule is to let the youth choose his own reading so long as it represents good taste in literature. As all others, he will drop a book that does not suit his intellectual level or stir his imagination.

Information about Books   The library committee of the Independent Schools Education Board has issued a basic list, *3,000 Books for Secondary School Libraries,* published by R. R. Bowker Co., New York. The books are especially appropriate for college-bound students and those enrolled in advanced-placement programs in high school.

By graduation, advanced students should be familiar with the chief sources of published book reviews. The reader of professionally written reviews may be inspired to try his own hand at book reviewing for the school paper or a local newssheet. The sooner he gets experience of this kind, the earlier will he discover whether or not journalism or professional writing promises to be an interesting career for him.

The advanced student, with the guidance of teachers and libraries, becomes conversant with current materials—the daily papers and monthly and weekly periodicals. In current newssheets, he will find many ideas for editorial work on his own school paper, literary magazine, or yearbook.

Films for enrichment of the study of the humanities are available from the Encyclopaedia Britannica Company.

Improvement of Skill in Reading   Previous sections have emphasized the value of reading for the gifted, both the ability to read fluently with full understanding and wide acquaintanceship with books. A gifted student whose primary interest lies in science experiments, music practice, or art expression might not think reading skills are important; however, if he expects to study theoretical aspects of these subjects, he needs to be an expert reader. This requires the ability to read rapidly, to find the meaning of new and specialized terms without difficulty, to read with maximum comprehension, to remember what he has read, and to extract the salient points for his records and reports. Critical reading, that is, the ability to evaluate an author's ideas, is essential.

A talented youth may have reading deficiencies that can be overcome through remedial work. A student who shows scholarly promise but lags behind in reading skills should first have diagnostic testing to appraise his needs, and then be given intensive drill on an individual basis.

Programmed instruction, with or without mechanical devices, comes to the rescue of the bright student who needs drill for improvement in reading. Graded exercises and drill materials to improve vocabulary and speed up reading can be adapted to the individual's particular requirements. The student makes his own assignment, keeps his improvement records, and charts his progress through a set of lessons.

For more information about English instruction for the gifted in high school, consult the following references:

Bennett, Paul L.: A Reading and Writing Program for the Talented Student, *English Journal*, 44:335–339, 1955.

English for the Gifted: Report of the Committee on Honors English, Alice A. Wright, chairman, *High Points*, 24:42–53, 1942.

La Brant, Lou: *We Teach English*, Harcourt, Brace & World, Inc., New York, 1951, chap. 10.

Mearns, Hughes: *Creative Youth: How a School Environment Set Free the Creative Spirit*, Doubleday & Company, Inc., Garden City, N.Y., 1925.

Program for Gifted Children: English and Literature Classes for Exceptionally Endowed Students in the High Schools of Portland, Oregon, Curriculum Publication GC 5 of the Portland, Oregon, Public Schools, February, 1957.

Rock, Mildred, and Robert R. Gard: *Enriching the English Program for the Academically Talented Student*, National Education Association, Washington, D.C., 1960.

Strang, Ruth M.: Creative Writing, chap. 7 in Louis A. Fliegler (ed.), *Curriculum Planning for the Gifted*, Prentice-Hall, Inc., Englewood Cliffs, N.J., 1961.

Teaching Reading for the Gifted in Secondary Schools: Bulletin of the National Association of Secondary School Principals, part 1, 39:5–73, 1955.

BIOGRAPHY AS ENRICHMENT FOR THE GIFTED

The reading of biography is an illuminating experience in which young people meet personalities they would like to emulate. In biography the young reader comes to identify himself with persons of intelligence and learning. Reading about noble deeds may not of itself produce noble character, but such reading is undoubtedly a source of inspiration.

Bright children like biographical material in their reading; as early as the age of nine, they can enjoy reading about Pocahontas and Capt. John Smith, Eli Whitney and the cotton gin, Fulton and his steamboat, Mark Twain learning to become a pilot on the Mississippi, Daniel Boone and his place in our history. Dr. Leta S. Hollingworth described the great interest shown by elementary school children in the study of famous lives (see Chapter Nine).

Biographies appeal strongly to the teen-ager who is going through the hero-worship stage, longing to go farther afield in his explorations, dreaming of a great career. He enjoys Muir of the California mountains; the life of Louis Agassiz, the great naturalist; George Westinghouse, the inventor. The story of Lewis and Clark, the career of Albert Schweitzer or of Florence Nightingale, John F. Kennedy's *Profiles in Courage*—all are thrillers for unusual young people. Surveys have shown that biography is the favorite reading of many students.

The ambitious young person who is fond of reading finds enchantment in the lives of people who overcame obstacles to achievement through dint of hard effort. Gifted young scientists enjoy reading about great discoveries in the words of the discoverers themselves. Here is a source of motivation toward unusual achievement.

Eminent persons have ascribed the shaping of their goals to the guidance of a wise parent or teacher who introduced them to biography. Norbert Wiener, of cybernetics fame, said that as a child he enjoyed reading the lives of naturalists. Yuri Gagarin, the first man into space, was greatly influenced by reading biographies and the reports of real-life heroes. Pasteur was once interested only in art, but on reading the lives of great scientists in the school library, he determined to go into science.

Through reading the life story of a creative worker, the serious student gains a fuller understanding of the creative process. He will be impressed by the account of Luther Burbank's early interest in plants and the endless experimentation needed to create a better fruit or vegetable, a lovelier flower. In *Electrical Genius: The Life of Nikola Tesla*, Arthur J. Beckhard tells the story of a boy who at the age of five decided to become a titan among scientists, persevering until he reached his goal.

The young person gains a more-realistic conception of the inventor, the scientist, the leader he hopes to become by reading the lives of remarkable people. He may also acquire a set of values that deepens the meaning of life. He will read about Galileo who was punished during the Inquisition for teaching and defending

Copernican theories. He will find in Booker T. Washington a great man who made the most of his educational opportunities for a life of service. He will read the stories of cripples and invalids who did not let handicaps, even blindness, stand in the way of achievement. He will discover that a shabby fellow named Jean Henri Fabre lived in poverty all his life, but became recognized as one of the world's greatest naturalists, that Mme. Curie gave little thought to her personal comfort. He will read about boys and girls who overcame the handicap of poverty—Hans Christian Andersen and the singer Marian Anderson, for example. The *Diary of Anne Frank* can be an inspiration to any child who scarcely realizes how generously all his wants are supplied.

Biography cuts across all subject-matter areas, enriching every subject and curriculum unit. The great educator, Comenius, recommended several hundred years ago that students read the lives of illustrious persons of all times and countries as inspiration for noble deeds. Here are the great figures of history and of today whose lives are more remarkable than fiction. Students should be encouraged to browse among the biographies on the library shelves, making their own selections, and reading for pleasure as well as for class projects. In social studies classes, one teacher suggests that the student first read source material of the period being studied, and then read biographies of historical characters.

Teachers should not underestimate the ability of young people to read and enjoy well-written adult biographies. Also, many of the best adult biographies now appear in abridged editions with some control of vocabulary and simplified sentence structure for younger children. Teachers need to inform themselves of the most useful biographical sources, children's book lists, book reviews, and the names of leading authors of juvenile biography.

The Biography Index of the H. W. Wilson Company, New York, is the most comprehensive source. Any good library for children contains many of the best biographies in print, and the staff is prepared to supply further information.

Social Studies

Most schools make the social studies—history, physical geography, economics, sociology, and civics—a central core of work throughout the grades. These studies provide a fuller understanding of human life and the universe in all its immensity than young people can possibly grasp incidentally or from general reading.

What can be done to enrich the social studies for the gifted? The best recommendation is to provide a top-notch program in the first place, and then to count on flexibility and the teacher's skill to enrich the program for individual students of exceptional ability.

Mentally advanced students become concerned about many important social topics, such as capital punishment, the waste of war, civil rights, the causes of unemployment, the role of the UN, the use of atomic energy, the place of automation in our modern economy. The following questions furnish good topics for unit studies:

How can this community solve its traffic problems?
How are health and sanitation protected in this community?
How can people be educated to make the best use of their leisure time?
What can you do as a citizen to help prevent a third World War?
What can our community do to improve intergroup relations?
How can we overcome hate and malice in human living?

A topic such as the emergence of new nations in the twentieth century cuts across a range of subject areas—various social studies, science, literature, and even philosophy—and it is well suited to the alert minds of junior high school pupils. In many instances social studies provide an enriched background for work on individual projects.

High school seniors should have advanced work in areas such as American foreign policy, civil rights, European and Latin American history, sociology, contemporary problems in economics. Courses in world culture and the humanities are now offered in some high schools. Instead of grinding away at assigned lessons and cramming for tests, unusual students in high school social studies classes should pursue their studies in seminars, forums, debates, panel discussions, dramatic presentations, field trips, community studies, collateral reading, book reviewing, critical use and analysis of mass media of communication, individual research projects, and the writing of reports.

The National Secondary Schools Principals Association recommends that able students from several grades be offered an elective social studies seminar dealing with issues in the fields of history, geography, economics, and sociology. In an advanced section of the seminar, students can move at a faster pace or take college-level work, using advanced textbooks along with other materials.

ECONOMICS

High school students need to study economics not only to prepare for citizenship in a democratic society, but also to learn something about the socioeconomic situation here and in other countries. The study of economics is emphasized today because a growing number of gifted people find employment in posts requiring extensive background in this field.

Personal economics is a practical and enriching study for gifted students in the upper grades and high school. Such topics as costs of food and clothing, the value of various objects, prices, savings, services, bargains, shopping, merchandising, care of belongings, and the broader subject of conservation of resources are taken up in junior high school. As the students become more mature, they study budgeting and personal accounting, the checkbook, receipts, insurance, loans, income taxes.

Learning in this field requires the study of organized material in textbooks as well as wide reading in journals, bulletins, and newspapers. These resources should be accessible to high school students either in the school library or on the seminar-room shelves. Good use can also be made of educational television programs.

Valuable suggestions for enriching social studies for the gifted are given in *Education for the Gifted* (1958). This yearbook of the National Society for the Study of Education includes a report on study resources for teachers and students, creative activities for the gifted, and suggestions for the exploration of ideas in this area. See also the following list of excellent source material:

Gavian, Ruth (ed.): *The Social Education of the Academically Talented,* National Council for the Social Studies, Curriculum Bulletin 10, Washington, D.C., 1958.

Kenworthy, Leonard S.: *Guide to Teaching the Social Studies,* Wadsworth Publishing Co., San Francisco, Calif., 1962. A comprehensive guide, including good illustrations of unit study problems.

Klein, Milton M.: *Social Studies for the Academically Talented Student in the Secondary School,* National Education Association, Washington, D.C., 1960.

Michaelis, John U.: *Social Studies for Children in a Democracy,* 3d ed., Prentice-Hall, Inc., Englewood Cliffs, N.J., 1963.

Social Studies for the Academically Talented Student, National Education Association, Washington, D.C., 1960.

Torrey, Robert D.: Citizenship Education for the Gifted Adolescent, *Progressive Education,* 33:78–84, 1956.

Science and Mathematics

All gifted students in high school should have a good background in science and mathematics, no matter what careers they plan to follow. For those with unusual mathematics and science talent, the high school years provide the essential foundation for advanced and professional study.

Improvements in teaching and facilities during the past decade have resulted in larger numbers of able students enrolling for chemistry, physics, mathematics, and biology. Science scholarship contests have stirred tremendous interest among high school youth. Increased impetus to the improvement of science and mathematics teaching has come from the National Defense Education Act, which supplies funds for training science teachers and for equipment.

The application of mathematics to science receives special attention today; statistical information relevant to various topics in the curriculum is introduced to children in the upper grades and junior high school. Study is extended through club activities, contests, and conferences with specialists. The use of high-grade instructional films for science and mathematics teaching is recommended for schools in which one teacher must handle a broad range of courses. These films can be accompanied by lesson assignments, supplementary readings, and laboratory experiment kits. Results can be checked with periodic tests.

SCIENCE

Secondary schools have moved toward multiple-track plans in teaching foundation science courses. School authorities recommend that the ablest students be selected by means of prognostic tests, that they be grouped together either in separate classes or in cluster groups within a regular classroom, that seminar and laboratory sections be set up for advanced students. The most talented should be admitted to honors courses and special laboratory sections.

A study by Witty and Bloom over ten years ago showed that considerable progress had already been made in science instruction. The most capable students were being identified early and were being given continuous guidance all the way through school; they were enrolled in advanced courses, engaged in research in science clubs, and taking advantage of community resources related to science (1955). A study of science talent search winners by H. H. Morgan (1952) proved that the awards reflected the interest that individual science teachers had taken in their best students.

Selection of gifted science students in the Evanston Township High School is guided by the following criteria:

Consistently high grades in science courses

Evidence of early and sustained interest in science as a pastime

An IQ of 125 or higher

Intention to take three years of science and three years of mathematics

Expression of interest in a career in mathematics or science

Recommendation from teachers who are acquainted with the student as a prospective scientist

Students who show unusual aptitude should be guided so that they retain their interest and develop their skills, learn new techniques, move on to more advanced levels, and make plans for college study.

Goals of science teaching for the gifted are essentially as follows:

To emphasize ideas, concepts, and relationships in scientific thought

To develop ideas in the student's mind, stir up curiosity, encourage constant seeking for answers to problems

To stimulate the desire to study; to give training in study habits

To provide problem-solving experiences; to increase the student's understanding of scientific processes

To develop skills

To encourage initiative and give play to creativity

Science experts point out the contrast between teaching science as a process of conveying facts and doctrines and teaching science as a way of thought. The development of critical thinking is more likely to lead to creativity than the mere accumulation of knowledge. If young students are to understand the scientific method, they should learn science through problem solving according to scientific methods rather than through observing the teacher's demonstrations or through doing the science experiments outlined in textbooks. The talented science student does not need direct preplanned instruction so much as he needs freedom to explore, to try out ideas, even if he experiences some failures and comes upon some wrong answers.

Putting science on a problem-solving basis is sure to yield better understanding of science terms and processes. Gifted students who are trained in problem solving make better use of reference works, library resources, and the instructor than do those not so trained, judging from reports of teachers who have worked with various teaching methods.

The problem-solving approach is one means of individualizing instruction so as to capitalize on the student's special interests. The method requires teacher-pupil planning for projects and experiments.

Science work with gifted students centers around problems and experimental procedures for solving them. For example, in biology, such problems as the following may be explored scientifically:

People say that milk is a perfect food. Can you prove it?

How do plants absorb nitrates from the soil?

Is Lysol the best disinfectant for use around the house?

How can the efficacy of new drugs be tested?

The students learn that the constructive and destructive uses of science affect the entire world.

With their attention focused on original problem solving, students still in their teens have conducted experiments leading to important discoveries. A high school junior in Boise, Idaho, succeeded in changing the sex of a chicken while it was still in the embryo stage. If the method is applicable on a wide scale, it will mark a great step forward for commercial poultry raisers. A boy on the West Coast produced synthetic emeralds indistinguishable from the genuine article.

A teacher noted that those who win science awards and scholarships at the end of high school do so without expensive laboratories or elaborate equipment. The thing that matters most is the student's attitude and his intense desire to learn. When he is shown how to experiment, he can go on learning for himself.

One expert science teacher says that he calls upon gifted students to take charge of the class from time to time—to take the teacher's place for a demonstration or to coach other students. Sometimes the class is divided into interest groups with a student leader for each group.

Forest Hills High School The best-known work in high school science is the program developed by Dr. Paul Brandwein at Forest Hills High School, New York (1955). At this school students of unusual promise in science and mathematics are clustered as a small group in a regular classroom. They are given differentiated assignments or honors problems; they use different textbooks; and they are given opportunities to work on original projects in the science laboratory. In mathematics these students may prepare their own problems. They may also be scheduled for laboratory periods in which they apply mathematics to engineering and industrial problems. Senior students are given college-level courses in chemistry, physics, and mathematics which earn advanced standing in college. (Other provisions for gifted students in science were described by Brandwein in *Education for the Gifted,* part 2, 1958.)

Students with special aptitudes in mathematics and science enter a group running parallel to other sections for all their years in high school. The special group investigates the scientific method and works on various projects. A separate homeroom may be set up for capable students who have expressed an interest in becoming mathematicians or scientists.

A flexible high school program extends the range of science and mathematics teaching through science clubs, tutorial groups, seminars, and special lectures. Science study is supplemented by science fair exhibits put on by students, science assemblies, and field trips. The Forest Hills High School sponsors fourteen clubs in science and mathematics for students interested in biology, chemistry, physics, natural science, mathematics, photography, and science journalism. These clubs enroll students capable of doing advanced work and carrying on individual projects in their specialties. Another school has clubs for students interested in astronomy and in mathematical games. Many school science clubs are affiliated with a national organization, Science Clubs of America.

Considerable concern has been expressed about the failure of gifted girls to elect advanced high school courses in science. Unless they do, it is impossible for them to undertake major science programs in college and the university. To increase the interest of girls in science, the Forest Hills High School has set up an all-girl section in physics. By this means, more girls are enticed into science than formerly, and there is no competition with boys who tend to get a head start in the earlier years. The results have been highly favorable. The percentage of girls passing the New York State Regents' examination in physics has generally been higher than the percentage of boys.

A description of the Phoenix, Arizona, plan of instruction for high school students talented in science has been given by Witty and Bloom (1955). Science classes for the exceptional student in

Portland, Oregon, have been described by Wilson and others (1957).

Learning to Work As a Scientist   To become a scientist, the student needs to learn to think and work as a scientist. He must have opportunities for independent research and project development in order to try out ideas.

Steps in scientific problem solving include:

Locating the problem, formulating the question, setting up a hypothesis

Gathering and sifting data

Suspending judgment until sufficient factual information is at hand

Weighing evidence

Comparing statements and reports from different sources

Citing authority for answers

Drawing conclusions

The student selects his own research problem, and then sets to work to solve it. He decides on ways of exploring the problem, looks up relevant material, discovers meanings, and draws conclusions. The final step is preparing his report.

Out-of-school Science Aids   A number of out-of-school programs were described in the preceding chapter. In some communities, local scientists participate in science club groups for advanced students which meet one evening a week or for weekend sessions. In other cases, the local college or university conducts classes and supervises laboratory work on Saturdays for a few outstanding science students.

Career conferences about positions in science, trips to representative industries, leadership of science squads by science professionals in the community—all are excellent means of creating interest in science and are within the reach of most schools.

During the past decade there has been a marked increase in science books for young people and in the number of young people who read them. The Traveling High School Science Library Program was initiated by the American Association for the Advancement of Science in 1955 under the direction of Hilary Deason, with a grant from the National Science Foundation. When the program was concluded in 1962, it had served nearly 6,000 public and private secondary schools throughout the United States and the Armed Forces dependents' schools abroad. Teen-agers joined with scientists to select the books, about 360 titles. Space travel, aviation, and exploration are popular themes, along with some stiff reading in classical science. The academically talented are eager to read about the great discoveries of science in the words of the scientists themselves. A good science resource book for the teen-ager is the publication by UNESCO listed at the end of this section (1958).

MATHEMATICS

Because of the intimate relationship between science studies and mathematics, many of the points made in the foregoing section apply also to instruction in mathematics. Students are sectioned according to ability in advanced mathematics, algebra, and geometry. The sectioning is done on the basis of mental test ratings, past achievement in mathematics, and the teacher's recommendations.

In the Bronx High School of Science, talented mathematics students take an enriched mathematics sequence throughout four years. At Phillips Andover Academy, superior students take a full course of analytical geometry and calculus in the senior year, following three years of algebra, geometry, and trigonometry. A combination of algebra and geometry is recommended for students who have excelled in geometry and trigonometry. In these courses students work on unusual problems in original ways.

EXPERIMENT WITH ADVANCED PLACEMENT
AT THE BRONX HIGH SCHOOL OF SCIENCE

The Bronx High School of Science was one of the seven schools selected for the pilot study of the Ford Foundation known as the School and College Program of Admission with Advanced Standing. College-level courses in English literature, mathematics, biology, chemistry, and physics were offered for selected senior year students in classes of twenty to thirty students. Fifty-two students were finally selected for the various courses. All had earned grade averages of 90 or better. Some took four of the courses; a few chose only one.

Breinan made a follow-up study of these fifty-two graduates of the Bronx High School of Science who participated in the School and College Program of Admission with Advanced Standing (1956). The finding that all were accepted at leading colleges, that forty obtained New York Regents' scholarships for four years of college study, and that ten others were awarded scholarships by the institutions they attended indicated the high caliber of the group. A number of the students did not ask for college credit or advanced placement for the college-level courses taken in high school. Most of the students gave enthusiastic endorsement to the program. Only ten said they needed some special attention as a result of having the advanced courses, and only six said that they were experiencing some difficulty as a result of participation in the program. Only five thought that their decision to take college courses in high school was not a wise one. Many reported favorably on their college work. Twenty of the students said that they had had some difficulty in the senior high school year because of taking advanced courses; for example, they regretted the curtailment of extracurricular activities.

OTHER AVANCED-PLACEMENT PROGRAMS

Several methods of enriching junior high school mathematics in Cheltenham, Pennsylvania, were investigated by Passow, Goldberg, and Link under the auspices of the Talented Youth Project of Teachers College, Columbia University (1961). The research plan involved three different programs of enrichment: (1) concepts of modern mathematics added to the existing course of study, (2) acceleration through the traditional mathematics sequence, and (3) focus on more-difficult and complex problems of the regular mathematics courses. Three comparable matched groups were set up: average IQ, 132–133; average arithmetic achievement, grade 9.2–9.3; average reading achievement, grade 9.4–9.8.

In the ninth grade the accelerated class completed the algebra 2 course normally taught to bright tenth graders. Another class was accelerated by completing units in the University of Illinois mathematics program for high school students: equations, graphs, and relations and functions. The enriched class completed the standard course in elementary algebra modified to permit the teaching of three enrichment units. The control class completed the standard course in elementary algebra and began the algebra 2 course.

At the end of the ninth grade after three years of instruction according to these different plans, the two accelerated groups did consistently better than the enrichment and control groups on the measures used to evaluate results, the Stanford Achievement battery, and a teacher-made test of thirty items. These outcomes suggest that early introduction of more difficult content and increased tempo of instruction result in greater mathematical competence and in somewhat more positive attitudes toward mathematics than the other instructional approaches used. The authors concluded that acceleration and enrichment are not opposing concepts; on the contrary, acceleration is a means of providing students with meaningful and enriching experiences. Enrichment becomes meaningful only when students deal with more advanced and more difficult concepts.

The reader is referred to the following books and articles for more information and suggestions on the teaching of science and mathematics:

Albers, Mary E., and May V. Seagoe: Enrichment for Superior Students in Algebra Classes, *Journal of Educational Research,* 40:481–495, 1947.

Brandwein, Paul F.: *The Gifted Student As Future Scientist,* Harcourt, Brace & World, Inc., New York, 1955.

Brandwein, Paul F.: Secondary School Programs, chap. 12 in *Education for the Gifted: Fifty-seventh Yearbook of the National Society for the Study of Education,* part 2, The University of Chicago Press, Chicago, 1958.

Brudick, John G.: Secondary School Science, chap. 8 in Louis A. Fliegler (ed.), *Curriculum Planning for the Gifted,* Prentice-Hall, Inc., Englewood Cliffs, N.J., 1961.

Coe, Burr D.: Ungraded Classes for Superior Pupils, *The Mathematics Teacher,* 37:81–83, 1944.

Mathematics for the Academically Talented Student, National Education Association, Washington, D.C., 1959.

Nelson, Willard H., and others: NSF–FSU Math Campers: Evaluations of and by Campers, *Mathematics Teacher,* 54:149–154, 1961.

Passow, A. Harry: Developing a Science Program for Rapid Learners, *Science Education,* 41:104–112, 1957.

Passow, A. Harry, Miriam L. Goldberg, and Francis R. Link: Enriched Mathematics for Gifted Junior High School Students, *Educational Leadership,* 18:442–448, 1961.

Salisbury, Muri B.: Science Seminars for Talented Secondary School Students, *The Science Teacher,* 26:150–193, 1959.

Science for the Academically Talented Student, National Education Association, Washington, D.C., 1959.

Seeger, R. J.: Mathematical Science and the Manpower Problem, *The Mathematics Teacher,* 50:10–18, 1957.

UNESCO (comp.): *700 Science Experiments for Everyone,* Doubleday & Company, Inc., Garden City, N.Y., 1958.

Wilson, Robert C., and others: *Science Classes for Exceptionally Endowed Students in the High Schools of Portland, Oregon,* Portland, Ore., Public Schools, 1957.

Witty, Paul A., and Samuel W. Bloom: Conserving Ability in the Sciences, *Exceptional Children*, 22:10–16, 46–47, 1955.

Zim, Herbert S.: Opportunities for Pupils with Unusual Science Talent, *Bulletin of the National Association of Secondary Principals*, 37:156–165, 1953.

Foreign Languages

Studying a modern foreign language in high school not only equips the gifted student with a useful tool for a career that may take him abroad, but it serves as a means of intellectual enrichment through the reading of prose and poetry reflecting life in another culture. As a general principle, every academically talented student should have a working knowledge of a second language by the time he is through high school, with the prospect of carrying advanced language studies in college.

Advanced students with a good foundation can enjoy the study of foreign literature without translation in classes conducted entirely in the foreign language. These students are often able to pass examinations for advanced placement in foreign languages on entering college.

Bright students show divergent attitudes toward foreign language study. Some are intensely interested; others consider it a waste of time, perhaps because they have not seen the relevance of language study to their current interests and career prospects. But another reason is that traditional methods of teaching are boring and tedious when centered on textbook lessons stressing minor grammar points of no great significance in using the language.

Since the study of foreign languages in high school is usually optional, some screening takes place automatically. Teachers have observed the great difference between a class of selected students with intellectual curiosity and sincere interest and an unassorted class. Girls usually show more interest in language study than boys because of the social asset of knowing another language, but boys respond just as well as girls once their interest is aroused. The opportunity to study a foreign language should be offered to every gifted student, but he should not be forced to continue if he loses interest. College-bound students tend to enroll in foreign language classes because most colleges require language credits for admission.

In large schools, students are sectioned primarily on the basis of previous work in a foreign language, general academic ability, and evidence of linguistic aptitude. Some use has been made of language prognosis tests as a predictor of future success, but results have not proved to be very satisfactory.

What language should be offered? French is usually most popular, with Spanish a close second. German has tended to decline in popularity in recent years. This is unfortunate, because German is used even more widely than French as a second language among the common people in many parts of Europe, and it is essential for advanced study in scientific fields.

METHODS OF INSTRUCTION

In the best schools and colleges, foreign language study is no longer an intellectual exercise—the study of grammer in formal fashion. Instead, there is practice in conversation and drill on speech patterns from the first lessons; then, with training in written expression, the new language becomes a practical tool.

There is a growing belief that modern foreign language study, by its very nature, should not be treated as other subjects in the high school curriculum. Foreign language study is actually a skill subject at first, more on a par with music and art than academic subjects. Experts who hold this view recommend that modern foreign language study be taken out of the regular curriculum and considered an appreciation study or a school activity. They recommend teaching foreign language in small club groups' or circles in order to provide a maximum of teacher-student and student-student contact. There can be full, active participation in speaking and dramatization, with more individual attention from the teacher or leader, and with students using the language informally, just as they use their mother tongue.

For oral work, the best instructional device is the teacher's demonstration. Although phonograph records go too fast for beginners, good use can be made of text with accompanying records. A well-equipped language laboratory is a boon for the gifted student who is eager to work independently in language practice.

The Foreign Language Association of America recommends that the gifted take a minimum of four years of foreign language study in high school, or continue with the same language for six years in junior and senior high school. Better still would be ten years of continuous language study, beginning in the elementary grades. Few schools are able to come up to these standards, because of the pressure from other curriculum areas for their share of the student's time; also, the students themselves would not care to devote this much time to a single field of study. If students could make constant use of their foreign language outside of school, as in Europe, they would need less school time to master it.

Mme. Jane Browne, French teacher at the Lincoln School of Teachers College, New York, and now at the New Lincoln School, says that she has obtained the best results when high school students begin language study in grade 7, at age eleven or twelve, and continue through a full six years. The next best schedule is to begin in grade 9 and continue with the same language for four years. Results are better with students who use their own language well and have excellent reading ability. Alert, interested students actually push the teacher for extended practice. Madame Browne recommends that the entire first year, grade 7, be spent on oral work without recourse to textbooks or practice in reading and writing.

With a continuous, sequential study program, capable students can acquire satisfactory command of the language in every aspect. Reading and writing the foreign language are learned more easily if the student has first learned to speak and comprehend it. Students should have a thorough grounding in one language, at least three to five years, before beginning another.

Gifted students in language classes can carry on research studies that relate to subject areas: science, music, art, intercultural relations. They can use foreign language newspapers, journals, and books. The study of language is enriched through trips, museum visits, art exhibits, the cinema, and the theater. Talented language students will be interested in staging plays and in writing their own scripts for dramatization and various programs.

As an integral part of his foreign language study, the student should become acquainted with the cultural background of native users of the language. Corresponding with "pen pals" in foreign cities is one device for enriching cultural awareness.

A number of American schools have arranged for student exchanges in which selected students go as "ambassadors" to foreign cities, while their counterparts abroad come to America for a year's stay. These students, with the open mindedness of youth, benefit tremendously from their contacts with the people and culture of another country where not only the language but the customs are different from their own. A graduate of the Garden City, New York, six-year French program spent a year in Aix-en-Provence, France, as representative of his city. A student of Spanish from the same school, after completing college, was selected by a South American poetess as her assistant in making English translations.

For more information on the teaching of modern foreign languages, see the following publications:

Méras, Edmond A.: *A Language Teacher's Guide*, Harper & Row, Publishers, Incorporated, New York, 1962.

Parker, William R.: *The National Interest and Foreign Languages*, 3d ed., U.S. Department of State, Washington, D.C., 1961.

Soffietti, James P.: Foreign Languages, chap. 9 in Louis A. Fliegler (ed.), *Curriculum Planning for the Gifted*, Prentice-Hall, Inc., Englewood Cliffs, N.J., 1961.

Starr, Wilmart H., Mary P. Thompson, Donald D. Walsh (eds.): *Modern Foreign Languages and the Academically Talented Student*, National Education Association, Washington D.C., 1960.

CLASSICAL LANGUAGES

Most of the current discussion about foreign language teaching relates to modern foreign languages. Latin has gone the way of Greek in the public secondary school curriculum since it has ceased to be required for college entrance. Now we are advancing into a new cycle in which school people recognize that Latin and Greek have enrichment values for the superior student. A young college instructor said that she regretted not having had the classical languages in high school or college; in her teaching of comparative literature courses, she felt that a knowledge of both Latin and Greek was essential. High schools enrolling a substantial number of college-bound and professionally oriented students should make classical languages available, at least on an optional elective basis.

Music and Art

With respect to the fine and applied arts, gifted students divide into two groups: those who benefit from music and art as enrichment of personal living, and the highly talented who plan to become professional artists or musicians. The question of art talent in relation to high general learning aptitude was discussed in Chapter Three.

Academically talented students may undervalue work in the arts because they consider this area lacking in academic discipline. This attitude reflects ignorance of the true value of the arts for a liberal education as well as an overconcern for college entrance credits. Music and art add a new dimension to the other curriculum areas, particularly when they provide enrichment for units in history, literature, science, and mathematics. A great scientist finds that his early experience in design enables him to construct a piece of equipment or to supervise its construction. Music is a release from emotional tension for the brain worker as well as a source of personal satisfaction.

The discovery of talent in the arts is not so simple as it seems, even in the case of the child who plays the piano expertly, draws and paints well, or shows unusual poise and artistry on the stage. Expert performance by an adolescent may be more the result of habit and enforced training than a sign of genuine interest and desire to "reach the heights." Tests of art aptitude, pitch discrimination, etc., may do little more than indicate the student's present level of achievement.

Indications of potentiality in the arts are the student's voluntary interest in perfecting his skills, in learning as much as possible about the theoretical and academic aspects of his chosen art field, his ambition for an art career, his aptitude for advanced study, the amount of information he has amassed in his chosen field, and his energy level.

Certainly, no adolescent should be encouraged to seek a career in the arts if he does not measure up favorably in most of these traits. To be a competent performer is not enough. The student must exhibit high educability to become a thoroughly trained professional.

For the instruction of talented music and art students who are beyond the rudimentary stages, the school needs excellent equipment: a music studio with high-grade instruments and musical literature, an art studio with proper lighting and equipment, a well-equipped stage for theatricals.

Workshops in music and art should be conducted several periods a week for the most promising students. Art instruction defeats its purpose when the members of a class are given uniform instruction according to a set pattern. In music there is less danger of uniform group teaching, except for theory, singing, certain demonstrations, and explanations.

Hunter College High School   Hunter College High School in New York has developed an experimental integrated course in five art areas (Woolcock, 1962). The course is presented in three double periods a week. Two of these periods are spent in laboratory workshops where students obtain firsthand experiences in at least two of the art categories, learning techniques and developing their own ideas creatively. In the remaining core period an attempt is made to integrate the study and to interrelate the activities of the various workshops. An important part of the course is required reading in each of the five art areas.

Art experiences extend beyond the classroom; the students attend plays, operas, concerts, hear guest speakers, visit museums, and view art films. A listening room is available where students can listen to music related to their studies.

Through this course, the students gain a fuller appreciation of achievement in the arts. Participation in art activities has increased, and learning in all areas of the curriculum has been enriched. As a result, the students show more awareness of art and culture in their environment. They are finding in art experience a new outlet for creative imagination; in fact, their whole view of life has been enlarged.

THE GRAPHIC ARTS

Cleveland, Ohio, has established special classes for talented students in the graphic arts; and Ontario, Canada, has conducted classes for art-talented adolescents for a number of years. Instruction is not limited to traditional lessons in painting and drawing; rather, students experiment with various media, surfaces, and instruments for expressing their feelings in art form. Work with clay in the lower school leads on to ceramics and sculpture as students gain skill in modeling and decoration.

Photography serves as an interesting art medium for clever high school youths who lack skills in expressive art media and are inclined to scorn artwork. Interior decorating, which requires a solid foundation in art education, provides another form of expression for art-talented students.

For further information on art education, see the references at the end of this section, page 400.

MUSIC

The majority of capable teen-agers participating in musical events in high school are not thinking of becoming professional musicians; for them, music is simply one of life's satisfying personal experiences. The tremendous upsurge of enthusiasm for music in all its varied forms can be attributed in large part to the stepped-up production of mechanical devices for music making: the phonograph (some 400 companies in America alone now manufacture phonograph records), the radio (nearly every household has two or three sets), and now television in even the lowliest cottage or crowded apartment.

Since the time of Dr. Carl Seashore's studies of musical aptitude some fifty years ago, attention has shifted from trying to discover children with inborn musical talent to sifting out those who show the most promise of profiting from a musical education. Musical aptitude tests such as those Seashore and others have devised serve this purpose to some extent. The fact that musical talent is not solely a matter of inborn gifts is proved by the tremendous increase in the number of expert young musicians in the United States within the past forty years. Today a wealth of musical talent is active in community life and in schools, colleges, and churches. According to the latest count, there are over 1,100 local symphony orchestras in the United States and at least 15,000 youth orchestras.

Enthusiasm has also been stimulated by the growth of high-standard music schools with liberal scholarships for the most promising students. Prizes and contests stir up enthusiasm for excellence in musical performance. When children continually come under the influence of good music and receive expert training, the number of excellent performers increases phenomenally. A few emerge as outstanding musicians or even musical geniuses.

Today, more than in any preceding period, public school instruction in music is producing well-trained young musicians. In the larger high schools musical organizations are among the most popular. A considerable proportion of students participate in the school chorus or glee club, in an orchestra, band, or ensembles, and in music clubs. There are contests with other schools both within and between states. Summer music camps such as those at Chautauqua, New York, and Interlaken, Michigan, extend the student's musical training through the summer months.

A new trend in high school music instruction is to have students work in a music laboratory that has much the same equipment as a foreign language or speech laboratory. Here the students listen to tapes and recordings and make tapes to study their own performance.

Experts describe the specially talented music student as one who has the ability to hear and distinguish melody, a strong sense of rhythm, and a superior tonal memory that enables him to reproduce what he hears. Such a student needs counseling in order to make long-range plans for his musical education and to prevent narrow specialization. The best work is done when the most talented are placed together in small groups and when they are encouraged to work out their own ideas independently.

Outstanding student musicians should practice with small ensemble groups, not only as soloists with large groups. In this way they cover more music literature and develop more initiative away from teacher supervision. Talented students should have experience in planning musical programs and preparing program notes; they should study music history and read the lives of celebrated musicians. They gain maturity by conducting rehearsals, working with groups, taking responsibility for the music library, and coaching other children.

The typical high school lacks space for individual and small-group work in music. Some of the newer schools have met this problem with a music suite consisting of large and small rehearsal and practice rooms. Another problem is the cost of maintaining a supply of music and high-quality instruments that the students can use both at school and at home. Since few public high schools are able to meet the needs of highly talented student musicians, the schools should try to work out cooperative arrangements with private music teachers or music schools so that students can get in the intensive daily practice they must have.

The High School of Music and Art in New York City is a public school for selected young people who are headed for careers in the arts. The School of Performing Arts, also in New York, gives selected students training in dramatic arts.

For further information on the subject of music and art education for the talented, see the following references:

Brittain, W. Lambert: Creative Art, chap. 10 in Louis A. Fliegler (ed.), *Curriculum Planning for the Gifted*, Prentice-Hall, Inc., Englewood Cliffs, N.J., 1961.

Capruso, Alexander: Music, chap 11 in Louis A. Fliegler (ed.), *Curriculum Planning for the Gifted*, Prentice-Hall, Inc., Englewood Cliffs, N.J., 1961.

D'Amico, Victor E.: *Creative Teaching in Art*, International Textbook Company, Scranton, Pa., 1942.

Hartshorne, William C. (ed.): *Music for the Academically Talented Student*, National Education Association, Washington, D.C., 1959.

Knuth, William E.: Creative Dramatics, chap. 12 in Louis A. Fliegler (ed.), *Curriculum Planning for the Gifted*, Prentice-Hall, Inc., Englewood Cliffs, N.J., 1961.

Lowenfeld, Viktor: *Creative and Mental Growth*, 3d ed., The Macmillan Company, New York, 1957.

Music for the Academically Talented Student, National Education Association, Washington, D.C., 1960.

Ziegleld, Edwin (ed.): *Art for the Academically Talented Student in the Secondary School,* NEA Project on the Academically Talented Student, National Education Association, Washington, D.C., 1961.

Technical Studies

The recommendation that the academically talented should take five solid subjects during all four years of high school is open to question. Such a program would crowd out practical studies under school auspices and would be especially unfortunate for the youth whose home background offers little opportunity for training and experience in manual work. Practical studies add a cultural dimension to a program of academic work. With early mastery of manual skills, the gifted will be all the more ready to handle the technical problems they encounter in their academic studies, such as, making a piece of laboratory equipment or drafting a set of plans. As a teacher and educational leader, Booker T. Washington found his early work experience and later technical training at Hampton Institute, Virginia, of inestimable value in helping him to understand workers and the world of work.

A gifted high school student or a college youth may well pride himself on his diversified skills when he can drive a car or truck and perhaps repair it, when he knows something of carpentry and household repairs, when he knows enough horticulture for gardening, can make or repair a radio set, is a competent photographer, and so on. His female counterpart will know how to cook a meal and make clothing; usually she, too, can qualify as a chauffeur.

Handcrafts are not beneath the dignity of academic-minded students. As John Dewey pointed out, students will encounter in manual work some of their best opportunities for critical thinking and problem solving. The problems to be met in technical studies are as challenging and as intellectual in their ramifications as the problems arising in academic studies.

If the gifted student cannot find time in his crowded school schedule for practical studies, there is the possibility of learning technical skills in out-of-school clubs, on weekends with recreation and hobby groups, or in summer camp. Wise parents who themselves have practical skills can become the child's best teachers.

Should terminal vocational studies be excluded from the secondary school curriculum for the academically talented? The answer is "Yes," as a general principle, because gifted students are not going to enter the trades, nor will their academic education terminate when they graduate from high school. There is no contradiction between these statements and the recommendation that the gifted student obtain as much manual training and work experience as possible during vacation periods, weekends, or after school.

Gifted and Talented Students in the Junior High School (Ages Eleven to Fourteen)

The junior high school offers a wider array of studies suited to children in the early adolescent years than can be provided in the typical elementary school. This is an excellent time for the budding teen-agers to try out new interests and develop their special aptitudes. By this time they are able to read well enough for independent study and have the basic skills of arithmetic needed for advanced work in science. In junior high school, students have new opportunities for participating in the life of the school, for recreation, club groups, and hobby interests.

The junior high school has the same responsibility as the other divisions in the school system for identifying children with unusual academic aptitude or special talent. Individual guidance begun at this period, if not before, will assist exceptional children in developing their aptitudes.

In the junior high school period, the range of individual differences becomes more apparent because the children come together from a number of different elementary schools. Variations in educability for academic studies now become more apparent.

Here are snapshots of two gifted children who are about to enter junior high school.

Ronald is eleven years old, the largest child in the sixth-grade class from which he is graduating this June. His IQ is 136. The boy did outstanding work in the class project, Niagara Falls, in which he was looked upon as a leader, as he directed the work of less-talented children. He enjoys science and spends much of his spare time reading on this topic. His classmates respect his vast fund of knowledge and listen to his suggestions. He is far ahead of the group in fundamental skills. Teachers say he has an excellent mind, his arguments are logical, his manner persuasive. He has been skipped twice, one term in the second grade, again at the end of the third grade. Here is a boy of unusual promise who should have special opportunities in junior high to develop his aptitudes.

Greta, now ten years, eight months, of age with an IQ of 148, is also completing sixth grade this June. She is an alert child, interested in everything, one of the recognized leaders of her class. She goes at a tremendous pace in carrying out her inventive plans and ideas. She constantly seeks an audience, is ambitious, takes pride in her work, sets high standards for herself, has keen powers of observation, is highly creative in working with materials, shows persistence and a will to work. She is far ahead of her class in arithmetic and enjoys writing original stories.

Greta tries to impose her ideas on everyone, especially her less-gifted classmates. She becomes impatient with the other children and does not respect their ideas and opinions. No wonder she is not considered a good sport. She loves power and will fight for a position of leadership. Recently she has developed an increasingly intolerant attitude toward her classmates, who "ganged up" so that they could have their own way about the class party. One child exclaimed, "Can't we ever do anything that Greta doesn't try to run?"

Here is a child who is far ahead of her classmates in originality and leadership capacity. Placed in a regular junior high school class with a traditional program, she will not be challenged, and the unfavorable qualities that are daily becoming more apparent may be exaggerated. What opportunities can a junior high school offer this child to absorb her energy and help her develop more wholesome relationships with her classmates?

SPECIAL PROVISIONS FOR THE GIFTED IN GRADES 7 THROUGH 9

This period intermediate between the elementary school and the senior high school has something in common with both. In the junior high school organization, there will be ability grouping in general courses, special classes for the academically talented, honors classes, and seminar groups. In a large New York City junior high school there may be as many as fifteen or even twenty sections in one grade, with the students grouped somewhat according to general ability and all-around achievement. School studies are largely departmentalized as in senior high school.

TELESCOPING THE JUNIOR HIGH SCHOOL YEARS

Capable junior high school students may speed up their progress through school by taking an extra course or by completing the three years of work in two or two and a half.

The change from the 8-4 plan that formerly prevailed in school organization to the present-day 6-3-3 plan means that the high school years are now divided into two separate units that have little in common, at least in large city high schools. This complicates program making for children who are able to accelerate a year or more during the combined junior-senior high school period. School authorities agree that considerable time can be saved by the most capable students in the intermediate years, ages eleven to fourteen. Three years in junior high school is too long for a rapid learner; but trying to compress two years into three causes strain. Covering six years of high school work in five provides for a smoother transition into college. In some schools the six-year span of high school study is planned for bright students on an accelerated basis.

A growing trend in both city and suburban communities is to terminate junior high school at the eighth grade, and then to begin the senior high school sequence at the ninth grade, grouping the young adolescents with the older teen-agers rather than with the younger children.

Saving time in the junior high school period should not cause a student to miss out on important areas of study or prevent his full participation in the life of the school. The gifted student who has already covered the basic seventh-grade studies may be put ahead into the next grade after full consideration of his abilities and status.

ENRICHMENT OF STUDIES

The tendency for efforts at enrichment to become trivial can only be offset by concerted planning for a full, stimulating program in which individual talents can be developed. Many of the practices for enriching and accelerating the work of gifted students in senior high school described above are also applicable to the junior high school. The suggestions for enrichment in the elementary school given in Chapter Nine apply equally well to the junior high school period.

The typical junior high school program cut up into 45-minute periods has never been very satisfactory. The periods are too short for consecutive work; individual work and integration of several subject areas for unit studies are virtually impossible. The better plan is to place students in the charge of one teacher for a double period, and then to send certain students to special teachers for science, arts and crafts, and other talent interests.

Bright boys and girls entering adolescence need to have a larger share in planning and conducting their own education than heretofore; they should be able to choose from an array of learning opportunities in harmony with current interests. At the same time, they should be sharing experiences in the social group and learning to work cooperatively to achieve group goals.

Junior high school students undertake a study theme such as "Our Water Supply," "Ships Are the Lifeline," "Exploring the Universe," or "Life in the Orient" with enthusiasm. The program for the gifted should feature special projects and reports, science field studies, algebra, and advanced science. There may be talent classes in journalism, mathematics, art, music, foreign languages, and other studies. Bright children should be encouraged to exercise their imagination by play writing, using current themes of home, school, and life experience.

In some schools, pupils are expected to work alone on their own projects. One student concentrated on coal mining. Another made a specialty of intricate stage lighting that was turned to good account in all the school's dramatic performances. One child became so interested in studying bees that he was soon a recognized authority on the subject. Now in college, he is continuing his interest in biological research with the promise of a successful career as a scientist.

In social studies the students concentrate on American history and its European backgrounds; they may do some history writing themselves. In ninth grade they work on selected topics in world history, going into a particular topic or period in depth, tying in the study with other curriculum areas such as literature, art, music, dramatics, and creative expression in various media.

In enrichment courses as much goes on outside of school as during class sessions. The students may take a city tour or concentrate on certain features of urban life for an extensive study.

If time permits, a double period of time daily might well be reserved for work on hobby projects. The Brighton Junior High School, Long Island, has club day twice a week on Tuesday and Friday for various talent groups.

In Westport, Connecticut, junior high school teachers give classes assignments via dictaphone machines so that they have more time with individual pupils.

This is the ideal time for students to begin the study of a foreign language for the full six-year sequence. Their studies in history and geography have given them considerable familiarity with, and curiosity about, other lands and people. At this age, too, students are keenly interested in working with the devices that language study now employs: tapes, recordings, movies, and filmstrips.

Practical studies are particularly valuable at this time in enriching life experience. Junior high school students in one community were given real work experience in tree surgery. The mechanics club worked on an old automobile; the radio club constructed a radio with the materials they assembled; the writer's club turned out the school paper.

The curriculum for the gifted is strengthened by stepping up the difficulty level of the courses, particularly in mathematics, science, and foreign languages. Today advanced junior high school students take courses formerly given only in senior high school. Students with special interest and aptitude in science are offered courses in biology, physics, and chemistry instead of general science. Instruction in basic skills, such as note taking, rapid reading, preparation of reports, and research techniques, receives full attention.

A new departure in the junior high school is the use of teacher teams working with the same group of students over a three-year period in English, social studies, mathematics, and science. The team makes for more-coherent and sequential learning, ensuring more opportunity for continuous teacher-pupil contacts.

Excessive homework assignments create a serious problem in junior high school. Some schools get around the difficulty by providing more time for study during the school day.

SPECIAL PROGRESS AND SPECIAL TALENT CLASSES IN NEW YORK CITY

New York City has operated a system of special progress classes for intellectually gifted students in the junior high school for nearly forty years. Enrollment in these classes on a selective basis enables a bright boy or girl to complete the three-year junior high school curriculum in two years. The classes were originally set up to offer bright children more challenge and to curb the tendency of young adolescents to coast along with verbal glibness.

Students admitted to the special progress classes, beginning with grade 7, must have an IQ rating of 130 or higher on standard tests, a reading grade level of at least 8.5, a mathematics grade of 8.0 or higher, and a minimum chronological age of eleven years. The student is expected to have the social maturity of a twelve-year-old, and he must be in good health. Both the principal's recommendation and the parents' consent are required for enrollment in these classes.

In the fall of 1960, a three-year junior high school program for children of high IQ was developed as an alternative to the speeded-up two-year classes, providing more enrichment in advanced studies than in regular classes and more opportunity for individual work. This change was introduced in the belief that young bright students might feel lost socially among physically more mature students when they entered the senior high school. Children entering the special progress classes are often a year or two accelerated to begin with. The two-year rapid-progress plan resulted in too many children's going on from junior high school with shortcomings in basic skills and gaps in general knowledge. In the new three-year enriched program, gifted students have plenty of intellectual challenge. With three years for junior high school there is more time for depth in studies, experimentation, special trips, foreign languages, and other desirable learning experiences suited to the young teens.

In some districts of New York City, a choice may be made of either plan, but more children are now tending to follow the three-year sequence of studies, according to Dr. Joseph O. Loretan, associate superintendent in charge of junior high schools. An occasional remarkably bright child may still go through junior high school at his own fast pace. In some cases these children earn advanced credit in mathematics or foreign languages for senior high school. Isolation of special-class students from others in the school is prevented by their participation in schoolwide programs.

In addition to the special progress classes, there are also special talent classes in New York. For admission to these classes the chief criterion is evidence of special talent in art, music, writing, mechanics, and so on. The selection of students is made by the teachers of the classes. Since no minimum mental ability level is required, the children in a class of this type range widely in intellectual ability. One child, according to his teacher, has a modest IQ, and has difficulty keeping up with his academic subjects, but he plays a "mean trumpet." There may be some better plan for taking care of children with special talents who cannot compete with brighter children academically.

References

Baughman, W. Dale: Challenging the Talented in Junior High School, *Elementary School Journal,* 61:246–253, 1961.

Breinan, Alexander: The School and College Program of Admission with Advanced Standing, *High Points,* 38:13–23, 1956.

Conant, James B.: *Recommendations for the Junior High School Years,* Educational Testing Service, Princeton, N.J., 1960.

Drews, Elizabeth M. (ed.): *Guidance for the Academically Talented Student,* NEA Project on the Academically Talented Student, National Education Association, Washington, D.C., 1961.

Everett, Samuel (ed.): *Programs for the Gifted: A Case Book in Secondary Education,* John Dewey Society Yearbook, Harper & Row, Publishers, Incorporated, New York, 1961.

56 Practices for the Gifted from Secondary Schools of New York State, University of the State of New York, Education Department, Albany, N.Y., 1958.

Fliegler, Louis A. (ed.): *Curriculum Planning for the Gifted,* Prentice-Hall, Inc., Englewood Cliffs, N.J., 1961.

The Gifted Child in the Junior High School, a report of the Junior High School Principals Association of New York City, 1958.

Jewett, Arno, J. Dan Hull, and others: *Teaching Rapid and Slow Learners in High School,* U.S. Department of Health, Education and Welfare, Office of Education, Washington, D.C., 1954.

Laycock, Samuel R.: *Gifted Children: A Handbook for the Classroom Teacher,* The Copp-Clark Publishing Company, Toronto, Canada, 1957.

Mearns, Hughes: *Creative Power: The Education of Youth in the Creative Arts,* Doubleday & Company, Inc., Garden City, N.Y., 1929.

Mearns, Hughes: *Creative Youth: How a School Environment Set Free the Creative Spirit,* Doubleday & Company, Inc., Garden City, N.Y., 1925.

Michael, Lloyd S.: Secondary Programs, chap. 12 in *Education for the Gifted: Fifty-seventh Yearbook of the National Society for the Study of Education,* part 2, The University of Chicago Press, Chicago, 1958.

Morgan, H. H.: A Psychometric Comparison of Achieving and Nonachieving College Students of High Ability, *Journal of Consulting Psychology,* 16:292–298, 1952.

Shertzer, Bruce: *Working with Superior Students,* Science Research Associates, Inc., Chicago, 1960.

Smilansky, Moshe: Israel, chap. 5 in Educational Research in Countries Other than the United States, *Review of Educational Research,* 37:280–293, 1962.

Willis, Margaret: *The Guinea Pigs after Twenty Years: A Follow-up Study of the Class of 1938 of the University School at Ohio State,* Ohio State University Press, Columbia, Ohio, 1961.

Wilson, Robert C., and others: *Science Classes for Exceptionally Endowed Students in the High Schools of Portland, Oregon,* Portland, Ore., Public Schools, 1957.

Woolcock, Cyril: *The Hunter College High School Program for Gifted Students,* Vantage Press, New York, 1962.

Chapter Fourteen

GUIDANCE OF GIFTED AND TALENTED STUDENTS

Guidance services have long proved their value in helping school authorities and parents to understand the behavior and problems of individual students. The experienced guidance counselor brings professional expertness to bear on the special problems of the gifted. Through personal guidance and counseling, aptitudes are discovered and explored, and interests are directed. The student is advised to think of himself as a scholarly person who may one day be distinguished because of unusual performance and accomplishments.

Guidance and Counseling Services

Guidance programs for the gifted are concerned primarily with the following services:

Educational counseling, selection of courses and programs, underachievement, college advisement

Personal counseling concerning problems of adjustment in everyday situations, at home and elsewhere

Prevocational and career counseling affecting decisions leading to investment of unusual abilities

The total counseling effort includes collating and analyzing records; conferring with parents, students, and teachers; gathering information needed for decisions and recommendations; making adjustments in school programs; and relating the student's program to the entire school curriculum. Counselors serve as liaison personnel between teachers and the school administration.

The counselor, in working over the cumulative records and test data for the entire school, can often make tentative identification of the gifted and talented. Guidance people have been successful in identifying potential failures among promising youths, catching them before their interest in study evaporates or before inferiority feelings become deep-seated, directing them toward unusual opportunities, helping them to understand themselves, and assisting them in planning for high-level careers. By directing the student in his own self-appraisal, a counselor can help him discover where his special aptitudes lie and how best to direct his energies to achieve his personal goals. Thus a student may discover that he has some talent in the creative arts or that his understanding of social issues can be broadened through study of current affairs. He may be directed toward enriching experiences outside the classroom in fields he has not yet explored such as art or science.

The guidance counselor can also help students improve their attitudes toward themselves, their classmates, the school, and the teachers. When the gifted student becomes hypercritical of a teacher, the guidance counselor can explain the teacher's point of view and perhaps make it more acceptable.

There may be special problems of motivation or difficulties in social adjustment. Gifted students from lower socioeconomic levels may require extra attention to realize the full development of their powers and to offset the negative effect of unfavorable influences. Advising parents is another aspect of counseling the gifted.

A counselor can be instrumental in advising the school about the wisdom of accelerating a gifted child or keeping him with his age-mates, of placing him in advanced sections and honor courses, of encouraging him to continue a certain course or field of interest or to choose another. Working out a financial-aid program for worthy students in high school—with the school authorities or local business people—may properly become part of the counselor's functions.

In a guide for rating a school's provisions for the gifted prepared by Passow and Brooks (1960), a number of points relate to guidance and counseling:

Educational, vocational, and personal counseling are planned specifically for the gifted.

Counselors and teachers participate regularly in conferences to consider the academic, physical, social, and emotional development of gifted students.

Counseling is provided for talented students with emotional or social difficulties or with a marked discrepancy between potential and achievement.

Talented students are referred to community service agencies when this is advisable.

Financial aid is sought for talented students when this assistance is needed for furthering their education.

Periodic conferences are arranged with the parents of talented students to review school progress and to consider special needs.

Follow-up study of the progress of graduates is made regularly to aid the school in evaluating its program for the talented.

Each talented student is assigned to a teacher and a counselor for study and assistance.

To provide adequately for individual counseling, there should be at least one full-time guidance counselor for every 250 or 300 high school students. These specially trained people supplement rather than supplant the teacher, who is necessarily concerned with the personal welfare of each of his students.

Continuity in counseling and guidance is the key to improved services for the gifted. The best plan is to have one counselor responsible for the supervision of gifted children, beginning in the elementary school and continuing through high school. In a small community this counselor will probably serve on a part-time basis in a single school. Under such an arrangement, comprehensive continuous records and an articulated program for every exceptional child can be developed. The unusual student is not so apt to become submerged when the same counselor keeps in touch with him year after year.

The need for better guidance and counseling services in the high school is being met through the National Defense Education Act of 1958. This act provides financial support not only for guidance programs in junior and senior high schools but also for training programs for guidance workers and counselors.

The high school years are a golden period for individual counseling. The students are more mature and are better able to understand and articulate their needs and problems in and out of school. Their interests are taking a more definite direction. They are ready for long-range planning. By this time, too, the counselor has sufficient background information on individual students to provide a sound basis for personal counseling.

DEVICES FOR COUNSELING

Two publications to assist teachers in studying and appraising their pupils have special application to work with the gifted. These are *The Teachers' Guidance Handbook*, by Kough and DeHaan, published by Science Research Associates, Inc., Chicago, 1955, and Flanagan's *Guidance Bulletin*, University of Pittsburgh. A third useful publication for high school guidance purposes is *Your Educational Plans* prepared by Stouffer of Harvard University and published by Science Research Associates, Inc., Chicago. This is a diagnostic tool consisting of thirty-one multiple-choice questions to be answered by the student. The questions provide insight into the student's attitudes and motives as well as information about social, family, and economic forces that may affect him. A second part of the form is the counselor's work sheet for summarizing the student's responses. This checklist device has been effective in discovering and analyzing the ambitions of teen-age students and their attitudes toward higher education and future work.

Counselors make use of all the techniques for gifted student identification and appraisal described in Chapter Six, plus their own personal judgments based on observations and conferences. Standard test results can be used to good effect in counseling both the students and their parents.

The basis of all effective counseling is the maintenance of comprehensive and continuous records for every child, beginning not later than age eleven or twelve and continuing through senior high school. These records provide a fair picture of the student's aptitudes and abilities. The gifted student's biographical inventory, which is a record of his family background, his educational progress, his behavior, interests, and aspirations, furnishes the raw material for personal advisement.

Educational Counseling

Educational guidance for the gifted includes choosing courses and arranging individual programs, sectioning students for advanced courses and rapid sections, planning a balanced school day, advising in cases of poor achievement, and assisting students with reading and study habits. Giving advice about college and other technical and preprofessional training, holding potential dropouts in high school, giving advice about participation in school life, and answering students' questions relating to the development of their special talents and interests are other aspects of counseling.

The decision as to what program to follow in high school is too often taken lightly. Bright students need guidance in choosing high school courses that will challenge their minds and prepare them for college. A counselor can advise students about the advantages of honors courses and other curriculum offerings designed especially for the gifted. The academic inventory referred to in an earlier chapter serves as a check on the suitability of the student's program of studies to his abilities (Conant, 1959).

The gifted student may occasionally need reassurance about his learning capacity. For example, he might begin the study of a foreign language in high school, but on reaching a difficult phase lose interest and decide that he lacks the special aptitudes the study requires. With advice at the crucial moment, he might surmount the difficulty and become an outstanding language student.

Students interested in science careers must be reminded that long years of training lie ahead of them. Achievement in science requires a large measure of maturity, stability, objectivity, and detachment, together with a sense of dedication.

THE DROPOUT PROBLEM

Over 50,000 students drop out of high school each year. Some of these are students of exceptional ability. A youth with an IQ of 118 from a poor home in the Midwest dropped out of school at the age of sixteen. He had always done well in school and had never been a problem to his teachers; but his older brothers and the other boys in his crowd dropped out before graduation, and he, consequently, had no incentive to continue. He had some special talent in art, but the high school atmosphere was impersonal, and the boy found the courses uninteresting. Had he received special guidance, he might have been encouraged to stay in school.

The dropout problem requires special attention. Undoubtedly many capable youths drop out of school because of the indifferent attitude of their parents, the lure of a job providing spending money, and the negative pull of peer-group associates.

INTERPRETING TEST RESULTS

Interpreting the results of intelligence and scholastic aptitude tests to teachers, parents, and students is usually one of the counselor's duties. Rather than stating numerical figures, IQs, percentile ranks, standard scores, and other technical terms, the counselor indicates what the results imply for modes of learning, school success, special talents and aptitudes, college prediction, future careers, etc. For example:

"Your child has a level of scholastic aptitude which should enable him to complete regular schoolwork more quickly than others."

"This is a student who can be expected to succeed with academic work in selected groups in high school and to carry a normal study program in college."

"This student shows more strength in mathematical reasoning than he does in vocabulary and language."

"With his ability, he should be able to pursue a course of study leading to a high-level profession."

"This student can succeed in one of the learned professions if he undergoes suitable training. He would probably be bored with routine office work."

PLANNING FOR COLLEGE

Advising students about college plans has become an important responsibility of high school counselors, one that requires study of the student's potentiality as well as knowledge of the requirements of the colleges. The transition from high school to college affects students in different ways; when problems arise, a counselor who is an authority on these matters can help to ease the transition.

Youths, along with their parents, should be counseled early about college opportunities and the wisdom of planning for advanced education. In a typical high school graduating class, from one-fifth to one-fourth of the students are "college material." Standardized intelligence and achievement tests administered to students in grades 8 and 9 predict college success about as well as tests given in senior high school. This is a good argument for testing early and using the results for counseling purposes.

Students who have little incentive to go to college may become interested through personal counseling. More of the students who attended the Major Work classes in Cleveland, Ohio, went on to college than did equally competent students who were not enrolled in these classes, because the former heard more about the advantages of college and learned more about college work and life.

Should every bright student be advised to attend college? Some school people advise that the bright student should not be permitted to entertain doubts concerning the wisdom of attending college. Others suggest that the decision should be made by the youth and his parents on the basis of objective information furnished by the counselors or school administrators. Certainly every capable student should be advised of the values of college training; but the fetish of a college degree, even for the gifted, becomes absurd in the light of other possibilities for career training. It is simply that in our present society college study is the main avenue to professional careers and managerial positions.

There will always be some youths of outstanding ability and good educational background who have no desire to go to college and might not be successful if they were required to do so. The promising student who is wavering about college plans should be helped to fix his sights on long-range goals. In some cases a period of work experience between high school and college may be the best plan.

Better counseling about career opportunities is the key to increasing the number of promising young people who go to college. A strong talking point with parents who want an academically talented son or daughter to go to work immediately after high school is the assurance that greater career opportunities as well as better salaries are open to the college-trained person. This is also a strong point with reluctant students.

One bright girl expressed an interest in following the general course in high school, with the prospect of getting an office job upon graduation. Her rating on the mental aptitude tests taken by all students placed her at the 91st percentile for the entire class. On the counselor's advice she took the college preparatory course, became an honor student, and won a college scholarship.

High-ranking students should not make final vocational choices too early. A talented student, capable of doing college work, might be sidetracked by specialized terminal training in senior high school. A bright boy who takes an electronics course in trade school that prepares him for a job in a large manufacturing and industrial plant immediately upon graduation may never get to college. Business and industrial firms contribute to the problem by sending representatives to the high schools to seek out bright students in the graduating class for jobs at good starting pay. In some cases the industrial firm grants college scholarships to promising boys, but such opportunities cannot be assured. A study in New Jersey revealed that the chief factor associated with choice of technical and vocational courses in high school was the occupation of the student's father.

The counselor's task in college advisement is not to ensure that selected students get into the "right college," but rather to encourage promising students to make college plans and to see that the school and the community give support as needed. High school counselors should have up-to-date information about college scholarships.

One of the newer ideas in precollege counseling is to sketch for prospective students a profile of the freshman class of the college for which they are applying: the ability of the entering class, the types of students enrolled, the nature of the freshman program, the amount of required reading, the college-life opportunities open to freshmen, and so on.

For information about talent search programs and college-going tendencies of high school graduates, see Chapter Sixteen.

Career Counseling

Every thoughtful student is concerned about the role he will play as an adult, about his function as a citizen and his status as a worker or employee. Although a few young people make their career plans early and stick to them, not many youths by the age of fifteen or sixteen have definitely decided what they want to be. In senior high school, students are usually eager for information about certain careers and their chances for success.

As experts in vocational counseling have pointed out, vocational choice is a developmental process. A young person's ideas change as new vistas open up and new opportunities arise. The tendency of modern-day youth to enter occupations other than those of their fathers is an index of life in a democracy with opportunities in every field open to all. Few youths in this day of rapid industrial change, with an interval of military training, follow the vocational interests they expressed in high school or in the first years of college. Even among the highly talented graduates of the Bronx High School of Science in New York City relatively few become practicing scientists.

Although parents and teachers should be on the lookout for talents that foreshadow a promising career, they should avoid making premature deductions. Quite diverse patterns of early ability are consistent with success in a given career or profession.

College youths appear to decide on a career less early than formerly, both because there are more highly specialized careers to choose from and because the program of studies in typical American colleges no longer prepares directly for a few specific professions. A relatively late decision about a career is not disadvantageous if the individual has accumulated a good background of general education. The possibility of entering a high-level career is largely determined by the type of advanced training a young person receives rather than by his particular "bent" or early expression of interest.

Career guidance in high school is largely a matter of acquainting the students with the nature of various professions and occupations, opportunities within the professions, and the type of training and educational background needed; students can then size up career opportunities for themselves.

The gifted young person needs job opportunities that challenge his intelligence and originality. He is certain to become bored with routine office work or an overly organized situation. The student must become aware of his own aptitudes, interests, and talents to learn whether he really has the combination of traits that make for successful work in a given field and the sustained interest that will carry him through both the training and initial experience on the job. Parents may do their children a disservice if they pressure them to follow some favored career or "high-prestige" profession.

There is considerable value in providing students with reading material on various occupations, but this should be supplemented by talks and conferences with people in the community and representatives of colleges, by visits to plants and institutions. The student will make his own decisions in the long run, but he will appreciate advice from "the experts."

Counseling Youths with Personal Problems

Gifted children manifest the same types of personal problems found in a cross-sectional population of similar age, plus difficulties peculiar to themselves. Their problems are different because they stem from different causes. Although the older notion that precocious children usually become neurotic and unstable has been dispelled, individual gifted children may experience unusual mental or physical strain, and the tension outlets they seek may be uncommon. The gifted young person with a reflective turn of mind who sets high standards for himself may be assailed by excessive doubt and feelings of inadequacy when he falls short of his goals.

Personal counseling—talking over a problem, whether major or minor, with a sympathetic adult—benefits any student. A gifted student with a speech impediment or a poor home background may be in serious need of understanding, but objective, advice.

A bright girl of fifteen said that she was accustomed to taking her personal problems to the school counselor. The counselor's role is to listen sympathetically and to lead the student tactfully to a clear understanding of his problems. Parents, too, are urged to seek guidance when they are perplexed over their children's problems and needs.

Personal guidance is intimately related to educational and prevocational counseling, because failures in achievement may be linked to the student's emotional problems.

In some communities, particularly in the larger cities, there are child-guidance clinics with specialists in psychiatry and psychology who can supplement the school's personnel in dealing with the problems of the gifted. Although these clinics are more often called upon to help slow learners or disturbed youths, school authorities will find the clinic staff equally interested in the problems of rapid learners and highly talented young people.

REPORTS OF ADJUSTMENT PROBLEMS

Hollingworth listed five problems that gifted children encounter (1942). These were:

To find enough challenge in schoolwork

To learn to "suffer fools gladly," that is, to be tolerant of the less-able and their views

To keep from becoming negativistic

To avoid becoming a recluse or an isolate, that is, to avoid the "hermit complex"

To avoid the formation of habits of extreme chicanery

Adjustment problems observed in students at the Lincoln School of Teachers College, Columbia University, New York, centered around emotional and social immaturity, irresponsibility, and failure to work up to expectations in terms of ability. The problems of the boys seemed more obvious than those of girls. Problems of the gifted reported by DeHaan and Kough (1955) were aggressive maladjustment, withdrawn maladjustment, the potential school dropout, and the underachiever.

A further problem is created for the gifted child when he is mistaken for an *older* child and is expected to perform up to the level of his apparent age.

Isolation and Solitariness   Isolation and loneliness in a gifted child are traits especially apparent in adolescence, a stage in which most young people become highly socialized and feel strange without like-age companions. A gifted child immersed in studies that satisfy his fantasies may build an imaginary world and retreat into books and daydreaming to the point of reclusiveness. Deeply immersed in his hobby—photography or studying insects—he may not really be concerned about social isolation. The danger here is that later on he may be blocked in his efforts to achieve satisfactory social relationships with other young people.

These bright, studious youngsters can be guided in the direction of social participation, but it would be a mistake to push them toward a more active social life. Psychological loneliness should not be confused with the isolation the genius seeks for his work. A great genius, seeking seclusion for his work, could be a thoroughly socialized person in his family and community life.

Feelings of Inferiority   The bright student who finds himself grouped with children older than himself, who is also smaller and less mature physically, may be disturbed by feelings of inferiority. This problem was considered in Chapter Ten as an aspect of acceleration. The preadolescent boy or girl in high school is competing socially with youths of full adolescent physical development and social interests. This means that he may be excluded from social affairs and leadership positions in school affairs as well as in outside club life. The shy bright child is at some disadvantage, particularly if he is rather young for the group, because typical young people expect everyone to be outgoing, dynamic, interesting.

Excessive Arrogance   The reports discussed in Chapter Four have shown that bright children are well accepted by their classmates if they are personable and outgoing, but not if they are show-offs, arrogant, domineering, impatient, and intolerant. A clever child, on occasion, becomes impatient with his associates when they fail to appreciate his visionary ideas, his rapid insights, or his large vocabulary; he may become aggressive toward others, wanting to run the game or boss the show. The student who is overimpressed with himself needs to gain an appreciation of the vastness of human knowledge and capabilities and the talents of other people.

Conformity versus Deviant Behavior   Every highly intelligent young person has to face the problem of conformity versus self-expression, submitting to the tryanny of the group or escaping from it for greater freedom of choice and action. So high a premium is put on conformity and group cooperation in our overorganized world that individualistic tendencies are looked upon with suspicion. If the gifted individual pulls far apart from the group, he may be shunned. Here is the dilemma: Can an individual who is so different from the crowd that he is not easily understood by them, but seems too original or "off beat," ever be a "well-adjusted" person—stable, efficient, cooperative, an understanding leader? How far should parents and teachers go in trying to strike a balance in training for conformity and encouragement of individuality? No one ever did creative work who did not deviate from the norm, but the people who get along best are successful in group interaction.

Gifted children need to be helped to understand why they seem different from others, and how, without sacrificing their individuality entirely, they can find "protective coloring" in the crowd. They, as other children, can overcome doubts of their abilities to realize their dreams.

Reading good books about children with perplexities similar to their own is one means of self-understanding.

CASES OF MALADJUSTMENT IN THE GIFTED

Several cases of maladjustment in highly gifted individuals will serve to illustrate the types of problems that occur in childhood and youth.

Henry is the son of college-educated parents; he is six years old, an only child, and exceptionally bright. He learned to read largely by figuring things out for himself. His handwriting, however, is poor, because he is left-handed. Reports of his adjustment in kindergarten were unfavorable. The boy disliked the school and seemed unable to share or communicate with the other children. He was bent on having his own way and displayed a know-it-all attitude. At home the picture is that of a "spoiled child" who has everything except firm parental control. He is rebellious and domineering, and his mother is unable to manage him. Now in first grade, he hates school and is impossible to control except through isolation from the other children. Recently, in a fit of anger, he slapped the teacher. Further isolation resulted in more hatred of school, of the teacher, of all authority. The parents are bewildered by the charge that this bright boy is unmanageable. They wonder about the future of a child who is bright but rejects instruction and refuses to submit to school discipline.

A teacher made the following report of a gifted boy who has been attending culturally enriched classes in a junior high school under the Higher Horizons Program. This boy, now thirteen, is good-looking and healthy. His IQ on a recent Otis intelligence test was 130, his reading level grade 11.8, and his mathematics grade score 10.5. His schoolwork is extremely poor, and his conduct is so bad that he is the terror of the school. The boy's mother and father appear to be intelligent people. But the father, who is a drill instructor in the Marines, is the punitive type who deals out punishment the moment reports come in that the boy has "stepped out of line." The parents tend to exaggerate both his successes and his failures. The mother, in contrast to the father, is a rather weak, submissive type of person. The boy has been torn between the extreme personalities of his parents all his life and has frequently been the victim of their arguments. These conflicts are causing the boy more of a struggle now that he is entering adolescence. Teachers recognize that this boy has the making of a natural leader; in fact, he has become the leader of a gang of the worst children in the school and neighborhood. He is in a constant state of rebellion against his father and his male teachers. The guidance counselor has been working on the case all year. What does the future hold for this boy?

A gifted youth, as other adolescents, may become involved in serious delinquencies. Recently a seventeen-year-old honor student in a suburban high school, a science winner in a national contest, was arrested when he was caught stealing money from the principal's office. Apparently he committed the theft for the thrill of it, since he had ample funds of his own.

Reports of maladjusted gifted girls are less frequent than those of boys, perhaps because girls' problems are more generally ignored.

Jane, an only child whose parents are professional people, has made poor adjustments in and out of school. She has been accelerated in school and now at seventeen is entering the sophomore year at a local college. She is awkward socially; her friendships are immature because she has never had normal child companionship; and she displays childishness in relationships with her mother who is excessively ambitious and overprotective. The girl is a competent pianist as the result of enforced instruction from an early age. Her great interest at present is reading, and she devotes most of her time to huge tomes on philosophy and religion. Apparently she is groping in books for some understanding of herself and of life which she might have gained in a more normal adolescence.

THE ASSOCIATION BETWEEN MENTAL AND PHYSICAL HEALTH

The close association between mental and physical health is generally recognized. Keeping physically fit is basic to good adjustments in life and work. This rule is doubly important for the gifted whose intellectual interests keep them indoors when other children are enjoying sports and recreation. The capable, educated person owes it to himself and his associates to keep in excellent condition so that he can withstand the stresses and strains of daily living and accomplish his best work.

Helpful suggestions for counseling the gifted are found in the pamphlet edited by Drews (1961). See also the article by Rothney and Klopman in *Education for the Gifted* (1958), an article on counseling services for the talented by Peters (1960), and the other references at the close of this chapter.

On the Trail of the Underachiever

The bright student who used to be called a loafer is now known as an underachiever. The term applies to students whose school achievement does not come up to their high potential, the ones who receive low or mediocre grades in spite of high IQs.

In some schools the underachiever is one who stands in the upper third or quarter of his class in ability as measured by objective tests, but falls in the middle or lower segment in achievement, either in a particular subject or in his schoolwork as a whole. Although slow learners who work below ability can also be called underachievers, the term has been most commonly applied to the bright or talented.

Concern about underachievement among bright children reflects the concern about waste of potential talent and leadership. The bright student may fail to qualify for college because of low marks. Both parents and teachers are perturbed when a youth who can learn easily fails to perform up to par. Teachers feel that these "failures" reflect adversely on their capacities as instructors.

Underachievement in high school is reported to average 15 per cent in some schools and to run as high as 40 per cent in others. The question has been raised whether a student can actually be considered gifted if he does not distinguish himself in schoolwork, and considerable research effort has been expended in attempting to analyze the causes of chronic underachievement.

IDENTIFYING THE UNDERACHIEVER

How do we reach the conclusion that an individual pupil is an underachiever? One method is to obtain scores of ability and achievement on standard tests and then to compare the two sets of measures in terms of standard scores, stanines, or percentiles. Another is to compute the student's grade index for his class marks, convert the index into a percentile or standard score, and then compare the results with his standing on aptitude tests.

What constitutes "success" in schoolwork? Marks in four or five subjects may be considered the sole criterion; if contribution to school life, originality, social adjustment, and participation in school affairs are considered, however, the judgment may be quite different. But there is no use dodging the issue here: The concern over the underachiever relates primarily to class standing in school marks.

There appear to be no studies of underachievers outside the area of academic achievement; for example, there are no reports concerning the child who is not so creative as he might be or who has more musical ability than he is developing.

THE GIFTED CHILD AS A SCHOOL LAGGARD

The general tendency of the "test-high" gifted to rate below the expected level in school achievement was first pointed out by Dr. Leonard S. Ayres, who referred to these children as "school laggards." From his earliest studies, Dr. Terman recognized that achievement below capacity was a characteristic of young scholars.

In the early 1920s, Dr. W. A. McCall proposed the use of the AQ, or accomplishment quotient, to indicate the ratio of achievement to ability as measured by standard tests of mental capacity and school achievement. The mentally slow and retarded children tended to be "overachievers"; that is, their achievement rated higher than their ability; whereas the mentally accelerated or bright children were generally below expectation.

Theoretically, students should live up to their high IQs in school accomplishment, but actually they do not and cannot; one reason is that their achievement is being compared with that of older boys and girls who are farther along in school. A ten-year-old with an IQ of 150 could scarcely be expected to equal a fifteen-year-old high school student in academic achievement, because he lacks the maturation and cumulated experience of the older child with whom his achievements are compared.

SPURIOUS JUDGMENTS OF UNDERACHIEVEMENT

Before jumping to the conclusion that an individual student is an underachiever, the bases on which this decision is reached should be explored. When achievement measures fall below capacity indices, the discrepancy between the two sets of measures is assumed to indicate the amount of underachievement. But there is no reason to assume that a perfect correspondence exists between measures of academic achievement and measures of aptitude or academic talent. Imperfections in measurements of ability and achievement lead to false assumptions about the relation between achievement and ability. The discrepancy between the two measures may be due to inaccuracy in equating the two sets of scores. The alleged underachiever has fallen victim to errors of measurement. This matter is discussed at further length in publications by Thorndike (1963) and Dyer (1960).

Studies comparing the relationship between a single IQ rating based on a standard test some years past and ratings of current achievement in schoolwork based on a set of marks show wide discrepancies, as shown by the follow-up study of French children (1943–1952) reported in Chapter Five. Comparisons between ratings on a single group intelligence test and subjective class marks measuring a combination of behavior traits and academic achievement are certain to show considerable discrepancy. One reason is that IQs on standard tests are indices which eliminate the influence of differences in age among the students compared, whereas school marks do not take the age factor into account. Furthermore, end-of-the-term marks represent only a limited appraisal of the student's total school achievement. Marks in formal courses seldom reflect a student's spontaneous original thinking or his ability to deal with ideas or materials creatively. A universal finding in our high schools is that girls earn higher marks on the whole than boys of comparable ability.

SUGGESTED CAUSES OF UNDERACHIEVEMENT

Assuming that a gifted student is actually an underachiever, judged from all reliable evidence, what is the cause? Every possible influence that could affect a bright child's progress has been suggested: traits of the student such as lack of interest in school, indifference to marks, inferiority feelings; factors in the background such as inferior home conditions, parental negligence; failures in the school instructional program such as an antagonistic teacher or formal methods that make little appeal to bright students.

Lack of Effort   The plain fact is that high achievers work better at their school tasks than low achievers of equal ability. A youth who shows an indifference to serious study or fails to put forth his best effort can scarcely expect to match one who sets high standards for himself.

A bright student may tackle a job enthusiastically enough and then not complete it as difficulties arise that call for concentrated study. Bright children who have never extended themselves fail to develop good study habits, particularly self responsibility for study tasks. Another point to consider is that bright students are verbally facile, a talent that covers up superficial work.

Lack of Challenge   Bright students lose interest if they are not sufficiently challenged. Why study for a course when there are more vital things to think about? The student may have lacked guidance in choice of studies, or he may have received wrong guidance. The result is falling interest and neglect of study.

A particular course may be uninteresting because it is taught in a perfunctory way. Perhaps the student's abilities are not fully tapped by routine textbook study and examinations. No matter how eager he may be to get into a good college, the student with an original mind finds routine learning irksome.

New Challenge in High School   The child who did well in elementary school without much effort may find intellectual challenge in high school that he is not prepared to meet. Students who got along easily in the lower schools may not realize that success in academic work at higher levels entails persistent, concentrated effort; possibly, they have never learned to study. Now in high school the work is more demanding, and there is more competing talent.

A teacher became concerned about a girl who earned an IQ of 125 in the lower school and was considered bright in school studies. In high school, however, she became a mediocre student. One explanation was that the high school students with whom she was compared were a brighter group than her elementary school classmates, and she would have to work much harder to keep ahead of them.

A bright child might have got off to a poor start in the lower grades, so that he never was able to prove his true abilities later on. In some cases, underachieving students are deficient in basic skills on which more advanced learning depends.

Gifted children who have no way of recognizing their own abilities may not set their sights high enough. The teacher may fail to recognize the superior talents of an unusual child, particularly if he is young for the grade. Also, with the rather abrupt changes produced by adolescence it is reasonable to assume that fluctuations in school achievement might be characteristic of this period.

Adolescent Attitudes   Underachievement is associated with emotional and social influences that interfere with study and concentration. In some cases it may reflect the child's rebellion against authority at home or at school.

Underachievement can also be due to the student's undervaluing high achievement, his fear of ridicule if he shines before the class. The student may be satisfied to work just enough to satisfy the teacher and earn a "gentleman's" average mark. The bright teen-ager fears being called a "brain"; he wants to be accepted as a "regular guy" like the others. A boy who was admitted to an honors class in high school said that now for the first time he could display his intelligence and not be ashamed of it. Older girls fear that being thought bright will diminish their popularity.

Some students are deeply concerned about getting good marks; they want personal recognition, or they want to please their folks. Others show no such concern when their parents do not.

Conflict of Interests   Sometimes the student is torn between school assignments and his own absorbing projects: invention, reading, music. Intense interest in a single study may reduce application to others in the curriculum.

Matthew, now fifteen, with an IQ of 164, is a one-sided genius. Although he is outstanding in mathematics (average grade 100), he has failed in almost all other subjects. In mathematics he makes up problems that his teacher cannot solve, and then calmly proceeds to demonstrate the proof. He is an avid reader of mathematical journals and books. Everything his French teacher did to interest him in foreign language study, however, was fruitless. Outside class he talks with his teachers about adult novels he has read; he discusses existentialism, surrealism, art, and philosophy with considerable insight. He uses an extraordinary vocabulary, and freely reveals his lack of interest in any school subject except mathematics. Recently he participated in picketing a shop where discrimination in employment prevailed. The boy seems indifferent to the fact that his allover grades are not high enough for membership in Arista, the school honor society.

An infatuation with baseball or with girls can throw a young man off the academic track temporarily; the need to study, girls say, interferes with their social life. When the bright child's time is overscheduled, he may find little time either for study or for hobby interests. A high school student from a low-income home may be working after school, or his home may be too crowded for study.

Apparently, underachievement is not a temporary condition that comes and goes, but a fairly consistent trait starting even before high school.

How Students View the Problem   Bright students interviewed by Strang gave four main causes of underachievement (1952).

They thought they were brighter than they actually discovered themselves to be. They assumed they would not have to study, so they did not learn good study habits. As a result, they fell down on examinations.

They feared that other students would not like them, that if they revealed their high abilities, they risked unpopularity.

They become interested in one or two subjects and neglected others.

They were inclined to monkey around instead of settling down to business. They lacked sufficient motive and purpose for serious study.

A college student confessed that he had not done well in high school because he fooled around too much, worked only on the studies that interested him, and rejected all the rest. Now in college, he has buckled down and tackled the distasteful along with the interesting subjects and is making excellent grades.

WHAT RESEARCH SAYS ABOUT THE UNDERACHIEVER

A number of studies have attempted to analyze the causes of underachievement by comparing the traits, behavior, and backgrounds of underachievers with those of equally bright children who achieve up to expectation. Most of these studies relate to senior high school students.

Underachievers at De Witt Clinton High School   Goldberg and associates made an extensive investigation of underachieving boys at De Witt Clinton High School in New York City, beginning in 1958 (1959). All the students were tenth graders with IQs above 125; they were divided into three levels of achievement, high, medium, and low, on the basis of school marks in all subjects. The students in different achievement levels were matched, and all were then tested with the same measuring instruments.

The only significant difference found between high and low achievers was in the family-background pattern. Fathers of underachievers were more frequently absent from home. There was less disruption in the home life of the high achievers. Poor achievers tended to be rather childish and babyish compared with high achievers. Underachievers participated more fully in the life of the school. The low grades were in mathematics and languages, possibly because of poor teaching in the junior high school. Underachievement was twice as prevalent among boys as among girls, a finding that is universal throughout the public schools.

Although special attention was given to the underachievers, with the students assigned to a special teacher for an hour a day, at the end of three years there was no measurable difference between these students and comparable control cases not specially tutored. The study disclosed, however, that there were at least two measures that would help to overcome the condition: identification with a supportive teacher who was interested in the student, and assistance in mastering the basic skills of learning in different subject areas.

Underachievers in Quincy, Illinois   In another study, the top 30 per cent in intellectual ability of the tenth- and twelfth-grade students in the Quincy, Illinois, public schools were divided into high and low achievers on the basis of ability in relation to school marks

(Pierce and Bowman, 1960). The groups were further divided according to sex and grade level. High-achieving boys scored higher than low-achieving boys on motivation scores at both grade levels, but there was no difference between high- and low-achieving girls on this test. The measure of strength of educational motivation differentiated in all cases, with high-achieving students scoring higher on this measure. The high-achieving students were better adjusted as measured by the California Psychological Inventory, except in the case of twelfth-grade girls. The high-achieving students also scored higher on leadership skills as measured by teachers and fellow students. The low-achieving tenth-grade students scored higher on aggression and withdrawn maladjustment. Twelfth-grade high-achieving boys were seen by their peers as more aggressive.

Different life-style patterns characterize high and low achievers among able high school students. In interviews, the high-achieving students reported that they had been more active in school-related activities at the junior high school level. On a test of values, high-achieving boys and girls valued the concepts "school," "work," and "imagination" more highly than did their low-achieving peers. The girls tended to score higher than boys on this test, and the tenth graders higher than the twelfth graders. High-achieving boys and girls named the father as an important influence in their lives significantly more often than did their low-achieving peers. High-scoring students were more active in religious groups than the low achievers.

Parents of high achievers were better educated than parents of low achievers. The mothers of high achievers held higher educational aspirations for their children, and more often these mothers reported their children to be responsive and independent. High achievers were engaged in more education-related activities—music, science, etc. More high-achieving students were first-born or only children; small families produced proportionately more high achievers than did large families.

Other Studies   A comprehensive study of underachieving elementary school pupils in Champaign, Illinois, has been reported by Mellon and his associates (1961). Under- and overachievers with IQs of 120 and above on the Stanford-Binet test were compared. There were forty-one children in each category. The study attempted to discover the relationship of a number of variables to academic achievement. The results disclosed that parents of overachievers were less authoritarian, less hostile-rejecting in their attitudes, and inclined to express favorable attitudes toward their children. The overachievers perceived themselves as more accepted and intrinsically valued by their peers. They were more realistic in their self-concept and higher in creative ability. There was no difference in the social maturity of the two groups.

In another study Drews and Teachan used a parental-attitude scale of thirty items to determine the attitudes of mothers of high and low achievers in terms of permissiveness, protectiveness, and domination (1957). There were two groups of students whose mothers' attitudes were explored, in each case half boys and half girls, matched for age and IQ. One group consisted of mothers of forty junior high school students of gifted intelligence, IQ 130 or above on the Stanford-Binet scale. Half of the children had been high achievers for at least two years, and the other half were low achievers. Another group was composed of mothers of twenty-eight students of average or high-average intelligence, IQs of 93 to 120. Mothers of high achievers in both groups were more authoritative and restrictive in the treatment of their children. Mothers of low achievers were overly permissive. Parents of high achievers of gifted intelligence also seemed to have more punitive attitudes with respect to child rearing. The results of this study indicate that the attitude of the mother is a factor in determining a student's motivation to achieve.

Attitudes toward scholarship and the intellectual life affect the quality of the student's academic accomplishments and his decision about college, according to Dr. David C. McClelland of the University of California. A strong desire to achieve appears to contribute to good marks in high school. High achievers are higher in achievement drive or motivation.

Tannenbaum investigated the attitudes of adolescents toward academic brilliance in a cross section of the high school population. Although brilliance in itself proved not to be a stigma, nonstudiousness as a trait seemed to be favored by the average adolescent (1961).

In their attitude toward study and intellectual accomplishments youths reflect their home training. Parents of high achievers prize excellence in achievement. Winterbottom attempted to determine how parents, particularly mothers, produced a strong interest in achievement in their sons (1953). "Need for Achievement" scores were first obtained for twenty-nine eight-year-old boys; then, interviews were conducted to determine whether mothers of "high-need" children differed from others. Mothers of high-need children were found to set higher standards for their sons and expect self-relevant mastery at an earlier age.

Underachievement appears to be anchored in peer-clique associations. Morrow and Wilson compared the traits of forty-nine underachieving boys with those of high-achieving matchees (1961). Significantly more underachievers described themselves as impulsive, irresponsible, and belonging to cliques. They had negative attitudes toward school achievement, showed opposition to authority, and were restless, excitement-seeking types.

In a study by Nason, low achievement in high school was found to be associated with a lack of positive influences in the student's background (1958).

Ausubel studied the relationship between performance in school and personal prestige (1951). His conclusion was that personality factors affect performance in academic work. Surveys of the Cleveland Major Work class graduates have shown that the best-achieving students among the gifted tended to show the best all-around adjustment. No doubt good adjustment aids stability, which makes for better achievement, but there are exceptions to this general finding.

In still another study of factors associated with the achievement of superior high school students, Musselman of Baltimore discovered a substantial lag between intellectual promise and school performance in general (1942). The achievement ratio for superior boys tended to be higher than for superior girls. Poor personality adjustment was found to be associated with highest achievement ratio, and best personality adjustment was found to be associated with high average achievement ratio. Superior students of high socioeconomic status had an advantage in achievement ratio over those of low socioeconomic status. The lag between promise and performance was less for superior students of foreign extraction than for the native born. There was a positive association between achievement ratio and the amount of formal education of the student's father. The association between achievement and the mother's education was not so marked. Superior students from small families had an advantage in achievement ratio over students from large families. Girls from metropolitan areas had an advantage over those from rural areas. Stricter home discipline was accompanied by higher achievement ratios. Good study habits were associated with high achievement ratios, but the association was not marked.

In a study of ninth-year students who rated an IQ of 130 and over in thirty-nine New York City high schools, Krugman and Impellizzeri reported that 50 per cent of the students were not functioning up to expected level in schoolwork. Each case proved to be unique, and no generalizations were possible from a study of these students compared with a "control" population (1960).

A recent study by Norman, Clark, and Bessemer pertains to pupils of elementary school age (1962). The subjects were sixth graders in Albuquerque, New Mexico, all with IQs of 130 or more on the California Test of Mental Maturity. Among the girls, 18 were designated as underachievers, and 22 as achievers; among the boys, 32 cases were underachievers, and 27 achievers, according to the statistical standards that were set up. Finally, both groups were restricted to 45 cases each, 27 boys and 18 girls. Disregarding achievement, both boys' and girls' groups were exactly at age for grade. The chief difference found between achievers and under-achievers was in chronological age. The mean age of the achievers was lower than that of underachievers. The achievers were much more consistent in their performance than the underachievers, a fact that might suggest better adjustment among the former. The underachievers proved to be backward in the mechanics of English and in spelling.

Evidence Concerning Poor Study Habits   Experts have emphasized poor study habits as a disturbing symptom among underachievers. Gifted children who come up through school at a rapid pace largely work out their own study methods. Judging from results on assignments and examinations, these self-devised approaches are woefully inefficient.

Incentive to achieve develops fairly early in life; in fact, the years five to ten are a crucial period for developing strong interest in intellectual activities. Positive attitudes toward scholarly work are being shaped even in the elementary grades. Shaw and McCuen found significant differences in factors affecting the achievement of gifted boys going back to third grade; for girls the differences showed up by the beginning of the ninth grade (1960). Under-achievers in the ninth grade tended to have poor work habits. In Evanston, Illinois, underachievers were found to spend an average of 8 hours on homework during the week, whereas high achievers spent 11 hours. Parents of underachievers were reported to be less interested in the child's achievement, yet inclined to put pressure on him. A senior who earns consistently high marks said he could scarcely do it without homework assistance from his mother, a college professor. High-ranking students report that their parents regularly help them with homework but do not do the work for them.

There is a rumor that children of professional parents are more apt to be underachievers than others, an astonishing statement. If true, it could be explained on the ground that the professional parent is a bright person who has full confidence in his child and lets him alone; or it may be that professional parents are too busy or too tired to supervise the child's homework.

SANE ATTITUDES TOWARD UNDERACHIEVEMENT

A parent commented, "My child tests high, but he receives poor marks. Why should we be concerned since he enjoys school life and his outside undertakings?" In speaking of his own bright thirteen-year-old boy with an IQ of 133, who was making an undistinguished B average in junior high school, a level-headed schoolperson said that he was not disappointed because the boy was happy at school, beginning to enjoy social activities in a "mixed crowd," participating actively in sports, and busy with his hobbies. This boy is particularly fond of swimming and outdoor excursions. He also carries his share of household responsibilities. Technically he is an "underachiever," but for all practical purposes he is a marked success, an interesting, attractive young person. There is always the danger that in our concern over school marks we will undervalue some remarkable traits and accomplishments of an adolescent that do not contribute directly to academic success.

One way to deal with the underachiever is to accept him as he is so long as there is no serious failure impending. This means permitting him to choose his own pace, tolerating the interests his maturing mind seems to dictate so long as his achievement in the self-selected activities is worthy of his talents. Underachievement may be a temporary condition that will disappear with fresh stimulation from one source or another.

Unevenness in Achievement   It is unrealistic to assume that a bright high school youth should make an equally good showing in all his studies, although a few remarkable children do. A teacher asked, "Why isn't it all right for a gifted child to be mediocre in a required subject that he dislikes? Why can't he even fail in it without recrimination?" To eliminate the underachiever problem it would be necessary for every student in the super-sigma range, 115 IQ and over, to earn grades of B⁺ or A in all subjects. It is asking too much to expect a bright child with special interests to excel in every subject or to work zealously at all subjects, even those he dislikes.

Children who are bright but young for the grade can easily be overstrained by requiring "achievement up to ability" in all school subjects. This is particularly apt to be the case for a child with strong creative interests. A bright youth who pours his energies into dramatic art might be excused from mediocre achievement in academic work until he himself is motivated to improve.

GUIDANCE OF THE UNDERACHIEVER

Since the specific causes of underachievement are complex and difficult to isolate, common sense suggests that individual guidance is the best solution. This means that the counselor must first of all become fully acquainted with the student's special aptitudes and purposes.

Teachers and others agree that the incidence of underachieving students could be reduced through class discussion and individual counseling. Evaluation of the child's effort by the teacher, the student himself, and his classmates can help him to gain a realistic picture of his accomplishments.

The bright are more capable of critical appraisal than others of the same age. They should consider: Is this the best I can do? If not, why not? What can I do to improve? There may be some value in giving a gifted high school youth some material to read about the desirability of making the most of school opportunities.

Remedying underachievement depends upon early diagnosis and attention from a sympathetic counselor, a teacher, or a parent. David, a boy of good potential, made marks that pleased his parents for a year or so after entering high school; then be began to slump, and the difficulties mounted when he attempted a heavy program of solid subjects in large classes. His parents took him in hand for homework supervision, the mother checking for Latin and written work, his father straightening out difficulties in mathematics. By the end of the term the picture had changed. The boy made good marks, and he was able to maintain his higher level of performance throughout high school. He entered the college of his choice, made a good record, and graduated with Phi Beta Kappa honors.

Several years ago the New York State Education Department put out a "study guide" for high school students, emphasizing nine points:

Keep healthy; get the right nourishment, rest, and sleep.

Make a study time budget or schedule.

Know how to prepare for and take examinations.

Take good notes.

Develop a good memory.

Become a skillful reader; improve your reading.

Know how to use the library for reference and research work.

Write correctly; learn to organize ideas and express your thoughts well.

Have the right attitudes toward your studies and studying.

Perhaps these suggestions seem most appropriate for the slow student, but they are sound advice, too, for a bright student who needs to improve his schoolwork.

Bright children, as all others, need to be self-motivated to work at routine, uninteresting tasks; this is not easy for those who learn with little effort.

The nature and quality of teaching will largely determine whether or not the capacities of a bright child are fully engaged in school studies. If the teacher is enthusiastic about his subject, bright students are more likely to take a lively interest in it. A chemistry teacher who happened to catch an unruly boy's interest found that the boy soon began to study harder.

Young people will do better work if they know they will receive some sort of tangible reward as a result, possibly a prize or scholarship or inclusion on the honor roll.

A more favorable attitude toward intellectual achievement will come about when the school itself shows that it values intellectual talent—by providing honors programs and opportunities for independent study for gifted students, by encouraging original and creative ideas, and by rewarding achievement by other means than marks (see Chapters Twelve and Thirteen).

There seems to be no way of allaying parental concern about marks in high school so long as admission to college remains highly competitive. The time is approaching, however, when remarkable traits other than high achievement reflected in class marks will be more fully considered by college admissions committees. A number of studies exploring this question are presently under way.

Instead of pressing for perfect correlation between IQ and school marks, it seems more sensible to appraise the gifted youth generously in terms of his many-sided developmental accomplishments. Even with intelligent guidance, he will still have a profile and not a straight line.

References

Ausubel, David P.: Prestige Motivation of Gifted Children, *Genetic Psychology Monographs*, 43:53–117, 1951.

Barman, A. B., and A. Klein: A Personality Study of Maladjusted Pupils of Superior Mentality, *High Points*, 24:57–63, 1942.

Boardman, Rhea K., and Gertrude Hildreth: Adjustment Problems of the Gifted, *Understanding the Child*, 17:41–44, 1948.

Burnside, Lenoir H.: Psychological Guidance of Gifted Children, *Journal of Consulting Psychology*, 6:223–228, 1942.

Carroll, Herbert A.: *Genius in the Making*, McGraw-Hill Book Company, New York, 1940.

Conant, James B.: *The American High School Today*, McGraw-Hill Book Company, New York, 1959.

DeHaan, Robert F., and Jack Kough: *Helping Children with Special Needs*, vol. 2, Elementary School Edition, Science Research Associates, Inc., Chicago, 1955.

Dowd, Robert J.: Underachieving Students of High Capacity, *Journal of Higher Education*, 23:327–330, 1953.

Drews, Elizabeth M. (ed.): *Guidance for the Academically Talented Student*, NEA Project on the Academically Talented Student, National Education Association, Washington, D.C., 1961.

Drews, Elizabeth M., and John E. Teachan: Parental Attitudes and Academic Achievement, *Journal of Clinical Psychology*, 13:328–332, 1957.

Dyer, Henry S.: A Psychometrician Views Human Ability, *Teachers College Record*, 61:394–403, 1960.

Edelston, H.: Educational Failure with High Intelligence Quotient, *Journal of Genetic Psychology*, 77:85–116, 1950.

Endicott, Frank S.: *Guiding Superior and Talented High School Students*, Luna Press, Minneapolis, 1961.

Fornwalt, Russell J.: *Scholarship Information Sources for Educational and Vocational Counselors*, Big Brother Movement, Inc., New York.

Goldberg, Miriam L., and associates: A Three Year Experimental Program at De Witt Clinton High School to Help Bright Underachievers, *High Points*, 41:5–35, 1959.

Gowan, John C.: Dynamics of the Underachievement of Gifted Students, *Exceptional Children*, 24:98–107, 122, 1957.

Guidance for the Underachiever with Superior Ability, U.S. Department of Health, Education and Welfare, Office of Education, Washington, D.C., 1961.

Hollingworth, Leta S.: *Children above 180 I.Q. Stanford-Binet: Origin and Development,* World Book Company, Tarrytown-on-Hudson, N.Y., 1942.

Johnson, H. G.: Does the Gifted Child Have a Low A.Q.? *Journal of Educational Research,* 35:91–99, 1942.

Krugman, Morris, and Irene H. Impellizzeri: Identification and Guidance of Underachieving Gifted Students, *Exceptional Children,* 26:283–286, 1960.

Mellon, E. H., and staff: *Study of Underachievement in Champaign, Ill.,* Champaign, Ill., Public Schools, 1961.

Morrow, W. R., and R. C. Wilson: The Self-reported Personal and Social Adjustment of Bright High-achieving and Under-achieving High School Boys, *Journal of Child Psychology, Psychiatry,* 2:203–209, 1961.

Musselman, J. W.: Factors Associated with the Achievement of High School Pupils of Superior Intelligence, *Journal of Experimental Education,* 11:53–68, 1942.

Nason, Leslie: *Academic Achievement of High School Students,* University of Southern California Press, Los Angeles, 1958.

Norman, Ralph D., Betty P. Clark, and David W. Bessemer: Age, Sex, I.Q. and Achievement Patterns in Achieving and Nonachieving Gifted Children, *Exceptional Children,* 29:116–123, 1962.

Passow, A. Harry, and Deton J. Brooks, Jr.: *A Guide for Rating Provisions for the Gifted,* Bureau of Publications, Teachers College, Columbia University, New York, 1960.

Passow, A. Harry, and Miriam L. Goldberg: Study of Underachieving Gifted, *Educational Leadership,* 16:121–125, 1958.

Peters, Herman J.: Counseling Services for Talented High School Students, in Bruce Shertzer (ed.), *Working with Superior Students: Theories and Practices,* Science Research Associates, Inc., Chicago, 1960.

Pierce, James V.: Personality and Achievement among Able High School Boys, *Journal of Individual Psychology,* 17:102–107, 1961.

Pierce, James V., and Paul H. Bowman: Motivation Patterns of Superior High School Students, in *The Gifted Student: Cooperative Research,* U.S. Department of Health, Education and Welfare, Office of Education, Washington, D.C., 1960.

Rothney, John W. M., and Norbert E. Klopman: Guidance of the Gifted, chap. 14 in *Education for the Gifted: Fifty-seventh Yearbook of the National Society for the Study of Education,* part 2, The University of Chicago Press, Chicago, 1958.

Shaw, Merville C., and John T. McCuen: The Onset of Academic Underachievement in Bright Children, *Journal of Educational Psychology,* 51:103–108, 1960.

Strang, Ruth: Guidance of the Gifted, *The Personnel and Guidance Journal,* 31:26–30, 1952.

Tannenbaum, Abraham: *Adolescents' Attitudes toward Academic Brilliance,* Teachers College, Columbia University, New York, 1962; also in *Dissertation Abstracts,* 21:20–27, 1961.

Thistlethwaite, Donald L.: Effects of Social Recognition upon Educational Motivation of Talented Youth, *Journal of Educational Psychology,* 50:111–116, 1959.

Thorndike, Robert L.: *The Concepts of Over- and Underachievement,* Bureau of Publications, Teachers College, Columbia University, New York, 1963.

Winterbottom, Marion R.: *The Relation of Childhood Training in Independence to Achievement Motivation,* unpublished doctoral dissertation, University of Michigan, Ann Arbor, Mich., 1953.

Witty, Paul A.: A Genetic Study of 50 Gifted Children, in *Intelligence: Its Nature and Nurture: Thirty-ninth Yearbook of the National Society for the Study of Education,* part 2, Public School Publishing Company, Bloomington, Ill., 1940.

Witty, Paul A.: Guidance of the Gifted, *Personnel and Guidance Journal,* 33:136–139, 1954.

Zorbaugh, Harvey: How May the Community Utilize Its Gifted Children? *Mental Hygiene,* 24:1–16, 1940.

Chapter Fifteen
EXPLORATIONS
OF
CREATIVITY

Creative thinking that generates new ideas of a high order is among the rarest and most valuable of human traits. As William James remarked in his statement on "Leadership":

Mankind does nothing save through initiatives on the part of inventors, great or small, and imitation by the rest of us—these are the sole factors active in human progress. Individuals of genius show the way, and set the patterns, which common people then adopt and follow.[1]

Inventive and original minds created civilization and changed the face of history. The master architects of great ideas brought about

[1] William James, *Memories and Studies,* Longmans, Green & Co., Inc., New York, 1911.

modes of life, although their inventions may have been rejected
neglected by their contemporaries.

Today there is growing concern that the creative spark in
youth be developed and conserved through all the means at our
disposal, with the expectation of increasing the world's resources
of creative power. During recent years, questions such as the following have been explored: What is the nature of the creative process?
What are the components of creative thinking? What cultural and
educational forces foster creativity? How does the creative impulse
originate? What is the relation of academic training to the development of the creative mind?

Other questions concern the criteria that distinguish the creative from the noncreative person. What is the creative person like?
What does he do? How does he work? What is there about his
product that distinguishes it as "creative"? What circumstances
generate creative thinking? Can creativity be learned and trained?

This chapter is concerned particularly with the nature of the
creative process, traits of creative people, signs of creativity in
children and young people, and the possibility of releasing imaginative and creative thinking through education.

The Nature of Creative Thinking

The essence of creativity is the production of something new, some
original idea or invention, or the reconstruction and reintegration
of existing products or ideas. The creative person is an innovator
because of his capacity for fresh, spontaneous, original thinking.
The world's knowledge can be found stored in a library, but not
the new truth that will fill blanks in that knowledge.

The creative mind avoids the clutch of stereotypes; it springs
away from standard patterns and established modes of response
just as a great artist breaks away from established artistic traditions
to experiment with new ideas.

Creativity is essentially a mental process, involving a larger
element of abstract reasoning and generalizing than of physical
manipulation of material or technical proficiency. Contrary to the
general opinion, creative work is done in the mind, not at the
piano, at the easel, or the writing desk, and not necessarily even
in the scientist's laboratory. The idea for the original painting or
for the invention develops in the artist's or in the inventor's mind

long before he ever starts to put brush to canvas or starts construction.

Creativity is intensely individual. Invention in the initial stages is most often the product of one person working alone, rather than the accomplishment of a group.

DIFFERENT LEVELS OF CREATIVITY

Products of the inventive mind differ in value and significance. Not all creative thinking is world-shattering in its effects on human progress. There are modest levels of invention as well as the rare heights of creative genius; but creativity at any level has the mark of newness, of fresh discovery or invention. Although relatively few people are intellectually creative, even ordinary folks have a flair for self-expression in one direction or another; for instance, thinking of a new way to arrange flowers, putting a new twist in a cooking recipe, devising improvements in children's clothing, thinking up useful inventions or gadgets such as an improved mousetrap or can opener. Without doubt, however, innovations of great consequence or lasting value to mankind are recognized as more valuable than technological improvements that are quickly outmoded.

DIFFERENT FORMS OF CREATIVE ACHIEVEMENT

Although creativity is most commonly identified with achievements in the arts, every area of human endeavor—medicine, engineering, teaching, all the professions—affords possibilities for creative work.

Mechanical inventions furnish spectacular illustrations of the creative mind at work: the telescope and microscope; the steam engine, moving with one giant stride ahead of transportation by horse, the power loom, the cotton gin, the linotype printing press, harvesting machines, even the bicycle, the vacuum cleaner, and the sewing machine, to name just a few inventions that have launched a new era of industrial efficiency. Accounts of the people who thought up these inventions fill the pages of biographical dictionaries.

Not all creative ideas and new inventions are distinctly new. Some of the greatest writers, artists, and musicians have been accused of plagiarism, among them, Shakespeare, Longfellow, Poe, and Raphael. These and other cases prove that innovators may draw their inspiration from the work of others who have gone before. A good idea may be the source of a greater one for an original thinker.

The form of expression creativity takes reflects the prevailing culture. The remarkable literary productivity of the nineteenth century, the work of brilliant novelists and gifted poets, derived from the enlarged social contacts as well as the new intellectual movements and aspirations of the period. The century was more remarkable for creativity and invention than any previous era, "charged with restless intellectual energy," in the words of one writer.

THE CREATIVE PROCESS:
THE ORIGIN AND DEVELOPMENT OF CREATIVE IDEAS

Obviously quite different mental processes are at work when people merely acquire existing knowledge or imitate and when they discover or invent. William James concluded that it was extraordinary capacity to perceive in an unhabitual way, to perceive analogies not readily apparent to the ordinary mind, that distinguished the creative genius from ordinary mortals. Sensing and recognizing a problem is a prerequisite to creative accomplishment. Posing a good problem is the initial step. According to Guilford, creativity is essentially problem solving in which the worker finds new problems to solve or works out new solutions to old problems (1952).

The creative thinker begins with a tentative idea relating to some unsolved problem. He works from a hypothesis: Such and such circumstances or operations probably account for certain phenomena. Then he makes observations, or something strikes his attention. He begins to classify and to arrange the data; then he draws a deduction or reaches a tentative conclusion, with the new idea as the crystallization of all the relevant facts. During the process the creator exercises his imagination, obtains relevant information, becomes active in exploration, exercises judgment in selection and organization of material, and, after arriving at a conclusion, makes a record of his discovery.

Suppose we wish to explain a phenomenon that everyone can observe: Kindergartners learn to speak a second language more easily than older children and adults. A hypothesis concerning learning and mental processes is first set up, and then facts are marshaled in an attempt to prove the tentative hypothesis. Suppose we start with the assumption that since the child's nervous system is immature, his mind and tongue are more flexible and pliable than the adult's; or the child is less easily embarrassed over the errors he makes; most often he does his learning in a different setting from that of the adult; and so on.

The stages in creative thinking as described by Ghiselin are (1952):

Background of preparation

Stage of reflection

Inspiration in problem solving

Productivity in working out the idea

Paulhan vividly described the mental processes of Charles Darwin in developing his theory of natural selection (1930). First, the scientist drew up his basic hypothesis, and then he made observations or noted facts that came to his attention. The facts were classified and arranged. Then Darwin drew deductions from the facts and arrived at his conclusion, with the resulting crystallization of his thought on the tremendous concept.

INTUITIVE THINKING IN CREATIVITY

Problem solving is done either through logical reasoning or through flashes of intuition. In intuitive thinking, the ideas seem to come in a moment without premeditation, and the creative thinker may make a remarkable discovery without conscious intent. The popular idea is that all creative ideas and inventions are sheer inspirations—they pop into the inventor's head from nowhere. The inventor is envisaged as a happy-go-lucky fellow who just happened to hit upon a clever idea that paid off. This conception of the creative act does have some basis in the spontaneous origination of novel ideas.

Ralph Waldo Emerson was said to be a thinker who arrived at his conclusions by intuition. Beethoven commented, "You will ask me where I get my ideas. They come unsummoned—in the open air, in the woods, at dawn." Mozart's experience was similar. He said in response to a question about the origin of his ideas, "When I am, as it were, completely myself, entirely alone, and of good cheer—say traveling in a carriage, or walking after a good meal, or during the night when I cannot sleep; it is on such occasions that my ideas flow and most abundantly. Whence and how they come I know not, nor can I force them."[2]

When Eli Whitney's hosts on a Southern plantation expressed concern over the laborious, time-consuming process of extracting the seeds from cotton bolls by hand, the idea for the cotton gin came to his mind almost immediately. George Westinghouse was concerned about the problem of bringing a string of railroad cars to a simul-

[2] Marcia Davenport, *Mozart*, Charles Scribner's Sons, New York, 1956.

taneous stop. The solution—sending compressed air to an air brake—flashed into his mind while he was observing a train of cars one day. By chance, Daguerre hit upon photography when he was engaged in some chemical experiments, without any idea of inventing a light-sensitive plate of film.

The noted biologist, Dr. Szent-Györgyi, says that he has rarely found the solution to any problem by conscious thinking; the solution comes at a time when the mind is otherwise occupied. Dr. Melvin Calvin, recent Nobel prize winner, described how the prize-winning idea came to him suddenly in a matter of seconds as he was sitting at the wheel of his car.

THE EVOLUTION OF A CREATIVE IDEA

The shrewd guess, the fertile hypothesis, is only the beginning of creativity. Although a unique idea sometimes occurs in a flash, a long period of time may elapse before the idea is brought to fruition. Henry Ford sought to conserve physical energy by putting a gasoline motor on a bicycle or a carriage, but he spent a long time failing and succeeding before marketing his first gasoline buggy. The Provençal poet, Frédéric Mistral, described the inception of his great epic poem "Mireille." The idea, he said, came to him in a flash: "One evening when sowing was on, watching the ploughmen who sang whilst they followed the plough, I broke, glory be to the Highest, into the first song of Mireille." Then he spent seven years completing the poem. Louis Pasteur carried on long hours of exacting work day after day until he succeeded in proving the efficiency of his cure for rabies. Similarly, Dr. Salk's discovery of a polio vaccine required exacting toil for several years.

Picasso's great picture "Guernica" symbolizing the Spanish Civil War, one of the most significant paintings of our time, started as a tremendous inspiration in the mind of the artist, but the picture reached completion only after a long series of experiments.

Accounts that inventors, artists, writers, and others have written of their own creative achievements, the inception of creative ideas in intuitive guesses, and the struggle to bring the ideas to fruition have been brought together in a book by Ghiselin (1952).

Studies of Creative People

Some observations on creativity were published over thirty years ago by Prof. Carl Spearman, of the University of London, who made statistical analyses of the creative mind based on test data.

About the same time, Dr. June E. Downey in this country was collecting information on flexibility in behavior and creative imagination. In the late 1940s and the 1950s psychologists and educators brought new approaches to bear on the subject. Dr. J. P. Guilford and his associates at the University of Southern California took the lead in calling attention to the need for explorations in creativity, and outlined a research program. Considerable attention has been given to the construction and validation of tests of originality and divergent thinking in an effort to measure the components of creativity.

Scholarly interest in this subject has been expressed in conferences held at university centers, particularly those organized during the past few years in Minnesota and Utah. The National Science Foundation sponsored conferences in 1955 and 1957 to consider problems in the study of creative scientific talent.

The National Merit Scholarship Corporation, a group that distributes many of America's grants for education received from industry, is seeking measures that will distinguish among the applicants all bright young people who show creative promise.

TRAITS OF CREATIVE PEOPLE

In discussing creative power, Dr. Samuel Johnson described the creative genius as having "a mind of large general powers accidentally determined in a particular direction." Creative people unquestionably have certain traits that distinguish them from others: a rare combination of intellect, mental energy, intensity of purpose, strong drive, and other unusual traits of character and temperament. The creative person's thinking is free from inertia, adaptive, and flexible as applied to problems in a special field. Freud's theory was that creative persons have easier access to primary processes and therefore less repression. As a result they have more available psychic energy. Creativity requires imagination beyond the average, a mind that is stimulated by challenging problems, and dynamic personal traits that bring great ideas to fruition and make them accessible to others. Creative urges and drives come from within the individual; they cannot be imposed from without or even drawn out by any formal set of educative experiences. Freud believed that the only way to make discoveries was to focus one's ideas exclusively on one central interest. There is a deep personal element in all artistic creativity. Vincent Van Gogh had a passionate commitment to art. Robert Schumann wrote of his "indescribable joy" in composing.

Creative ideas emerge under conditions of freedom and absence of external evaluation according to fixed standards of excellence, such as "very good" or "bad" in style or composition. Yet there has been orderliness in the original thinker's training and in his manner of working and handling his data, rather than carelessness or indifference.

Remarkable achievements are not the work of the intellect alone, but of the individual's total personality. Creative thinking appears to be motivated by the inner urges and strivings of a person who is in a state of unrest. The creative thinker senses the lure of chasing a problem around to see how the solution will come out, speculating on the outcome of his experiments, working with zeal to test his hunches.

A mild degree of tension appears to be an asset to the creative thinker. Feelings of tension act as a spur, but the tension is not strong enough to disrupt mental effort. Instead of being discouraged by failure the inventor tries a new tack.

DIMENSIONS OF GIFTEDNESS, TALENT, AND CREATIVITY

The Work of Dr. J. P. Guilford   Guilford and his associates at the University of Southern California explored characteristics of scientific creativity through the method of factor analysis. They analyzed intellect into five categories: cognitive thinking, memory, divergent thinking, convergent thinking, and evaluation (1952). Traits isolated by Guilford in his analyses of creativity were ability to see problems, fluency of ideas and expression, originality, variability in thinking, flexibility; ability to redefine, to improvise, to use familiar objects in new ways; and the ability to elaborate. This list of traits tells nothing about emotional constituents, such as motivation, drives and incentives, persistence, patience, and the energy output required to accomplish a chosen goal.

Guilford and his associates investigated three dimensions of creativity: uncommonness, remoteness, and cleverness. Results of tests showed that uncommonness and cleverness of responses were more closely associated with originality than was remoteness. Highly creative people in all fields were found to be overwhelmingly intuitive.

The Work of Dr. Donald W. MacKinnon   At the Institute of Personality Assessment and Research connected with the University of California, an intensive and wide-ranging research program on creativity has been conducted for a period of years under the direction of Dr. Donald W. MacKinnon, director of the institute (1960, 1962). Hundreds of persons known to be creative in a variety of fields have served as subjects of the investigation to determine the personality, background influences, and intellectual qualities that account for creativity.

This research group has described the creative person as intelligent, independent, curious, skeptical, emotionally committed to his work, energetic, aesthetically sensitive, introverted, a nonconformist in behavior, and occasionally egotistical. Although primarily independent in his thinking, he is not irresponsible. Regardless of the person's profession, his life has little in common with that of ordinary people.

Confirming the findings and observations of others, MacKinnon concluded that creative people are highly intuitive. They are ever alert to what could be a step ahead of what now is. These people show a strong trend toward reflective thinking. Their attention centers on the thinking through of intellectual problems. A person with creative talent is less concerned with the details, the concrete and practical aspects, than with the meanings, implications, and symbolic expression of ideas. Creativity is fostered by freedom in achieving objectives; the creative individual must either be free of frustrating problems or be able to ignore them.

Other Studies of Creativity   In analyzing the traits of 153 living artists and writers of established reputation, Drevdahl and Cattell (1958) reported that these people differ from the normal adult population in being more intelligent and having greater verbal fluency, flexibility, originality, and emotional maturity. They are dominant, adventurous, emotionally sensitive, unconventional, radical, self-sufficient, and of high-energy tension level. They are scholarly people who work with singleness of purpose to achieve their goals. They think originally, trying out new ideas, experimenting with problems, and making coherent records of their experiments. They think and reason with scientific objectivity, are painstaking, good at perceiving and noting details, tenacious, and not easily discouraged from their purposes. The creative person is inclined to isolate himself for study, work, and reflection.

In another study, Stein and Heinze of New York University, found that the more and less creative career people did not differ in intelligence, but the more-creative men were more autonomous and more dynamic than the less-creative (1960). The creative person is more flexible in entertaining and playing with ideas, but he also knows how to discipline himself in his investigations and his attack on problems. He works out his solutions through careful, painstaking marshaling of evidence.

Dr. Viktor Lowenfeld concluded that creativity in the arts has elements in common with creativity in science, as reported by Guilford. Tests of creativity developed at Purdue University measure traits of fluency, flexibility, and originality.

All this evidence suggests that the world's creative thinkers live and work quite differently from other people. In fact, creative work imposes conditions for which most people are temperamentally unsuited. The creative person must withdraw from the ordinary concerns of life to a certain extent; he needs to be free of distraction in order to carry out his experimenting, data checking, and writing. He comes to accept isolation, even neglect and rejection, as a necessary circumstance of creative work. Tchaikovsky is a notable example. Another is Jean-Jacques Rousseau, who throughout his lifetime, enjoyed the enchantment of solitude. He described himself as a persistent daydreamer; his whole life, he said, was "a long reverie." There is something about long, lonely walks that seems to stimulate the creative thinking of writers, musicians, and philosophers, Rousseau among them.

Highly creative persons are not well-rounded individuals because concentration on special interests does not permit the spread of attention required to be well-rounded. Whether or not a creative individual is a happy, contented person depends more on his attitudes toward life than on the fact that he is obsessed with original ideas.

INTELLIGENCE AND CREATIVITY

Is there high correlation, little correlation, or no positive relationship between high intelligence and traits recognized as signs of high creativity? This question has been the subject of considerable discussion; some research on it has been done through factor analysis.

The current theory is that creativity, instead of being independent of high intelligence, is actually rooted in superior cognitive powers—thinking, inductive reasoning, the ability to generalize, to deal with principles, and to work with abstract symbols, whether words, mathematical formulas, or musical notation. Spearman, who proposed a theory of *general* intelligence in contrast to the theory of special unrelated mental traits, believed that high general intelligence was an essential factor in all creative achievement in the arts and sciences (1931). He concluded on a priori grounds that no separate or special creative power exists apart from a high level of G, or general intelligence. Highly creative persons tend to be highly intelligent, but the converse is not necessarily true. According to Spearman, exceptional creativity would be impossible without unusual intelligence.

MacKinnon and his associates found that creative people were intelligent, but that the level of intelligence did not determine the quality of the person's creativity. Although a certain high threshold of intelligence is necessary for creativity, somewhere around the level represented by 120 IQ, there is little relation between creativity and a person's level of intelligence above this point. The scholastic records of some of the most highly creative people ranged around a B average. Highly creative persons may not be recognized as unusual in school if they are not interested in getting high marks.

Creative ability is not synonymous with academic intelligence since it involves certain temperamental characteristics. Not every intelligent person or everyone with a high IQ wishes to become a creative artist or could become one even if he tried. The reason that relatively few of the high-IQ chaps in the June graduating class will produce original ideas of unusual significance is not due to lack of correlation between traits of creativity and high intelligence, but because creativity demands so much more of a person than intelligence alone.

INVENTIVENESS AND THE ALERT, PREPARED MIND

Louis Pasteur said, "Chance favors the prepared mind." Central in all original thinking is the capacity to see the implications and relevancy of facts in problem solving. The creative thinker's sensitivity to significant details is keen, his powers of imagery most exceptional, due both to inclination and to training.

New ideas and inventions originate as often as not in observations of situations available to everyone. Stock examples are Archimedes and the bathtub, Newton and the falling apple, Galileo watching the swinging pendulum of the cathedral clock, Watts observing steam pressure in his mother's teakettle.

The ancients observed ships sinking below the horizon as they passed from view, but it took a genius to conclude at last that the earth was round and had a gravitational pull. The discovery of the doppler effect of sound waves—that lower pitch is associated with a receding body—was based on a set of observations that anyone could make at a railroad station or on a busy highway.

Murphy, of the Menninger Foundation, believes that the creative act is rooted in experience (1958). Creativity is shown only by well-informed people with remarkable intellect and unusual capacity for mental imagery. Originality depends on organized knowledge. "Facts are needed for thinking," as John Dewey pointed out. The creative thinker has his facts well in hand not only in his own specialty, but in related fields.

AGE AND SEX AS FACTORS IN CREATIVITY

The ideas and discoveries that have profoundly affected social progress have been the work of comparatively young people—and almost exclusively of men. The most original work is done and masterpieces are produced early rather than late in life; as a rule, according to a long series of reports by Lehman, the greatest productivity comes in the late twenties and early thirties for persons in the arts and sciences, and a little later for persons in literature and philosophy (1953). When Dr. Wernher Von Braun, the German-born rocket expert now in the United States, was captured at the close of World War II, he was considered by his captors "too young, too fat, and too jolly" to be Germany's greatest scientist. Great inventions and masterpieces in art, science, literature, and music are predominately the work of men. Although a woman novelist won the Pulitzer prize in 1942, the award was not given to another woman until 1951.

CLUSTERING OF CREATIVE PEOPLE IN TIME AND PLACE

That creative workers have appeared in clusters in different periods of history and in certain geographical areas suggests the strong influence of a stimulating and congenial environment for creative work. Clustering appears more frequently in a society where there is cultural ferment, accessibility to intellectual ideas, and the stimulus of new movements.

Glorious Greece produced at least twenty-five illustrious figures in a short span of 200 years; Italy produced scores of masters of painting and sculpture during the High Renaissance period of the fifteenth century. There were 40 per cent more people of remarkable ability in the first half of the seventeenth century than in the second half. The French painters of the late nineteenth century and the early twentieth seemed to have a stimulating influence on one another, and out of this stimulation new art movements arose. England of the nineteenth century was noted for its great statesmen, Germany for a remarkable clustering of musicians, while the New England intellectual ferment a century or more ago centered about Emerson's circle in Concord. Dr. James McKeen Cattell noted that eminent scientists tended to come from certain centers of higher education where the faculty recognized and supported creative-minded students.

"STAR-TOUCHED" GENIUS

The term "genius" is reserved for those to whom history has accorded the palm for superlative achievement of lasting value. The great works of genius are unique, inimitable; they stand the test of time.

On the thirteenth of December, 1962, a famous lady left Paris, France, for her first trip to America. She sailed on the new liner *France,* having been escorted from Paris to LeHavre by the director of the Louvre and a strong police guard. The captain of the vessel himself met her at the pier and carried her on board where she was installed in a first-class suite. Who was this personage so signally honored? It was not a human being, but one of the most valuable pieces of canvas in existence, none other than the "Mona Lisa," "La Gioconda," painted in the late fifteenth century by Leonardo da Vinci.

The poet Heine drew a thumbnail sketch of genius. "The genius," he said, "lives a very full, often a carefree life, producing his great work casually and effortlessly as part of his daily activity. He mixes with people, enjoys good meals, is careless of money, works impulsively, may die very early because of the very fullness of his life."

Geniuses have been remarkable not solely for their original products, but also for their powerful personalities. Cox found that historical geniuses had not only high intelligence, but a strong desire to excel, persistence in the face of obstacles, and zeal in applying their unusual abilities (1926). These eminent people followed an arduous path to fame and glory, mobilizing all their energies in the direction of their special goals and overcoming enormous obstacles in the way.

The discoveries of a genius are far ahead of his time. The laws of probability were discovered by Pascal 300 years ago. Jules Verne not only described rocket trips to the moon nearly a century ago, but even located the launching pads in Florida. Scientist Ernest Lord Rutherford's comment on hearing someone say, "Lucky fellow, Rutherford, always on the crest of the wave," was, "Well, I made the wave, didn't I?"

Talent versus Genius   Through the ages, thousands of gallons of paint have been spread on canvas and paper to create works of art, but few paintings show the elusive quality of a Cézanne water color, the work of highest creative imagination. Picasso did a mother and child drawing with a few deft strokes that created a unique masterpiece. The famous "Mother" by Whistler is a simple "arrangement in gray and black," as he himself described it, but the unique creation of a genius.

Plenty of capable writers, professionals and amateurs alike, scribble away, but scarcely one in a century produces a Gettysburg Address or a Wordsworth sonnet.

The difference between talent and genius is that talent is expert in technique, without the originality of genuine creativity. The artist Rubens composed a masterpiece, but his talented assistants filled in the painting.

MANY-SIDED GENIUS

Although narrow specialization is more common than manysidedness in people of genius, history affords numerous examples of remarkable versatility in creative people. Leonardo da Vinci is perhaps the best illustration of a universal genius—painter, sculptor, architect, engineer, inventor, poet, and musician. He excelled in all. Chaucer was known as a many-sided genius. So was Thomas Jefferson, who was described by the writer, James Parton, as "a gentleman of 32 who could calculate an eclipse, survey an estate, tie an artery, plan an edifice, try a case, break a horse, dance a minuet and play the violin."

After three centuries, no French writer is more alive than Blaise Pascal, a blend of poet, mathematician, scientist, and theologian who lived a short thirty-nine years. Goethe was not only one of the world's greatest poets, but also an eminent scientist and statesman.

Neglect and Martyrdom of Genius   Society is hostile to bold original minds. The creative thinker too far ahead of his times is looked upon as a visionary. Heine reflected on the malediction that men of genius suffer: Why must ill luck curse the noblest spirits while it exempts low-level mediocrity?

The true value of creative products may not be recognized in a creator's lifetime, because the judgments are made by the society of which the work is a part. As the saying goes, "The only good painter is a dead one." Van Gogh could not sell a single painting in his lifetime, but all his work is highly valued today.

Someone has said that no genius is ever normal, but then, neither is a masterpiece. The myth that the genius is a screwball, highly unstable, a drug addict or paranoid, is difficult to dispel. Unfavorable publicity only exaggerates traits that in an ordinary person would pass unnoticed.

Creativity in the Childhood Years

All normal young children are by nature curious and spontaneous in behavior. Indications of originality and inventiveness and of rich fantasy and lively imagination are typical of the young child's play life. These traits facilitate learning and adjustment to the environment.

If creativity is the capacity to imagine something new or different from the accepted patterns, then countless kindergartners are creative. Young children show originality in block building; they draw unusual designs and experiment with soap carving, with inclined planes, with kites and rockets, and with the number system. They explore all the possibilities in paints, clay, and paper, in weaving, in rhythms and dancing, and in tunes and rhymes.

Although originality and inventiveness are most commonly observed in bright, energetic youngsters from family backgrounds that encourage independence and self-expression, all children find satisfaction in fantasy and imagination in their play life. The end product is not what counts, no matter how remarkable it may seem, but the imaginative thinking that goes into it and the satisfaction the child derives from his accomplishment.

When the subject of childhood creativity arises, the illustrations most commonly given are of original work in the graphic arts and in writing. Observers are less often sensitive to children's creativity in music, in science and mathematics, or in mechanical invention. The reason must be that childish exploits in art and writing leave a product that can be displayed and admired.

CHILDHOOD INVENTION AND ADULT CREATIVITY

A number of questions arise concerning the relationship between creativity in childhood and that in the adult years. The term "creativity" is applied indiscriminately to original behavior of children and adults alike. Perhaps the inventive activities of young children would be more appropriately termed "forms of self-expression."

Is there any connection between the early exploratory efforts of the unformed mind and the creativity of youth and adulthood? Before adolescence, traits such as originality, ingenuity, and inventiveness, perhaps precreativity, are shown, but early evidence of these traits, which most young children have in some measure, does not necessarily predict adult creativity, which is of a different order. The chief difference between the two is that the child's creativity is rooted in his inexperience and ignorance. All the world is new to him, and exploration is his chief mode of learning. A young child who invents new words or original spellings is revealing that he has not yet mastered standard forms of expression. But when lexicographer Samuel Johnson invented new words and devised some original spellings for English words in the hope of improving English spelling and usage, he drew upon his vast classical learning. A young child drawing or finger painting is expressing his emotional feelings and playing a game with new media. This activity is scarcely comparable with the brilliant projections of Mr. Arthur Wyatt at his easel. The child who hits on something interesting in his experiments with paper, paint, or clay is naïve rather than a mature artist. The upper-grade schoolchild no longer does fraction problems in an original way because he has learned to do them efficiently by school-taught methods. The child's original ideas arise spontaneously during his play; the adult's are the result of considered judgment and sustained research.

Beyond age nine or ten, it is true, children show more inventiveness based on knowledge and experience in problem solving, but until early youth a child seldom has both the range of experience and the reasoning powers that genuine creativity requires. The characteristic inventiveness of childhood originates in sensory-motor experience; that of the creative adult derives from reflective, intellectual processes, primarily conceptual thinking requiring the manipulation and interpretation of symbols. These observations lead to the conclusion that there may be little connection between childhood inventiveness and the high creativity of adults.

Although the chief value of self-expression in childhood is that it adds to the child's satisfaction in his fantasies and play life, it may also have propaedeutic value for creative work later on.

DECLINE IN CREATIVITY AND INVENTIVENESS WITH MATURITY

Why does the originality of children gradually fade out? Many explanations have been given. Possibly the children are only naïve and unsophisticated, not really creative. In the course of growing up, they learn the standard behavior patterns of their culture and prefer going with the crowd to being original. They find that uncritical thinking is simpler and more congenial than experimenting with new ideas. Spontaneity seems to die down as school and family pressures exert their molding influence. Furthermore, the child's interests may shift as he matures. An eight-year-old who does remarkable writing is not necessarily destined to become a prizewinner in literature as an adult, because his interests may shift to some other type of work.

Some critics blame the schools for stifling spontaneity and originality. Formal, perfunctory teaching, they say, leaves little opportunity for independent thought or action; if children were given more time for free and independent exploration in problem solving, they would continue to be creative throughout the school years and into adult life.

The difficulty with this argument is that schools have always exerted a conserving and conforming influence; they must necessarily do so if they are to pass along the cultural heritage of the race. Without minimum standards, a measure of uniformity, and some pressure, this could not be accomplished.

Two lines of evidence provide some information about the relationship between childhood and adult creativity and about the effects of schooling on the emergence of high creativity. These include reports of the behavior of creative adults in childhood and studies of the products of various kinds of educational systems.

STUDIES OF CHILDHOOD CREATIVITY

Until recent years studies of childhood creativity have been comparatively rare. In the early 1920s Simpson devised a number of tests of creative imagination, which were tried out on school children (1922). Simpson recommended that such tests be used to supplement standard tests of intelligence, since the latter did not measure creative productivity and originality. At about the same time, Hargreaves in England also reported the results of a series of tests of creativity given to schoolchildren (1927).

Hollingworth, in her last studies of high-IQ children, gave some attention to creativity. She reported that a third of the children, or twelve cases among thirty-six, testing over 180 IQ showed signs of creativity (1942). A recent study attempted to identify creativity in adolescents by means of Guilford's tests (Piers, 1960).

A number of experimenters have devised performance tests as measures of creativity, and some use has been made of rating scales and trait checklists. The sociometric approach has also been used in identifying creative children: "Who in the class has the best new ideas?" "Who thinks of the craziest ideas?"

The Getzels-Jackson Study   Getzels and Jackson of the University of Chicago investigated the traits of high school youth who showed signs of high creativity (1960, 1962). From a group of 449 students attending the University of Chicago laboratory schools, two distinct groups were selected on the basis of IQ measures and the mean of five measures of divergent thinking.

Group I, the high-creativity group, included 26 students in the top 20 per cent in creativity, but not in the top 20 per cent in IQ. Group 2, the high-intelligence group, included 28 students in the top 20 per cent in intelligence, but not in the top 20 per cent in creativity. Students who rated high in both sets of traits were eliminated from the study. A wide range in creativity scores and ratings was found among these students.

The results of the Getzels-Jackson study, as reported in 1960, are as follows:

	Total population	High-IQ group	High-creativity group
Mean IQ	132	150	127
School achievement	49.91	55	56.27
Teacher preference ratings	10.23	11.20	10.54
Need for achievement scores	49.81	49	50.04

The high-IQ, noncreative group tended to converge upon stereotyped meanings, to perceive personal success by conventional standards, to move toward the model provided by the teacher, to seek out careers that conformed to what was expected of them. By contrast, the high-creativity group tended to diverge from stereotyped meanings, to move away from the model provided by teachers, to seek careers that did not conform to what was expected of them. The high-IQ adolescents tended to favor convergent modes of problem solving, and the high-creativity group tended to favor divergent modes.

The groups were equally superior in school achievement. Teachers exhibited a clear-cut preference for the high-IQ child.

In making judgments, the creative group rated high marks, IQ, and items such as pep and energy, character, and goal directedness lower than did members of the highly intelligent group. The creative group placed a higher value on sense of humor than the high-IQ group.

Members of the high-IQ group were different from the creative group in the degree to which they aspired for "success" in adult life. The high-IQ student's self-idea was consonant with the one he believed teachers would most readily approve. This was not true of the creative child.

The children in the two experimental groups were asked to write four-minute stories in response to six pictures flashed on a screen. In their responses to the pictures, the creative students exhibited a degree of imagination and originality unmatched by the high-IQ students. These results, the authors believe, suggest that a distinction should be made between high-IQ children who are fast learners and students who are distinctly creative.

Other Studies   Weisberg and Springer reported that children with expressive and nondominant parents scored higher than others on tests of originality, curiosity, fluency, flexibility, and other traits associated with creativity (1961). Environmental factors were judged essential in the development of creativity.

In a study of creative talent in writing, Witty collected over 2,000 compositions of school children in 80 classrooms in 34 cities. The children were asked to complete the story of a film entitled *The Hunter and the Forest* (1956). About 10 per cent were judged to be outstanding and to suggest potential creative ability. Some of the most creative compositions were written by pupils in the 115 to 130 IQ range.

The Work of Dr. E. Paul Torrance   Using performance tests of originality and divergent behavior, Dr. E. Paul Torrance and his associates at the Bureau of Educational Research at the University of Minnesota have studied tendencies toward creativity in over 15,000 boys and girls from nursery school through grade 6. In one study Torrance asked pupils to remodel toy play kits to make them more fun to play with (1962). These improvement tests were administered to 20 fifth graders of typical middle-class background in the public schools of Bloomington, Minnesota.

In responding to tests of originality and inventiveness, boys demonstrated twice as many creative ideas as girls, and the suggestions of the boys were more valuable. The experiment showed that gifted children in special classes had more confidence in their ability to be creative than children of comparable ability in regular classes. The two highest scorers on the creativity tests had the lowest IQs and their academic ratings were mediocre.

The key signs of creativity as reported by Torrance were:

Curiosity

Flexibility

Sensitivity to problems

Self-feeling (child works independently on own problems; merely following instructions bores him)

Originality

Insight[3]

Through further tests and observations Dr. Torrance found that children aged three to five are highly creative, but that a sudden drop in creativity occurs when children enter the first grade. A new creative period appears in grades 2 and 3, and then another drop occurs toward the end of third grade and the beginning of fourth. By the age of nine or ten, most children have lost the typical spontaneity and curiosity of the earlier periods. Torrance concluded that most children cease to do creative thinking in the middle grades and beyond because of social pressures to conform, especially the influences of the school. He believes that if educators were more concerned about the identification and motivation of innovating, nonconforming individuals, more children would retain their zest for experimentation and innovation.

The Question of the Validity of Creativity Tests   Are tests that start with something already manufactured, which a child is asked to improve upon, a true measure of creativity? In tests of this kind, the child has no chance to think up his own problems and to work out original solutions. The ready-made product may not be congenial to the child's interest or in line with his imaginings. Furthermore, these tests do not necessarily measure the kind of creative behavior that a student might exhibit in the laboratory, on a field trip, or in the normal classroom setting. As Thorndike points out, the validity of the tests currently available is also questionable because of the low correlation between subtests and between the various tests themselves (1963).

THE RELATIONSHIP BETWEEN CHILDHOOD CREATIVITY AND INTELLIGENCE

There has been a good deal of confused thinking about the relationship between evidences of creativity in children and ratings of general intelligence. Popular articles on the subject, presumably

[3] E. Paul Torrance, *Guiding Creative Talent*, Prentice-Hall, Inc., Englewood Cliffs, N.J., 1962. Used by permission of the author and publisher.

based on research, seem to say that creative ability is one thing and high intelligence quite another. A teacher called attention to two boys who were involved in a map-making project. One boy who was very bright drew his map to scale with mathematical precision, but the other boy, not so bright, did a more original job, showing relief effects and cleverness in coloring and lettering.

What do research studies actually disclose about childhood creativity and the IQ? Spearman, in his interpretation of Hargreave's study of child creativity referred to above, found that the tests of creativity were highly saturated with G, that is, general intelligence. The children rating high on creativity tests tended to be among the most intelligent.

The Getzels-Jackson study is most frequently cited as evidence that IQ tests do not single out the young student with unusual originality and depth. The IQs of the creative children have been referred to in popular journals as "relatively low." As a matter of fact, both groups were far superior in IQ to the general population of upper-grade and high school students; the groups were virtually equal in school achievement, as the data cited on page 456 indicate. Students who rated high on both tests were eliminated from the study to begin with.

Torrance concluded that the creative child—the one who rated high on the creativity tests—tended to have good intelligence as well. High creativity was not often found among low-IQ children, but above the 115 to 120 IQ range, creativity test scores were uncorrelated with intelligence. If children were to be identified as creative on the basis of high intelligence or scholastic aptitude test scores, Torrance concluded that approximately 70 per cent of the most creative would be missed.

Simpson and Martinson reported from their studies in California that children selected on the criterion of high intelligence showed great virtuosity and great variety in their talents (1961). These findings refute the conclusion of Getzels and Jackson that the high-IQ criterion identifies only those narrowly oriented toward conforming academic superiority.

A substantial relationship between intellectual level as measured by intelligence tests and creativity in writing as judged by evaluation of children's writing in response to the film *The Hunter and the Forest* was reported by Miller (1962). Two-thirds of the intellectually superior children were rated as highly creative in at least one area; a number were creative in more than one area. The highly gifted children were also superior in imagination and abstract thinking as measured by the Kahn Test of Symbol Arrangement. The mentally superior children surpassed others in dramatic creativity, though there were cases of high creativity in nonsuperior children.

In a study of high school students, Holland reported that creative performance occurred more frequently among students who were independent, intellectual, expressive, social, consciously original, and who had high aspirations (1961).

The "Guinea Pig" follow-up report referred to in Chapter Five throws further light on this question of creativity and intelligence, though the data are for ratings of adults. The Adult Guinea Pigs were classified in quintiles on the basis of intelligence tests administered while they were in high school. When their protocols were analyzed for evidences of creativity, the highest concentration of the trait was found in the top quintile; the least creativity was found in the two lowest quintiles.

There are statistical pitfalls in interpreting results of tests measuring creativity and intelligence. The low IQ-creativity correlations for the Getzels-Jackson study may be due to the restricted IQ ranges of the samples. Torrance reported a correlation of 0.03 (virtually no correlation) between Stanford-Binet IQs in the range from 132 to 186 and scores on measures of creativity (1962). However, performance tests of creativity, such as those used in Torrance's study, lack the "ceiling" of typical intelligence tests; hence, scores in the upper ranges remain undistributed. Brief tests of any trait tend to be more unreliable than longer tests; hence, their intercorrelations tend to be low.

The conclusion to be drawn is that high intelligence is certainly an element in creative thinking of unusual quality, but having a high IQ does not guarantee high creativity. None of the studies conducted in recent years, however, warrant the conclusion that there is no correlation between intelligence as measured by mental tests and scores on creativity tests. In our present state of knowledge it is not possible to draw any final conclusion concerning the relationship between test intelligence and test creativity.

THE EMERGENCE OF CREATIVENESS

The prospect of increasing the number of creative young people rests upon studies of the origin and development of creativity. The individual's creativity is not the product of any one type of environmental conditioning, familial influence, or schooling; nor is it an instinctive trait that predestines a person to do original thinking regardless of his background or circumstances. Recent research suggests that originality is learned behavior that varies with the antecedent conditions affecting the individual. Originality is the end product of a type of intellect and certain habits of mind, scholarly ways of working and thinking, together with significant experiences.

Can we spot among the children in our midst today the creative thinkers of tomorrow? Are there significant behavior traits in childhood that foreshadow the future creative genius? These questions point up the mystery concerning the origins of adult creativity. The educational world is seeking predictive measures of creativity in young people and guidelines for cultivating creativity through school instruction. Instead of bewailing the loss of spontaneity in the growing-up process, we could more profitably study the early careers of creative adults for clues to their development.

Prediction of Creativity   Although children may show early evidences of creativity, originality of thinking, persistence in problem solving, and other likely symptoms, whether or not they will become creative adults can scarcely be determined until they meet the challenges of adolescence and adult life. Brief creativity tests are unreliable alone as predictors because responses to such tests tell nothing about the traits of the individual: drive, concentration in work, talent for experimentation and research, indifference to external evaluation of behavior and achievement. Young people with marked capacity for originality and inventiveness may lack the energy, opportunity, inspiration, stimulation, or determination to develop exceptional gifts.

Pressey believes that a practicing genius is produced by giving an able youngster early encouragement, intensive instruction, and continuing opportunity as he advances, a congruent stimulating social life, and cumulative experience of success (1955). These points are well exemplified in the lives of the creative persons mentioned in the following pages. People who become highly creative in adult life are the product of circumstances and influences reaching back into childhood. The type of early experience and the instruction a young person receives apparently have a cumulative effect.

Although there is not much reliable information concerning creative people as children, there are enough indications to suggest that their childhood was distinctly different from the average even if this fact was not recognized at the time. The unoriginal young person performs as he was taught, but not the child with unusual imagination. The creative individual escapes the clutch of conformity. Even in youth he prefers to go his own way; in fact, he will insist on doing so, and resist the temptation to yield to prescriptions in his area of special interest. The youthful scientist begins early to isolate himself for work on an absorbing problem, arranging his collection, experimenting with chemicals, studying rocks or shells.

The life histories of creative adults indicate that by age eleven or twelve, in many cases even earlier, they exhibited a remarkable capacity for original thinking, a trait that persisted throughout life. Sir Edwin Landseer, the British painter of notable animal pictures, showed originality and lack of stereotyping in his childhood sketches. He exhibited his work at the Royal Academy in London when he was twelve, and by age twenty-two had attained full success as a mature artist. At the age of eleven, the artist Doré had a set of lithographs published in his native city of Strassburg. Picasso won his first prizes for art in his childhood, and had a one-man showing at the age of nineteen.

Most of the famous poets were precocious as children. At the age of twelve, John Milton was devouring the classics. At the age of six, Goethe began to arrange and conduct plays on a miniature stage. Before he was eight he developed a passion for writing poetry. William Blake, who is recognized today as one of the greatest figures in British poetry and art, showed talent in art at the age of ten and began writing poetry at fourteen. Byron also began writing poetry very early, and Poe composed a remarkable poem, "To Helen," while still in his teens.

The Brontë sisters were authors in childhood, writing novelettes before they were in their teens. Selma Lagerlöf decided at the age of seven to write stories when she grew up; at ten she was directing other children in dramatic presentations. Louisa May Alcott, considered by her father the most creative of his four children, felt impelled to read all the good books in Mr. Emerson's library while still a child.

Many noted historians and philosophers have shown childhood precocity. At the age of nine, Edward Gibbon studied Phaedrus and Nepos, was acquainted with Pope's *Homer* and the *Arabian Nights*. Soon he was reading Dryden's *Virgil*, Ovid's *Metamorphoses*, and many volumes of English poetry, romance, history, and travel. Between the ages of fourteen and sixteen he continued to read widely in ancient, modern, and universal history. By his fifteenth year he had stumbled on to Oriental history, and was soon reading everything he could find on this subject. The idea for his great work originated on a visit to Rome in his late teens. John Dewey, as a high school youth, became enamored of studies in philosophy.

The childhood precocity of the great scientists has been documented in many biographies. Galileo made his famous observation of the swinging pendulum when he was seventeen. Blaise Pascal worked out the major laws of geometry for his own amusement by the age of eleven, and when he was twelve wrote a treatise on acoustics. Carl Friederich Gauss was another gifted child mathematician. John Ericsson, a Swedish boy, discovered the principle of the screw propeller when he was nine while playing with boats on a stream that ran through his father's farm. At the age of thirteen he was put in charge of a 600-man work crew. Edison began his career as an inventor at the age of ten. Nikola Tesla, a genius in electric power with 700 inventions to his credit, was often so far ahead of his contemporaries that his patents had expired before the inventions could be put to practical use; he had made the decision to become an inventor by the age of five. As a small boy, Luther Burbank showed unusual interest in his mother's house plants and took charge of them. He made little discoveries now and then —for example, about the effects of climate on plant growth.

The early life of Dr. Lee De Forest, who was known as the father of radio at the time of his death in 1961, showed all the hallmarks of one who was destined for an unusual career in science and invention. In childhood he became interested in experimenting with tools. He designed a new type of farm gate and built a locomotive. At the age of fifteen he insisted on studying electricity. After graduation from preparatory school he enrolled in Sheffield Scientific School at Yale University.

Dr. Robert B. Woodward, one of the country's leading chemists today, began experiments at the age of ten. By twenty he had completed his Ph.D. in chemistry at Massachusetts Institute of Technology.

The persistent questions are: Why do relatively few children develop originality in thought and action that continues through later childhood and the adolescent years? Which ones among all the capable, interesting children growing up in all parts of the world today are destined to catch and retain the creative spark? There is no possibility of answering these questions in our present state of knowledge. Eventually, detailed biographical records should provide the answers.

OUT-OF-SCHOOL INFLUENCES

The creativity of gifted children is shown most characteristically out of school, perhaps because this is the larger and freer part of the youth's world. Out-of-school life, particularly influences in the home, may count for more in stimulating creative imagination than the formal or informal learning experiences of the school, provided the youth has time to read, explore, and experiment.

The Goertzels' study indicates that there are distinctive family influences that foster the traits from which adult creativity emerges (1962). The brother of Dr. Ernst Meumann who wrote up the distinguished psychologist's life concluded that a "creative school" was not so essential in the production of original thinking and scholarship as the type of home life in the early years and university or other advanced training later.

Parents who foster creativity set the child on his way, but they do not impose undue restrictions or dictate procedures to be followed. Instead of exacting conformity, they view independence of thinking as a highly desirable childhood trait. Although adults in the household may give full support to a child's urge to think and achieve imaginatively, they are not necessarily aware that he is creative, nor do they exert any pressure to make him so.

The children are given freedom to range and to engage in self-initiated projects during their out-of-school life. Self-responsibility is expected in the early years, but limits are set to freedom in terms of age and understanding. The child's enthusiasms, no matter how ephemeral they may seem, are welcomed and shared. The home atmosphere is congenial to the child's questioning and his urge to investigate.

Roe's study of scientists revealed that early family experiences inclined a youth toward a science career, whether or not the parents were scientists (1953). The father's influence has most to do with budding science interest, along with the influence of stimulating teachers. Dr. Szent-Györgyi, the Hungarian-born scientist, believed that his drive toward creative research came from growing up in a family of scientists and an intellectual atmosphere, so that intellectual creativity became his highest aim, the one thing worth striving for; his brothers, however, did not share his interest in scientific research.

During free play or while working at hobbies, children display the greatest evidence of original thinking. Lewis Carroll showed his inventiveness early in games he devised for his young brothers and sisters. A hobby in the field of science or technology is a first indication of interests that may lead to creative work. This was true of the boy Edison and other inventors. During his youth, Pierre Loti (Louis Marie Julien Viand) had his own study and maintained a museum at the top of his parents' house.

The young person is more likely to do creative thinking if he has a quick intellect, unusual powers of observation, a fine memory for details, interest in investigation related to problem solving, the urge to seek out new facts, a tendency to engage in theoretical speculation, interest in laboratory work and field studies.

The older boy or girl who is bent on genuine experimenting in his spare time, whether it is with photography, electrical equipment, mathematics, costume design, or ballet, should be encouraged. Early signs of creativity may be seen in products that are off the beaten track, that show cleverness and humor, or that may even seem silly and farfetched.

FORMATIVE INFLUENCES OF THE SCHOOL

There is no doubt that the school can be a powerful agent in fostering habits and attitudes that give students a new outlook, that stir the imagination and equip young people for original work. During his brief hours with a superior teacher, a child may catch insights that challenge to the full his interest in working creatively on a hobby or some special problem.

Some people who have been recognized as highly creative have had extensive formal education; some have had an informal and limited education; some have had almost no schooling at all. Certainly it is possible to overestimate the role of formal schooling in shaping the creative mind. Shevchenko, an artist and the leading poet of the Ukraine, was a lowly serf who had no formal education, but he learned to read in early childhood from a church cantor in his village, and went about to other villages seeking people who would teach him to paint. Michael Faraday, the discoverer of electromagnetic properties, was a blacksmith's son who received no formal education; but he quickly acquired a background of knowledge as a bookbinder's apprentice, and then went on to become laboratory assistant to Sir Humphry Davy in London.

Today the question of the type of schooling that is most likely to foster creativity in young people is seriously debated. Is child interest-centered education more apt to strike the spark than a formal-drill type of school? Does permissiveness or authoritarianism in teaching encourage creativity?

The complaint is heard that traditional methods of teaching by authority tend to strangle the inquiring minds of children, to destroy their natural curiosity, to penalize invention in the interest of conformity.

The assumption generally made is that educational experiences of the type sponsored by the Progressive Education Association and the child-centered schools of former years are more likely to foster creativity than are formal curriculum and teaching methods. This assumption is questionable, because some highly creative people have survived the rigors of formal, classical education, whereas creative-minded children have not blossomed perceptibly in a permissive atmosphere.

The Effects of Too Much Rigidity   Standard lesson learning with its emphasis on working the problems according to the method of the book may seriously interfere with the development of intuitive thinking. In fact, the teacher's directives may be less productive of thinking than the student's original ideas about what to study and observe. Throttling of original talent occurs when teachers put a premium on answer getting instead of encouraging experimentation in problem solving. Suppressing the urge to experiment, particularly among adolescents, may cause the original thinker to lose interest in school studies. Too often formal teaching procedures cut off all possibility of a student's raising pertinent questions concerning the cause and meaning of things. How can original thinking be stimulated if the student's questions are promptly answered for him? All too frequently in the typical classroom, a punitive attitude is adopted toward the lively-minded youth with original ideas who fails to produce the accepted answers to the teacher's questions: the child who shows originality is considered refractory, if not definitely abnormal. Even in college, high marks usually go to the conforming student rather than to the original thinker.

The Other Side of the Picture   Creative thinkers, reflecting on their early school experiences, have attributed their success to their rigorous intellectual training at the hands of capable teachers. Some have said that they suffered as they pegged away at Latin and Greek or mathematics, but that, in the end, they earned the reward. A century ago, formal classical education was the only intellectual training to be had, yet creative minds kept appearing on the scene.

The historian Arnold J. Toynbee, a distinguished and original thinker, says that he had the supreme good fortune to receive an uncompromisingly classical education, and Sir James Frazer, the great ethnologist, observed that young students preparing for the university in his day had no freedom in choice of subjects whatsoever. The great scientists were not only trained in the scientific method, but they were thoroughly schooled in pertinent scientific work carried to the highest level of abstract thinking and problem solving. The artists were thorough masters of their specialties, even often in the teens, as a result of early apprenticeships.

EVIDENCE ON TYPE OF SCHOOLING AND CREATIVITY

During the 1920s and 1930s traditional formalities in education gave way in experimental schools to new methods of instruction, in which learning through discovery and firsthand experiencing had a large place. The pupils themselves, along with the teacher, took a part in planning their learning experiences. The graduates of these experimental schools are now adults, whose creative contributions can be evaluated. Is there any evidence that a "creative curriculum" produced an exceptional number of creative adults in comparison with students of similar background and ability who graduated from the more traditional elementary and college preparatory schools?

Records of Graduates from Experimental Schools   The Lincoln School of Teachers College, Columbia University, New York, was one of the best representatives of the new era in education. There were some remarkably talented children in the school who responded fully to the unusual opportunities afforded them. There were incentives to creativity in the curriculum and instructional materials, there were close personal contacts between pupils and master teachers, and extensive use was made of the cultural advantages of New York City. Upper elementary school pupils had a "creative work period" once a week in which they could pursue their special hobby interests. There were courses labeled "creative music" and "creative writing." The facilities of shops and studios, on a par with the best in the country, provided incentives for experimentation in every subject area and every medium of expression. Teachers tried to stimulate the children to creative effort through indirect guidance and suggestion: watching for signs of original thinking, encouraging initiative, stimulating expression, offering suggestions and criticism. A graduate of the school observed, "The teachers really did try to release the creative abilities of the students. They made you feel that you could tackle anything."

Although there has been no recent survey of the Lincoln School graduates (the school closed in 1948), information gained from former teachers and others who have kept in touch with the graduates has furnished a partial picture of these people in adult life. Today a considerable number of the graduates are recognized as leaders in their callings throughout the world. Some have made brilliant records in music, writing, university teaching, government, business, and industry. They have won prizes and honors for signal accomplishments with more than average frequency.

Of all the graduates from 1922 onward, what proportion has been notable for creative achievements in the arts and sciences, for invention and the discovery of new knowledge? Although the proportion of those who have earned high distinction for original contributions is small, perhaps 5 per cent of the graduates, the number who have shown creativity in their approach to problem solving in a wide range of occupations is much higher, possibly 25 or 30 per cent, according to estimates of graduates who have kept in touch with their classmates. The effects of the exceptional features of the Lincoln School curriculum are observed in the social sensitivity of the graduates, their competence and leadership in managerial posts, in the professions, and in home and community life rather than in overwhelming demonstration of high creativity.

Creativity of the "Guinea Pigs"   The Ohio State University School, famous for the Guinea Pigs who wrote up an account of their school experiences, had much in common with the Lincoln School of Teachers College. It was a campus school enrolling bright children of superior social status for the most part, a substantial number of whom were children of university faculty members. This school, like Lincoln, was a member of the "Eight-year Study," a group of thirty leading high schools in the country conducting an experimental program, freed from traditional college entrance requirements. The Lincoln School population was somewhat less homogeneous than that of the Ohio school, and the stay of the typical Lincoln graduate was shorter than that of the "Guinea Pigs," all of whom attended their school for a full six years.

There was marked similarity between the Ohio students and the Lincoln School graduates of the same era in expressiveness and self-responsibility, in ability to communicate, and in interests.

As at Lincoln, the curriculum and teaching at the Ohio School featured student experimentation and self-direction. According to the statement of the philosophy and purposes of the school, for every curriculum area, "The School should provide experiences which demand novel adjustments to situations rather than routine and repetition" (Willis, 1961). The write-up of the high school program for the Eight-year Study prepared by the faculty indicated that creativity was fostered by much the same means as at the Lincoln School. The students were encouraged to use their intelligence creatively in the free-reading program and other areas. The fact that the first graduating class produced a published document of high merit, *Were We Guinea Pigs?* attests to the originality of the class members.

In the follow-up study of the Guinea Pigs twenty years later, when they were in their mid-thirties, evidences of "creativity" were sought along with other outcomes of the program. For purposes of the follow-up questionnaire and interviews, creativity was defined as "a spontaneous expressive inquiring reaction toward living." The term was closely allied with "self-direction" and self-realization" as used in the early statement of the school's philosophy and purposes, as well as with "the method of intelligence" or open-minded inquiry developed in problem solving.

In the published report of the follow-up study, a section of the chapter entitled The Achievement of Purposes is devoted to evidences of creativity. On the basis of the protocols, ratings of creativity were as follows:

Number	Rank	Per cent
13	Very high	28.9
12	High	26.7
13	Some	28.9
7	Little or very little	15.5

Reprinted from *The Guinea Pigs after Twenty Years: A Follow-up Study of the Class of 1938 of the University School at Ohio State,* by Margaret Willis. Copyright 1961 by the Ohio State University Press. Used by permission of the author and the publisher.

These results indicate that, with a broad definition of "creative living," well over half of the graduates earned a high creativity rating. As in the case of the Lincoln School graduates, these people demonstrated their original thinking in unusual sensitivity to human relationships, the development of breadth of view, leadership, and competence on the job and in the community. Without a comparison study of comparable high school youths graduating from other types of schools, there is no way of knowing to what extent and in what ways the school program of itself contributed to the creativity of the graduates.

In Conclusion   So far there is no clear-cut proof that opportunities for self-expression, an informal permissive classroom atmosphere, and guidance in individual problem solving are more likely to develop creativity of a high order than traditional curriculum organization and teaching practices.

It is fatuous to assume that "free activities" twice a week or even that provision for pupil initiative and expression interwoven with studies throughout the school day can kindle the creative imagination of all students or have lasting effects.

The uniqueness of creativity in itself precludes the possibility of training to develop the trait. No formula can be worked out because no education program can ever control all the influences that produce the creative mind.

Whether instruction is formal or not is less pertinent than whether the student derives from it something that kindles his imagination or supplies knowledge and skills essential to creative development and whether the instruction offers a serious challenge to an unusual mind. In the arts as well as in the sciences, whether the student ultimately becomes a creative career person depends more upon how far he continues his studies than upon whether his schooling was formal or informal, obtained en masse or highly individualized.

As a matter of fact, few children are the product of only one type of school today. A child seldom continues even as long as two years with the same teacher or group of teachers. A student who graduates from a certain high school can scarcely be said to be the product of that particular school alone. Because of the high mobility of the population, children are in and out of several different schools before they graduate. Furthermore, the school term is too brief, the school day too short, the school experience necessarily too restricted, contained as it is largely within a boxlike structure and cubicles of rooms, to have great influence one way or another in developing original thinking and problem solving.

The Mentor   One factor persistently shows up as highly significant in shaping a youth's creative bent—the influence of a mentor, perhaps a teacher, who excites the student and makes him want to keep on exploring even after the closing school bell rings. In all times, in varied circumstances, children have been awakened by inspiring teachers who allied themselves with the child's interests and who could enter fully into the child's enthusiasms. They not only had an understanding and appreciation of originality in children, but were able to spur them on to new aspirations, to arouse the inner depth of feeling upon which true creativity depends. Although this is more likely to occur in the upper high school years or in college or university, there is evidence that the teacher's influence in developing the spirit of creativity may begin much earlier.

The gifted teacher opens up new avenues of interest for eager young scholars. He demonstrates new techniques of working or performing and suggests that his students discover how great minds have tackled their intellectual problems. This mentor-teacher knows how to evaluate a child's attempts at problem solving and how to guide his embryonic research efforts without imposition or dictation. This is just the opposite of teaching by fiat: "These are the facts you must learn. Do this, do that to get your answer."

At a certain stage a child of ten, thirteen, or sixteen may be ready with plans for his original production, whether a new way of recording the passage of time or the draft of an original story. It is at this point that the student needs encouragement to continue with his plan; it is the time, too, when he is most in need of instruction.

A devoted teacher in intimate contact with a promising young student can produce exceptional results, as the following case illustrates. Professor Frank Jewett, head of the chemistry department at Oberlin College many years ago, on the occasion of the fiftieth anniversary of his graduation from Yale, remarked that his most noteworthy discovery in science had been a young man by the name of Charles M. Hall. Charles was a white-headed boy of fourteen or so, a student in the preparatory department of Oberlin College and keen about chemical research when he first approached Professor Jewett for some needed supplies. He commented that he liked to work with chemical apparatus. Repeated observations confirmed Professor Jewett's impression that here was a youth of unusual promise who would one day make his mark in the world. The boy was industrious, always questioning and investigating, fond of reading, dreaming of discoveries that would benefit the world. When Charles entered college, Professor Jewett took him into his own private laboratory where they discussed problems from day to day. The youth continued working on what he called his "schemes." One day Professor Jewett happened to remark in class that anyone who discovered a process by which aluminum could be produced on a commercial scale would bless humanity and make a fortune for himself. The young student declared then and there that he would "go after it." At the age of twenty-two, shortly after graduation from college, the discovery was made in young Hall's own home laboratory with materials lent him by the college, thus laying the foundation for the aluminum industry.

A plaque at the entrance to the physics building at Columbia University commemorates the fact that Prof. Michael Idvorsky Pupin, physicist and inventor, was "a true guide to the perplexed." The same thing could be said of academician Ivan Pavlov, Nobel prize winner, Russia's great physiologist.

Teaching That Encourages Creativity

All children are better off when they have freedom for self-expression and experimental learning through firsthand contacts, whether or not these learning experiences develop new depths of original thinking. Aside from the advantages for physical well-being and mental health, there is always the chance that some students will develop traits of distinctive originality.

Questions to consider are:

What can the teacher do to stir up initiative, to stimulate imagination and independent thinking?

How can a teacher make full use of the child's interest in doing unusual things?

Can young people do creative thinking, make original contributions, and still meet the usual standards of the school curriculum?

Certain features of the educative process, particularly of the teacher-pupil relationship, contribute to creative thinking. Practically everything that John Dewey said about leading children to think about the questions they themselves raise and the problems they discover in their own occupations has a bearing on this subject. Through manual activities and firsthand experimenting, handling tools and manipulating materials, the creative-minded youth tries out his ideas. Some of his experiments are based on ideas gained from reading or observing demonstrations.

Schoolchildren can be made aware of the contrast between working in a standard conventional way and thinking up a new approach. In the making of mobiles or maps, for example, there is one standard method, but there may be dozens of new ideas to be tried out. The student must acquire courage and self-confidence in his ability to do distinctive work by constant encouragement of his effort to think independently and exercise initiative.

What a remarkable thing it is to see a classroom teacher turning everything to account in arousing the children's curiosity and drawing out their original thinking. There are precious opportunities for composing poems, creating songs, designing bookcovers, or decorating a screen. What ideas do the children have? Opportunities for expressive writing, for creative dramatics, for improvising dances and creating costumes are always present when a group of children come together. Who has good ideas to try out? This is the basis of creative teaching.

Dr. Kemp of Michigan State University reported on an experiment he undertook to free students from formal training and encourage more flexibility. The children were a class of fifth graders, all with IQs above 120, attending a six-week summer school. A permissive atmosphere loosened up the group and tended to overcome the rigidity in their thinking. They became freer in expression, made more decisions for themselves, and showed more independence. The rewarding results were due largely to the teacher's attitude in encouraging the children to seek solutions to problems for themselves, instead of memorizing answers to stereotyped questions.

In the Winnetka, Illinois, schools, under the direction of Dr. Carleton Washburne, creativity was not a compartmentalized experience in the curriculum or limited to work on isolated hobbies; rather, it derived from all areas of study in the curriculum and blended with them (1963). There were opportunities for creative expression and originality in democrative citizenship, economic enterprises, the school newspapers, programs, as well as in dramatic expression, art, and music. A topic such as Egyptian culture in the fourth grade gave children outlets for their energy and original ideas.

Dr. Torrance has made the following suggestions for encouraging creativity in children (1962):

Do not discourage fantasy.
Do not interfere with a child's creative tendencies or hold him back.
Make creative efforts rewarding.
Avoid the sex stereotype—boys do this, girls do that.

Do not judge a child by his success in reading and writing. A creative child
   may lag behind.
Allow freedom to experiment in getting answers.
Help a child to use his creativity in social situations.[4]

Creativity in the arts, music, painting, writing, science, and mathematics can scarcely be taught, but it can be encouraged by alert teachers who recognize and value free, original expression.

School experiences should involve the children more dynamically in the whole process of education—in planning their studies, raising questions, discovering exciting problems, searching out materials, consulting the teacher without fear of ridicule or punishment.

Practices of Doubtful Value   Some of the assignments intended to make children "more creative" are of doubtful value. For example, lists are sometimes drawn up of things children can work on for "creativity" credit. A trivial assignment such as, "Look out the window and see how many things you can observe that no one else notices," may arouse children from a state of lethargy, but contributes little to original thinking. In one class the children were told, "Old light bulbs are usually thrown in the trash can. How many different uses can you think of for an old light bulb?" It might have been safer not to mention trash can light bulbs to this class.

Opportunities for Independent Projects at School   Since invention and originality often trace back to a youngster's early hobby interests, time and place during the school day should be allocated for work on individual projects. In the past these have most often taken the form of activities in the arts and crafts, but today they cover practically the entire gamut of children's interests. The time required for independent projects cannot always be predicted in advance, nor will the projects fit into a standard time schedule. The teacher is advised to set up a flexible, workshop type of classroom with an informal atmosphere that encourages exploration and independent problem solving.

Elaborate equipment is not necessary to spark creative ideas. The "tea cup–rubber band" scientists came up with some remarkable observations, and so can children, if only their thinking is stimulated.

[4] E. Paul Torrance, *Guiding Creative Talent*, Prentice-Hall, Inc., Englewood Cliffs, N.J., 1962. Used by permission of the author and publisher.

Teachers are advised to:

Make more use of ideas the children get from out-of-school projects and suggest that the children work at home on some of the interests developed at school.

Reward independence of thought and action; praise creative effort. Encourage imaginative thinking in the areas of problem solving in which the student's strengths and talents lie. Stress the discovery angle in study projects: how to improve the school paper, ideas for the class play, choice of reading material for a social studies report. Accept any valid ideas, whether or not they furnish the anticipated correct answer.

Deemphasize class marks if children are not to be discouraged from attempting original thinking. Give full credit for original ideas, but do not grade the children on "creativity."

Instead of giving ready-made answers, require the children to discover answers to their own questions. The children should be asking original questions as evidence that they are thinking closely. When Dr. Isadore Rabi, the famous physicist and Nobel prize winner, was a schoolboy, his mother would inquire on his return from school, "Did you ask any good questions today?"

Avoid overscheduling the children's time at school or at home so that scant time remains for their own plans and ideas.

Draw on gifted resource people in the community to assist the children with their original ideas in art, story writing, science experiments, photography, and so on.

Avoid overstressing the mechanics of expression at the expense of content and originality. Avoid demanding artwork that conforms to traditional standards. George Gershwin never would have succeeded with his original musical creations if he had conformed to accepted standards in composition.

Provide inquiring minds with full library resources and a materials center where serious scholarly work can be carried on. Suggestions are given in Chapter Thirteen for organizing independent studies, seminar work, and studio opportunities.

Avoid formal restrictions and external standards of judging so far as possible. No matter how far-fetched an idea about how to frame a picture or weave a mat seems, it may be a good one, even better than the teacher's.

Good suggestions for encouraging creativity in the school environment have been given by Conant, Strang, and Witty (1959), Klausmeier (1961), and Torrance (1962).

References

Anderson, Harold H. (ed.): *Creativity and Its Cultivation,* Harper & Row, Publishers, Incorporated, New York, 1959. Interdisciplinary Symposia on Creativity, Michigan State University, 1957–1958.

Barkan, Manuel, and Ross L. Mooney (eds.): *The Conference on Creativity: A Report to the Rockefeller Foundation,* Ohio State University, Columbus, Ohio, 1953.

Conant, James B., Ruth Strang, and Paul A. Witty: *Creativity of Gifted and Talented Children,* Teachers College, Columbia University, New York, 1959.

Cox, Catherine M.: *Genetic Studies of Genius,* vol. 2, *The Early Mental Traits of Three Hundred Geniuses,* Stanford University Press, Stanford, Calif., 1926.

Davenport, Marcia: *Mozart,* Charles Scribner's Sons, New York, 1956.

Downey, June E.: *Creative Imagination,* Harcourt, Brace & World, Inc., New York, 1929.

Drevdahl, J. E., and R. Cattell: Personality and Creativity in Artists and Writers, *Journal of Clinical Psychology,* 14:107–111, 1958.

Gallagher, James J.: *Teaching the Gifted Child,* Allyn and Bacon, Inc., Boston, 1963.

Gerber, Barbara W.: Creativity: A Frame of Reference for Teachers, *New York State Education,* 48:14–15, 1960.

Getzels, Jacob W., and Philip W. Jackson: *Creativity and Intelligence,* John Wiley & Sons, Inc., New York, 1962.

Getzels, Jacob W., and Philip W. Jackson: The Study of Giftedness: A Multidimensional Approach, in *The Gifted Student: Cooperative Research,* U.S. Department of Health, Education and Welfare, Office of Education, Washington, D.C., 1960.

Goertzel, Victor H., and Mildred G. Goertzel: *Cradles of Eminence,* Little, Brown and Company, Boston, 1962.

Ghiselin, Brewster (ed.): *The Creative Process,* University of California Press, Berkeley, Calif., 1952.

Guilford, J. P.: *Creative Intelligence and Education,* Educational Research and Guidance Association, Los Angeles, 1958.

Guilford, J. P.: Creativity, *The American Psychologist,* 5:444–445, 1950.

Guilford, J. P.: Factors That Aid and Hinder Creativity, *Teachers College Record,* 63:380–392, 1962.

Guilford, J. P.: Three Faces of Intellect, *The American Psychologist,* 14:469–479, 1959.

Guilford, J. P., R. C. Wilson, and P. R. Christensen: *A Factor Analytic Study of Creative Thinking,* University of Southern California Reports, no. 8,

Psychological Laboratory, University of Southern California, Los Angeles, 1952.

Hargreaves, H. L.: The Faculty of Imagination, *British Journal of Psychology Monograph Supplement,* Cambridge University Press, London, 1927.

Holland, John L.: *Creativity and Academic Performance among Talented Adolescents,* National Merit Scholarship Corporation, Evanston, Ill., 1961.

Hollingworth, Leta S.: *Children above 180 I.Q. Stanford-Binet: Origin and Development,* World Book Company, Tarrytown-on-Hudson, N.Y., 1942.

Intelligence and Creativeness, *Childhood Education,* 39(8), 1963.

Klausmeier, Herbert, J.: *Learning and Human Abilities,* Harper & Row, Publishers, Incorporated, New York, 1961, chap. 7.

Lehman, Harvey C.: *Age and Achievement,* Princeton University Press, Princeton, N.J., 1953.

MacKinnon, Donald W.: The Highly Effective Individual, *Teachers College Record,* 61:367–378, 1960.

MacKinnon, Donald W.: The Nature and Nurture of Creative Talent, *American Psychologist,* 17:484–495, 1962.

Mearns, Hughes: *Creative Power: The Education of Youth in the Creative Arts,* Doubleday & Company, Inc., Garden City, N.Y., 1929.

Mearns, Hughes: *Creative Youth: How a School Environment Set Free the Creative Spirit,* Doubleday & Company, Inc., Garden City, N.Y., 1925.

Merry, Frieda, K., and Ralph Vickers Merry: *The First Two Decades of Life,* Harper & Row, Publishers, Incorporated, New York, 1958, chap. 14.

Miller, Vera: Creativity and Intelligence in the Arts, *Education,* 82:488–495, 1962.

Murphy, Gardner: *Human Potentialities,* part III, Basic Books, Inc., Publishers, New York, 1958.

Olsen, Fred, and others: *The Nature of Creative Thinking,* New York University Press, New York, 1957.

Patrick, C.: *What Is Creative Thinking?* Philosophical Library, Inc., New York, 1955.

Paulhan, Fr.: *Psychologie de l'invention,* 4th ed., Alcan, Paris, 1930.

Peet, Harriet E.: *The Creative Individual,* The Ronald Press Company, New York, 1960.

Piers, Ellen V., Jacqueline M. Daniels, and John F. Quackenbush: The Identification of Creativity in Adolescence, *Journal of Educational Psychology,* 51:346–351, 1960.

Pressey, Sidney L.: Concerning the Nature and Nurture of Genius, *Scientific Monthly,* 81:123–129, 1955.

Progressive Education Association, Commission on the Relation of Schools and College, *Thirty Schools Tell Their Story,* Harper & Row, Publishers, Incorporated, New York, 1943.

Rees, M. E., and M. Goldman: Some Relationships between Creativity and Personality, *Journal of General Psychology*, 65:145–161, 1961.

Reid, J. B., F. J. King, and P. Wickwire: Cognitive and Other Personality Characteristics of Creative Children, *Psychological Reports*, 5:729–737, 1959.

Roe, Anne: *The Making of a Scientist*, Dodd, Mead & Company, Inc., New York, 1953.

Sagen, H. B., and K. Yamamoto: The Minnesota Studies of Creative Thinking: Implications for High School Counselors, *Minnesota Counselor*, 1:21–24, 1961.

Simpson, R. M.: Creative Imagination, *American Journal of Psychology*, 33:234–243, 1922.

Simpson, Ray E., and Ruth A. Martinson: *Educational Programs for Gifted Pupils: A Report to the California Legislature*, State Department of Education, Sacramento, Calif., 1961.

Spearman, Carl: *The Abilities of Man*, The Macmillan Company, New York, 1927.

Spearman, Carl: *The Creative Mind*, Nisbet, London, 1931.

Stein, Morris L., and Shirley J. Heinze: *Creativity and the Individual*, The Free Press of Glencoe, New York, 1960.

Szent-Györgyi, Albert: *New York Times Magazine*, July 30, 1961.

Taylor, Calvin W.: *Research Conference on the Identification of Creative Scientific Talent*, University of Utah Press, Salt Lake City, Utah, 1955, 1956.

Taylor, Calvin W. (ed.): *The Third University of Utah Research Conference on the Identification of Creative Talent*, 1959, University of Utah Press, Salt Lake City, Utah, 1962.

Terman, Lewis M.: *Genetic Studies of Genius*, vol. 1, *Mental and Physical Traits of a Thousand Gifted Children*, Stanford University Press, Stanford, Calif., 1925.

Thorndike, Robert L.: The Measurement of Creativity, *Teachers College Record*, 64:423–424, 1963.

Thurstone, L. L.: Creative Talent, in L. L. Thurstone (ed.), *Applications of Psychology*, Harper & Row, Publishers, Incorporated, New York, 1952.

Torrance, E. Paul (ed.): *Creativity: Second Minnesota Conference on Gifted Children*, Center for Continuation Study, University of Minnesota, Minneapolis, 1960.

Torrance, E. Paul: *Creativity: What Research Says to the Teacher*, American Educational Research Association, Washington, D.C., 1963.

Torrance, E. Paul: *Guiding Creative Talent*, Prentice-Hall, Inc., Englewood Cliffs, N.J., 1962.

Washburne, Carleton W., and Sidney P. Marland: *The History and Significance of an Educational Experiment*, Prentice-Hall, Inc., Englewood Cliffs, N.J., 1963.

Weisberg, Paul S., and Kayla J. Springer: Environmental Factors in Creative Function: A Study of Gifted Children, *Archives of General Psychiatry*, 5:554–564, 1961.

Wertheimer, Max: *Productive Thinking*, Harper & Row, Publishers, Incorporated, New York, 1959.

Whiting, Charles: *Creative Thinking*, Reinhold Publishing Corporation, New York, 1958.

Willis, Margaret: *The Guinea Pigs after Twenty Years: A Follow-up Study of the Class of 1938 of the University School at Ohio State*, Ohio State University Press, Columbus, Ohio, 1961.

Wilson, Robert C.: Creativity, in *Education for the Gifted: Fifty-seventh Yearbook of the National Society for the Study of Education*, part 2, The University of Chicago Press, Chicago, 1958.

Witty, Paul A.: The Use of Films in Stimulating Creative Expression and in Identifying Talented Pupils, *Elementary English*, 33:340–344, 1956.

Chapter Sixteen

THE SUPERIOR STUDENT IN COLLEGE

Colleges and universities are today the chief sources of specialized manpower. Advanced intellectual training in the liberal arts and sciences is viewed as the best way for youth to gain the depth of understanding needed to deal with problems and to exert leadership in all fields. In college, the student's powers of thinking, his judgment, and his social sensitivity are raised to new heights through contacts with stimulating professors. Although a college education does not guarantee that one will be a leader or a success in his chosen career, the advantages of higher education are many, and may even outweigh obvious disadvantages in early life.

The purpose of higher education is not to create a new class of intellectuals, remote from the common people and their problems, but rather to give capable young people the insights needed for dealing with people in every occupation and all walks of life. In modern society there is more scope for the ideas of people with well-trained minds than in the day when power and decision making were in the hands of relatively few individuals.

There are more high-level occupations today demanding specialized training than ever before. The General Electric Company alone employs about 23,000 college graduates. College people man the research laboratories in every industry from soap and paint to airplanes and rockets. Those with university training can look forward to careers not only in all the older professions, but also in the new and growing fields of government and industry, social science, commerce, and international affairs.

Stepped-up College Attendance

Young people who have the capacity for higher education should be discovered and encouraged to continue their education. This has become a matter of worldwide concern as new nations emerge lacking sufficient trained leadership for social and economic development.

Fortunately, college-going rates in the United States are steadily rising. In 1900 only 4 per cent of young people of college age were enrolled in colleges of the United States. Of these, 70.7 per cent were men. According to data for 1960, approximately 1,700,000 were students graduated from high schools throughout the United States, and about 45 per cent of them continued their education in colleges or other institutions. Of the 23 per cent of high school graduates who entered academic colleges in 1961, about half were expected to graduate. Economists and others believe that our college rates are still not high enough to meet increasing demands for highly trained manpower.

Abroad, university matriculation tends to be the continuation of a selective process that begins with the student's entrance to the secondary school. In 1963, 8 in 100 young Britons had access to full-time higher education; however, if recommendations for the establishment of new colleges are carried out, the proportion will soon rise to 17 in 100. Although a substantial proportion of Gymnasium and *lycée* graduates in other foreign countries, age nineteen or twenty, go on to the university, the total number of young people who enter these institutions is relatively small. Abroad, university students constitute from 1 to 8 per cent of the college-age group (Bowles, 1963). The United States produces more than eight times as many college graduates in proportion to the youth population as Germany, but that country produces twice as many Ph.D.s as the United States.

In making comparisons between American colleges and foreign universities the fact that foreign students are usually a year or two older at university entrance, more on a par with American juniors than freshmen, must be taken into account.

In Ontario during the years 1946 to 1958, statistics indicated that 34 of every 100 students entering the elementary school completed the high school course through grade 12; 15 of the 34 survivors completed grade 13, a junior college year in high school; 10 of the 34 entered the university; and only 6 received a first degree. No doubt there were many reasons other than lack of ability to account for the dropouts (Brehaut, 1962).

Today in the United States, institutions of higher learning— four-year colleges, state universities, two-year community colleges, and technical-training institutions—are more generally accessible than ever before. The state of Kansas alone has 43 institutions of higher learning, including 24 four-year colleges and universities and 19 junior colleges. Of these, 21 are public institutions. The continuing trend toward urbanization means that institutions located in urban areas are within reach of a large youth population, with motorized transportation enabling thousands of commuters to obtain a higher education without having to leave their home-town.

The state of Pennsylvania has drawn a master plan for tripling the capacity of its higher-education system by 1970; enrollment in all the state-supported institutions is expected to reach 35,000, with 10,000 of these in the freshman and sophomore years. The plan will bring public higher-degree institutions and technical-institute programs within commuting distance of 97 per cent of the state's population.

Problems relating to the improvement of higher education opportunities for the gifted fall into several categories:

Deciding who should go to college

Identifying the most promising students and counseling them about college opportunities

Ensuring continuity between studies in secondary schools and the college or
   university
Creating new programs and special opportunities for the most promising college
   students

These topics will be discussed in this chapter and the one that follows.

Who Should Go to College?

Should everyone with a high school diploma be encouraged to enter college if he wishes to, or should college opportunities be restricted to those with recognized aptitudes of high order? In the past, collegiate education has been lavished on those who could afford to pay for it regardless of their intellectual capacities. Now with public tax-supported institutions for higher education coming to the fore, this question must be given more serious consideration.

Some leaders in higher education believe that secondary school education should be terminal for most youths. Although 15 to 20 per cent might plan to go on for two years at a community junior college or some other type of institution, not more than 5 per cent should be invited to undertake the four-year academic college sequence. Mediocre students who seek college admission merely for the prestige of a diploma or for social reasons should be excluded. The economics of the situation must be considered. College training is the most costly phase of education in terms of salaries of instructors, housing, laboratories, libraries, equipment for experimental work, and other expenditures.

The state universities, public tax-supported institutions, have been plagued with the problem of whom to admit in view of the widespread demand that every high school graduate in the state be permitted to enter if he cares to do so. Eleven state universities are obliged to admit anyone holding a diploma from an accredited high school in the state. Ten others have long-standing liberal admission policies for public relations reasons. The problem is complicated by the fact that virtually everyone can obtain a high school diploma today.

A state university dean observed that with the broad admissions policy at his institution, the freshman class is almost as diversified as a class of high school graduates, with the result that 30 to 40 per cent of the freshmen flunk out before the end of the year. As in high school, the welfare of the most competent is sacrificed when classes include a motley array of mediocre students.

Some authorities think that, instead of increasing the size of existing universities, it would be wiser to limit the student body to the most capable and ambitious students, those most likely to succeed. Bestor, of the University of Illinois, has urged rigorous selection policies to ensure that only those of superior intellect are admitted to higher education (1956). He argues that college instruction is too expensive to waste on students who are unable to keep up with difficult courses. Bestor and others urge colleges to seek out the best students and then make it possible for all of them to enter.

The present plan in California is to admit to the state university only the highest-standing high school graduates, those in the top one-eighth of the graduating class. Those next in rank are admitted to the four-year state colleges. Others are admitted to the state's junior colleges. This means that virtually any high school graduate can have a chance to try out his abilities in some type of higher institution in California.

Other educators hold the view that advanced training in a college atmosphere is so valuable that as many young people as possible, not only those with the best brains, should be admitted. More education for everyone has been the slogan that has kept the American education system burgeoning through the years.

Instead of contending that everyone who cares to go to college has a right to do so, many educators feel that the sounder viewpoint is that everyone should have the right to tertiary education that will enhance his skills and make him a more capable citizen. This would mean that those of modest abilities could take advantage of a variety of practical and enriching educational opportunities quite distinct from the stiff academic demands of high-level college and university programs. High school graduates lacking the academic aptitude required for four years of academic work in college could enter technical schools where they could learn a skill. Training institutes where girls learn office procedures or interior decorating or where boys learn professional photography or electronics would fill the bill. Junior colleges would meet the needs of students who wished to have some college experience but were not intent upon a four-year academic course.

Summing up, the outlook seems to indicate extension of the junior college idea and new developments in community adult education through the schools, library programs, and institutes, rather than opening doors of the four-year colleges to an avalanche of ambitious youths regardless of their intellectual capacity, background of knowledge, or purposes in wanting to go to college.

Selectivity of the College Population

Colleges, public and private, have always been selective institutions. Before the day of competitive entrance examinations, required academic high school credits sifted out the more able students. Without setting up high admission standards, our leading colleges could never turn out the excellent product that gives a college its high rating.

The new developments in college admissions policy today are, first, planned selection, with criteria for admission carefully set up to identify the best talent, and, second, the equalizing of college opportunities for all youth who can meet the established admissions criteria, without regard for social distinctions.

In former years, whether or not a youth went on to college was largely a matter of family tradition. The picture of a presentable youth automatically entering the college of his parents' choice following graduation from prep school has been radically altered.

Today the leading colleges admit students on a competitive, selective basis through an extensive system of examinations and collection of records concerning the student's past school achievement, his experiences, background, purposes, and personality traits. Admission to the leading institutions is slanted more and more toward young people of high promise who have prospects of going on for graduate study.

Entrance examinations for foreign universities screen secondary school graduates for the specific faculty or department in which they desire to specialize professionally. The policy is to admit all *lycée* graduates who wish to attend. For various reasons, some of these young people are poorly equipped for university work. Although a *lycée* graduate enrolling for preprofessional courses in the university hopes to obtain a diploma, few students actually receive degrees. This is in direct contrast to the situation in American institutions where a third to a half of college entrants remain to graduate.

RECORDS OF HIGH SELECTIVITY

The fact that selective admission on the basis of scholastic aptitude, prediction of probable success in college, and career promise works very well is supported by the correlations reported between selection criteria and follow-up data. Little reported that students at the University of Wisconsin who entered as freshmen in 1949 and continued until graduation tended as college entrants to rank in the highest fourth of the class both on the Henman-Nelson Test of Mental Abilities and in class rank (1959). These students tended to come from large high schools, and, in general, their parents held professional or executive positions.

Colleges differ in their intellectual demands. Some colleges enroll only the top 5 per cent in the college age group, whereas others accept students in the upper 50 per cent. A student's success tends to be relative to the ability level of the college population with which he is competing. A good student might have a struggle in a college with high selectivity, whereas he might be a top student in a less-selective school.

COLLEGE PREDICTION FROM SCHOOL MARKS AND IQS

When grading standards at different high schools are put on a common scale, exceptionally good predictions of college success as measured by freshman grades can be made from high school marks combined with achievement test results, according to a report of Spaulding (1960).

The IQ most frequently stated as the average in a typical college is 120, although, it may be around 116, about ten points above the general high school average in the freshman class of a less highly selective institution. The entire college population in the grade A institutions tends to be mentally gifted in comparison with like-age young people in the general population. The median score of University of Chicago students on the American Council on Education Psychological Examination is around the 90th percentile. If an estimated 5 per cent of all college students are in the superior-ability class, this means that out of the 600,000 freshmen who enter college in the United States each year, 30,000 merit attention as truly remarkable young people. Carefully selected students entering college today are by no means a homogeneous group. Among any freshman class there is tremendous diversity in talents and interests as well as in tentative career plans.

Which Students Seek a College Education?

Who goes to college? Of those who should go to college how many actually go? Why do some qualified students fail to attend? These questions are being asked by all high school and college authorities who are concerned about the conservation of superior talent.

Although failure of the potentially gifted to continue in school is only one source of educational waste, it looms as one of the most significant in view of the need for greater reserves of trained manpower everywhere around the world.

Talent loss is broadly defined as the failure of any young person to achieve in terms of his potential. The educator's concern is largely with the waste that ensues from the failure of highly promising students to continue in college or professional schools, and the failure of outstanding scholars to undertake graduate work. The percentage of loss is defined in terms of the cutoff point arbitrarily chosen to distinguish exceptionally capable students.

The most insistent problem in higher education today is to bring into institutions of higher education those of outstanding ability who are now barred by social-class distinctions or other chance factors. The colleges are eager to extend the privileges of higher education to youths of all social strata without any restrictions save evidence that they have the ability and ambition to study for a college degree.

Some years ago, Dr. Walter V. Bingham, whose army experience included mental testing of over 10 million men, reported that more than a million men in the top intellectual levels, with strong leadership potential, had not completed high school, much less gone on for further training. Even today an estimated 200,000 of the country's most promising youths fail each year to obtain any education beyond high school. Another significant finding is that fewer girls than boys go on to college or remain to graduate. The proportion is about 5 to 7.

In France, a twenty-year-old youth of superior intelligence from an impoverished farm family was recently discovered through military recruitment screening tests. From the age of fourteen, this youth had been working as a laborer on his family's farm. He not only made the highest score the officials had ever seen on the French army test, but completed the test at record speed. Instead of being required to enter the armed forces, the youth was sent to a high school where in five months he completed the equivalent of a six-year course. His memory is said to be prodigious; in fact, his remarkable abilities were recognized by his teachers in the early grades.

The questions "Who goes to college?" and "Who should go to college?" have been pondered for many years. In 1935 Dr. Herbert A. Toops of the Ohio State University inaugurated a series of studies of the college-going tendencies of Ohio high school graduates. The results were summarized in a series of *College Realization Bulletins, 1936–1937*. The per cent of Ohio high school graduates who were most likely to succeed in college, according to the principals' estimates of those who actually entered college, was 37.24 of a total of 2,793 students.

In 1949 a commission was appointed by the Conference Board of the Associated Research Councils, Washington, D.C., to determine how well the nation was using its resources of talent and intellectual ability. This was the beginning of a period of increasing attention to manpower problems. The commission studied the supply of persons in the natural and social sciences, the humanities, the professions, and other fields of high-level specialization, including growing demands both here and abroad for specialists in every field, and analyzed the potential supply of new talent.

This work was continued and extended in 1951 by a commission headed by Dr. Dael Wolfle that sought (1) to identify in the first two decades of life young persons who were likely to become outstanding in various fields and (2) to advance research concerning the achievement of the gifted and their contributions to society (1954). Attention centered on the subsequent educational careers of high school graduates.

The published report revealed a shocking loss of high-level intellectual resources. Fewer than half of the upper 25 per cent of American high school graduates went on to college; only six in ten of the top 5 per cent obtained university degrees. Of those in the top 2 per cent in intelligence who were also in the top fifth of their classes in high school, nearly 40 per cent did not go on to college. Although about 25 per cent of all eighteen-year-old youths were found to have IQs of 110 or over, 60 per cent of these bright young people did not go on to college; in fact 20 per cent of them did not complete the secondary school.

Another research project involving extensive studies of the nation's manpower resources was conducted by Dr. Douglas Bray, Dr. Eli Ginsberg, and their associates under the auspices of the Columbia University Graduate School of Business in the 1950s.

Bridgman published figures on college attendance compiled for the National Science Foundation (1959). Of the top 30 per cent of all high school students qualified for college work, 45 per cent of the young men graduated from college. Of the other 55 per cent, two-fifths entered college but did not finish, and one-fifth did not finish high school. Fewer girls than boys completed college, and more dropped out. Of 100 girls in the top 30 per cent of high school youth, 30 graduated from college. Of the remaining 70, about 10 failed to finish high school, 40 finished high school but did not attend college, 20 entered college but did not graduate. The number of talented youths in this category who drop out of school and college is well over 400,000 a year.

In Bridgman's study, data showed that college entrance and retention rates were higher for the top 10 and 5 per cent in intelligence. Of the top 10 per cent (in intelligence) of high school students, about 55 per cent of the boys and 40 per cent of the girls graduated from college, but dropouts in this category were well over 100,000 a year.

Although 40.4 per cent of Kansas high school graduates went to college in 1955, only 61 per cent of the valedictorians and salutatorians did so. Many capable students do not attend college even though they are within easy reach of a good institution.

Chambers made a follow-up study of 341 men and women who were formerly students in St. Louis, Missouri, high schools in the 1920s, all with IQs on early tests of 135 and over (1956). Results showed that of 150 with top-ranking IQs, not more than 75 per cent went on to college, and only 60 per cent graduated. One person who was interviewed said that he had not known about college scholarship opportunities.

A distinction should be made between capable youths who fail to complete high school or do not continue in college through lack of incentive and the nonacademic individuals of limited scholastic promise who fail in high school and could not succeed with the standard college curriculum.

FACTORS THAT INFLUENCE COLLEGE ATTENDANCE

About half of the capable young people who do not go on with their education say they are not financially able to do so. Others are not interested in going on because other opportunities seem more attractive.

A few years ago the Educational Testing Service under the sponsorship of the National Science Foundation made a national survey of the college-going plans of a carefully chosen sample of public high school seniors (Stice, Mollenkopf, and Torgerson, 1956). The survey sought to determine how many students had no college plans, the most effective means of counseling students with respect to college, the kinds of school programs and courses that would motivate interest in going to college, and the use of college scholarship information.

According to this report and others, factors besides lack of financial resources that deter qualified high school graduates from attending college are the significant attitudes of youths and their families toward higher education, the greater appeal of job opportunities, a disinclination to set up and follow through on long-range goals, a lack of educational and career guidance in high school, and the social and cultural background of the student.

Reports of Studies of Student Plans   More attention is now being paid to the social and cultural factors that influence attitudes toward higher education. Studies of high school students' future plans and attitudes have brought to light basic social problems. Youths from homes of low economic status less often go to college, not necessarily because they cannot afford to, but because their home and community life offers little incentive for them to "better themselves." This is often true of Negroes in urban centers as well as children of immigrants. The proportion of those who do not go on to college differs according to cultural and social background as well as the student's sex.

In a survey of 34,151 Wisconsin high school seniors, a very high proportion of those in the top 3 per cent in ability planned to attend college; but of the top 15 per cent, 23 per cent of the boys and 47 per cent of the girls had no college plans (Little, 1959). Boys lacking college plans come from families with average or below-average income and with low occupational status. They had attended small schools and had taken less interest in their studies than the average student.

Statistics prove that students in the following categories are more likely to go to college: boys, though the proportion of girls is rising; those with higher IQs; those from homes of relatively higher economic status; and those living in cities or suburbs, rather than in small towns and rural areas. Certain ethnic groups are not well represented in the college population because of the attitudes of parents. Rural youths, minority groups, and girls are inadequately represented. Among immigrant groups the economic factor is linked with negative parental attitudes.

In 1958, 1,000 graduates of Indiana high schools ranking in the top 10 per cent of their classes were asked why they did not intend to continue their education (Wright and Jung, 1959). Among boys the chief reasons were the desire to earn money immediately, the idea that high school is terminal, or another compelling interest. Among girls the chief reasons were marriage and indifference to further schooling.

The University of New Mexico began a study in 1952 under a Ford Foundation grant to determine whether bright students not attending college because of lack of funds would complete college with scholarship aid (Paschal, 1960). Of the 62 students who were awarded college scholarships 25 came from non-English-speaking homes: 23 of them were from Spanish-speaking homes, and 2 were Indians. The careers of these and other students in subsequent years were followed. Out of 193 students, 83 failed to complete college. Although 17 of the dropouts were doing better than average work, they left college for lack of interest. Lack of motivation was also a cause in a number of academic failures. The conclusion was reached that lack of orientation toward higher education, due to cultural factors, may be a greater barrier to attending and completing college than financial need.

In high school and even more so in college, continuing in school is not seen as furthering the goals of girls. The low priority given to higher education for young women reflects the notion that college is of little use to girls who will soon marry and raise families, that it may even lessen their chance of marriage. The girls are expected to assist the family financially while the boys go on with their education.

Claudette, an adolescent girl with a high IQ, told her English teacher that she intended to get a job as a secretary immediately following graduation from high school. When the question of college was raised at home, the girl's mother reminded her that she would have to help support her four younger brothers. The teacher has been trying to persuade the girl that she should enter the local public college for which she is eligible.

Although the proportion of girls in college today is almost as high as that of boys, girls more frequently drop out before completing a four-year course; they are not so apt to take intellectually demanding courses, and they less often go on for graduate work. Top-level womanpower cannot be effectively developed until more girls go on to college with serious purposes in mind.

The matter of motivation and attitude is particularly baffling to college authorities. College must seem a remote, unreal world, an impractical ambition to a family totally lacking in college background. Unfortunately, the movies give a distorted picture of college as a sort of hangout for rich boys with time on their hands.

The Relation of Socioeconomic Status to College Attendance   Surveys of students' backgrounds invariably disclose the influence of socioeconomic status on college-going rates. A report by Havighurst showed that whereas 85 per cent of top-ranking boys from good homes went on to college and 70 per cent of the girls, not more than 10 per cent of boys and 5 per cent of girls of equally high ability but of low economic status continued their education beyond high school (1960).

College attendance at the leading private institutions is still largely weighted in favor of those who can afford the staggering tuition and living expenses, although large scholarship and loan funds are available to high-ranking students. In the United States almost half the population of the Ivy League colleges are graduates of independent private schools enrolling a mere 2 per cent of all high school students in the country. The state universities with modest fees and the municipal colleges and universities with nominal fees are crowded with students who wish to obtain a college education at small cost.

In low-income families, a student's educational ambitions tend to reflect the father's level of education and the father's occupation, regardless of the individual's career potential. The mother's status and ideas on the subject appear to have less influence on college-going attitudes.

Personal Motivation and College Attendance   Whether or not a promising youth continues his education beyond high school depends largely on personal motivation. Those who are strongly motivated will make every effort to go to college. Others may be diverted by outside pressures from thinking of the possibility. The problem is complicated by the fact that these young people are of legal working age and have attractive job opportunities open to them.

A promising youth is more apt to plan for college if a teacher or counselor actively encourages him to do so. Dr. Walter H. Bingham once said that as he was nearing the end of high school with no thought of continuing his education, one of his teachers urged him to apply for college. Young people who talk about college with their parents and friends are more likely than others to attend.

The Junior College   The junior college serves as an intermediate institution for high school graduates who are not certain of their plans or for those who are reluctant to leave the community to launch into a four-year program of college studies. A mushrooming junior college may be instrumental in unearthing hidden talents; it may reveal students of unexpected powers who can be persuaded later to transfer to a four-year institution. This is one way, too, of taking care of the less socially mature students who finish high school early but are not quite ready to leave home.

Identifying Outstanding Students

College admissions officers have not discovered or invented any perfect device identifying outstanding college applicants. The requirement that the student complete 16 units in academic courses is no longer considered a valid criterion of probable success in college because these units have no uniform value from school to school, and their completion does not necessarily signify that the student has the requisite intellectual capacity for college studies. The Eight-year Study proved that there is no close relationship between curriculum patterns and courses of study in high school and later college success (Aikin, 1942).

The record of members of the Armed Forces selected for advanced officer's training in college primarily on the basis of allover competence proved the fallacy of relying on the student's previous schooling as an indicator of college aptitude; rather, it proved the validity of objective appraisal of academic ability.

High school marks are not infallible predictors of college success. Top-ranking students in high school may make B grades in college and even drop out before graduation, according to the report of Little (1959). Over and above the ability to earn high marks, the trait of true scholarliness is indispensable for high-standard college work.

College selection is most frequently based on results of standard competitive aptitude tests combined with evidence of competence in academic studies furnished by school marks and other records through four or six years. Scores on the most reliable college aptitude tests have considerable predictive capacity for the student's later showing in college, even his degree of success in a particular college. The results of the College Entrance Examination Board tests evaluated in the light of the student's total school record are considered the best indicator of aptitude for college success; but personal traits also count, especially motivation, drive to excel, continued interest, stamina, effective study habits, and social intelligence.

The Biographical Inventory   More attention is now being paid to the student's biographical inventory from the time of high school entrance, his special talents and interests, hobbies, activities, and occupations, in addition to his academic record. The use of the biographical inventory for screening the gifted was mentioned in Chapter Six.

Anastasi, of Fordham University, New York, has evaluated the use of the comprehensive biographical inventory in appraising the aptitudes of young people and predicting college success (1960). Validation of the biographical inventory proved that the device differentiated better among three groups varying in college adjustment than did aptitude, achievement, personality, and interest tests.

Other Indicators of Outstanding Ability   The National Merit Scholarship Corporation conducts research in the identification of talent, the forecasting of college achievement from secondary school records, and the conservation of talent. A study by Weir (1963) explored the characteristics of scholars selected primarily on the basis of comprehensive achievement and scholastic aptitude tests. The report disclosed that more finalists came from families of higher socioeconomic status than was the case in a random sampling of college students that served as a normative comparison group. More were males, more received college honors (71 per cent were on the dean's list), more finalists planned to go ahead with graduate study (two out of three), and more tended toward research and academic careers. Working with ideas and having the opportunity to be original and creative appeal to these young people more than to the average college student. They are less interested in security than in opportunity for leadership.

With the wealth of talent knocking at their doors, the leading colleges are now seeking something more in their applicants than ability to go through college with a good record. They are also looking for evidence of career success that will reflect credit on the college. "Potential for leadership" is a trait that is considered, along with other essential criteria for college admission today, the trait that tends to predict the distinctive "American career style," as it is known abroad.

The traits sought in winners of Rhodes scholarships according to the statement of the founder, Cecil Rhodes, are qualities of distinction whether of intellect or character, truthfulness, courage, devotion to duty, sympathy, kindliness, unselfishness, fellowship, moral force of character, capacity for learning, and an interest in others. This list reflects the ultimate in qualification for "greatness" in students of college age.

Planned Talent Search in the Secondary School

One of the measures that has been taken to counteract the waste of our human resources is the planned talent search. Programs have been set up in schools, in departments of education, by private foundations, and by other agencies to seek out the ablest young people while they are still in high school.

Colleges are seeking applicants with the combination of qualities college work requires regardless of the students' educational plans, financial condition, racial background, or any other chance factors. If the college could carry on this search on a nationwide scale, it would constitute the greatest advance ever taken in higher education. The planned talent search in secondary school as the basis for honor awards and college scholarships has become a nationwide program and is one of the most promising features of the present educational scene. The expectation is that these programs will discover more future talent for government posts as well as for private industry and the professions; that more bright youths will plan to attend college; that more of the nation's womanpower will be salvaged for service in public life; and that more youths of all minority groups will be located and enabled to extend their education.

High school and college authorities point to the success of athletic talent scouts in recruiting promising athletes for college teams. Here is a model for recruiting top scholars for the colleges, provided there is sufficient financial and alumni support.

Along with the talent search movement has gone the necessary accompaniment, extensive scholarship aid for all worthy students on the basis of financial need. The prize for scholarship winners is not only a free college education, but usually excellent job opportunities after graduation as well.

THE PROCESS OF TALENT SEARCHING

The chief questions confronting the talent searchers are what traits to look for, what techniques to use in exploring high aptitude and talent in young people, and what educational guidance to give the young people after they have been located. The whole process is complicated by the different levels of student ability found in various colleges and the unequal requirements for admission; a few selective "status" colleges receive the lion's share of applications.

Recruitment of talent is the joint responsibility of the secondary schools and the colleges. Although the process of sifting for gifted college material is a task for secondary school administrators and guidance officers, the standards of selection are set up by the colleges. For this reason, there must be close liaison between the high schools and the colleges to which students seek admission. This involves exchange of information about the quality of student applicants and the academic goals and instructional standards of the colleges. Suggestions concerning college advisement for high school students and their parents are given in Chapter Fourteen. One recommendation is that "talent scout" committees be set up in the high schools to consider all matters pertaining to the identification of exceptional students. Instead of the individual college doing its own talent scouting, the trend is toward broader programs set up on a statewide or national basis to establish pools of talent. These enterprises are headed by experts with trained staffs.

Organized talent search programs have been concerned primarily with locating the ablest high school students in science and mathematics, yet only a few students have the interest and aptitude to train for top-level careers in science. Educators have warned that science talent scouting may be overdone; other specialties are equally important.

In the opinion of Dr. Roger Lennon, director of the Division of Test Research and Service, Harcourt, Brace, & World, Inc., the search for mathematics and science talent should be but one phase of a comprehensive program for the discovery and development of all sorts of talent.

In spite of the manifest advantages of talent search programs conducted by schools and other agencies, these programs run the danger of depending too largely on superficial group testing, not enough on long-range study of individuals. Critics point out that ratings of traits such as creativity are neglected; talents and aptitudes not revealed in school achievement remain undiscovered, and knowledge of the genuine intellectual traits of the selected students is inadequate. The role of self-motivation and other personal traits in the emergence of talent is little understood.

Personal traits other than intellectual superiority shown by outstanding college students provide clues to the qualities that are desired in college applicants. In the judgment of Morgan, who explored the traits of achieving and nonachieving college students (1952), these include:

Maturity and seriousness of purpose

Awareness and concern for others

A sense of responsibility

Dominance, persuasiveness, and self-confidence

Motivation to succeed

Dr. Henry Chauncey of the Educational Testing Service urges that talented youths be identified before adverse environmental circumstances operate to lessen their chances of success in advanced education. This means that search for promising students must begin in the early high school years.

In 1950 representatives of the Markle Foundation expressed concern about the identification of persons in the first two decades of life who would be most apt to become outstanding in various fields of endeavor, and asked the Social Science Research Council to study the problem. A committee was organized to conduct research on the factors related to achievement and the contributions of gifted individuals to society. The report of this committee headed by David C. McClelland was entitled *Talent and Society* (1958). It contains an excellent chapter on the identification of talent, as well as theoretical discussions of the nature of talent.

College Talent Search Programs   The oldest college talent search program, that of the College Entrance Examination Board, has been operating for over half a century. Other programs are organized on a national, statewide, or private basis.

Beginning in 1942, Science Service inaugurated the national talent search for Westinghouse science scholarships to discover youths with exceptional science talent and to ensure their future education.

The science talent search, conducted annually by the Science Clubs of America, is open to secondary school seniors. The students take a difficult scientific aptitude test and also submit written descriptions of science research projects they have undertaken.

A number of states have instituted statewide testing programs for evaluating the aptitudes of all high school youth to provide the state-supported colleges and universities with information about applicants. These programs have been conducted annually, in some cases for a period of years. Ohio, Iowa, Minnesota, and Oregon are illustrations. One purpose of these programs is to obtain evidence to support the granting of college loan funds.

Minnesota has for many years operated a statewide testing program in which results of standard aptitude and achievement tests, grades in high school courses, and rank in the senior class in high school are combined to yield a "college ability rating" on every student graduating from a Minnesota high school. These data are furnished to the state university and to other public and private colleges within the state.

Indiana University has established a program to help high schools of the state locate and counsel talented secondary school students. The talented student is defined as one who is superior to his peers in general intelligence and in talent for work in any useful area of learning. Many high schools of the state now participate in this program.

New York State conducts a Regents' scholarship contest annually in which the winners, all residents of New York State, receive college scholarships. Pennsylvania has a plan to award state scholarships ranging from $100 to $1,000 to the top 5 per cent of high school graduates in the state on the basis of scholarship and academic talent. The Engineering Experiment Station at the University of Wisconsin has launched a long-range research program to discover students of superior ability for careers in engineering and science as well as in the liberal arts.

In Florida, the state university conveys information concerning its program for gifted students to the high schools of the state through conferences with educational leaders, county superintendents, and state education officials.

A growing number of communities now conduct their own "Go to College" programs, assist in the selection of candidates, and conduct campaigns for scholarship funds for worthy students. The Scientech Club of Indianapolis, whose members are all leading engineers and scientists in that city, formed an education committee to explore ways of encouraging students with potential engineering talent to continue their education.

The proposal has been made that the separate states in the United States set up a central registry for all gifted young people comparable to the registration of blind or handicapped persons in some states. The chief difficulty is deciding on standards of giftedness for inclusion of individuals in the register.

Broad-band Youth-assessment Programs and College Prediction Several youth-assessment programs now under way in the United States and Canada are accumulating extensive comparative records on all aspects of achievement and performance that will be invaluable in college talent recruitment. The comprehensive exploration of the talents and achievements of high school youth that was begun in 1960 under the direction of Dr. John C. Flanagan was referred to in Chapter Six. In the spring of 1960 nearly 500,000 students in over 1,000 junior and senior high schools, a sampling of one-twentieth of the nation's schools, took an extensive series of tests measuring aptitudes, abilities, achievement, and background factors. This census of a cross section of young people will produce new evidence concerning the extent to which capable youth go on to college, as well as the extent of talent loss when those who rate in the upper 10 per cent of high school graduates fail to continue their education.

The study of all the high school graduates in the province of Ontario, Canada, known as the Atkinson Study of the Utilization of Student Resources, was mentioned in Chapter Five. This study originated in concern over the waste of talent in high school and the high failure rate in the first year of the university. Educational leaders in Ontario, as elsewhere, were expressing growing concern about questions such as: Who goes to college? Who should go to college? Why do some promising young people fail to enter college? As a result of the Atkinson study, more attention has been given to guidance in the high school and to financial aid for worthy students. University admission practices have also been influenced by these studies.

RECRUITING DISADVANTAGED STUDENTS FOR COLLEGE

Among the students both here and abroad who do not continue their education through high school and college are many who have been handicapped from early youth by poverty, racial discrimination, cultural deprivation, or other social disadvantages. An intensive effort is now being made to free exceptional young people from the limitations that have prevented full recognition and fostering of talent wherever it may be found.

With the assistance of a grant from the Rockefeller Foundation, Antioch College has embarked on a program to discover talented Negro students and to help them qualify for college. Although this college has always been open to Negroes, the authorities are convinced that there are many more Negro youths of college caliber than the small proportion applying for admission from year to year represents. The program seeks to identify, encourage, and assist able students who have not planned on attending college, and to devise methods of appraising qualities of young people who lack some of the standard skills.

As noted above, National Merit Scholarship winners have come largely from homes of superior socioeconomic status. In a New York City junior high school in a slum area enrolling 1,400 students, tests and ratings located only 50 in the ninth grade who could be considered "college caliber." The leaders of talent promotion projects hope that by supplying cultural advantages now lacking in the homes and communities where these children live, more will be able to continue in school and take advantage of college opportunities. Large financial support for this effort has come from both public and private sources.

The Higher Horizons programs described in Chapter Twelve represent an effort through educational leadership to lift the sights of underprivileged youth who might never think of aspiring to a college education, much less prepare for it. By starting early, the school hopes to compensate for negative factors in the child's life and upbringing so that the most capable will be more nearly on a par with children from more fortunate homes who are sent to college as a matter of course.

The disadvantages cannot be made up suddenly at the point of college entrance. There are study habits to be learned, gaps in common information to be made up, handicaps in vocabulary and English expression to be overcome, attitudes toward college to be changed. Part of the developmental program involves convincing parents who might interfere with a gifted youth's educational plans. The leaders of the movement feel that the program is worth the effort no matter how limited its initial success may be.

With the establishment of urban colleges, a more representative clientele is able to continue their education—boys and girls who live at home, possibly working their way through college, and young people who are second- or third-generation Americans rather than "old stock." They are of all races and creeds, often members of minority groups, some from disadvantaged slum homes. This is the best thing that could happen in any nation so long as reasonably high standards for college admission are maintained.

Brooklyn College of the City University of New York has

been working through a talent search committee with personnel of the local high schools to locate bright students of limited socio-economic background and to encourage them to enroll in college following high school graduation, provided they meet the standards for admission.

Aspira is a private educational agency in New York City set up to further the aspirations of young Puerto Ricans who may be interested in going ahead for professional study after completing high school. Aspira clubs have been formed in several high schools with the cooperation of the board of education. Thus the Puerto Rican youth of ability finds new opportunities open to him. A number of college scholarships have been granted through this organization.

Negro students have been severely handicapped because of restrictions set up by some schools and colleges as well as some state governments. In the Southern states, in particular, where educational institutions for Negroes and whites have been separate, only about 60 per cent as much money is spent for the higher education of Negroes as is spent for whites. Yet the gifted Negro student's vocational future depends largely on whether or not he goes on to college.

The National Association for the Advancement of Colored People, in collaboration with other agencies and foundations, is conducting a persistent talent search to ensure that a larger proportion of youths in minority racial groups receive the advantages of higher education. There are foundations offering medical scholarships and other study opportunities for Negroes beyond the undergraduate level. The National Scholarship Service and Fund for Negro Students has enabled a record number of promising high school graduates of the Negro race to obtain college education in recent years. It also finances the education of Southern Negroes in Northern college preparatory schools. Ford Foundation funds have supported the work of this organization. The results of the program have been highly satisfactory. This service has published a booklet to help communities seek out and assist able young Negroes who might not otherwise have an opportunity to attend college (Plaut, 1957).

SCHOLARSHIP AID FOR PROMISING STUDENTS

College training at public expense is now recognized as a sound educational policy. But until such a policy can be instituted,

scholarship aid is necessary in thousands of cases if the most tal
ented of our high school graduates are to continue their education.
Students from all but the most wealthy families are out-priced
in the expensive private colleges unless there is generous scholarship
aid. Even students attending local colleges and living at home
may need financial aid. Poverty, the high school and college
authorities note, however, is not a deterrent in recruiting athletic
talent for the colleges.

The past decade saw more developments to assist the gifted
in going to college than any previous period in educational history.
Most of the regional and national scholarship programs have been
established since 1950. As a result of these efforts, there has been
a marked increase in the number and value of college scholarship
awards.

The National Science Foundation established by Congress in
1950 awards approximately 700 fellowships a year to science students who compete for the awards in a nationwide contest. The
present Federal government program of loans and scholarships for
college is certain to be greatly extended in the future. Scholarships
are now available under the National Defense Education Act of
1958, and in the education act of 1961 there was provision for
a five-year program of Federal grants and loans to promote higher
education. About 40,000 Federal scholarships for college students
are provided annually.

The proposal has been made that a nationwide system of
centers be set up where able students could register for Federal
scholarships. Colleges and universities participating in this plan
would apply for funds, $700 for each student, limited to 10 per
cent of the freshman class. Students would be selected from those
enrolled at one of 50 or more scholarship centers, one in each
state. Each student registering would file his high school records,
financial status report, results of college aptitude test scores, and
other pertinent information. Some authorities advocate that Federal
funds be allocated for stipends to worthy students of high caliber
beginning in the upper years of high school and continuing through
college.

In the spring of 1961 Governor Nelson Rockefeller of New
York signed a bill that provided scholarship grants to New York
State high school graduates who qualify for the college of their
choice. As a result, college scholarships in amounts up to $700
annually for four years were awarded to 16,242 graduating high
school seniors in New York State during the first year.

Other Sources of Scholarship Aid   Many big business firms grant liberal scholarship aid to colleges for qualified students who otherwise could not afford to attend. The Westinghouse Company pioneered in awarding college scholarships and fellowships to winners in national science contests. Other organizations that now maintain large scholarship programs, not necessarily limited to science, include General Motors, the Sears-Roebuck Foundation, the Ford Foundation, the Union Carbide and Carbon Corporation, Merck and Co., Du Pont, Bell Telephone Laboratories, Gulf Oil Corporation, Eastman Kodak Company, E. I. Lilly Company, and Time, Inc. The Texas Company recently launched an "aid-to-education" program by offering 160 scholarships and 140 unrestricted grants-in-aid of $1,500 each to colleges and universities.

Communities everywhere have set up local college scholarship funds to which business, industry, and other organizations contribute. Through the talent search project started in Hartford, Connecticut, sponsored jointly by the Hartford Board of Education, the Hartford Foundation for Public Giving, and the National Scholarship Service and Fund for Negro Students, financial assistance is to be given to selected talented students without reference to race or creed.

Support from the Ford Foundation   The Fund for the Advancement of Education, which was established by the Ford Foundation in 1951, decided at its first board meeting to institute a program of college scholarships for able students who had not yet graduated from high school, with the expectation that they might complete college before entering military service. In 1955 the Ford Foundation made 20 million dollars available to establish the National Merit Scholarship Organization, which also receives assistance from the Carnegie Corporation, as well as from business and industrial firms. About 1,000 scholarships are awarded annually to high school graduates through the National Merit Scholarship Program. The size of the grant generally depends upon the financial need of the student; there is no ceiling on the amount to be granted. The average four-year scholarship is about $6,000; the college that the student attends makes an additional grant about equal to the student's tuition. According to a report of Stalnaker, a substantial majority of the first winners in the National Merit Scholarship Program have graduated from college with outstanding records (1961).

In some communities in England the local education authorities have adopted the policy of paying the tuition fees and maintenance of any of their students who are selected for admission to a university. The Ministry of Education has also increased the number of state scholarships.

The public colleges and universities that charge only nominal tuition and cater to students who, for the most part, live at home are also beginning to offer scholarship incentives to help deserving students of high promise remain in college.

A pamphlet on scholarship opportunities, prepared by Fornwalt, *Scholarship Information Sources for Educational and Vocational Counselors,* may be obtained from the Big Brother Movement, Inc., 33 Union Square West, New York 3, New York.

Scholarship Aid for Graduate Students   Graduate scholarships and fellowships in all fields are available for well-qualified students. One illustration is the scholarship program of the Woodrow Wilson Foundation to prepare graduate students for college teaching. Applicants for graduate scholarships are expected not only to have good undergraduate records, but also to show traits of self-discipline and originality.

Scholarships for Study Abroad   Scholarships available to American students for study abroad had their inception in 1902 with the Rhodes scholarship program for study at Oxford University. More recently international exchanges have tremendously increased these opportunities on a worldwide basis. Proposals have been made that organizations such as NATO and SEATO finance educational grants for promising bright students on an international basis as one means of matching the output of trained personnel in the Soviet Union.

References

Aikin, Wilford M.: *The Story of the Eight-year Study,* Harper & Row, Publishers, Incorporated, New York, 1942.

Anastasi, Anne, M. J. Meade, and A. A. Schneiders: *The Validation of a Biographical Inventory as a Predictor of College Success,* Educational Testing Service, Princeton, N.J., 1960.

Bestor, Arthur: *The Restoration of Learning,* Alfred A. Knopf, Inc., New York, 1956.

Bond, Horace Mann: *The Search for Talent,* Inglis Lecture, The Graduate School of Education, Harvard University, Cambridge, Mass., 1957.

Bowles, Frank H.: *Access to Higher Education; The Report of the International Study of University Admissions,* Columbia University Press, New York, 1963.

Brehaut, Willard: *The Atkinson and Carnegie Studies of Student Talent in Ontario,* Department of Educational Research, The University of Toronto, address at the American Educational Research Association, Atlantic City, N.J., February, 1962.

Bridgman, Donald S.: *Losses of Intellectual Talent from the Educational System Prior to Graduation from College,* National Science Foundation, Washington, D.C., 1959.

Chambers, Catherine P.: *A Follow-up Study of Gifted St. Louis Pupils of the 1920's,* unpublished doctoral dissertation, Washington University, St. Louis, 1956.

Edgerton, H. A., and S. H. Britt: The First Annual Science Talent Search, *The American Scientist,* 31:55–68, 1943.

Havighurst, Robert J.: *American Higher Education in the 1960's,* Ohio State University Press, Columbus, Ohio, 1960.

Hoffman, Benesh: Some Remarks concerning the First Annual Talent Search, *The American Scientist,* 31:255–262, 1943.

Hollingshead, Byron S.: *Who Should Go to College,* Columbia University Press, New York, 1952.

Little, J. Kenneth: The Persistence of Academically Talented Youth in University Studies, *Educational Record,* 40:237–241, 1959.

Little, J. Kenneth: The Wisconsin Study of High School Graduates, *Educational Record,* 40:123–128, 1959.

McClelland, David C., and others: *Talent and Society: New Perspectives in the Identification of Talent,* D. Van Nostrand Company, Inc., Princeton, N.J., 1958.

Morgan, H. H.: A Psychometric Comparison of Achieving and Nonachieving College Students of High Ability, *Journal of Consulting Psychology,* 16:292–298, 1952.

National Manpower Council: *A Policy for Skilled Manpower,* Conservation of Human Resources Project, Graduate School of Business, Columbia University, New York, Columbia University Press, New York, 1954.

Paschal, Elizabeth: *Encouraging the Excellent: Special Programs for Gifted and Talented Students,* The Fund for the Advancement of Education, New York, 1960.

Plaut, Richard L.: *Blueprint for Talent Searching,* National Scholarship Service and Fund for Negro Students, 1957.

Selection and Guidance of Gifted Students for National Survival, Report of the Twentieth Conference, Educational Records Bureau, American Council on Education, Washington, D.C., 1956.

Spaulding, Geraldine: *The Application of Secondary School Cumulative Record Data to the Prediction of College Success,* Educational Records Bureau, New York, 1960.

Stalnaker, John M.: Recognizing and Encouraging Talent, *American Psychologist,* 16:513–522, 1961.

Stice, G., W. G. Mollenkopf, and W. S. Torgerson: *Background Factors and College-going Plans among High Aptitude Public High School Seniors,* Educational Testing Service, Princeton, N.J., 1956.

Strodtbeck, F. L.: Family Interaction Values and Achievement, in David C. McClelland and others, *Talent and Society: New Perspectives in the Identification of Talent,* D. Van Nostrand Company, Inc., Princeton, N.J., 1958.

Weir, W. D.: Research and the Talented, National Merit Scholarship Corporation Report, *The Superior Student,* 5(3):7–8, 1963.

Wolfle, Dael: *America's Resources of Specialized Talent,* Harper & Row, Publishers, Incorporated, New York, 1954.

Wright, Wendell W., and Christian Jung: Why Capable High School Students Do Not Continue Their Schooling, *Bulletin of the School of Education, Indiana University,* 35:1–78, 1959.

Chapter Seventeen

PROGRAMS
FOR
SUPERIOR
STUDENTS
IN
COLLEGE

Education at the college level is concerned with arousing the spirit of scientific inquiry through which students may gain new insights into the physical world and into the relationships in society and government that have influenced world progress. This is accomplished by bringing students into contact with great ideas that have dominated thinking through the centuries, ideas that the student gains from communication with his instructors and through wide reading. As a result, the individual is equipped to approach new problems with mature insight and skill.

The four-year academic colleges, by focusing on liberal education in the arts and sciences, graduate young people of broad culture and humanitarian sympathies rather than narrowly trained specialists in a particular field. Preparation for the learned professions—medicine, law, architecture, social work, the ministry, etc.—tends to be concentrated in the graduate school. Preparation for teaching begins in the last year or two of college and continues in postgraduate study. Engineering education, formerly the study of technical subjects, now requires a foundation of liberal arts and sciences with emphasis less on the practical application of science than on theoretical concepts. College-trained people with versatile minds are equipped to deal with all sorts of problems for which they have not been specifically prepared.

Studies of college graduates do not show a close correspondence between the undergraduate major and the area of career specialization. According to a recent study, 62 per cent of college-educated executives were in occupations unrelated to their undergraduate majors. Training for the work was gained on the job or through a series of different jobs.

Young people in increasing numbers enter such fields as advertising, public relations, industrial management, government, and civil service. Dr. Ralph Tyler, director of the Center for Advanced Study in the Behavioral Sciences of Stanford University, has estimated that more than 50 per cent of the occupations this year's college graduates will enter did not exist when these young people were born.

BRIDGING THE GAP BETWEEN THE ARTS AND SCIENCES

The widening gulf between the liberal arts and scientific studies in college has caused growing concern both here and abroad. C. P. Snow, in *Two Cultures and the Scientific Revolution,* suggested that the remedy for the schism is to be found in liberalizing and broadening the college curriculum for students specializing in either field. Anton Chekhov once said he knew of no better training for a writer than to spend some years in the medical profession.

Focus on the Gifted Student in College

Education today is showing a devotion to high scholarship that is reminiscent of the time when colleges were primarily concerned with intellectual training. Although college students represent a highly selected group of young people, the standard college curriculum is unsuitable for the most superior students. In college, as in the secondary school, the superior student needs to avoid wasteful repetition. He should have challenging work that engages his full powers of imagination and encourages creative thinking and independence of thought and action. As the head of a leading foreign university expressed it, "Students are not bottles to be filled but lamps to be lighted."

Since the early 1950s, the leading institutions have taken definite steps to provide a variety of experimental programs and instructional procedures for superior students. The objectives are not only to enrich college life, but to enable students to achieve more for themselves independently and to advance more rapidly in their studies. Such programs include the following types of provisions:

Admission of qualified students to college before high school graduation—the early-admissions programs

Advanced placement at college entrance; admission to advanced standing on the basis of high school record and exemption examinations, waiving standard prerequisites

Provision of an administrative unit for the gifted, a "college within a college"

Sectioning students on the basis of aptitude and achievement records in particular subjects; offering special sections of courses that make greater intellectual demands on the students than the standard syllabus

Special work and study groups for students capable of advanced work in particular courses

Seminar courses with tutorial instruction for honors students

Independent study supervised by faculty members; the assignment of gifted students to selected professors who are released from part or all of their other teaching assignments

Pursuit of studies in special areas, for example, foreign languages for students inclined toward the foreign service

Exemption from the usual class attendance requirements to enable students to work independently of class requirements

High-speed progress groups for the exceptionally able

Graduate-level studies in the upper college years

Citation of students for awards, dean's list honors, and other forms of recognition for high scholarship

Personal and career counseling for the gifted student by the college personnel office and instructors in tutorial programs

Special assistance for underachievers among students of superior ability

The use of standard, objective-type aptitude and achievement tests has sharpened the entire college picture; first at the admissions level, then for exemptions from common required courses, and, finally, for placement in special programs, particularly honors work and independent study.

In 1953 the University of Florida undertook to provide for gifted students through the following means (Davidson, 1956):

Setting up special sections in English, biological sciences, humanities, American institutions, and other courses so that the rate of progress and breadth of coverage could be adjusted to the capacities of superior students

Developing two new general education courses, one in laboratory sciences and another in mathematics, for nonscience students of superior ability

Emphasizing the study of foreign languages, ancient and modern, throughout the college years so that students could achieve full access to another culture

Assigning a permanent faculty adviser to every superior student from a panel of advisors in the college of arts and sciences from the time of the student's entrance until his graduation

Providing an independent study plan for the superior student in his area of specialized study; permitting some degree of freedom from standard departmental requirements

Offering a reading and discussion seminar in the philosophy of human values to give the superior student fuller awareness of basic interrelations of liberal arts subject matter and the need for standards to guide the individual in his life and work

The most up-to-date information about special programs for talented college students will be found in *The Superior Student*, the bimonthly newsletter of the Interuniversity Committee on the Superior Student. The bulletin is supported by a grant from the Carnegie Corporation. It contains reports of honors programs, scholarship grants, college opportunities for foreign students, college liaison efforts on behalf of the talented, and many other topics.

Acceleration through School and College Articulation

The problem of articulation between the end of high school and beginning of college is crucial because of the waste of time and effort that ensues when students remain in school longer than is necessary. The educational lockstep which holds all students, good, poor, or mediocre in a tight, standard grade sequence does actual harm to the bright, ambitious student. Some unusual students may even be lost to college unless they can move ahead more rapidly than the standard curriculum permits. The findings of the Eight-year Study sponsored by the Progressive Education Association over twenty years ago (Aikin, 1942) disclosed a large amount of duplication and overlapping of high school and college work.

The traditional "sheep skin curtain" between the secondary school and the college is beginning to disappear. Today the high schools and colleges are working together to identify the bright students, to encourage them to go to college, and to save the students' time in bridging over from one level to the next. The School and College Study of The Fund for the Advancement of Education found that gifted students in selected schools could complete the present eight-year secondary school–college sequence in seven years (*Bridging the Gap between School and College,* 1953).

The slack is taken up in one of two ways: The student has the alternative of taking advanced work in high school so that he can save as much as a year in college by entering with advanced standing, or he can enter the freshman year in college on completion of his junior year in high school. Some authorities argue strongly in favor of retaining the gifted for the full high school course and abbreviating or telescoping college programs. Others cite studies of the success of early college admission for selected students. Both the secondary schools and the colleges tend to favor advanced placement over early admission, unless the student is within easy commuting distance of a good college that will accept him.

EARLY–ADMISSIONS PROGRAMS

Admission of occasional students lacking four full years of high school credits has been a policy with some colleges for years. As early as 1919, the University of Chicago precollege schools fed into the university a number of students who were saved a year of regular preparatory work. A highly gifted student could combine his senior year in high school with the first year in college.

In the fall of 1932 President Walter Dill Scott of Northwestern University proposed that half a dozen precocious boys and girls, thirteen to fifteeen years of age, who could meet the entrance requirements be admitted to the freshman class instead of having to wait till the usual age of seventeen or eighteen. The president's experience with an occasional early entrant had proved to be satisfactory.

In 1942 the University of Chicago adopted the policy of admitting students who had not yet completed high school. Although this may have been a wartime emergency, it marked the beginning of wholesale experiments in a redetermination of the best age and other qualifications for entering college.

Program of The Fund for the Advancement of Education   The initial project for saving time for gifted students through closer articulation between the schools and the colleges supported by The Fund for the Advancement of Education was called the "School and College Study of General Education." The organizers of the project realized that there was needless overlap between the curriculum of several of the leading independent preparatory schools and the universities the students tended to enter, as well as discontinuity between the studies undertaken in high school and college. Four years in preparatory school seemed to be a needlessly long period for able students.

In 1951 the fund sponsored an experiment for a school-college plan of acceleration for young people who had not completed four years of high school, although they were mentally and scholastically advanced enough to enter college. This was known as the Early Admissions to College Program. The young people selected for the experiment were sixteen years of age or younger and had completed at least the tenth grade in high school. Twelve cooperating colleges admitted 362 such students in the fall of 1951, and 415 in 1952. These scholars were somewhat brighter to begin with than typical college freshmen, judging from results of scholastic aptitude tests. They were offered scholarships at the colleges they chose to enter.

Each college developed its own program of courses and services for these early-admissions students. Most of the participating colleges gave them the same academic treatment as any other entering freshmen, even to the extent of not identifying them to faculty members.

Outcomes of Early Admission   The Educational Testing Service of Princeton, New Jersey, assisted the fund officers and the colleges in evaluating the outcomes of the program. The accelerated students were compared with those of equivalent ability who had entered college at the same time after completing secondary school. The first report of this program, *Bridging the Gap between School and College,* was published by the fund in 1953. In 1957 a more comprehensive report was published, *They Went to College Early,* summarizing outcomes from the experiment up to that time. (See the end of this chapter for complete references.)

Of the early entrants, 76 per cent were boys and 24 per cent girls; 29 per cent entered before sixteen years of age, and 14 per cent were seventeen years of age; 42 per cent had completed only the tenth grade or sophomore year of high school, 51 per cent the eleventh grade, and 7 per cent the twelfth. Thus the age of the group was about two years lower than the standard college entrance age. Only 9 per cent came from private schools; 84 per cent were from public high schools; 7 per cent came from rural schools. Some 76 per cent of the students came from families of professional, government, and business occupations; the rest came from homes of laborers or farmers. Of the 1952 scholars who graduated, 76 per cent planned to enter graduate work, whereas only 58 per cent of the comparison group had graduate work in mind.

The results indicated that students with as little as ten or ten and a half years of schooling held their own with respect to grade point average. In general, they tended to make excellent records in college. In terms of physical health, mental health, and overall adjustment to college there were no appreciable differences between those who went to college early and the normal entering students, judging from the extensive data that were analyzed. In extracurricular affairs, athletic as well as nonathletic, the early-admissions students were as active as others, in some cases more so. They earned the respect of their teachers; they expressed satisfaction with their college experiences. In most of the participating colleges relatively few of these accelerated scholars withdrew because of academic and general adjustment failures.

At Yale, Columbia, and elsewhere a number of these scholars have been winners of the highest scholastic awards and graduate scholarships. In a number of individual cases they have become outstanding leaders in their colleges. Lack of preparation in terms of specific senior high school courses did not appear to hamper their success.

At Goucher College, of twelve early-admissions scholars who graduated in 1955, five won Phi Beta Kappa honors out of a total of eleven students selected for this honor. Four were presidents of their residence houses on the campus; six were dean's scholars in their junior year, four as early as their freshman year. As a group, their grade point average was 3.99 against 3.51 for the class as a whole. They also held positions of leadership in campus organizations. The final summing up of results for the 800 scholars admitted to the program in 1951 and 1952 showed that, year by year, the scholars outstripped their comparison matchees. Ninety per cent of both the scholars and the comparisons were rated by the faculty as having made "excellent," "good," or "moderately good" overall adjustments, but there was a consistent although slight tendency for more of the scholars to receive "poor" or "very poor" adjustment ratings.

Of the sixty scholars in the first year at the University of Chicago, all but six engaged in campus activities. At Goucher College, despite their youth, the scholars participated as extensively as the matching students in nonathletic campus activities and were far more active in athletics. Moreover, three of the nine elective offices of the freshman class were filled by scholars.

When the participating colleges and universities were asked their judgment as to the wisdom of the early-admissions program, 76 per cent responded in favor, 17 per cent gave divided opinions, and 6 per cent said they considered the policy unwise.

In the senior year, when students were asked their opinion as to whether the early-admissions program was profitable, 75 per cent said yes, very much so; and 15 per cent said yes, with reservations. Personal and social problems were more acute among the scholars than among the older comparison group, but the scholars felt that their difficulties could be overcome through an effective orientation program.

The experience of the colleges is that care must be exercised in the selection of early-admissions scholars to make sure that only the more mature young students are sent to college early. Careful selection is necessary to ensure that they have good health and sufficient stamina as well as maturity.

One impediment in the way of students entering college at the end of the junior year in high school is that they may not be able to qualify for most of the scholarship grants mentioned in Chapter Sixteen, but must be provided for in special accelerated-student assistance programs.

CONCLUSIONS FROM EXPERIMENTS IN EARLY ADMISSION

Fear was expressed in the beginning that early entrance to college would be a disastrous shock to youths below the standard admission age, that they would be misfits socially, and intellectually overstrained, that they might be deprived of opportunities for leadership because of their social immaturity. After a study was made of the social and emotional adjustment of the scholars, the conclusion was reached that the scholars adjusted as well as comparison students and classmates, and that the reasons for the failures among them were the same as for college students in general.

LATER DEVELOPMENTS IN EARLY ADMISSION

The program originally supported by The Fund for the Advancement of Education expanded right along and in 1955 was taken over by the College Entrance Examination Board (CEEB). The leading colleges and universities are now sponsoring their own programs as the result of the success of the original experiment. By 1958, thirty colleges and universities had announced early-admissions programs.

The University of Connecticut has put into operation a program of enrichment and acceleration for the state's superior high school students. These students may be admitted to the university after three years in high school, or they may enter with advanced standing on the basis of college-level courses taken in high school.

In 1958, Brooklyn College initiated a program enabling selected high school seniors to enroll in a college course while still attending a local high school. These students are required to show superior achievement in high school courses and superior scores on the scholastic aptitude tests of the College Entrance Examination Board. High school counselors work with the college authorities in selecting the students.

In the first four years of the program the students successfully completed 115 courses. The records of these students show that 90 of the grades earned in the courses taken were A or B, 24 were C, and there was only 1 D. Seventy-seven courses were completed in foreign languages, twenty in mathematics, seventeen of them at the calculus level and beyond. The remaining courses were divided among social sciences, sciences, and other humanities courses. The first student to enter Brooklyn College under the early-admissions policy attained the highest score of any candidate for the New York State awards for medical study the year he graduated from college.

Advanced–placement and Exemption Programs

In the better colleges today, the freshman program of a decade ago has become obsolete; about half of the highly selected freshman class are beyond the traditional first-year courses in chemistry, physics, English, and history. A substantial proportion have already covered the first semester's course in calculus, even though this course is now offered on a more advanced level than in previous years. Students also enter college today better prepared in foreign languages and science. The prediction is that by 1970 an estimated 200,000 college entrants will begin work at the present sophomore level.

ADVANCED PLACEMENT FOR SUPERIOR STUDENTS

College-level courses in high school through which superior students gain credit for college work on entering college were described in Chapter Fourteen. Students also qualify for exemption credits by taking summer courses or through individual study and tutoring.

Advanced placement has come to be accepted as an economical means of accelerating gifted students through college. With several exemptions and extra courses or summer work, a student can finish college in three years instead of four. Students who begin their college work in the sophomore year can save a year toward graduate study.

PROGRAM OF COLLEGE ENTRANCE EXAMINATION BOARD

The program known as the School and College Study of Admission with Advanced Standing conducted by the College Entrance Examination Board was originated in 1952 by President Gordon Chalmers of Kenyon College and Dr. William Cornog, principal of Central High School, Philadelphia. This study accomplished several objectives. The program:

Provided for assistance in the organization of new college-level courses in a group of cooperating high schools

Conducted examinations for students who completed these courses

Worked out an agreement whereby the cooperating colleges gave college credit and advanced placement to students successfully passing the examinations

Sponsored conferences for teachers in high school and college to improve articulation between these two educational divisions

The exemption examinations were constructed by a joint group of school and college faculty members and were conducted by the Educational Testing Service of Princeton, New Jersey. Mathematics and modern languages have accounted for the largest number of exemptions.

A survey showed that participants in the program graduated from college 1.2 years younger than average; the dropout rate was less than half that of a control group. These students were also more likely to continue on into graduate school. Subsequent evidence has proved the soundness of giving college credit by exemption examination. Students who take a second course after being exempted from the first make higher grades than those who actually took the first course (College Entrance Examination Board, 1954, 1956).

Students taking examinations for exemption from college courses increased from around 1.5 per cent of all entering students in 1955–1956 to 13 per cent in 1960–1961. In 1959 over 10,000 students from 800 schools took tests given by the College Entrance Examination Board to qualify for college credit for advanced courses taken in high school. There are now over 700 secondary schools that cooperate with more than 300 colleges in which students who have taken college-level courses in high school are given exemption from these courses in the freshman year.

POLICIES AND PRACTICES IN THE COLLEGES

Each college is autonomous in its policies concerning the granting of credit for advanced courses. Some colleges give credit automatically to students who have received a grade of 3 or higher on the CEEB Advanced Placement Examination, and also give some consideration to those receiving a lower mark. Some colleges grant a full year of credit, some a half year, and others grant no advanced credit.

Harvard College has experimented with admission of advanced high school graduates to sophomore standing since 1956. In 1960, approximately 42 per cent of Harvard freshmen applied for advanced placement in one or more courses, and about 8 per cent were eligible for full sophomore standing. Results of a seven-year study of Harvard College students who took college-level courses in high school and consequently gained as much as a year's time in college showed that almost half of them earned degrees with high honors or with highest honors. The percentage was even higher, over 80 per cent, for students who went from high school directly into sophomore standing on the basis of work done before entering college.

Mr. R. N. Cunningham, headmaster of the Moses Brown School, Providence, Rhode Island, reported the case of one brilliant boy who as a high school sophomore moved ahead rapidly in mathematics. On entering Harvard College he went directly into junior-year mathematics and also carried advanced work in physics, receiving a straight A average in his work. Another boy took college-level history courses in high school. As a freshman at college he took a course for upper classmen and graduate students in which he did excellent work.

A revised program introduced for undergraduates at Yale reduces the study time required of bright students by granting credit for work done in high school. Columbia College grants up to six points of college credit for college-level courses taken in high school.

In spite of the generally favorable results of advanced-placement courses and programs, a number of criticisms have been voiced against them. There is criticism of:

The lack of uniformity in the policies and practices of the participating colleges and universities

The reluctance of some colleges to grant credit or advanced placement for work done in the secondary school

The lack of publicity informing secondary schools about these programs

The lack of communication and assistance between the participating secondary schools and colleges

Special Programs and Courses for Superior Students

ACCELERATION THROUGH COLLEGE

For the superior student with drive who is well advanced when he enters college, spending four years on the baccalaureate degree is a waste of time. The most capable, as their younger brothers in high school, can telescope or skip some of the standard requirements without any loss in intellectual training. A number of colleges are experimenting with compressed courses or sections for superior students of demonstrated maturity.

At George Washington University the program in effect from September, 1963, does away with the traditional four-year college sequence. All students are designated as introductory, intermediate, or advanced. Placement and movement of students through these three forms is based on individual achievement. Thus an entering student might be technically a freshman, but intermediate in French and advanced in physics.

Columbia College has formulated a program that encourages the best students to move ahead as rapidly as their abilities permit.

At Dartmouth College special classes for gifted students are set up in mathematics for the first two years to permit the most talented students to go at a faster pace than the average. The students are separated according to ability on the basis of previous records.

Yale has scrapped its regular mathematics course and is now offering a new series of courses developed for students of varying levels of competence. This plan prevents competent students from repeating work taken in high school, and advances the talented more rapidly.

Hofstra College, Hempstead, New York, has set up an experimental program for advanced freshmen that will enable them to finish in two and a half years. A group of 120 selected entering students is organized in a separate unit that will compress the first two years of college into one. About 2 per cent of entering freshmen are in this group. The academic year is extended from Labor Day to July 4; the academic week is four days.

At the University of North Carolina superior students are allowed to register for upper college after only a year's study. The university has inaugurated a special program for a group of superior students in the entering class who are selected on the basis of high school records and placement tests. These students stay together as a class in four of the five subjects they take, English, mathematics, philosophy, and social science, with the level of instruction adjusted to the pace of the group.

As the result of favorable outcomes of these experiments, the standard four-year liberal arts program is on the way out for the ablest students.

Summer study of collegiate level has always enabled students to make up credits or to take advanced work. Today there is a greater effort to provide special summer offerings for gifted college students that will enable them to save a year's time.

The publication by Paschal summarizes the achievements of college programs sponsored by The Fund for the Advancement of Education (1960).

Honors Work and Independent Study

The thing that counts most in the college experience is not the size of the buildings or the cost of furnishings, but the intimate contact between the student and a sympathetic teacher who has the insight to discern talent and the skill to develop it. A wise mentor inspires the student to study and releases him from routine assignments for original work.

Honors Programs   The first honors seminars in an American college were instituted by Dr. Frank Aydelotte at Swarthmore College in 1921 to provide more intellectual stimulation for superior students. Dr. Aydelotte, then president of the college, believed that the nation's colleges were not getting the best work from their students because all were subjected to the same curriculum and standards without regard to differences in scholarship and competencies.

Since that time, a steadily increasing number of colleges and universities have offered honors programs for selected students. According to a survey of the Interuniversity Committee on the Superior Student, 171 institutions in 1960 were offering honors programs for undergraduates, with 41 others exploring the possibility. By 1962, 335 programs were being conducted in all types of institutions. At that time there were over 200 full four-year honors programs in colleges all over the country. In typical colleges the proportion of students enrolled in honors courses is about 5 per cent of the total enrollment in upper classes.

Honors programs are the chief means of introducing greater flexibility into the college curriculum and of enabling superior students to investigate subjects with more depth and scope. This type of study makes fuller use of library facilities, fosters cooperation between departments, and elevates the tone of intellectual life on the campus.

Honors programs that are open to superior students beginning in the sophomore year or above replace the usual sequence of college courses with seminars, colloquies, independent research work in library or laboratory, and field work experience. Honors programs in colleges usually involve independent study, with many features of tutorial programs.

Originally, honors work was largely confined to the senior year; it is now increasingly offered in all four years of college. The newer plan is to set up honors programs for carefully selected entering freshmen who will continue in the program throughout their undergraduate years.

The type of honors program developed depends upon the local situation. Each department in the college or university develops its own program. Usually a director, appointed to coordinate all the honors work in the institution, works with a committee or council of staff members representing the various departments.

Since college honors work is offered in the separate subject areas, a student might do honors work in one subject, for example, English literature, but not in others.

Selection of honors students is made on the basis of excellent academic records plus indications of general intellectual superiority, seriousness of purpose, maturity, and sense of responsibility. Students who succeed best in honors work have superior intellectual qualities, the capacity to be self-directive, and the ability to work independently. Individualized counseling is continuous throughout the program.

In *The Superior Student,* the newsletter of the Interuniversity Committee on the Superior Student, January 1961, an inventory was given of honors courses offered in four-year colleges and universities in America, with some indication of the offerings in each of the colleges that sent in a report of its program.

Reports of Honors Programs   The Directed Studies Program at Yale University inaugurated in 1946 is one of the older honors programs. Many of its features are found in the programs of other colleges. The program provides for students who have anticipated college work while in the secondary school and may wish to shorten the usual four-year college span. Both science and mathematics are required along with the humanities. Students enrolled in special honors courses are permitted to study much as they please instead of having to take formal courses, provided they pass examinations in their studies. New interdepartmental honors courses at Yale feature seminars, a syllabus of required reading, and a set of comprehensive examinations rather than formal courses. This program is limited to 10 to 20 students. A super-honors group consisting of 12 selected students works in the same areas as the Directed Studies Program, but in the humanities the group works together in separate discussion classes.

Students at Swarthmore who choose to "read for honors" devote their last two years almost exclusively to independent study and research, attending no formal classes and using the faculty as a resource. Oberlin College has added to its well-established honors program a senior scholar's project, which permits highly qualified students to devote their entire time to independent study during the last year of college. Students who have had outstanding records during previous years in college are nominated for this opportunity by faculty members and are selected by the college committee on honors. The student plans his program with a faculty adviser and consults with other faculty members concerning his work.

An honors program was established at Michigan State University in 1956 to provide gifted students with advanced and enriched studies. Students are invited to enter the program at the freshman or sophomore level. Once in the program, the student is assigned to an adviser who assists him in planning independent study, individual research, seminars, graduate courses, and credit for courses by examination. The student, after admission, has no requirement other than completion of the total hours required for graduation and maintenance of a 3.2 grade index.

Beginning in 1959, the University of Illinois, after some years of experience with honors courses, formally recognized the honors program by appointing a director and faculty honors council to select and guide honor students from their freshman year. These students major in the field of their choice and follow an enriched plan of studies. Students qualify for the program on the basis of high school record and results of aptitude and achievement tests at the time of entering the university. Virtually every academic division has some kind of program for superior undergraduates.

The Fund for the Advancement of Education has supported the new Seattle University honors program for the first two college years. Students are selected for the program on the basis of academic ability and personal characteristics. A senior seminar is available for those who have not taken the freshman honors work.

Brooklyn College Honors Work   There are several varieties of honors work at Brooklyn College of the City University of New York. These include honors courses in all major departments open to qualified junior and senior students, exemption examinations available for elective as well as required courses, and honors projects or independent study undertaken in addition to regular course work under an instructor's sponsorship in virtually every department. The students are excused from regular class attendance, and work space in the library is allocated to them. A grade of A or B in any of the areas of honors work is noted in the student's record as an honors grade. Honors courses are open to qualified juniors and seniors who are admitted to the program by the department chairman on recommendation of staff members. One out of eight graduates has taken one or more honors courses.

At Brooklyn College the emphasis in honors work is on independent study. In the college physics laboratory there is no prescribed work; there are no required experiments. Students are told: "These are the areas we should cover. Here is the apparatus. We'll help you if you need assistance." The experiments are open-ended; there is no "right" answer to be obtained. In economics, during the last year in college, students with the highest ratings receive individual advisement from an economics professor.

Students and instructors say that the advantage of honors work in English is that there is greater opportunity for writing thoughtful and coherent essays. In some cases, the honors program requires the writing of a thesis which combines research work with cogent summary and exposition of the results. Furthermore, the honors instructor is in a better position than regular class instructors to evaluate all the written work of the honors students.

Brooklyn College Scholars' Program   Brooklyn College began operating the Scholars' Program in 1961 with a grant from The Fund for the Advancement of Education. The program frees 2 or 3 per cent of the entering freshman class from formal course requirements to pursue an individualized program. Each student completes the requirements for the baccalaureate degree at his own pace, with increased reliance on independent study. The students also participate in the work of regular classes. Most of them complete their college work in three years. Virtually all these students are headed for graduate studies.

Here are a few examples of work at advanced levels: Five students, in large measure independently, are working through a calculus course that probes deeply into theory and emphasizes rigor in proofs; a group of four students meets once a week to deal with special problems arising out of or related to their work in physics 1.5; two freshmen are pursuing courses normally taken by juniors and seniors, one in biology and one in French. By midterm three students had completed the first term's work in English, and they all enrolled in the next course. Some students accelerate by taking an increased credit load.

City College   A Selected Student Program was inaugurated at City College, the City University of New York, in the fall of 1960. In the evaluation of the program at the end of the first year, participants referred to the extent to which their interests had been broadened and their intellectual curiosity aroused. The program was not "all work and no play" because the students also participated in extracurricular activities at the college.

Some Problems in Honors Work   The introduction of honors work in the colleges raises a number of questions. Does sectioning and the forming of honors groups and seminars of selected students contribute to intellectual snobbishness, clannishness, or solitary habits? These results are unlikely when the students live among other students and participate fully in college life.

A critical problem in the colleges and universities is the dropout rate for honors students, in some cases half the students who enter the programs. This fact raises some question about the criteria for admitting students to the program. A report from the University of Arkansas revealed that successful students in honors work had the capacity to work alone and the ability to formulate problems and possible solutions independently; they had intellectual curiosity and sufficient drive to concentrate on tasks involving long-range goals.

The system of A, B, C grades is inapplicable to college honors work because the lower end of the distribution in scholastic ability is cut off, and there is no provision for "super" grades. This necessitates some system of indicating that grades were earned in honors courses.

INDEPENDENT STUDY AND TUTORIAL PLANS

For many years independent study on a tutorial basis has been the most frequent device for adjusting the college curriculum to the superior student, for putting the student more fully on his own and giving him more latitude for working on his particular study interests.

In independent study, students pursue special topics or develop individual projects under the guidance of faculty members outside of organized courses.

The students themselves recognize what is most worth learning and proceed to acquire it under faculty guidance. Today over a fourth of American institutions of higher learning make some provisions for independent study, usually as a feature of honors work.

Values of independent study for gifted students may be summarized as follows:

The opportunity to undertake advanced studies

The development of initiative and originality in research

The opportunity to link college study with special interests

The necessity of summarizing outcomes of the study in a comprehensive report

Close rapport between students and faculty members

Independent study includes library or laboratory research or field work on a particular research topic. Guidance is provided by a faculty member who advises the student throughout his study and evaluates the final report.

At the University of Illinois, selected students of high ability known as James scholars in honor of a former president follow independent programs of study in chosen fields. The results of the work done by these scholars is now being studied.

The Distinguished Student Program at the University of California at Los Angeles is designed to enrich the work of superior students. Although the students remain in regular sections in all courses, their work goes beyond that of regular class requirements.

Study abroad affords a unique kind of enrichment. The leading colleges now offer a year abroad for work in language study, art, music, and other fields. Gifted students who are interested in opportunities for college study abroad are referred to *Study Abroad–Études à L'Étranger,* a book published by UNESCO, Paris.

GRADUATE AND PROFESSIONAL STUDIES

On attaining the baccalaureate degree, scholarly young people go on preparing for professional careers in graduate school; others continue their preparation in government agencies and industrial firms. Whether or not a college graduate continues his study depends largely upon the advice and support he receives from his college advisers.

A number of experiments are now under way in engineering, medicine, and other fields to speed the progress of the most capable students through the long term of combined undergraduate and graduate training. There is evidence that the seven or eight years now required can be reduced to six, and that in the process a larger number of well-qualified professionals can be turned out. Leading colleges and universities are now starting a six-year medical course for gifted students beginning in the freshman year.

The able student who takes his undergraduate work at a college within a university can telescope his studies to some extent by combining work in the last year of college with the first year of graduate study. At Columbia, students in the last year of college are permitted to take 24 of the 30 points required for the M.A. degree. This might be called advanced placement in graduate school. Radcliffe College juniors in the Special Standing Program may apply for course load reduction to carry on individual work, and in some cases to take courses in the Graduate School of Arts and Sciences. Five hundred American colleges and universities have been asked to participate in a survey of graduate studies being conducted by the National Science Foundation as part of the nation's effort to conserve and develop its scientific manpower.

CONTINUING EDUCATION FOR COLLEGE WOMEN

A new plan rapidly gaining acceptance is that of continuing education for mature college women. Talented women who originally planned to enter the learned professions but were sidetracked by marriage can now fulfill their original ambitions. With their children grown, these women are taking advantage of new opportunities for refresher work at the graduate level in colleges and universities.

Radcliffe College and other institutions now provide graduate studies on an independent basis for women college graduates of former years who are interested in returning to school to extend their knowledge in special fields. The student receives a stipend during a year or two of study to prepare to undertake careers in teaching and other professions. Douglass College of Rutgers University gives refresher training in mathematics for college women graduates who wish to prepare for teaching or other work in which specialized knowledge of mathematics is required. This movement is spreading rapidly throughout the country and is receiving support from many sources.

The College Student and Work Experience

The scholarly student usually prefers to finish college, go through graduate school, and enter upon his career without paying much attention to actual work experience along the way; however, educational authorities have long considered work experience under educational auspices desirable for virtually all college-going youths. Without some work experience the bright young intellectual may be "all thumbs" when it comes to anything involving practical skills, and his attitudes toward ordinary work may be unsound.

COOPERATIVE WORK–STUDY PROGRAMS

For many students, including those of unusual ability, combining study toward a college degree with actual work experience is better than spending four straight years in college remote from the world of business and industry.

The University of Cincinnati conducted the first cooperative work-study program with engineering students in 1906. Today the university enrolls co-op students who attend classes for seven weeks and then work for the next seven. Other students may take night classes and work in the daytime. Antioch College led the way in requiring a combined program of school and work experience for all students for the purpose of acquainting them with the world of work and preparing them to step directly into paying positions on graduation.

The colleges are finding that cooperative work-study programs not only enrich the students' education in many respects, but enable the colleges to accommodate many more students who alternately study and work for a period away from the campus. In some cooperative college-work programs, pairs of students alternate in college study and the job they hold in business or industry.

The Berea College program requires two hours of manual work a day combined with a full program of academic work. With such a program, the students not only have the basic equipment to serve more fully in any calling, to live more efficiently, but also to understand the manual worker's life and tasks. In the Soviet Union, students are required to combine their advanced technical training with work experience, with few exceptions.

Today it has become fairly common for students to interrupt their studies and take a leave of absence, either for work experience or for some other type of study not necessarily related to the college program. Recessing gives the student an opportunity to reassess himself and his objectives without actually giving up his college plans. After a leave he is likely to return to his studies with more enthusiasm, as did many young people whose college careers were interrupted by World War II.

Counseling the Gifted in College

Through counseling services in college, superior students can be advised about special arrangements the college has made for them. The dropout of high-ranking students results in a heavy talent loss, which can be prevented in some measure by effective guidance. Counseling of gifted students in college is a continuation of counseling in secondary schools within the same three areas: education, career, and personal problems. Students seek advisement concerning the wisdom of remaining in college, selection of courses, underachievement, study problems, career opportunities, and so on.

The intellectually gifted student's problems of personal adjustment and happiness in college life outside of study may revolve around the fact that he is younger than his classmates. Younger boys have more social problems than girls unless they are willing to date high school girls. These difficulties loom larger during the first year in college than later, when the gifted young person has won friends among those who share his special interests.

The failure of many girls to remain in college and to graduate presents a major problem for college authorities. It is difficult to convince attractive girls of nineteen or twenty that there is plenty of time ahead for marriage and that there is more chance of success in interesting careers if they remain in college. The colleges find that girls who can finish college by age twenty remain to graduate in larger proportion than older entrants.

Another complaint is that girls who take difficult courses in college and prepare for careers do not turn out as well as men, although the girls are reassured that they are just as good as the men. The problem stems from differences in career motivation and professional employment opportunities for women and men. This is primarily a social-cultural problem. Recent legislation prohibiting employment discrimination against women simply because they are women is an interesting sidelight on the problem, and may prove helpful in its solution.

References

Advanced Placement Program, College Entrance Examination Board, New York, 1956.

Aikin, Wilford M.: *The Story of the Eight-year Study,* Harper & Row, Publishers, Incorporated, New York, 1942.

Aydelotte, Frank: *Breaking the Academic Lockstep,* Harper & Row, Publishers, Incorporated, New York, 1944.

Barnette, Warren L., Jr.: Advanced Credit for the Superior High School Student, *Journal of Higher Education,* 28:15–20, 1957.

Bonthius, Robert H., F. J. Davis, and J. G. Drushal: *The Independent Study Program in the United States,* Columbia University Press, New York, 1957.

Bridging the Gap between School and College, Evaluation Report no. 1, The Fund for the Advancement of Education, New York, 1953.

Briggs, Leslie J.: Intensive Classes for Superior Students, *Journal of Educational Psychology,* 38:207–215, 1947.

College Admission with Advanced Standing, The School and College Study of Admission with Advanced Standing, College Entrance Examination Board, New York, 1954.

Davidson, R. F.: A Program of General Education for the Superior Student, *Basic College Quarterly,* 2:12–19, 1956.

Drews, Elizabeth M. (ed.): *Guidance for the Academically Talented Student,* NEA Project on the Academically Talented Student, National Education Association, Washington, D.C., 1961.

Howell, Bernice M.: Academic Performance and Personality Adjustment of Highly Selected College Students, *Genetic Psychology Monographs,* no. 55, 1957.

Lewis, Lanora G., in cooperation with J. Ned Bryan and Robert Poppendieck: *Talent and Tomorrow's Teachers: The Honors Approach,* New Dimensions in Higher Education, no. 11, U.S. Department of Health, Education and Welfare, Office of Education, Washington, D.C., 1963.

MacLean, Malcolm S., and Robert B. Carlson: College and University Programs for the Gifted, chap. 13 in *Education for the Gifted: Fifty-seventh Yearbook of the National Association for the Study of Education,* The University of Chicago Press, Chicago, 1958.

Mayhew, L. B.: How Can the Colleges Meet More Adequately the Needs of Talented Youth? *North Central News Bulletin of the Committee on Liberal Arts Education,* 15:1, 1956.

Meister, Morris: Cooperation of Secondary Schools and Colleges in Acceleration of the Gifted, *Journal of Educational Sociology,* 29:220–227, 1956.

Paschal, Elizabeth: *Encouraging the Excellent: Special Programs for Gifted and Talented Students,* The Fund for the Advancement of Education, New York, 1960.

Pearson, Richard: The Students' View of Early Admissions, *College Board Review,* 8:10–13, 1956.

Robinson, Edgar E.: *Independent Study in the Lower Division of Stanford University: 1931–37,* Stanford University Press, Stanford, Calif., 1937.

Snow, C. P.: *Two Cultures and the Scientific Revolution,* Cambridge University Press, London, 1959.

Stedman, Edith: *The Gifted Student and Student Personnel Services in Colleges and Universities,* Monograph, Western Personnel Institute, 1956.

The Superior Student, bimonthly newsletter of the Interuniversity Committee on the Superior Student, Boulder, Col.

They Went to College Early, Evaluation Report no. 2, The Fund for the Advancement of Education, New York, 1957.

Chapter Eighteen

TEACHERS
OF THE
GIFTED

The teacher is the most powerful out-of-home influence in a child's life. As the careers of leaders and eminent persons have shown, good teachers were in large measure responsible for their exceptional achievements.

All teaching is creative work in which the basic materials are the minds and aspirations of impressionable youngsters. A high school teacher, Mr. William S. Lane of Vashan Island, Washington, expressed the view that what bright youngsters need most is someone to guide their educational course. He says that he searches the freshman class as a prospector looking for uranium. Mr. Lane finds that too many "brainy kids" have no sense of their own abilities and no knowledge of their opportunities.

A gifted teacher inspires his students and guides them in making the most of their opportunities. Henry Adams remarked, "A teacher affects eternity. You never can tell where his influence stops." A relevant statement was made by Goethe when he said: "If you treat an individual as he is, he will stay as he is, but if you treat him as if he were what he ought to be and could be, then he will become what he ought to be and could be."

QUALIFICATIONS OF TEACHERS OF THE GIFTED

There is no question that all students should have well-qualified teachers. What are the special qualifications and competencies required for work with the gifted?

Skill in teaching is the first essential. As the students themselves say, their respect can be won and held only by a teacher with lively intelligence who can stimulate their thinking.

In earlier chapters, a number of suggestions were made for teaching the gifted. In Chapters Seven, Nine, and Fifteen, particularly, reference was made to the need to encourage original thinking and intelligent problem solving and to the importance of providing a superior classroom environment. Teachers of the gifted need to understand how the gifted student learns and conceptualizes, thinks and reasons. With this understanding, he is able to guide the student's development in learning and study.

More skill is required of the teacher who listens to the children's questions and helps them seek answers than of one who asks ready-made questions based on the text and checks outcomes of learning with an achievement test. The teacher of the gifted must be able to go beyond the textbook in directing the gifted in their studies.

Good teaching has much in common with intelligent conversation, questioning and answering between two people. Socrates taught Plato by this method in the Grove. Teachers of the gifted need to develop skill in group discussion and in instructing students to conduct discussion so that orderly group processes are followed and the students gain experience in group leadership.

Only an ingenious person is qualified to work with the gifted student, because one can never predict in what direction discussion may lead, what questions may arise, what type of assistance may be demanded. The teacher must be prepared to drop a hint, raise an appropriate question or answer one, perhaps demonstrate a new technique or make alternative proposals for solving a problem.

Breadth of training is needed by the teacher who works with the gifted: The teacher of science should have thorough grounding in the humanities, and the teacher of humanities needs to be well versed in science; otherwise, special aptitudes in these diverse areas of study may go unrecognized.

Teachers who discern their own special interests and talents in children—for example, mechanical ability or music—are quite likely to arouse the children's interest in developing their talents. This is particularly true when the teacher displays marked enthusiasm for his particular specialty or hobby. Those who are fully informed about modern instructional devices—particularly audiovisual equipment, the language laboratory, programmed instruction—who are competent to use these devices and to instruct students in their use have an advantage over the teacher who relies on traditional methods.

Somewhat different skills are required in class management when the gifted are taught as a cluster group or as individuals in the regular classroom rather than in a separate class composed of highly gifted children. The teacher who knows how to make the best use of specialists in such fields as science and mathematics, foreign languages, the arts and crafts, and other areas is prepared to give talented students a richer learning experience (see Chapter Nine).

Viewpoints of the Experts   Throughout the years of experimentation with the gifted, attention has always been given to the question of teacher qualifications. Dr. T. S. Henry, who collaborated with Dr. Guy M. Whipple in appraising results of special-class instruction for the gifted fifty years ago, listed some conclusions about teaching gifted children in the elementary school (1920). He observed that the teacher must possess a large fund of general information, have energy, enthusiasm, and an inspiring personality; he must be able to draw out pupil initiative and be less concerned about discipline than independently controlled learning activities. These qualities are equally desirable in all teachers, but certainly they must never be lacking in the teacher of the gifted.

Desirable qualifications commonly mentioned by respondents to a questionnaire used by Dr. Katherine G. James of the Southern Connecticut State College in a study of teacher preparation for work with the gifted in the elementary school were (1960):

High intellectual capacity and love of learning

Broad and scholarly knowledge in academic areas

Keen understanding of children, including understanding of and sympathy for children of high ability

Professional competency beyond the average

The principals of elementary schools in New York City conducting special classes for gifted children were asked what qualities they looked for in teachers. The traits deemed most essential were dynamic personality, warmth and human insight, emotional stability, mature skill in teaching, superior educational background, creativeness, initiative, originality, talent in art, music, languages, and the ability to inspire young learners. High school teachers need, in addition, greater breadth of knowledge, mastery of methods of teaching, and skill in developing desirable attitudes. They must be able to think clearly and to work with sustained effort.

High school honors sections and special groups make unusual demands on the teacher because the students are intellectually mature, sometimes highly specialized in their interests, and preparing to enter college. Only a teacher with extensive scholarship in his field can keep up with the eager demands for specialized knowledge made by the gifted students in senior high school courses.

Traits of Teachers Mentioned by Honors Class Students Honors students in New York City high schools who were asked to name the traits they appreciated most in their teachers mentioned the following:

1. Knowledge of the subject: "He is a walking encyclopedia. The class will lose confidence if the teacher does not know the field."

2. Skill in presenting the subject: "He has to know how to arouse interest in the subject." The teacher must be able to stimulate group discussion, get the students to think, and keep things going on a high level.

3. Relationship with students: willingness to be part of the class, to be a guide instead of a dictator, to give students responsibilities, to control students in an adult way.

4. Understanding of students: insight into their emotional life. The teacher should exhibit patience and be interested in students as people.

5. Personality: extra spark, "more on the ball."

6. General knowledge, not merely book knowledge: "They should know as much as we do about many subjects." They must be able to discuss more than their own field.

7. Interest in and enthusiasm for the subject: "Makes things interesting, believes in what he is doing, expects us to respect the subject and to enjoy it."

Traits of Gifted Science Teachers   A study by Brandwein, at the Forest Hills High School, New York, indicated that the teachers were the most influential factor in the remarkable achievements of gifted science students (1955). The teachers were exceptionally well versed in science; they had themselves undertaken scientific research and published articles summarizing their findings. They were active, alert people with good health, a wide range of hobbies, interested in athletics, vigorous in manner, and decisive in character. They had a sense of humor and engaged in a wide range of activities outside the world of science. They often came to school early to work with students individually or to prepare special work for them. All were inspiring master teachers, splendid demonstrators, and experimenters. All were in some way associated with efforts to improve instruction. They were all vitally interested in science and in other intellectual pursuits. Invariably, they enjoyed working with children.

These teachers were highly admired by their students; they were persons the students desired to emulate. They served as guides, counselors, friends, and father-confessors. They were sensitive to human problems, considerate of others, and showed respect for the goals and dreams of the children.

CRITERIA FOR THE SELECTION OF TEACHERS FOR THE GIFTED

Superior intellectual and personal qualities are basic. Dr. Walter B. Barbe recommended the following additional criteria as guides in the selection of specialized teachers:

Demonstrated teaching ability in the regular classroom

Expressed interest in teaching the gifted

Willingness to attend training classes

Receptivity to supervisory assistance

TEACHER–PUPIL RELATIONSHIPS

A congenial teacher-pupil relationship is the key to all successful teaching. The gifted in particular thrive under a teacher whom they genuinely like and admire. The teacher who is friend and counselor, not a dictatorial drillmaster, helps the bright child emerge from a state of uncertainty and aimlessness toward full confidence in his abilities.

A teacher who lacks deep human understanding may show resentment toward a pupil with fresh perceptions and originality. The unquestioning youth may be commended whereas highly observant and ultracritical children are perceived as aggressive and rebellious, and those who show unusual curiosity or a keen sense of humor are considered impudent or disrespectful. One teacher became enraged at a boy who started an argument over some fine point in the lesson and threatened to fail him. The pupil who asks unusual questions may be ridiculed by his teacher and classmates. Einstein, as a high school youth, was scolded by his teachers for asking too many questions. Dr. Genevieve Coy discovered that teachers tended to be envious of a gifted child, for fear of being "shown up."

Some Illustrations of Problems   The case of a nine-year-old boy with an IQ around 150 was referred to the counselor for diagnosis. The conference went like this:

"What is your problem, Bernie?"

"The teacher can't pronounce."

"Can't pronounce what?"

"Oh, lots of things. The teacher said 'Magdelan College'—at Oxford, you know. I said, 'In England they call it Madlen College.' The teacher wrote a note home saying I was rude and disorderly. She does not like me."

In a primary class the teacher directed the children to pantomime to the music, "Row, Row, Row Your Boat," but bright Bobbie refused, explaining, "Putt-Putt, I'm in my outboard motor boat."

Another child refused to read the story in the text entitled "Little Brown Dog," explaining that his own dog was a black spaniel and that he would like to tell the class a story about his dog or write it out for them.

Unexpected witticisms can throw a teacher off balance unless he himself is lively and quick-witted. To encourage promptness, a primary grade teacher pointed to the famous picture of Sir Galahad hanging on the wall. "Yes, but you can see he had a horse," was the quick rejoinder of a child scarcely out of kindergarten.

A teacher reported that a child of eleven in the sixth grade deliberately gave wrong answers merely to attract attention. Thinking up "good" wrong answers was an easy trick for him. Another child, a boy in grade 5, obsessed with his superior abilities, habitually called out when he finished his work well ahead of the others. The distracted teacher inquired, "What can I do with a nuisance like that in the class?"

The teacher who feels threatened by a student's high-powered thinking and questioning may tend to suppress or to reject the student—for instance, when a student gets the answer to a mathematics problem intuitively, and then is unable to explain how he did it.

Many a bright student is actually better informed than his teacher on special topics such as astronomy, nuclear fission, or magnetism. A bright youngster who is highly specialized in some topic through reading and independent study expects the teacher to be equally conversant in the subject, without realizing that no one can be an expert in all areas.

The child who is sure he "knows it all" may have difficulty accepting instruction. One bright youngster commented, "I know everything the teacher talks about, so I don't have to do any of the work." Another has decided not to ask any more questions of the teacher because this seems to confuse and embarrass her. Instead, he takes his problems to the school principal.

Can a teacher learn to accept children who can think faster and make a better suggestion than he thought of himself? This is a crucial question in work with the gifted and talented. What attitude should the teacher take when the gifted student knows more than the teacher in some area of specialized knowledge? In the answer to this question lies the test of a true teacher. He sees this situation as an opportunity to guide the student in making new discoveries and in utilizing his specialized knowledge in class and school projects.

The Question of Rotating Teachers Some schools adopt the policy of rotating teachers in and out of special classes for the gifted to equalize the opportunities of teachers in working with what are considered "more favored groups." Regular class teachers are rewarded for good results by giving them a gifted class for a change. The disadvantage of this policy is that a teacher's special competencies and valuable experience may be lost.

A teacher who was shifted in and out of gifted classes, even from a slow-learner class to a gifted group, said that she found the new adjustment difficult each time. The better plan is to allocate this work regularly only to those who have had special training.

LEARNING TO WORK WITH THE GIFTED AND TALENTED

Working with the gifted and talented excites the imagination of young people entering the teaching profession as well as those who are already experienced teachers. Here are unique opportunities for the courageous and talented.

The objective in training teachers to work with the gifted is no different from the main objective of teacher education in general: to provide the best possible education for every child in the light of his individual aptitudes and special talents.

Those who plan to work primarily with the mentally exceptional should, first of all, obtain the general background of preparation required of all teachers; then on this foundation they can build the superstructure of special preparation, preferably in a fifth- and sixth-year graduate program of training and internship experience.

Every teacher should have some knowledge of gifted deviates as part of his general preparation whether or not he expects to specialize in this work. Such knowledge serves to correct misconceptions about the gifted, the talented, and the creative genius.

The time may come when special certificates will be required of those who work with the gifted, comparable to the special licenses of teachers of other types of exceptional children. The state of Pennsylvania now issues a certificate for teachers of the mentally advanced.

TRAINING PROGRAMS FOR TEACHERS OF THE GIFTED

A graduate course for preparing teachers of the gifted was offered at Teachers College, Columbia University, in the early 1920s. Gradually other colleges and universities both here and abroad began offering training programs for this special field.

Since 1954, when Romaine P. Mackie and Lloyd M. Dunn of the United States Office of Education published a report of college and university programs for the preparation of teachers of the gifted, training opportunities have been greatly expanded.

Although there is a growing tendency for those who are ambitious to work with the gifted to "take the course" at a local college or university, beyond that point not much else has been required. Wilson queried city superintendents of schools concerning specific training for teachers of the gifted (1953): 29 per cent favored special training for teachers in the elementary schools and 31 per cent for those in secondary schools. In actual practice, however, only a small proportion of schools were requiring such training.

In-service courses for teachers and others who work with the gifted are offered on two levels: first, a course that provides general background in the field and, second, intensive courses in various areas that provide more specific training, such as work in science and mathematics or with young children in the self-contained class-room.

In the Portland, Oregon, program for the gifted, special attention has been given to the selection and training of teachers. Teachers receive training in workshops as well as assistance from consultants and supervisors. The improvement of classroom teaching is considered a continuing part of the program (*The Gifted in Portland*, 1959).

Proposed Courses   Fliegler has proposed training courses for teachers of the gifted in five steps (1961):

The psychology and education of gifted children

The curriculum and programs of instruction of gifted children

Practice in the education of gifted children; observation and student teaching of the gifted; field experience

Special courses in the content areas: science, mathematics, social studies, English, foreign languages, and so on

Research problems in the education of the gifted[1]

Some differentiation in terms of the future teacher's level of interest, whether in the elementary school or in junior or senior high school, is necessary. Those preparing to work with the gifted need special training in curriculum planning, in the unified program and core curriculum, in the adaptation of teaching methods to individualized instruction, and in guidance and counseling. In addition to courses in the psychology of the gifted and in curriculum making, field experience (observation and practice teaching) should be required, supplemented where possible with some clinical experience. Laboratory schools attached to colleges and universities have furnished some of the best opportunities for this experience.

Most people engaged in teacher training would agree with Fliegler that preparation for teaching the gifted should begin at the graduate level. This would ensure a tryout in the general field of education and a background of liberal education before the prospective teacher undergoes specialized training.

A Study of Training Programs   James made a survey of training programs for teachers of the gifted in teacher-training institutions throughout

[1] Louis A. Fliegler (ed.), *Curriculum Planning for the Gifted*, Prentice-Hall, Inc., Englewood Cliffs, N.J., 1961, chap. 13: Curriculum Implementation. Used by permission of the author and publisher.

the country (1960). Responses from 81 colleges showed that 31
offered a separate course in work with the gifted, 19 others offered
a unit on the gifted, 3 provided a sequence of courses, and 9
provided practice in student teaching with the gifted. Although
a number of colleges offered courses pertaining to the gifted at
the undergraduate level, the consensus was that the requirement
of maturity and previous experience with children made it advisable
to offer the major portion of the sequence at the graduate level.

Important elements in the program of teacher preparation
were:

Breadth and depth in general education

A broad basis of psychology

Experience with gifted children

Provision for development of professional competencies

As a result of her study, James recommended a sequence of
courses covering knowledge of the gifted child; material and techniques of teaching the gifted; reading, mathematics, and science
for gifted children; and experience in teaching the gifted.

In New York City and vicinity practically all the colleges
enrolling a substantial proportion of teacher trainees offer at least
a one-semester graduate course on the psychology and teaching
of the gifted. Graduate students may choose additional electives,
such as literature, psychological testing and evaluation, speech improvement, guidance, mental hygiene, dramatics. Hunter College
provides supervised practice teaching with gifted children.

Plans have been made in the state of Illinois to set up thirty-six
school demonstration centers for work with the gifted. The first
of these centers was established at Evanston Township High School,
where experienced teachers of honors and advanced-placement
courses in various subject areas are given some released time
for conferences with visitors who are interested in the program.
Special conferences are also held during the year to help schools
organize programs for gifted students, to develop courses of study,
and to explore unique problems in various subject areas.

Summer School Opportunities Summer workshops have become increasingly popular for the orientation of teachers preparing for
work with the gifted. These may be as short as two weeks in
duration or as long as the full college summer term. Summer
seminars for study of the gifted have been a feature at George
Peabody College, Nashville, Tennessee, since 1953.

An experimental program to give teachers a better understanding of the gifted child was inaugurated at Brooklyn College, the City University of New York, during the summer term of 1962. The program, conducted by Dr. Hilary Gold of the Education Department, combined class instruction with a demonstration class for bright children. In addition to attending theoretical courses in the psychology of the gifted and curriculum making for the exceptional, each teacher enrolled in a practicum that afforded him an opportunity to become intimately acquainted with at least one child and to observe the whole class daily. Teachers also observed individual testing of children in the educational clinic.

The demonstration class was in session daily during the month of July.

The unifying theme of the children's studies during the month of the demonstration class was "The Far East." The teachers who participated in the program joined with the teacher of the demonstration class and the children in planning the curriculum for the program. Usually the participating teachers worked with the individual children assigned to them for half an hour to an hour daily. They were thus able to observe the beginnings of the creative process as they followed and guided the children's projects.

In this work, the participating teachers were supervised by the instructors of the practicum. Other instructors in the college, as well as the librarians and service personnel, assisted in the program either by talking to the demonstration class or through the selection and loan of resource materials.

At the close of the term each participating teacher prepared a report of the intensive study of his assigned pupil, including a summary of the activities the child had carried on, the results of tests given, and recommendations for future guidance of the child. These statements were forwarded to the heads of the cooperating schools. Gold concluded that the demonstration had been of great value to the participating teachers because of the fortunate combination of theory and practice that gave them new understanding of unusual children (1962).

OTHER ASPECTS OF TEACHER PREPARATION

The teacher builds up his own cultural background through wide reading, college courses, travel, and the utilization of cultural resources of his community.

In addition to studying research reports and textbooks, teachers preparing for work with the gifted can read biographies of eminent people, especially those furnishing details of the childhood years, as source material about the developmental characteristics of giftedness and creativity. By keeping a file of this material, the college instructor soon has a valuable collection of material for use with advanced students.

The training of teachers of the gifted at the graduate level should not be limited to a course on the gifted or to education and psychology courses. Many departments offer courses that enrich the teacher's background in understanding the gifted and talented. Teachers can also attend service training workshops conducted in their own schools or districts, go to lectures given by experts, and attend conferences on the gifted child.

Teachers assigned to work with the gifted can get assistance from the school principal or, in a large high school, the department chairman. In some cases honors course coordinators assist teachers in securing special materials. In conferences and staff meetings a principal or coordinator may present findings or discuss new developments in the education of the gifted. At informal meetings the teachers may discuss such topics as attitudes toward the gifted child, enrichment of school subjects, the teacher's role in guidance, working with parents.

For further information on teacher training for work with the gifted, see the writings of Prof. Frank Wilson, formerly of Hunter College, New York, and other references at the end of this chapter.

A SYLLABUS OUTLINE FOR THE "GIFTED" COURSE

The syllabus for a graduate course on the education of the gifted at Brooklyn College, City University of New York, prepared by the author, is as follows:

Education 325: The Education of the Gifted Child. A study of the nature and needs of gifted children and youth; educational provisions of these children at all levels of instruction.

Course Outline and Study Guide
1. *The conservation of human resources:* The gifted in modern society. The nation's resources of specialized talent.

The talent search: Growing respect for high-level intellect, talents, and remarkable accomplishments. Some issues and problems in the identification and education of the gifted. The question of selective education in a democracy. *Historical background of interest in the gifted child:* The work of various leaders.

2. *Definitions:* Who is the gifted child? The talented individual? Older and newer viewpoints. Broad versus narrow interpretations. Changing conceptions of the gifted child, his nature and needs, his potential role in society. *Incidence of these children in the general population.*

3. *Traits of the gifted:* Types of gifted and talented children. Mental and physical characteristics. Personal traits and qualities, abilities, accomplishments. Correlation of traits. Backgrounds of gifted children. Findings of research studies.

   Traits of the creative person.

   The child prodigy, quiz kids, the pseudogifted child.

   Early promise and subsequent achievement: Findings of follow-up studies. The relation of ability to achievement.

4. *Identification of the gifted and talented:* Methods and techniques for identification of the gifted in a wide age range. Developmental data, behavior records, tests and ratings of performance, aptitudes, etc.

   Problems and practical recommendations.

5. *Education of the gifted at all school levels:* Some issues and problems. Speeding up, special educational provisions, articulation throughout the entire school career.

   Learning with understanding: Learning about the learning process. Developing powers of thinking and problem solving, learning research methods and use of research tools. Training for self-responsibility and self-discipline. Education for creativity.

   A. *Elementary school years*

   Acceleration in age-grade status, various means of acceleration.

   Special classes and homogeneous grouping. Partial segregation, small-group work, clubs, etc.

   Individual projects, curriculum studies and units.

   Enrichment in regular classes.

   Interrelationships between these provisions. Gifted children in special schools.

   Skills and fundamentals. Creative work in arts, crafts, dramatics, written expression.

   B. *Junior high school*

   The question of acceleration, means of acceleration.

   Special progress classes, special courses.

   Enrichment projects in regular classes.

   The contribution of the integrated program, curriculum units.

   Skills and fundamentals.

   Foreign language study.

   Arts and crafts, literature, dramatics.

   Individual guidance.

C. *Senior high school*

    Special programs and courses, rapid-advancement sections.

    Provision for advanced courses, laboratory work.

    Individual projects, e.g., mathematics, science, literature, and arts.

    The arts, literature, dramatics, foreign language.

    Educational and prevocational guidance.

    College counseling.

    Early admission to college.

    Gifted children in independent and private preparatory schools.

D. *General*

    The library in the education of the gifted.

    Extracurricular activities.

    Working at hobbies and special interests.

    Out-of-school influences in the training of the gifted.

    Social institutions and the gifted.

    The use of community resources and agencies.

    Schoolwide and community planning for the gifted.

    Reports of experimental plans and projects.

    Providing for the gifted in rural areas.

    Benefits to the gifted of general improvements in schooling.

6. *Personal adjustments of the gifted:* Self-understanding and evaluation of attitudes.

The mental hygiene of the gifted: Character development.

The problem of motivation: Underachievers at all educational levels. The question of class marks.

The gifted from lower-class homes and neighborhoods, in minority groups.

7. *Home cooperation in the education of gifted children:* Parent-child relationships, parental attitudes, home-school relationships.

8. *The art of teaching the gifted and talented:* Qualifications of teachers. Teacher selection and training. In-service training programs. The teacher's role in school and community planning for the gifted.

9. *Literature on the psychology and education of the gifted and talented:* Résumé of scientific studies.

    An extensive bibliography of current reference materials is included with each copy of the syllabus.

Recommended Activities   Recommended study activities for the course include:

    Reading of assigned material on various topics. The student is urged to develop some kind of personal note taking for ready reference.

    Oral participation by means of individual reports, panels, symposiums, etc.

Writing a statement of educational ideas concerning the education of the gifted. The nature of this assignment will be cooperatively developed by the class members and the instructor.

Extensive study of significant research findings in the student's particular subject-area interest.

Preparation of several research abstracts on the education of the gifted, both recent and earlier findings. The form for reporting is given in class.

Organizing a school program for the gifted. Possible plans for initiating a program in a class and the school.

A description of an action research project carried on in the classroom and the school dealing with some aspect of programming for the gifted and talented.

Investigation of curriculum bulletins and other school-produced materials on the education of the gifted prepared by school systems in the United States.

A study of the work of community agencies and professional organizations in the New York area providing special programs and facilities for the gifted.

Participation in clinical case studies, systematic observation of gifted children.

Building a Professional Library   Teachers or college students undertaking a serious study of the gifted are advised to begin building a library of professional reading on the subject. In view of the tremendous array of literature that has been accumulating for over forty years, the selection of a handful of the "best" books becomes something of a problem. Some books are general; others are highly specialized. The various chapters in this book include basic references, both specialized and general, on every phase of the subject.

Parents as Teachers of Gifted Children

Parents are inevitably teachers and counselors; the first and the strongest influences on a child are those of his parents and the home background. A child's home environment will largely determine the course of his development. In some cases the guidance and training of wise parents have offset the disadvantages of poor schooling and a meager environment.

The childhood of people who developed unusual creative talent suggests that the bright and talented flourish in homes where parents encourage original thinking, questioning, and experimentation without being overdemanding. The mother's influence is great, but studies show that the father's influence can be an even stronger force in shaping children's intellectual tastes and interests.

Congenial family living fosters sound emotional and social development in any child; in the case of the gifted, normal family life can forestall traits such as onesidedness, bossiness, selfishness, or solitariness. A gifted youth of seventeen had this to say about parental influences: The thing that helps most is not coercion or great concern about school marks, but the creation of an atmosphere that helps develop one's special abilities.

KNOWING THE CHILD'S ABILITIES

Parents often ask, "How shall I help my gifted child?" One answer is: Know his capacities so that you can make reasonable demands of him. The mother of a gifted four-year-old said to the child's teacher, "Since you told me that my child was mature, more like a six-year-old, I have experimented with giving her more responsibility and more freedom in choices. She now does simple errands for me, takes care of her things better, helps other children, and seems happier than formerly. She gets into mischief less because she is proud of her new duties and takes her responsibilities seriously. Temper tantrums and negative behavior have disappeared."

PARENTAL ATTITUDES TOWARD THE BRIGHT CHILD

In handling a bright child, parents seem to go to one of two extremes: either they neglect or belittle the child, laugh at what strikes them as absurd in the child's questions or behavior, and fail to understand why he is different from others, or they exploit the child's exceptional traits at every turn and push him beyond normal limits.

Parents may not realize the extent to which they identify themselves with their gifted child, finding in the child's precocity compensation for their lack of education or intellectual achievement. As a parent of a child in a gifted class once put it at a parents' meeting, "These parents think they're the gifted children."

Parents seem more aware of spectacular talents than of high intelligence in their children, and they think of these talents as God-given or inherited, if not wholly inexplicable. Some parents cling to the older notion that a gifted child is doomed to become a neurotic failure. Parents are not invariably the best judges of their children's aptitudes and talents in comparison with other children because they are not sufficiently acquainted with the range of abilities in the like-age population. A bright child might be wholly overlooked in an exceptionally gifted family or considered odd by parents of average ability. Laycock advises informing parents that gifted children are apt to show unevenness in different aspects of growth (1956).

If the intellectual atmosphere of the home and the influence of educated parents play so large a role in the early years of childhood, why aren't parents of younger children given suggestions about making their influence count for more? One answer is that, if the parent has to have the matter brought to his attention instead of recognizing it spontaneously, then probably the suggestions would not be of great value. On the other hand, young parents may welcome the suggestion that they respect the child's growing capacity for independence of thought and action and show tolerance, if not warm support, of his original ideas.

Parents who "show off" the precocious youngster make him obnoxious to others. It is poor taste, to say the least, to brag about a child's accomplishments or to enter him in "quiz kid" shows. Worst of all is the parent who exploits the child's marketable talents for money. The gifted child fares best if his parents keep him in proper perspective and avoid the "genius complex," the wishful thinking about his superiority, and the premature "forcing" of talents. The child fares best who is allowed to be himself; he can then enter more fully into normal, wholesome contacts with other children.

HOME EDUCATION OF THE GIFTED

At home, the child obtains an education in human living, in intellectual exploration, in practical mechanics, in the arts, and especially in social interactions. Wide reading in the home library, interesting conversation with older persons, informative answers to eager questions round out the child's formal education. Records of eminent and distinguished people prove that their parents held learning in great respect and hoped to see their children excel in scholarship.

When the home encourages learning and questioning, when children are surrounded with good books and are permitted to experiment in construction, science, dramatics, writing, art, and other hobby interests, then children are well started on independent and creative thinking. In the absence of favorable home influences, the school can accomplish less for a mentally advanced or talented child. It is unfortunate, indeed, when the child has a neglectful parent or one who mercilessly exploits him. Although a gifted child's parents may not be highly educated, they can still exert a favorable influence on his intellectual development.

Some parents show intuitive understanding of their gifted child—his need for freedom and independence, along with reasonable direction and controls. As a good teacher, the thoughtful parent gives the alert, curious child a chance to try out his own ideas. He supplies materials and then sensibly leaves the child to his own devices (within the bounds of personal safety) when he observes the child's preoccupation with plans and inventions. The child is free to set up his own work center, to arrange and use it in any way he wishes for projects in science, amateur theatricals, reading, and writing.

An eager, ambitious parent must remember to keep his hands off the child's work, to avoid dictation or domination. The child's ideas will often be fresher, freer, more original, and more interesting than his parent's.

The thoughtful parent lends support to a child's emerging talents and hobby interest at the right moment. When Robert's parents observed the boy's interest in earth science, they provided him with a globe and two atlases. Another type of parent may actually thwart a child's interest in some new activity. Ruth, a young girl with special interest in papier-mâché work, told her teacher that she couldn't do this work at home because her mother objected to her soiling her dress.

The talented boy or girl who lives his own child life from year to year without undue pressures will be better prepared for normal adulthood than one who is pushed and exploited. As Brumbaugh remarked, a gifted child is growing best to the extent that he is being made independent of his parents and teachers (1959).

Parents are advised to take advantage of educational features in the community to supplement the child's formal education. Possibilities include membership in the local library and in community clubs suited to the child's age group. There may be a museum to visit, parks, the zoo, youth concerts, not to mention the cinema programs. The parents' adult friends may be willing to share with the children their interest in stamp collecting, photography, coins, or art.

The gifted boy or girl needs to grow up in a household where there is intimate "give and take" with healthy children of different ages. He learns from the older ones; in turn, he learns by instructing the younger ones. The child who develops friendships with other children, instead of isolating himself or associating mainly with adults, tends to develop healthy social attitudes.

Parents Help with Reading   Parents can get their child off to a good start in reading by reading aloud to him from books that he chooses in the picture-story collection; then when school days begin, they can supply the youngster with good reading material in line with his emerging interests—cowboys, railroads, rocket ships, sports, and lives of heroes. The parent is advised to keep in touch with the activities of the local library, to visit book fairs with the child, to check on reviews of juvenile books, and to select good books as gifts. Many a parent has whetted a young child's love of literature through storytelling and frequent reading aloud. Parents appreciate advice about books to give children as gifts as well as reports about the school's program in reading and literature.

The home has direct influence on the formation of study habits. Several outstanding high school boys and girls who were asked whether their parents helped them with homework said, "Yes"; then they went on to say that their parents gave help, but did not do their homework for them.

THE DANGER OF OVERSCHEDULING BRIGHT CHILDREN

One problem that concerns parents and teachers alike is the overloaded programs of children, particularly young teen-agers. School hours and out-of-school time are so filled with a number of things—ballet lessons, music studies, sports, movies, television, museum visiting, going on trips, riding lessons, foreign language tutoring or speech work, party going and giving, club mettings, scouts, not to mention time out for the orthodontics—that one begins to wonder why more children do not openly rebel. A mother of several bright children became so indignant about the situation that she published an article entitled "Our Conscripted Children," written from the point of view of the parent who would like to see something of her children now and then, or at least give them some free time for their own self-devised occupations.

COUNSELING PARENTS OF THE GIFTED

Since education is a joint responsibility of school and home, exchange of ideas between parents and teachers should be mutually helpful, a means of resolving many problems. When the parents keep in touch with the child's school program, home training can reinforce and supplement the teacher's efforts.

Virtually all parents benefit from interpretations by the teachers and school authorities of modern theories of education and new departures in the local schools. Their understanding and cooperation are indispensable in helping a child derive the most benefit from his schooling.

Parents who think they observe traits of precocity in their children are advised to consult with the child's teachers and the school authorities. They are entitled to ask whether the school is cognizant of children of unusual abilities and what is being done about them. Before taking the child to a private consultant for diagnosis of superior abilities or special talent, parents should consult the school authorities in order to determine whether pertinent information is already at hand.

Counseling the parents of the gifted parallels the school's guidance program for the students. The purposes of counseling are:

To prevent exploitation of a gifted child

To prevent neglect and underappreciation

To make home training more fruitful In developing the child's interests and talents, equipping his mind, developing his personality

To interpret the school's plans and programs

To advise parents about the child who is not achieving up to his capacity in schoolwork

Parents of high school youths should be advised about college prospects for superior students, whether or not they seek advice of the school. They may need to be cautioned about prejudicing the youth's choice of college and a career.

When the school discovers that a child is gifted or specially talented, it must exercise caution in advising parents. Instead of telling a parent outright that the child is highly gifted, the teacher can suggest that the child has some unusual qualities. Advice may then be given in response to the parent's questions. Instead of stressing the fact that the child is superior to others of his age, the counselor can talk about the parents' responsibility toward a child who learns rapidly and is able to carry advanced work.

Instead of talking to parents in terms of IQ test scores and percentiles, the counselor can give them a picture of the child's potentials and talents, along with some indication of what a child with this type of potential should be able to accomplish as he goes through school. Parents must realize that a high IQ derived from an intelligence test is nothing more than a tentative indication of academic potential which may or may not be borne out in the child's future development; much depends upon his response to school and his home training. The parent's consent is usually required for "skipping" a child or placing him in a special class.

During group meetings and individual conferences, parents are advised of the ways in which they can support the school's efforts. If a child in the primary school comes home reporting that she is bored because schoolwork is too easy, the parent's first step is to consult with the teacher to ascertain the facts.

One parent may require advice concerning the dangers of exploitation; another, concerning the dangers of neglect and underappreciation. Most parents benefit from advice about home training suited to the child's special abilities and talents.

The sibling problem frequently arises in the home of a gifted child whose brothers and sisters are not equally gifted or talented. If the bright child is selected for special programs at the school and his siblings are not, they may become anxious and envious. These problems can best be handled by giving equal recognition to each child's accomplishments.

Some Leading Questions for Parents   The parent who inquires, "What can I do to help my gifted child?" might well consider the implications of the following questions:

Does your child have responsibilities that build independence of thought and action? Does he have regular household tasks to perform? Does he take pride in taking care of his things? Is he assured that when he tries things for himself, help will be there when needed?

Does the child have a regular schedule for daily routines such as eating, sleeping, recreation?

Do you listen to the child's questions and seek to answer them or direct him how to find the answers?

Do you give the child some personal attention every day? Does the child's father give him as much attention as possible?

Do you talk with the child, drawing out his ideas on various subjects?

Do you encourage the child's interest in learning, in questioning, in thinking independently?

Do you arouse and sustain the child's interest in reading through giving him good books, seeing that he has a library card, reading aloud to him, encouraging him to discuss what he has read, suggesting that he read aloud to younger children?

Do you take the child to places of interest about the city or community? Does he have an opportunity to hear good music? Do you supervise his TV watching so that he does not get an unbalanced diet of cheap, sensational drama?

Do you pay sufficient attention to the child's school progress? Visit the school? Confer with teachers? Join parent discussion groups? Attend the children's school performances?

Do you recognize the danger of overweighing the child's mind with intellectual cramming at the expense of recreation and free choice of activity?

If you do not know how to help the child with his homework or think he needs more help at school, do you speak to his teachers?

Do you realize that every child needs to learn to respect rules made for the general good and to learn the value of discipline for the common good?

A number of excellent books and pamphlets have been written primarily for parents of the gifted and talented. Recommended publications are the books by Brumbaugh and Roshco (1959), Cutts and Moseley (1953), Hurlock (1937), and Strang (1960).

Helpful pamphlets have been prepared by Witty (1952), Carson (1959), and experts at Kent State University (1957). Laycock has prepared a useful article on counseling parents of gifted children (1956).

References

Brandwein, Paul F.: *The Gifted Student As Future Scientist,* Harcourt, Brace & World, Inc., New York, 1955, chap. 5.

Brumbaugh, Florence N., and Bernard Roshco: *Your Gifted Child: A Guide for Parents,* Holt, Rinehart and Winston, Inc., New York, 1959.

Carroll, Herbert A.: *Genius in the Making,* McGraw-Hill Book Company, New York, 1940.

Carson, Ruth: *Your Child May Be a Gifted Child,* Public Affairs Pamphlet, no. 291, Public Affairs Pamphlets, New York, 1959.

Cutts, Norma E., and Nicholas Moseley: *Bright Children: A Guide for Parents,* G. P. Putnam's Sons, New York, 1953.

DeHaan, Robert, F.: *Guidelines for Parents of Capable Youth,* Project of Superior and Talented Students, Science Research Associates, Inc., Chicago, 1961.

Epstein, Mary: Teachers Look at Gifted Children, *Peabody Journal of Education,* 31:26–34, 1953.

Fliegler, Louis A. (ed.): *Curriculum Planning for the Gifted,* Prentice-Hall, Inc., Englewood Cliffs, N.J., 1961, chap. 13: Curriculum Implementation.

The Gifted in Portland: A Report of Five Years of Experience in Developing a Program for Children of Exceptional Endowment, Portland, Ore., Public Schools, 1959.

Gold, Hilary: *Report on the Practicum: The Psychology and Education of the Gifted,* unpublished staff report, Brooklyn College, 1962.

Henry, T. S.: *Classroom Problems in the Education of Gifted Children: Nineteenth Yearbook of the National Society for the Study of Education,* part 2, Public School Publishing Company, Bloomington, Ill., 1920.

Hurlock, Elizabeth B.: *Modern Ways with Children,* J. B. Lippincott Company, Philadelphia, 1937.

James, Katherine G.: *A Report of the Study in the Preparation of Teachers for the Gifted in the Elementary School,* summary of doctoral thesis on file in the library of the School of Education, New York University, New York, 1960.

Laycock, Samuel R.: Counseling Parents of Gifted Children, *Exceptional Children,* 23:108–110, 134, 1956.

Mackie, Romaine P., and Lloyd M. Dunn: *College and University Programs for the Preparation of Teachers of Exceptional Children,* U.S. Department of Health, Education and Welfare, Office of Education, Bulletin no. 13, Washington, D.C., 1954.

The Role of the Parent in the Education and Training of the Mentally Superior Child, Department of Special Education, Kent State University, Kent, Ohio, 1957.

Schiefele, Marion: *The Gifted Child in the Regular Classroom,* Bureau of Publications, Teachers College, Columbia University, New York, 1953.

Selvi, Arthur: Preparing Teachers for the Education of the Gifted, *Educational Administration and Supervision,* 39:493–494, 1953.

Strang, Ruth: *Helping Your Gifted Child,* E. P. Dutton & Co., Inc., New York, 1960.

Wilson, Frank T.: The Preparation for Teachers of Gifted Children, chap. 15 in *Education for the Gifted: Fifty-seventh Yearbook of the National Society for the Study of Education,* part 2, The University of Chicago Press, Chicago, Ill., 1958.

Wilson, Frank T.: Preparation for Teachers of Gifted Children in the United States, *Exceptional Children,* 20:78–80, 1953.

Wilson, Frank T.: Suggestions for the Preparation of Teachers of Gifted Children, *Elementary School Journal,* 52:157–161, 1951.

Wilson, Frank T.: Teacher Education and the Gifted, *Journal of Teacher Education,* 6:263–267, 1955.

Witty, Paul A.: *Helping the Gifted Child,* Science Research Associates, Inc., Chicago, 1952.

APPENDIX

Checklist for Gifted Children (*ages 10 and over*)

Child's name_____ _____

Age_____Birthdate_____Sex_____

Nationality and race_____

Parent_____

School_____

Grade_____Date_____

Evaluations made by_____ _____

CHARACTERISTICS

EVALUATION

I. Mental Traits, Intellectual Qualities

1. Is considered old for his years, "long-headed"; regarded as gifted by family and friends

2. Enjoys the challenge of intellectual tasks, excels in performance of difficult mental tasks; displays capacity for organized thinking, reasoning, and judgment beyond his years

3. Shows intellectual curiosity, desire for knowledge; questioning attitude regarding sources and causes; seeks reasons and explanations

4. Has keen powers of observation, excellent memory for items and topics of interest to him

5. Possesses a large fund of general knowledge and information

6. Is inventive, creative; shows imagination, originality in working on plans and projects

7. Shows maturity in comprehending and carrying out instructions

<table>
<tr><td>CHARACTERISTICS</td><td>EVALUATION</td></tr>
</table>

CHARACTERISTICS   EVALUATION

8. Shows preference for games requiring concentrated thinking, involving rules and system; introduces more complexity into games

II. Command of Language

9. Shows maturity beyond his age-mates in use of oral language, fluency in speaking, giving oral reports, etc.

10. Has effective choice of words in speaking, command of vocabulary typical of older children or adults; enjoys using long words

11. Shows maturity and facility in grasping meanings in oral communication

12. Shows maturity in written expression; fluency, accuracy, originality in stating ideas; effective use of words

13. Shows talent in composing original stories, essays, poems, plays, material for school projects, etc.

14. Speaks, reads, and writes a second language with considerable fluency

III. Academic Skills and Attainments

15. Learns easily and quickly at school; needs less explanation and repetition than his age-mates

16. Has progressed through school more rapidly than other pupils his age; placed in rapid-advancement sections or honors classes

17. Likes to study, considered a studious child; capable of independent study; has received academic honors

18. Is advanced in independent use of library facilities; wide acquaintance with library resources

19. Has reading skills above average for age level; enjoys reading books for older children or adult literature; uses advanced or adult reference materials

20. Handles mathematics processes easily; long division, fractions, decimals, percentage,

CHARACTERISTICS   **EVALUATION**

measurement, algebra, geometry, according to opportunity to learn; uses computation devices, slide rule, mathematical tables, etc.; handles written problems in mathematics with quick understanding, shows ingenuity in mathematical problem solving

21. Has wide fund of information in the sciences; understands the processes of scientific thinking; uses science tools—magnifying glass, telescope, magnets, dissecting instruments—with ability beyond his years

22. Has wide fund of information in social studies: history, geography, civics; grasps principles in social science; does reading beyond his years in these areas. Uses maps, globe, atlas; works with charts, graphic and tabular material

23. Takes an interest in current events and political situations, government and world affairs; does critical thinking on issues of the day; reflective attitude toward ideas of a social and philosophical nature

IV. **Special Interests, Aptitudes, Talents**

24. Shows many-sided interests and aptitudes; versatile

25. Spends a considerable part of his spare time working alone at his hobbies and self-devised projects

26. Shows initiative, enthusiasm, originality, persistence, sustained attention in working on favorite projects; strong drive to attain goals; good planning and execution of self-devised projects; has received recognition, prizes resulting from hobby interests

27. Shows marked interest in science topics; enjoys discussion of science, mathematics, astronomy, etc.; shows preference for reading on these subjects; has a considerable fund of information in one or more of these subjects

CHARACTERISTICS   EVALUATION

28. Is interested in working with mechanical devices and apparatus; shows mechanical ingenuity and inventiveness in mechanical construction; enjoys discussing and reading about mechanical devices and inventions; has a considerable fund of information in this area

29. Has shown special talent for music; well advanced in musical studies; has given recitals, received special recognition for exceptional performance, prizes, scholarships, etc.; has a considerable fund of information about music

30. Has shown special talent in graphic arts: painting, drawing, sculpture, handicrafts; work has been exhibited, recognized by prizes, scholarships, etc.; has a considerable fund of information in this area

31. Has shown special talent in expressive and performing arts: dramatics, dancing; has given recitals, received recognition, prizes, scholarships, etc.; has a considerable fund of information in this area

32. Has made unusual achievement in athletics, sports, games, physical contests; has won recognition, medals, prizes, etc.

33. Sets high standards of workmanship, has high degree of self-criticism, not easily satisfied with his achievement; strives for accuracy and precision

34. Reads and uses books—a favorite activity

35. Enjoys looking up facts, seeking out items of information, using classified sources of information, dictionary, encyclopedia, almanac, etc.; enters contests requiring a fund of information

36. Makes collections of a systematic, orderly type, reflecting special interests

37. Keeps a diary or journal; keeps systematic or periodic records related to his studies and interests

38. Has indicated intention of entering a

CHARACTERISTICS   EVALUATION

high-level profession requiring college education or professional training beyond high
school

V. **Personal and Social Traits, Character Qualities**

39. Prefers companionship of older children,
or association with adults

40. Is socially adaptable; adept at dealing
with others in personal relationships

41. Seems naturally to assume leadership;
chosen by associates as leader in class activities, school and club affairs; is looked up
to as an authority by other children; is asked
to take charge or to organize activities; his
decisions are respected

42. Is considered "different" or "a brain" by
other children; expresses impatience with
those who respond more slowly than himself;
shows aggressive or dominating attitude toward age-mates

43. Shows rebellious attitude when situation
offers no challenge or requests made of him
seem unreasonable

44. Makes mature response to authority, respects and observes rules and regulations

45. Shows concern for the welfare of others;
thoughtful, unselfish; shows desire to be of
service, interested in social service programs

46. Has mature ethical sense; understands
and exemplifies justice and fair play in his
conduct; resents injustice

47. Is trustworthy, dependable; has high
sense of responsibility

48. Shows modesty in rating his abilities and
accomplishments; respects the achievements
of others; disclaims having abilities higher
than others

49. Enjoys humor with an intellectual flavor;
shows cleverness in originating jokes

50. Has mature physique for his age; good
physical stamina, endurance, strength, agility,
motor coordination

CHARACTERISTICS   EVALUATION

VI. Background and Early Development

51. Was known as precocious child before school age; showed accelerated mental development at an early age

52. Was advanced in the use of language by age 2 or 3; used sentences, original expressions, invented words

53. Showed manipulative ability ahead of his years before school age, shown in handwork, building, using tools and mechanical toys, cutting, pasting, sewing, weaving, clay modeling, etc.

54. Showed early evidence of artistic or musical talent

55. Showed early interest in picture books and reading aloud; retentive memory for characters, stories, rhymes, etc.; learned to read informally at home before entering school

56. Learned to read at school easily; attained level of functional reading skill (grade level 4.5) well before typical age of 9 or 10 years

57. Learned to write name, numbers, simple words before school age; early mastery of the alphabet

58. Showed early interest in numbers, counting, computation; advanced in arithmetic, knowledge of money, stamps; interest and knowledge ahead of his years in time, distances, clocks, calendar, etc.

59. Was advanced in knowledge of common objects, their names and uses, operation

60. Was ahead of age-mates in written expression by age 9; showed interest in composing stories, drafting letters

61. Showed early interest in table games involving rules, system, scorekeeping

62. Enjoyed solitary play of his own invention in early childhood years; tended to invent imaginary companions or an imaginary world

63. Entered first grade before 5 years, 9

## CHARACTERISTICS											EVALUATION

months of age; second grade before 7; made rapid progress on entrance to grade 1; skipped one or more terms in the primary grades

64. Comes from home of relatively high literacy level and intellectually stimulating environment

65. Parents encourage child's interests and activities, without coercion or overstimulation; parents encourage freedom of expression, independence, self-responsibility

INDEX

Ma